Cases in European Marketing Management

The Irwin Series in Marketing

Gilbert A. Churchill, Jr., Consulting Editor
University of Wisconsin, Madison

Alreck & Settle
The Survey Research Handbook, 1/e

Arens & Bovee
Contemporary Advertising, 5/e

Belch & Belch
Introduction to Advertising and Promotion: An Integrated Marketing Communications Approach, 2/e

Bernhardt & Kinnear
Cases in Marketing Management, 6/e

Bonoma & Kosnik
Marketing Management: Text & Cases, 1/e

Boyd & Walker
Marketing Management: A Strategic Approach, 1/e

Boyd, Westfall & Stasch
Marketing Research: Text and Cases, 7/e

Burstiner
Basic Retailing, 2/e

Cadotte
The Market Place: A Strategic Marketing Simulation, 1/e

Cateora
International Marketing, 8/e

Churchill, Ford & Walker
Sales Force Management, 4/e

Cole
Consumer and Commercial Credit Management, 9/e

Cravens
Strategic Marketing, 4/e

Cravens & Lamb
Strategic Marketing Management Cases, 4/e

Crawford
New Products Management, 4/e

Dillon, Madden & Firtle
Essentials of Marketing Research, 1/e

Dillon, Madden & Firtle
Marketing Research in a Marketing Environment, 3/e

Engel, Warshaw & Kinnear
Promotional Strategy, 8/e

Faria, Nulsen & Roussos
Compete, 4/e

Futrell
ABC's of Selling, 4/e

Futrell
Fundamentals of Selling, 4/e

Hawkins, Best & Coney
Consumer Behavior, 5/e

Kerin, Hartley, Rudelius & Berkowitz
Marketing, 4/e

Lambert & Stock
Strategic Logistics Management, 3/e

Lehmann
Market Research and Analysis, 3/e

Lehmann & Winer
Analysis for Marketing Planning, 3/e

Lehmann & Winer
Product Management, 1/e

Levy & Weitz
Retailing Management, 1/e

Mason, Mayer & Wilkinson
Modern Retailing, 6/e

Mason, Mayer & Ezell
Retailing, 5/e

Mason & Perreault
The Marketing Game!, 2/e

McCarthy & Perreault
Basic Marketing: A Global-Managerial Approach, 11/e

McCarthy & Perreault
Essentials of Marketing: A Global-Managerial Approach, 6/e

Patton
Sales Sim, 1/e

Peter & Donnelly
A Preface to Marketing Management, 6/e

Peter & Donnelly
Marketing Management: Knowledge and Skills, 3/e

Peter & Olson
Consumer Behavior and Marketing Strategy, 3/e

Peter & Olson
Understanding Consumer Behavior, 1/e

Quelch & Farris
Cases in Advertising and Promotion Management, 4/e

Quelch, Dolan & Kosnik
Marketing Management: Text & Cases, 1/e

Smith & Quelch
Ethics in Marketing, 1/e

Stanton, Buskirk & Spiro
Management of a Sales Force, 8/e

Thompson & Stappenbeck
The Marketing Strategy Game, 1/e

Walker, Boyd & Larréché
Marketing Strategy: Planning and Implementation, 1/e

Weitz, Castleberry & Tanner
Selling: Building and Partnerships, 1/e

CASES IN EUROPEAN MARKETING MANAGEMENT

John A. Quelch
Harvard University

Kamran Kashani
and
Sandra Vandermerwe
International Institute for Management Development

Irwin
McGraw-Hill

Boston, Massachusetts   Burr Ridge, Illinois   Dubuque, Iowa
Madison, Wisconsin   New York, New York   San Francisco, California   St. Louis, Missouri

Irwin/McGraw-Hill

A Division of The **McGraw·Hill** *Companies*

Executive editor: Rob Zwettler
Editorial assistant: Geri L. Smith
Project editor: Mary Conzachi
Production manager: Diane Palmer
Designer: Mercedes Santos
Art manager: Kim Meriwether
Compositor: Bi-Comp, Inc.
Typeface: 10/12 Times Roman
Printer: R. R. Donnelley & Sons Company

Library of Congress Cataloging-in-Publication Data

Cases in European marketing management / John A. Quelch, Kamran
  Kashani, and Sandra Vandermerwe.
      p.   cm.—(Irwin series in marketing)
   ISBN 0-256-15722-7
      1. Marketing—Europe—Case studies.   2. Marketing—Europe-
-Management—Case studies.   3. Marketing research—Europe—Case
studies.   I. Quelch, John A.   II. Kashani, Kamran.
III. Vandermerwe, Sandra.   IV. Series.
HF5415.12.E8C37   1994
658.8′0094—dc20   93–41069

Printed in the United States of America
  4 5 6 7 8 9 0 DO 1 0 9 8

PREFACE

This book represents a collaboration between faculty at two leading business schools, which have long been at the forefront of developing field-based case studies that illustrate important management problems and decision-making. Given the ever-increasing interest in management education in Europe, both among executives and on university campuses, we believe that this compilation of well-crafted, challenging case studies on marketing problems in Europe is especially timely. In addition, the interest in nondomestic cases for the US market has increased dramatically in recent years. The book should be of interest as a companion volume to those instructors wishing to offer nondomestic cases for courses in marketing management, marketing strategy, or global marketing.

Books are rarely the product of a single individual. Ideas, thoughts and suggestions from many sources all contribute to ultimately shaping a final product. With casebooks, this is even more true. Cases would not be possible without the close cooperation between industry and academia. For us, these relationships have been forged over the years and we are extremely grateful to those executives who have so generously shared with us their time, insights and experiences. It is their "real-life" marketing challenges in the diverse and increasingly competitive European markets that we have attempted to capture in this compendium so as to provide a practical setting for the understanding, learning and application of sound managerial principles across a variety of situations.

Cases demonstrate principles continuously defined, challenged and refined in business school classrooms. For their thoughts and comments, we would like to extend our gratitude to our colleagues who have read through and taught these cases, and so enriched them as learning vehicles. We also wish to thank our faculty colleagues at Harvard Business School, IMD and elsewhere for permitting us to use case studies they prepared. They include Robert Buzzell (Harvard Business School), Michele Costabile (SDA Bocconi, Italy), Kyoichi Ikeo (Keio Business School), Ilkka Lipasti (formerly Helsinki University of Technology), Jon Martinez (Universidad Adolfo Ibanez, Chile), Jose Luis Nueno (IESE, Spain) and Dominique Turpin (IMD). In addition, our thanks goes to our research assistants who worked long and hard to gather and compile information and prepare drafts of the cases themselves. These include, at IMD, Alex Bloom, James Henderson, Robert Howard, and Marika Taishoff; and, at Harvard Business School, Greg Conley, Nathalie Laidler, Geoffrey Smith, Susan Smith, and Julie Yao.

Finally, we wish to thank Rob Zwettler and Geri Smith at Richard D. Irwin for their enthusiasm and editorial support.

John Quelch   **Boston, Massachusetts**
Kamran Kashani   **Lausanne, Switzerland**
Sandra Vandermerwe   **Lausanne, Switzerland**

CONTENTS

SECTION IV

PRODUCT POLICY

PART I THE MARKETING MIX

INTRODUCTION

1

THE SKISAILER

Early in 1987, David Varilek was given the bad news about the worldwide sales of his invention, the Skisailer. The management at Mistral, the company which had invested in David's innovation, informed him that the first-year sales of Skisailer had failed to match the target and that the future of the product was in doubt. Only 708 Skisailers had been sold in the first season the product was on sale. Mistral, who manufactured and marketed the product worldwide, had already invested more than half a million dollars in the project. The management was seriously considering dropping the product from its line next year.

Realizing that such an initial setback could jeopardize the future of his four-year-old invention, in March 1987 David asked a group of MBA students at a leading international school of management in Switzerland to study the market potential for Skisailer and recommend what needed to be done to revive sales. The students had recently completed the first phase of the project. They had presented David with their findings, and the 23-year-old inventor was reviewing the information.

The Invention

Skisailer was based on a concept that combined downhill skiing and windsurfing in a new sport: skisailing. As a Swiss native, David Varilek considered himself "born on skis." However, he had always been frustrated by not being able to ski on the flat snow fields that surrounded his home in the winter season.

In 1983, in his own garage, David invented a connection bar which could be fixed onto regular skis while still allowing them to be directed with great flexibil-

---

This case was written by Professors Dominique Turpin and Kamran Kashani. Copyright © 1991 by the International Institute for Management Development (IMD), Lausanne, Switzerland. Not to be used or reproduced without permission. IMD case 396

ity. A windsurfing rig, consisting of a connecting bar and a sail, could then be installed on the connection bar, and, with enough wind, flat snow surfaces could become great fun for skiing. The idea was subsequently patented under the Swiss law. A major feature of the invention was that the Skisailer's unique design also allowed "windskiers" to use regular downhill skis and almost any type of wind-

EXHIBIT 1

Illustration of Skisailer from product brochure

The SKISAILER™

Invented by David Varilek and developed in conjunction
with Mistral Windsurfing AG, Bassersdorf, Switzerland

Contact

Mistral Windsurfing A.G.
CH - 8303 Bassersdorf/Zürich
Switzerland
Telephone 01/836-8922
Telex 59 266 MWAG CH

Photos: O.Pfeiffer - F.Bertin

EXHIBIT 1 (*continued*)

FREEDOM: With the Skisailer, Mistral has developed the ultimate marriage of wind and snow, ski and sail. All the thrills of skiing without the need of mountains or ski-lift passes. More sport and pleasure per hour invested. The boring, grey, winter afternoons, when all you can do is gaze at surf photos in the magazines and remember the sunny days on your funboard, are over. Mistral Skisailer—That's funboard surfing in the snow and ski-holidays hanging on the boom.

EASE: Once you have fixed the small rails to your skis in front of the toe-bindings, you are free at any time to "fly" across the snow-covered countryside, simple and easy to assemble, the equipment stores neatly in a back-pack, leaving you free to ski should you wish to switch from wind-power to gravity-power.

FUNCTION: The principal advantages of the Skisailer derive from the basic concept and the light, strong construction of the equipment. The multidirectional freedom of movement of the mast-foot plate allows for all normal ski manoevers (edging, turning etc.) while the optimum positioning of the mast in relation to the skier allows the manoevers of sailboarding (jibing, jumping, snow-starts!).

SAFETY: There is no limit to your striving for always more speed, longer jumps and more radical manoevers. The security of the sport is assured by the triple release security system: the conventional ski bindings, the mast-foot plate connectors and the mast-foot.

FREEDOM: Mit dem Skisailer lässt Mistral den Traum vom Windsurfen im Pulverschnee Wahrheit werden. Vergessen Sie endlose Warteschlangen am Lift und überfüllte Pisten. Die langweiligen, grauen Winternachmittage, an denen die Erinnerungen an die Surferlebnisse des letzten Sommers nur noch beim Betrachten der Fotos in den Magazinen wach werden, sind vorbei. Mistral Skisailer—Fundboardfahren im Pulverschnee, Skivergnügen am Gabelbaum.

IT'S SO EASY: Montieren Sie einfach die Funktionsteile vor Ihrer Skibindung. Und los geht's: Snowstart, Raumshots über verschneite Wiesen, Take-Off an einer Bodenwelle, weiche Landung, Slalom zwischen den Schneeflocken, Duck-Jibe, . . . Hawaii ist vergessen. Wenn der Wind nachlässt, schalten Sie um von Windkraft auf Schwerkraft, und gehen normal skifahren. Die nicht mehr benötigten Teile passen in Ihren Rucksack.

THE CONCEPT: Der Vorteil des Mistral Skisailers liegt in der superleichten, robusten Konstruktion der Funktionselemente und in der Wirkungsweise des Prinzips. Die allseitige Bewegungsfreiheit der Mastfussplatte ermöglicht Kanteneinsatz und Schwungauslösung wie beim normalen Skilauf. Durch die optimale Positionierung des Riggs auf den Skiern, funktionieren die Funboardmanöver im Schnee bald genauso gut wie auf dem Wasser.

SAFETY FIRST: Ihrem Drang nach immer mehr Speed, noch weiteren Sprüngen und noch heisseren Manövern können Sie freien Lauf lassen. Selbst bei spektakulären Stürzen schützt Sie ein dreifaches Sicherheitssystem: Ihre Skibindung, der Mastfuss und die Mastfussplatten-Verbinder sind auslösende Konstruktionselemente.

LIBERTE: Avec le Skisailer, Mistral réalise enfin le mariage du vent et de la neige, du ski et de la voile. Tous les avantages du ski, sans les inconvénients de la foule et des remontées mécaniques, donnent un rapport plaisir/temps investi incomparable. Fini l'ennui des gris après-midi d'hiver où la seule distraction était de lire des magazines de surf et de se souvenir. Le Skisailer de Mistral c'est du funboard sur neige, des vacances d'hiver accroché au wishbone.

FACILITE: Une fois les petits rails de fixation installés à l'avant des butées, plus rien ne peut vous empêcher de "voler" à travers les plaines enneigées, de jiber sur une bosse de neige ou si le vent vous lâche, de ranger votre matériel dans un sac à dos et de skier comme tout le monde.

EXHIBIT 1 (*concluded*)

TECHNICITE: La conception mème du Skisailer en est son atout majeur. Les articulations multidirectionnelles de la plaque de soutien du mât permettent une totale liberté de mouvement des skis (prise de carre, virage etc . . .). D'autre part, la position optimale du mât sur les skis permet de faire toutes les manoeuvres de funboard (snow starts, jibes, sauts).

SECURITE: Celle-ci est assurée en cas de choc par un déclanchement à trois niveaux: aux fixations de ski conventionnelles, aux articulations de la plaque de soutien et au pied de mât. Ainsi toutes craintes dissipées, vos progrès en saut, vitesse et manoeuvres seront encore plus rapides.

surfing rig, an innovation that limited the buyer's expense. The connection bar and the sail were easy to install. Lateral clamps used for attaching the connection bar to the skis did not damage them in any way except for small grooves on the side of each ski. Only 5 cm (2 inches) of the ski's length were held rigid, and the rest retained normal flexibility. Safety had also been an important consideration when developing the Skisailer; three self-releasing safety mechanisms were installed on the product. (Refer to Exhibit 1 for an illustration of the Skisailer.)

The Skisailer could be used on either smooth slopes or flat surfaces. The ideal surface for skisailing was on the kind of hard-packed snow usually found on groomed ski slopes, but the Skisailer could also be used on ice where it could achieve speeds of up to 100 km/h.[1] Skisailing in deep snow or slightly uphill required stronger wind. For use at high speeds, a safety helmet was recommended.

According to David Varilek, skisailing was as much fun as windsurfing even though it had to be done in cold weather. "For identical sensations, skisailing is easier to learn and handle than windsurfing," David claimed. "You can get on and get off the Skisailer easily, and you are always on your feet. Another great thing with the Skisailer is that you can take advantage of the terrain to perform the same kind of loopings as on sea waves. The Skisailer is a great vehicle for discovering variety in the surroundings."

Mistral Windsurfing AG

In 1987, Mistral Windsurfing AG was a company affiliated with the ADIA Group. ADIA, a $1 billion conglomerate with headquarters in Lausanne, Switzerland, had its activities centered around ADIA Interim, a company providing temporary personnel to companies around the world.

In 1980, ADIA had acquired Mistral as part of its diversification strategy. The acquisition was seen as an opportunity to enter a rapidly growing industry. Consistency in marketing and product policy over the past 10 years had made Mistral a leader in the worldwide windsurfing industry. This success was grounded in technological competence, permanent innovation, high quality standards, a

---

[1] 1 kilometer = .62 mile.

selective international distribution policy, and strong financial backing. Thus, in a fiercely competitive market for windsurfing equipment, characterized by the rise and fall of brands and manufacturers, Mistral was occupying a leading position. To Martin Pestalozzi, the president of ADIA, the Skisailer represented a good opportunity to extend Mistral's product line, at a time when Mistral management was increasingly concerned about the future of the windsurf market.

Mistral and the Windsurf Market

The fathers of the modern windsurf were two Californians, Hoyle Schweitzer and James Drake, who had developed the concept and registered the Windsurfer brand. They had applied for and received a patent in 1970 for their device, which was a cross between a surfboard and a sailboat.

In the early 1970s, Schweitzer bought out Drake and developed his firm, Windsurfing International, from a living-room operation into a multimillion-dollar corporation with branches in six countries. Due to its North American patents, Windsurfing International was able to hold a virtual monopoly in the United States and Canada until 1979, when a number of other firms entered the market.

Meanwhile, competition in the European windsurfing equipment market was years ahead of North America. First introduced to the European market by Ten Cate, a Dutch firm, windsurfing enjoyed an unprecedented growth, particularly in France and Germany. Even as the industry matured in the mid-1980s, it maintained growth in terms of dollar volume though not in units. Interest in windsurfing had grown from a small pool of enthusiasts to a large and growing population, an estimated 2–3 million people internationally.

Established in 1976 in Bassersdorf near Zurich (Switzerland), Mistral rapidly won an international reputation among windsurfers. Its success was enhanced by two promotional strategies. First, from the start, Mistral had signed up Robby Naish, a young Californian who had won all the major distinctions and titles in this sport. Using Mistral equipment, Robby Naish had become the 1977 World Champion at age 12 and had dominated this sport ever since. In 1986, he won the world title for the 10th time in a row. Second, Mistral had promoted its brand by supplying several hundred windsurfs free of charge to such leisure organizations as Club Méditerranée that gave the brand visibility around the world.

Mistral also enjoyed an advantage over other windsurf manufacturers by concentrating on the upper price and quality range of the market. Worldwide, Mistral's equipment was considered the best. Robby Naish's name and the high quality and reliability of Mistral's products had helped build an extensive network of distributors in 30 countries. In 1980, the company had its own subsidiary in the United States where it generated about one-third of its global sales and market share. Mistral was also directly represented in a number of European countries such as France, Germany, and the Benelux. For the rest of the world, Mistral used exclusive agents who were responsible for selling Mistral products in specific regions.

Recent Market Developments in Windsurfing

Recently, a number of factors had combined to dampen the sales of windsurfs in the US market. Patent infringement fights had led to the forced withdrawal of Bic and Tiga, both French manufacturers, from the market. With total sales of 16,000 units, the two companies were among the major brands in the United States. Meanwhile, a number of European manufacturers had gone bankrupt, thus reducing even further the supply of and marketing expenditures on windsurfing equipment. Market saturation had also contributed to the decline of sales from 73,000 units in 1985 to 62,000 in 1986.

In Europe, where windsurfing had grown at spectacular rates over the years, the market was showing the signs of a slowdown. According to the French market research group ENERGY, windsurfing equipment sales in France had risen from less than 600 units in 1974 to more than 115,000 units in early 1980s. However, cool weather conditions as well as general market saturation had reduced French sales to 65,000 units in 1986. In Germany, the second largest market after France, sales had also declined to below 60,000 units from the high levels of early 1980s. Sales had leveled off in Italy at around 35,000 units, in Holland at 45,000 units, and in Switzerland at 15,000 units.

European sales were dominated by European brands. In France, for example, Bic and Tiga together accounted for 45,000 sales. Mistral was the top imported brand. In Germany, Klepper was the leading local brand; Mistral was a distant fourth in market share. In 1986, the distribution of Mistral's global sales of 45,620 units was: the United States, 25%; Europe, 30%; and the rest of the world, 45%. Windsurfing equipment accounted for 60% of the company's $52 million sales, while the rest was divided between sportswear (20%) and spare parts and accessories (20%).

The Skisailer and Mistral's Diversification Policy

Mistral Windsurfing AG had contacted David Varilek at the beginning of 1984 after ADIA management learned about the Skisailer from a four-page article in a major Swiss magazine. David Varilek was interested in establishing a relationship with Mistral, as the company was the world leader in windsurfing equipment.

The Skisailer seemed an appropriate product diversification for Mistral. The Skisailer could also fit in with the new line of winter sportswear and other ski-related products that Mistral's management was planning to develop. Mistral had full support from ADIA to launch the project.

In the spring of 1984, a contract for development, manufacturing, and distribution of the Skisailer was formally signed between David Varilek and Mistral. For the duration of the agreement, all Skisailer patent and trademark rights would be transferred to Mistral, but David would serve as technical adviser to the company and would receive in return a 2% royalty on sales. It was also agreed that David would demonstrate the Skisailer in competitions and exhibitions where Mistral was participating. Should total sales fall short of 5,000 units by the end of 1986, either party could terminate the agreement, with trademarks and patents reverting back to David Varilek. Mistral could also counter any competitive offer made to David, a so-called "first right of refusal."

Introducing the Skisailer

During the summer of 1984, two prototypes of the Skisailer were developed at Mistral for presentation in November at ISPO, the largest European sports exhibition, held annually in Munich, Germany. Between May and November 1984, the engineers developed several innovations that were added to the Skisailer. For example, the connecting bar and mounting blocks were strengthened to resist shocks and low temperatures. The equipment was also modified to accommodate the Mistral windsurf sailing rig.

In Munich at ISPO, the Skisailer was widely acclaimed as a truly innovative product which would certainly win public enthusiasm. However, at this early stage of development, the product still lacked promotional support. No pamphlet, video, or pictures had been developed to present the product and educate potential users. David thought that the pictures used to introduce the product to Mistral's distributors were not attractive enough to trigger interest and buying. Nevertheless, some distributors liked the product and placed immediate orders.

The formal launch of Skisailer got under way in 1986. Mistral produced 2,000 Skisailers—consisting of a mast foot, sail (available from its standard windsurf line), and the connecting bar. They were to be distributed worldwide through the company's network of wholesalers and independent sports shops in large and medium-sized cities. For example, in Lausanne, Switzerland, a city of 250,000 inhabitants with 30 ski shops and three windsurf equipment stores, Skisailer was sold in three locations. Of the three stores, two specialized in ski equipment and the third sold windsurfing products.

Skisailer was priced $410 at retail; the price included the bar connection and its mounting blocks, but excluded the sail and mast—which cost an additional $590. Retail margins on the Skisailer and its rig were set at 35%. The wholesale margins were also 35%. Skisailer cost Mistral $85 per unit to produce and ship to distributors; the cost for the sailing rig was around $200.

It seemed to David that the 1986 promotional budget of $15,000 set for Skisailer was too low. Mistral management had already turned down a $35,000 proposal from David to produce a promotional video showing Skisailer in action. Nevertheless, David decided to arrange for the shooting of such a video on his own at Mammoth Lake, California. Mistral later refunded David the $10,000 which the video had cost him.

As of early 1987, Mistral had invested more than half a million dollars in Skisailer:

Development Costs	
Engineering and tooling	$214,000
Other costs	74,000
	$288,000
Inventory—Assembled and Spares	
At central warehouse	$180,000
At distributors	68,000
	$248,000
Total	**$536,000**

Market Research Findings

Because of his concern about the future of the Skisailer, David had commissioned the group of MBA students to study the global market for Skisailer and report on their findings. By early fall, the students had completed the first phase of their study, which dealt with estimating the market potential for Skisailer; competing products; ski market developments; and a survey of buyers, retailers, and wholesalers. A summary of the findings follows.

Potential Market

Based on interviews with buyers of the Skisailer, the team had learned that the potential customers were likely to be those who did both skiing and windsurfing. Building on industry reports suggesting a total worldwide population of 2 million windsurfers and 30 million skiers, the team estimated that a maximum of 60% of windsurfers, or a total of 1.2 million individuals, were also skiers. The "realizable market" for the Skisailer, according to the MBA students, was far below this maximum, however. They identified at least four "filters" that together reduced the realizable market potential to a fraction of the maximum.

Filter 1: Customer Type.   As a relatively new sport, Skisailer appealed to a group of enthusiasts whom the MBA students referred to as "innovators." Their study suggested that these buyers were in the 15–25 age bracket, liked sports but, for the most part, could not afford the price tag of the Skisailer. The next most likely group of buyers, called "early adopters," were older, less sporty, and more image conscious. For this segment, price was not a major factor. The team believed that sufficient penetration of the first segment was necessary before the second group showed any interest in the new product.

Filter 2: Location.   Users of the Skisailer reported that ideal skisailing conditions, such as flat ice or snow-covered fields, were not always accessible. This location factor, the team believed, tended to reduce the potential for the product.

Filter 3: Climate.   Climate, according to the MBA students, was another inhibiting factor. The Skisailer required not only suitable snow or ice, but also a good wind. The minimum required wind speed was around 20 km/h. The study identified a number of regions as meeting both the needed snow and wind conditions: Scandinavia and central Europe, certain parts of North America, and parts of southern Australia.

Filter 4: Competing Products.   Four similar products were identified, but, according to the student report, all lacked brand image, wide distribution, and product sophistication. Although information on competing products was scanty, the students had assembled the following information from different sources:

Brand (Origin)	Retail Price	Total Units Sold	Main Sales Area
Winterboard (Finland)	$395	4,000	Finland, United States
Ski Sailer (Australia)	90	3,500	Australia, United States
ArticSail (Canada)	285	3,000	Canada, United States
Ski Sailer (United States)	220	300	United States

Based on their initial estimate of the maximum size of the potential market, as well as the limiting effects of the four "filters," the students arrived at an estimate of 20,000 units as the total realizable market for Skisailer. This volume, they believed, could grow by as much as 10% per year. (Refer to Exhibit 2 for an estimate of the market potential and Exhibit 3 for the levels of sales the students believed Skisailer could achieve over the next five years.)

EXHIBIT 2

Skisailer market potential

Market	Size	%	Filters
Potential market	1.2 million	100%	• Customer type
Available market	800K	66%	• Location • Climate
Qualified market	80K	7%	• Indirect competition (monoski, skates, etc.)
Served market	40K	3.5%	• Direct competition (Winterboard, Articsail, etc.)
Realizable market	20K	1.7%	• Customer type

SOURCE: MBA Student Report.

EXHIBIT 3

Skisailer achievable sales estimate

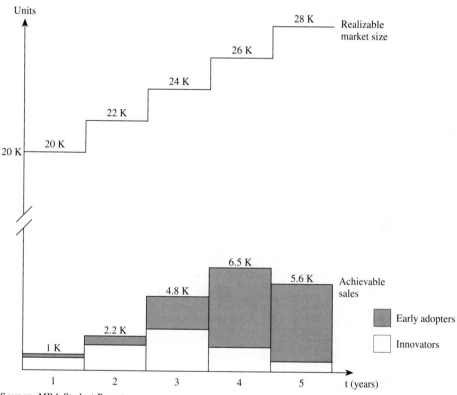

SOURCE: MBA Student Report.

Competing Products

Winterboard.   Winterboard, a light windsurfing board with skis, had been invented in Finland. It could be used on both ice and snow, and its performance was said to be impressive. Some rated the Winterboard as the best performing windski after the Skisailer. In terms of sales, Winterboard had been the most successful windski product. Over the last five years, 4,000 units had been sold, mainly in Scandinavia and the United States, in regular sports shops. Winterboard was being sold at a retail price of $395, excluding the sailing rig. Retail margins were at 40%. The skis were already integrated into the board and did not need to be purchased as an extra.

According to the research team, Winterboard's management believed that prices, retail margins, and advertising expenditures were relatively unimportant in their marketing strategy. The key to success was organizing events, as people wanted sportive social gathering on weekends in the winter. When they had to go out snowsailing in the cold by themselves, they quickly lost interest.

Australian-made Ski Sailer.   This product was essentially a simple bar with a mast foot on it which could be attached to normal ski boots and used with either conventional skis or roller skates. The Ski Sailer had an equalizing slide and joint mechanism, so maneuvers such as parallel turns, jump turns, and snowplowing were possible. Any sailing rig could be fitted to the Ski Sailer's mast post.

The US distributor for this product reported cumulative sales of about 3,000 units (30% through ski shops, 70% through surf shops) at a retail price of $90 each. But he admitted that he had lost interest in the product when he realized that only customers who were tough and resistant to the cold enjoyed windsurfing in the wintertime. This meant a much smaller customer base than for his other leisure/sportswear products.

ArticSail Board.   This product was essentially a W-shaped surfboard for use on snow, ice, or water. It was distributed by Plastiques LPA Ltd. in Mansonville, Quebec, Canada, approximately 50 miles from the US–Canadian border.

The ArticSail was especially designed for snow and ice, but it could also be used on water, in which case the rear filler plates would be replaced by two ailerons, also supplied with the board. Adjustable footstraps, included with the board, also had to be repositioned for use on water. The product was made of a special plastic, usable at both normal and very low temperatures. The producer warned users to watch for objects which could damage the underside of the sled.

The company reported a cumulative sales of approximately 3,000 units (600 estimated for the winter of 1987–88), mostly in Canada at a retail price of $285 (including a 38% retail margin). Promotion expenses were about 15% on Canadian and US sales, mainly spent on a two-man team demonstrating at skisailing resorts.

American-made Ski Sailer.   Yet another Ski Sailer had been invented by a young Californian, Carl Meinberg. The American Ski Sailer also used a small board mounted on skis and was similar to the product developed by David Varilek. On his own, the inventor had sold about 50 Ski Sailers retailing at $220 each. During the winter season, Carl Meinberg toured a number of ski resorts, demonstrating the Ski Sailer; he spent the rest of the year selling his invention.

Recent Developments in the World Ski Market

As background to their study, the research team also obtained information on the ski market. (The 1986 sales of downhill, also called Alpine, and cross-country skis are given in Exhibit 4.)

The total world Alpine skiing population was estimated at 30 million people in 1987. Competition in the ski market was intensive, and production capacity exceeded demand by an estimated 25–30% in 1987. Prices for skis were under pressure, and retailers used discounts to build traffic. Retail profits were mostly made on sales of accessories and skiwear.

In distribution, specialty shops were losing market share to the large chains. Production was concentrated, with seven manufacturers controlling 80% of the market. The falling exchange rate for the US dollar had put the large European producers such as Fischer and Kneissel at a disadvantage in the US market.

Exhibit 4   World Market of Alpine and Cross-Country Skis (1985–86 Season)

	Pairs Sold
Alpine Ski Sales	
Austria, Switzerland, Germany	1,450,000
Rest of Europe	1,550,000
United States and Canada	1,600,000
Japan	1,100,000
Other countries	300,000
Total	6,000,000
Cross-Country Ski Sales	
Austria, Switzerland, Germany	700,000
Scandinavia	800,000
Rest of Europe	400,000
United States and Canada	750,000
Other countries	150,000
Total	2,800,000

Marketing skis depended heavily on successes in world championships and the image associated with the winning skis. In the mid-1980s, customers in the United States appeared to be losing interest in skiing, but these signs had not been observed in Europe and Japan, where the sport remained popular at a stable level.

A new innovation in skiing was the snowboard, a product with increasing popularity among younger customers. A snowboard was essentially a single large ski with two ski bindings positioned in a similar way as the footstraps on a windsurf.

The board had been available in the United States for many years, but had only recently been introduced in Europe. Snowboard's worldwide sales had doubled every year, reaching an estimated 40,000 in the 1986 season. One US manufacturer, Burton, accounted for 50% of the market. Many manufacturers of winter products had taken advantage of the opportunity and had started producing their own versions of the snowboard. The product was very popular in the European distribution channels, and expectations for further growth were high.

Buyers' Survey

The research team had interviewed a small number of Skisailer customers in Germany, Austria, the Benelux countries, the United States, and Canada. Highlights of their comments on the advantages and disadvantages of the Skisailer were:

Advantages of the Product

- Sure, skisurfing in winter is great; it's a lot of fun.
- You can do quick maneuvers, nice turns, beautiful power turns, and fast changes of the grips. It [the Skisailer] gives a good opportunity to train

for windsurfing, as you have to drive the way you surf—with the pressure on the inner ski.

- I did not have any problem with turns.
- It is not difficult to learn if you have some feeling for sailing.
- It simulates surfing in your backyard.
- It is the right device if you want to do something on Sunday afternoon (with no time to drive somewhere in your car).
- Fun, different, new, good.
- It is the only thing with a mountain touch that you can use on the plain.
- It turns. That makes it much more fun than the other products on the market. You can do jives, curve jives, jumps . . . It is close to sailing a shore boat . . . It's a lot of fun.
- If the conditions are ideal, it's a lot of fun.

Disadvantages of the Product

- The feet get twisted; sailing on the wind requires exceptional twisting of the legs and knees.
- Both of the white caps at the end of the bar came off, and it was virtually impossible to get spare parts.
- Difficult in heavy snow.
- Difficult to find the perfect conditions.
- You use it three or four times a season. For this, the price is too high.
- It is uncomfortable to use. You have to loosen up your boots; otherwise the rim of the shoe cuts into your twisted leg.
- If the snow is too deep, you cannot use it. What you want is strong wind.
- The price is too high.
- My problem is that there is hardly any wind in winter.
- In the beginning, I was getting stiff in the unnatural position and my knees hurt, but later I got more relaxed and with time you have a lot of fun.
- In midwinter, it is too cold to use it; spring is ideal.

Retailers' Opinions of the Mistral Skisailer

A dozen retailers of the Skisailer—in Germany, Canada, Austria, and France— were also surveyed. Highlights of their comments were as follows:

Advantages of the Product

- You could sell a lot of them in the first year, but I do not see it as the absolute "barnstormer."
- It is a first-year novelty.
- It is a lot of fun in the snow . . . and for people with a lot of money. It is a new gimmick.
- It combines two favorite sports . . . skiing and windsurfing.

- It is better than all self-built products . . . You have full movability.
- Easy to use. It is an original idea.
- You can use your ski; it is flexible and easy to store.
- Very thoroughly constructed, very stable.

Disadvantages of the Product

- Unhappy product. Usable only under specific weather conditions.
- It is only a fad.
- You just don't drive with your ski to a lake and try it on the ice.
- Maybe it sells better in a winter shop.
- Your position on the skis is abnormal—the snowboard is a better alternative.
- We do not think that it will be a fast-turning product . . .
- Impossible to sell—nobody tried it.
- In my environment, there is no space to do it, no lakes, no fields.
- For a backyard product, the price is too high. Even Mistral's good image doesn't help. Maybe this will change if the product is better known.
- Customers watched the video with enthusiasm, but when they learned the price, enthusiasm was nil. We are offering our last piece now at a discount of 40%.
- If you ski and windsurf, your hobbies cost you a lot of money. Often the early user is the sportive freak with a low income. How will you convince him about the product?

Distributors' Comments

The research team interviewed Mistral distributors in 10 different countries in Europe and North America. Highlights of comments from five distributors were:

- We first learned about the Skisailer at ISPO in Munich and ordered some.
- From Mistral we got some folders and the video. If you see it on the video, you want to use the Skisailer right away.
- We did not support the retailers very much because we felt that the Skisailer's marketing was not done professionally from the beginning. For instance, Skisailer deliveries were late.
- The product would have potential if the price were lower and the promotion were done professionally all the way through.
- We bought the Skisailer, which is good for use in our winter climate, after Mistral contacted us in 1985.
- The product is expensive and not really functional.
- Promotion was not good at all, only a few folders and a video which was not free of charge. When there were product breakdowns, spare parts were not available.

- A Finnish competitor now has captured the market with a product that looks like a surfboard with two skis fitted into it. We have the right places for skisailing here!
- We used all our contacts and spent approximately $7,500 in mid-1987 to promote this product on television.
- The retail price is too high for a product to be used only a few weekends in the winter.
- The snowboard, especially made for surfing on ski slopes, is much more fashionable.
- Surf and ski shops make higher margins on clothing and accessories that are sold in larger quantities.
- You don't create a product first and then look for the market; this is the wrong way around. The Skisailer is more a product for Scandinavia and similar regions in America or Canada.

France

- We didn't know the product but found the demonstration film to be convincing. Therefore, we organized ski resort demonstrations in the French Alps at racing events where there are many spectators. We also pushed about 40 Skisailers in several retail shops.
- For this product, finding suitable locations where you can have a training session with wind and snow is necessary.
- We estimate that the retailers have sold about half their inventory, but we do not want to get more involved and have the rest sent back to us. Retailers are looking for customer demand, which is lacking.

Canada

- I cannot see further sales of the Skisailer without more product support. At low temperatures the rubber joints failed, but when we asked for replacements, there was no reply from Mistral. In the end, we had to strip other Skisailers to get the spare parts.
- We have good skisailing conditions (in South Ontario/Quebec) and a group of interested enthusiasts here. The product has been promoted to thousands of people! The folder and video are very good.
- On a trade show in Toronto, the product was well received except for the price, which is a problem.

Conclusion

In reviewing the research team's report, David was searching for clues which could explain the Skisailer's poor performance in its first selling season. Was it the product design which needed further refinement? Or the Skisailer's price which was perceived by some as being high? Was the absence of high promotional support, which he had always suspected to be a problem, a key factor? Or maybe Mistral's selective distribution was the core issue? What else could explain why his invention had failed to match everybody's expectations?

An additional piece of information had heightened the need for immediate action. David had just received the final sales and inventory figures for the Skisailer from Mistral—while 708 units had been sold to the trade, only 80 units had been bought at retail:

	Unit Sales		
Country	*To Distributors*	*To Retailers*	*To End Users*
United States/Canada	233	98	45
Germany	250	50	10
Switzerland	42	30	1
France	56	40	20
Benelux	60	0	0
Others	67	12	4
Total shipped	708	230	80

David knew that Mistral management was about to review the future of the Skisailer. He feared that without a convincing analysis and action plan from him, the Skisailer would be dropped from Mistral's line. He was therefore impatiently waiting for the MBA research team's recommendations based on the data already collected.

2

GALLO RICE

In March 1992, Sig. Cesare Preve, managing director of F&P Gruppo, marketer of the Gallo brand of rice, was reviewing his company's current market position. Specifically, he was evaluating how to penetrate further the retail rice markets in three countries: Italy, where the Gallo brand had been present for over a century and held a 21% volume share; Argentina, where Gallo had been established in 1905 and held a 17.5% volume share; and Poland, where Gallo had been distributed in small quantities for three years and held less than a 1% volume share in 1992.

Preve wondered what experience, information, and insights gained in one market could be transferred to other markets and where to focus management time and effort. Should the company attempt to consolidate its position in large, mature, slow-growth markets, or should the newer high-growth-potential markets receive a higher proportion of managerial time and marketing effort in the future? In order to assess the marketing requirements of each country and the potential sharing of experience across markets, Preve compiled a summary of the comparative country data. See Table A.

Company Background

Focused on the production of value-added rice, F&P Gruppo described itself as "the rice specialist" and was one of only a few companies in the world involved in the entire process from growing and milling to the packaging and marketing of branded rice. The company added value through research and development of new and improved strains of high-quality rice, proprietary manufacturing pro-

This case was prepared by Research Associate Nathalie Laidler under the direction of Professor John Quelch. Copyright © 1993 by the President and Fellows of Harvard College. Harvard Business School Case 563-018.

TABLE A   Market Characteristics of Italy, Argentina, and Poland (1990)

	Italy	*Argentina*	*Poland*
Population (millions)	57.7	32.3	38.4
Age distribution: 0–14, 15–59, 60+	18%, 63%, 19%	30%, 57%, 13%	26%, 60%, 14%
Percentage urban population	67%	85%	60%
Annual population growth	0.1%	1.0%	0.4%
GNP per capita	$15,652	$2,134	$2,500
Per capita expenditures on food	$2,170	$465	$256
GDP breakdown: agricultural, industrial, services	4%, 33%, 63%	13%, 41%, 45%	14%, 36%, 50%
Inflation rate	6.5%	17%*	600%
Cereal imports (tons)	6,699	4	1,550
Rice is a major crop	Yes	Yes	No
Television set penetration	1 per 3.9 persons	1 per 4 persons	1 per 3.9 persons
Radio penetration	1 per 3.9 persons	1 per person	1 per 3.6 persons
Literacy rate	98%	92%	98%
Advertising expenditures per capita	$116	$13	N/A
Advertising expenditures: percentage breakdown by medium	Print = 59% TV = 35% Radio = 2.5% Cinema = 0.2% Outdoor = 3.3%	Print = 45% TV = 31.3% Radio = 8.8% Cinema = 0.8% Outdoor = 14.1%	N/A
Number of consumers per retail food outlet	182	1,318	724
Distribution concentration: percentage of retail sales through supermarkets	56%	56%	15%

* Argentina inflation rate estimated for first quarter 1992, down from 3,000% in 1989.

cesses, and packaging. Gallo had resisted the temptation to manufacture or market any food products other than rice. The goal of the company was to achieve market share leadership through bringing differentiated, higher margin products to an increasingly segmented marketplace. A higher percentage of the resulting profits were, in turn, reinvested in research and development. It was a company objective to ensure that 35% to 40% of total gross margin was derived from products that were not in the product line five years before.

F&P Gruppo was a private, family-owned company dating back five generations. It owned production facilities in Italy, Germany, Argentina, and Uruguay and sold throughout Europe and South America. The group comprised wholly owned subsidiaries in the above four countries as well as Switzerland and Brazil, plus a joint venture in the United Kingdom.

The Gallo brand name and Gallo rooster logo were used consistently across geographic markets and product lines. In 1991, Gallo marketed white rice, parboiled (partly boiled) rice, and brown rice. The company had also recently introduced dehydrated, quick-cooking rice and dehydrated mixes in many of its more developed markets. These branded, top-of-the-line products delivered to the company as much as 50 times the profit margin achievable through the sale of the same quantity of bulk white rice.

The Rice Industry

In 1991, world production of rice was around 500 million metric tons, and consumption, which varied significantly by geographic area, was around 350 million metric tons on a milled basis. Only 12 million tons were traded internationally.

There were two main strains of rice: Indica grains—long and thin, fluffy when cooked, and more popular in northern Europe; and Japonica grains—shorter and more absorbent, creamier when cooked, and more popular in southern Europe. In recent years, Spain and italy had increased their production of Indica rice; as a result, imports of rice into Europe had decreased.

Rice reached the consumer in many forms:

- Paddy rice was the raw material harvested from the field, with only primary cleaning and drying.
- Cargo rice resulted from an initial milling process, whereby the hulls (accounting for 20% of the raw rice weight) were removed.
- White rice was the product of the final milling process and could be refined to varying degrees.
- Brown rice was similarly milled, but the bran layer was retained on the kernel during the milling process.
- Parboiled (i.e., partly boiled) rice was a response to the consumer's desire for more convenience. Its production involved a special milling process, whereby paddy rice was soaked in hot water, cooked with steam pressure, and then dried. During this process, the starch was gelatinized such that the vitamins migrated into the interior of the grain. This made the rice grains harder and almost impossible to overcook, resulting in a nonsticking final product.
- Precooked or quick-cooking rice was an increasingly popular niche product, processed by a freeze-thaw method. Regular milled rice was soaked in water to increase moisture content, boiled, cooled quickly with cold water, then allowed to freeze and thaw slowly. The end result was a rice kernel that absorbed water more readily, thereby reducing the necessary cooking time.

Exhibit 1 shows the breakdown of rice consumption by end use and type in a typical developed country such as the United States. Domestic consumption, calculated from domestic production plus imports minus exports, included three primary use categories: processed food production (for breakfast cereals, for example); beer production; and direct food use. Of direct food use volume, most was eaten at home after purchase through food retailers. It was in this channel that branding of rice played an important role. Most retail rice sales were of basic milled white rice, with parboiled white rice being the second most important subcategory.

Gallo milled rice consistently earned the highest of six quality grades. In 1991, Gallo handled 200,000 tons of milled rice worldwide, valued at six times the average world crop price of cargo rice. In the 1980s, many other companies tried

EXHIBIT 1

Distribution of US milled rice volume, 1992

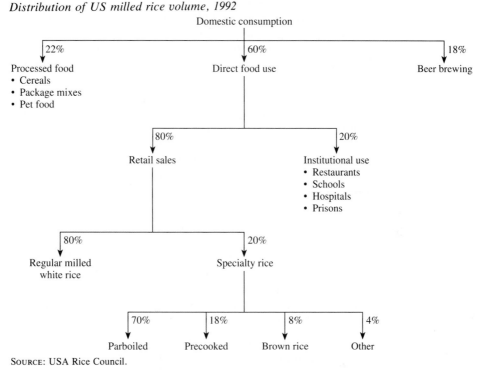

SOURCE: USA Rice Council.

to enter the market for value-added, branded rice products. Although this caused some price pressure, price-insensitive consumer segments were identified for certain higher value products such as brown rice and dehydrated risotto mixes (rice mixed with dehydrated ingredients such as peppers, mushroom, chicken, and spices).

Italy

Market Characteristics

Rice was a staple of the Italian diet. Used by 98% of the Italian population in 1991, per capita consumption averaged 5 kg[1] per annum. Some regional differences existed, with consumption being closer to 8 kg in the north (Italian rice production was concentrated in the Po valley, in the north of the country) and 3 kg in the south.

---

[1] 1 kg = 2.2 lbs and 1 ton = 2,000 lbs.

Of the 320,000 tons of rice sold in Italy in 1991, approximately 70,000 tons were sold through food service establishments and 250,000 tons were sold through grocery stores. Retail sales in 1991 were 85% white rice and 15% parboiled by volume, and 70% white rice and 30% parboiled by value. Sales of both parboiled rice and special rices (less than 5% of the market by value) were growing at 8% and 12% per annum, respectively. White rice was losing share at 1% to 3% per annum.

Rice was seen as quick and easy to prepare, versatile, healthy, easily digested, and an alternative to pasta. Brand choices were based on quality, habit, availability, and packaging. Typically, rice was sold through stores in 1-kg cardboard boxes, although a small percentage was sold from bulk bins and in 5-kg plastic bags. Legal restrictions in Italy required each variety of rice to be sold separately; the result was extended product lines since different rice varieties could not be mixed.

Gallo in Italy

Present in Italy since the 19th century as a rice miller, Gallo products accounted for 21% of Italian retail rice volume in 1991, 2% higher than in 1990. The Gallo logo, a cheerful rooster, was widely recognized and symbolized a trustworthy, good-quality, albeit somewhat traditional brand. As the overall market share leader, Gallo offered three product lines:

- The basic *Riso Gran Gallo, white rice* line was offered in nine varieties (ranging from simple white rice to superfine white rice), reflecting regional preferences and different recipe requirements. For example, Gallo Padano, popular in Milan, was used mainly in soups. Six of the nine varieties were long-grain, more absorbent rice suitable for risotto dishes.[2] In 1991, this line accounted for 64.4% of Gallo's total Italian sales volume and 51% of its total lira sales. Gallo's volume share of white rice sales in Italy was 17.3% in 1991. Product package illustrations appear in Exhibit 2.

- The *Blond* line of parboiled rice included three parboiled nonstick products and one dehydrated quick-cooking rice (also parboiled). The three parboiled products were Orientale, white rice that cooked light and fluffy; Risotti, a larger grain rice suitable for risotto recipes; and Integro, a "natural" brown rice that retained important ingredients and fiber sometimes depleted in the milling process. A dehydrated quick-cooking product, Meta'Tempo (half time), was included in the line in 1990 and cooked in five to seven minutes. In 1991, this line accounted for 34.4% of Gallo's Italian volume sales and 48% of its lira sales. Gallo's volume share of parboiled rice sales in Italy was 35.4% in 1991. Product package illustrations appear in Exhibit 2.

---

[2] Risotto dishes were rice-based meals that included meat and/or vegetables.

EXHIBIT 2

Product package illustrations for the Gallo product lines in italy

- The *Grandi Risi del Mondo* (great rices of the world) was a superpremium line introduced in 1989 in five varieties (Long and Wild, Basmati, Arborio, Carnaroli, and Patna). Although this line carried the familiar Gallo chicken logo on the front package panels, the line was marketed through a separate sales force and specialty store distribution. In 1991, this line accounted for just 1.2% of volume sales and 1.5% of lira sales. Product package illustrations appear in Exhibit 2 on the previous page.

Most Gallo products were sold to retailers through a network of 60 agents and brokers, not by a company sales force. These agents carried other food products but no other rice brands. Due to its brand strength, Gallo received excellent push marketing efforts from its agents. A sales incentive program rewarded those who grew the Gallo business. In 1991, Gallo was carried in stores accounting for 80% of Italian grocery sales, more than any other brand. A typical supermarket carried two of Gallo's white rice varieties and three of the four parboiled items; the higher priced Orientale was least widely distributed.

Competition

The Italian retail rice market was fragmented, with many local and regional millers selling under their own brand names. Grocery retailing was also fragmented but rapidly consolidating. In 1991, supermarkets and hypermarkets accounted for 60% of all rice value sales and 64% of Gallo's value sales, up from 57% and 59% in 1989. In 1991, private labels held a 17% share of rice retail sales volume, up from 13% in 1990. Gallo also competed against three major national brands:

- *Flora,* a subsidiary of BSN, the French food conglomerate, marketed only parboiled rice and competed directly with Gallo's Blond line.[3] Flora offered four varieties: Integral, Orientale, Risotti Blond, and Rapido. Combined, these items held a 41% volume and a 46% value share of the Italian parboiled market in 1991.

  Flora television advertising was upbeat and depicted the lifestyles of four target segments, one for each item in the line. For example, the Integral commercial showed a health-conscious woman working out, while the Rapido commercial featured a successful businesswoman. The "lifestyle" commercials were modern, light, and appeared to be targeted at younger women. Flora also used five-minute television "infomercials," which included viewer call-in games to promote the brand. In 1990, Flora spent 20% more on advertising than Gallo. A recent consulting study estimated that manufacturer gross margins on Flora were 30% compared to Gallo's margins on the Blond line of 35%.

- *Curti-Buitoni* was acquired in 1985 by Nestlé, the Swiss food company. The Nestlé sales force provided the Curti brand with excellent distribution, but the brand was not heavily advertised. Curti-Buitoni offered both

---

[3] In Italy, BSN was also a strong player in branded pasta.

basic white rice and parboiled products and held a 10.2% and 5.6% volume share of these markets, respectively.

- *Scotti* was a family-owned regional firm. Its product line was restricted to basic white rice. Scotti held a 7.5% volume share and had been approached by F&P Gruppo and others as a possible acquisition target.

Exhibit 3 summarizes market shares and brand awareness data for the four principal national brands in 1990–91. Exhibits 4 and 5 compare Gallo and competitor market shares for white rice and parboiled rice and their relative retail prices.

EXHIBIT 3   Market Shares and Awareness Levels for Gallo and Competitors in Italy, 1990

	Volume Market Shares (%)		1991 Awareness Levels (%)		
	1990	*1991*	*First Mention*	*Unaided*	*Aided*
Gallo	19.1	21.1	37	62	91
Flora	8.1	8.8	14	28	52
Curti-Buitoni	10.5	9.2	15	30	79
Scotti	5.9	6.1	8	14	64

EXHIBIT 4   White Rice in Italy: Gallo and Competitor Market Shares and Relative Retail Prices, 1990 and 1991

	Volume Market Shares (%)		Relative Retail Prices ($)	
	1990	*1991*	*1990*	*1991*
Riso Gallo	16.4	17.3	1.00	1.00
Curti-Buitoni	11.1	10.2	0.98	0.97
Scotti	7.0	7.5	0.98	0.98
Private label	15.5	17.3	0.78	0.78

EXHIBIT 5   Parboiled Rice in Italy: Gallo and Competitor Market Shares and Relative Retail Prices, 1990 and 1991

	Volume Market Shares (%)		Relative Retail Prices ($)	
	1990	*1991*	*1990*	*1991*
Riso Gallo	31.3	35.4	1.00	1.00
Curti-Buitoni	7.8	5.6	1.03	0.98
Flora	43.3	40.9	1.05	1.04
Private label	14.2	12.2	0.74	0.69

Communication Strategy

Gallo's marketing expenditures had been increased from 13% of sales in 1988 to a planned 15% in 1992. Actual promotional and advertising expenditures for 1991 and planned expenditures for 1992 are detailed in Exhibit 6. In 1991, Gallo's television advertising was divided evenly between spot commercials and five-minute promotional infomercials. Television commercials for the Blond line depicted different consumers winning cooking competitions thanks to Gallo rice. Each commercial depicted a nervous individual waiting in the wings holding a dish of rice, being called to the stage to receive an award, then being congratulated and applauded. The commercial cut back to the product, and an announcer explained that the award was won thanks to the Gallo brand of rice. Print advertisements in magazines often included a recipe, a photograph of the product, and detailed information on the differences of rice varieties. Exhibit 7 shows a typical print advertisement, and Exhibits 8 and 9 (on pages 30 and 31) show other Gallo magazine print advertisements. Consumer promotions included in-store sampling and continuity programs, advertised on packages and in magazines, whereby consumers could redeem Gallo box tops for pottery and other merchandise. Gallo accounted for 33% of total category media advertising in 1991.

In 1992, television advertising planned for the Blond line would focus on the nonstick benefit. Specific print advertising for Integro and Meta'Tempo products would communicate nutritional value and quick cooking time. An umbrella print advertising program, in both national and regional newspapers and magazines, would portray Gallo as serious and reliable and focus on the brand's tradition and culture.

EXHIBIT 6   Gallo Advertising and Promotion Expenditures in Italy

	Millions of Lire*	
	1991 (Actual)	1992 (Planned)
Media advertising:	9,466	9,210
TV ads for Blond		5,000
Gallo umbrella ads in magazines		1,150
Magazine ads for Blond Integro		200
Magazine ads for Blond Meta'Tempo		700
Supermarket magazines		180
Fees and production costs		980
Consumer promotion	3,039	2,300
Regional marketing	300	265
New product launch	789	350
Trade and sales force incentives	6,047	7,950
Total	19,641	20,075

* $1 = 1,272 lire.

SOURCE: Company records and estimates.

EXHIBIT 7

Gallo Italy: Typical print advertisement

LO SPECIALISTA DEL RISO

Il "riso bianco" non è tutto uguale. Comprende molte varietà che si differenziano tra loro per grandezza e forma del chicco, per trasparenza, contenuto in amido, tenuta in cottura, capacità di assorbimento dei condimenti. Conoscerle significa sfruttare al meglio le caratteristiche di ognuna per avere in cucina risultati eccezionali.

La gamma più completa presente sul mercato è firmata Riso Gallo che, con le due linee Gallo e Gran Gallo, propone nove varietà di riso bianco tra le quali troviamo: Gran Gallo Roma, con una grana lunga e grossa che assorbe molto bene i condimenti; dà grandi soddisfazioni se usato per risotti "ricchi" di ingredienti.

Gran Gallo Arborio, nato ad Arborio nel 1946 è il riso italiano con i chicchi più grandi e perfetti: ideale per i risotti più classici e raffinati.

Gran Gallo Baldo, è il riso con la struttura più cristallina e compatta, molto resistente in cottura, va benissimo per i risotti, ma è perfetto per le insalate di riso, i timballi, il riso in teglia.

Il segreto: per ogni piatto saper scegliere il riso bianco adatto e, con Riso Gallo, il migliore.

Ricettario

RISOTTO CON FUNGHI PORCINI E ANIMELLE

Ingredienti per 4 persone. 250 gr di Riso Gran Gallo Arborio - 200 gr di animelle - 100 gr di funghi porcini - 1,2 l di brodo di pollo leggero - 25 gr di cipolla - 10 gr di scalogno - 2 dl di vino bianco - 1 cucchiaio di estratto di carne - 10 gr di dragoncello - 50 gr di burro - 50 gr di parmigiano grattugiato - olio di semi - sale e pepe q.b.

Lasciare spurgare le animelle per 5 ore sotto acqua corrente fredda. Sbianchirle per 5 minuti in acqua bollente salata e lasciarvele raffreddare. Una volta fredde sgranarle, liberandole dalla pellicina e spezzettarle. Pulire i funghi porcini e tagliarli a cubetti. Farli saltare, con 10 gr di burro, in una pentola antiaderente, salarli e peparli. Aggiungere e far dorare le animelle. A parte fare ridurre 2 dl di vino bianco con lo scalogno finemente tritato, l'estratto di carne e un po' di burro. Per il risotto far sudare la cipolla tritata con 10 gr di burro, aggiungere il riso e farlo tostare fino a quando non inizierà a scoppiettare. Bagnare con vino bianco, farlo evaporare e portare il riso a cottura bagnandolo a poco a poco con il brodo bollente. Togliere il riso dal fuoco e mantecarlo con burro e parmigiano grattugiato: disporlo sui piatti e guarnirlo con le animelle, i funghi porcini e il dragoncello tritato. Macchiare la superficie del piatto con il fondo, di consistenza sciropposa, ottenuto con l'estratto di carne.

RISOTTO DEL DI' DI FESTA

Ingredienti per 4 persone: 250 gr di Riso Gran Gallo Roma - 1 litro di brodo - 1 cipolla - 2 peperoni gialli - 2 peperoni rossi - 1 ciuffo di basilico - 200 gr di pomodori pelati - 5 cosce di pollo - 1 bicchiere di vino bianco secco - prezzemolo tritato - olio, burro, sale q.b. - 1 foglia di alloro

Rosolare la cipolla tagliata sottile e aggiungere le cosce di pollo tagliate in tre pezzi. Far colorire, aggiungere il vino bianco secco e lasciarlo evaporare. Mettere i peperoni tagliati a listarelle e i pelati, dopo 10 minuti versare il brodo bollente e cuocere per 50 minuti. Aggiungere il riso e finire di cuocere. Completare con prezzemolo e basilico tritati e una foglia di alloro.

EXHIBIT 8

Gallo Italy: Print advertisement for the Grandi Risi del Mondo line

TRACCE DI RISO.

Quanta strada da fare in cucina, con "I grandi risi del mondo". Seguire le loro tracce, sarà un'avventura. Dall'India il Basmati, quasi una leggenda. In Thailandia è il Patna, l'orgoglio nazionale. Dal Nord America, il Long & Wild: chicco bianco e chicco nero. Dall'Italia infine il fiore. Fiore di Arborio per i risotti di grande tradizione, Fiore di Carnaroli, il re dei risi, per ricette d'autore. Sono loro "I grandi risi del mondo". L'avventura da portare a tavola. La ricetta per girare il mondo.

DA GALLO, LO SPECIALISTA DEL RISO.

EXHIBIT 9

Gallo Italy: Print advertisement with consumer promotion ("Win a Car with Blond Rice")

Issues

In considering how to further penetrate the branded rice retail market, Preve had to decide whether to create an entire new dehydrated line around the Meta'Tempo sub-brand. Consumers perceived Meta'Tempo to be superior to simple parboiled rice, and some thought that the product could be the base of a whole new dehydrated product line, particularly since Gallo had a competitive advantage being further down the learning curve in dehydrated technology than competitors. Sales of Meta'Tempo were growing rapidly, and dry rice mixes (such as risottos) were selling at three to four times the retail price of normal white rice.

Gallo's Naturis company produced dehydrated quick-cooking rice and supplied both BSN's Flora Rapido and Gallo's Blond Meta'Tempo. Flora's Rapido had been the only brand of quick-cooking rice on the market between 1988 and 1990. Gallo's Meta'Tempo was launched as a freestanding product in 1990, but had to be withdrawn due to poor sales and the high cost of promotional support. It was quickly repositioned within the Blond line, and, by 1992, sales of Meta-'Tempo equaled those of Rapido. It was rumored that BSN was thinking of opening its own dehydrated rice manufacturing plant, and Preve wondered whether to attempt to keep supplying BSN with the rice it used to make Flora's Rapido.

Preve also wrestled with several questions regarding the 1992 communications budget. First, he wondered if the competitive situation called for a substantially higher budget than in 1991. Second, he wondered whether Gallo should continue to put all its advertising behind the parboiled Blond line or allocate more support to the core white rice line.

There was also some concern that Gallo was not as strong as Flora in the growing supermarket/hypermarket retail segment. Actual retail trade margins were around 7% on Flora compared to 1% on Gallo's Blond line. Preve believed that the Gallo brand was often used as a traffic builder and that consumers who purchased Gallo branded rice were also more likely to purchase higher value products, with greater retailer margins. In addition, Preve argued that Gallo products had a higher turnover than many other food products and that F&P Gruppo allowed retailers generous payment terms. Despite this, Preve was concerned that chains would be motivated to develop their own private-label lines of rice products.

Argentina

Market Characteristics

In 1991, an estimated 140,000 tons of rice were sold through retail stores and a further 40,000 tons through food service establishments. Per capita consumption approached 5 kg per annum, with 92% of Argentine households consuming rice at least once a week and 30% consuming rice at least three times a week. Sales of branded rice had decreased from 85,000 tons in 1990 to 81,000 tons in 1991, due to the increasing price of paddy rice relative to other food products such as meat. In July 1989, the retail price of 1 kg of meat was equal to the retail price of 5.4 kg of rice. By November 1991, the equivalent was only 2.7 kg of rice. Parboiled rice accounted for 18.2% retail sales volume in 1991, compared to 16.1% in 1990; the remaining sales were of white rice, with brown rice accounting for an estimated 2% of sales volume. Exhibit 10 gives an estimated breakdown of rice consumption by volume.

During the 1980s, the Argentine economy had suffered from cycles of strong growth and consumption, followed by ever longer periods of recession. A new economic plan launched in 1991 aimed to tame inflation, initiate deregulation, privatize public enterprises, and liberalize trade restrictions and import duties. In 1992, inflation was estimated at 17%.

Rice was distributed primarily through supermarkets, which accounted for 63% of all retail rice sales in 1990; large, medium, and small stores accounted for 10%, 14%, and 13%, respectively. The volume of rice sold in different packages was 72% for plastic pillows, 19% for cardboard boxes, and 9% for triangle-shaped packages. Most packages were either 1 kg or 500 grams in weight.

EXHIBIT 10

Distribution of Argentine milled rice volume, 1991

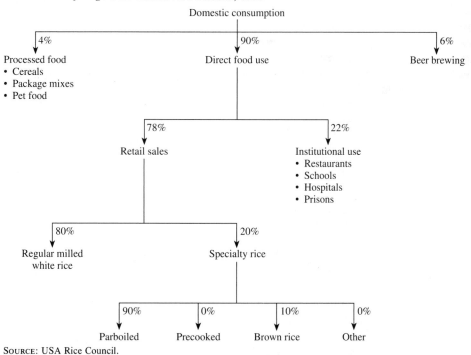

SOURCE: USA Rice Council.

Gallo in Argentina

The first rice mill in Argentina was established by Arrocera Argentina, a subsidiary of F&P Gruppo, in 1905. In 1991, the Arrocera Argentina mills were running at 85% capacity, milling rice grown in Argentina. All of the output was processed into Gallo-branded products. Sales of Gallo-branded rice were $30 million in the fiscal year April 1991 to March 1992. In 1991, Gallo held a 17.5% volume share and a 23.7% value share of the total retail rice market, up from 15.7% and 22.8%, respectively, in 1990. In addition, Gallo held a 48% share in greater Buenos Aires, which accounted for 30% of the country's population. Solely focused on the rice market, Gallo was both the market share and product innovation leader.

The Gallo line included the following items:

- Gallo *Grano Largo Fino* and Gallo *Doble,* long-grain and European long-grain rice, were long, wide types of rice known as *doble* because each grain was double the length of an ordinary grain of rice. They were the original products in Gallo's Argentine product line and were targeted at traditional homemakers who enjoyed the art of cooking and described themselves as "knowing how to cook" and "using the brand that my mother used." Packaged in 1-kg and ½-kg cartons, this line accounted for 28% of Gallo's sales by volume in 1991, compared to 32% in 1989.

- Gallo *Oro,* long-grain and European long-grain parboiled rice, was positioned as a quality rice that did not stick or overcook and was easy to prepare. The line was targeted at the modern, middle-income working consumer, aged 25 years and over, who wanted ease of preparation without sacrificing taste. The line included doble and boil-in-the-bag products in both 1-kg and ½-kg carton packages. The first parboiled product had been introduced in Argentina in 1963, and by 1991 this line accounted for 59% of Gallo's sales volume, compared to 62% in 1989.

- Gallo *Integral,* a long-grain parboiled brown rice, was positioned as a health and fitness product with a high nutritional value based on high levels of fiber, vitamins, and minerals. It was targeted at middle-income men and women, 18 years and older, who led a healthy, natural, and sporty lifestyle and wanted a balanced diet without sacrificing good taste. It was sold in 500-gram and boil-in-the-bag formats as well as the standard 1-kg box. Sales of this product represented 5% of Gallo's volume in 1991, the same percentage as in 1989.

- Gallo *Risotto* dry mixes, made of European long-grain parboiled rice, came in four flavor varieties. The rice was mixed with dehydrated ingredients such as peppers, mushroom, chicken, and spices and was targeted at middle-income consumers aged 25 and over, seeking tasty, easy-to-prepare meals. Launched in 1984 and sold in 300-gram boxes, it represented 1% of Gallo's sales volume in 1991, as in 1989, and held an 87% share of the Argentine risotto market in 1991.

**EXHIBIT 11   Arrocera Argentina Product Line: Shipments, Margins, and
Package Sizes, 1991**

	Shipment (Tons)	*Manufacturer Margin (%)*	*Package Sizes*
Gallo Grano Largo Fino (long-grain)	1,875	35	1 kg
Gallo Doble (European long-grain)	3,891	44	1 kg
Gallo Oro (long-grain parboiled):			
Regular	11,173	38	1 kg
Boil-in-bag	361	41	½ kg
Gallo Doble Oro (European long-grain parboiled)	761	45	1 kg
Gallo Integral (long-grain brown)	786	51	1 kg
			½ kg
			boil-in-bag
Gallo Risotto (European long-grain parboiled dry mixes)	104	60	300 gm
Nobleza Gaucha:			
Long-grain	711	21	1 kg
European long-grain	256	35	
Long-grain parboiled	575	29	
Integral	44	43	

Exhibit 11 reports shipments, manufacturer gross margins, and package sizes for each item in the product line. Gallo was one of the only companies selling rice packaged in cardboard boxes (only two other minor competitors also packaged in boxes). Product packages for the four lines are depicted in Exhibit 12 on page 36.

Three-quarters of Gallo's retail sales were through supermarkets. There was a trend toward consolidation in food retailing in Argentina, with the large supermarkets (of 350 square meters or more) increasing their market share from 34% in 1989 to 38% in 1991. Gallo was weaker in the medium and smaller stores, which represented 27% of retail volume rice sales but accounted for only 15% of Gallo's retail sales volume. Approximately 90% of sales were made through a company sales force, while 10% was sold through agents serving remote areas. In 1991, the Gallo line was present in stores representing 77% of the country's retail food sales with an average of seven items per retail outlet. On average, large supermarkets carried between five and seven different brands of rice.

Competition

The Argentine retail rice market was fragmented and regional. The four major national brands accounted for only 45% of total retail sales volume in 1991. Gallo faced one major and two minor competitors:

- *Molinos* food products, a subsidiary of Bunge Corporation, a large Argentine conglomerate, held 10.1% of the rice retail market by volume in

EXHIBIT 12

Product package illustrations for the Gallo product lines in Argentina

Long Grain Parboiled Rice

European Long Grain

Long Grain Rice   European Long Grain Rice

1991, up from 8.8% in 1990. It seriously challenged Gallo in 1990 with its Maximo brand of parboiled long-grain rice.

Maximo, sold in triangle packages, held a 5.3% volume share of retail sales in 1990 and was the only Molinos brand that was not the market leader in its category. In 1991, Molinos spent twice as much as Gallo on advertising Maximo, despite the fact that the Argentine economy was depressed, promoting the brand as ''oro puro of Molinos'' on radio and television and in magazines. To gain market share, Maximo was priced 12% under equivalent Gallo products, and, by the end of 1991, Maximo had increased its retail volume market share to 7.5%. Molinos had difficulty achieving quality control on its doble and brown rice entries, and these were marketed under the brand name Condor. Distribution coverage for Molinos was still lower than for Gallo, and the company was not particularly strong in any one region.

Gallo had responded to Maximo with a fighting brand called Nobleza Gaucha. Also sold in triangle-shaped packages, it came in four varieties: long-grain, long-grain parboiled, European long-grain, and Integral. In 1991, this line was priced around 25% below equivalent Gallo-branded products and around 12% below Maximo. Within one year the Nobleza Gaucha brand accounted for 7.7% of Gallo's sales volume and held a 1.1% share of total retail rice sales by volume in 1991. The brand was sold by Gallo sales force, but supermarkets accounted for 65% of sales compared to the 75% for the Gallo brand.

- *Mocovi* and *Moneda* were smaller, regional players in the long-grain and doble market segments, with shares of 4.2% and 4.4%, respectively. Mocovi, a family-owned company, successfully focused on marketing its Mocovi Doble brand and was the leader in the doble market segment. Moneda's products included both the Moneda and Doble Moneda brands.

Exhibits 13 and 14 summarize overall market shares for the four brands from 1989 to 1991 and the volume and value shares of their specific product lines in 1991. Exhibit 15 compares the relative retail prices and percentage distribution penetration of these brands in 1991.

EXHIBIT 13   Rice Brand Market Shares in Argentina, 1989–91

	Percentage of Total Retail Volume		
	1989	*1990*	*1991*
Arrocera (Gallo and Nobleza Gaucha)	17.7%	15.7%	17.5%
Molinos (Maximo)	8.2	8.8	10.1
Moneda	4.3	4.7	4.4
Mocovi	7.2	5.4	4.2

EXHIBIT 14   Rice Brand Market Shares in Argentina by Product Line, 1991

	Percentage of Total Rice Market	
	Retail Volume Share	*Retail Value Share*
Dobles and Long-Grain		
Arrocera:		
Gallo	5.2%	7.6%
Nobleza Gaucha	0.7	0.7
Molinos:		
Condor	2.6	3.3
Mocovi	4.2	6.9
Moneda	4.4	5.9
Parboiled		
Arrocera:		
Gallo	9.8	12.5
Nobleza Gaucha	0.4	0.4
Molinos:		
Maximo	7.5	10.3
Integral		
Arrocera:		
Gallo	1.2	2.0
Risottos		
Arrocera:		
Gallo	0.2	0.5

Communication Strategy

Advertising expenditures on the Gallo brand in 1991 were the equivalent of $562,000, only 50% that of Maximo, and were used exclusively to back Gallo Oro. Television commercials included demonstrations of how to prepare and serve rice (particularly boil-in-the-bag products) and "slice-of-life" depictions of family scenes. For example, one commercial showed children sneaking into a kitchen to eat the rice their mother just prepared, while a second depicted a daughter making the same dish for her mother that her mother used to make for her when she was a child. Other promotional programs in 1991 included consumer promotions and sales force incentives.

Exhibit 16 on page 40 summarizes marketing expenditures for Gallo and Nobleza Gaucha in 1991 and planned expenditures for 1992. The budget for 1992 was $1.9 million, to be divided as follows: $726,000 on a new Gallo Oro television campaign; $400,000 on print advertising for the whole Gallo line; $220,000 on Gallo Oro radio advertising; $57,000 on consumer promotions; and $173,000 on sales force incentives.

Competitive television commercials focused on displaying the cooked product in different forms. A typical Maximo television commercial stressed quality,

EXHIBIT 15 **Relative Retail Prices and Distribution Penetration of Argentine Rice Brands, 1991**

	Retail Price ($ per kg)	Index	% Distribution Penetration
Long-Grain			
Arrocera:			
Gallo Grano Largo Fino	$1.30	1.00	32%
Nobleza Gaucha Long-grain	1.07	0.82	12
Molinos:			
Condor long-grain	1.26	0.95	35
Mocovi:			
Long-grain	0.98	0.75	10
Moneda:			
Long-grain	1.20	0.92	15
Doble			
Arrocera:			
Gallo Doble	2.54	1.95	51
Nobleza Gaucha European long-grain	1.61	1.24	8
Molinos:			
Condor Doble	2.06	1.58	37
Mocovi:			
Doble	2.05	1.58	47
Moneda:			
Doble	1.82	1.40	29
Parboiled			
Arrocera:			
Gallo Oro	1.68	1.29	75
Gallo Doble	2.30	1.77	40
Nobleza Gaucha	1.30	1.00	26
Molinos:			
Maximo	1.48	1.14	59
Integral			
Arrocera:			
Gallo	2.16	1.66	45
Risottos			
Arrocera:			
Gallo	6.70	5.15	42

price, and ease of preparation. The commercial was fast paced with a musical background and depicted a number of meals that could be prepared with Maximo rice. A Moneda television commercial depicted a woman hosting a dinner party explaining that when she used to cook rice "nothing happened" but that now, with Moneda, she was able to serve flavorful meals. Exhibits 17 and 18 show examples of Gallo print advertisements in Argentina, and Exhibit 19 gives an example of a Maximo print advertisement.

EXHIBIT 16   **Advertising and Promotion Expenditures for Arrocera Argentina, 1991–92**

	Dollar Amount (000s)	
	1991 (Actual)	*1992 (Budget)*
Media Advertising		
Television commercials:		
Gallo Oro	$342	$ 762
Doble Gallo		194
Risotto		
Others		84
Print advertising:		
Gallo Oro		
Doble Gallo		
Risotto		80
Others		320
Radio advertising:		
Gallo Oro		220
Doble Gallo		52
Promotions		
Consumer promotions:		
Gallo Oro	35	
Doble Gallo	25	26
Others	60	31
Trade promotions		25
Sales force incentives	100	173
Total	$562	$1,931

Issues

First, Arrocera Argentina managers were debating how to respond to a market that was eroding due to a difficult economic climate and high product prices relative to other food products. Preve was hesitant, however, to implement price reductions on the high-end products despite a drop in raw material costs of approximately 63% between 1988 and 1991. Second, the issue as to whether Gallo should attempt to match Maximo's level of advertising was raised. Third, Gallo was committed to introducing new products and planned to launch Meta'Tempo quick-cooking rice under the brand name *Gallo Quick* in 1992. A key question was how the brand should be positioned and priced in the Argentine market, and the proportion of total marketing expenditures that should be allocated to its launch.

Since it would be the first brand in the precooked segment of the Argentine market, Arrocera Argentina executives believed that Gallo Quick could be positioned to enhance Gallo's product leadership and market share. They suggested pricing the product at a 60% premium to Gallo Oro.

EXHIBIT 17

Gallo Argentina: Print advertisement for the risotto line

Risottos Cremosos...Deliciosos...

Disfrute de los mejores risottos
con *Gallo Todo Resuelto*.
En cualquiera de sus 4 variedades: a la Normanda,
a la Piamontesa, a la Española y Primavera.
Su exquisito sabor proviene de la utilización
de verduras frescas deshidratadas de primera calidad
(sin el agregado de sustancias químicas ni conservantes)
y de la utilización del mejor arroz: Doble Gallo Oro.

EXHIBIT 18

Gallo Argentina: Two separate print advertisements for Gallo Integro

EXHIBIT 19

Gallo Argentina: Print advertisement for the Maximo competitor brand

Poland

Market Characteristics

With the demise of Communist control, Poland underwent rapid cultural and political change in the late 1980s. After 1989, Poland was flooded by imported goods of all kinds, mainly from Germany, Italy, and France. To deal with these imports, private wholesale and retail chains emerged in 1991 to replace the state-owned stores. Although in 1992 the Polish economy was still suffering from inflation and low wages, consumers were becoming increasingly sophisticated in the quality of products they demanded. With the advent of advertising and private companies, Poland was believed to be evolving from a market dominated by commodities to one where branding would become important.

Prior to 1989, rice had been imported in bulk by the state from Vietnam, Thailand, China, and Indonesia. It was of variable quality, often dirty and broken, and was sold in low-quality paper bags. Traditionally used as a substitute to potatoes, as a booster in soups, in cabbage rolls, or for rice pudding, rice had a low-quality image. Traditionally, imported food such as rice had been subsidized by the state. The end of these subsidies in 1989 resulted in price increases on imported food of around 1,100%.

In the 1980s, distribution of branded Western products, including branded rice, had been controlled by a state-owned company called Pewex with a network of approximately 800 stores. Purchases could only be made in US dollars. The stores enabled the state to obtain hard currency from consumers who received it from family members living outside Poland. In 1989, the Polish currency (the zloty) was tied to the US dollar. An additional 800 private exchange stores and markets sprung up to distribute imported foods. Sales of such products by entrepreneurs through makeshift street stalls and open-air car trunk markets also became common. These were later organized into covered market halls. In 1991, private food retail outlets began to emerge, although there were no dominant supermarket chains as yet. In 1992, 70% of retail food sales were made at open markets and market halls, 15% at supermarkets, and 15% at small grocery stores.

In 1988, total rice consumption in Poland was 64,000 tons, or 1.5 kg per capita. By 1991, per capita consumption reached 2.3 kg per annum. Used by 65% of the population, 80,000 tons were sold through retail stores in 1991. Of this volume, 90% was standard white rice; parboiled rice was a novel product for Polish consumers. Exhibit 20 shows the breakdown of rice volume in Poland in 1991.

Gallo in Poland

In 1988, Arrocera Argentina started exporting to the Polish market through an agent who received a commission on sales to Pewex. Gallo rice was sold in 200 Pewex shops in packages with both Argentine and Polish labeling at an average retail price of $1 per kg. In 1991, with Pewex in decline, Arrocera's agent established a private distribution company, Argentyna Ltd., to import and distribute

EXHIBIT 20

Distribution of milled rice volume in Poland, 1992

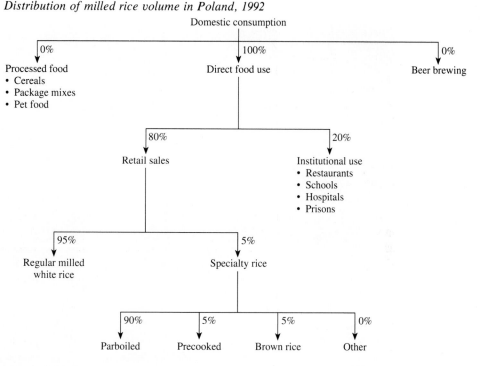

the products he had previously handled for Pewex. In addition to rice, Argentyna Ltd. imported and distributed tea, beverages, and soups. Argentyna did not handle other brands of rice.

Between March 1990 and January 1991, 59 tons of Gallo Oro (parboiled) and 9 tons of Gallo risottos, both imported from Argentina, were sold through Pewex. Initial package labels carried Spanish text to which a Polish sticker had been added; subsequent packages carried bilingual Spanish–Polish labeling. From February 1991 to February 1992, 70.5 tons of Gallo Oro parboiled white rice were imported exclusively through Argentyna Ltd. from Gallo's German factory, P&L Rickmers. Prior to 1991, P&L Rickmers had experienced excess capacity. These 1-kg carton box packages carried the bilingual label. In 1992, Gallo expected to sell 100 tons of Gallo Oro in 1-kg cartons, less than one-quarter of 1% of the retail market volume.

In 1992, Argentyna Ltd. had a central warehouse in Warsaw and distributed 65% of Gallo's product volume directly to retailers in the Warsaw area. The remaining 35% of sales were made through four secondary distributors that served the major cities of Krakow, Sczeczin, Poznan, and Lodz. The Gallo brand was available in 200 supermarkets and upscale grocery stores, which accounted for 30% of all grocery sales volume in Warsaw and 5% in Poland. In 1992, Rickmers' gross margin averaged 21% of its selling price. The Argentyna Ltd. margin averaged 40%, while secondary distributors made about 20% margin on Gallo products. Retailer margins were 15%. Exhibit 21 shows photographs of three food

EXHIBIT 21

Photographs depicting three food retail stores in Poland. From top to bottom: Upscale, middle, and lower-end outlets

stores, at the high, medium, and lower range, retailing rice in Poland in September 1992.

Competition

Gallo's main competitor was the Uncle Ben's brand owned by Mars Co., distributed in Poland since 1991. In addition, several German and Belgian brands of both white and parboiled rice had entered the market at lower price points. In mid-1992, it was estimated that 95% of the market was unbranded white rice, packaged in paper bags, which retailed at an average price of 8,000 zlotys ($0.58).

Uncle Ben's sold long-grain parboiled rice and brown rice in 1-kg cartons, ½-kg cartons, and boil-in-the-bag packages. In just over a year, Uncle Ben's had penetrated 90% of the supermarket and grocery outlets in Warsaw. Initially, the company had supplied its products to retailers on credit and accepted returns of unsold product. The launch was supported with $500,000 of expenditures on television commercials, print advertising, and point-of-sale displays.

Uncle Ben's used a North American television commercial translated into Polish. It depicted a rural picnic in the southern United States, where an African-American community was preparing to welcome home a young soldier. Considerable consumer confusion existed between the Gallo and Uncle Ben's brands; increased advertising by Uncle Ben's resulted in an increase in sales for Gallo and other imported brands. In 1992, Uncle Ben's was expected to sell over 200 tons of rice. It was believed that Uncle Ben's was losing money in Poland but that the company's strategy was to increase brand awareness and build long-term market share.

Britta, Doris, and *La Belle Caroline* were other major foreign rice brands distributed in Poland. Usually priced lower than Uncle Ben's or Gallo, these brands were not advertised. Exhibit 22 summarizes the relative prices of different brands in February and September 1992.

EXHIBIT 22   Relative Retail Prices of Major Rice Brands in Poland, February and September 1992

	February 1992		September 1992	
	$/Kg	*Index*	*$/Kg*	*Index*
Parboiled				
Gallo Oro	$2.28	1.00	$1.78	1.00
Uncle Ben's	3.50	1.54	2.24	1.26
Doris (Belgian)	1.27	0.56	1.23	0.69
White Rice				
Local brand (in plastic bags)	$0.72	0.32	$0.56	0.33
Local brand (instant rice flakes)	1.50	0.65	1.32	0.75
Britta (German)	1.50	0.65	1.31	0.73
La Belle Caroline (French)	n.a.*	n.a.	1.23	0.69

* n.a. = Not available.

Consumer Research

A consumer research study in September 1990 indicated that a basic meal in Poland consisted of meat, potatoes, and a vegetable. Rice was seen as an occasional substitute for potatoes. There was little knowledge of different types of rice and rice recipes, little understanding of nutrition, and little exposure to foreign foods. Homemakers were used to buying what was available and preparing meals every two or three days that could be stored in refrigerators; most Polish households had access to refrigerators in 1990.

In product trials of Gallo products, parboiled rice was enthusiastically received. Ease of cooking (aided by clear cooking instructions), taste, and ability to store once cooked were cited as the main benefits of Gallo Oro. One drawback, however, was that consumers found the rice too firm for use in soups. Savory rice (with mushrooms added) was not well received; it had an unfamiliar taste and smell, had to be watched when being prepared, and was higher in price. Brown rice was viewed negatively; most consumers felt that a good-quality rice should be long-grained and white and, lacking in nutritional awareness, were unwilling to pay a price premium. Consumers suspected the boil-in-the-bag concept because it involved cooking in plastic. Cartons were the preferred form of packaging, and Polish labels were deemed necessary. Gallo managers wondered whether all these perceptions would continue or whether an investment in consumer education by Gallo and other foreign brands would change them.

Communication Strategy

Gallo's initial plan was to superimpose a Polish voice on an Argentine television commercial of a Chinese cook demonstrating how to prepare Gallo Oro. A variety of dishes that included rice were shown during the commercial, and the nonstick properties and taste of the rice were stressed. Testing revealed that the pace of the commercial was too quick and that the central message and product benefits were not well understood. The commercial was never aired. In addition, television advertising was becoming increasingly expensive, and radio was therefore considered as an alternative medium.

From February 1991 to February 1992, Gallo spent $3,000 on promotional support and point-of-sale displays. In September 1992, $6,000 was spent on print advertising in women's magazines. A full-page advertisement, to be placed in one magazine for three consecutive months, pictured a Gallo Oro carton and included a description of the product and a suggested cooking recipe. A total of $20,000 was budgeted for 1992, and Exhibit 23 outlines the proposed breakdown of expenditures.

Gallo's agent believed increased advertising expenditures were essential. He explained:

> Gallo's product quality is better than the other cheaper brands but consumers don't know this. We are caught between Uncle Ben's, perceived as a premium product, and brands such as Britta and Doris that compete on price. People do not know that Gallo is high quality and we need to create this perception of the brand.

<table>
<tr><td>**EXHIBIT 23**</td><td>**Proposed Gallo Communication Budget in Poland, 1992**</td></tr>
</table>

Advertising	
Newspaper ads	$ 4,000
Women's magazines	6,000
Promotion	
Point-of-purchase material	5,000
Three promotion reps	2,500
Other	2,500
Total	$20,000

EXHIBIT 24   Gallo Product Line by Country

	Italy	*Argentina*	*Poland*
White Rice			
• Round, short-grain	Riso Gallo Originario		
• Semi-long, "pearl"	Riso Gallo Padano		
• Round, fat grain	Riso Gallo Vialone Nano		
• Long-grain Italpatna	Riso Gran Gallo Europa		
• Long-grain	Riso Gran Gallo Ribe	Gallo Doble and Nobleza Gaucha	
• American long-grain	Riso Gran Gallo S. Andrea	Gallo Grano Largo Fino and Nobleza Gaucha	
• Semi-round Japanese	Riso Gran Gallo Roma		
• Crystalline	Riso Gran Gallo Baldo		
• Large-grain Italian	Riso Gran Gallo Arborio		
• Brown		Gallo Integral and Nobleza Gaucha	
Parboiled			
• Long-grain	Blond Risotti	Gallo Oro and Nobleza Gaucha	Gallo Oro
• Long-grain brown	Blond Integro		
• Long-grain Patna	Blond Orientale	Gallo Doble Oro	
• Dehydrated long-grain	Blond Meta'Tempo	Gallo Quick	
Risottos			
• Parboiled dry mixes		Gallo Risotto	

Issues

Preve wondered how to establish the Gallo brand in Poland. Specifically, which lines should be introduced and in which order? How should the products be positioned and priced? What level and types of advertising and promotion would be needed? Could the Polish market be expected to evolve like Argentina and, subsequently, like Italy? If so, how rapidly would this evolution take place? To assess the potential transfer of products and expertise from one country to another, Preve reviewed the Gallo line in the three countries (see Exhibit 24).

3

HEINEKEN NV: BUCKLER NONALCOHOLIC BEER

As he spoke, Jerome de Vries, in charge of marketing at Heineken Netherlands, looked first at Hans Brinker, the European corporate marketing manager, and then at the rest of the team sitting around the room. "Since this time last year, Bavaria Malt has grabbed 30% of our market share. Its prices are one-third of ours, but, on top of that, 60% of the customers say that they prefer the taste of Bavaria Malt. So, we either have to change our taste or drop our price."

It was July 1990, and the European brand team was holding its first meeting at Heineken's corporate headquarters in Amsterdam. The function of the group, consisting of two members from Corporate Marketing, one from Export, and six from the operating companies, was to coordinate European activities for Buckler nonalcoholic beer.

Brinker hesitated a moment before answering de Vries. "It would be easy, Jerome, to react on a local level and pull down prices if we're only after market share. But that would lead to other problems. There are bigger things at stake."

For the first time, Heineken had developed and launched a Pan-European product from its very beginning, one that was centrally managed and highly standardized. This was part of a larger corporate goal initiated by Mr. Gerard van Schaik, CEO of Heineken, "to make Heineken a truly European company which happens to have a head office in the Netherlands, rather than a Dutch company which does business in Europe."

Buckler was first introduced into Spain and France in 1988 and then was extended to other European countries. The brand had been highly successful for Heineken. By 1990, only two years after its launch, Buckler had attained a 15% share of the European nonalcoholic beer market even without entering the two largest markets, the United Kingdom and Germany.

This case was prepared by Research Associate James Henderson under the direction of Professor Sandra Vandermerwe. Copyright © 1991 by the International Institute for Management Development (IMD), Lausanne, Switzerland. Not to be used or reproduced without permission. IMD case 377.

"We had a similar problem in France, Jerome, just after we launched Buckler," said Claude Pelletier, responsible for marketing in France. "BSN reacted by offering a one-litre bottle, cutting prices, and repositioning Tourtel. This slowed us down, I can tell you. We didn't even make budget in the first year. But we stuck it out, and now we have over 15% of the segment. I would say we've got a good product here."

De Vries replied, "Well, I can tell you that if we don't do something quickly, we won't be in the Dutch market much longer. We can't just sit back and enjoy a technological advantage the way we used to. Our competitors are too quick to respond. We've got to move fast to hold our share."

"I understand your position, Jerome, but I think you are overemphasizing local market share. The nonalcoholic beer segment is growing as a whole in Europe. Last year alone it jumped by 55%. So, I say that if we stick to our strategy, we should get a 25% growth per year."

"It is all very well for you to say, 'Stick to a European strategy,'" said Emilio Fernandez, marketing manager in Spain. "But we have to deliver bottom-line results. I am worried, too. At first I thought we would be OK, but in the last few months, three brands have come into Spain, including Tourtel. I also expect a local brand, Laiker Sin, to be launched any day, and it could very well be priced much lower than our brand!"

Background: Heineken NV

G. A. Heineken founded Heineken NV in 1864 by purchasing de Hooiberg (the Haystack), a brewer which had been operating in the centre of Amsterdam since 1592. By 1990, Heineken, still in the hands of the Heineken family, had become one of the world's largest international beverages group, producing and distributing leading brands of beer, soft drinks, spirits, and wine. In addition to Heineken, its world-famous brand, there were other well-known names: Amstel, Sourcy, Royal Club, and, more recently, Buckler. The company also carried a variety of national and regional brands in several markets.

Heineken, like other international brewing companies, followed several distribution strategies for its global brands: exporting, brewing under license, and, finally, either wholly acquiring or taking a minority position in other breweries.

Exporting.   This strategy had the initial advantage of providing the breweries with another market. The product, as an import, could also be marketed as a premium brand. However, with an export strategy, the brewery's transportation costs were increased, and, without a substantial distribution network, its market share was limited.

Licensing.   Another common strategy was for a brewery to license its recipe to another brewery. In this way, a company could obtain a steady stream of profits and an increased market share through the licensee's distribution network. However, breweries complained about the lack of control over marketing the brand.

Acquisition. With this strategy, beer companies would either take a minority position or would wholly acquire other breweries. The brewers then had the choice of exporting the global brand with the distribution being handled by the operating company or having the product produced locally by the operating company. However, when acquisitions in other countries were made, the brewery added numerous local brands from that company to its portfolio. In addition, the acquired company needed to have a sufficiently wide network to ensure successful distribution of the global brand. In the 1960s and 1970s, several UK beer companies acquired German and Belgian breweries. The strategy failed because these two markets were too fragmented.

The following table shows Heineken's distribution strategy for each European country:

TABLE A   Distribution Strategies in Europe

Exporting	Licensing	Acquisition (Operating Companies)
Belgium	United Kingdom	Spain (El Aguila)
Portugal	Norway	France (Sogebra)
Switzerland	Sweden	Italy (Birra Dreher)
Germany	Finland	Greece (Athenian Brewery)
Austria		Ireland (Murphy Brewery)
Denmark		Netherlands (Heineken Neth.)

With this setup, the company's European strategy was to have a portfolio of international brands such as Heineken and Amstel, along with local brands produced by the operating company, among the leaders in each market segment. For example, Heineken's operating company in France, Sogebra SA, produced a local brand, "33" Export, for the mainstream lager market and imported the Heineken brand for the premium import lager market. The company was most successful with its global brands in the countries where there was an operating company and was less successful in countries where it exported.

The Heineken Organization

The Heineken organization was managed by a five-person executive board which included the president, van Schaik, and the four regional coordinating directors (Europe, Asia/Australia, Africa, and Western Hemisphere). At Heineken Corporate, the organization was divided into six main areas: Marketing and Licensees, Technical Affairs, Social Affairs, Exports, Finance, and finally Regional Coordination. These four regional coordinating directors were given strategy and coordinating responsibilities for the operating companies in their respective regions. (For an organization chart of Heineken NV, refer to Exhibit 1.)

The issue of centralisation versus decentralisation often arose in the company. The executive board realized that the complexity and diversity of the operating companies made central control difficult. As well, they felt that local breweries that were left as autonomous business units rather than incorporated into an overall Heineken structure would be better positioned to exploit domestic market situations. Heineken Corporate, then, had a service and coordinating function: assisting the operating companies with managing operations, technical problems, marketing services, and logistics.

However, certain areas were centralised, for example, policies on finance, technology, and, to a lesser extent, marketing. The amount of centralisation in the marketing function had increased over time. Corporate Marketing, in trying to maintain a consistent international image for the corporate brands, developed stricter marketing guidelines, which reduced the opportunities for local creativity.

EXHIBIT 1A

Organization chart, Heineken corporate

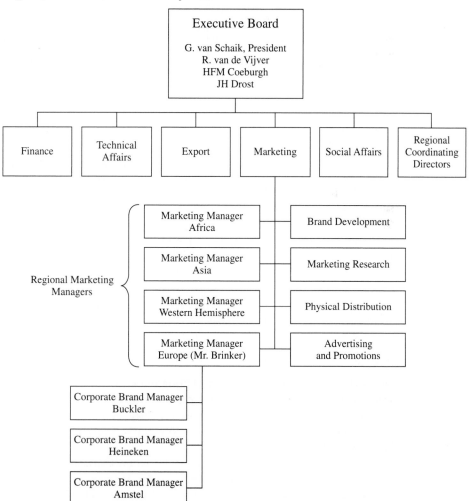

EXHIBIT 1B

Organization chart, regional coordination

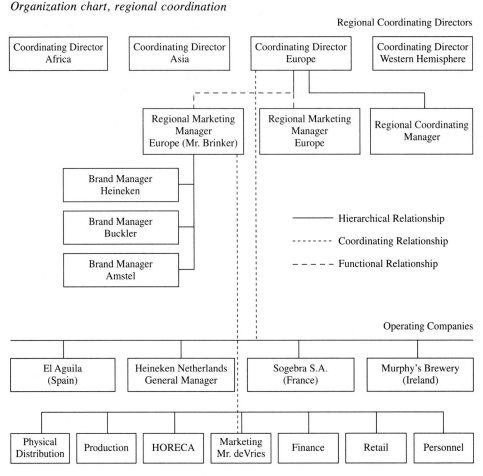

Operating companies were therefore left to market their own domestic brands and to operate on a day-to-day basis.

Corporate Marketing

Hans Brinker, as the regional marketing manager for Europe, was well aware of the tensions between centralisation and decentralisation. For the corporate brands (Heineken, Amstel, and, more recently, Buckler), Brinker was instrumental in trying to find ways to standardise marketing strategy without dampening local marketing initiatives.

One such example occurred in 1990, when Corporate Marketing appointed one Pan-European advertising agency for the Heineken brand. Historically, each operating company had had its own local agency. Therefore, each communications strategy was developed through discussions with the operating company and Corporate Marketing. With the new arrangement, Brinker set up a European brand team for Heineken consisting of two members from Corporate Marketing, six marketing managers from the operating companies, and an export manager to develop the Pan-European communications strategy. In this way, he could include local ideas and opinions.

The Nonalcoholic Beer Industry, 1986–1990

The Product

Nonalcoholic beer was part of the $45 billion European beer industry, which in turn fell into the $134 billion European drinks industry. While the beer industry was stagnating and sometimes even declining during the 1980s, nonalcoholic beer was enjoying a moderate to fast growth in sales. (For details on sales volumes of nonalcoholic beer, refer to Exhibit 2.)

The first introductions of nonalcoholic beer took place in Switzerland and Germany after World War II. The production process at that time, called *vacuum distillation*, removed the alcohol after fermentation. Since then, other production methods had been developed, including a special fermentation process where alcohol was not produced.

Nonalcoholic beer usually contained some alcohol; the amount depended on a country's legal limit for alcohol in nonalcoholic drinks. In Germany, for example, nonalcoholic beers could contain up to the legal limit of 0.5% alcohol, whereas in France the limit was 1%. It was often referred to as alcohol-free or low-alcohol, which were simply more specific descriptions. Alcohol-free beer contained traces of alcohol, whereas low-alcohol contained a little less than the legal limit.

EXHIBIT 2   Sales Volumes of Nonalcoholic Beer by Region (in hectolitres)

Countries	1985	1987	1988	1989
Saudi Arabia	400,000	300,000	250,000	225,000
West Germany	400,000	750,000	1,100,000	1,500,000
France	200,000	330,000	450,000	600,000
Spain	180,000	250,000	350,000	600,000
Netherlands	15,000	25,000	50,000	250,000
Belgium	10,000	20,000	50,000	165,000
United Kingdom	150,000	400,000	600,000	800,000
Switzerland	80,000	80,000	85,000	85,000
United States	625,000	750,000	795,000	850,000
World	3,000,000	4,000,000	4,800,000	6,000,000

SOURCE: Heineken estimates.

The Market

The drinkers of nonalcoholic beer were those who liked the taste of beer but were avoiding alcohol for some reason. Most often, the reason was medical (i.e., pregnancy, diabetes, etc.), and some consumers were also concerned about drinking and driving or felt guilty about drinking too much alcohol.

However, the taste of nonalcoholic beers put regular beer drinkers off. Research findings showed that the product had a watered-down negative image among traditional beer drinkers. As one Heineken executive explained, "A person would describe it as a perfect drink for the neighbour who drinks too much beer. And, in return, the neighbour would say that it's the perfect drink for *his* neighbour because he does not know anything about beer!"

During the 1980s, two market trends created more demand for the product: increasing health consciousness and social pressure regarding alcohol abuse. From the statistics, regular beer companies could see the decline in their share of the total drinks market as more "healthy" beverages including nonalcoholic beer were consumed. In Europe, governments were becoming increasingly tougher in their laws against drinking and driving. Fines and police monitoring had increased substantially. For example, in the United Kingdom, fines ranged from $500 to $4,000 with drivers' licenses often being taken away. As a result, police checks, breathalizer tests, and criminal charges all caused the public to shun drinking and driving. Moreover, it had become socially unacceptable to be drunk in a public situation. Therefore, moderate drinking and diluting drinks (for example, beer with lemon-lime) took place more often. Much of the slack in alcohol consumption was replaced by mineral water, soft drinks, and fruit juices.

These trends also affected the proportion of the market who drank nonalcoholic beer because of feeling guilty about consuming too much alcohol. These people consciously gave up some taste in order to not have alcohol in their beer.

The Introduction of Buckler Beer

Nonalcoholic beer was nothing new at Heineken. As early as the 1930s, there had been discussions about introducing a product in the United States during the prohibition period. By the 1980s, the company already had two nonalcoholic products, Amstel Brew and Aguila Sin, in the Saudi Arabian and Spanish markets. However, both suffered from poor taste, as did many nonalcoholic beer brands at the time. Therefore, neither one was ever considered for an international rollout.

Top management felt that the nonalcoholic beer market was too small to warrant a full-scale product development effort to make the taste right. Corporate Marketing, however, continually monitored the activities in some of the larger nonalcoholic beer markets, such as Switzerland and the United States, in order to be up-to-date on any new developments. The executive board did not become really interested until 1986, when Guinness introduced Kaliber alcohol-free beer.

Heineken quickly provided financial support for a full-fledged product development and commercialization program. In February 1987, the company formed a working team consisting of the brand development manager from Corporate

Marketing, a technical manager from HTB (Heineken Technical Beheer, the research and development arm), and the production and marketing managers from Heineken Netherlands, the Dutch operating company. The objective was to develop, by December of that year, a better tasting non-alcoholic beer than the existing competing brands and to introduce it first in Europe and, later, throughout the world. The time period for development gave the working team a formidable challenge, as such a project usually took around two years to complete.

In April 1987, during a meeting of the general managers of the European operating companies, the general manager of Spain announced, coincidentally, that his organization was going to develop an upgraded version of its nonalcoholic beer, Aguila Sin. The brand's market share had continued to decline at the expense of the only other brand in the country, Cruz Campo Sin. When Heineken's president learned that Spain was interested in a better tasting nonalcoholic beer, he jumped at the opportunity. Because Spain needed a replacement brand urgently and because that country's operating company already had marketing experience with nonalcoholic beer, the president suggested that it be given a "lead country" role, that is, be the "locomotive" for getting the process going. One week later, the marketing manager for Spain joined the working group.

Developing a Marketing Strategy

The team was excited by the opportunity to launch the brand in several countries. They instinctively believed that nonalcoholic beer drinkers tended to be the same everywhere. They were people who liked the taste of beer but could not or did not want to have alcohol. The consensus was that a standard marketing strategy for the brand could be used with only minor local changes. (Refer to Exhibit 3 for the expected level of standardization in the marketing mix elements for Buckler.)

EXHIBIT 3   Level of Standardization for Buckler's Marketing Mix Elements

Marketing Mix Elements	Level of Standardization*
Brand name	5
Product name	4
Product	5/4
Design	5
Positioning	5
Packaging	4
Pricing	4
Advertising	5/4
Sponsoring	5/4
Sales promotions	3/2
Public relations	3/2
Customer service	2
Expiry date	5/4

* 5 = Highly standardized, 1 = Highly localized.

Product Development

The working group felt that developing a nonalcoholic lager would be most appropriate, as its taste in regular beer was most widely accepted in Europe. They agreed to an alcohol content of around 0.5%, which was the average amount in nonalcoholic beers on the market. During the five months of development, a friendly rivalry grew between the technical manager from HTB and the production manager from Heineken Netherlands as to who could produce the best-tasting nonalcoholic beer. The Spanish organization also got involved. Both processes—fermentation without alcohol or removing alcohol after fermentation—were explored. In the end, a special fermentation process was developed and kept a tight-lipped secret.

The group soon realized that the more alcohol the product had, the better it tasted. They had always assumed that nonalcoholic beer drinkers would want the taste to be as close to traditional lager as possible. This product was therefore slightly altered (0.9% alcohol) for the Spanish and French markets, where the legal limit was 1%. For the rest of Europe, the alcohol content was kept at the accepted 0.5%.

Positioning

Previous research findings showed that two positioning strategies were possible for Buckler: to be either a nonalcoholic adult drink or a beer with no alcohol. In both cases the object was to increase the consumption of nonalcoholic beer, only the approach was different. The first implied being a substitute for all soft drinks, and the second offered an alternative beer to beer drinkers.

The group debated the pros and cons of each strategy. As a nonbeer drink, the potential market was enormous. But, the competition for soft drink substitutes was vast; there were colas, mineral water, fruit juices, coffee, and each had its own positioning and marketing strategy. They agreed that using that strategy was too risky.

The group therefore decided to follow the second option. From the market research that had previously been performed in Switzerland, they knew that the majority of the existing nonalcoholic beers were positioned as beer products rather than as nonbeer products.

They also decided to pursue their idea to develop a beer as close to the typical lager beer as possible. They did not want to move too far from a regular beer taste or image because they wanted the consumers to feel they were getting the "real thing" without alcohol rather than something inferior. (Refer to Exhibits 4 and 5 for positioning maps used by the company for competitive brands and substitute products.)

Target Group

The aim was to reach the upper- and middle-income class groups because, the group felt, they would be the first to reduce their alcohol intake. Regular Heineken beer drinkers were between 20 and 35 years of age. Buckler, the group decided,

EXHIBIT 4

Positioning chart of nonalcoholic beer with other drinks

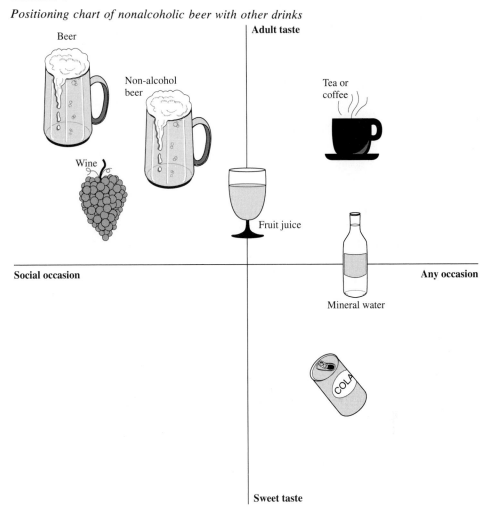

would be directed at consumers 25 to 40 years old, the age category where people were more apt to be concerned about alcohol consumption.

At the beginning, the team did not really know whether they should target the heavy or light drinker. Some believed that heavy drinkers had a greater need. But others disagreed and said lighter users were more rational about alcohol intake. The debate was left unresolved. The final marketing strategy, though, did take heavy users into account.

Pricing

The group decided to introduce Buckler at a premium price even though it cost less to produce due to savings in excise duties. They believed that the product

EXHIBIT 5

Positioning chart of Buckler and competing beer products

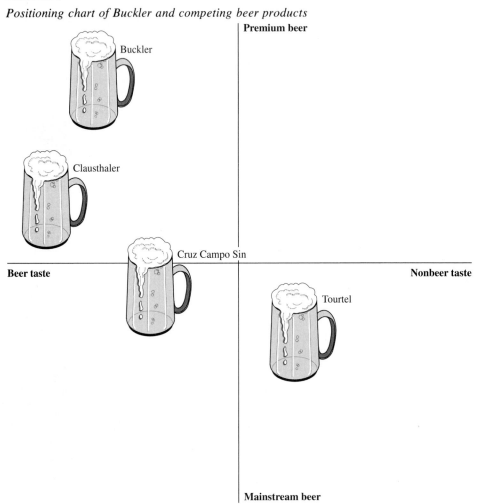

would then have more credibility, and they wanted it to be seen as a premium image brand, especially after the poor quality of nonalcoholic beers in the past. They also wanted to reinforce the taste quality and make consumers feel as if they were gaining something—taste with no alcohol—instead of making a sacrifice when buying the product.

Branding

A debate also centered around whether the product should be a line extension of an existing brand or have a totally new name. Although the company had extended both the Heineken and Amstel brands (Amstel Gold, Amstel Light, Heineken Old Bruin, etc.), all these extensions contained alcohol. Some argued that nonalcoholic beer had a negative connotation; therefore, by extending an existing brand name, the company would not only jeopardize the success of the standard brand but also confuse the consumer. Others, however, pointed out that some line extensions had performed quite well in their local markets. Swan Special Light, an extension of Swan Export, a mainline lager, took a market share of approximately 40% in the Australian market. Cruz Campo Sin, an extension of Cruz Campo, also enjoyed a 40% market share in the Spanish nonalcoholic beer market.

   Having decided to use a new name, the group briefed an international agency, Interbrands, to develop something "beer sounding." After several months of consumer preference tests, as well as language and legal checks on 25 proposed names, the agency came up with two: Buckler and Norlander. Two design agencies were asked to develop different beer labels, some contemporary and some more traditional. (As the illustration in Exhibit 6 shows, the group decided on a more traditional label.)

EXHIBIT 6

Examples of the Buckler labels

Market Research

After developing the product, settling on a positioning strategy, and choosing a traditional label, the two names—Norlander and Buckler—were finally tested. Both qualitative and quantitative tests were done in four countries: the Netherlands, Spain, the United States, and France. The qualitative surveys consisted of focus group discussions on the attributes of nonalcoholic beer. The quantitative research asked participants to compare the taste and image of Buckler and Norlander with competing products: in Spain against Cruz Campo Sin, the market leader; in France against Tourtel, also the market leader; in the United States, against an import called Kaliber; and in the Netherlands against Clausthaler, the imported market leader.

Results of the qualitative test confirmed that nonalcoholic beer was perceived as not tasting very good. However, the participants were pleasantly surprised during the taste tests. In general, both Buckler and Norlander performed better than the competition. Consumer preference did not differ significantly between the two names, so they arbitrarily decided to choose the name *Buckler*.

The Product Launch

The brand development manager, from Corporate Marketing, sent a memo to each operating company in early November informing them of the proposed marketing plan for Buckler beer. The paper included reasons why the group had made the various decisions on the different elements of the marketing mix: product, packaging, price, target group, positioning, and communications strategy. (Refer to Exhibit 7 for highlights of the marketing plan.)

EXHIBIT 7

Highlights of the marketing plan on nonalcoholic beer

Memorandum

To: Marketing Managers
From: Peter Meijer, Corporate Brand Development
Date: Nov. 11, 1987
Subject: Introduction of Buckler

The objective is to participate in the growing beer market with the recently developed Buckler product as an international brand and to gain a leading role. The priority is to introduce the product in all European countries where we have Operating Companies; introduction is planned April/June, 1988. Furthermore, our aim is to have the product available for export elsewhere and/or license it to other countries.

Product:
The product is a lager type beer with the following characteristics:

Original Gravity: + 5 P°
Alcohol Content: 0.4 vol %–0.9 vol %
Bitterness: 21 EBE
Colour: 7 EBC

EXHIBIT 7   (*continued*)

The product may vary in alcohol content; this depends on the local situation given by the law. When a higher alcohol content is possible, this is preferred (better taste). The differences in taste, due to the different alcohol content, are small and therefore acceptable. The .5% alcohol beer will be brewed in the Netherlands whereas the .9% alcohol beer will be produced in Spain. The Spanish version will be exported to France and the Dutch version will be exported to all other European countries, first with Operating Companies and then ones without.

Product Benefits:
A nonalcoholic beer (alcohol percentage the same or lower than other nonalcoholic drinks like fruit juices)

• a tasteful (nonsweet) refresher/thirstquencher
• an adult drink
• a healthy drink (natural ingredients)
• low in calories (50% less than regular beers)
• an acceptable alternative for beer
• a better lager beer taste than the competition.

Target Group
The following segmentation has to be made:

1. Nonalcoholic beer as an occasional drink (at lunch/after sport/before driving)
   • medium/heavy beer drinkers
   • male
   • 25–45 years
2. Nonalcoholic beer as a tasteful thirstquencher (in competition with mineral water/soft drinks)
   • light/medium beer drinkers
   • male and female
   • 20–45 years

Positioning
In theory, two concepts are possible: a beer without alcohol concept or a nonalcohol refresher with an adult taste concept. For the time being the beer concept seems to be the most realistic; motivations and drinkers are more or less coming from regular beer. Beer is the reference. However, it is necessary to develop an own identity for the nonalcoholic beer and to avoid a too strong beer-minus approach.

In general, people are very skeptical about the taste of nonalcoholic beer (watery/flat); after tasting, the product appears to be better than expected. The taste of Buckler is better (more lager taste) than the competition. Although nonalcoholic beers try to be similar to regular beers, they won't be the same due to the lack of alcohol. Nonalcohol beers have to be valued in their own nonalcoholic context against other nonalcoholic drinks, not against regular beers.

Brand Name
Since nonalcoholic beer could be considered as beer-unfriendly, it has been decided to develop a new brand name, instead of a line-extension of Heineken/Amstel. But, above all, a new brand name is desired to establish the proper identity which is felt to be important for this new segment.

The criteria for the development of the brand name were: a good lager beer taste (not watery), social, refreshing, healthy, safe, high, quality, international, masculine, not to be ashamed of. To give it authority, it is possible to use Heineken sourcing (a Heineken product).

Packaging/Label
The packaging is a beer bottle (brown/returnable or one way). The label is, in principle, a beer

---
EXHIBIT 7   (*concluded*)

label; however, the colours (blue/yellow and white/silver) give it a character of its own (nonalcoholic). No draught beer will be provided.

Pricing Strategy

The pricing will be a 20% premium above regular beer or more, the latter if exported. When the product is imported it will be higher due to the higher costs of transport. The pricing throughout Europe will be within a range to avoid parallel imports.

Communications Strategy

The communications strategy will be to position the product as a premium brand with a good quality beer taste. An international communication concept is striven for (with possible local adaptation); the reason behind this international concept is that the background for the development of nonalcoholic beer in different countries is felt to be more or less the same for each country.

The executive board decided to proceed with a product launch in late December 1987. Corporate Marketing was somewhat surprised when the operating companies showed a mixed reaction to the plan. Ideally, they wanted to introduce the product throughout all the operating companies in Europe. However, the divisions in France and Spain were the only ones interested in introducing the product immediately. The Netherlands division stalled because it was introducing a similar product, Amstel Light, on the Dutch market and did not want to confuse the consumer. In addition, the management did not strongly support the product because the Netherlands had only a small nonalcoholic beer market at that time. In Ireland, the organization was introducing Amstel and felt there were not enough resources to introduce two brands at the same time. The Italian operating company felt there was no market in Italy and so was resistant. In Greece, the company did not feel that the association between healthy living and less alcohol consumption had caught on yet, so they also rejected the brand.

Developing a Communications Strategy

Corporate Marketing was therefore left with only Spain and France where they could introduce the brand and develop a communications strategy. Despite the fact that France was the only country really interested in having an advertising campaign, Corporate Marketing still wanted to pursue a Pan-European communications strategy, with a consistent message to all Europeans.

The First Campaign

FHV, a Dutch agency used by Heineken Corporate, was briefed on the product. The agency proposed the slogan "Sometimes you drink beer, sometimes you drink Buckler." This concept was shown to the marketing managers of the operating companies in a meeting in Amsterdam. It was not received warmly by anyone, especially the managers from France and Spain. Spain did not like the message because it seemed to focus too much on developing the nonalcoholic beer category and not enough on the brand; the Spanish nonalcoholic beer market was already well established. The meeting ended with no decision being made. The Spanish and French divisions were left to create their own advertising.

These two operating companies discussed their respective proposals for advertising copy before deciding on the French one. In Spain, some changes were made. For example, in a television advertisement using a hang glider, in the French advertisement nothing was written on the sail, whereas the Spanish ad had the word *Buckler* on the sail.

The Second Campaign

The executive board got involved in the fall of 1988. They concluded that the brand required a consistent communications strategy for the whole of Europe. This time, however, the general manager of the Spanish operating company was appointed to develop the Pan-European communications strategy for Buckler beer. With the aid of a selection agency, the general manager and members of Corporate Marketing chose the international advertising agency Lintas, because of the concept they proposed: "So much taste you won't miss the alcohol." (Refer to Exhibit 8 for an illustration of the concept.)

The general manager, along with Corporate Marketing, decided to take a more objective stand with the operating companies. First, they were shown the briefing to the advertising agencies, which they accepted. Then, before discussing

EXHIBIT 8

Example of second advertising concept

BUCKLER LAGER BEER. SO MUCH TASTE YOU WON'T MISS THE ALCOHOL.

the actual campaign with the operating companies, Corporate Market Research tested it in the various countries to determine the response. If positive, the operating companies would have to accept it. If negative, they could run their own campaign. Managers at the French operating company objected because they did not want to give up their original hang glider campaign. Therefore, Corporate Market Research tested both campaigns to show that the second one, a story of a journalist's day on the run, was more successful. In the other countries, Spain, Ireland, and the Netherlands, the tests also proved successful.

One year later, the second campaign with the journalist advertisement was still being used by each operating company, including Spain, France, the Netherlands, Ireland, and then, in 1990, by Italy and Greece (the last two operating companies to take on the product).

Brand Developments in Three Countries

The Netherlands

The competitive situation in the Netherlands was quiet before the introduction of Buckler in the fall of 1988. Clausthaler, an imported German brand, virtually owned the market, which was only approximately 20,000 hectolitres.

Because of this small market, the Dutch operating company did not have much faith in the Buckler brand. The management was more interested in Amstel Light, a low-calorie product introduced several months earlier. Therefore, in 1989 the operating company budgeted for only 15,000 hectolitres, with no advertising support. However, in that year, the brand achieved a 60% market share, or 100,000 hectolitres, virtually destroying Clausthaler. When they saw the sales increase so impressively, management at Heineken Netherlands quickly allocated G 13 million[1] for the European advertising campaign.

In the beginning of 1989, the Buckler brand began to notice some competitive activity. At that time, a local brewery called Bavaria started selling Bavaria Malt (originally exported to the Middle East markets) in the Netherlands at discounted prices. Grolsch and Allied, other local breweries, then entered with "me too" products, Stender and Classe Royale, respectively. The Bavaria Malt brand consistently won in blind taste tests. Test participants considered it "milder, less bitter than the lager taste of Buckler, and easier to drink than regular lagers." In addition, Bavaria Malt was priced 30% lower than the Buckler brand. By the middle of 1990, Bavaria Malt had stolen 40% market share, and Buckler was down to 30%. (Refer to Exhibit 9 for more details about the Dutch market.)

----

[1] G = Dutch guilders

EXHIBIT 9   Nielsen Report on the Dutch Nonalcoholic Beer Segment, 1989, 1990

	Apr./May	*June/July*	*Aug./Sept.*	*Oct./Nov.*	*Dec./Jan.*	*Feb./Mar.*	*Apr./May*
Market Shares Retail							
Buckler (Heineken)	66.3	62.9	62.7	62.2	46.2	33.2	28.0
Clausthaler (Binding)	10.8	9.6	6.0	4.8	3.4	2.2	2.2
Bavaria Malt (Bavaria)	19.8	25.3	28.9	30.4	34.5	43.3	45.8
Birell (Huerlimann)	2.2	1.4	1.0	1.0	0.5	0.4	0.3
Strender (Grolsch)	0.0	0.0	0.0	0.0	14.3	20.1	23.1
Percentage of total beer market	2.4	3.8	3.0	4.1	5.2	6.4	7.0
Weighted Distribution*							
Buckler	98%	95%	98%	98%	98%	98%	98%
Clausthaler	94	91	90	88	92	86	89
Bavaria Malt	27	29	44	49	54	71	85
Birell	18	19	17	17	15	13	13
Stender	0	0	0	0	27	76	87
Price per Litre (in Guilders)							
Buckler	2.95	2.97	2.99	2.96	2.98	3.00	3.02
Clausthaler	5.38	5.36	5.42	5.38	5.13	5.02	4.71
Bavaria Malt	2.00	1.90	1.94	1.93	1.94	1.95	2.00
Birell	3.24	3.51	3.46	3.51	3.44	3.68	3.63
Stender	n.a.[†]	n.a.	n.a.	n.a.	2.83	2.78	2.79

* Weighted distribution: 20% of the stores carrying the product sell *x*% of the total product sales.

[†] n.a. = Not available.

SOURCE: Nielsen Food Index, the Netherlands.

Spain

The competitors in Spain before the introduction of Buckler were Cruz Campo Sin, the market leader with 60% market share, followed by Aguila Sin, with a declining market share. El Aguila's original plan was to introduce Buckler with no advertising support, along with Aguila Sin. The intent was to slowly remove the old brand, but Buckler sold so well both in retail and on-premise that Aguila Sin was removed after only two months.

Despite low advertising and marketing support, Buckler began gaining approximately 1% market share per month, even with the 20% premium over Cruz Campo Sin. No changes had been made to the Cruz Campo Sin brand. However, other competing brands had already appeared in the Spanish market, including Tourtel (BSN), Dansk LA (Carlsberg), and Malt Beer (Grupo Damm, a regional brewery). Soon, Laiker Sin, developed by Mahou, another regional brewery, would be introduced as well. (Refer to Exhibit 10 for more details about the Spanish market.)

EXHIBIT 10   **Nielsen Report on the Spanish Nonalcoholic Beer Segment, 1989, 1990**

	Apr./May	*June/July*	*Aug./Sept.*	*Oct./Nov.*	*Dec./Jan.*	*Feb./Mar.*	*Apr./May*
Market Share							
Retail and Bar							
Buckler	40.6	40.6	41.7	44.5	44.0	46.0	45.9
Aguila Sin	1.7	1.7	1.1	0.8	0.9	1.2	1.2
Cruz Campo	51.4	50.1	46.3	41.8	39.3	37.2	35.7
Other (Tourtel,							
Dansk LA)	6.3	7.6	10.9	12.9	15.8	15.6	17.2
Numeric and							
Weighted							
Distribution*							
Buckler	19%/34%	21%/36%	22%/39%	22%/38%	23%/39%	25%/40%	26%/42%
Aguila Sin	2/3	1/3	1/2	1/2	2/2	1/1	1/1
Cruz Campo	20/34	22/36	21/34	21/34	20/35	20/33	20/34
Average Price							
per Litre as							
Index vs. Cruz							
Campo Sin							
"Bar" Price							
(Cruz Campo							
"Bar" = 100)							
Retail							
Buckler	61	61	62	62	64	66	66
Aguila Sin	58	50	58	53	54	51	51
Cruz Campo Sin	56	56	57	58	58	61	61
Other	60	62	65	64	65	66	68
Bar							
Buckler	107	97	98	102	102	100	100
Aguila Sin	95	102	104	104	108	105	108
Cruz Campo Sin	100	100	100	100	100	100	100
Other	102	106	111	112	110	116	109

* Numeric distribution: % of Nielsen audited stores carrying product.
Weighted distribution: 20% of the stores carrying the product sell *x*% of total product sales.
SOURCE: Nielsen Food and Bar Index.

The success of the product sales in Spain also caused some worry. Could the growth be maintained? What would stop another competitor from repeating the same experience that had happened with Bavaria Malt in the Netherlands? The company waited in anticipation.

France

In France, before the introduction of Buckler, there had been only one dominant brand, Tourtel, a product that had been in the market for 20 years. Positioned as

---

EXHIBIT 11   Nielsen Report on the French Nonalcoholic Beer Segment

---

	Apr./May	June/July	Aug./Sept.	Oct./Nov.	Dec./Jan.	Feb./Mar.	Apr./May
Market Share Retail							
Buckler	12.4	16.1	16.6	15.4	14.8	16.4	17.3
Tourtel	79.8	76.8	77.0	77.8	78.6	77.5	75.3
Celta	n.a.*	n.a.	4.0	4.9	4.7	4.6	5.1
Others	7.8	7.1	2.4	1.9	1.9	1.5	2.3
Numeric and Weighted Distribution†	%	%	%	%	%	%	%
Buckler	23/70	23/74	28/77	27/76	27/77	33/79	37/84
Tourtel	65/96	66/96	70/96	68/97	66/97	66/96	67/96
Average Price in French Francs							
Buckler	9.08	8.90	8.91	8.89	8.93	9.12	9.10
Tourtel	6.90	6.97	7.04	7.12	7.22	7.24	7.48

---

* n.a. = Not available.

† Numeric distribution: of Nielsen audited stores carrying the product.

Weighted distribution: 20 of the stores carrying the product sell *x* of total product sales.

SOURCE: Nielsen Food Index.

an adult drink rather than a beer, and with an extensive distribution, the brand commanded a 90% market share.

The immediate competitive reaction to Buckler's entry by BSN, the brewers of Tourtel, was to try to block distribution by dropping its prices below Buckler, changing the labeling, revising the product composition, and positioning Tourtel as a beer competitor rather than as a substitute adult drink. Furthermore, BSN offered more types of packaging (a one-litre bottle) and introduced two umbrella brands: Tourtel Brune and Tourtel Amber Gold.

These competitive actions caused the Buckler brand to have a slow start in France relative to the two other countries. Retail chains were hard to penetrate as they demanded huge listing fees and some proof of a successful product. After the first year, sales of Buckler were below budget. Blind taste tests showed a 50% preference for Buckler and 50% for Tourtel. However, by the middle of 1990, the company had attained a 15% market share. (Refer to Exhibit 11 for more details about the French market.)

The Decision

Hans Brinker had a problem. The executive board had made a decision to make Buckler Pan-European, and he personally felt that this was a breakthrough for the company. He was convinced that the original Buckler marketing strategy was sound but that the long-term earning potential would be jeopardized if a change were made now in midstream.

He was not particularly worried about the local brands. The real competition, he believed, were the Pan-European brands like Tourtel. Since Buckler's introduction in France, BSN continued to react by introducing Tourtel in other countries such as Belgium, Switzerland, the United Kingdom, Spain, and, more recently, Italy and Greece. BSN also had several operating companies with wide distribution power. In addition, more was being spent for advertising on Tourtel than on Buckler, and Tourtel's price was also lower. (Refer to Exhibit 12 for details about the Tourtel brand.) At the same time, something had to be done for the operating companies, as they were entitled to have a fair share of the market.

EXHIBIT 12   Marketing Mix Details, Tourtel

Marketing Mix	France	Belgium	United Kingdom	Spain	Switzerland
Brand name	Tourtel	Tourtel	Tourtel	Tourtel	Tourtel
Packaging	Almost the same over the different countries, with slight differences in text: green bottles.				
Product composition	Alcohol: 0.7%	Alcohol: .35%	n.a.*	Alcohol: .75%	Alcohol: .4%
	Wort: 6.9	Wort: 6.9		Wort: 7.0	Wort: 6.9
	Colour: 7.5	Colour: 8.0		Colour: 7.5	Colour: 8.0
	Bitterness: 20	Bitterness: 22		Bitterness: 19	Bitterness: 20
Positioning	Drink more	Drink more	n.a.	Drink more	n.a.
	Personal care	Personal care		Taste	
Price proportion with mainstream beer	106	122	n.a.	153	129
Advertising theme	Tourtel, you can drink it all night long.	Tourtel, you can drink it all night long.	n.a.	Tourtel, you can drink it all night long.	n.a.
Advertising agency	BDDP	Booster/BDDP	n.a.	BDDP	n.a.
Media choice	Television	Television, print billboard	n.a.	Television, print	n.a.
Entry strategy	Locally produced	Import	Import	Import	Import
Distribution intensity	Intensive	Intensive	n.a.	Intensive	Intensive
Target group	n.a.†	Age group: 25–34	n.a.	Age group: 25–34	n.a.
		Sex: male, female			
				Sex: male, female	
		Beer/nonbeer drinker		Beer/nonbeer drinker	
Market share	75%	61%	n.a.	5%	n.a.

† n.a. = Not available.

II COMMUNICATIONS POLICY

CLUB MED ESPAÑA

Jean-Michel Landau, the newly appointed managing director of Club Med Spain, was eager to proceed with his plans to launch a full-scale marketing and sales effort for the Spanish market. It was February 3, 1992, and in less than two weeks Club Med would be holding a press conference in Madrid to announce its first major communications campaign aimed at Spanish holiday travelers. With vacation spending rising at an annual rate of 32%, Spain was one of Europe's fastest growing markets for package holidays. In fact, some managers at "the Club" feared that they had waited too long to exploit the Spanish market and that sales opportunities had been lost; consequently, there were high expectations that, once a formal communication campaign was launched, sales in Spain would quickly blossom.

Jean-Michel's communications budget for the Spanish market was limited. Jean-Michel knew that he would have to employ an effective mix of communication techniques in order to promote the product, while at the same time generating enough sales over the next few seasons to continue funding his marketing efforts. Should he emphasize the unique Club Med concept through media advertising? Or should he focus directly on his distributors and target customers? What was the most effective means of reaching his target audience? How effectively would he be able to measure the results as the season progressed so that he could modify his strategy appropriately for the next season?

As he considered these issues, Jean-Michel thought back on his successful years as marketing manager for Club Med's biggest market—France. "Spain is a different kind of challenge," he said, "but here in Spain, I have a brand-new

This case was prepared by Research Associate Alex Bloom under the direction of Professor Dominique Turpin. Copyright © 1992 by the International Institute for Management Development (IMD), Lausanne, Switzerland. Not to be used or reproduced without permission. IMD case 431 (Revised 1993).

market, and there are no constraints on how I operate. I can build this organization from the bottom up.''

Background

Club Méditerranée was founded in 1950 by George Blitz, who, along with a group of friends, developed the Club as an association devoted to sports and seaside vacations. Originally, the Club was a nonprofit organization, and during their travels the members adhered to a set of principles encompassing rustic communal life. By 1954, as the organization grew increasingly popular, Blitz asked Mr. Gilbert Trigano, whose family business supplied the Club with tents, to take over management of the Club. Trigano accepted, and sensing the commercial potential of the Club's concept, he transformed the organization into a profitable enterprise.

The Club Med Concept

The Club's venue began to evolve when, in 1954, Club Med under Trigano's management opened its first straw-hut village. Social life at the village also took its formal shape. Customers were named *gentils membres* (GMs), or ''nice members,'' and staff were referred to as *gentils organizateurs* (GOs), or ''nice organizers.'' The GO's role in the village was, in the words of the Club, that of a ''friend rather than a servant.'' Much of the Club's appeal stemmed from the daily games and sports activities that the GOs would organize and the nightly amateur entertainment that the GOs would perform, often with the GMs themselves participating. Each resort was run by a *chef de village,* who was responsible for village operations as well as for hosting and entertaining the GMs. These *chefs de village,* who would move from village to village each season, soon attained fame both within Club Med and among its loyal GMs.

The Club Med vacation was sold as an all-inclusive package, including transportation, food, entertainment, sports, and activities. This was integral to the Club's principles of egalitarianism and communal interaction at the village. For example, instead of using money, GMs would pay for any extras (usually drinks) with beads taken from a necklace, and at mealtimes, GMs and GOs alike would sit together at tables of eight. Furthermore, the ''hassles'' of modern civilization—such as telephones, televisions, and even newspapers—were not provided or allowed in the villages.

Globalization

As Club Med's unique vacation concept attained fame and success, the company expanded its operations by opening new villages at prime locations around the world. The first snow village was opened in Switzerland in 1956, and over the next decade villages were opened throughout Europe and North Africa. In 1968, a village was opened in Guadeloupe in the Caribbean; in 1979, villages opened in

South America, New Caledonia, and Malaysia. The first village in the United States was opened in 1980, and the first one in Japan was opened in 1987. By 1990, Club Med operated over 100 villages in 33 countries around the world and employed over 24,000 people.

Sales had also expanded around the world. Countries like Belgium, Italy, and Germany had provided strong customer bases from early on in the Club's history; North and South American markets were cultivated during the 1970s, and, more recently, sales had been growing rapidly in Japan and the Far East. Club Med's target in Japan was ambitious: 200,000 members by 1999 from 50,000 in fiscal year 1989. By 1990, with sales offices in 26 countries, Club Med's global revenues had reached FF 8.2 billion.[1] Sixty-two percent of their customers came from Europe, 20% from North America, and 12% from Japan and the Far East. France, with 431,700 GMs, was still the Club's largest single market, providing over 35% of its total customer base.

Global expansion was not painless, however. As sales grew outside of France, it became apparent that village operations had to be modified to accommodate the demands of non-French GMs. Consequently, GOs were hired from different nationalities in order to address any cultural or language problems which might arise, menus were modified to cater to non-French tastes when necessary (Japanese GMs, for example, expected seaweed for breakfast rather than croissants), and bookings were controlled in order to balance the mix of nationalities at the villages. GOs and GMs from around the world mixing together in Club Med villages gave the product an "international" character but created a complex logistical tangle between marketing and operations.

Sales and Marketing

New markets were typically launched by opening a Club Med agency (or "boutique") which would sell directly to the public while serving as a base for operations. In the larger, more highly penetrated markets, the bulk of the sales were made through independent travel agents; the boutiques continued to play an important role, however, serving as information outlets and reinforcing the Club's image through their presence in metropolitan centers. Besides, sales made through the boutiques normally yielded better margins than those made through travel agencies.

Club Med focused on providing outstanding service to its GMs. A sophisticated customer feedback survey, known internally as the *baromètre* (or "barometer"), was used to monitor GM satisfaction, and the results of the survey were used to measure the performance of the village managers and their GO teams. Consequently, the repeat purchase rate for Club Med products was typically high (the repeat purchase rate in France, for example, was 70%), and many GMs returned to the Club year after year for their holidays.

---

[1] 1990 average market exchange rate: $1 = FF 5.4453.

Product Evolution and Diversification

While much of the early Club Med concept remained as an integral part of the village experience, attention to GM satisfaction and changing tastes had led to an evolution of the product. "Upscale" activities (such as golf) were added, special facilities were created to accommodate children, and the product line now ranged from straw-hut villages and bungalows to luxury resorts. Most villages now had locks on the rooms, and the Club had become sensitive to criticisms of being "over-organized."

In addition to its village holidays, Club Med had begun to diversify into other, related activities. Club Med villages were marketed to corporate customers for seminars, conferences, and incentive trips through the Club Med Business program; a luxury yacht (the *Club Med One* and *Club Med Two*) offered cruise packages in the Mediterranean and the Caribbean or the Pacific. A City Club was opened in downtown Vienna, and Club Med subsidiaries operated timeshare holiday villas.

Club Med in Spain

Club Med's presence in Spain began in 1962 when the company opened a hut village in Cadaquès on the Costa Brava, a resort area on the Mediterranean Sea. Since then, four more villages were opened, bringing total capacity to over 4,000 beds. The most recent village, an upscale resort hotel in Ibiza, was opened in 1990. Two of the villages were operated during both the summer and winter seasons, while the remaining three operated as summer villages only.

Club Med began selling its holiday packages to Spanish vacationers in the mid-1970s through Club de Vanguardia, a local tour operator. In 1982, the Club opened a boutique in Barcelona, where most of its customers were concentrated. The boutique sold Club Med holidays directly to the Spanish public, while at the same time serving as a base for managing village operations in Spain. Parallel to the opening of the Barcelona boutique, Club Med made its products available for distribution by most leading travel agencies in Spain. Promotion of the product was left to word of mouth and to the travel agents, who received a standard commission (5–8% on the retail price) for every sale.

Sales during the 1990–91 season alone totaled 2,200 bookings, representing about 8,000 customers with revenues reaching Pta 450 million.[2] Thirty-nine percent of these revenues were from group sales to companies using Club Med villages for conferences, seminars, or incentive trips. Awareness of the product (1.5% in 1990) remained low in Spain, but the unfostered growth in sales led Club Med management in Paris to conclude that the Club Med vacation should be marketed more actively to the Spanish market. Italy was cited as an example of a

---

[2] 1990 average market exchange rate: $1 = Pta 101.90.

country where, some years earlier, conditions had been similar to those currently existing in Spain; Italy had since grown to become Club Med's largest market in Europe outside France.

Jean-Michel Landau

Jean-Michel Landau, 42, was a veteran Club Med manager. Born in southern France, he grew up in North Africa, where he joined Club Med at the age of 19. He soon became a *chef de village* and eventually moved into management, heading Club Med country offices in Mexico, Tunisia, Italy, and Canada. Prior to taking over the Spanish office in October 1991, he had spent six years as head of marketing and sales activities in France. Under Jean-Michel, sales in France were the highest they had ever been for Club Med, reaching revenues of FF 2.3 billion in 1989.

"As marketing manager in France," explained Jean-Michel, "you are not allowed any mistakes. One percent loss of market share in France represents a tremendous amount of money to the Club." In contrast to the 300-person organization he managed in France, Club Med's office in Spain employed only 25 people, but Jean-Michel felt this gave him the freedom and flexibility he needed to tackle a new market launch. Because of his success in France, Club Med senior management felt that Jean-Michel was ideal for building up the marketing organization in Spain. Sales potential in Spain was felt to be high, and Paris wanted to develop the Spanish market as quickly as possible. Christian Remoissenet, who had been with Club Med in Spain since 1989, was appointed sales and marketing

EXHIBIT 1

Organization chart of Club Med Spain

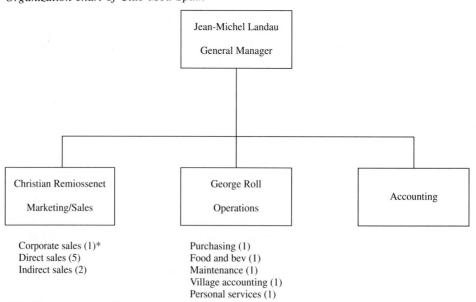

* Numbers in parentheses denote number of employees.

manager by Jean-Michel, and together the two of them would oversee the day-to-day activities of marketing the product. (Refer to the organization chart in Exhibit 1.)

The Spanish Tourist Industry

By 1990, more than half of Spain's population of 39 million traveled on holiday each year. While this figure had not changed dramatically through the 1980s, holiday spending had increased at an average yearly rate of 32%, with 1989 expenditures (excluding international transportation) reaching Pta 365 billion. Spaniards were thus among the fastest growing holiday spenders (average growth around the world was only 18% for the same period), and by 1990 Spain ranked 15th among nations in terms of overall vacation spending.

Most Spaniards spent their holidays in Spain. By the late 1980s, however, the number of Spaniards traveling abroad for their holidays began to increase rapidly, growing from 7% of vacationers in 1985 to 19% by 1990. (Exhibit 2 shows a

---

EXHIBIT 2   Excerpts from a Survey of the Spanish Tourist Market

Motivations for Tourist Travel within Spain

Diversion and change of environment	41.6%
Visit family and friends	31.5
Health and relaxation	16.1
Visit new places	13.6

Motivations for Tourist Travel to Foreign Countries

Tourism	49.3%
Tourism and other	31.5
Visit family	13.8
Cultural curiosity	10.5

Preferred Activities

Cultural activities	86.0%
Relaxation	49.4
Night life	27.4
Cuisine	25.6
Rural tourism	14.0

Principal Foreign Destinations*

France	30.3%
Italy	19.0
Portugal	17.8
Andores	14.0
Germany	7.2
Switzerland	6.1
United Kingdom	6.0

* NOTE: Some respondents listed two destinations—total may be greater than 100%.

SOURCE: *Le Marché Touristique Espagnol—Guide Pratique* (Maison de la France, 1990).

breakdown of foreign destination by geographical origin for Spanish travelers and lists the key travel incentives for Spanish holiday makers.)

Club Med's Spanish GMs represented the upper end of the vacation market. An analysis of the 1987 season showed that over 75% of Spanish GMs were professionals or executives, most were between the ages of 30 and 50, and most traveled as singles or couples, with less than 20% of the bookings consisting of families. In contrast to the overall market, Club Med customers preferred to vacation abroad, with nearly two-thirds of the GMs choosing non-Spanish destinations (although only one-third chose destinations outside the Mediterranean basin—refer to Exhibit 3). The Club also achieved a higher-than-average volume of low-season sales, with 26% of its GMs traveling during the winter.

In preparation for the marketing campaign, Jean-Michel commissioned a customer satisfaction study with Metra-Seis, a market research firm in Barcelona. The study, which was based on interviews with selected GMs, indicated that certain aspects of Club Med's products conflicted with Spanish expectations.

EXHIBIT 3   Customer Profile

1. Club Med Spain Customer Profile, Summer 1989 Season

Sales by Destination—Individuals:

Spain	35%
Mediterranean basin (Morocco 19%, Tunisia 7%, Turkey 5%, Greece 4%, others)	35
Nearby destinations (France 6%, Portugal 4%, Italy 3%)	13
Exotic islands (Caribbean 6%, Polynesia 2%, Mauritius 1%, Maldives 1%, Phuket 0.7%, Bali 0.7%)	13
Long-distance destinations (Mexico 2.5%, Brazil 1%, Malaysia 0.25%, Senegal 0.25%)	4

2. Survey of Current and Potential Customers Who Contacted the Barcelona Boutique, November 1989

First Heard of Club Med through:

Friends, acquaintances	70%	(80% for potential customers)
Brochure	22	
Media	4	
Mailing	4	

Principal Motivations for Purchase of Club Med:

Sports activities	35%	(40% for potential customers)
Meet new friends	19	
Rest/relaxation	16	
Social activities	16	
Destination country	11	
Exoticism	3	

Travel status:

Couple	30%
Family	26
Couple with children	18
Friends	15
Alone	11

Exhibit 3   *(concluded)*

3. Club Med Customer Analysis, 1987 Season

Profession:	
Heads of enterprises	36%
Executives	19
Liberal professions	27
Employees	11
Students	5
Other	2
Departure Status:	
Alone	44%
Couple	38
With family or friends	18

SOURCE: *Evaluation du Marché du Tourisme Espagnol et Stratégie de Développement* (Charles Riley Consultants International).

Complaints focused on the quality of accommodations, the inflexibility of time schedules, the high degree of organization, and the fact that French was the principal language of the Club; some also felt that the Club concept was not adequately explained in either the brochure or at the point of sale. However, overall satisfaction with the Club was high. Positive comments particularly emphasized the sports activities, the children's activities, and the food.

Competitive Package Holiday Products

Club Med's principal competitors in Spain were the major tour operators who developed and sold inclusive package holiday products. Sales of package holiday products had been growing in Spain, from 900,000 packages sold in 1985 to 1.5 million packages in 1990. (Travel agent revenues for 1990, *including* transportation, reached Pta 900 billion; with nearly one-third of this amount estimated to be attributed to package holiday sales.) The typical package holiday comprised transportation and accommodation, often including one or more meals and sometimes consisting of excursions to multiple destinations. The most common package holiday products sold to Spanish vacationers were to local sun/sea destinations in Spain, followed by European and North African sun/sea destinations during the summer and winter seasons, and European snow destinations during the winter; less common were excursions to the Americas and the Far East.

By 1990, there were 284 tour operators developing package holiday products in Spain. Tour operators distributed their products through independent travel agencies, which operated more than 3,000 travel agency outlets throughout the country. (An "independent" typically owned an average of 1–3 outlets, all in one particular city or region, and sold holiday packages on behalf of the tour operators on a commission basis.) The larger tour operators, however, generally operated their own outlets as well. Wagons-Lits and Viajes Melia, the two largest such companies, operated 150 and 120 outlets, respectively. Both of these companies were typical of the large international travel groups which had been expanding globally, primarily through acquisition of local travel agent chains. Wagons-Lits, a French conglomerate, had worldwide revenues of FF 16.1 billion in 1990, while Viajes Melia, a Spanish company which had been bought by an Italian group in 1987, had revenues of Pta 33.9 billion.

Jean-Michel estimated that the retail price of Club Med holidays averaged 30% higher than those of available package holidays to comparable destinations. Club Med believed that this premium price reflected the unique characteristics of the product and that the organized activities, the entertainment, and the GO spirit at a Club Med village were features that were not to be found in the standard inclusive packages. In other countries, Club Med often justified its higher prices by claiming that the additional activities at the Club yielded higher value for money and that just the transportation, accommodation, food, and activities would cost the consumer much more if purchased separately than through a Club Med package.

Club Med's Strategy for Spain

Jean-Michel's goal was to build up the GM customer base in Spain from the current 8,000 customers to 50,000 customers and to raise national awareness for the Club from 1.5% to 40% over a five-year period. According to Club Med España's estimates, a target of 50,000 customers represented about 10% of the 500,000 Spaniards who took package holidays comparable in value to the average Club Med product. Jean-Michel expected marketing efforts to result in a doubling of both group and individual sales for the 1991–92 season, and he expected growth to continue steadily over the next few years as the product gained recognition.

An advertising and public relations campaign would be launched within the month. This, along with the Club Med brochure, would be critical in building the Club s image in Spain. An effective distribution network would also have to be created. Selected travel agencies would have to develop a good understanding of the product, and incentives would have to be provided to sell Club Med over other package holiday products.

Target

Club Med España aimed at targeting the most affluent segment of the Spanish population, particularly liberal professionals—doctors, lawyers, property owners, businesspeople, and so on. Charles Riley Consultants International had estimated Club Med's potential market in Spain in 1990 to be 375,000 customers.

Product Offering

In 1991, Club Med España wanted to offer its Spanish customers a whole range of products and destinations through three versions of the company's brochure, the *Trident:*

- The winter ski catalog offered nine destinations to French ski resorts, one in Italy, and nine in Switzerland.
- The winter sun catalog destinations introduced 12 destinations in Europe and Africa—Spain, France, Israel, Ireland, Morocco, Portugal, Senegal, Tunisia, and the Caribbees (Antilles); 13 in the Carribean or America—Bahamas, the French Carribean, Haiti, Brazil, Mexico, and the United States; and 8 in Asia, Polynesia, and other faraway places—Indonesia, Malaysia, the Maldives, Tahiti, New Caledonia, Mauritius, and Thailand.
- The summer catalog introduced 32 villages in Europe and Africa—4 in Spain and Turkey, 5 in France and Morocco, 3 in Greece, Tunisia, and Italy, 1 in Ireland, Israel, Portugal, and Senegal; 16 destinations in the Americas—5 in Mexico, 3 in the French Carribbean, 2 in Brazil and the Bahamas, 1 in the United States, the Turks and Caicos, and Haiti; and 6 destinations in Asia and Polynesia—Indonesia, Malaysia, the Maldives, Mauritius, Thailand, and Tahiti.

Communication

A poll conducted by Dym SA (a market research organization which had developed a holiday and travel-oriented omnibus) found that only 1.5% of the population in Spain had heard of Club Med. (In contrast, the awareness level for France was 90%; results of the Spanish survey are shown in Exhibit 4.)

Advertising would be developed by the local offices of RSCG, an international advertising agency based in Paris, which handled all of Club Med's advertising for Europe. RSCG planned to use existing Club Med material from its archives in Paris but to design advertisements specifically targeted to a Spanish audience. (Exhibit 5 on page 83 shows preliminary advertisements developed by RSCG for the Spanish campaign.) Jean-Michel had run two series of trial tactical advertisements in Barcelona's daily *La Vanguardia* in December of 1991. The test, which was timed to coincide with the Christmas holidays, seemed to have produced successful results, with more bookings requested than could be accommodated.

RSCG would also be used to produce the Club Med brochure, the *Trident*, as it was called within the company, in reference to the Club's logo. The *Trident* was distributed to travel agents, who displayed it on shelves, redistributed it to customers, and used it as a reference to the Club's products. Brochures were also distributed to customers directly by Club Med, both at the boutique, and, when new brochures were printed, through direct mailings to previous GMs. Historically, Club Med gave away 4 brochures for every direct booking and 10 brochures for every indirect booking. A total of 50,000 brochures had been printed and distributed in Spain during the two 1990–91 seasons, and another 30,000 brochures had already been printed for the winter season of 1991–92.

A major decision that Jean-Michel had to make was to determine the size of the communications budget. Since Club Med España was spending very little on communications before he took over his new position, Jean-Michel had to start from scratch to figure out an appropriate budget for the Spanish market. During 1990–1991, Club Med España had spent the equivalent of FF 26,000 in

<hr>

EXHIBIT 4   Results of the DYM Survey, November–December 1991
Questions

Q1: "Have you ever had the occasion to hear about Club Med?"
Q2: "If 'yes,' tell me please, what is the principal activity of Club Med?"

Results

	Total	Age			Status*				Sex	
		16–30	*31–45*	*46–50*	*A + B*	*C1*	*C2*	*D*	*M*	*F*
Q1:										
Yes	1.5	1.3	2.1	1.1	3.3	0.8	1.6	0.9	1.5	1.5
No	98.5	98.7	97.9	98.9	96.7	99.2	98.4	99.1	98.5	98.5
Q2:										
Vacation club	10.6	—	25.3	—	12.9	53.7	—	—	13.2	8.0
Travel agency	3.7	11.6	—	—	12.1	—	—	—	—	7.5
Club Mediterranée[†]	3.3	—	7.9	—	10.7	—	—	—	6.6	—
Residences w/activities	—	—	—	—	—	—	—	—	—	—
Conglomerate	2.5	—	—	9.5	—	—	6.4	—	—	5.0
Sports facilities	11.9	26.8	7.9	—	27.8	—	8.6	—	6.6	17.3
Sports/football	4.3	13.4	—	—	13.9	—	—	—	—	8.6
Food company	9.7	9.5	9.7	10.0	8.4	24.9	10.5	—	13.3	6.1
Other	26.9	11.0	33.2	36.4	7.9	21.4	48.1	17.8	12.3	41.5
Don't know	31.3	41.0	15.9	44.0	20.4	—	26.4	82.2	47.8	14.7

* The socioeconomic status classification is defined as follows:

Social Status		*Head of Household's Occupation*
A	Upper middle class	Higher managerial, administrative, or professional
B	Middle class	Intermediate managerial, administrative, or professional
C1	Lower middle class	Supervisory, clerical, junior managerial, administrative, or professional
C2	Skilled working class	Skilled manual workers
D	Working class	Semi- and unskilled manual workers

[†] Club Med had recently changed its name in Spain from "Club Mediteranée" to "Club Med."

advertising, FF 132,000 in promotion, FF 975,000 in brochures, and FF 352,000 in commissions to travel agents. He knew that his major local competitor had spent Pta 300 million on communications during the past year. However, such a budget was well over what he could afford. In any case, any budget he would present to the Paris headquarters had to be fully justified.

Distribution

By 1990, only one-third of Club Med's individual sales in Spain were made through 40 travel agents. Club Med España expected that agents would make about two-thirds of its sales by 1995–96. Jean-Michel's objective was to obtain national coverage by increasing this number to 150–200 agents. Travel agents

EXHIBIT 5

Tactical advertisements developed by RSCG for Club Med, Spain (published in La Vanguardia, *December 1991)*

would be key to a successful marketing effort, however, and because of his experience as marketing manager for France, Jean Michel was particularly concerned about developing the distribution channels properly in Spain. "In France," he explained, "99% of our indirect sales are made by one agency—a competitor of ours, Havas Voyages. We account for 30% of their gross turnover, and they account for 30% of ours. We fight a lot, but we can't live without them, and they can't live without us. I don't want a situation like this in Spain—it leaves you with no control over the distribution."

Consequently, Jean-Michel planned to spread the risk of indirect distribution over several of the more prestigious independent travel agents in Spain, which would be selected based on gross turnover (candidates should average about Pta 400 million per year), geographical location, and their previous track record selling Club Med. Selected agents would be groomed as "Club Med Experts." Employees from "Expert" agencies would be sent to Club Med villages, would receive extensive training on Club Med's products and selling techniques, and would eventually be granted more favorable commissions than normal travel agencies.

The boutique was still the most critical point of sale, with two-thirds of the GMs currently booking their trips directly through Club Med. Jean-Michel was preparing to open a second boutique in downtown Madrid by the end of February, in time for the beginning of summer bookings. Start-up costs for the Madrid boutique had been budgeted at Pta 36 million, of which Pta 25 million represented a one-time "rental-rights" payment, while the remaining Pta 11 million had been used for construction and decorating. With a rent of Pta 300,000 per month, Jean-Michel estimated that the direct costs of operating the Madrid boutique would amount to about 5% of its gross sales within two years of operation. A third boutique was planned for Valencia, the third largest city in Spain, but no time frame had been set; boutiques located outside Madrid, however, were expected to incur significantly lower rental and rights costs.

Options

Commercial activity for Club Med Spain was measured by headquarters in Paris on a sales-driven system whereby the Spanish office received a 15% commission for each booking. "Profitability" of the office was then affected by two main factors; transportation margins and the cost of sales. Since transportation was included in every Club Med booking, the office bought seats on charter flights and resold them to its GMs; profit margins from this activity averaged 20–25% for the Spanish office, and Jean-Michel estimated that transportation would soon be accounting for 35–40% of gross revenues. Cost of sales comprised travel agent commissions, overhead for boutiques, and the cost of advertising and promotion. (Village operations for Spain, which also fell under Jean-Michel's management, did not represent a factor in measuring commercial activity of the Spanish office; Spanish villages were booked worldwide, and Jean-Michel was only responsible for their cost of operations.)

The communications budget would be based on loss-making sales during the initial years of the marketing plan. As a budgetary guideline, Jean-Michel had agreed with Club Med headquarters in Paris to maintain gross operation costs (not including village operations) at 30–35% of revenues for about three years—beginning with the 1991–92 season—until operations could become profitable.

While Spain showed every indication of providing Club Med with a strong market, Jean-Michel faced the dilemma of allocating his limited budget between promoting the product and pushing it through the distribution channels. Furthermore, the right products had to be sold to the right customers; otherwise, the initial marketing effort could backfire through client dissatisfaction.

The Cost of Advertising

Advertising represented the most expensive component of the communications campaign. RSCG proposed an advertising schedule that focused on print media in Barcelona and Madrid and that would cost the Club an estimated Pta 34 million, including Pta 2.3 million for design and layout. (The schedule and a summary of advertising rates are shown in Exhibit 6.) The RSCG proposal was for a series of double-page color advertisements to be run in selected daily and weekly newspapers during the summer season. The proposal also included periodic tactical advertisements for promoting specific destinations and included advertisements in two travel-oriented specialty magazines. Lead times for reserving

EXHIBIT 6   RSCG Proposed Advertising Schedule

Double-Page, Color, Image Advertisements, Newspapers

Sunday Supplements	Weeks of	Total Cost (Pta 000,000)
La Vanguardia	16/3, 4/5, 18/5, 1/6	10.0
El Periodico	16/3, 22/5	4.5
ABC	18/5, 1/6	5.3
El Mundo	16/3, 25/5	4.0
El Pais	4/5	6.4

Double-Page, Color, Image Advertisements, Magazines

Periodical	Month of	Total Cost (Pta 000,000)
GEO	May	1.5
Viajar	June	1.2

Quarter-Page, Tactical Advertisements, Newspapers

Leading Dailies	No. Ads	Total Cost (Pta 000,000)
La Vanguardia	8	3.3
El Pais	8	3.9

advertising space limited the extent to which advertising could be modified as the season progressed. Jean-Michel also planned to repeat the Dym survey at least once per year (at a cost of Pta 200,000 per poll) in order to monitor the awareness level as the advertising campaign proceeded.

The advertising campaign would be coordinated with public relations activities, including a press conference scheduled for mid-February to announce the launch of Club Med's advertising campaign. A public relations firm, Gene Associates, had been contracted to manage all of Club Med's public relations activities in Spain for a fee of Pta 500,000 per month; the firm's responsibilities included organizing press conferences and feeding stories to the press, as well as organizing any special events. Jean-Michel was considering sponsoring some events (such as golf tournaments) that would promote the Club and generate news coverage; in addition to the public relations firm's fee, such activities typically cost the Club about FF 40,000 per event.

A New Brochure

Since Spaniards were unfamiliar with the Club, the *Trident* would play a critical role in promoting the product and generating sales. The current Spanish *Trident* was similar to the "European" *Trident* produced every season in Paris and translated into the appropriate languages for Club Med's other marketing organizations in Europe. A brief introduction described the Club, after which the villages were listed by country, with one to two pages and a few photographs used to describe each village; a separate insert listed the prices of each destination. (Refer to Exhibit 7.)

Three decisions had to be made regarding the *Trident:* the number of different *Tridents,* the number of copies, and the content. RSCG estimated the cost of producing three separate brochures (summer, winter–sun, and winter–ski) to be

---

EXHIBIT 7   Summary of the Introduction from the Club Med Spanish Trident Sol–Invierno 91/92 ("Sun–Winter 91/92")

The introduction consists of seven pages of text, interspersed with pictures of scenes from Club Med villages. The text is divided into the following subtitled sections:

Life in the Club
  The Village
  Freedom
  The GOs
  The Food
  The Necklace Bar
  Entertainment
The Best Sports School in the World
The Paradise of Children
Enrich Your Knowledge, Discover
Club Med One

EXHIBIT 7 *(continued)*

EXHIBIT 7 (*concluded*)

INDICE

EUROPA - AFRICA

AMERICA - OCEANIA

ASIA - OCEANO INDICO

Clud Med Diagonal, 503 - 08029 Barcelona
Tel. (93) 439 57 02 - Fax: (93) 405 33 46
Horarios de apertura: De Lunes a Viernes de 9'30 h. a 20 h., Sábados de 9'30 h. a 14 h.

Pta 3 million for layout and design, plus Pta 173.7 per copy for printing. As with advertising, RSCG would use photographs from Paris in the production of the new Spanish *Tridents*. Layout and text would be different, however, with the aim of targeting Spanish GMs and better explaining the Club concept. Targeting included the emphasis placed on the individual villages. Popular Club Med destinations for Spaniards, for example, could be displayed more prominently, and the least visited villages would have their description omitted entirely (although the full product line would be included in the price list).

Finally, direct mailings to previous customers were conducted to distribute newly published brochures and to announce special offerings. A direct mailing to the current customer base cost approximately Pta 600,000; several mailings would have to be conducted during the 1991–92 season.

Prices and Quotas

Each village had a basic price which was set by Club Med's headquarters in Paris. Jean-Michel could adjust the price seasonally, so long as the basic price remained the annual average. In addition to setting prices based on time of year, special promotions were often used to fill certain destinations or if bookings were slow. (Promotions could be in the form of price discounts or special deals such as free accommodation for children, etc.)

Price setting, however, had to be balanced between Spanish seasonal holiday patterns and a complex quota system imposed by Paris which limited the bookings that Jean-Michel could make for each village. Club Med attempted to manage the mix of GMs at the villages by assigning each country a fixed number of booking slots for each destination, and countries like Spain did their best to fill these slots by adjusting their marketing efforts. These quotas were primarily in place to ensure adequate supply for France, Club Med's biggest market; consequently, quotas during the high-season months were rarely adequate for the other countries. Jean-Michel did not expect this to affect 1991–92 sales, but he did expect the quota system to become problematic relatively soon, since Spanish holiday patterns were heavily concentrated in the month of August.

The Travel Agent Network

The standard travel agent commission in Spain was 5–8% of the retail price. Club Med Experts were expected to promote the Club because of the training they received and because of the expected volume that Club Med sales would generate for them. (Jean-Michel expected Experts to eventually reach 10% of their gross turnover through Club Med sales.) Initial training costs were minimal—about Pta 5,600 per agent. Commissions could be adjusted, however, either temporarily as an incentive to fill specific destinations or on a permanent basis to push the Club through specific agencies. (Above-average commissions were typically set at 10%.)

While travel agent incentives were particularly critical during the initial stages of the marketing strategy, the demand for Club Med could be expected to increase on its own once the product gained notoriety. Thus, Jean-Michel had to determine the optimal number of agencies to include in the Club Med Expert program and set an incentive policy which would generate sales effectively until the advertising campaign began to pay off. Furthermore, in order to maximize selling margins, Jean-Michel wanted to maintain a 65% direct-sales ratio (including group sales); the direct-sales ratio was currently much higher than 65%, but an increase in demand for the product combined with a successful travel agent program was expected to increase the level of indirect sales over the next few years.

The next three years, then, would be a busy time for Jean-Michel and his staff, as they faced the intricacies of growing their customer base as quickly as possible with a limited budget and within the constraints imposed by Club Med headquarters. Would the advertising campaign be successful in conveying a positive image of the Club? What should Jean-Michel's communications budget be? Would awareness increase fast enough? Would distribution be effective? The upcoming season's sales—by which Paris would ultimately judge them—would go a long way in answering these questions.

EXHIBIT 8   Basic Information on Spain

Superficy	505,000 km²
Population	
Total	39,217,000
Active	14,700,000
Working	12,000,000
Unemployed	2,700,000
Unemployment rate	18%
Major Cities	
Madrid	3,400,000 inhabitants
Barcelona	1,900,000
Valencia	800,000
Sevilla	660,000
Bilbao	400,000

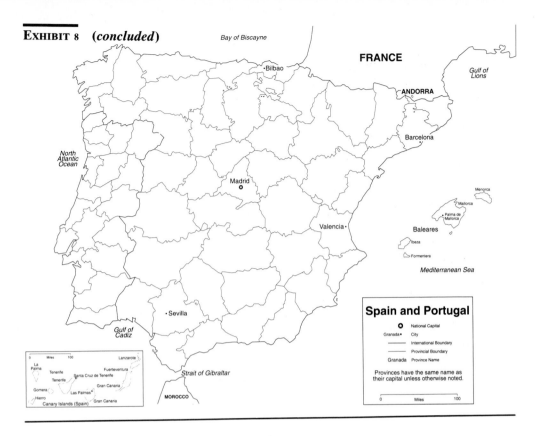

EXHIBIT 8   *(concluded)*

EXHIBIT 9

Pro forma income statement

	A	B	C	D	E	F	G
1							
2							
3		90/91	91/92	92/93	93/94	94/95	95/96
4	Number of Customers (GM)						
5	Number of Bookings						
6							
7							
8	Revenues (Millions Ptas)						
9	Of Which:						
10	Transport. (35%)						
11	Transport. Margins (23%)						
12							
13	Villages (100%–35%)						
14	Villages Margins (15%)						
15							
16	Total Gross Margins						
17	Cost of Sales (%)						
18	Cost of Sales						
19	Net Profit/(Loss)						

EXHIBIT 10

Budget

	A	B	C	D	E	F	G
20							
21							
22							
23							
24		90/91	91/92	92/93	93/94	94/95	95/96
25	Bookings						
26							
27	SALES (Million Pta.)						
28	Of Which:						
29	Boutique (%)						
30	Of Which:						
31	Barcelona (%)						
32	Madrid (%)						
33	Total Boutique (Mill. Pta.)						
34	Travel Agency (Mill. Pta.)						
35							
36	EXPENSES (Million Pta.)						
37	Overheads Boutique Barcelona						
38	Overheads Boutique Madrid						
39	Indirect Commissions (8%)						
40							
41	PR Agency (Fees/year)						
42	No. of PR Events/Year						
43	Cost/Event						
44	Total PR						

EXHIBIT 10 (*concluded*)

	A	B	C	D	E	F	G
45		90/91	91/92	92/93	93/94	94/95	95/96
46	Advertising Layout (Pta.)						
47	Advert. Space (Summer)						
48	Advert. Space (Winter)						
49	Total Advertising						
50							
51	No. of brochures/year						
52	Brochure Layout (Pta.)						
53	No. of copies						
54	Printing cost/brochure						
55	Total Printing						
56	Total Cost for Brochures						
57							
58	Market Survey (once/year)						
59							
60	No. of Direct Mailings						
61	Cost of Direct Mailings						
62	Total Direct Mail						
63							
64	Other Expenses:						
65							
66							
67							
68							
69							
70	Total Expenses						
71	Budgeted Cost of Sales (%)						
72	Budgeted Cost of Sales						
73	Budget Surplus (Overrun)						

5 | BRITISH AIRWAYS

On Sunday, April 10, 1983, a six-minute commercial for British Airways (BA) was aired in the middle of a weekend talk show. The commercial included a statement by Lord King, BA's chairman, and highlighted BA's achievements during the previous two years. The commercial also included the inaugural showing of a 90-second advertisement known as "Manhattan Landing." This advertisement and three others formed the basis of an unprecedented £31 million advertising campaign designed to promote BA's brand name and corporate image worldwide.[1]

British Airways

By many criteria, BA was the largest international airline in the world. In 1982–83, BA carried 11.7 million passengers on 130,728 international departures, well ahead of Air France, which carried 9.6 million international passengers. In terms of international passenger miles, BA's 37 billion a year comfortably surpassed Pan Am. BA flew to 89 cities in 62 countries outside the United Kingdom during 1982–83. Forty-two percent of BA sales were made in the United Kingdom, 25% in the rest of Europe, and 33% in the rest of the world.

BA was a state-owned enterprise, formed as a result of the 1972 merger of British European Airways and British Overseas Airways Corporation. The economies of scale in the work force that many expected from the merger were slow to materialize. Partly as a result, BA continued to record annual losses throughout the 1970s. BA's financial performance was aggravated by increases in the price of fuel oil stemming from the 1973–74 energy crisis. In addition, greater price competition, especially on transatlantic routes, resulted from the deregulation of

---

This case was prepared by Professor John A. Quelch. Copyright © 1984 by the President and Fellows of Harvard College. Harvard Business School case 585-014 (Revised 1991).

[1] BA's fiscal year ran from April 1 to March 30. At the time of the case, £1 was equivalent to about $1.50.

international airfares. An example of this trend was the advent of the low-price, no-frills Laker Airways Skytrain service on the lucrative transatlantic route in 1979.

The election of a Conservative government in the United Kingdom in 1979 prompted a change in approach toward the management of BA. The new administration was determined to reduce the losses, which almost all state enterprises showed each year and, in many cases, to restore these enterprises to private ownership. A new chairman, Sir John (later Lord) King, was appointed to head BA in 1980. He initiated programs to improve BA's products and services along with a hiring freeze and an early retirement program to reduce the size of the work force. By March 1983, BA's work force had been reduced to 37,500 people from 59,000 just three years earlier. In addition, BA showed a profit in 1982–83 for the first time in 10 years, compared to a £500 million loss in 1981–82 (see Exhibit 1).

EXHIBIT 1 **British Airways: Income Statement, April 1, 1982–March 31, 1983**

	Million £
Sales Revenues	
Passengers on scheduled services	1,771
Passengers on charter services.	86
Freight	151
Mail	36
Ground arrangements for package tours	100
	2,144
Expenses	
Staff	593
Aircraft	101
Engineering	107
Operations	863
Marketing	205
Accommodation, ground transport and administration	159
Recoveries	(158)
Ground arrangements for package tours	102
	1,972
Operating surplus	172
Plus Operating surplus from nonairline activities*	18
Plus Other income†	20
	210
Less Cost of capital borrowings and tax	149
Profits before extraordinary items	51
Plus Profit on sale of subsidiaries	26
Profit	77

* Including BA helicopters, BAAC, and IAC.

† Investments in other companies, interest earned on cash deposits, surplus from a disposal of assets.

Industry observers believed that BA would have to sustain this improved performance if stock was to be offered to private investors by the end of 1984. So the programs of product and service improvement continued, together with further labor cutbacks. Recently introduced Boeing 757s were added to the fleet in 1983, a quality control division was established, and the UK Super Shuttle was introduced.[2]

The turnaround in performance was recognized when BA received the 1983 Airline of the Year award, based on a survey of business travelers. However, although costs were reduced and the quality of service improved, BA's public image remained weak. Along with other nationalized industries, BA continued to share a reputation for inefficiency and incompetence. Accordingly, Lord King stated that one of his main objectives was "to make the airline proud again."

Advertising during the 1970s

During the 1970s, BA country managers had revenue responsibility for BA's marketing and operations in their individual markets. The advertising agencies with which they dealt were appointed by BA headquarters. Foote, Cone & Belding (FCB) had held the BA account in the United Kingdom since 1947, and, as a result, many country managers outside the United Kingdom also used FCB subsidiaries or affiliates.

In 1978, British Airways appointed FCB as its worldwide agency, meaning that all country managers *had* to deal with the FCB subsidiaries or affiliates in their countries. The purpose was to achieve a more favorable commission rate from FCB rather than to increase centralized control of advertising content around the world. Indeed, in the United States, where the BA account moved from Campbell Ewald to FCB, the BA advertising theme built around Robert Morley was retained intact since it had only recently been launched (see Exhibit 2). Although the Morley campaign was considered a success, building as it did on Britain's favorable reputation in the United States for old-fashioned hospitality, the campaign nevertheless caused problems for BA executives in the United States. In the words of one, "It overpromised on customer service; every time something went wrong, my phone would ring off the hook."

Prior to the appointment of FCB as the worldwide agency, BA country managers were not required to submit their proposed advertising copy to headquarters for approval. There were certain loosely defined guidelines governing the presentation of the BA logo, but beyond that, local country managers and their agencies were free to determine their own advertising copy. Major advertising campaign concepts did, however, require headquarters' approval. Following the appointment of FCB as the worldwide agency, this procedure changed. Each December,

---

[2] Four shuttles operated between London and Manchester, Glasgow, Edinburgh, and Belfast. Tickets could be purchased in advance or on board, and flights typically left every hour during the day.

EXHIBIT 2

Robert Morley campaign magazine advertisement

Britain Salutes
New York 1983
NEW YORK INTERNATIONAL ARTS FESTIVAL

"We're up in the air
before most airlines
even wake up!"

We can beat the experience

British Airways beats Pan Am's experience five times a day. After all, we have more business seats to London than Pan Am and TWA combined.

You'd like a 10 a.m. flight? Of course we have it…we've had it for years. And British Airways offers something really special on it. First Class and Super Club® passengers receive a voucher worth £20 (about $33) for dinner in any one of four exclusive restaurants. Tourist passengers receive a voucher for a choice of one of five evenings of cabaret entertainment with dinner.*

British Airways has the very first flight out daily (9:30 a.m. Concorde). So we're up in the air before most airlines even wake up. We also have the last daily flight out (10:00 p.m.) and three

flights in between. And British Airways Super Club seats are by far the world's widest business class seats.

Need we go on? We could mention our free helicopter service,** or our preferred hotel and car rental rates for business travelers, or our longstanding commitment to our 10 a.m. flight. And you'll be pleased to note that your flight miles between the U.S. and London will count as credit toward the A Advantage® travel award plan.

So you see, British Airways has no trouble beating the experience. It's experience like ours that makes us the world's favourite airline. That's why British Airways flies more people to more countries than anyone else. See your travel agent or corporate travel department.

DEPARTURE	AIRCRAFT	FREQUENCY
9:30AM	Concorde	Daily
10:00AM	TriStar/747	Daily
1:45PM	Concorde	Daily
7:00PM	747	Daily
10:00PM	747	Daily

British airways
The World's Favourite Airline™

*Offer valid April 15-October 31, 1983 and subject to government approval. For full fare USA originating passengers only. See vouchers for details.
**Helicopter service free for Concorde, First Class and Super Club passengers

BA country managers would submit to headquarters requests for advertising funds for the following fiscal year as part of the annual planning process. Once the commercial director at headquarters had allocated these funds, each country manager would then brief the local FCB agency or affiliate and develop the advertising copy for the coming year. Country managers in the larger markets would submit their advertising copy to the commercial director in London more as a courtesy, while the smaller countries were required to submit their proposed copy for approval. Headquarters required changes in about 5% of cases, typically on the grounds that the advertising overstated claims or was inconsistent with the image BA wished to project.

Whatever the intent, the result of this process was inconsistent advertising from one country to another. First, campaigns varied across markets. The Robert Morley campaign was only considered suitable for the United States. And a recently developed UK campaign in which a flight attendant emphasized the patriotism of flying the national flag carrier could likewise not be extended to other countries. Second, commercials and advertising copy promoting the same service or concept were developed in different markets. There were limited procedures within BA and the agency for ensuring that the best ideas developed in one market were transferred to other markets. Finally, the quality of FCB's subsidiaries and affiliates varied significantly from one country to another, aggravating the problem of inconsistency.

BA advertising during this period, like the advertising for most other major airlines, tried to persuade consumers to choose BA on the basis of product feature advantages. Rather than attempting to build the corporate image, BA advertising emphasized superiority and differentiation in scheduling, punctuality, equipment, pricing, seating, catering, and/or in-flight entertainment. Advertising typically focused on particular products such as the air shuttle, BA tour packages, route schedules, and classes of service (such as Club[3]). The impact on sales of many of these product-specific and tactical advertising efforts could be directly measured. In addition, the commercial director responsible for BA advertising worldwide insisted that a price appear in all advertisements in all media. Frequently, BA advertisements compared the prices of BA services to those of competitors. The commercial director's insistence on including price information in each advertisement frequently caused problems. For example, in the United States, the APEX fare[4] to London from New York differed from that from Boston or Chicago, so different commercials had to be aired in each city.

The 1982–83 advertising budget of £19 million was allocated almost entirely to advertising of a tactical or promotional nature. Only the patriotic "Looking Up" campaign in the United Kingdom made any effort to develop BA's corporate image. About 65% of the 1982–83 budget was allocated by the commercial director to the International Services Division (ISD); about 30% to the European Services Division (ESD); and about 5% to the Gatwick Division, which handled BA air tours, package holidays, and cargo business in the United Kingdom.[5] BA

---

[3] The BA equivalent of business class.

[4] Advance purchase excursion fare.

[5] The geographical coverage of the ISD and ESD mirrored that of the old BOAC and BEA.

EXHIBIT 3   Comparative Data for 14 Markets

	BA 1982–83 Worldwide Passenger Revenues	1982–83 Advertising Expenditures (£ 000)	Principal BA Competitors	BA's Market Share versus Principal Competitor	% Business/ % Pleasure BA Passengers
United Kingdom	42.0%	6,223	British Caledonian* Pan American	Similar	42/58
United States	14.0	5,773	Pan American TWA	Lower	26/74
Germany	5.0	228	Lufthansa British Caledonian	Lower	50/50
Australia	3.0	967	Qantas Singapore Airlines	Similar	6/94
France	3.0	325	Air France British Caledonian	Lower	52/48
Japan	3.0	393	Japan Airlines Cathay Pacific Airways	Lower	30/70
Gulf States	2.0	134	Gulf Air Kuwait Airlines	Lower	12/88
Canada	2.0	991	Air Canada Wardair	Lower	11/89
South Africa	2.0	331	South African Airways TAP (Air Portugal)	Lower	15/85
Italy	2.0	145	Alitalia Dan Air	Lower	50/50
New Zealand	1.0	125	Air New Zealand Singapore Airlines	Similar	3/97
Egypt	0.5	53	Egyptair Air France	Similar	26/74
Zimbabwe	0.4	41	Air Zimbabwe KLM	Higher	8/92
Trinidad	0.3	77	BWIA	Higher	7/93

* These are BA's principal competitors on international routes. BA's main competitors on domestic United Kingdom routes were British Midland Airways and Dan Air.

advertising expenditures during 1982–83 for 14 representative countries are listed in Exhibit 3, together with other comparative market information.

Saatchi & Saatchi Appointed

In October 1982, the Saatchi & Saatchi (S&S) advertising agency was asked by Lord King to explore the possibility of developing an advertising campaign that would bolster BA's image and that could be used on a worldwide basis. S&S was one of the first agencies to espouse the concept of global brands. In newspaper advertisements such as that shown in Exhibit 4, S&S argued that demographic and cultural trends, and therefore the basic factors underlying consumer tastes

EXHIBIT 4

THE OPPORTUNITY FOR WORLD BRANDS.

Nowadays, life for branded goods manufacturers is not as straightforward as it once was.

Many years ago manufacturers first recognised that advertising could provide a key foundation for their business growth.

They realised that while their customer was the retailer, the actual 'consumer' was the public; that advertising could enable them to build a solid position in their market by building the goodwill of their real customer – the 'consumer.'

They also saw that if they, the manufacturers, did something to move their goods from retailers' shelves as quickly as they arrived on them, trade would be brisk and everyone would be satisfied.

Thus the manufacturer became the advertiser of 'branded' products, the retailer became the purveyor of 'brands' and advertising became a conspicuous feature of the age.

This happy cycle produced 'brands' of startling endurance and longevity, as the table below shows.

US BRAND LEADER

1923	CURRENT POSITION
SWIFT PREMIUM, BACON	NO. 1
EASTMAN-KODAK, CAMERAS	NO. 1
WRIGLEY, CHEWING GUM	NO. 1
NABISCO, BISCUITS	NO. 1
EVEREADY, BATTERY	NO. 1
GOLD MEDAL, FLOUR	NO. 1
LIFE SAVERS, MINT CANDIES	NO. 1
SHERWIN-WILLIAMS, PAINT	NO. 1
GILLETTE, RAZORS	NO. 1
SINGER, SEWING MACHINES	NO. 1
COCA-COLA, SOFT DRINKS	NO. 1
CAMPBELL'S, SOUP	NO. 1
IVORY, SOAP	NO. 1

SOURCE: ADVERTISING AGE

Brand Character

Nowadays, when probed deeply, consumers describe the products they call brands in terms that we would normally expect to be used to describe people. They tell us that brands can be warm or friendly; cold or modern; old-fashioned; romantic; practical; sophisticated; stylish and so on.

They talk about a brand's persona, its image and its reputation – and this 'aura' or 'ethos' is what characterizes a brand.

It follows that all brands, like all people, have a 'personality' of one kind or another. But like the strongest individuals, the strongest brands have more than mere personality – they have 'character' – more depth, more integrity, they stand out from the crowd.

Note the importance that one major marketer attaches to this concept.

> *"My acid test on the issue is whether a housewife intending to buy Heinz Tomato Ketchup in a store, finding it to be out of stock, will walk out of the store to buy it elsewhere or switch to an alternative product."*
>
> A J O'REILLY, PRESIDENT & CEO, H J HEINZ

This explains why the best marketers try to develop powerful brand characters. They make them less vulnerable in the market-place. They help a higher quality product to be perceived as such by consumers.

Today, the establishment of such strong and enduring brands is rather more difficult.

- ☐ Static populations mean static markets which means increased competition for market share.
- ☐ Product quality is converging, with increasing technological parity among major marketers.
- ☐ The influence of the retailer and retailers' own store brands is growing in many parts of the world.
- ☐ Marketing expenses are growing, as manufacturers respond to the ever-higher cost of reaching the consumer.

All in all, the pressures on manufacturers' brands are immense.

Superior Product Quality

Serious marketers know that in the face of these pressures the success of their brands can only rest on superior product quality.

They know that as the consumer views more products as commodities, it becomes harder to establish a meaningful point of difference for their products. They know that clever marketing and promotion of cosmetic differences cannot paper over this.

They know that the longevity of their brands is helped by good marketing, but is founded on superior product performance and this in turn is founded on their ability to produce a *higher quality product at a lower cost.*

Which is why market leaders' priorities are now focusing on a common objective which was not among their priorities in previous decades – to work diligently to be the *low-cost producer* in their market.

Low costs provide the means to achieve that happiest of all situations – higher product quality ... fewer price increases ... and more advertising.

Low costs are the priority as a sound base for all the other steps needed to build growth.

Thus, the competitive intensity of maturing packaged goods markets around the world has brought to the fore the economic logic of world brands – *the opportunity for international economies of scale as the basis of long-term strategic security.*

Today, the most thoughtful companies are adopting a new approach to international marketing.

These companies are moving through the five basic stages in the life of a multinational corporation as seen in the chart below.

And as they pass through stages 4 and 5 the need for pan-regional and world marketing is emerging at the heart of their business strategy.

> *"The globalization of markets is at hand. With that, the multinational commercial world nears its end, and so does the multinational corporation.*
>
> *The global corporation operates as if the entire world (or major regions of it) were a single entity; it sells the same things in the same way everywhere.*
>
> *Corporations geared to this new reality can decimate competitors that still live in the disabling grip of old assumptions about how the world works."*
>
> PROFESSOR THEODORE LEVITT, HARVARD UNIVERSITY

A New Approach

After the vicissitudes of the 1950s and 1960s, more companies are now reaching the status of having acquired 'critical mass' in various regions of the world. They are now starting to turn from primary concern about 'return on acquisition investment' and 'overhead recovery' towards getting to grips with long-term franchise building across each world region.

At the same time the progressive harmonization of 'headquarters' and 'local' management culture and style, evolving from more frequent two-way movement of personnel, is enhancing the likelihood of successful adoption and execution of pan-regional business strategies.

And meanwhile in Europe, management's strategic thinking is beginning to broaden to match the dimensions of the Common Market as legislative harmonization focuses attention on pan-European issues.

International Growth Priority

Companies have passed through the bygone age when many of them treated 'Overseas Division' as the poor cousin of the organisation, struggling to compete in foreign markets with strongly established indigenous competitors.

The international divisions of many companies are now beginning to 'come of age' and receive their rightful allocation of corporate resource, if only for the practical reason that corporate earnings growth in many multinationals is today often provided by non-domestic markets.

Business System Economics

The strategic value of pan-regional branding lies in the scale economies it affords across the company's business system – to help make the company the low-cost producer.

Where the economies arise will vary by product category, and may include research and development, materials purchasing, manufacturing, distribution and advertising.

The optimum business system for a European beer, for example, is markedly different to that for chewing gum, but the principle is the same. Secure, franchise-protected volumes at the regional scale can allow a company to *build a price/cost/value structure which will eventually put it out of reach of competition.*

All these factors set the conceptual framework within which a truly pan-regional brand can exist in the years ahead. The international need is the starting point. Research will be conducted to look for market similarities between countries, not to seek out differences. Similarities will be the new fuel for growth.

The creative process will still be as vital as ever; marketers in each location will still be dependent on the intuitive creative judgement of locally based creative management, but this effort will be marshalled to a single-minded overall advertising strategy.

Marketing Learning Curve

There is then a real marketing learning curve that allows the progressive refinement of a success formula, as the pan-regional brands broaden their experience country by country.

The best creative brains are given an opportunity to develop advertising for an entire region of the world, and not simply for one market – to find a real advertising idea *so deep in its appeal* that it can transcend national borders previously thought inviolate.

Consumer Convergence

In the past, the successes in world branding have been few, and have been achieved by virtue of the sheer will and far-sighted commitment of managements who stayed consistently with a long-term vision for the business. Procter & Gamble is a company in this category that comes to mind.

In the future, the only winners in cross-country branding will be companies who have seen that social developments are making redundant the old idea that differences between nations are decisive in framing marketing strategy.

The most advanced manufacturers are recognising that there are probably more social differences between Midtown Manhattan and the Bronx, two sectors of the same city, than between Midtown Manhattan and the 7th Arrondissement of Paris. This means that when a manufacturer contemplates expansion of his business, consumer similarities in demography and habits rather than geographic proximity will increasingly affect his decisions.

Demographic Convergence

Trends of vast significance to consumer marketing, such as ageing populations, falling birth rates, and increased female employment are common to large segments of the modern industrial world.

Consumer convergence in demography, habits and culture is increasingly leading manufacturers to a consumer-driven rather than a geography-driven view of their marketing territory.

Decline of the Nuclear Family

Some of the most telling developments spring from the same source – the decline of the nuclear family. Observers have attributed this to various causes – the rapid pace of technological development; higher labour productivity which reduces hours of work; and other more metaphysical notions such as the emergence of a 'liberal' philosophy, which increasingly recognizes that a woman's role can exist outside the home.

DECLINE OF THE FAMILY UNIT

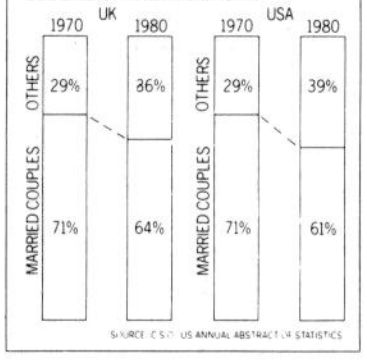
UK
USA
1970
1980
1970
1980
OTHERS
MARRIED COUPLES
29%
36%
29%
39%
71%
64%
71%
61%

SOURCE: C.S.O. US ANNUAL ABSTRACT OF STATISTICS

Whatever the causes, the effects in terms of household composition have been dramatic. There are now less children per household, and a declining proportion of households which conform to the two-adult-two-children pattern.

The result is the erosion of the traditonal family unit and its clarity of role and relationship. The effects have been illustrated by the decline of formal meal-taking and the corresponding increase in the sales of 'instant' and 'convenience' foods. The multinational expansion of fast-food franchises like McDonalds is another manifestation of the same trend.

Changing Role of Women

The table below shows the change in the role of women in the working population over the past decade. The fact that the majority of women in most modern societies now have a job requires a major adjustment to current ideas on communicating with a consumer group that no longer conforms to the home-centred stereotype of yesteryear.

MORE WORKING WOMEN

	%CHANGE 1970–1979 WORKING POPULATION	WORKING WOMEN
USA	+ 24.4	+ 37.6
BELGIUM	+ 8.3	+ 24.7
NETHERLANDS	+ 10.1	+ 24.6
ITALY	+ 8.1	+ 22.8
FRANCE	+ 7.7	+ 17.3
UK	+ 4.5	+ 15.1
GERMANY	- 1.6	+ 3.5

SOURCE: EUROSTAT

Associated with this change, there has been a well documented trend to lower marriage rates and higher divorce rates. This trend has led one group of social scientists to invent the phrase "serial monogamy" to describe what they forecast to be the nature of relationships in the 1980s and beyond. They suggest that there will be an increasing tendency for couples to live together for a number of years, then to change their partners and set up home afresh, changing again after a few years, and so on. This discontinuity in formal relationships, especially where children are involved and re-marriages occur, will have profound effects on family relationships.

MORE DIVORCES, LESS MARRIAGES (1970=100)

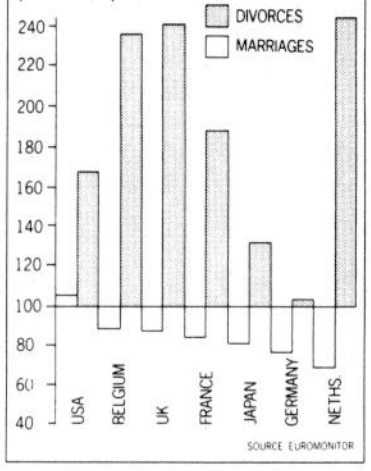
DIVORCES
MARRIAGES
240
220
200
180
160
140
120
100
80
60
40
USA
BELGIUM
UK
FRANCE
JAPAN
GERMANY
NETHS

SOURCE: EUROMONITOR

Static Populations

Population growth is now almost zero in the western world. All modern industrial countries are forecast to produce population growth of much less than 1% per annum over the next 20 years. It is hardly surprising that within this static population, the age structure is undergoing a transformation. The over 65s are a growing group relative to the 25–65s, and that group is growing relative to the fourteen and unders.

STATIC POPULATIONS

	% GROWTH PER ANNUM 1960–70	1980–2000 ESTIMATE
AUSTRALIA	2.0	0.8
CANADA	1.8	0.8
USA	1.3	0.7
SPAIN	1.1	0.7
JAPAN	1.0	0.6
FRANCE	1.0	0.4
ITALY	0.6	0.3
UK	0.5	0.2
GERMANY	0.9	0.1

SOURCE: WORLD DEVELOPMENT REPORT

ORGANISATIONAL PROGRESS TO WORLD BRANDS

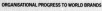

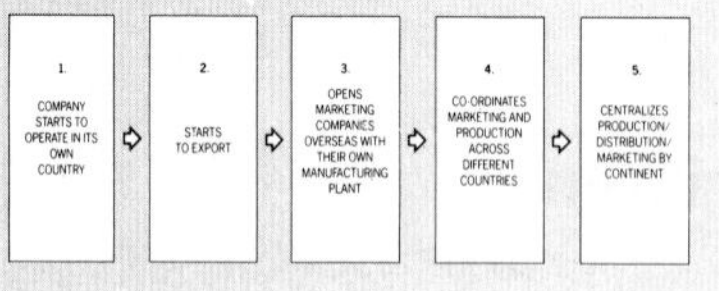
1. COMPANY STARTS TO OPERATE IN ITS OWN COUNTRY
2. STARTS TO EXPORT
3. OPENS MARKETING COMPANIES OVERSEAS WITH THEIR OWN MANUFACTURING PLANT
4. CO-ORDINATES MARKETING AND PRODUCTION ACROSS DIFFERENT COUNTRIES
5. CENTRALIZES PRODUCTION/ DISTRIBUTION/ MARKETING BY CONTINENT

ECONOMIC PROGRESS TO WORLD BRANDS

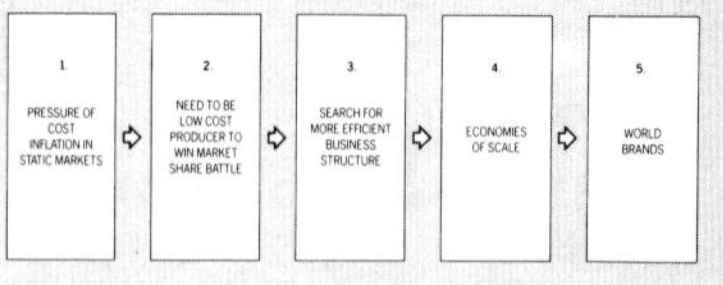
1. PRESSURE OF COST INFLATION IN STATIC MARKETS
2. NEED TO BE LOW COST PRODUCER TO WIN MARKET SHARE BATTLE
3. SEARCH FOR MORE EFFICIENT BUSINESS STRUCTURE
4. ECONOMIES OF SCALE
5. WORLD BRANDS

EXHIBIT 4 (*concluded*)

Higher Living Standards

In most western countries, improvements in the material standard of life have resulted in a growing demand for consumer durables and for more leisure. This is reinforced by shorter working weeks that accompany technological progress and productivity growth.

The entry of women into the labour market itself creates a demand for consumer durables to ease the strain of 'keeping house'.

HIGHER LIVING STANDARDS	
	GROWTH IN REAL PERSONAL CONSUMPTION 1970–82
USA	+ 42%
UK	+ 26%
FRANCE	+ 60%
GERMANY	+ 34%
JAPAN	+ 65%
	SOURCE: HENLEY CENTRE

Cultural Convergence

At the same time as demography is converging, television and motion pictures are creating elements of shared culture. And this cultural convergence is facilitating the establishment of multinational brand characters. The worldwide proliferation of the Marlboro brand would not have been possible without TV and motion picture education about the virile rugged character of the American West and the American cowboy – helped by increasing colour TV penetration in all countries.

Observers believe that cultural convergence will proceed at an accelerated rate through the next decade – particularly with the deployment of L-SAT high-power TV satellites throughout Europe.

EUROPE'S NEW SUPER STATIONS

These developments will reduce cultural barriers as countries exchange their media output through satellite networks – for the first time allowing viewers freer access to international television without the barrier of language.

Marketing Timetables

Analysis of all these demographic, cultural, and media trends is allowing marketers to define market expansion timetables. Essentially, marketers will be tracking trends which indicate when a region is ready for attack via programmes they have tested elsewhere.

For example, current changes in European laundry practices were foreshadowed by similar trends in the US during the late '60s and early '70s. Thus a US manufacturer of low-suds detergent would examine the growth in the penetration of front-loading washing machines in the UK to assess the ripening potential for his own product.

MARKET EXPANSION TIMETABLES
% OF HOUSEHOLDS OWNING FRONT LOADING WASHING MACHINES

Consider also Europe's soap powder manufacturers. Driven by improved washing machine technology and the increased popularity of relatively fragile synthetic and coloured fabrics, European laundry habits have converged. Every major nation now washes a majority of its wash loads in under 60°C water. This has created a common need for a product which performs well under these circumstances.

The result has been the marketing of single brands with a common brand name, product formulation, and positioning across the whole of Europe.

In the future, the only winners in cross-country branding will be companies who do a lot of things right and synthesise their efforts effectively around three golden rules:

1. To market clearly differentiated products that either drive, or capitalize on, real convergences in consumer habits and tastes.

2. To create a dedicated management value system that mirrors the vision of a pan-regional branded business.

3. To monitor their brands' character on a consistent, continuous, comparable basis across geography and over time.

The opportunity for world brands is there to be seized but only for those companies with the long-term determination to meet these stringent requirements.

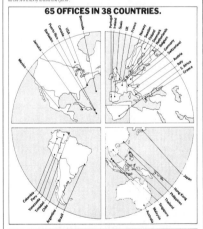

Here are two other examples of the global approach in action – for British Airways and Procter & Gamble's Pampers. The Pampers brand was introduced in the US in the late 1960s. Pampers created the disposable diaper market by providing a product that was more convenient and more absorbent than cloth diapers at a price consumers were willing to pay. Pampers is now Procter & Gamble's largest brand and is sold on a similar strategy almost all over the world. If the Pampers business was a separate company, it would rank in the top one-third of the 'Fortune 500' list.

Does a global advertising campaign have to be bland? Not according to the South China Morning Post which described B.A.'s new worldwide campaign as "*unique and imaginative*"; or the Sydney Morning Herald – "*a radical departure from the usual formula*"; or Newsweek – "*a tour de force*"; or the Wall Street Journal – *the most ambitious attempt so far ... to use a one world campaign*"; or the London Sunday Times – "*a flash of inspiration.*"

The Agency is now working on a similar exercise on Silk Cut for American Brands/Gallaher – a Company whose marketing was recently described by the Financial Times as "*an object lesson for its competitors on the rewards of brand discipline.*"

65 OFFICES IN 38 COUNTRIES.

THE UK AGENCY WORKS WITH 6 OF BRITAIN'S TOP 10 ADVERTISERS.

THE US AGENCY HANDLES MORE No. 1 BRANDS THAN ANY OTHER AGENCY IN AMERICA.

THE INTERNATIONAL NETWORK WORKS WITH 44 OF THE WORLD'S TOP 200 ADVERTISERS.

Impact on Agency Structure

What are the implications of these trends for the advertising industry?

Business service companies, such as agencies, benefit from the increasing complexity of problems in their areas of expertise. Knowledge has value, and there is a greater 'value-added' during periods of turmoil and change in the business environment.

Most observers believe that the trend to pan-regional or global marketing will have a marked impact on the structure of advertising agencies... because world brands require world agencies.

A HANDFUL OF WORLDWIDE AGENCY NETWORKS WILL HANDLE THE BULK OF \$125 bn WORLD ADVERTISING EXPENDITURE FOR MAJOR MULTINATIONALS.

Many expect to see the advertising industry moving in the same direction as accounting, banking, financial services, etc. – a polarization between worldwide networks servicing global corporations, and strong local firms handling domestic clients in their own country.

SOME OF THE AGENCY'S CLIENTS IN 3 OR MORE COUNTRIES	
ALLIED LYONS	IBM
AMERICAN BRANDS	JOHNSON & JOHNSON
AMERICAN MOTORS	NABISCO BRANDS
AVIS	NESTLE
BLACK & DECKER	PEPSICO
BRITISH AIRWAYS	PROCTER & GAMBLE
BSN-GERVAIS DANONE	PLAYTEX
CADBURY SCHWEPPES	ROWNTREE MACKINTOSH
CHESEBROUGH-POND'S	TIMEX
DU PONT	UNITED BISCUITS

This is pleasant for the business prospects of those agencies who can serve this global requirement, but leaves open one important question – whether this trend will result in *better* advertising? On this question opinions differ.

Some agency managers are fond of saying that they would rather operate a solid, disciplined international network than run the best creative agency in the world.

Meantime, others declare that they would rather have high creative standards than succumb to the arthritis of international management structures.

Both these viewpoints ignore the possibility of combining discipline and creativity in one international organisation. This is because it is hard to do.

IN 1982, OUR UK AGENCY WON MORE TOP UK ADVERTISING AWARDS THAN ALL THE OTHER MAJOR MULTINATIONAL AGENCIES PUT TOGETHER.
SOURCE: GOLD AND SILVER AWARDS IN THE CAMPAIGN PRESS AWARDS, D&AD AND BRITISH TELEVISION ADVERTISING AWARDS.

The Company has always aimed to create the *one type of agency which has somehow eluded the grasp of those few men and women who have tried to achieve it* – a large agency, certainly, with all the stability that gives to employees and all the back-up that provides for clients – but one which at the same time also succeeds in being progressive, youthful and innovative in approach.

The fact that this combination has so rarely been achieved in our industry increases the sense of purpose with which we continue to pursue it as our goal.

This has been the fundamental spur to our growth over the years.

HIGH CREATIVITY ACROSS A DISCIPLINED WORLD NETWORK. THE COMPANY'S CONSISTENT STRATEGIC GOAL.

Last month Saatchi & Saatchi Company PLC, the parent company of the worldwide agency network, announced its results for the year ended September 30th 1983. It was the Company's 13th successive year of profit growth. In the year pre-tax profits rose by 103%, earnings per share by 40%, dividends per share by 45%.

Over the last five years the Company has shown a compound average growth of 43% in pre-tax profits, 33% for earnings per share, and 37% for dividends per share.

If you would like a copy of the Chairman's Statement on these results please write to the Company Secretary, Saatchi & Saatchi Company PLC, at 80 Charlotte Street, London W1A 1AQ, or 625 Madison Avenue, New York, New York 10022.

SAATCHI & SAATCHI COMPTON WORLDWIDE.

and preferences, were converging. In addition, S&S noted a growing spillover of media across national borders, fueled by the development of satellite television. Given these trends and the increasing level of international travel, S&S viewed the concept of global brands employing the same advertising themes worldwide as increasingly plausible.

Following its appointment, S&S set up a Central Policy Unit (CPU) to plan and coordinate work on the worldwide BA account. This unit included a director aided by specialists in research, planning, and budgeting. Over a two-month period, the CPU developed into a complete account team, one section of which handled advertising in the United Kingdom and Europe, while the second handled advertising in the rest of the world. The account team included a creative group and a senior media director with international experience.

After winning the BA account, S&S had to resign its business with British Caledonian, Britain's principal private airline. This business amounted to £3.5 million in media billings in 1982. Three S&S offices in other countries had to resign competitive airline accounts. Of the 62 countries in which BA had country managers, S&S had wholly owned agencies in 20 and partly owned agencies in 17. In the remaining countries, S&S retained a local agency, in some cases an FCB affiliate, to continue to handle the BA account. S&S did not permit its overseas affiliates to collect commissions on locally placed media billings as compensation for working on the local BA account. Rather, each affiliate received a fee or share of the commission for the services it performed from S&S headquarters in London. S&S billed BA headquarters for all of its services worldwide, except in the case of markets such as India where legal restrictions inhibited currency transactions of this nature.

The relationship between S&S affiliates and headquarters was closer than it had been when FCB handled the BA account. A BA country manager would work with the local S&S agency to develop an advertising copy proposal, which would be submitted to BA headquarters in London on a standard briefing form. The BA headquarters' advertising manager would then decide whether to approach the S&S account team in London to develop a finished advertisement to be sent back to the BA country manager. Under this system, neither BA country managers nor their local agencies were involved in the design of advertising copy except in terms of working requests, stating objectives, and suggesting content. According to S&S executives, the frequency with which certain types of advertisement were requested meant that it might, in the future, be possible to develop standard "ad mats." BA country managers and their local agencies would simply fill in the relevant destination and fare information on these ad mats and would not have to submit them to London for approval.

The system described above varied somewhat from one country to another. BA country managers and their local agencies in the five most important long-haul markets (United States, Canada, Australia, South Africa, and Japan) had slightly more autonomy than their counterparts in less important markets. Although all advertising had to be approved in London prior to use, finished copy could be developed in the local market by the local agency in conjunction with the BA country manager.

An early example of how commercials might be developed for use in more than one country under the S&S approach occurred at the end of 1982. The US country manager developed an advertising proposal for the "Inbound" line of package tours from the United States to the United Kingdom. Members of the US agency creative team and BA executives from New York came to London to develop proposed scripts for the commercials. These were then approved by the US country manager, but the commercials were shot in the United Kingdom so that British scenery could be included. These same commercials were subsequently used in South Africa and the Caribbean with different voiceovers; these countries' budgets could not be stretched to fund their independent production of television commercials of this quality.

Meanwhile, organization changes occurred at BA. Following the appointment of Mr. Colin Marshall as managing director in February 1983, the three divisions were replaced by eight geographic market centers, which handled BA's basic passenger business, and three additional business units handling cargo, air charter services, and package tours. These 11 profit centers reported to Mr. Marshall through Mr. Jim Harris, marketing director.[6] Mr. Harris also supervised a central marketing services staff involved with strategic planning, advertising, market analysis, and market research. An advertising manager who reported to the general manager for marketing services was responsible for agency relations and for the review and implementation of advertising by BA country managers. One of his assistants handled relations with the UK and European country managers; a second handled relations with the remaining country managers.

Under this new organization, BA country managers submitted their annual marketing plans, including proposed advertising and promotion budgets, to the appropriate market center manager in London. The country managers were informed in 1983 that their future budget proposals would have to provide detailed objectives and research support. In particular, country managers would have to forecast how their overall sales and profits would be affected by particular advertising and promotion programs. The total advertising budget would be allocated among the country managers according to the quality of the proposals and according to which markets were designated for maintenance or development spending levels.

If a country manager required additional advertising funds during the fiscal year or wished to offer special consumer price deals and travel agency commissions above the norm applicable to the countries in his or her market center, she or he could apply to the market center manager in London. The marketing director held a reserve fund to deal with such contingencies. He also reserved the right to reallocate funds designated for one market to another during the fiscal year if, for example, foreign currency fluctuations altered the attractiveness of one market versus another as a holiday destination.

---

[6] The marketing director performed the tasks previously undertaken by the commercial director. The latter title was no longer used.

Development of the Concept Campaign

The S&S creative team was charged with developing an advertising campaign that would restore BA's image and prestige, and not necessarily by focusing on specific BA products, services, and price promotions. The agency described the qualities of the ideal advertising concept for the campaign: "It had to be simple and single-minded, dramatic and break new ground, instantly understood throughout the world, visual rather than verbal, long-lasting, likable, and confident." S&S executives believed that the type of product-feature-based advertising that was used by BA and traditional in the airline industry could not satisfy these objectives. First, an airline competitor could easily match any product-based claim BA might make. Second, such advertising only affected that portion of the target market who viewed the benefit on which superiority was claimed (e.g., seat width) to be particularly important. The agency believed that only a brand concept campaign could focus consumers on the permanent and essential characteristics of BA which transcended changes in product, competitive activity, and other market variables.

The agency established five objectives for the worldwide BA concept campaign:

- To project BA as the worldwide leader in air travel.
- To establish BA as the world's most successful airline.
- To demonstrate the superiority of BA products.
- To add value in the eyes of passengers across the whole range of BA products.
- To develop a distinctive, contemporary, and fashionable style for the airline.

The account team had the benefit of consumer research that S&S had conducted in July 1982 with business and pleasure travelers in the United Kingdom, United States, France, Germany, and Hong Kong to understand better attitudes toward, and preferences for, particular airlines. Based on these data, S&S executives concluded that consumers perceived most major airlines to be similar on a wide array of dimensions. To the extent differences existed, BA was viewed as a large, experienced airline using modern equipment. However, BA was rated poorly on friendliness, in-flight service, value for money, and punctuality. In addition, BA's image varied widely among markets; it was good in the United States, neutral in Germany, but weak in France and Hong Kong. The name of the airline and the lack of a strong image meant that consumer perceptions of its characteristics were often a reflection of their perceptions of Britain as a country.[7] BA was often the carrier of second choice after a consumer's national flag airline, particularly among consumers taking a vacation trip to the United Kingdom.

---

[7] In addition, some BA executives believed that BA was perceived more favorably in countries that had previously been served by BOAC than those previously served by BEA.

EXHIBIT 5

"Manhattan Landing" storyboard

By November 1982, BA had developed in rough form a series of 11 television commercials around the theme "The world's favorite airline." The lead commercial of the concept campaign, known as "Manhattan Landing,"[8] was to be 90 seconds long with no voiceover during the first 40 seconds and with a total of only 35 words of announcer copy. It would show the island of Manhattan rotating slowly through the sky across the Atlantic to London accompanied after 70 seconds by the statement that "every year, we fly more people across the Atlantic than the entire population of Manhattan."[9] Ten other commercials known as the "preference" series showed individuals (from an Ingrid Bergman look-alike in Casablanca to members of a US football team) receiving airline tickets and being disappointed to find that they were not booked on BA. International celebrities such as Peter O'Toole, Omar Sharif, and Joan Collins were shown at the end of each commercial checking in for a BA flight. The announcer copy for all the preference commercials was identical. Storyboards for Manhattan Landing and one of the preference commercials are presented as Exhibits 5 and 6. The intention was to air these commercials in all BA markets worldwide with changes only in the voiceovers.

In November, the BA board of directors approved production of "Manhattan Landing" and three of the preference commercials. Production costs for these four commercials were estimated at £1 million.[10] S&S executives were asked to have the finished commercials ready for launch by April 1983, a very tight schedule given the complexity of the executions.

---

[8] The "Manhattan Landing" commercial was originally conceived as a corporate advertisement to be shown exclusively in the United Kingdom to support BA's privatization effort. When it became clear that the offering of BA stock to the public would be delayed until at least the end of 1984, it was decided to include it in the worldwide concept campaign.

[9] BA flew 1.5 million passengers across the Atlantic to the United Kingdom in 1982–83, more than Pan Am and TWA combined. The population of Manhattan was 1.4 million.

[10] Recent BA television commercials had cost about £75,000 to produce.

Exhibit 6

Casablanca Preference Campaign storyboard

While the commercials were being produced, members of the S&S account team and BA headquarters advertising executives traveled to each BA market. Their purpose was to introduce and explain the worldwide concept campaign at meetings attended by each BA country manager and his or her staff along with representatives of the local BA advertising agency. These visits occurred during January and February 1983 and involved the presentation of storyboards rather than finished commercials.

Reactions to the Concept Campaign

Reactions varied. The concept campaign was well received in the United States, although the BA country manager was concerned about its dissimilarity from the existing Robert Morley campaign, which emphasized traditional British values. In India, there was some question as to whether Manhattan would hold any significance for the local audience. In other countries, including former British colonies, the claim "the world's favorite airline" was met with reactions such as "You must be joking!" The claim seemed to lack credibility, particularly in those markets where BA was in a relatively weak share position versus the national flag carrier. In other markets, such as France and Kuwait, only the state-owned airline was allowed to advertise on television, so the BA concept commercials could only be used in cinema advertising.

Questions about the proposed campaign were also raised by S&S affiliates. Since the parent agency had built its reputation on the importance of developing clear-cut positioning concepts, the proposed commercials seemed inconsistent with the philosophy of the agency. Even though the preference commercials were each planned to be 60 seconds long, some agency executives argued that they were too cluttered and tried to achieve too many objectives.

In particular, the 90-second "Manhattan Landing" commercial was greeted by some with amazement. One agency executive commented: "The net impact of three 30-second commercials would surely be greater." The South African agency requested a 60-second version of the commercial because the South African Broadcasting Company would not sell a 90-second piece of commercial time. S&S management had to decide whether to accommodate this request.

Other BA country managers were concerned that the concept campaign would reduce the funds available for local tactical advertising presenting fare and schedule information specific to their particular markets. One BA manager, after seeing the proposed campaign, commented, "Where are the smiling girls, the free cocktails, and the planes taking off into the sunset?" Another asked, "Will this campaign sell seats?" The BA proposal to spend half of the worldwide 1983–84 advertising budget of £26 million on the concept campaign meant that the amount available for local tactical advertising would fall from £19 million to £12 million. Preliminary BA concept and tactical advertising budgets for 14 representative countries are presented in Exhibit 7. Partly in response to the country managers' concerns, the total budget was raised to £31 million in April when BA's 1982–83 operating results were known. Forty percent of the new budget was allocated to the worldwide concept campaign, 60% to tactical local market advertising.

Some country managers complained that their control over advertising would be reduced and that a corporate advertising expenditure in which they had no say would be charged against their profits. BA headquarters executives responded

EXHIBIT 7   BA Concept and Tactical Advertising Budgets: Initial 1983–84 Plan (£ 000)

	Concept Campaign			Tactical Campaigns	Row Total
	April–September	October–March	Total		
United Kingdom	4,700	1,200	5,900	3,200	9,100
United States	2,600	750	3,350	2,450	5,800
Germany	450	450	900	607	1,507
Australia	500	100	600	350	950
France	150	200	350	269	619
Japan/Korea	200	70	270	400	670
Gulf States	0	35	35	190	225
Canada	900	200	1,100	400	1,500
South Africa	300	75	375	250	625
Italy	150	100	250	225	475
New Zealand	100	0	100	100	200
Egypt	50	0	50	30	80
Zimbabwe	32	0	32	25	57
Trinidad	18	0	18	27	45
Other	n.a.*	n.a.	860	3,220†	4,080
Total	10,150	3,180	14,190	11,740	25,930

* n.a. = Not available.
† Includes contingency fund.

that while the country managers were required in 1983–84 to spend 40% of their budgets against the concept campaign, they were free to determine the media allocation of concept campaign expenditures in their markets and the weight of exposures given to each of the four executions. They were also free to spend more than 40% of their budgets on the concept campaign if they wished.

Despite such concessions, the Japanese country manager remained adamantly opposed to adopting the concept campaign. On the London–Tokyo route, Japan Air Lines held a 60% market share compared to BA's 40%. Of the traffic on the route, 80% originated in Japan, and 80% of those on board BA flights were tourists on package tours. The Japanese country manager rejected the concept campaign as inappropriate. He presented market research evidence showing that his main challenge was selling Britain as a destination rather than developing consumer preference for BA.

The April 10 Launch

Some S&S executives had hoped that BA would commit almost all of its 1983–84 advertising budget to the concept campaign. However, local marketing requirements highlighted by the country managers necessitated the continuation of tactical advertising, albeit at a reduced rate. The logo and slogan from the concept campaign were, however, to be incorporated in BA tactical advertising, and the requirement that tactical creative copy be developed by S&S in London ensured that this would be the case.

Despite all the reservations they had encountered, BA and S&S executives in London felt that they had sold the campaign effectively to most of the BA country managers. Thus, an invitation was mailed by Lord King to all BA employees in the United Kingdom to view the introductory television commercial on April 10. Videocassette copies of this six-minute commercial were mailed to BA offices around the world. BA country managers invited representatives of the travel industry to attend preview parties timed to coincide with the launch of the new concept campaign in their respective countries.

The campaign was launched in the United Kingdom on April 10 as planned and, within two weeks, was being aired in 20 countries. For two reasons, few country managers adopted a wait-and-see attitude. First, the marketing of package tours for the summer season had already started (in the northern hemisphere). Second, many country managers had exhausted their 1982–83 advertising budgets by the end of January, with the result that consumers had not been exposed to any BA advertising for several months.

The Concept Campaign in the United States

The United States was one of the countries in which the concept campaign was launched on April 10. The BA country manager welcomed the campaign since consumer research indicated that BA's size was not recognized by most consumers in a country where, for many, bigger meant better. When asked to name the airline that carried the most passengers to the United Kingdom, more respondents cited Pan Am and TWA than BA. The results of the survey, conducted in New York and Los Angeles in March 1983, also showed the following:

- Unaided awareness of BA as a leading international carrier was 41% in New York (Pan Am, 85%; TWA, 74%) and 33% in Los Angeles (Pan Am, 76%; TWA, 74%).
- Unaided recall of BA advertising was 21% in New York and 17% in Los Angeles.
- BA was mentioned as one of the three largest airlines in the world by 15% of New York respondents and 13% of Los Angeles respondents.
- BA was mentioned as one of the three best international carriers by 11% of New York respondents and 9% of Los Angeles respondents.

The BA country manager viewed the concept campaign as a means of addressing some of these deficiencies. Since the claim "the world's favorite airline" was well documented, the US country manager did not anticipate a legal challenge from Eastern Airlines, which used the slogan "America's favorite way to fly."

The media plan for the concept campaign (Exhibit 8) called for a combination of spot television in BA's six key gateway cities, national network television, and

EXHIBIT 8   Media Budget and Schedule of the British Airways Concept/Brand Campaign in the United States ($ Millions)

	April–June 1983		September–October 1983	
	# Spots	Expenditures	# Spots	Expenditures
Spot television (in 6 gateway markets)*	686	$2,900	175	$572
Network television†	4	1,040	—	—
Cable television	40	104	25	58
	730	$4,044	200	$630

	Reach/Frequency	
	April–June 1983	September–October 1983
Gateway cities	86%/8.7 times	63%/3.3 times
Remainder of United States	45%/1.2 times	—

Audience Composition	% of Those Reached	Index††
Adult men	48	102
Adult women	52	99
Age 25–54	73	137
Household income $30,000+	47	169

* New York, Washington, Boston, Miami, Chicago, and Los Angeles.

† Only the Manhattan Landing execution was shown on network television. It was targeted at the 78% of US households not reached by the spot television advertising.

†† Each index figure represents the percentage degree to which the audience reached included more or fewer people than the US population at large.

commercials on Cable News Network. The ''Manhattan Landing'' commercial was scheduled to be shown four times on national network television. Management argued that this would provide BA with exposure in important markets near gateway cities and would also excite the BA sales force and the travel industry. Four exposures were deemed sufficient given the commercial's creative originality. They would reach 45% of the US adult population an average of 1.2 times.

The budget for the concept campaign from April to June was $4 million. Nevertheless, during this period, the BA country manager expected to be outspent by Pan Am and TWA in BA gateway cities. In 1982–83, Pan Am and TWA advertising expenditures for domestic and international routes combined approximated $65 million and $50 million, respectively.

In addition to the concept campaign, the BA country manager had also developed a business campaign and a leisure campaign for 1983–84.

Business Campaign

Recent consumer research indicated that Pan Am and TWA were perceived as superior to BA on attributes important to business flyers. BA advertising directed at businesspeople had not significantly improved these perceptions. (BA and TWA advertisements targeting the business traveler are presented as Exhibits 9 and 10.) However, the perceptions of BA among its business passengers were much more positive than those of non-BA passengers, indicating significant customer satisfaction. BA's US marketing director concluded that BA had a substantial opportunity to increase its share of the transatlantic business travel market.

The following three objectives were established for the 1983–84 business advertising campaign:

1. Increase awareness of the name *Super Club* as a service comparable to (or better than) TWA's Ambassador Class and Pan Am's Clipper Class.
2. Increase the business traveler's awareness and knowledge of the features of all three BA business travel services: Concorde, First Class, and Super Club.
3. Maximize the ''halo'' benefits of BA's Concorde in marketing efforts directed at First Class and Super Club consumers.

The media schedule for the business campaign (Exhibit 11) emphasized national magazines and both national and local newspapers. Magazines were selected that had higher than average percentages of readers in BA's gateway cities. Newspapers with strong business sections were given preference.

Leisure Campaign

BA advertising targeting the leisure traveler had traditionally focused on BA's hotel, car rental, and package tour bargains. Despite high consumer recall of these ''bolt-on'' features, consumer perception research indicated that BA lagged its competitors on attributes such as ''good value for money'' and ''good deal for

EXHIBIT 9

BA business campaign magazine advertisement

CUT HERE for Pan Am's 18½″ Clipper Class seat.

CUT HERE for TWA's 20⅞″ Ambassador Class seat.

WORLD'S WIDEST AIRLINE SEAT CUTS OTHER AIRLINES DOWN TO SIZE.

British Airways Super Club*
When you're travelling on business, we offer you the widest seats in the air. We give you 24 inches between armrests — more room than TWA or Pan Am!* You'll always be next to an aisle or a window, and you have almost a foot of work space between you and the next passenger.

American Airlines AAdvantage* Program
Show us your number at check-in and your flight miles on British Airways between the U.S. and London will count towards your AAdvantage travel award plan.

First Class Comfort
Lean back in luxury in our sumptuous First Class, with its sleeperseats and impeccable British service.

The Ultimate: Concorde
If you want to reach London in half the usual time, there's only one way — our Supersonic Concorde.

It's no wonder that British Airways fly more people to more countries than anyone else. After all, we're the World's Favourite Airline. Call your travel agent or corporate travel department.

British airways
The World's Favourite Airline™

*Measurements are inside armrest to inside armrest. British Airways has a few Super Club seats only 22″ wide due to structural requirements. However, all Super Club seats are wider than our competitors.

EXHIBIT 10

TWA business segment magazine advertisement

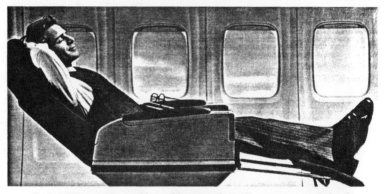

TWA.
Our First is foremost.

**Only TWA has First Class Sleeper-Seats™ on every widebody.
For First Class comfort.**

First and foremost, there are our First Class Sleeper-Seats.

They are available on every 747, every L-1011, and every 767, everywhere we fly in the U.S., Europe and the Middle East. So you can rest easy every time you fly TWA.

Just settle into a Sleeper-Seat, and you'll be impressed with its incredible comfort and legroom. Then settle back—the seat stretches out with you.

**Royal Ambassador℠ Service.
First Class service in a class by itself.**

TWA's Royal Ambassador Service is available on every transatlantic and transcontinental route we fly, as well as selected shorter domestic flights.

We offer a gourmet menu with a choice of entrees like Chateaubriand. Vintage wines from California and France. A selection of fine liqueurs and cognac. All cordially offered to you in a warm, personal manner.

We even cater to your needs before you take off. In major airports, you'll find a special First Class desk to speed you through check-in. And a special lounge for transatlantic passengers to relax in before flight time.

So call your travel agent, corporate travel department, or TWA.

Because for First Class service that's second to none, there's only one choice. TWA.

You're going to like us ╱TWA

Source: *New York Magazine*, March 7, 1983.

leisure travelers.'' Accordingly, BA's advertising agency suggested that these bolt-on features be subordinated to the objective of creating a general impression of value for money through advertising an airfare bargain along with BA's expertise in things British.

The objectives for the 1983 summer campaign were the following:

1. Capitalize on BA's reputation as a marketer of good vacation buys, reinforcing consumers' willingness to arrange their European vacations with BA.

EXHIBIT 11   Media Budget and Schedule of the British Airways Business Campaign in the United States ($ Millions)

	December 1982–March 1983*		April–June 1983		September–October 1983	
	# Insertions	*Expenditures*	*# Insertions*	*Expenditures*	*# Insertions*	*Expenditures*
22 magazines	8	$121	30	$ 745	22	$674
3 newspapers (*Wall Street Journal, New York Times, L.A. Times*)	9	563	13	371	17	276
	17	$684	43	$1,116	39	$950

	Reach/Frequency: Men 25–54	
	December 1982–June 1983	*September–October 1983*
Gateway cities	73%/7.4 times	65%/5.4 times
Remainder of United States	67%/6.3 times	55%/3.5 times

Audience Composition	*% Reach to Those Planning Foreign Travel for Business*	*Index*
Adult men†	72	147
Age 25–54	69	126
Attended/graduated college	64	197
Household income $35,000+	55	284

* No insertions prior to February 1983

† In 1982–83, about 10% of transatlantic business travelers were women.

2. Promote awareness of and demand for BA's summer transatlantic leisure-oriented fare of $549 roundtrip.

A BA summer campaign newspaper advertisement and a Pan Am advertisement targeting the leisure traveler are reproduced as Exhibits 12 and 13 on pages 114 and 115. BA executives were planning on developing print advertisements targeting the leisure market which would mirror the commercials in the concept campaign if it proved successful.

The media schedule for the leisure campaign (Exhibit 14) emphasized spot television and the travel sections of local newspapers. Their late advertising deadlines meant that fare changes could be quickly communicated to consumers.

EXHIBIT 12

BA leisure segment print advertisement

Great Britain Great Price

$549

round trip
(and only $18 a day for a hotel*)

With British Airways' fantastic fares and today's incredible dollar exchange rate, there's never been a better time to visit Britain. Plus, British Airways offers "London Hotel Bargains" including the modern, convenient Kennedy Hotel for only $18 per night (includes private bath and continental breakfast); the Regent Palace for $13 a day (without private bath but a stone's throw from Piccadilly); and "Britain Car Rental" offering a Ford Fiesta with unlimited mileage for only $17 a day. Call British Airways or your travel agent for more information on these and other great deals now!

"Good show"

Britain Salutes
New York 1983

British airways

Airfare valid for travel through September 14. Tickets must be purchased 21 days in advance.
Minimum stay 7 days. Maximum stay 6 months. There is a weekend surcharge. Car and hotel rates
valid through October 31. Petrol and tax not included with car.
*Hotel rates per person, double occupancy and include VAT and tax.

British Airways, P.O. Box 10010,
Dept. H.T. Long Island City, NY 11101
Dear Mr. Morley:
Please send me the following brochures:
☐ DollarSaver* Holidays in London
☐ Fly/Drive Holidays in Britain

Name _____

Address _____

City _____

State _____ Zip _____

EXHIBIT 13

Pan Am leisure segment print advertisement

EXHIBIT 14   Media Budget and Schedule of the British Airways Leisure Campaign in the United States ($ Millions)

	December 1982–March 1983		April–June 1983		September–October 1983	
	# Spots, Insertions	Expenditures	# Spots, Insertions	Expenditures	# Spots, Insertions	Expenditures
Spot television (10 markets)	—	—	450	$795	—	—
Local newspapers (11 markets)	3–4/market	$641	3–7/market	620	4–6/market	$550

Reach/Frequency

	December 1982–March 1983	April–June 1983	September–October 1983
Average market	40%/2.0 times	75%/5.0 times	47%/2.9 times

Audience Composition	% Reach to Those Planning a Foreign Vacation	Index
Adult men	45	96
Adult women	55	105
Age 25–54	60	114
Household income $30,000+	49	175

Conclusion

As BA and S&S executives implemented the worldwide concept campaign and the biggest advertising effort in BA history, they contemplated several issues. First, if awareness, recall, and sales data indicated that the campaign was not having the desired impact in a particular market, would BA headquarters permit the country manager to curtail the concept campaign? Second, if the campaign was successful, how long could it be sustained before becoming "tired"?

A third issue was how competitive airlines would respond to the BA concept campaign. Believing that the major carriers wished to avoid a new worldwide competitive price war, BA executives believed that they would adopt a wait-and-see attitude. However, market share losses would make retaliation inevitable, particularly in markets like the Far East where Singapore Airlines and Cathay Pacific held high market shares and were extremely price competitive. In such a situation, should BA steadfastly continue to spend 40% of its advertising budget on the concept campaign, or should some of these funds be diverted to tactical advertising in particular local markets? The probability of such diversion of funds depended partly on the emerging profit picture during the fiscal year and partly on the level of unspent tactical advertising funds. It was therefore more likely to become an issue toward the end of the fiscal year.

A further related issue was the appropriate budget split between the concept campaign and tactical advertising in 1984–85. Some BA executives argued that if the concept campaign were successful, it would be possible to reduce expenditures on the campaign to a maintenance level and proportionately restore tactical advertising. They maintained that such a move would shift control of the advertising budget from S&S back to BA. But agency executives argued strongly that the concept campaign should be centrally administered from BA headquarters and that expenditures on the campaign in each country should not, unlike tactical advertising, be regarded as a route operating cost. They also argued that the concept campaign was essential to BA's long-term effectiveness and should not be sacrificed to short-term operational requirements.

6

MAISON BOUYGUES

In November 1990, M. Jean Gallet, Maison Bouygues's vice president of marketing, reviewed his marketing budget for 1991. As France's largest builder of single-family homes, Maison Bouygues (MB) had not escaped the effect of an ongoing economic slump. MB's home sales to date in 1990 were 20% below forecast. Further, the company was projecting a 15–20% drop in total new-home sales in France in 1991.

Reviewing the marketing budget (Exhibit 1) led Gallet to consider the sales and marketing strategy that MB had employed in recent years. To stimulate demand, MB used direct marketing to a much greater extent than any of its competitors. Gallet wondered if this strategy was still appropriate during a recession. In a recent management meeting, discussion about the 1991 marketing budget had become quite heated. Claude Figneron, MB's vice president of sales, had stated, "We must boost marketing spending during the recession to maintain our 1990 sales level . . . That will also position us for the inevitable postrecession boom." Marie Suchet, MB's vice president of finance, had completely disagreed. She believed that marketing, like other departments, had to cut its costs during the recession.

Thus, Gallet had to determine whether to recommend increased, decreased, or constant total marketing spending during the economic downturn. Further, he had to consider whether MB's marketing funds should be allocated differently during tough times.

This case was prepared by doctoral Candidate Greg Conley under the direction of Professor John A. Quelch. Copyright © 1991 by the President and Fellows of Harvard College. Harvard Business School case 592-059 (Revised 1993).

117

EXHIBIT 1 **Maison Bouygues Marketing and Sales Budgets (Actual 1989, Estimated 1990, and Proposed 1991)**

	1989	1990*	1991
Category			
Salesperson-months[†]	2,922	2,903	3,134
New-home sales objective (in units)	3,653	3,472	3,650
Medium (in 1,000 FF)			
Marketing budget:			
Television	10,000	0	5,000
Radio	0	6,000	0
Agency fees	1,911	2,565	2,842
Catalogs	3,509	4,708	3,129
Merchandising: point of sale	1,396	1,489	1,122
Market research	55	0	48
Total marketing budget	16,871	14,762	12,141
Sales budget:			
Advertising:			
Local newspapers	1,453	1,261	1,007
Free circulation newspapers	4,281	4,399	3,926
Regional magazines	979	535	484
National magazines	9,662	9,690	9,523
Technical fees	112	170	172
Direct mail:			
Bulk (not stamped)	6,462	5,506	5,424
Stamped	1,430	1,268	796
Telephone listings: Yellow Pages	250	363	293
Subtotal	24,629	23,192	21,625
Promotion:			
New-home exhibitions:			
Cocktail parties in new homes	575	874	948
Shopping mall booths/trade shows	5,200	5,625	4,852
Sales promotions:			
Sales incentives	795	941	688
Hosts/hostesses in exhibition homes	620	696	782
Commercial:			
Trade shows	967	956	1,063
Referrals: finders' fees	202	249	437
Subtotal	8,359	9,341	8,770
Reserves and contingencies	0	0	449
Total sales budget	32,988	32,533	30,844
Grand total marketing and sales	49,859	47,295	42,985

* Estimate based on actual spending for January through October and estimated spending for November and December.

[†] One salesperson-month equals one salesperson working for one month.

The French Home Construction Industry

The home construction industry was one of the largest and most visible industries in France. Total spending on new homes in 1989 approximated FF 90 billion.[1]

The home construction industry was greatly affected by the number of households and by population mobility. Between 1982 and 1990, the number of households in France had increased from 20 million to 22 million. In 1990, the majority (55%) of these households occupied homes, while the balance (45%) lived in apartments. Three-quarters of the households living in homes were owners, and one-quarter were renters. Table A summarizes single-family home sales for 1979 and 1989:

TABLE A	Single-Family Home Sales in France (in Units)	
	1979	*1989*
Homes sold	320,000	275,000
New homes sold	290,000	185,000
Preowned homes sold	30,000	90,000

NOTE: New homes sold includes both individual homes (140,000 in 1989) and homes in housing developments (45,000 in 1989). Condominium sales are not included.

Population mobility in France increased during the 1970s and 1980s. The days of the extended family living in close proximity to one another were fading as offspring often moved to distant cities when they grew older. Thus, it became increasingly common for preowned homes to go on the market rather than be occupied by the next generation of the same family. Many of these preowned homes had been built during the building boom of 1960–1980. (Since the Second World War, 6 million new homes had been built.)

Political developments also affected the housing market during the 1980s. The French government gradually reduced funding for mortgage assistance programs throughout the decade. A 1986 law enabled the remaining government aid to be used for either new or preowned homes; before 1986, government aid could be used only for new homes. Hence, it became harder for lower- and middle-income households to purchase new homes. In 1983, 70% of MB home buyers benefited from government aid, yet by 1989, only 30% of MB home buyers qualified for such aid.

Changes were also occurring in the types of homes people were buying. The average size of new homes sold increased steadily during the 1980s. In 1986, only 24% of new homes sold were larger than 120 square meters. By 1989, this percentage had risen to 38%.

There were also marked regional differences in the French home market. Growth rates and architectural styles varied greatly. For example, new home

---

[1] $1.00 was equivalent to 5.5 French francs (FF).

sales in Auvergne-Limousin were 52% lower in 1990 than in 1982, while in Alsace, sales were 5% higher. Further, in some areas there were deficits of homes, while in others there were surpluses.

Maison Bouygues

MB, the largest builder of single-family homes in France, was a subsidiary of the Bouygues Group, a company founded in 1952 by Francis Bouygues to bid on industrial and construction projects in greater Paris. The Bouygues Group went public in 1970, but the Bouygues family maintained control. In 1979, the MB subsidiary was created to address the growing new-home market.

Initially, MB focused on building small, basic homes for middle- and lower-income households. During the mid-1980s, the company shifted its focus to the higher end of the single-family housing market. During the same period, MB's main competitors were targeting the lower end of the new-home market. MB managed the design and marketing of new homes and subcontracted all aspects of construction. MB had an in-house quality control department, which selected such subcontractors and inspected homes under construction.

In 1990, MB's sales were FF 1.4 billion compared with total sales for the Bouygues Group of FF 60 billion. In the Bouygues Group 1989 annual report, chairman and CEO Martin Bouygues declared:

> In the field of catalog homes, Maison Bouygues confirmed its number one position as the largest builder of single-family homes in France by delivering some 3,200 units during the year. This remarkable performance was achieved despite a shrinking market caused by tighter consumer credit, renewed interest in city accommodations, and strong and highly fragmented competition. To meet this challenge, Maison Bouygues modified its product offering and put the emphasis on top-range products and services.

The Bouygues Group's values were stated in its annual report:

- The work force: our most precious resource.
- The customer: our reason for being.
- Youth: the future of the company.
- Quality: the root of satisfaction.
- Technical innovation: the foundation of our number one rating.
- Creativity: the wellspring of major projects.
- Training: the means to broaden our skills.
- Promotion: based on merit.
- Challenge: the driving force behind progress.
- Company spirit: the basis of our dynamism.

Competitors

Maison Bouygues's principal competitors changed significantly during the 1980s. Several national companies went out of business because of poor cost control and the decline in new-home sales. Gallet commented, ''Paradoxically, we find it more

---

EXHIBIT 2   New-Home Sales by Four Largest French Home Builders: 1979–1989

	New-Home Sales (in Units)		
	1979	*1984*	*1989*
Maison Bouygues	Founded	4,000	3,200
Maison Phenix	15,000	7,500	1,800
Maison Familiale	8,000	3,000	1,200
Bruno Petit	3,000	2,800	600

SOURCE: Company records.

EXHIBIT 3   Number of New Homes Built by Size of Builder (1989)

	Number of Homes Built in 1989				
	1–20	*21–50*	*51–100*	*101+*	*Total*
Number of builders	5,150	500	110	69	5,829
New homes built	40,850	19,500	7,100	23,550	91,000
Percentage of new homes built	45%	21%	8%	26%	100%

NOTE: To be read: 5,150 builders built between 1 and 20 homes in 1989. In 1989, 91,000 new homes were built by "referenced" builders—those with exhibition homes, one or more salespersons, or, at least, a listing in one telephone Yellow Pages. About 49,000 other new homes were built by unlisted "one-man shops" or by homeowners themselves.
SOURCE: Company records.

difficult to organize our marketing effort when there are few obvious national competitors.'' Exhibit 2 reports sales levels for the top four new-home builders in France.

MB competed in the small, medium, and large new-home markets. The nature of competition differed depending on the size of the home. In the small-home market, MB's primary competition was another national home builder, Maison Phenix. In the market for medium and large homes, MB's main competitors were typically smaller regional and local builders who often offered customized homes. Competing against these smaller builders was challenging; many had cost structures which were 10–15% less than MB's, allowing them to offer low prices. Further, some small builders did not have a clear understanding of their costs, which also led to low price quotes. Many small builders were going out of business at the end of the 1980s as the economic recession made it more difficult for them to secure project financing from banks.

Barriers to entry in the home-building industry were low. The market was fragmented and included thousands of builders, as shown in Exhibit 3. It was not uncommon for a salesperson to leave an existing builder to start his or her own company. An entrepreneur could subcontract the building of a home, then pay subcontractors 90 days after the work was completed. However, a new law taking effect in 1991 would require that builders pay subcontractors within 30 days of completion of contracted work. This law was expected to cause financial difficulties for many small builders.

Customers

Most new-home buyers did not want to design their homes totally from scratch. Instead, 85% of buyers were happy to choose from a range of model homes, then customize the home to their wishes. Almost all new homes were bought by couples, and, typically, both spouses had equal influence in the home-buying decision. Moreover, most couples were not greatly influenced by advice from family or friends. In France, 80% of households had two or fewer children, so 90% of new homes had four or fewer bedrooms.

MB sold homes to customers from a broad range of demographic backgrounds. To learn more about its changing customers, MB conducted an extensive customer research study every three years. Exhibit 4 reports key findings from the 1990 study. Exhibit 5 (on page 126) reports the results of another MB study on unaided and aided brand awareness; MB had the highest unaided brand recognition of any new-home builder in all regions of France.

Product Line

In 1986, MB had offered eight home models with unique exterior design styles in a narrow price range. By 1989, MB's product line had grown to 25 models grouped into three price/size levels. Exhibit 6 (on page 126) shows average sales prices and average gross margins for each level. Each home model was available in four to six different floor plans. One of MB's strengths was its ability to take a range of basic models and adapt those models to the various regional styles of architecture. In addition, MB offered numerous equipment and interior decoration options that enabled buyers to customize their homes. These options included different window shutters, garage doors, skylights, kitchen cabinets, and floor coverings. MB guaranteed a delivery date at the agreed-upon price, and all MB homes were sold with a 10-year warranty on construction and a 2-year warranty on mechanical equipment.

By 1989, MB was introducing and dropping four new-home models each year. Each new model adapted to each geographic region by a new product team that included Gallet, senior marketing and sales executives from the region, an architect, and a technical manager from headquarters. The new-product development process, which typically lasted four months, was as follows:

1. For brand-new-product concepts, a qualitative study of the needs of the region was undertaken. Interviews were conducted with prospective buyers to learn about customer preferences.

EXHIBIT 4   1990 New-Home Buyer Usage and Attitude Survey

The sample comprised 520 couples throughout France between the ages of 25 and 40 who had purchased a newly built home within the past six months. The sample was balanced such that roughly 25% of respondents were in each of four buyer groups: MB, multiregional builders, regional/local builders, and craftsmen. Data were collected through a one-hour interview with each couple.

4A. Buyer Characteristics

- Habits of buyers of newly built homes included the following:
  - —Do not visit cinema, theater, and restaurants frequently.
  - —Avid television watchers. Average: three hours/day.
  - —Value spending time with friends.
  - —Frequently read newspapers and television magazines.
- The average monthly household income of MB buyers was FF 15,300, the same as for all buyers in the sample.
- 24% of the sample had owned their previous residence. 66% had previously lived in a house as opposed to an apartment.

4B. New-Home Characteristics

	1987	1990
Average home size (in m²)*	106	126
Average home price (not including land)	FF 387,000	FF 480,000
Average land site price	FF 189,000	FF 240,000
Homes with two or more bathrooms	22%	44%
Homes with two or more stories	47%	62%
Traditional design	43%	24%

* Square meters.

4C. Maison Bouygues versus Other Suppliers: New-Home Characteristics (1990)

	MB Buyers	Multiregional	Regional or Local	Craftsmen
Average home price (in 1,000 FF)	448	425	477	513
Average land price (in 1,000 FF)	228	228	250	246
Average size (in m²)	111	114	132	140
Homes with two or more bathrooms	39%	29%	47%	54%
Homes with two or more stories	59%	51%	62%	66%
Average monthly salary of buyer (in FF)	15,300	14,200	16,000	15,500

4D. Land Plot Procurement

	MB Buyers	Multiregional	Regional or Local	Craftsmen
Plot suggested by builder	75%	58%	46%	10%
Plot procured independently by buyer	25%	42%	54%	90%

4E. Information Search

- 36% of MB home buyers, compared with 17% of non-MB home buyers, reported receiving information about new homes via mail.
- 62% of all buyers reported that their initial contact with their builder was either at an exhibition or over the phone.

EXHIBIT 4 *(continued)*

- Only 3.5% of MB buyers, compared with 10% of non-MB buyers, reported that they were referred to MB by a friend or associate.
- Among non-MB buyers, 28% had seen an MB catalog; 27% had visited an MB home; and 24% had met with an MB salesperson.
- 66% of MB buyers developed their first financing plan with MB.
- 66% of craftsmen home buyers developed their first financing plan with a bank.

4F. Selling Process

- 10% of non-MB buyers in the sample had received an MB home price quote.
- 33% of all buyers considered no alternative price quotes to that of the builder they bought from; 36% considered one alternative price quote; 31% considered two or more.
- Average time from initial contact to closing the sale was 9.5 weeks for non-MB buyers and 7.5 weeks for MB buyers.

4G. Buyer Motivations

- The most frequently stated reason for buying a new home:
  "To acquire a home where we can feel comfortable—a place that we will own, not rent."
- The second most frequently stated reason for buying a new home:
  "A home which we can pass on to our children."
- Warranties expected by buyers (in order of frequency of mentions):
  1. Proper construction warranty.
  2. Building delay warranty.
  3. Builder bankruptcy warranty.

4H. Maison Bouygues' After-Sale Service

- 28% of MB buyers were dissatisfied with after-sale service, compared with 18% of all buyers.

4I. Maison Bouygues Brand Image: 1987 versus 1990*

	1987	1990
All new-home buyers	6.3	5.7
MB new-home buyers	8.0	5.7
Multiregional buyers	6.1	6.1
Regional/local buyers	6.0	5.2
Craftsmen buyers	n.a.†	5.6

* 10 = High, 1 = Low.
† n.a. = Not available.

4J. Customers' Builder Selection Criteria

Stated as Most Important Criteria	Total Sample (%)	MB Buyers (%)	Multiregional (%)	Regional or Local (%)	Craftsmen (%)
Low price	9	6	10	10	10
Quality of builder	30	23	29	29	38
Floor plan	9	7	9	10	11
Most space	8	8	6	10	7
Maximum warranties	20	35	24	16	6
Competent salesperson	13	10	11	13	17
Other*	11	11	11	12	11

* Includes "Best Equipped Home" (2% for MB) and "Best Land Plot" (7% for MB).

EXHIBIT 4 *(concluded)*

4K. Market Segmentation

1. Wealthy Savers (24% of sample)
   MB Presence Index:* 123%
   - Able to make large down payment.
   - Often owned previous home.
   - Prefer to buy land site from builder.

   - Average size of new home: 135 m².
   - Average salary: FF 18,100.
   - Average age: 36.

2. Wealthy Spenders (16%)
   MB Presence Index: 44%
   - Able to make large down payment.
   - Comfortable using debt/credit.
   - Very dependent on builder.

   - Average size of new home: 143 m².
   - Average salary: FF 19,700.
   - Average age: 36.

3. Autonomous Independents (19%)
   MB Presence Index: 53%
   - High social level.
   - Often former renters.
   - Often beneficiaries of family money.
   - Value oriented.
   - Want input on design.

   - Average size of new home: 136 m².
   - Average salary: FF 16,600.
   - Average age: 33.

4. New Anxious (25%)
   MB Presence Index: 138%.
   - Qualified hard workers.
   - Often renters who want to stop renting.
   - Do not have much money.
   - Develop financial plan with builder.
   - Use builder for land site selection.
   - Want to leave property to children.
   - Demanding on warranties, price, and quality.
   - Need to be reassured and assisted during buying process.

   - Average size of new home: 109 m².
   - Average salary: FF 12,700.
   - Average age: 33.

5. New Responsible (16%)
   MB Presence Index: 123%
   - Intermediate professionals.
   - Hard workers.
   - Younger.
   - Shoppers. Compare builders.
   - Want to leave property to children.
   - Sensitive to warranties.
   - Value-oriented.

   - Average size of new home: 112 m².
   - Average salary: F 14,000.
   - Average age: 33.

---

* MB Presence Index = (% of MB unit sales from segment)/(% of total industry unit sales from segment). The higher the index, the greater MB's presence in that segment.

EXHIBIT 5   **Unaided and Aided Brand Awareness: Major Builders (1984–1989)**
Unaided Awareness

Question: "What are the names of the individual home builders that you know?"

Builder	Nov 84	Dec 85	Dec 86	Dec 87	Dec 88	Dec 89
Maison Phenix	39%	37%	34%	33%	31%	28%
Maison Bouygues	20	24	32	50	48	49
Bruno Petit	15	11	13	22	12	11
Maison Familiale	9	8	9	8	7	6

Aided Awareness

Question: "On this list (of major builders), what names of individual home builders do you recognize?"

Builder	Nov 84	Dec 85	Dec 86	Dec 87	Dec 88	Dec 89
Maison Phenix	85%	84%	87%	88%	85%	88%
Maison Bouygues	58	61	71	84	85	84
Bruno Petit	47	44	49	59	56	49
Maison Familiale	50	34	39	35	43	30

SOURCE: Company records.

EXHIBIT 6   **Maison Bouygues Product Line (1990)**

Home Size	Living Area (in m²)	Number of Models	Average Price	Average Gross margin	Percentage Sales (Units)
Small	80–100	8	FF 360,000	FF 140,000	55%
Medium	101–145	11	448,000	162,000	35
Large	146–200	6	650,000	200,000	10

NOTE: Average prices do not include land prices and taxes.
SOURCE: Company records.

2. Photographs of attractive houses of the region were reviewed by the new-product team.

3. Drawings and small models were developed by the architect. From these, one or more models were selected to be added to the product line. No sample full-scale homes were built before this selection occurred.

4. After a new model was selected, MB analyzed its costs and set the selling price. MB had greater experience building small homes and thus was able to estimate costs for these homes more precisely. Occasionally, a finished home was built to gather cost data; this home was then used as a combination exhibition home/MB sales office.

Pricing

Maison Bouygues's prices were nonnegotiable. Prospective buyers received the same price quotes for MB homes regardless of the salesperson or region. All prices were computed using a sophisticated in-house software package. The total price of the new home depended on the home model and on each exterior and interior equipment option selected by the customer.

Services

Maison Bouygues did not offer financing to its customers. Instead, customers were responsible for securing their own home loans. However, one of France's largest banks was a large shareholder in the Bouygues Group. Consequently, MB was able to facilitate customer loan applications made at this bank. This bank typically loaned money to MB customers at interest rates ½% below normal rates.

Ninety percent of new homes were purchased with bank loans. The standard down payment on a new home was 10% of the purchase price. Yet 30–40% of new-home buyers bought with less than 10% down. Banks were able to borrow at a 1% lower interest rate when they used their money for new-home loans.

MB did not provide the land for the home. Buyers were responsible for securing their own plots of land. However, MB did offer a free land referral service whereby each sales office maintained an updated database of plots available in its area. Approximately two-thirds of MB customers used this land referral service, while the other one-third found their own plots. This service was more important to customers at the low end of the market.

Marketing Communications

As indicated in Exhibit 1, Maison Bouygues used a variety of marketing communications techniques to raise brand awareness, to stimulate interest in buying a new home from MB, and to identify prospects. The management of marketing communications was divided between the director of sales and the national marketing manager, both of whom reported to Gallet. The director of sales managed all advertising relating to the regions, which included all direct marketing. The national marketing manager was responsible for all "image" advertising. This manager was in charge of the brand, merchandising, television and radio advertising, catalogs, market research, and public relations.

Catalogs.   MB was the only home builder in France to develop and distribute catalogs. MB, working with its advertising agency, produced two catalogs covering product line and equipment. The product line catalog contained pictures, drawings, and descriptions of all available home models. MB developed a unique product line catalog for each of its 12 regions.

The equipment catalog contained all available materials and components. For example, the catalog presented 15 types of tiles that could be used in an MB bathroom. The equipment catalog was 100 pages long and was updated every two years. This catalog cost FF1 million to develop.

Direct Marketing.   MB ran the most sophisticated direct marketing program of any home construction firm in France. While it would build anywhere in France, MB's direct marketing covered 80% of the country. The direct marketing program included mailings and magazine inserts which emphasized that it was possible for consumers to obtain the home of their dreams that they thought they could not afford. In addition to general information on MB and pictures of young families enjoying MB homes, the mailings invited recipients to complete a questionnaire profiling the features of their ideal home, which they could mail to MB for a no-obligation consultation. Consumers requesting information by completing a mailing or magazine insert coupon became sales prospects. MB was considering developing a television direct marketing advertisement which would include a toll-free phone number that viewers could call for information about MB. Exhibit 7 presents an MB direct mail piece. For comparison, Exhibit 8 presents a similar direct mail piece by Maison Phenix, one of MB's main competitors.

Advertising.   MB first used television advertising in 1987 to communicate that it was no longer just a builder of small homes but also had the skills to build larger homes. Understanding that its key competitors for larger homes were small local builders, MB emphasized its quality control and building expertise. In 1989, MB spent FF 10 million on ''image'' television advertising. In 1990, MB spent FF 6 million on national radio to launch the new equipment catalog and did not advertise on television. For 1991, MB planned to invest FF 5 million in a recently developed ''Egyptian'' television advertising campaign. MB placed print advertisements in regional newspapers throughout France. In addition, MB was the only builder that advertised in national magazines.

Promotion.   MB also used various promotional approaches to raise brand awareness and generate sales prospects. First, MB homes were offered twice a year as grand prizes in sweepstakes and contests sponsored by French consumer goods companies and advertised on the principal television channel; MB absorbed part of the cost of the new home in return for the publicity. Second, MB sponsored cocktail parties in recently completed MB homes. New buyers were treated by MB to a party at which they could show their new home to friends and neighbors. Guests were informed that the new home had just been built by MB and were encouraged to pick up MB information packages. Third, MB appeared at all the major French home shows and maintained exhibition booths at shopping malls throughout the country. The distinctive MB orange-and-blue exhibition booth was a landmark outside many supermarkets. Fourth, MB sponsored sports teams to increase brand awareness. In 1989 and 1990, the company sponsored a Formula 3000 racing car which competed throughout Europe. From 1986 to 1988, MB had been the exclusive sponsor of the successful Marseille soccer team.

EXHIBIT 7
Sample Maison Bouygues direct mail piece

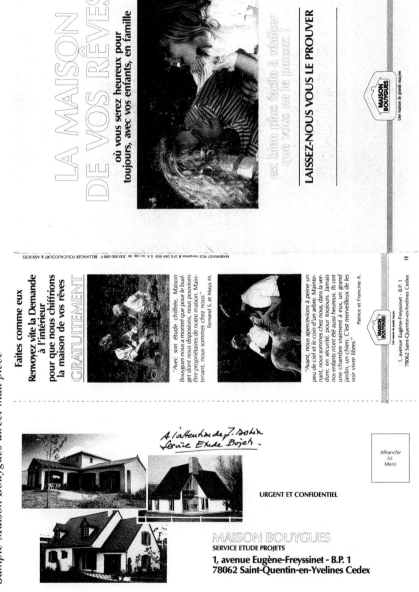

EXHIBIT 7 (*concluded*)

EXHIBIT 8

Sample Maison Phenix direct mail piece

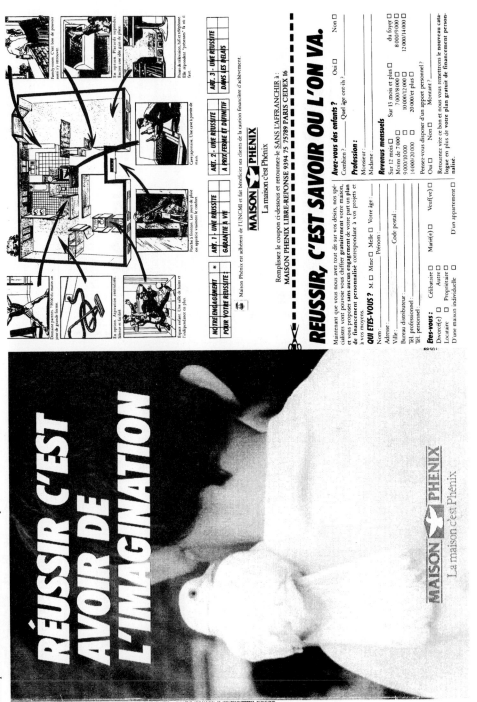

131

EXHIBIT 8 (concluded)

VOICI "ARC EN CIEL" LA FORCE DE L'IMAGINATION

Modèle "Arc-en-ciel" à deux niveaux.

Arc-en-ciel, c'est une maison exceptionnelle qui bouleverse complètement toutes les idées reçues sur le confort.

Arc-en-ciel, c'est un nouveau savoir-vivre, une nouvelle façon de vivre l'espace maison. Maison Phénix l'a pensée pour qu'elle devance vos désirs, réponde à tous vos besoins.

C'est une maison pleine d'imagination en plain-pied ou à étage qui va vous surprendre : plus de pièces, une annexe en sous-sol, un garage, des combles aménageables, c'est un choix. Regardez-la bien, vous n'avez pas fini d'être étonné. L'espace est à vous, vous en jouez comme vous voulez.

Arc-en-ciel, c'est vraiment la force de l'imagination.

FAMILY-ROOM
LE RENDEZ-VOUS SOLEIL DE LA FAMILLE

Les portes et les murs coulissent, et vous, vous choisissez. Un jour vous pouvez préférer un grand espace familial avec une cuisine, bien séparé du salon, et le lendemain avoir envie d'un grand séjour pour recevoir vos amis autour d'un verre. C'est vous qui décidez selon votre humeur. C'est votre maison.

DOMAINE PARENTS
L'ESPACE-PRIVÉ

Ça aussi, c'est comme vous voulez. Cet espace est conçu comme un appartement dans la maison, la chambre peut s'ouvrir sur la salle de bains et devenir un véritable espace de mise en forme. C'est la totale liberté pour les parents.

Info financement

N°VERT 05 30 10 30
APPEL GRATUIT

MAISON PHENIX
La maison c'est Phénix
10, rue Pergolèse - 75016 PARIS

ESPACE ENFANT
L'ESPACE-LIBERTÉ

Pour jouer, lire, rêver, à eux l'indépendance.
Chacun sa chambre, et une salle de bains comme les grands. Chacun chez soi mais jamais éloigné : les enfants peuvent au choix s'isoler ou s'inviter. Vivre chaque pour une nouvelle maison, c'est une chance.

NOUVEAU
ARC-EN-CIEL
LA MAISON
PLEINE D'IDÉES

REUSSIR, C'EST FAIRE LE BON CALCUL.

Calculez l'argent que vous perdez en payant chaque mois un loyer à fond perdu, alors que vous pourriez utiliser cet argent pour devenir propriétaire, prenons l'exemple d'un loyer moyen à 2.450 F par mois :

2.450 F x 180 = 441.000 F

VOTRE LOYER — NOMBRE DE LOYERS D'UA REGLÉS (soit 15 ans) — VOICI CE QUE VOUS AVEZ D'UA DEPENSE

REUSSIR, C'EST DEVENIR PROPRIETAIRE.

"ARC EN CIEL" LA FORCE DE L'IMAGINATION

Modèle "Arc-en-ciel" de plain-pied

Arc en Ciel, c'est plus qu'une maison, c'est une idée.
Maison Phénix la construit pour vous, vous la modulez au quotidien.

Arc en Ciel, c'est une maison vivante, inventive et étonnante qui vit au rythme de la famille d'aujourd'hui, et qui laisse une grande place à votre imagination. Vous modulez l'espace selon vos besoins ou votre humeur. Arc en Ciel, c'est la nouvelle maison Phénix, la maison à idées.

BOW-WINDOW

Un élargissement sur l'horizon qui donne une clarté exceptionnelle. La luminosité dans la maison est toujours au maximum de l'ensoleillement.

Il fait toujours beau dans une maison Phénix.

CAVE JAPONAISE

C'est l'invention la plus malicieuse : une cave à porter de main, sans empiéter sur l'espace. La cave japonaise cachée sous le plancher permet de se constituer une vraie cave de connaisseur.

RANGEMENTS MULTIPLES

Une maison claire, c'est aussi une maison dégagée, ordonnée. Avec les placards coulissants l'encombrement et le désordre n'existent plus. C'est un gain de place fantastique. Avec les placards coulissants, tout est à sa place, la maison est toujours en ordre. Une idée bien pratique.

REUSSIR, C'EST SATISFAIRE SES REVES.

Décrivez-nous la maison de vos rêves, allez jusqu'au bout de vos ambitions, n'hésitez pas à voir grand, à voir beau. Maison Phénix aura toujours une réponse adaptée à vos exigences.

A quel endroit désirez-vous faire construire ?
Localité :
Département :
Possédez-vous un terrain ? Oui □ Non □
Désirez-vous que nous vous proposions un terrain ?
Oui □ Non □
De combien de chambres avez-vous besoin ?
1 □ 2 □ 3 □ 4 □ 5 et plus □
A quelle surface habitable pensez-vous ?

Une maison à étage □   Une terrasse □
Une façade avec volumes décalés □   Un garage □
Un séjour avec mezzanine □   Une cheminée □
Un sous-sol □   Des combles aménageables □

NOS SPECIALISTES CHIFFRERONT GRATUITEMENT ET SANS ENGAGEMENT DE VOTRE PART L VOTRE PROJET.
Coût total :   Soit par mois :

MAISON PHENIX
La maison c'est Phénix

TL05

Sales Organization

Headquartered in Paris, MB was organized into 12 geographic regions. In each region, MB maintained a regional sales and marketing office. Gallet was based at headquarters yet spent a great deal of time visiting the regional offices. Gallet directed the marketing strategy, managed the marketing budget, and supervised the 12 regional marketing managers.

The vice president of sales directed the sales organization through 12 regional sales managers. Reporting to them were 65 chiefs spread across the 12 regions who were each responsible for managing a group of three to five salespersons. A chief's job was primarily managerial and was not expected to include any direct selling. A chief controlled the flow of prospects (leads) to salespersons in his or her group. Each chief received a base salary of FF 11,000 to FF 16,000 per month and earned FF 2,000 for each sale for his or her group above a monthly quota of three sales per sales group. The chiefs and their groups operated out of storefront offices on the high streets of the principal French towns. The MB logo (in the shape of a house) and other store insignia were standardized in MB's orange, white, and blue colors.

MB employed 250 salespersons who were expected to devote themselves entirely to selling and customer contact. Typically, each salesperson received 35 sales prospects per month from his or her chief, which he or she worked to convert into sales. Many of MB's salespersons were former insurance or car salespersons, 80% of whom were aged between 25 and 35. Only 5% of MB salespersons actually lived in an MB home.

MB did not have a national salesperson-recruiting program. Instead, each regional office handled its own hiring. New hires traveled with an experienced salesperson for their first few weeks to learn the job. During training, MB videotaped some of a new recruit's initial sales calls. Later the regional sales manager, chief, and trainee reviewed the tapes to identify areas for improvement. Antoinette Daveu, MB regional sales manager, noted, "One frequent failing of a new salesperson is that he or she tries to screen out prospects too quickly and scares customers away."

A salesperson's financial compensation comprised roughly half salary and half commission. Base salaries ranged from FF 6,000 to FF 8,000 per month plus commission of about FF 6,000 per unit sold. In addition, each salesperson was entitled to a company car, which displayed the company name and came in white with orange and blue pinstriping. Occasionally, a regional office held a sales contest to motivate its salespersons. The prizes for these regional contests ranged from free dinners to new VCRs. MB did not sponsor any national sales contests.

Salesperson turnover averaged 120% per year. Of the salespersons leaving the company, approximately two-thirds resigned and one-third were asked to leave. MB's competitors experienced comparable salesperson turnover.

New salespersons who sold 45 homes during their first 24 months of employment were awarded the title of commercial engineer. Working conditions for commercial engineers and other salespersons were similar. Further, chiefs did not give special treatment to commercial engineers. However, commercial engineers earned FF 10,000 per month and FF 7,500 per sale. In addition, commercial engineers received higher-grade automobiles. Commercial engineer turnover averaged 25%. Of MB's 250 salespersons, 60 had earned the title of commercial engineer.

Prospecting and the Selling Process

In 1989, Maison Bouygues achieved one sale for every 24 prospects generated (4.2%). Ten years earlier, prospect yields had been significantly higher. Specifically, in 1979, MB had realized one sale for every 12 prospects (8.3%).

MB tracked the origin of each sale; that is, for each sale, it traced how the initial prospect had been generated (i.e., attended an exhibition, answered a print ad, etc.). The number of prospects generated by each communications medium and the number of sales (second signings) for 1989 and 1990 are shown in Exhibit 9. The cost per prospect and cost per second signing are presented in Exhibit 10 (calculated by dividing Exhibit 1 amounts by Exhibit 9 figures).

EXHIBIT 9   Prospects Generated and Second Signings by Communications Medium (Actual 1989, Estimated 1990, and Planned 1991)

Medium	Number of Prospects			Number of Second Signings		
	1989	*1990*	*1991*	*1989*	*1990*	*1991*
Advertising:						
Local newspapers	1,721	1,330	878	46	30	40
Free circulation newspapers	4,573	4,689	5,345	165	113	140
Regional magazines	803	596	915	15	12	20
National magazines	35,707	36,281	32,515	920	821	860
Technical fees	0	0	0	0	0	0
Direct mail:						
Bulk (not stamped)	8,583	9,851	10,609	267	265	280
Stamped	3,175	3,312	1,910	71	85	85
Telephone listings: Yellow Pages	0	0	0	0	0	0
Subtotal	54,562	56,059	52,172	1,484	1,326	1,425
Promotion:						
New-home exhibitions:						
Cocktail parties in new homes	719	1,164	1,803	38	73	38
Shopping mall booths/trade shows	13,709	12,178	10,284	343	278	370
Sales promotions:						
Sales incentives	0	0	0	0	0	0
Hosts/hostesses in exhibition homes	0	0	0	0	0	0
Commercial:						
Trade shows	0	0	0	0	0	0
Referrals: finders' fees	3,132	2,388	3,398	515	402	440
Subtotal	17,560	15,730	15,485	896	753	848
Unsolicited	20,029	21,235	21,851	1,273	1,393	1,540
Total	92,151	93,024	89,508	3,653	3,472	3,813

NOTE: Commercial trade shows contribute to unsolicited prospects and unsolicited second signings.

EXHIBIT 10   Cost per Prospect and Cost per Second Signing by Communications Medium (Actual 1989, Estimated 1990, and Planned 1991)

	Cost per Prospect			Cost per Second Signing		
Medium (in FF)	*1989*	*1990*	*1991*	*1989*	*1990*	*1991*
Advertising:						
Local newspapers	844	948	1,147	31,587	42,033	25,175
Free circulation newspapers	936	938	735	25,945	38,929	28,043
Regional magazines	1,219	898	529	65,267	44,583	24,200
National magazines	271	267	293	10,502	11,803	11,073
Technical fees	n.a.*	n.a.	n.a.	n.a.	n.a.	n.a.
Direct mail:						
Bulk (not stamped)	753	559	511	24,202	20,777	19,371
Stamped	450	383	417	20,141	14,918	9,365
Telephone listings: Yellow Pages	n.a.	n.a.	n.a.	n.a.	n.a.	n.a.
Promotion:						
New-home exhibitions:						
Cocktail parties in new homes	800	751	526	15,321	11,973	24,947
Shopping mall booths/trade shows	379	462	472	15,160	20,234	13,114
Sales promotions:						
Sales incentives	n.a.	n.a.	n.a.	n.a.	n.a.	n.a.
Hosts/hostesses in exhibition homes	n.a.	n.a.	n.a.	n.a.	n.a.	n.a.
Commercial:						
Trade shows	n.a.	n.a.	n.a.	n.a.	n.a.	n.a.
Referrals: finders' fees	64	104	129	392	619	993
Unsolicited	0	0	0	0	0	0

* n.a. = Not available.

The home sale was basically a one-time transaction. Almost no buyers returned to MB for a "repeat purchase." Hence, the salesperson and buyer usually never saw each other again after the sale.

The standard selling process at MB was as follows:

1. A salesperson received a sales prospect from his or her chief.

2. The salesperson then called and set up an initial meeting with the prospect at the prospect's home. The initial meeting was scheduled when both heads of the household were available.

3. The salesperson mailed the product line catalog to the prospect to arrive before the initial meeting.

4. Initial meeting. The salesperson presented MB's capabilities and discussed the prospect's wants and needs. The salesperson gave the equipment catalog to the prospect and explained various equipment and material options. By the end of the initial meeting, a specific project was discussed with the goal of setting up a second meeting at a land site, preferably within 48 hours.

5. Second meeting. At a specific site, the prospect "walked" the land, and the salesperson suggested homes that would fit the site. It was important

TABLE B   Maison Bouygues's 1989 Prospect Yields by Stage of Selling Process

	Percentage of Prospects Advancing to Stage
1. Prospect	100.0%
2. Initial meeting	70.0
3. Second meeting	30.0
4. Further meetings	10.0
5. First signing	6.0
6. Second signing	4.2

to review the land site, as all price quotes were "site specific." That is, the cost of the same model home varied by land site due to varying excavation costs.

6. Third/fourth meetings. Third and fourth meetings were held, if necessary, to discuss alternatives in detail. Salespersons were not encouraged to hold more than four meetings with a prospect. Additional meetings were held only at the prospect's request.

7. First signing. The first signing represented intent to purchase. At the first signing, MB and the prospect agreed on home model, equipment options, land site, and price.

8. Second signing. The second signing was the legal sale. Some "first signers" did not make it to the second signing due to permit problems, financing problems, or second thoughts.

MB tracked the percentage of prospects that advanced to each stage of the selling process, as shown in Table B above. In other words, 70 out of 100 prospects attended an initial meeting, 30 out of 100 prospects attended a second meeting, and so on.

The average time from the initial meeting to the first signing was nine weeks, and from the first signing to the second signing just four weeks. After the second signing, MB typically began construction six months later. Historically, 19% of second signings were canceled during this intervening period. Once construction began, it took MB about six months to complete the new home.

Conclusion

Gallet remained concerned about the total marketing budget and its allocation among different marketing programs for the coming year. He was scheduled to present his 1991 marketing budget to MB's president in two weeks.

7

Mediquip, SA

On December 18, Kurt Thaldorf, a sales engineer for the German sales subsidiary of Mediquip, SA, was informed by Lohmann University Hospital in Stuttgart that it had decided to place an order with Sigma, a Dutch competitor, for a CT scanner. The hospital's decision came as disappointing news to Thaldorf, who had worked for nearly eight months on the account. The order, if obtained, would have meant a sale of DM 2,370,000 for the sales engineer.[1] He was convinced that Mediquip's CT scanner was technologically superior to Sigma's and, overall, a better product.

Thaldorf began a review of his call reports in order to better understand the factors that had led to Lohmann University Hospital's decision. He wanted to apply the lessons from this experience to future sales situations.

Background

At the time, the computer tomography (CT) scanner was a relatively recent product in the field of diagnostic imaging. This medical device, used for diagnostic purposes, allowed examination of cross sections of the human body through display of images. CT scanners combined sophisticated X-ray equipment with a computer to collect the necessary data and translate them into visual images.

When computer tomography was first introduced in the late 1960s, radiologists had hailed it as a major technological breakthrough. Commenting on the advantages of CT scanners, a product specialist with Mediquip said, "The end product looks very much like an X-ray image. The only difference is that with

---

This case was prepared by Professor Kamran Kashani. Copyright © 1991 by the International Institute for Management Development (IMD), Lausanne, Switzerland. Not to be used or reproduced without permission. IMD case 395.

[1] For the purposes of this case, use the following exchange rates for the deutsche mark (DM): DM 1.00 = SF 0.85, $0.60, Ecu 0.50, £0.35.

scanners you can see sections of the body that were never seen before on a screen—like the pancreas. A radiologist, for example, can diagnose cancer of the pancreas in less than two weeks after it develops. This was not possible before CT scanners.''

Mediquip was a subsidiary of Technologie Universelle, a French conglomerate. The company's product line included, in addition to CT scanners, X-ray, ultrasonic, and nuclear diagnostic equipment. Mediquip enjoyed a worldwide reputation for advanced technology and competent after-sales service.

"Our competitors are mostly from other European countries," commented Mediquip's sales director for Europe. "In some markets they have been there longer than we have, and they know the decision makers better than we do. But we are learning fast." Sigma, the subsidiary of a diversified Dutch company under the same name, was the company's most serious competitor. Other major contenders in the CT scanner market were FNC, Eldora, Magna, and Piper.

Mediquip executives estimated the European market for CT scanners to be around 200 units per year. They pointed out that prices ranged from DM 1.5 million to DM 3.0 million per unit. The company's CT scanner sold in the upper end of the price range. "Our equipment is at least two years ahead of our most advanced competition," explained a sales executive. "And our price reflects this technological superiority."

Mediquip's sales organization in Europe included eight country sales subsidiaries, each headed by a managing director. Within each country, sales engineers reported to regional sales managers, who in turn reported to the managing director. Product specialists provided technical support to the sales force in each country.

Buyers of CT Scanners

A sales executive at Mediquip described the buyers of CT scanners as follows:

Most of our sales are to what we call the public sector, health agencies that are either government-owned or belong to nonprofit support organizations such as universities and philanthropic institutions. They are the sort of buyers that buy through formal tenders and have to budget their purchases at least one year in advance. Once the budget is allocated, it must then be spent before the end of the year. Only a minor share of our CT scanner sales goes to the private sector, profit-oriented organizations such as private hospitals or private radiologists.

Of the two markets, the public sector is much more complex. Typically, there are at least four groups that get involved in the purchase decision: radiologists, physicists, administrators, and people from the supporting agency—usually the ones who approve the budget for purchasing a CT scanner.

Radiologists are the ones who use the equipment. They are doctors whose diagnostic services are sought by other doctors in the hospital or clinic. Patients remember their doctors, but not the radiologists. They never receive flowers from the patients! A CT scanner could really enhance their professioal image among their colleagues.

Physicists are the scientists in residence. They write the technical specifications which competing CT scanners must meet; they should know the state of the art in X-ray technology. Their primary concern is the patient's safety.

The administrators are, well, administrators. They have the financial responsibility for their organizations. They are concerned with the cost of CT scanners, but also with what revenues they can generate. The administrators are extremely wary of purchasing an expensive technological toy that will become obsolete in a few years.

The people from the supporting agency are usually not directly involved with decisions as to which product to purchase. But, since they must approve the expenditures, they do play an indirect role. Their influence is mostly felt by the administrators.

The interplay among the four groups, as you can imagine, is rather complex. The power of each group in relationship to the others varies from organization to organization. The administrator, for example, is the top decision maker in certain hospitals. In others, he is only a buyer. One of the key tasks of our sales engineers is to define for each potential account the relative power of the players. Only then can they set priorities and formulate selling strategies.

The European sales organization at Mediquip had recently started using a series of forms designed to help sales engineers in their account analysis and strategy formulation. (A sample of the forms, called Account Management Analysis, is reproduced in Exhibit 1.)

Lohmann University Hospital

Lohmann University Hospital (LUH) was a large general hospital serving Stuttgart, a city of 1 million residents. The hospital was part of the university's medical school. The university was a leading teaching center and enjoyed an excellent reputation. LUH's radiology department had a wide range of X-ray equipment from a number of European manufacturers, including Sigma and FNC. The radiology department had five staff members, headed by a senior and nationally known radiologist, Professor Steinborn.

Thaldorf's Sales Activities

From the records he had kept of his sales calls. Thaldorf reviewed the events for the period between May 5, when he learned of LUH's interest in purchasing a CT scanner, and December 18, when he was informed that Mediquip had lost the order.

May 5.   Office received a call from a Professor Steinborn from Lohmann University Hospital regarding a CT scanner. I was assigned to make the call on the professor. Looked through our files to find out if we had sold anything to the hospital before. We had not. Made an appointment to see the professor on May 9.

May 9.   Called on Professor Steinborn, who informed me of a recent decision by university directors to set aside funds next year for the purchase of the hospital's first CT scanner. The professor wanted to know what we had to offer. Described the general features of our CT system. Gave him some brochures. Asked a few questions which led me to believe other companies had come to see him before I did. Told me to check with Dr. Rufer, the hospital's physicist, regarding the

EXHIBIT 1

Account Management Analysis forms (condensed version)

Key Account: _____

ACCOUNT MANAGEMENT ANALYSIS

The enclosed forms are designed to facilitate your management of:

1 A key sales account
2 The *Mediquip* resources that can be applied to this key account

Completing the enclosed forms, you will:

- Identify installed equipment, and planned or potential new equipment
- Analyze purchase decision process and influence patterns, including:
  —Identify and prioritize all major sources of influence
  —Project probable sequence of events and timing of decision process
  —Assess position/interest of each major influence source
  —Identify major competition and probable strategies
  —Identify needed information/support

- Establish an account development strategy, including:
  —Select key contacts
  —Establish strategy and tactics for each key contact, identify appropriate *Mediquip* personnel

---

KEY ACCOUNT DATA

☐ Original (Date: _____)   Account No.: _____   Type of Institute: _____

☐ Revision (Date: _____)   Sales Specialist: _____   Bed Size: _____

                                     Country/Region/District: _____   Telephone: _____

---

1. CUSTOMER (HOSPITAL, CLINIC, PRIVATE INSTITUTE)

Name _____

Street Address: _____

City, State: _____

2. DECISION MAKERS – IMPORTANT CONTACTS

INDIVIDUALS	NAME	SPECIALTY	REMARKS
Medical Staff			
Administration			
Local Government			
State Government			

EXHIBIT 1 *(concluded)*

3. INSTALLED EQUIPMENT

TYPE	DESCRIPTION	SUPPLIED BY	INSTALLATION DATE	YEAR TO REPLACE	VALUE OF POTENTIAL ORDER
X-ray Nuclear Ultrasound RTP CT					

4. PLANNED NEW EQUIPMENT

TYPE	QUOTE		% CHANCE	EST. ORDER DATE		EST. DELIVERY		QUOTED PRICE
	NO.	DATE		1980	1981	1980	1981	

5. COMPETITION

COMPANY/PRODUCT	STRATEGY/ TACTICS	% CHANCE	STRENGTH	WEAKNESS

6. SALES PLAN

KEY ISSUES	*Mediquip's* PLAN	SUPPORT NEEDED FROM:	DATE OF FOLLOW-UP/REMARKS

7. ACTIONS–IN SUPPORT OF PLAN

SPECIFIC ACTION	RESPONSIBILITY	DUE DATES			RESULTS/REMARKS
		ORIGINAL	REVISED	COMPLETED	

8. ORDER STATUS REPORT

REVISION DATE	ACCOUNT NAME AND LOCATION	ISSUES/ COMPETITIVE STRATEGY	ACTIONS/ STRATEGY	RESPON- SIBILITY	% CHANCE	EXPECTED ORDER TIMING	WIN/ LOSE

specs. Made an appointment to see him again 10 days later. Called on Dr. Rufer, who was not there. His secretary gave me a lengthy document on the scanner specs.

May 10.   Read the specs last night. Looked like they had been copied straight from somebody's technical manual. Showed them to our product specialist, who confirmed my own hunch that our system met and exceeded the specs. Made an appointment to see Dr. Rufer next week.

May 15.   Called on Dr. Rufer. Told him about our system's features and the fact that we met all the specs set down on the document. He did not seem particularly impressed. Left him with technical documents about our system.

May 19.   Called on Professor Steinborn. He had read the material I had left with him. Seemed rather pleased with the features. Asked about our upgrading scheme. Told him we would undertake to upgrade the system as new features became available. Explained that Mediquip, unlike other systems, can be made to accommodate the latest technology, with no risk of obsolescence for a long time. This impressed him. Also answered his questions regarding image manipulation, image processing speed, and our service capability. Just before I left, he inquired about our price. Told him I would have an informative quote for him at our next meeting. Made an appointment to see him on June 23 after he returned from his vacation. Told me to get in touch with Carl Hartmann, the hospital's general director, in the interim.

June 1.   Called on Hartmann. It was difficult to get an appointment with him. Told him about our interest in supplying his hospital with our CT scanner, which met all the specs as defined by Dr. Rufer. Also informed him of our excellent service capability. He wanted to know which other hospitals in the country had purchased our system. Told him I would provide him with a list of buyers within a few days. He asked about the price. Gave him an informative quote of DM 2,850,000—a price my boss and I had determined after my visit to Professor Steinborn. He shook his head, saying, "Other scanners are cheaper by a wide margin." I explained that our price reflected the fact that the latest technology was already built into our scanner. Also mentioned that the price differential was an investment that could pay for itself several times over through faster speed of operation. He was noncommittal. Before leaving his office, he instructed me not to talk to anybody else about the price. Asked him specifically if that included Professor Steinborn. He said it did. Left him with a lot of material about our system.

June 3.   Went to Hartmann's office with a list of three hospitals similar in size to LUH that had installed our system. He was out. Left it with his secretary, who recognized me. Learned from her that at least two other firms, Sigma and FNC, were competing for the order. She also volunteered the information that "prices are so different, Mr. Hartmann is confused." She added that the final decision will be made by a committee made up of Hartmann, Professor Steinborn, and one other person whom she could not recall.

June 20.   Called on Dr. Rufer. Asked him if he had read the material about our system. He had, but did not have much to say. I repeated some of the key operational advantages our product enjoyed over those produced by others, including Sigma and FNC. Left him some more technical documents.

On the way out, stopped by Hartmann's office. His secretary told me that we had received favorable comments from the hospitals using our system.

June 23.   Professor Steinborn was flabbergasted to hear that I could not discuss our price with him. Told him about the hospital administration's instructions to that effect. He could not believe this, especially when Sigma had already given him their quote of DM 2,100,000. When he calmed down, he wanted to know if we were going to be at least competitive with the others. Told him our system was more advanced than Sigma's. Promised him we would do our best to come up with an attractive offer. Then we talked about his vacation and sailing experience in the Aegean Sea. He said he loved the Greek food.

July 15.   Called to see if Hartmann had returned from his vacation. He had. While checking his calendar, his secretary told me that our system seemed to be the "radiologists' choice," but that Hartmann had not yet made up his mind.

July 30.   Visited Hartmann accompanied by the regional manager. Hartmann seemed to have a fixation about the price. He said, "All the companies claim they have the latest technology." So he could not understand why our offer was "so much above the rest." He concluded that only a "very attractive price" could tip the balance in our favor. After repeating the operational advantages our system enjoyed over others, including those produced by Sigma and FNC, my boss indicated that we were willing to lower our price to DM 2,610,000 if the equipment were ordered before the end of the current year. Hartmann said he would consider the offer and seek "objective" expert opinion. He also said a decision would be made before Christmas.

August 14.   Called on Professor Steinborn, who was too busy to see me for more than 10 minutes. He wanted to know if we had lowered our price since the last meeting with him. I said we had. He shook his head and said with a laugh, "Maybe that was not your best offer." He then wanted to know how fast we could make deliveries. Told him within six months. He did not say anything.

September 2.   The regional manager and I discussed the desirability of inviting one or more people from the LUH to visit the Mediquip headquarters operations near Paris. The three-day trip would have given the participants a chance to see the scope of the facilities and become better acquainted with CT scanner applications. This idea was finally rejected as inappropriate.

September 3. Dropped in to see Hartmann. He was busy but had time to ask for a formal "final offer" from us by October 1. On the way out, his secretary told me there had been "a lot of heated discussions" about which scanner seemed best suited for the hospital. She would not say more.

September 25. The question of price was raised in a meeting with the regional manager and the managing director. I had recommended a sizable cut in our price to win the order. The regional manager seemed to agree with me, but the managing director was reluctant. His concern was that too big a drop in price looked "unhealthy." They finally agreed to a final offer of DM 2,370,000.

Made an appointment to see Hartmann later that week.

September 29. Took our offer of DM 2,370,000 in a sealed envelope to Hartmann. He did not open it, but he said he hoped the scanner question would soon be resolved to the "satisfaction of all concerned." Asked him how the decision was going to be made. He evaded the question but said he would notify us as soon as a decision was reached. Left his office feeling that our price had a good chance of being accepted.

October 20. Called on Professor Steinborn. He had nothing to tell me except that "the CT scanner is the last thing I want to talk about." Felt he was unhappy with the way things were going.

Tried to make an appointment with Hartmann in November, but he was too busy.

November 5. Called on Hartmann, who told me that a decision would probably not be reached before next month. He indicated that our price was "within the range," but that all the competing systems were being evaluated to see which seemed most appropriate for the hospital. He repeated that he would call us when a decision was reached.

December 18. Received a brief letter from Hartmann thanking Mediquip for participating in the bid for the CT scanner, along with the announcement that LUH had decided to place the order with Sigma.

PRICING POLICY

8

DHL Worldwide Express

In July 1991, in Jakarta, Indonesia, the shouts of the *kaki lima* (street vendors) outside did little to soothe Ali Sarrafzadeh's concerns. Sarrafzadeh, DHL's worldwide sales and marketing manager, had spent the previous three days chairing the Worldwide Pricing Committee workshop at DHL's annual directors' meeting. On the following day, he was to present his recommendations on pricing to the conference's 300 attendees.

Some of the statements made during the workshop meetings were still ringing in his head:

> If I have P&L [profit and loss] responsibility for my region, then I'd better be able to set my own prices. If not, how am I supposed to impact profits? By managing my travel and entertainment account?
>
> Jurgsen Beckenbauer
> Regional Director—Central Europe

> Many of our large multinational customers have come to us and told us that they want a consistent worldwide pricing structure . . . If we don't offer worldwide prices and our competitors do, are we going to lose some of our largest accounts?
>
> Christine Platine
> Account Manager, Brussels Headquarters

> If our pricing structures were consistent across regions, it would be much easier to consolidate regional reports. With better reporting, we could gain valuable information about our costs . . . The simpler our pricing structure, the easier it is to manage hardware and software around the world.
>
> Adelina Rossi
> VP Systems, Brussels Headquarters

This case was prepared by Doctoral Candidate Greg Conley under the direction of Professor John A. Quelch. Copyright © 1992 by the President and Fellows of Harvard College. Harvard Business School case 593-011.

We are the only company which services some regions of Africa. Thus, we charge premium prices in these markets. If we are forced to charge the same rates as in other regions, we will only lose profits. Sales will not grow with lower prices.

Aziz Milla
Country Manager—Cameroon, Africa

Our prices have always been 20–40% higher than the competition's prices. We can command these premium prices by continuing to give more value to our customers . . . Our pricing must not encourage "cherry picking." We don't want customers to just ship with us on routes that are difficult to serve such as those to and from Africa.

Bobby Jones
Regional Director—United States

In his presentation the following day, Sarrafzadeh wanted to make recommendations on pricing strategy, structure, and decision making. On strategy, he viewed his options as recommending either a price leadership strategy or a market response strategy. The former meant DHL would charge premium prices and aim to deliver superior value-added services in all markets. The latter meant DHL would set prices independently in each country, according to customer usage patterns and competitive pressures.

If the principle of standardized worldwide pricing was pursued, what were the pricing structure implications? For example, should weight breaks (the parcel weights at which prices per pound rose or fell) be standardized across countries? Should DHL charge a weekly or monthly handling fee (a set fee in return for automatically visiting a customer each business day) in all countries? Should the same price be charged for shipments between any two cities, regardless of which was the origin and which the destination?

Regarding pricing structure, Sarrafzadeh had to address several additional questions. Should DHL have different pricing schedules for documents and parcels? Should DHL set different prices for different industries? For example, should prices be different for banking and manufacturing customers? Should DHL offer special prices to multinational corporations seeking to cut deals with individual shippers to handle all their express document and parcel delivery needs worldwide?

Another issue was the DHL discount program. Sarrafzadeh had to decide whether DHL should continue to offer volume discounts. If so, should they be based on units, weight, or revenue? Should they be based on projected or actual volume? Should they be based on the quantity picked up per stop or per week or month?

In addition, Sarrafzadeh wanted to recommend who should hold primary price-setting responsibility. He considered his three options to be a centralized, decentralized, or hybrid approach. A decentralized approach would continue the present policy in which country/region managers set all prices, and headquarters offered counsel and support. Under a centralized approach, a headquarters management committee would set all prices around the world. Country managers would be responsible for collecting data and making suggestions to headquarters. A third option was to establish multiple pricing committees, each including managers from both headquarters and the regions, and each responsible for setting prices for one or more specific industries.

Company Background and Organization

DHL legally comprised two separate companies: DHL Airways and DHL International. DHL Airways was based in San Francisco and managed all US operations. DHL International was based in Brussels and managed all operations outside the United States. Each company was the exclusive delivery agent of the other. Revenues for 1990 were split: $600 million for DHL Airways, and $1,400 million for DHL International. One DHL executive commented, "The main reason DHL is involved in domestic shipping within the United States is to lower the costs and increase the reliability of our international shipments. We would be at the mercy of the domestic airlines bringing our packages to the international gateways." In 1990, DHL accounted for only 3% of intra-US air express shipments but 20% of overseas shipments from the United States.

DHL was the world's leading international express delivery network. It was privately held and headquartered in Brussels, Belgium. The company was formed in San Francisco in September 1969 by Adrian Dalsey, Larry Hillblom, and Robert Lynn. The three were involved in shipping and discovered that, by forwarding the shipping documents by air with an on-board courier, they could significantly reduce the turnaround time of ships in port. DHL grew rapidly and, by 1990, serviced 189 countries. In 1990, revenues were approximately $2 billion. Profits before taxes were 4–6% of revenues. Exhibit 1 summarizes the growth of DHL operations from 1973 to 1990, while Exhibit 2 displays DHL's revenues by industry.

DHL used a hub system to transport shipments around the world. In 1991, the company operated 12 hubs as shown in Exhibit 3. Within Europe, the United States, and the Middle East, DHL generally used owned or leased aircraft to carry its shipments, while on most intercontinental routes it used scheduled airlines. In

EXHIBIT 1   DHL Operations Statistics: 1973–1990

	1973	*1978*	*1983*	*1990*
Shipments	2,000,000	5,400,000	12,400,000	60,000,000
Customers	30,500	35,000	250,000	900,000
Personnel	400	6,500	11,300	25,000
Countries served	20	65	120	189
Hubs	0	2	5	12
Flights/day	14	303	792	1,466
Aircraft	0	5	27	150
Vehicles	300	2,235	5,940	7,209

NOTE: Shipments included both documents and parcels. Hubs were major shipment sorting centers. Aircraft and vehicle data included both owned and leased equipment.

EXHIBIT 2   **DHL Worldwide Revenues by Industry (January–June 1991)**

Conglomerates	10%
High technology	8
Import–export	8
Banking	7
Transport	7
Heaving engineering	6
Chemicals	5
Precision manufacturing	5
Professional services	4
Foodstuffs	4
Textiles/leather	4
Other	32

1991, approximately 65% of DHL shipments were sent via scheduled airlines and 35% via owned or leased aircraft. The other leading shippers also utilized scheduled airlines but to a lesser extent than DHL. Federal Express (FedEx) relied on its own fleet of planes to transport all its shipments. Pierre Madec, DHL's operations director, noted:

> FedEx has a dedicated airfleet which ties up capital and limits the flexibility of its operation: Express packages are forced to wait until the FedEx plane's takeoff slot, which at major international airports frequently does not tie in with the end-of-the-day courier pickups. By using a variety of scheduled international carriers, DHL is able to optimize its transport network to minimize delivery times.

To strengthen its "open network," DHL, in May 1990, entered into an alliance with three companies: Japan Airlines (JAL), Lufthansa, and Nissho Iwai Corporation. The deal gave DHL additional access to shipping capacity on major routes between Europe, Japan, and the United States. In return, the three companies received equity stakes in DHL initially totaling 12.5%. The alliance could ultimately lead to the three partners owning 57% of DHL. (Before the alliance, all DHL equity had been held by the founders and senior managers.)

DHL was organized into nine geographic regions. Region managers oversaw the relevant country managers and/or DHL agents in their regions and held profit and loss responsibility for performance within their territories. Revenues and profits were recognized at the location in which a shipment originated. Only 70 people worked at DHL's world headquarters in Brussels. The main functions of the worldwide marketing services group, of which Sarrafzadeh was a member, were business development, information transfer, communication of best practice ideas, and sales coordination among the country operating units.

EXHIBIT 3

DHL hub system

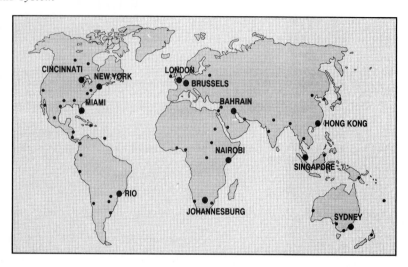

The word "Hub" derives from the image of a wheel with the spokes, the Hub is a sorting and redistribution centre and the spokes are flights in and out.

DHL routes material via Hubs, we do not use direct flights to every destination around the world. There are Hubs in every area of the world:

USA (Cincinnati, New York);   **AFRICA** (Johannesburg, Nairobi);

MIDDLE EAST (Bahrain);   **FAR EAST** (Hong Kong, Singapore);

AUSTRALIA (Sydney);   **EUROPE** (London, Brussels);

The routing of material through the Hubs passes on a saving of both time and cost for the customer.

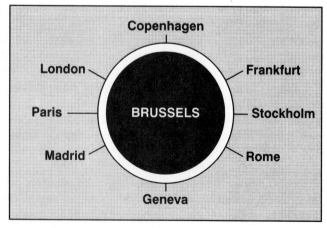

Of DHL's 60 million shipments in 1990, 50 million were cross-border shipments. DHL's worldwide mission statement, included in its 1990 annual report, read:

> DHL will become the acknowledged global leader in the express delivery of documents and packages. Leadership will be achieved by establishing the industry standards of excellence for quality of service and by maintaining the lowest cost position relative to our service commitment in all markets of the world.

DHL management believed that achievement of this mission required the following:

- Absolute dedication to understanding and fulfilling DHL's customers' needs with the appropriate mix of service, products, and price for each customer.
- Ensuring the long-term success of the business through profitable growth and reinvestment of earnings.
- An environment that rewards achievement, enthusiasm, and team spirit, and which offers each person in DHL superior opportunities for personal development and growth.
- A state-of-the-art worldwide information network for customer billing, tracking, tracing, and management information/communications.
- Allocation of resources consistent with the recognition that DHL is one worldwide business.
- A professional organization able to maintain local initiative and local decision making while working together within a centrally managed network.

DHL's annual report also stated that: "The evolution of our business into new services, markets, or products will be completely driven by our single-minded commitment to anticipating and meeting the changing needs of our customers."

The International Air Express Industry

Total revenues for the international air express industry were approximately $3.4 billion in 1989, and $4.3 billion in 1990. The air express industry offered two main products: document delivery and parcel delivery. Industry revenues were split roughly 75:25 between parcels and documents. In 1989, the parcel sector grew 40%, while the document sector grew 15%. The growth of parcel and document express delivery was at the expense of the air cargo market and other traditional modes of shipping.

The growth of the air express industry was expected to continue. One optimistic forecast for 1992 is presented in Table A on the following page. Other observers were concerned that shipping capacity would expand faster than shipments, particularly if economic growth slowed.

TABLE A   **Worldwide International (Cross-Border) Air Express 1992 Estimated Revenue Growth Rates**

Market	1992 Estimated Growth Rate
Europe	28%
Asia/Pacific	30
United States	25
Rest of the world	9
Total	25

NOTE: Growth rates are for time-sensitive documents/packages under 30 kilograms.

Acknowledging continuing progress toward completion of the European market integration program by the end of 1992, an article on the air express industry in Europe in *Forbes* (April 1991) noted:

> The express-delivery business in Europe is booming . . . Measured by revenues, the European express-delivery business is growing at a 28% compound annual rate. Big European companies are stocking products and parts in central locations and moving them by overnight express, instead of running warehouses in each country.

Competitors

Air express companies serviced a geographic region either by using their own personnel or by hiring agents. Building a comprehensive international network of owned operations and/or reliable agents required considerable time and investment and therefore acted as a significant barrier to entry.

DHL's principal competitors in door-to-door international air express delivery were Federal Express, TNT, and UPS. Exhibit 4 provides operational data for the top four competitors, while Table B summarizes their 1988 market shares:

TABLE B   **International Air Express Market Shares by $ Revenue (1988)**

Company	Market Share	Revenue (1988) (in $ Million)
DHL	44%	1,200
FedEx	7	200
TNT	18	500
UPS	4	100
Others	27	735
Total	100%	2,735

EXHIBIT 4   Major Air Express Competitors (1988)

	DHL	FedEx	TNT	UPS
International air express revenues (in $ million)	$1,200	$200	$500	$100
International air express employees	23,000	5,000	10,000	3,000
Countries covered	184	118	184	175
Total service outlets	1,427	1,135	800	1,700
Service outlets outside United States	1,207	278	750	465
Ratio of owned : agent country operations	2.00 : 1	0.53 : 1	0.77 : 1	0.36 : 1
Owned aircraft	49	38	17	3
Years of international experience	20	5	17	3
Document : parcel revenues	65 : 35	20 : 80*	50 : 50	20 : 80

* After FedEx's 1989 acquisition of Tiger International, Inc., its document : parcel revenue ratio remained relatively unchanged as Tiger concentrated on heavy air freight. However, postacquisition, document and parcel combined revenues represented a smaller portion of total revenues.

Founded in 1973, FedEx focused for many years on the US domestic market. During the late 1980s, the company began to expand internationally through acquisitions and competitive pricing, sometimes undercutting DHL published prices by as much as 50%. Between 1987 and 1991, FedEx invested over $1 billion in 14 acquisitions in nine countries: the United Kingdom, Holland, West Germany, Italy, Japan, Australia, United Arab Emirates, Canada, and the United States. FedEx also entered the international air freight business through the acquisition of Tiger International (Flying Tigers), which expanded further FedEx's global reach in document as well as parcel delivery, particularly in Asia. However, the challenge of integrating so many acquisitions meant that FedEx's international operations lost $43 million in 1989, and $194 million in 1990. Nevertheless, with 45% of the US air express market, 7% of the European market, and leadership in value-added services based on information systems technology, FedEx remained a formidable competitor.

According to FedEx's 1990 annual report:

> Federal Express offers a wide range of customized services for time-definite transportation and distribution of goods and documents throughout the world, using an extensive fleet of aircraft and vehicles.

The annual report noted that, as the air express market in the United States matured, customers were demanding increased value for their shipping dollars. As a result, FedEx launched a number of new services in 1990 which gave customers a broader menu of delivery time options at different prices. For example, customers wanting overnight delivery could pay a premium for early morning delivery or save money if they were willing to accept delivery later in the day.

Thomas Nationwide Transport (TNT) was a publicly owned Australian transport group which had historically concentrated on air express delivery of documents. TNT focused mainly on Europe and had a low profile in North America.

To participate in the North American market, TNT held a 15% stake in an American shipper, Airborne Freight Corporation. This stake could only be increased to a maximum holding of 25% under US aviation laws. During the late 1980s, TNT began to target heavier shipments and bulk consolidations to fuel its growth. In 1987, TNT placed an order for 72 new jets to augment its fleet in Europe. However, TNT proved unable to fill the added capacity, and the company was expected to report a loss for its fiscal year ending in June 1991.

TNT's objective, as expressed in its 1990 annual report, was: "To be recognized by customers, employees, and investors as being synonymous with excellence in all aspects of domestic and international transport—as 'The Worldwide Transportation Group.'"

United Parcel Service (UPS) was a privately held US company, most of whose equity was owned by its employees. UPS had traditionally been known as a parcel shipper that emphasized everyday low prices rather than the fastest delivery. Unlike DHL, UPS sometimes held a package back to consolidate several shipments to the same destination in the interest of saving on costs. UPS had historically tried to avoid offering discounts from its published prices.

UPS's 1990 annual report proclaimed the company's strategy as follows:

> UPS will achieve worldwide leadership in package distribution by developing and delivering solutions that best meet our customers' distribution needs at competitive rates. To do so, we will build upon our extensive and efficient distribution network, the legacy and dedication of our people to operational and service excellence and our commitment to anticipate and respond rapidly to changing market conditions and requirements.

In his 1990 letter to shareholders, UPS chairman and CEO Kent Nelson stated:

> Higher fuel costs took about $62 million dollars off our bottom line during the last two quarters of 1990. We decided to spare our customers the confusion of adjustable fuel surcharges, because we know how disruptive frequent rate changes are to their operations.
>
> After extensive studies, we have begun to change the way we price our services. We made adjustments in two principal areas: We restructured our ground rate chart to reflect higher costs associated with residential deliveries, and we developed more tailored rates and services for large shippers with shipment characteristics that create high revenue and low delivery costs.

In addition to the industry giants, there were many small shipping forwarders which concentrated on a specific geographic area or industry sector. In the late 1980s, many of these small companies were acquired by larger firms trying to increase their market shares. National post offices were also competitors in air express, but they could not offer the same service and reliability because they were not integrated across borders. That is, no national post office could control the shipment of a package from one country to another. One industry executive commented: "When we have internal competitive discussions on international business, the post offices just don't come up."

Finally, the regular airlines were minor competitors in door-to-door express delivery. British Airways operated a wholesale airport-to-door courier service called Speedbird in cooperation with smaller couriers that did not have international networks. Swissair serviced 50 countries through its Skyracer service in cooperation with local agents. In the heavy cargo sector, most airlines were allied with freight forwarders who consolidated cargo from different sources and booked space in aircraft. These alliances represented significant competition as DHL expanded into delivery of heavier shipments. Some airlines were reluctant to upset their freight forwarder customers by dealing with integrated shippers such as DHL.

Competition in the air express industry, aggravated by excess capacity, had resulted in intense price competition during the late 1980s.[1] DHL's chairman and CEO, L. Patrick Lupo, estimated that prices had dropped, on average, 5% each year from 1985 to 1990, with extreme price drops in some markets. For example, in Great Britain, DHL's list prices for shipments to the United States fell approximately 40% from 1987 to 1990. Some of the price reductions were offset, in part, by rising volume and productivity, yet Lupo noted, "There's no question that margins have been squeezed."

DHL Services

DHL offered two services: Worldwide Document Express (DOX) and Worldwide Parcel Express (WPX). DOX offered document delivery to locations around the world within the DHL network. DOX was DHL's first product and featured door-to-door service at an all-inclusive price for nondutiable/nondeclarable items. Typical items handled by DOX included interoffice correspondence, computer printouts, and contracts. The number of documents sent to and from each DHL location was, in most cases, evenly balanced.[2]

WPX was a parcel transport service for nondocument items that had a commercial value or needed to be declared to customs authorities. Like DOX, WPX offered door-to-door service at an all-inclusive price which covered DHL's handling of both the exporting and importing of the shipment. Typical items handled by WPX included: prototype samples, spare parts, diskettes, and videotapes.

DHL imposed size, weight, and content restrictions for all parcels. The size of a package could not exceed 175 centimeters in exterior dimensions (length + width + height), and the gross weight could not exceed 50 kilograms. Further, DHL would not ship various items such as firearms, hazardous material, jewelry, and pornographic material.

---

[1] DHL planes flew, on average, 85% full in 1990. FedEx and UPS planes on international routes were thought to be achieving only 60% capacity utilization.

[2] Canada was an exception. Low prices offered by FedEx and Purolator meant that the number of DHL inbound documents was greater than the number of outbound documents.

Table C compares DHL's parcel and document businesses for 1990:

TABLE C   DHL's Document and Parcel Businesses (1990)

	Total Revenues	Revenue Growth (1989–90)	Total Shipments	Total Weight	Gross Profits
Document	60%	+14%	70%	50%	70%
Parcel	40	+28	30	50	30

DHL offered numerous value-added services including computerized tracking (LASERNET), 24-hour customer service, and proof of delivery service. In addition, DHL offered Saturday, Sunday, and holiday service, and maintained express centers and drop-off boxes for consignments after normal business hours. DHL couriers used handheld laser scanners to transmit customer shipment information to DHL sort centers and to receive package pickup requests in their vans. For some large customers, DHL installed an on-site EasyShip computer system which enabled them to track and trace their own shipments, generate bills of lading and invoices, and analyze their shipping patterns. Customers could access DHL Express Parts Centers, custom-bonded warehouses that served as parts and equipment depots for customers throughout Europe and Asia. Customers could also tap the assistance of specialized industry consultants based in DHL regional offices. Such value-added services could enhance customer loyalty and increase DHL's share of a customer's international shipping requirements. However, such services were expensive to provide, and customers using them were often not always charged extra, particularly since they were also offered by key competitors such as FedEx.

DHL had 20 years of experience in dealing with customs procedures and, by 1990, was electronically linked into an international customs network. All shipments were bar coded, which facilitated computerized sorting and tracking. Thanks to a direct computer link between DHL and customs authorities in five European countries, customs clearance could occur while shipments were en route. In addition, DHL's staff included licensed customs brokers in 80 countries.

DHL had been cautious about differentiating itself on the basis of speed of service, and arrival times were not guaranteed. However, DHL executives believed that their extensive network meant that they could deliver packages faster than their competitors. Hence, in 1991, DHL commissioned an independent research company to send on the same day five documents and five dutiable packages from three US origin cities via each of five air express companies to 21 international destinations (three cities in each of seven regions). Exhibit 5 reports the percentages of first place deliveries (i.e., fastest deliveries) achieved by each competitor in each region. DHL had the highest percentage of first place results in six of the seven regions. The research also indicated that DHL was consistently able to deliver more dutiable items through customs in time for earliest business district delivery (before 10:30 AM) than any of its rivals. A similar intra-European

---

EXHIBIT 5   Results of Shipment Delivery Speed Tracking Study

	DHL	TNT	FedEx	UPS	Airborne
Western Europe	39%	34%	4%	26%	n.a.*
Eastern Europe	42	16	14	28	1%
Southeast Asia	34	16	18	6	27
Far East	56	11	21	3	9
Middle East	70	6	16	2	7
South America	28	10	32	9	21
Africa	62	9	13	10	7
All documents	55	15	13	13	6
All dutiables	40	14	21	11	14

NOTE: To be read, for example: Of the packages shipped on the five carriers to Western Europe, 39% of the packages that arrived first at their destination were shipped by DHL.
* n.a. = Not available.

study found that DHL also achieved the highest percentage of first place deliveries on packages shipped between cities within Europe.

DHL also commissioned independent research to ascertain how it was rated by customers against its key competitors. Table D reports the ratings on the two attributes considered by customers to be the most important in choosing an international air express service:

TABLE D   Ratings of Air Express Carriers

	DHL	TNT	FedEx	UPS
Reliability	8.4	7.7	7.8	8.1
Value for money	8.0	7.3	7.5	8.0

NOTE: Respondents rated each carrier on a 10-point scale.
SOURCE: Triangle Management Services Ltd. and IRB International Research, 1991.

The study also asked the customer sample which air express carrier they would turn to first when sending both a document and a parcel to destinations in each of four geographic regions. Results are presented in Exhibit 6 on the following page. The results of a comparative study of unaided brand awareness for the major international air express companies are summarized in Exhibit 7.

Customers

In the early years of air express, banks and finance houses were the major customers. For financial institutions, delays in delivery of checks and promissory notes could cause considerable financial losses. During the 1970s, most air express shipments were "emergency" in nature. Examples included an urgent

EXHIBIT 6   First Choice of Air Express Carrier by Final Destination

	DHL	TNT	FedEx	UPS
Documents				
Europe	32%	7%	8%	5%
North America	38	10	10	4
Middle East	35	14	6	5
Australia	38	10	7	5
Other	40	14	6	6
Parcels				
Europe	28%	5%	7%	7%
North America	32	7	12	8
Middle East	33	13	6	7
Australia	27	9	10	9
Other	32	10	4	9

SOURCE: Triangle Management Services, Ltd., and IRB International Research, 1991.

EXHIBIT 7   Unaided Brand Awareness for International Carriers of Documents and Packages

	DHL	TNT	FedEx	UPS
Documents				
All countries	87%	50%	23%	16%
France	77	27	20	20
Germany	90	71	25	20
Italy	91	45	19	15
United Kingdom	85	67	37	22
Parcels				
All countries	72%	58%	28%	29%
France	58	40	14	10
Germany	67	76	28	46
Italy	75	62	23	27
United Kingdom	72	58	43	35

SOURCE: Company records. Disguised data.

contract, a check or note that sealed a financial transaction, a computer tape, a replacement part, and a mining sample which had to be studied before drilling could begin. During the 1980s, many customers began to use air express more systematically. For example, companies that operated "just-in-time" inventory systems began to use express delivery services to deliver components.

In 1990, DHL had 900,000 accounts, of which the top 250 accounts represented 10% of revenues and 15% of shipments. DHL had only about 10 global contracts with customers (representing 1% of revenues), as few multinational corporation (MNC) headquarters had expressed interest in negotiating such agreements. Like DHL, most MNCs were decentralized. However, DHL did have many regional agreements with MNCs as well as contracts in individual country markets. Sarrafzadeh was not enthusiastic about encouraging global contracts, believing that they could only lead to pressure for lower prices.

Exhibit 8 shows how DHL segmented its US customers in 1990 by level of monthly billings, and it provides profile information on each segment. Tony Messuri, DHL New England area sales manager, noted:

> There are two principal types of customers. First, there are the people who know where they're shipping. They know where their international offices are located, and will ask overseas offices for feedback about shippers. These customers select a carrier that's well received and well respected by their own customers, both internal and external.
>
> Second, there are customers who cannot forecast where their future shipments will be going. They are more price sensitive but they can't give us enough information to enable us to set their discounts properly on the basis of anticipated volume. We are at more risk here of making a poor pricing decision. Sometimes a few months after we and the customer agree on a price and discount, the customer will conclude that it's overpaying, then seek more discounts from us or switch shippers.
>
> Customers are very service sensitive. The small customers tend to switch shippers more readily. Often it only depends on which company's sales rep visited most recently.

The parcel market was typically more price sensitive than the document market. For most companies, the total cost of shipping parcels was a much larger line item than the total cost of shipping documents. Further, the decision-making unit was often different for the two services. The decision on how to ship a document was frequently made by an individual manager or secretary. Whereas "documents went out the front door, parcels went out the back door." They were shipped from the loading dock by the traffic manager, who could typically select

EXHIBIT 8   Profile of DHL's US Customer Base (1990)

Customer Segment: Level of Monthly Billing International	Percent of Total Accounts	Percent of Total Sales	Percent of Total Profits	Typical Discount*	DHL Penetration†	Percent Using Only DHL††
$0–$2,000	15%	5%	45%	10–35%	70%	95%
$2,001–$5,000	40	15	20	30–40	70	80
$5,001–$15,000	35	30	25	40–50	60	60
$15,0001+	10	50	10	45–60	35	35
	100%	100%	100%			

* The exact discount was negotiated between DHL and the account. Percentages represent discounts off the published DHL tariff.
† Penetration means the percentage of all accounts in the segment that used DHL for at least some of their international shipping needs.
†† To be read: Percent of DHL customers who use only DHL for international shipping.
SOURCE: Company record.

from a list of carriers approved by the purchasing department. In some companies, parcel shipment decisions were being consolidated, often under the vice president of logistics. As one European auto parts supplier stated: "We view parts delivery as a key component of our customer service."

As a result, many shippers split their air express business among several firms. For example, all documents might be shipped via DHL, while parcels might be assigned to another carrier. Alternatively, the customer's business might be split by geographic region; a multinational company might assign its North American business to Federal Express and its intercontinental shipments to DHL. For the sake of convenience and price leverage, most large customers were increasingly inclined to concentrate their air express shipments worldwide with two or three preferred suppliers.

Pricing

Evolution of Pricing Policy

As DHL expanded service into new countries throughout the 1970s and 1980s, it developed many different pricing strategies and structures. DHL country managers had almost total control of pricing. They typically set prices based on four factors: what the market could bear, prices charged by competition (which was often initially the national post office), DHL's initial entry pricing in other countries, and DHL's then current pricing around the world.

DHL's prices were historically 20–40% higher than those of competitors. Exhibit 9 provides sample prices for DHL, TNT, FedEx, and UPS. In most countries, DHL published a tariff book which was updated yearly. Competitors who followed DHL into new markets often patterned their pricing structures after DHL's.

DHL had developed a sophisticated, proprietary software package called PRISM to analyze profitability. A PRISM staff officer at each regional office advised and trained country operating units on use of the software. The program could calculate profitability by route or by customer in a given country. However, PRISM could not consolidate the profits of a given customer across countries.

EXHIBIT 9   Sample Published List Prices on Selected Routes (1990)

Service	DHL	TNT	FedEx	UPS
1-kilogram document				
London–New York	$ 51	$ 47	$ 50	$ 44
2-kilogram document				
Brussels–Hong Kong	131	143	118	97
2-kilogram parcel				
Singapore–Sidney	120	120	39	34

EXHIBIT 10

Development and description of PRISM

DHL local management was judged on revenue and control costs. The contribution of each local operation was calculated by subtracting local costs from revenue. This measure of performance did not, however, consider the costs to other country operations of delivery and whether the selling price was sufficient to cover the cost of pickup, line haul, hub transfer, delivery, and headquarters overhead and management costs.

In 1987, all countries and regions analyzed their costs and provided DHL headquarters with detailed delivery, pickup, hub, and line haul costs. Using these data, headquarters developed the PRISM (Pricing Implementation Strategy Model) software package. The inputs to the model were cost data along with competitive price information. PRISM costs were based on historical data which had been consolidated and averaged.

Country organizations were provided with the PRISM software which enabled them to analyze their profitability at the country, customer segment, and individual customer levels. The methodology was refined further to take into account the scale economies large shippers provided to DHL.

PRISM was used for the following purposes:

- Analyzing the profit impacts of possible tariff adjustments, taking into account the competitive intensity of the route.
- Identifying low- or negative-margin customers whose yields should be managed upward.
- Settling price strategy for different customer segments.

Country and regional managers were still measured on local contribution (local revenues minus local costs). They were, however, encouraged to analyze profitability by account when developing their annual budgets and use PRISM when considering price revisions. The level of use of PRISM varied by region and country.

SOURCE: Company records.

(Exhibit 10 provides a fuller description of PRISM.) All profitability analyses had to be based on average costs due to the variability in costs associated with transporting a shipment. For example, a package from Perth, Australia, to Tucson, Arizona, might be consolidated seven to eight times in transit and travel on five to six planes. Further, every package from Perth to Tucson did not necessarily travel the same route. Exhibit 11 on the following page shows the revenues and costs associated with two sample lanes to illustrate the significant impact of geographical differences on costs and profitability.

PRISM was not used extensively by all DHL offices. As one country manager put it:

> We and the customer both want a simple pricing structure. PRISM just provides more information, adds to complexity and takes time away from selling.

Base Prices and Options

DHL's base prices were calculated according to product (service), weight, origin, and destination. The charge was higher for parcels than for documents due to increased costs for customs clearance, handling, packaging, and additional paperwork. FedEx charged the same for parcels and documents. Shipment weights were computed in pounds in the United States and in kilograms in all other

---

EXHIBIT 11   Revenue and Cost Lane Examples: DOX and WPX

	DOX (Document)	*WPX (Parcel)*
United Kingdom to United States (1990)		
Revenue	$5,723,000	$2,342,000
Outbound cost	2,392,915	667,712
Hub cost	596,608	490,436
Line haul*	1,121,882	647,915
Delivery	1,376,953	386,049
Margin	234,642	149,888
Margin percentage	4.1	6.4
Shipments	321,139	68,580
Revenue/shipment	$24.76	$34.15
Belgium to Hong Kong (1990)		
Revenue	$13,800,000	$6,660,000
Outbound cost	6,341,100	1,837,733
Hub cost	1,138,146	1,181,400
Line haul	2,926,662	1,837,733
Delivery	2,276,292	1,050,134
Margin	1,117,800	693,000
Margin percentage	8.1	10.5
Shipments	456,802	109,544
Revenue/shipment	$30.21	$60.25

* Line haul refers to the air segment of the shipment.

countries. Moreover, weight breaks varied among countries. For example, in Hong Kong, breaks were every half kilogram, and in Spain, every two kilograms. Some DHL executives believed that, for the sake of simplicity, DHL's weight breaks should be the same worldwide. Table E gives examples of base prices on routes from London:

TABLE E   DHL Sample Prices (1990)

From London	*First ½ Kilo*	*Each Additional ½ Kilo*
Document:		
To New York	£24.50	£1.60
To Switzerland	26.00	2.20
To Japan	26.50	2.50
Parcel:		
To New York	£27.00	£1.60
To Switzerland	32.00	2.20
To Japan	34.00	2.50

Customers elected whether or not to buy extra insurance coverage for their shipments. All shipments were automatically insured by DHL for up to $100.

Customers could purchase additional insurance based on the declared value of the shipment. For example, in the United States, customers could purchase extra insurance for $0.40 per $100.

Pricing Structures

In any country market, DHL followed one of three pricing approaches: monthly handling fee, frequency discount, and loaded half-kilo.

Under the first approach, DHL charged a flat monthly fee to customers who wanted to be included on its regular pickup route. DHL automatically visited such customers once each business day without the customer having to contact DHL for pickup. The purpose was to motivate customer usage of DHL's services and encourage customers to process all their shipments through DHL. Customers who elected not to be on DHL's regular route could either call for shipment pickup or drop off a shipment at a DHL office. Customers who called for pickup were charged a nominal pickup fee. Under the monthly fee structure, customers did not receive volume discounts.

Sarrafzadeh summarized his views on the problems with this approach:

> The monthly fee can work but only if it is properly marketed. Because it does not relate to a unit of value, customers resent it and salespeople can't defend it. As a result, it has often proved hard to raise the monthly fees as fast as the per shipment charges.

In some markets, including Great Britain, DHL offered a frequency discount structure under which a discount was provided based on number of units shipped. The more often a customer used DHL during a given month, the cheaper the unit shipment cost. Table F shows the frequency discount structure in Great Britain:

TABLE F	DHL Frequency Discount Structure in Great Britain (1990)
Shipments/Month	*Discount/Shipment*
1–4	£ 0
5–10	5
11–15	8
16–25	9
26–40	10
41–60	11
61–100	12
101–200	13
200+	14

The frequency discount was based on the total number of documents and parcels shipped. For example, if a customer purchased 10 document and 20 parcel shipments in a given month, a discount of £10 per shipment was given. Under the frequency discount structure, a customer did not pay a standard monthly route fee, and DHL only visited the account upon request.

The per shipment frequency discount was retroactive and was computed for each customer at the end of the calendar month. Conversely, FedEx's discounts were based on forecast demand rather than past performance and on revenues rather than unit shipments. FedEx monitored a new account's actual shipments for six months before the account qualified for a discount and then adjusted the discount upward or downward based on quarterly shipment data and shipment density.[3]

Sarrafzadeh was not enthusiastic about the frequency discount structure:

> Once you publish your frequency discounts, they're no longer discounts. They're expected. Though they may sometimes attract the small routine shipper, it's easy for competitors to discover what the discounts are and undercut them. Better to publish only the book prices and apply discounts as needed on a case-by-case basis.

The loaded half-kilo structure used in the United States resembled the frequency discount structure, except that discounts were based on total weight shipped during a given month rather than on the number of shipments. According to Sarrafzadeh:

> I think this is the best approach so long as the guidelines for discounting are appropriate.

Price Negotiations

The largest customers sought one- or two-year deals with shippers to handle their transport needs. Typically, when a current agreement was nearing its end, the customers put their businesses up for bid and solicited proposals from interested shippers. Proposals incorporated the following information: transit times, overhead rate structures and rates for specified countries, tracking capabilities, sample tracking reports, a sample annual activity report, and a list of international stations (indicating which were company owned versus run by agents). Most bid requests were made by the purchasing manager, yet the decision-making unit was often a committee comprising managers from the traffic, sales and marketing, customer service, and purchasing departments. The decision was complicated because the major shippers were organized into different regions and lanes, thereby hindering direct comparisons among proposals. Sophisticated accounts typically calculated the bottom-line cost of each proposal, while unsophisticated accounts based their decisions on comparisons on a few "reference prices" (e.g., New York–London).

The average term of shipping agreements was two years, with almost all ranging between one and three years. Fifteen percent of DHL agreements involved formal contracts, while the other 85% were "handshake" agreements.

---

[3] Shipment density referred to the number of items picked up per stop. The more items collected per stop, the lower the pickup cost per unit. DHL's information systems did not permit it to award discounts based on shipment density.

Some customers tried to renegotiate prices in the middle of an agreement, though most Fortune 2000 companies abided by their contracts.

DHL sales reps had significant flexibility when negotiating proposals. For example, the rep could tailor discount rates by lane such that an account would obtain large discounts on its most frequently used routes. DHL senior management typically gave only general direction to sales reps on negotiating discounts. For example, senior management might advise, ''Hold price on Asia, yet you can give some on the United States and Europe.'' Most proposals associated a monthly minimum level of billings (adjusted, if necessary, for seasonality of the business) with the offer of any discounts.

DHL sales reps could negotiate discounts from book prices up to 35%. District sales managers could approve discounts up to 50%, while discounts above 50% required the approval of a regional sales director. Further, discounts over 60% required approval from the vice president of sales. For all discounts over 35%, a sales rep had to submit a Preferred Status Account (PSA) report, which included a detailed analysis of the profitability of the account. As shown in Exhibit 12, the PSA used a computer model to calculate fixed and variable costs, net profits by geographic lane and product line, and overall contribution margins. When deciding on the discount, management considered not only the financial implications of the discount but also competitive and capacity factors.

Tony Messuri, DHL New England area sales manager, stated:

> It is good to have pricing flexibility. Managers at most companies are just looking for justification to use us. But they and DHL upper managers both know that we're not the only game in town . . . We can sit down with a customer and build our own rate table leaving the book prices aside. We can customize the table to the customer's needs. This customization really helps negotiations.

Sales and Advertising

DHL had a single sales force that sold both document and parcel services. Sales reps were organized geographically, and were evaluated primarily on monthly sales. Typically, sales reps had separate monthly sales objectives for international, domestic, and total sales, and received a bonus whenever they exceeded any one of the three. Sales managers were evaluated against profit as well as revenue objectives.

When a new account called for a pickup, that account was assigned an account number the next day and was called upon by a DHL sales rep within a week.[4] At large companies, sales reps targeted the traffic, shipping and receiving, and purchasing departments, while at small companies, they focused their efforts on line managers such as the vice president of marketing or vice president of international.

---

[4] In the United States, prospective accounts with less than $500 in annual express shipment expenditures were handled by DHL's telemarketing center in Phoenix.

EXHIBIT 12 Sample DHL Preferred Status Account (PSA) Annual Report

PSA analysis for:	Plasmo Systems
Number of pickup sites:	1
Stops per month:	20
Origin station:	Boston
Model date:	1/31/90
Costs date:	4/7/89

Margin by Lane (Note: Not all lanes included)

Service	Lane	Revenue	Pickup Costs	Ship Costs	Weight Costs	Net Profit	% Profit
DOC	A Europe	45.89	3.12	24.02	7.62	11.13	24.3%
DOC	B Europe	48.02	3.12	28.72	7.66	8.07	18.0
DOC	C Europe	31.99	3.12	24.59	4.94	−0.66	−2.1
DOC	D Europe	23.17	3.12	20.46	2.34	−2.75	−11.9
DOC	E Latin Am	38.01	3.12	20.92	4.32	9.65	25.4
DOC	F MidEast	40.79	3.12	22.08	7.26	8.33	20.4
DOC	G Caribbn	31.32	3.12	21.29	3.76	3.15	10.1
WPX	A Europe	44.95	3.12	38.61	4.44	−1.22	−2.7
WPX	B Europe	73.25	3.12	47.36	5.49	17.28	23.6
WPX	D Canada	25.49	3.12	29.24	3.51	−10.38	−40.7

Margin by Product Line

Service	Revenue	Pickup Cost	Ship Cost	Weight Cost	Net Profit	% Profit
DOC	743	46	535	90	72	9.7%
WPX	214	12	196	21	−15	−7.0

Fixed/Variable Cost Report

Service	Revenue	Variable Cost	Gross Margin	Fixed Cost	Net Profit	% Profit
DOC	743	476	267	195	72	9.7%
WPX	214	173	41	56	−15	−7.0

Contribution Report

Service	Revenue	US Cost	US Profit	International Cost	International Profit
DOC	743	494	249	177	72
WPX	214	173	41	49	−15

EXHIBIT 13

Sample US advertisement: Flying van

Our business took off 21 years ago, and we're flying higher than ever.

It's significant that the letters DHL stand for the names of three people (Dalsey, Hillblom and Lynn).

Significant, because it took their personal entrepreneurial vision to recognise a business need, and their personal energy to get the solution off the ground.

Today, however, it's even more significant that the letters DHL stand for over 23,700 names: the highly trained, highly motivated employees

DHL is as international as the United Nations. Our network spans 186 countries, states, territories and protectorates.

And from Ouagadougou to Wagga Wagga. Jakarta to Jeddah, there is not likely to be any city or town that you might wish to send something to, that does not feature on our list of 70,000 destinations served.

Most of all, however, the letters DHL have come to stand for two key words which mean so

If you're a major company you cannot afford anything less than total reliability when you air express your important documents and packages.

And as the world's largest international air express company, it is DHL's mission to provide it. Which we do.

It may be that your own company has an equally impressive growth story to tell. But old or new, large or small, please consider this.

and wouldn't you be better able to concentrate on your own job, if you allowed DHL to apply its expertise to your international air express needs?

167

EXHIBIT 14

Sample advertisement: Europe

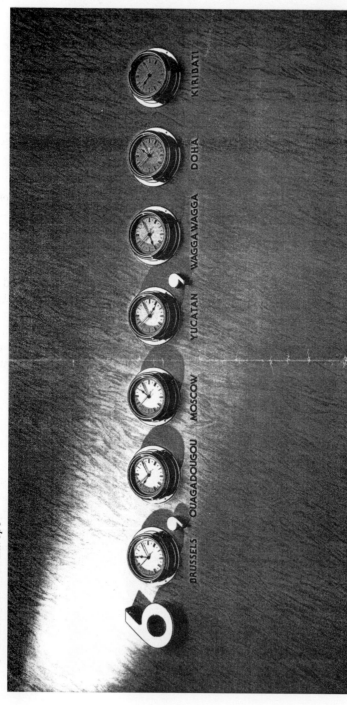

Sixty million deliveries a year around the world and around the clock.

London to Ouagadougou. Wagga Wagga. Yucatan. Kiribati — wherever. Take it from us that, with 70,000 cities and towns on our list, your air express destination is not likely to faze us.

Every 58 seconds, a plane takes off somewhere in the world carrying some of those 60,000,000 shipments.

190 of those planes are our own. Plus over 7,200 vehicles. Plus more owned-and-operated service centres in more countries than any of

Plus, above all, over 25,000 DHL employees. Trained in over 100 languages. But trained in the same company philosophy.

To think globally and act locally. To apply our global and group resources to each customer's advantage. To go that further mile which shows a customer that we're not just going through the motions — we care.

That care is demonstrated by the fact that we never use agents. We believe that if you want a

So if your concern is on-time delivery of your important documents and packages, you are unlikely to do better with any other operator.

But where you *definitely* will not be able to do better is with the total reliability which DHL provides.

From oil wells in Alaska to clinics in Africa, farms in South America to factories in China, people turn to DHL when they have to be sure. In some places, indeed, DHL is just about the

So please consider the implications of this for you and your business.

After all, such total reliability is hard to find these days.

Prior to 1984, DHL headquarters developed global advertising campaigns that the regions and countries could adopt or not as they saw fit. After 1984, each country operation could contract with its own local advertising agency. Headquarters approval of locally developed commercials was not required, though standard guidelines on presentation of the DHL name and logo had to be followed worldwide. In addition, headquarters marketing staff disseminated to all DHL offices commercials that had worked especially well in a particular market and might be worth extending to others.

DHL spent roughly 4% of worldwide sales on advertising. Between 1987 and 1989, DHL built its US advertising campaign around Gary Larson's comic ''The Far Side.'' Dick Rossi, DHL's director of marketing services, noted:

> We went to Larson primarily because we needed to get the DHL name out there. We needed a quick boost in our visibility, to increase awareness and enhance our image.

In 1990, DHL launched a new advertising campaign in the United States based on the slogan ''Faster to more of the world.'' This campaign, inspired by the fighter pilot movie *Top Gun,* featured flying DHL delivery vans. A sample advertisement is reproduced as Exhibit 13 on page 167. In the United States, the objectives of DHL's advertising campaign were threefold. First, DHL wanted to raise brand awareness. Second, DHL aimed to explain that shipping overseas required different capabilities from shipping within the continental United States. Third, DHL sought to convince consumers that DHL was the best at shipping overseas because of its experience, network, worldwide scope, and people.

DHL advertising in Europe used the slogan ''You know it's arrived the moment it's sent.'' A sample advertisement is shown in Exhibit 14.

Conclusion

As he pondered DHL's pricing options, Sarrafzadeh recalled the old adage ''The value of a thing is the price it will bring.'' Perhaps DHL's profits would be maximized if each country manager simply charged each customer ''whatever the market could bear.'' However, from a headquarters perspective, Sarrafzadeh believed a degree of order and consistency was necessary in DHL's pricing strategy, structure, and decision-making process. In particular, he wondered how pricing policy would enhance customer relationships, help to retain customers, and minimize their tendency to split their shipments among several air express carriers. Further penetration of existing accounts where DHL carriers were already making pickups and deliveries would, he was convinced, result in increased profits.

PHARMA SWEDE: GASTIRUP

Early in 1990, Bjorn Larsson, advisor to the president and the head of Product Pricing and Government Relations for Pharma Swede, in Stockholm, Sweden, was reviewing the expected consequences of "1992" on Gastirup in Italy. Gastirup was a drug for the treatment of ulcers. Since its introduction in Italy in 1984, this innovative product had achieved considerable success in its category of gastrointestinal drugs. However, the success had come as a result of pricing the drug at a significant discount below the prevailing prices for the same product in the rest of Europe. Higher prices would have disqualified Gastirup from the government reimbursement scheme, the system by which the state health insurance agency reimbursed patients for pharmaceutical expenditures. The government-negotiated prices for Gastirup in Italy were significantly lower than the average European price.

Bjorn Larsson was concerned that, with the anticipated removal of all trade barriers in Europe, Gastirup would fall victim to massive parallel trading from Italy to the higher-priced countries in the region. Furthermore, with the increased coordination among government health insurance agencies, also foreseen in the years following 1992, price differences among EEC countries were expected to narrow. This likely development highlighted the need for a consistent pricing policy throughout Europe.

As head of Product Pricing and Government Relations, it was Bjorn Larsson's responsibility to recommend the actions that top corporate and local Italian management should take to avert potential annual losses for Gastirup, projected in the $20–$30 million range. Among alternatives being considered, the most extreme was to forgo the large and growing Italian market altogether and concentrate the

This case was prepared by Professor Kamran Kashani, with the assistance of Research Associate Robert C. Howard. Copyright © 1991 by the International Institute for Management Development (IMD), Lausanne, Switzerland. Not to be used or reproduced without permission. IMD case 380.

product's sales elsewhere in Europe. The Italian market for Gastirup had grown to $27 million in recent years and accounted for 22% of European sales. Another option was to remove Gastirup from the Italian government reimbursement scheme by raising the prices to levels close to those prevailing in the higher priced countries. This action would most likely reduce the drug's sales in Italy by as much as 80%. Still another alternative was to take legal action in the European Court of Justice against the Italian government's reimbursement scheme and the related price negotiations as barriers to free trade. Finally, the company could take a wait-and-see attitude, postponing any definitive action to a time when the impact of 1992 was better known.

Company Background

Pharma Swede was formed in 1948 in Stockholm, Sweden; it concentrated solely in pharmaceuticals. In 1989, the company employed over 2,000 people and earned $50 million on sales of $750 million, distributed among its three product lines: hormones (20%), gastrointestinal (50%), and vitamins (30%). Gastirup belonged to the gastrointestinal product category and, as of 1989, accounted for roughly $120 million of Pharma Swede's sales. (See Exhibit 1 for a breakdown of Pharma Swede's sales.)

International Activities and Organization

As of December 1989, Pharma Swede had wholly owned subsidiaries in 11 countries in Western Europe, where it generated 90% of its sales. The balance of sales came from small operations in the United States, Australia, and Japan.

Due to high research and development (R&D) costs as well as stringent quality controls, Pharma Swede centralized all R&D and production of active substances in Stockholm. Partly as a result of these headquarters functions, 60% of the company's expenditures were in Sweden, a country that represented only 15% of sales. However, the politics of national health care often required the company to have some local production. Consequently, a number of Pharma Swede's subsidiaries blended active substances produced in Sweden with additional compounds and packaged the finished product.

Pharma Swede had a product management organization for drugs on the market (refer to Exhibit 2). For newly developed drugs, product management did

EXHIBIT 1   Pharma Swede Sales (in $ Millions)

Product Line	1987	1988	1989
Hormones	$ 90	$130	$150
Vitamins	175	205	225
Gastrointestinal	200	290	375
Total	$465	$625	$750

EXHIBIT 2

Pharma Swede: Partial organization chart

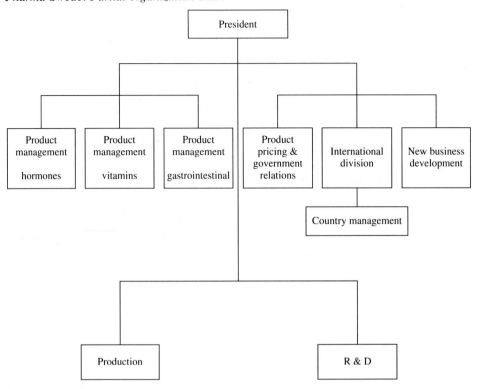

not begin until the second phase of clinical trials, when decisions were made as to where the new products would be introduced and how. (Refer to Exhibit 3 for the different phases of a new product's development.) Besides country selection, product management at headquarters examined different positioning and price scenarios, and determined drug dosages and forms. It had the final say on branding and pricing decisions, as well as basic drug information, including the package leaflet that described a drug's usage and possible side effects. As one product manager explained, the marketing department in Stockholm developed a drug's initial profile and estimated its potential market share worldwide. However, it was up to local management to adapt that profile to their own market.

As an example, in 1982 headquarters management positioned Gastirup against the leading anti-ulcer remedy, Tomidil, by emphasizing a better quality of life and 24-hour protection from a single tablet. To adapt the product to their market, the Italian management, with the approval of Stockholm, changed the name to Gastiros and developed a local campaign stressing the drug's advantages over Tomidil, the oral tablet that had to be taken two or three times a day.

As a rule, headquarters limited its involvement in local markets. It saw its role as one of providing technical or managerial assistance to country management who were responsible for profit and loss.

EXHIBIT 3

Pharma Swede: The development of a new drug

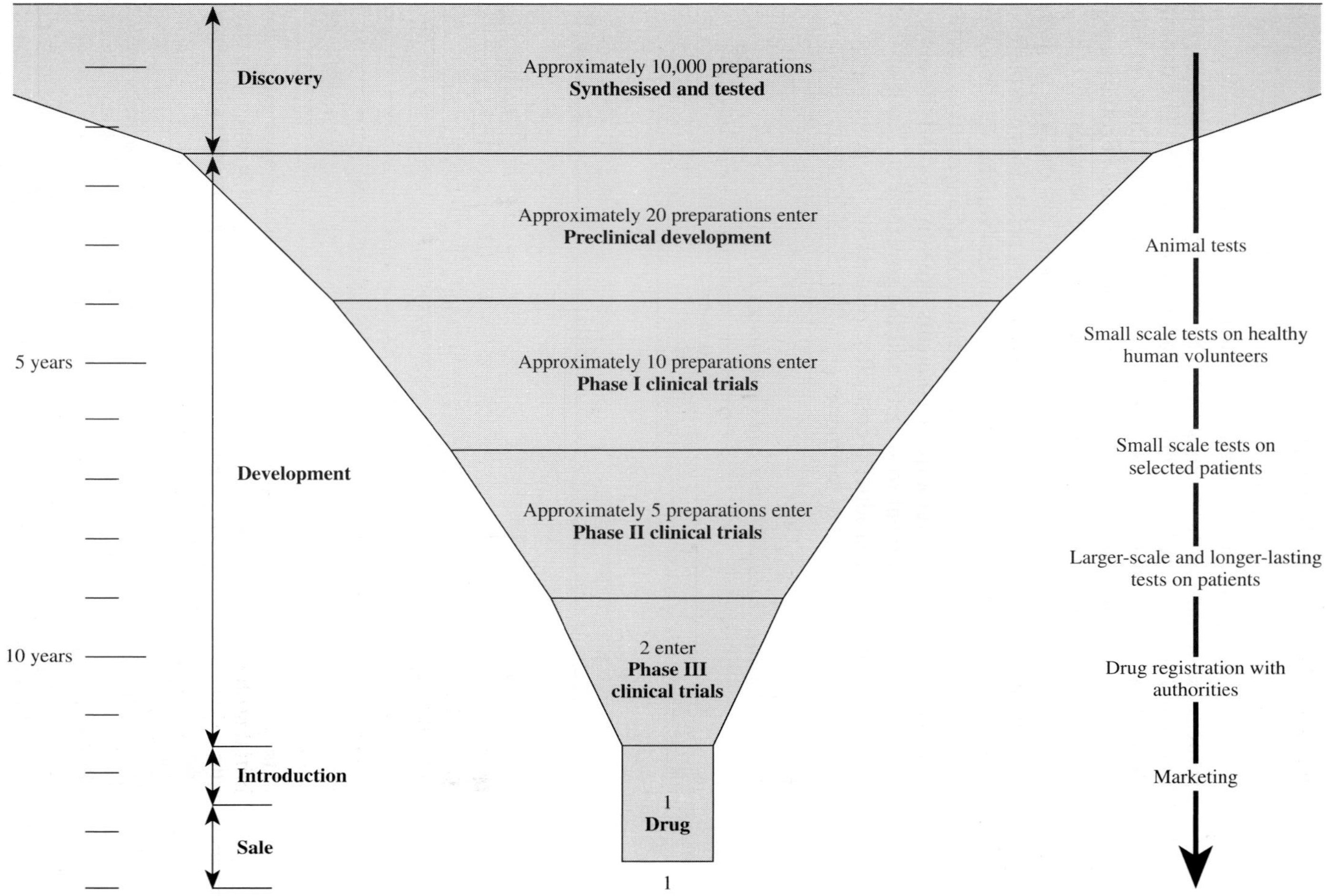

Animal tests

Small scale tests on healthy human volunteers

Small scale tests on selected patients

Larger-scale and longer-lasting tests on patients

Drug registration with authorities

Marketing

Approximately 10,000 preparations **Synthesised and tested**

Approximately 20 preparations enter **Preclinical development**

Approximately 10 preparations enter **Phase I clinical trials**

Approximately 5 preparations enter **Phase II clinical trials**

2 enter **Phase III clinical trials**

1 **Drug**

Discovery

Development

Introduction

Sale

5 years

10 years

Product Pricing and Government Relations

The Product Pricing and Government Relations department, located at the head-quarters, was a recently established function within the company. It prepared guidelines for subsidiary management to use in negotiating drug pricing and patient reimbursement policies with local government agencies. The department was divided into Government Relations and Product Pricing. Those in Government Relations followed ongoing political events and prepared negotiating positions on such issues as employment creation through local production.

The role of Product Pricing, headed by Bjorn Larsson, was to determine the ''optimum'' price for new products. An optimum price, Bjorn explained, was not necessarily a high price, but a function of price–volume relationships in each market. An optimum price also reflected the cost of alternatives, including competitive products and alternative treatments like surgery, and the direct and indirect costs of nontreatment to society and the government. Each of these criteria helped to quantify a product's cost effectiveness or, as government authorities saw it, its treatment value for money.

EXHIBIT 4

Pharma Swede: Product Pricing and Government Relations

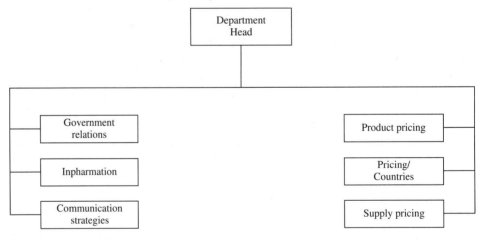

The Government Relations Group observed and recognized potential political problems for the division. When necessary, the group developed counterstrategies and oversaw their implementation.

Inpharmation gathered and managed all pharmapolitical information, on both a national and international basis.

The Communication Strategies group advised the division on product strategies and proposed communications programs.

During drug development, the Product Pricing group worked to secure drug registration, using economic and social data.

Pricing/Countries oversaw and helped build a favorable negotiating environment for pricing decisions.

Supply Pricing was responsible for administering prices and managing relationships with Pharma Swede's distributors.

SOURCE: Company records.

Using cost-effectiveness data in price negotiations was a recent development in the pharmaceutical industry and corresponded to the increasing cost consciousness among public health authorities. Economic exercises that were initially performed in Stockholm to measure a drug's treatment and socioeconomic benefits were repeated with local authorities during negotiations. In Bjorn Larsson's opinion, the latest measure of "nontreatment cost" was becoming an important factor. He explained that a thorough understanding of the direct and indirect costs of an illness had come to play a key role in whether or not a government was willing to pay for a product by granting it reimbursement status, as well as the magnitude of that reimbursement. according to industry observers, the task of marketing to governmental agencies had become crucial in recent years as public agencies were scrutinizing drug prices more carefully. (Refer to Exhibit 4 for an overview and further description of Product Pricing and Government Relations.)

The Pharmaceutical Industry

As of 1989, approximately 10,000 companies worldwide competed in the $180 billion pharmaceutical industry. Industry sales were concentrated in North America, Western Europe, and Japan, with the 100 largest companies in these areas accounting for nearly 80% of all revenues. Western Europe alone accounted for an estimated 25% of total volume.

The industry classified pharmaceutical products according to how they were sold and their therapeutic status. In the first instance, pharmaceutical sales were classified into two categories, ethical and over-the-counter (OTC). Ethical drugs, with four-fifths of all pharmaceutical sales worldwide and a 10% annual growth rate, could only be purchased with a doctor's prescription. These drugs were branded or were sold as a generic when original patents had expired. OTC drugs were purchased without a prescription; they included both branded and generic medicines such as aspirin, cough syrups, and antacids. At Pharma Swede, ethical drugs accounted for more than 90% of total sales.

Ethical drugs were also classified into therapeutic categories, of which gastrointestinal was the second largest, representing 15% of industry sales. Within the gastrointestinal category there were a number of smaller segments, such as anti-ulcer drugs, used to control and treat digestive tract ulcers; antidiarrheas; and laxatives. In 1989, the ethical anti-ulcer drug segment was valued at $7 billion worldwide and growing at 18% a year, faster than the total prescription market.

Trends in Europe

In parallel with worldwide trends, several factors were expected to play a role in shaping the future of the European pharmaceutical industry. Among these were an aging population, rising R&D and marketing costs, greater competition from generics, and government cost controls.

Aging Population.   Europe's stagnating population was gradually aging. The segment of the population over 55 years old was forecast to grow and account for between 33% and 40% of the total by the year 2025—up from below 25% in the mid-1980s. During the same period, the segment below 30 years of age was forecast to drop from about 40% to 30%. The "graying of Europe" was expected to have two lasting effects on drug consumption. First, low growth was projected in the sales of drugs normally used by children or young adults. Second, drug companies marketing products for age-related diseases, such as cancer, hypertension, and heart ailments, could expect growing demand.

Rising R&D and Marketing Costs.   Research and development expenses included the cost of identifying a new molecule and all the tests required for bringing that molecule to the market.

Generally, for every 10,000 molecules synthesized and tested, only 1 made it through the clinical trials to appear in the market. Product development costs were estimated to average $120 million per drug, from preclinical research to market introduction. Industry estimates for research and development expenses averaged around 15% of sales in the late 1980s, with some companies spending as much as 20% of sales on new drugs. Research in more complex diseases like cancer, as well as lengthy clinical trials and government registration processes, had raised these costs recently.

Marketing costs had also increased due to a general rise in the level of competition in the industry. In the early 1980s, pharmaceutical firms spent, on average, 31% of sales on marketing and administrative costs. By 1987, the ratio had increased to 35% and was still rising. Some companies were reported to have spent unprecedented sums of $50–$60 million on marketing to introduce a new drug.

Growth of Generics.   Generic drugs were exact copies of existing branded products for which the original patent had expired. "Generics," as these drugs were known, were priced substantially lower than their originals and were usually marketed by some firm other than the inventor. Price differences between the branded and generics could be as large as 10 to 1. Depending on the drug categories, generics represented between 5% and 25% of the value of the total prescription drug market in Europe, and their share was expected to grow. For example, in the United Kingdom, sales of generic drugs had grown to represent an estimated 15% of the total national health budget and were forecast to reach 25% by 1995. In line with efforts to contain costs, governments in many parts of Europe were putting increased pressure on physicians to prescribe generics instead of the more expensive branded drugs.

Government Role.   Governments were one of the strongest forces influencing the pharmaceutical industry in Europe, where, in conjunction with public and private insurance agencies, they paid an average of two-thirds of health care costs. In Italy, for example, 64% of all ethical pharmaceutical expenditures were covered by the public health care system. In Germany, France, and the United Kingdom, the respective shares were 57%, 65%, and 75%. These ratios had risen considerably throughout the 1960s and 1970s.

European governments were facing two opposing pressures: to maintain high levels of medical care while trying to reduce the heavy burden placed on the budget for such expenditures. Influence on pharmaceutical pricing, according to industry experts, had become an increasingly political as well as economic issue.

Not surprisingly, government agencies seeking to reduce health insurance costs increasingly encouraged the use of generics. In fact, before the advent of generics and official interventions, well-known branded drugs which had lost their patents in the 1970s, such as Librium or Valium, often maintained up to 80% of their sales for several years. In contrast, by the late 1980s, it was more likely that a drug would lose nearly 50% of its sales within two years after its patent expired.

Gastirup

Ulcers and Their Remedies

Under circumstances not completely understood, gastric juices—consisting of acid, pepsin, and various forms of mucus—could irritate the membrane lining the stomach and small intestine, often producing acute ulcers. In serious cases, known as peptic ulcers, damage extended into the wall of the organ, causing chronic inflammation and bleeding. Middle-aged men leading stressful lives were considered a high-risk group for ulcers.

Ulcers were treated by four types of remedies: antacids, H-2 inhibitors, anticholinergics, and surgery. Antacids, containing sodium bicarbonate or magnesium hydroxide, neutralized gastric acids and their associated discomfort. Some of the more common OTC antacid products were Rennie and Andursil. In contrast, H-2 inhibitors such as ranitidine reduced acid levels by blocking the action of the stomach's acid-secreting cells. Anticholinergics, on the other hand, functioned by delaying the stomach's emptying, thereby diminishing acid secretion and reducing the frequency and severity of ulcer pain. Finally, surgery was used only in the most severe cases, where ulceration had produced holes in the stomach and where ulcers were unresponsive to drug treatment.

In 1989, the world market for nonsurgical ulcer remedies was estimated at $8 billion, with most sales distributed in North America (30%), Europe (23%), and Japan (5%). Worldwide, H-2 inhibitors and OTC antacids held 61% and 12% of the market, respectively.

The Oral Osmotic Therapeutic System

Gastirup, introduced in 1982 as Pharma Swede's first product in the category of ulcer remedies, used ranitidine as its active ingredient. As of 1982, ranitidine was available as a generic compound, after having lost its patent protection in that year. The US-based Almont Corporation was the original producer of ranitidine and its former patent holder.

What distinguished Gastirup from other H-2 inhibitors, including ranitidine tablets produced by Almont and others, was not its active ingredient, but the method of administration called the oral osmotic therapeutic system (OROS). In contrast to tablets or liquids taken several times a day, the oral osmotic therapeutic system was taken once a day. Its tablet-like membrane was specially designed to release a constant level of medicine over time via a fine laser-made opening. By varying the surface, thickness, and pore size of the membrane, the rate of drug release could be modified and adapted to different treatment needs. Furthermore, the release of the drug could be programmed to take place at a certain point in time after swallowing the tablet. Consequently, drug release could be timed to coincide with when the tablet was in the ulcerated region of the upper or lower stomach. (Refer to Exhibit 5 for a diagram and brief description of OROS.)

Drugs supplied via OROS had certain advantages over the others. First, because of a steady release of the medicine, they prevented the "high" and "low" effects often observed with the usual tablets or liquids. Furthermore, the time-release feature also prevented overfunctioning of the liver and kidneys. In addition, because drugs contained in an OROS had to be in the purest form, they were more stable and had a prolonged shelf life. Pharma Swede management believed that drugs administered by OROS could lead to fewer doctor calls, less hospitalization, and reduced health care costs for insurance agencies and governments.

Because OROS was not a drug per se but an alternative method of drug administration, it was sold in conjunction with a particular pharmaceutical substance. By the end of 1989, Pharma Swede was marketing three drugs using

EXHIBIT 5

The oral osmotic delivery system (OROS)

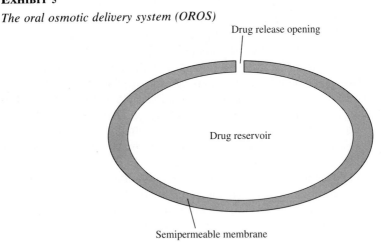

Although OROS looked like a normal tablet, the system used osmotic pressure as a source of energy for the controlled release of active substance. Water, present throughout the body, passed through the semipermeable membrane as long as the reservoir contained undissolved substance. An increase in reservoir pressure, caused by the influx of water, was relieved by releasing drug solution through the opening. Up to 80% of the drug was released at a constant rate; the remainder at a correspondingly declining rate. To guarantee the accuracy of the system, the opening had to comply with strict specifications. Hence, a laser was used to bore a hole through the membrane in such a way that only membrane was removed, without damaging the reservoir.

SOURCE: Company records.

OROS. Gastirup was the company's only OROS product in the gastrointestinal category; the other two were in the hormones category. The management of Pharma Swede characterized the use of OROS as an attempt to introduce product improvements which did not necessarily rely on new molecules but on new "software," leading to improved ease of use and patient comfort.

Ranitidine, the active ingredient in Gastirup, was not made by Pharma Swede because of its complex manufacturing process and the fact that since 1982 it was available from a number of suppliers both inside and outside Sweden. Gastirup OROS tablets were manufactured by the company in Sweden; final packaging, including insertion of the drug information sheet, was done in a number of European countries, including Italy.

Patent Protection

OROS was developed and patented by the Anza Corporation, a US company that specialized in drug delivery systems. In Europe, Anza had applied for patents on a country-by-country basis. Patent protection was twofold: OROS as a drug delivery system, and its use with specific drugs. The more general patent on OROS was due to expire in all EEC countries by 1991. The second and more important patent for Gastirup, covered oral osmotic therapeutic systems containing ranitidine. This latter patent, exclusively licensed to Pharma Swede for Europe, would expire everywhere on the Continent by the year 2000.

Although Pharma Swede sold more than one OROS product, it had an exclusive license from Anza for only the ranitidine–OROS combination. Over the years, a number of companies had tried to develop similar systems without much success. To design a system that did not violate Anza's patents required an expert knowledge of membrane technology, which only a few companies had.

Competition

Broadly speaking, all ulcer remedies competed with one another. But Gastirup's primary competition came from the H-2 inhibitors in general, and from ranitidine in particular. Since 1982, when ranitidine joined the ranks of generics, it was produced by a number of companies in Europe and the United States. Despite increased competition, ranitidine's original producer, the US-based Almont Corporation, still held a significant market share worldwide.

Almont had first introduced its Tomidil brand in 1970 in the United States. After only two years, the product was being sold in 90 countries capturing shares ranging between 42% and 90% in every market. Tomidil's fast market acceptance, considered by many as the most successful for a new drug, was due to its high efficacy as an ulcer treatment and its few side effects. The drug had cut the need for surgery in an estimated two-thirds of cases. Pharma Swede attributed Tomidil's success also to centralized marketing planning and coordination worldwide, high marketing budgets, and focused promotion on opinion leaders in each country. Although Almont was not previously known for its products in the ulcer market, and the company had little experience internationally, Tomidil's success helped the firm to grow into a major international firm in the field.

In the opinion of Pharma Swede management, Tomidil's pricing followed a "skimming" strategy. It was initially set on a daily treatment cost basis of five times the average prices of antacids on the market. Over time, however, prices were reduced to a level three times those of antacids. After 1982, the prices were cut further to about two times those of antacids. In 1990, competing tablets containing ranitidine were priced, on average, 20% below Tomidil for an equivalent dosage. In that year, Tomidil's European share of drugs containing ranitidine was 43%.

Pharma Swede management did not consider antacids and anticholinergics as direct competitors because the former category gave only temporary relief and the latter had serious potential side effects.

Results

Gastirup's sales in Europe had reached $120 million by the end of 1989, or 7% of the ethical antiulcer market. (Refer to Exhibit 6 for a breakdown of sales and shares in major European markets.)

EXHIBIT 6   Sales and Market Shares in Major European Markets*
1989 Sales (in $ Million)

Countries	Total Market (100%)	Gastirup (% Share)	Tomidil (% Share)	Others† (% Share)
Belgium	41	2 (5%)	16 (39%)	23 (56%)
France	198	15 (8%)	61 (31%)	122 (61%)
Germany	318	30 (9%)	51 (16%)	237 (75%)
Italy	394	27 (7%)	110 (28%)	257 (65%)
Netherlands	81	8 (10%)	25 (31%)	48 (59%)
Spain	124	5 (4%)	11 (9%)	108 (87%)
Sweden	34	10 (29%)	5 (15%)	19 (56%)
United Kingdom	335	18 (5%)	97 (29%)	220 (66%)
All Europe	1,673	120 (7%)	486 (29%)	1,054 (63%)

* All ethical anti-ulcer remedies.
† Includes branded and generic drugs.

Pricing

Gastirup was premium priced. Its pricing followed the product's positioning as a preferred alternative to Tomidil and other ranitidine-containing tablets by improving the patient's quality of life and providing 24-hour protection in a single dosage. While competitive tablets had to be taken two or three times daily, the patient needed only one Gastirup tablet a day. The risk of forgetting to take the medicine was thus reduced, as was the inconvenience of having to carry the drug around all the time. Because of these unique advantages, substantiated in a number of international clinical trials, management believed that using Gastirup ultimately resulted in faster treatment and reduced the need for surgery. Gastirup was priced to carry a significant premium over Tomidil prices in Europe. The margin over the generics was even higher. (Refer to Exhibit 7 for current retail prices of Gastirup and Tomidil across Europe.)

Pharmaceutical Pricing in the EEC

Drug pricing was a negotiated process in most of the EEC. Each of the 12 member states had its own agency to regulate pharmaceutical prices for public insurance reimbursement schemes. From a government perspective, pharmaceuticals were to be priced in accordance with the benefits they provided. Although the pricing criteria most frequently cited were efficacy, product quality, safety, and patient comfort, European governments were putting increasing emphasis on cost effectiveness, or the relationship between price and therapeutic advantages. Among diverse criteria used by authorities, local production of a product was an important factor. As a result of individual country-specific pricing arrangements, there were inevitably widespread discrepancies in prices for the same product across Europe.

EXHIBIT 7   Retail Prices in Europe
1989: Daily Treatment Cost

Countries	Gastirup	Tomidil	$\frac{Gastirup}{Tomidil}\%$
Belgium	$3.86	$2.47	56%
Denmark	5.96	3.94	51
France	3.69	2.12	74
Germany	5.31	3.54	50
Greece	3.43	2.36	45
Italy	2.40	1.35	78
Netherlands	5.66	3.11	82
Portugal	3.13	2.24	40
Spain	4.03	2.82	43
Sweden*	5.91	4.22	40
United Kingdom	5.40	3.10	74

* Not a member of the EEC.

For new products, price negotiations with state agencies began after the drug was registered with the national health authorities. Negotiations could last for several years, eventually resulting in one of three outcomes: no price agreement, a partially reimbursed price, or a fully reimbursed price. In the event of no agreement, in most EEC countries the company was free to introduce the drug and set the price, but the patient's cost for the product would not be covered by health insurance. In many EEC countries, a drug that did not receive any reimbursement coverage was at a severe disadvantage. Partial or full reimbursement allowed the doctor to prescribe the drug without imposing the full cost on the patient. Any price adjustment for a product already on the market was subject to the same negotiation process.

Once agreement was reached on full or partial reimbursement, the product was put on a reimbursement scheme, also called a *positive list*—a list from which doctors could prescribe. Germany and the Netherlands were the two exceptions within the EEC employing a *negative list*—a register containing only those drugs that the government would not reimburse. Drugs on the reimbursement list were often viewed by the medical profession as possibly better than nonreimbursed products. (Refer to Exhibit 8 for a summary of price-setting and reimbursement practices within the EEC.)

EXHIBIT 8   Price Setting and Reimbursement in the EEC

Countries	Price Setting	Reimbursement
Ireland	No price control for new introductions.	Positive list (prescription recommended). Inclusion criteria: • Efficacy/safety profile. • Cost-effectiveness profile.
	Prices of prescription drugs are controlled through PPRS (Pharmaceutical Price Regulation Scheme). Control is exercised through regulation of profit levels.	Positive list for NHS (National Health Service) prescriptions. Inclusion criteria: • Therapeutic value. • Medical need.
Belgium	Price control by the Ministry of Health on the basis of cost structure.	Positive list (Ministry of Health). Inclusion criteria: • Therapeutic and social interest. • Duration of treatment. • Daily treatment costs. • Substitution possibilities. • Price comparison with similar drugs. • Copayment: four categories (100%, 75%, 50%, 40%).
Greece	Price control by the Ministry of Health based on cost structure (support of local industry appears to be of importance).	Positive list (IKA, Social Security Ministry).

EXHIBIT 8 *(concluded)*

Countries	Price Setting	Reimbursement
Portugal	Price and reimbursement negotiations with the Ministry of Health and Commerce based on: • Local prices. • Lowest European prices. • Therapeutic value. • Cost effectiveness.	Positive list. Inclusion criteria: • Therapeutic value. • International price comparison. • Cost effectiveness.
Spain	Price control based on cost structure.	Positive list (Social Security System). Inclusion criteria: • Efficacy/safety profile. • Cost effectiveness.
France	No control for nonreimbursable products. Price negotiations with the Ministry of Health for reimbursed products.	Positive list (Transparence Commission and Directorate of Pharmacy and Pharmaceuticals, within the Ministry of Health). Inclusion criteria: • Price. • Therapeutic value. • Potential market in France. • Local R&D. • Copayment: four categories (nonreimbursable, 40%, 70%, 100%).
Luxembourg	Price control by the Ministry of Health. Prices must not be higher than in the country of origin.	Positive list. Inclusion criteria: • Therapeutic value. • Cost effectiveness.
Italy	Price control for reimbursed drugs by CIP (Interministerial Price Committee), following guidelines of CIPE (Interministerial Committee for Economic Planning) based on cost structure.	Positive list (Prontuario Terapeutico Nazionale) National Health Council. Reimbursement criteria: • Therapeutic efficacy and cost effectiveness. • Innovation, risk–benefit ratio, and local research also considered.
Germany	No direct price control by authorities.	Negative list; reference price system since January 1989. Principles: • Drugs will only be reimbursed up to a reference price. • Patient pays the difference between the reference and retail prices. • Copayment: DM 3 per prescribed product (1992: 15% of drug bill).
Netherlands	No price control by authorities.	Negative list; reference price system since January 1988.
Denmark	Price control based on: • Cost structure. • "Reasonable" profits.	Positive list. Inclusion criteria: • Efficacy/safety profile. • Cost-effectiveness profile.

Pricing Gastirup in Italy

Pharmaceutical pricing was particularly difficult in Italy. Health care costs represented 8% of the country's gross domestic product and one-third of the state budget for social expenditures. Government efforts to contain health care costs resulted in strict price controls and a tightly managed reimbursement scheme. Italy was considered by Pharma Swede management a "cost-plus environment" where pricing was closely tied to the production cost of a drug rather than its therapeutic value.

In May 1982, Pharma Swede Italy submitted its first application for reimbursement of Gastirup. The submitted retail price was $33 per pack of ten 400-milligram tablets. On a daily treatment cost basis, Gastirup's proposed price of $3.30 compared with Tomidil's $1.35. Although priced 25% lower than the average EEC price for Gastirup, Italian authorities denied the product admission to the positive list. They argued that Gastirup's therapeutic benefits, including its one-a-day feature, did not justify the large premium over the local price of Tomidil, which was already on the reimbursement scheme. Tomidil and another generic ranitidine-containing brand were produced locally, while Gastirup was to be manufactured in Sweden and only packed in Italy.

Despite the rejection by authorities, Pharma Swede chose to launch Gastirup in Italy without the reimbursement coverage. Management hoped to establish an early foothold in one of Europe's largest markets. Hence, early in 1983, Gastirup was introduced in Italy at a retail price of $37 for a pack of 10 units, and under the brand name Gastiros. This price translated into a daily treatment cost of $3.70, or 16% below the EEC average retail price of Gastirup and nearly three times that of Tomidil in Italy.

The response of the Italian market to Gastiros was better than management had expected. Following an intensive promotional campaign aimed at the general practitioners, sales reached $500,000 a month, or 2% of the market. Meanwhile, the number of requests for reimbursement received by the Italian health care authorities from patients and doctors was growing daily. Management believed that these requests were putting increased pressure on the authorities to admit the product to the positive list.

In a second round of negotiations, undertaken at the initiative of management nine months after the launch, Pharma Swede Italy reapplied for reimbursement status based on a price of $31 per pack of 10 units. This price represented a daily treatment cost of $3.10 and was 30% below the EEC average. Once again, the price was judged too high, and the request was rejected. In November 1984, management initiated a third round of negotiations, and in April 1985 Gastiros was granted full reimbursement status at $24 per pack, a price which had not changed since.

Gastirup's Italian sales and market share among H-2 inhibitors grew substantially following its inclusion in the reimbursement scheme. By 1989, factory sales had reached $27 million, representing a dollar share of 7% of the market. Gastirup was Pharma Swede Italy's single most important product, accounting for nearly a quarter of its sales.

In Italy, as in other countries, Pharma Swede distributed its products through drug wholesalers to pharmacies. Typical trade margin on resale price for pharmacies was 30%. Gastiros' factory price to wholesalers of $15 per pack of 10 tablets had a contribution margin of $3 for the Italian company, which paid its parent $1 for every 400-milligram tablet imported from Sweden. The transfer price was the same across Europe. In turn, the parent earned $0.70 in contribution for every tablet exported to its local operations. The variable cost of producing the tablets included raw materials and the licensing fees paid to Anza.

Lifting the Trade Barriers

As 1992 drew closer, Pharma Swede management believed that two important issues affecting the European pharmaceutical industry would be manufacturing location and drug pricing. In the past, many of the cost-constraint measures taken by authorities had, by design or coincidence, an element of protectionism and represented national trade barriers. For example, local authorities might refuse a certain price or reimbursement level unless the sponsoring company agreed to manufacture locally. Under current EEC regulations, such actions were considered barriers to trade and illegal.

As a countermeasure to such barriers, companies could take legal action against local agencies at the European Court of Justice. With the support of the European Federation of Pharmaceutical Industries Associations (EFPIA), drug firms could sue the agencies for violating the EEC regulations. Although the EFPIA had won 12 cases over the preceding decade, litigation processes lasted sometimes up to seven years, and the results were often partial and temporary in value. Nonetheless, industry participants were relieved that, after 1992, the element of local production linked to price negotiation would disappear.

Since December 1988, under a new EEC regulation called the Transparency Directive, government pricing decisions were open to review by the pharmaceutical companies. The directive served to eliminate any interference with the free flow of pharmaceutical products within the community caused by price controls or reimbursement schemes. It required state agencies to explain how they set drug prices in general as well as in each case. If not satisfied, companies that believed they had been discriminated against could appeal a ruling on price, first to local courts, thereafter to the EC Commission, and, ultimately, to the European Court of Justice.

In addition, the new law required that agencies act quickly when a new drug was approved for sale or when a company asked for a price adjustment. On average, it had taken Pharma Swede one year to reach agreement on a price for a new product. Price adjustments for old products, on the other hand, had taken as long as two years because of delays by local authorities.

Another development related to the creation of a single European market was the expected harmonization in pharmaceutical prices and registration systems among member states. Bjorn Larsson and others in the industry believed that, across Europe, pharmaceutical price differences would narrow in a two-stage process: initially as a result of the transparency directive, and thereafter as part of a more comprehensive market harmonization. Bjorn thought that harmonization was a gradual process and that the completion of a single European market would occur at the earliest between 1995 and 2000.

Aside from a narrowing of the differences in drug prices, possible outcomes for the post-1992 environment included a Pan-European registration system and harmonized health insurance. Some observers predicted that a harmonized drug registration system would be put in place sometime between 1992 and 1995, although the exact form it might take remained open. Pharma Swede management believed it was unlikely that such a system would discriminate against non-EEC firms. Harmonization of national health insurance systems, a longer-term consequence of 1992, was not expected before 1995. Industry analysts believed that, in the interim, the states would continue to press for cost containment on a national basis. Private Pan-European insurance offerings, on the other hand, were expected to increase with deregulation and the completion of the internal market.

The Problem

Prior to 1992, Europe's parallel trade in pharmaceutical products had been limited to less than 5% of industry sales. Each country had local language packaging and registration requirements that tended to restrict or prohibit a product's acceptance and distribution in neighboring markets. Furthermore, according to some Pharma Swede managers, products produced in certain countries, such as Italy or France, suffered a poor quality image in other markets, such as Germany and England. National sentiments aside, distributors seeking to capitalize on parallel imports had to have approval from local authorities, which often implied repackaging to meet local requirements.

Where parallel imports had been a minor problem in the past, they posed a serious challenge to drug firms, including Pharma Swede, in the post-1992 environment when such trade would be protected by law. Hans Sahlberg, the company's product manager for gastrointestinal drugs, explained that government insurance agencies were already examining price and reimbursement issues on a European-wide basis. For drugs already on the market, it was only a matter of time before authorities reimbursed on the basis of the lowest priced parallel import. As an example, this implied that Gastirup, priced at $2.40 per tablet in Italy and $5.40 in Germany, would be reimbursed in Germany at the lower price of imports from Italy. If this proved true, German revenue losses from Gastirup alone could amount to $17 million on current sales. Furthermore, if a system should emerge after 1992 mandating a single EEC price, Pharma Swede would have to revamp its entire price-setting policy.

Management Options

With the upcoming changes in Europe, Gastirup's pricing discrepancies had become a source of major management concern. If not carefully managed, Bjorn and his colleagues believed that the company could lose money, reputation, or both. (Refer to Exhibit 9 for relative prices of Gastirup in Europe.)

In looking for options to recommend to top management at headquarters and at the Italian operation, Bjorn and his staff developed four alternatives. The first, and the most extreme option, was to completely remove Gastirup from the Italian market and concentrate sales elsewhere in Europe. This action would be in defense of prices in the more profitable markets. This alternative was not Bjorn's first choice, as it implied sales revenue losses of $27 million. It also went counter to Pharma Swede's policy of marketing all its products in every European country. Bjorn feared that such a move would lead to heated discussions between headquarters and local management in Italy. It could even seriously damage the company's public reputation. "How," asked Bjorn, "could Pharma Swede, an ethical drug company, deal with public opinion aroused by the apparently unethical practice of denying Gastirup to the Italian market?"

As another alternative, Bjorn could suggest removing Gastirup from the reimbursement scheme by raising prices to levels closer to the EEC average. Such

EXHIBIT 9

Relative retail prices of Gastirup

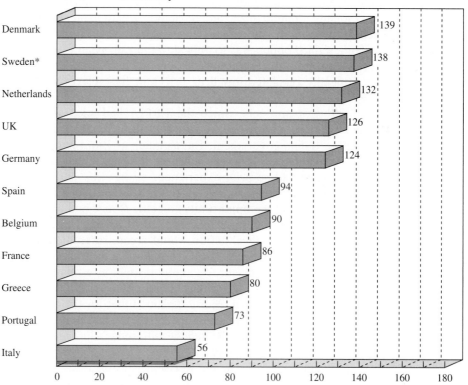

Average EEC Countries = 100

*Sweden not in EEC

action would place Gastirup in the nonreimbursed drug status and lead to an estimated 80% loss in sales. Since the magnitude of this loss was nearly as great as in the first option, headquarters did not believe the Italian management would be any more receptive. Moreover, if Gastirup were removed from the reimbursement scheme, both the product and the company might lose credibility with the medical profession in Italy. According to Bjorn, many doctors perceived the drugs on the reimbursement list as "economical" and "really needed."

Nonetheless, shifting the drug to nonreimbursement status would shift the financing burden from the government to the patient, thus coinciding with the Italian government's view that patients should assume a greater financial role in managing their health. With an increased emphasis on cost containment, such a proposal was liable to appeal to Italian authorities. Bjorn expected full support for this proposal from managers in high-priced markets whose revenues were jeopardized by low-priced countries such as Italy.

There was, however, a possibility that changing the reimbursement status might backfire. Hans Sahlberg recalled a case in Denmark where, after removing a class of cough and cold drugs from reimbursement, Danish authorities came under pressure from a group of consumer advocates and were forced to reverse their decision. If Pharma Swede requested that Gastirup be removed from the Italian reimbursement scheme and the government were forced to reverse that position, the company's public image and its standing with local authorities might be damaged.

Still, a third option was to appeal to the European Commission and, if necessary, start legal action before the European Court of Justice. As Bjorn explained, the artificially regulated low drug prices in Italy placed higher priced imported drugs at a disadvantage and hence acted as a barrier to the free movement of pharmaceutical products. Since the EFPIA had sued and won a similar case against Belgium, Bjorn believed that Pharma Swede might have a good case against the Italian government. But as much as Bjorn might want to pursue legal action, he recognized the risks inherent in using a legal mechanism with which Pharma Swede had no prior experience.

Headquarters management, on the other hand, looked favorably at this option, as it provided the opportunity to settle "once and for all" the conflict with the Italian government over pharmaceutical pricing. Local management, however, feared that any legal action would create resentment and sour the atmosphere of future negotiations. At any rate, legal action could take several years and might even jeopardize Gastiros's status in Italy as a reimbursed drug.

A fourth option entailed taking a wait-and-see attitude until the full effects of 1992 became better known. Bjorn explained that for the next two to three years, governments would continue to concentrate on price controls. After 1992, pressure for harmonization would reduce differences in drug prices, though it was impossible to project the direction the prices might take. As an estimate, the Product Pricing and Government Relations staff had calculated that uniform pricing translated to an EEC-wide general decrease of 10% in drug prices, although prices in Italy would probably rise by about 15%. Thus, for the next few years, management at Pharma Swede could monitor the changes within the EEC and prepare as carefully as possible to minimize any long-term price erosion. Bjorn felt this option argued for vigilance and "having all your ammunition ready." But he was not sure what specific preparatory actions were called for.

Conclusion

With the integration of Europe in sight, top management was deeply concerned about the impact that the changing regulatory environment might have on Pharma Swede's operations. Gastirup was the first product to feel the effects of harmonization, but it would not be the last. A decision on Gastirup could set the pace for the other products. In evaluating the alternative courses of action for Gastirup, Bjorn had to consider their likely impact on several stakeholders, including the country management in Italy, the management in high-priced countries and at headquarters, the Italian and EEC authorities, and the medical profession at large. Bjorn was not sure if any course of action could possibly satisfy all the parties concerned. He wondered what criteria should guide his proposal to the company president, who was expecting his recommendations soon.

10

WARNER-LAMBERT IRELAND: NICONIL

Declan Dixon, director of marketing for Warner-Lambert Ireland (WLI), examined two very different sales forecasts as he considered the upcoming launch of Niconil®, scheduled for January 1990. Niconil was an innovative new product that promised to help the thousands of smokers who attempted to quit smoking each year. More commonly known simply as "the patch," Niconil was a transdermal skin patch that gradually released nicotine into the bloodstream to alleviate the physical symptoms of nicotine withdrawal.

Now in October of 1989, Dixon and his staff had to decide several key aspects of the product launch. There were different opinions about how Niconil should be priced and in what quantities it would sell. Pricing decisions would directly impact product profitability, as well as sales volume, and accurate sales forecasts were vital to planning adequate production capacity. Finally, the product team needed to reach consensus on the Niconil communications campaign to meet advertising deadlines and to ensure an integrated product launch.

Company Background

Warner-Lambert was an international pharmaceutical and consumer products company with over $4 billion in worldwide revenues expected in 1989. Warner-Lambert consumer products (50% of worldwide sales) included such brands as Dentyne chewing gum, Listerine mouthwash, and Hall's cough drops. Its pharmaceutical products, marketed through the Parke Davis division, included drugs for treating a wide variety of ailments including heart disease and bronchial disorders.

Warner-Lambert's Irish subsidiary was expected to generate £30 million in sales revenues in 1989:[1] £22 million from exports of manufactured products to other Warner-Lambert subsidiaries in Europe and £4 million each from pharmaceutical and consumer products sales within Ireland. The Irish drug market was estimated at £155 million (in manufacturer sales) in 1989. Warner-Lambert was the

---

This case was prepared by Research Associate Susan P. Smith under the direction of Professor John A. Quelch. Copyright © 1992 by the President and Fellows of Harvard College. Harvard Business School case 593-008 (Revised 1993).

[1] In 1989, one Irish pound was equivalent to $1.58.

16th largest pharmaceutical company in worldwide revenues; in Ireland, it ranked 6th.

Dixon was confident that WLI's position in the Irish market would ensure market acceptance of Niconil. The Parke Davis division had launched two new drugs successfully within the past nine months: Dilzem, a treatment for heart disease, and Accupro, a blood pressure medication. The momentum was expected to continue. The Irish market would be the first country launch for Niconil and thus serve as a test market for all of Warner-Lambert. The companywide significance of the Niconil launch was not lost on Dixon as he pondered the marketing decisions before him.

Smoking in the Republic of Ireland

Almost £600 million would be spent by Irish smokers on 300 million packs of cigarettes in 1989; this included government revenues from the tobacco sales tax of £441 million. Of 3.5 million Irish citizens, 30% of the 2.5 million adults smoked cigarettes (compared to 40% of adults in continental Europe and 20% in the United States).[2] The number of smokers in Ireland had peaked in the late 1970s and had been declining steadily since. Table A presents data from a 1989 survey

TABLE A	Incidence of Cigarette Smoking in Ireland (1988–1989)	
Of adult population (16 and over)	30%	(100%)
By gender		
Men	32	(50)
Women	27	(50)
By Age		
16–24	27	(17)
25–34	38	(14)
35–44	29	(12)
45–54	29	(9)
55+	27	(19)
By Occupation		
White collar	24	(25)
Skilled working class	33	(30)
Semi- and unskilled	38	(29)
Farming	23	(17)

NOTE: To be read (for example): 27% of Irish citizens aged 16–24 smoked, and this age group represented 17% of the population.

---

[2] *Adults* were defined as those over the age of 15, and *smokers* as those who smoked at least one cigarette per day.

that WLI had commissioned in 1989 of a demographically balanced sample of 1,400 randomly chosen Irish adults. Table B shows the numbers of cigarettes smoked by Irish smokers; the average was 16.5 cigarettes.

TABLE B	**Number of Cigarettes Smoked Daily in Ireland** Based on 400 Smokers in a 1989 Survey of 1,400 Citizens
More than 20	16%
15–20	42
10–14	23
5–9	12
Less than 5	4
Unsure	3

Media coverage on the dangers of smoking, antismoking campaigns from public health organizations such as the Irish Cancer Society, and a mounting array of legislation restricting tobacco advertising put pressure on Irish smokers to quit. Promotional discounts and coupons for tobacco products were prohibited, and tobacco advertising was banned not only on television and radio but also on billboards. Print advertising was allowed only if 10% of the ad space was devoted to warnings on the health risks of smoking. Exhibit 1 shows a sample cigarette advertisement from an Irish magazine.

Smoking as an Addiction

Cigarettes and other forms of tobacco contained nicotine, a substance that induced addictive behavior. Smokers first developed a tolerance for nicotine and then, over time, needed to increase cigarette consumption to maintain a steady elevated blood level of nicotine. Smokers became progressively dependent on nicotine and suffered withdrawal symptoms if they stopped smoking. A craving for tobacco was characterized by physical symptoms such as decreased heart rate and a drop in blood pressure, and later could include symptoms like faintness, headaches, cold sweats, intestinal cramps, nausea, and vomiting. The smoking habit also had a psychological component stemming from the ritualistic aspects of smoking behavior, such as smoking after meals or in times of stress.

Since the 1950s, the ill effects of smoking had been researched and identified. Smoking was widely recognized as posing a serious health threat. While nicotine was the substance within the cigarette that caused addiction, it was the tar accompanying the nicotine that made smoking so dangerous. Specifically, smoking was a primary risk factor for ischemic heart disease, lung cancer, and chronic

EXHIBIT 1

Cigarette advertisement from an Irish magazine

SMOKING CAUSES CANCER

Irish Government Warning

pulmonary diseases. Other potential dangers resulting from prolonged smoking included bronchitis, emphysema, chronic sinusitis, peptic ulcer disease, and, for pregnant women, damage to the fetus.

Once smoking was recognized as a health risk, the development and use of a variety of smoking cessation techniques began. In *aversion therapy*, the smoker was discouraged from smoking by pairing an aversive event such as electric shock or a nausea-inducing agent with the smoking behavior, in an attempt to break the cycle of gratification. While aversion therapy was successful in the short term, it did not provide a lasting solution, as the old smoking behavior would often be resumed. Aversion therapy was now used infrequently. *Behavior self-monitoring* required the smoker to develop an awareness of the stimuli that triggered the desire to smoke and then to systematically eliminate the smoking behavior in specific situations by neutralizing those stimuli. For example, the smoker could learn to avoid particular situations or to adopt a replacement activity such as chewing gum. This method was successful in some cases but demanded a high degree of self-control. While behavioral methods were useful in addressing the psychological component of smoking addiction, they did not address the physical aspect of nicotine addiction that proved an insurmountable obstacle to many who attempted to quit.

Niconil

Warner-Lambert's Niconil would be the first product to offer a complete solution for smoking cessation, addressing both the physical and psychological aspects of nicotine addiction. The physical product was a circular adhesive patch, 2.5 inches in diameter and containing 30 mg of nicotine gel. Each patch was individually wrapped in a sealed, tear-resistant packet. The patch was applied to the skin, usually on the upper arm, and the nicotine was absorbed into the bloodstream to produce a steady level of nicotine that blunted the smoker's physical craving. Thirty milligrams of nicotine provided the equivalent of 20 cigarettes, without the cigarettes' damaging tar. A single patch was applied once a day every morning for two to six weeks, depending on the smoker. The average smoker was able to quit successfully (abstaining from cigarettes for a period of six months or longer) after three to four weeks.

In clinical trials, the Niconil patch alone had proven effective in helping smokers to quit. A WLI study showed that 47.5% of subjects using the nicotine patch abstained from smoking for a period of three months or longer versus 15% for subjects using a placebo patch. Among the remaining 52.5% who did not stop completely, there was a marked reduction in the number of cigarettes smoked. A similar study in the United States demonstrated an abstinence rate of 31.5% with the Niconil patch versus 14% for those with a placebo patch. The single most important success factor in Niconil effectiveness, however, was the smoker's motivation to quit. "Committed quitters" were the most likely to quit smoking successfully using Niconil or any other smoking cessation method.

There were some side effects associated with use of the Niconil patch, including skin irritation, sleep disturbances, and nausea. Skin irritation was by far the most prevalent side effect, affecting 30% of patch users in one study. This skin irritation was not seen as a major obstacle to sales, as many study participants viewed their irritated skin areas as "badges of merit" that indicated their commitment to quitting smoking. WLI recommended placement of the patch on alternating skin areas to mitigate the problem. Future reformulations of the nicotine gel in the patch were expected to eliminate the problem entirely.

Niconil had been developed in 1985 by two scientists at Trinity College in Dublin working with Elan Corporation, an Irish pharmaceutical company specializing in transdermal drug delivery systems. Elan had entered into a joint venture with WLI to market other Elan transdermal products: Dilzem and Theolan, a respiratory medication. In 1987 Elan agreed to add Niconil to the joint venture. Warner-Lambert planned to market the product worldwide through its subsidiaries, with Elan earning a royalty on cost of goods sold.[3]

Ireland was the first country to approve the Niconil patch. In late 1989 the Irish National Drugs Advisory Board authorized national distribution of Niconil but stipulated that it could be sold by prescription only. This meant that Niconil, as a prescription product, could not be advertised directly to the Irish consumer.

Health Care in Ireland

Ireland's General Medical service (GMS) provided health care to all Irish citizens. Sixty-four percent of the population received free hospital care through the GMS but were required to pay for doctors' visits, which averaged £15 each, and for drugs, which were priced lower in Ireland than the average in the European Economic Community. The remaining 36% of the population qualified as either low-income or chronic condition patients and received free health care through the GMS. For these patients, hospital care, doctors' visits, and many drugs were obtained without fee or copayment. Drugs paid for by the GMS were classified as "reimbursable"; approximately 70% of all drugs were reimbursable in 1989. Niconil had not qualified as a reimbursable drug; though WLI was lobbying to change its status, the immediate outlook was not hopeful.[4]

Support Program

While the patch addressed the physical craving for nicotine, Dixon and his team had decided to develop a supplementary support program to address the smoker's psychological addiction. The support program included several components in a

---

[3] A royalty of 3% on cost of goods sold was typical for such joint ventures.

[4] None of the products in the smoking cessation aid market was reimbursable through the GMS. Reimbursable items excluded prescriptions for simple drugs such as mild painkillers and cough and cold remedies.

neatly packaged box, which aimed to ease the smoker's personal and social dependence on cigarettes. A booklet explained how to change behavior and contained tips on quitting. Bound into the booklet was a personal "contract" on which the smoker could list his or her reasons for quitting and plans for celebrating successful abstinence. There was a diary, which enabled the smoker to record patterns of smoking behavior prior to quitting and which offered inspirational suggestions for each day of the program. Finally, an audiotape included instruction in four relaxation methods which the smoker could practice in place of cigarette smoking. The relaxation exercises were narrated by Professor Anthony Clare, a well known Irish psychiatrist who hosted a regular television program on the BBC. The tape also contained an emergency help section to assist the individual in overcoming sudden episodes of craving. A special toll-free telephone number to WLI served as a hotline to address customer questions and problems. Sample pages from the Niconil support program are presented as Exhibit 2.

While studies had not yet measured the impact of the support program on abstinence rates, it was believed that combined use of the support program and the patch could only increase Niconil's success. It had proven necessary to package the Niconil support program separately from the patch to speed approval of the patch by the Irish National Drug Board. A combined package would have required approval of the complete program, including the audiotape, which would have prolonged the process significantly. If separate, the support program could be sold without a prescription and advertised directly to the consumer. Development of the support program had cost £3,000. WLI planned an initial production run of 10,000 units at a variable cost of £3.50 per unit.

The support program could serve a variety of purposes. Several WLI executives felt that the support program should be sold separately from the nicotine patches. They considered the support program a stand-alone product that could realize substantial revenues on its own, as well as generating sales of the Niconil patches. Supporting this position, a pricing study completed in 1989 found that the highest mean price volunteered for a 14-day supply of the patches and the support program combined was £27.50, and for the patches alone, £22.00. The highest mean price for the support program alone was £8.50, suggesting a relatively high perceived utility of this component among potential consumers. There was a risk, however, that consumers might purchase the Niconil support program either instead of the patches or as an accompaniment to other smoking cessation products, thus limiting sales of the Niconil patches.

Another group of executives saw the support program as a value-added point of difference that could stimulate Niconil patch sales. This group favored wide distribution of the support programs, free of charge, to potential Niconil customers. A third group of WLI executives argued that the support program was an integral component of the Niconil product, which would enhance the total package by addressing the psychological aspects of nicotine addiction and improve the product's success rate, thereby increasing its sales potential. As such, these executives believed that the support program should be passed on only to those purchasing Niconil patches, at no additional cost.

Two options, not necessarily mutually exclusive, were under consideration for the distribution of the support programs. One option was to distribute them

Exhibit 2

Sample Pages from Niconil Support Program

The first step

Fill in the contract in your own words. Write down all the reasons that are most important to you for beating the smoking habit.

Then write down how your life will be better and more enjoyable without the smoking habit.

Finally, write down how you will reward yourself for your courage and hard work. You will deserve something very special.

Choose the day

Decide when to stop and put a ring round that date on your calendar.

Try to find a time when you are not going to be under pressure for a few days. The start of a holiday is good for two reasons. You will not have the stress of work and you will be free to change your routine.

Countdown

1. In the days leading up to your stop date see if you can get your partner or a friend to stop smoking along with you.

2. Ask a local charity to sponsor you or join a non-smoking group. Having other people to talk to who have kicked the habit can be a lifeline when your willpower gets shaky. They will know and understand what you are going through. Your doctor will be able to tell you what groups are running in your area.

3. The evening before your stop date, throw away all your cigarettes and get rid of your lighters and ashtrays. You will not need them again.

4. Read over your smoker's diary entries. Know your habit.
   - What are the most dangerous times?
   - Where are the most dangerous places?
   - What are the most dangerous situations?
   - Who do I usually smoke with?

CONTRACT

1. I, ... ,
   HAVE STOPPED SMOKING BECAUSE
   I WANT:

2. MY LIFE WILL BE BETTER WHEN I AM FREE OF SMOKING BECAUSE:

3. AFTER BEATING SMOKING FOR A MONTH I WILL CELEBRATE BY:

SIGNED:

DATE:

COUNT DOWN TO D-DAY				DAY 1	
Cigarette	Time of day?	Where were you?	Who were you with?	What were you doing?	How did you feel?
1					
2					
3					
4					
5					

WEEK ONE   *THE WINNER'S DIARY*

DAY

1. Today is the greatest challenge. If you succeed today, tomorrow will be easier. You can do it.

2. Well done. The first 24 hours are over. Your lungs have had their first real rest for years.

3. Remember: smoking is for losers. If you find yourself getting tense, use your relaxation tape.

4. Read your contract again. See how much better life is getting now that you are freeing yourself from this unpleasant addiction.

5. Your body says "thank you". It's feeling fitter already.

6. Don't forget to distract yourself at key cigarette times.

7. Well done. You're through your first week. Give yourself a treat. Go out for a meal or buy yourself something you've always wanted.

through doctors prescribing Niconil. A doctor could present the program to the patient during the office visit as he or she issued the Niconil prescription, reinforcing the counseling role of the doctor in the Niconil treatment. Supplying the GPs with support programs could also serve to promote Niconil in the medical community. A second option was to distribute the support programs through the pharmacies, where customers could receive the support programs when they purchased the Niconil patches. A disadvantage of this option was that a customer might receive additional support programs each time he or she purchased another package of Niconil. However, these duplicates might be passed on to other potential customers and thus become an informal advertising vehicle for Niconil.

Pricing

Because all potential Niconil customers would pay for the product personally, pricing was a critical component of the Niconil marketing strategy. Management debated how many patches to include in a single package and at what price to sell each package. In test trials, the average smoker succeeded in quitting with Niconil in three to four weeks (i.e., 21 to 28 patches); others needed as long as six weeks.[5]

As Niconil was essentially a tobacco substitute, cigarettes provided a logical model for considering various packaging and pricing options. The average Irish smoker purchased a pack of cigarettes daily, often when buying the morning newspaper. Fewer than 5% of all cigarettes were sold in cartons.[6] Because the Irish smoker rarely purchased a multiweek cigarette supply at once, he or she was thought likely to compare the cost of cigarette purchases with the cost of a multiweek supply of Niconil. WLI thus favored packaging just a seven-day supply of patches in each unit. However, Warner-Lambert subsidiaries in continental Europe, where carton purchases were more popular, wanted to include a six-week supply of patches in each package if and when they launched Niconil. Managers at Warner-Lambert's international division wanted to standardize packaging as much as possible across its subsidiaries and suggested as a compromise a 14-day supply per package.

Following the cigarette model, two pricing schemes had been proposed. The first proposal was to price Niconil on a par with cigarettes. The average Irish smoker smoked 16.5 cigarettes per day, and the expected retail price in 1990 for a pack of cigarettes was £2.25. WLI's variable cost of goods for a 14-day supply of Niconil was £12.00.[7] Pharmacies generally added a 50% retail markup to the price at which they purchased the product from WLI. A value-added tax of 25% of the retail price was included in the proposed price to the consumer of £32.00 for a 14-day supply. In addition, the consumer paid a £1.00 dispensing fee per prescription.

[5] Smokers were advised not to use the patch on a regular basis beyond three months. If still unsuccessful in quitting, they could resume use of the patch after stopping for at least a month.

[6] A carton of cigarettes contained 20 individual packs of cigarettes; each pack contained 20 cigarettes.

[7] This cost of goods included Elan's royalty.

Under the second pricing proposal, Niconil would be priced at a premium to cigarettes. Proponents argued that if the Niconil program was successful, it would be a permanent replacement for cigarettes and its cost would be far outweighed by the money saved on cigarettes. The proposed price to the consumer under this option was £60.00 for a 14-day supply.

Competition

Few products would compete directly with Niconil in the smoking cessation market in Ireland. Two small niche products were Accudrop and Nicrobrevin, both available without a prescription. Accudrop was a nasal spray that smokers applied to the cigarette filter to trap tar and nicotine, resulting in cleaner smoke. Anticipated 1990 manufacturer's sales for Accudrop were £5,000. Nicobrevin, a product from the United Kingdom, was a time-release capsule that eased smoking withdrawal symptoms. Anticipated 1990 manufacturer's sales for Nicobrevin were £75,000.

The most significant competitive product was Nicorette, the only nicotine-replacement product currently available. Marketed in Ireland by Lundbeck, Nicorette was a chewing gum that released nicotine into the body as the smoker chewed the gum. Because chewing gum in public was not socially acceptable among Irish adults, the product had never achieved strong sales, especially given that its efficacy relied on steady, intensive chewing. A second sales deterrent had been the association of Nicorette with side effects such as mouth cancer and irritation of the linings of the mouth and stomach.

Nicorette was sold in 10-day supplies, available in two dosages: 2 mg and 4 mg. Smokers would chew the 2-mg Nicorette initially, and switch to the 4-mg gum after two weeks if needed. In a 1982 study, 47% of Nicorette users quit smoking versus 21% for placebo users. A long-term follow-up study in 1989, however, indicated that only 10% more Nicorette patients had ceased smoking compared to placebo users. The average daily treatment cost to Nicorette customers was £0.65 per day for the 2-mg gum and £1.00 per day for the 4-mg gum. Nicorette, like Niconil, was available at pharmacies by prescription only, so advertising had been limited to medical journals. Anticipated 1990 manufacturer sales of Nicorette were £170,000; however, the brand had not been advertised in three years.

Forecasting

Although Nicorette was not considered a successful product, WLI was confident that Niconil, with its less intrusive nicotine delivery system and fewer side effects, would capture a dominant position in the smoking cessation market and ultimately increase the demand for smoking cessation products. Precise sales expectations for Niconil were difficult to formulate, however, and two different methods had been suggested.

The first method assumed that the percentage of smokers in the adult population (30% in 1990) would drop by one percentage point per year through 1994. An estimated 10% of smokers attempted to quit smoking each year, and 10% of that number purchased some type of smoking cessation product. WLI believed that Niconil could capture half of these "committed quitters" in the first year, selling therefore to 5% of those who tried to give up smoking in 1990. Further, they hoped to increase this share by 1% per year, up to 9% in 1994. Having estimated the number of customers who would purchase an initial two-week supply of Niconil, WLI managers then had to calculate the total number of units purchased. Based on experience in test trials, WLI anticipated that 60% of first-time Niconil customers would purchase a second two-week supply. Of that number, 20% would purchase a third two-week supply. About 75% of smokers completed the program within six weeks.

A more aggressive forecast could be based on WLI's 1989 survey. Of the 30% of respondents who were smokers, 54% indicated that they would like to give up smoking, and 30% expressed interest in the nicotine patch. More relevant, 17% of smokers indicated that they were likely to go to the doctor and pay for such a patch, though a specific purchase price was not included in the question. A rule of thumb in interpreting likelihood-of-purchase data was to divide this percentage by 3 to achieve a more likely estimate of actual purchasers. Once the number of Niconil customers was calculated, the 100%/60%/20% model used above could then be applied to compute the total expected unit sales.

Production

Under the terms of the joint venture with Elan and using current manufacturing technology, production capacity would be 1,000 units (of 14-day supply packages) per month in the first quarter of 1990, ramping up to 2,000 units per month by year-end. WLI had the option to purchase a new, more efficient machine that could produce 14,000 units per month and reduce WLI's variable cost on each unit by 10%. In addition, if WLI purchased the new machine and Niconil was launched in continental Europe, WLI could export some of its production to the European subsidiaries, further expanding its role as a supplier to Warner-Lambert Europe. WLI would earn a margin of £2.00 per unit on Niconil that it sold through this channel.[8] Estimated annual unit sales, assuming a launch of Niconil throughout Western Europe, are listed in Table C.

TABLE c   Estimated Unit Sales of Niconil in Western Europe

Year	Units
1	100,000
2	125,000
3	150,000
4	175,000
5	200,000

---

[8] Warner-Lambert's European subsidiaries were likely to consider purchasing this new machine themselves as well.

Warner-Lambert management aimed to recoup any capital investments within five years; the Niconil machine would cost £1.2 million and could be on-line within nine months.

Marketing Prescription Products

Prescription products included all pharmaceutical items deemed by the Irish government to require the professional expertise of the medical community to guide consumer usage.[9] Before a customer could purchase a prescription product, he or she first had to visit a doctor and obtain a written prescription which specified that product. The customer could then take the written prescription to one of Ireland's 1,132 pharmacies and purchase the product.

The prescription nature of Niconil thus created marketing challenges. A potential Niconil customer first had to make an appointment with a doctor for an office visit to obtain the necessary prescription. Next, the doctor had to agree to prescribe Niconil to the patient to help him or her to quit smoking. Only then could the customer go to the pharmacy and purchase Niconil. This two-step purchase process required WLI to address two separate audiences in marketing Niconil: the Irish smokers who would eventually use Niconil and the Irish doctors who first had to prescribe it to patients.

Niconil's potential customers were the 10% of Irish smokers who attempted to give up smoking each year (2% of the total Irish population). Market research had shown that those most likely to purchase Niconil were aged 35–44 and in either white-collar or skilled occupations (18% of Irish smokers). Smokers under the age of 35 tended to see themselves as "bullet proof"; because most were not yet experiencing the negative health effects of smoking, it was difficult to persuade them to quit. Upper-income, better-educated smokers found less tolerance for smoking among their peers and thus felt greater pressure to quit. Research had also indicated that women were 25% more likely to try Niconil as they tended to be more concerned with their health and thus more often visited the doctors from whom they could learn about Niconil and obtain the necessary prescription.

The most likely prescribers of Niconil would be the 2,000 general practitioners (GPs) in Ireland. The average GP saw 15 patients per day, and 8 out of 10 general office visits resulted in the GPs writing prescriptions for patients. Although 10% of Irish doctors smoked, virtually all recognized the dangers of smoking and rarely smoked in front of patients. A *Modern Medicine* survey of 780 Irish GPs indicated that 63% formally gathered smoking data from their patients. GPs acknowledged the health risk that smoking posed to patient health, but they were usually reluctant to pressure a patient to quit unless the smoker was highly motivated. Unsolicited pressure to quit could meet with patient resistance and result, in some cases, in a doctor losing a patient and the associated revenues from patient visits. Smoking cessation was not currently a lucrative treatment area for GPs. Most would

---

[9] Drugs and other pharmaceutical products that did not require a written prescription from a doctor were called over-the-counter (OTC) drugs.

spend no longer than 15 minutes discussing smoking with their patients. To the few patients who asked for advice on how to quit smoking, 92% of GPs would offer "firm, clear-cut advice." Fewer than 15% would recommend formal counseling, drug therapy, or other assistance. GPs were not enthusiastic about Nicorette due to poor results and the incidence of side effects.

WLI was confident that Niconil would find an enthusiastic audience among Irish GPs. As a complete program with both physical and psychological components, Niconil offered a unique solution. In addition, the doctor would assume a significant counseling role in the Niconil treatment. It was anticipated that the GP would initially prescribe a 14-day supply of Niconil to the patient. At the end of the two-week period, it was hoped that the patient would return to the doctor for counseling and an additional prescription, if needed.

Marketing Communications

WLI intended to position Niconil as *a complete system that was a more acceptable alternative to existing nicotine replacement therapy for the purpose of smoking cessation.* Niconil would be the only smoking cessation product to address both the physical dimension of nicotine addiction through the patch, and the psychological dimension through the support program. Compared to Nicorette gum, Niconil offered a more acceptable delivery system (Niconil's transdermal system vs. Nicorette's oral system) and fewer, less severe side effects. WLI planned to promote these aspects of the product through a comprehensive marketing program. The Niconil launch marketing budget, detailed in Exhibit 3, followed the Warner-Lambert standard for new drug launches. Several WLI executives felt that this standard was inadequate for the more consumer-oriented Niconil and pressed for increased communications spending.

Advertising

Because Irish regulations prohibited the advertising of prescription products directly to the consumer, Niconil advertising was limited to media targeting the professional medical community. Three major publications targeted this audience: *Irish Medical Times, Irish Medical News,* and *Modern Medicine.* WLI planned to advertise moderately in the first year to raise awareness of Niconil in the medical community. After that it was hoped that the initial momentum could be maintained through strong public relations efforts and personal testimony to the products efficacy. Exhibit 4 summarizes the proposed 1990 media advertising schedule for Niconil.

WLI's advertising agency had designed a distinctive logo for Niconil that would be used on all packaging and collateral materials such as No Smoking placards. These would feature the Niconil logo and be distributed to doctors' offices, hospitals, and pharmacies to promote the product. Ideally, the logo would become sufficiently well recognized that it could be used eventually on a stand-alone basis to represent Niconil to the end consumer without the brand name. This would allow some flexibility in circumventing Irish advertising restrictions to

EXHIBIT 3   Niconil First-Year Marketing Budget (£ 000)

Advertising

Ad creation	£ 4
Media advertising	28
Total advertising	£ 32

Promotion

Development of support programs	£ 3
Production of support programs	35
Training/promotional materials	44
Direct mailing to GPs	2
Total promotion	£ 84

Public Relations

Launch symposium	£ 5
Roundtable meeting	2
Press release/materials	1
Total public relations	£ 8
Market research	3
Sales force allocation	23
Product management allocation	50
Total budget	£200

EXHIBIT 4   1990 Niconil Media Advertising Schedule

Publication	Frequency	Circulation	Cost/1,000	Placements
Irish Medical Times	Weekly	5,200	£154	13
Irish Medical News	Weekly	5,100	137	11
Modern Medicine	Monthly	3,700	176	5

reach the end consumer. Sample logos and packaging are illustrated in Exhibit 5 on the following page. The agency had also developed alternative concepts for a Niconil advertisement, which are summarized in Exhibit 6A-B on pages 204 and 205.

Direct Mail

A direct mail campaign to Ireland's 2,000 GPs was planned in conjunction with the Niconil product announcement. Two weeks prior to launch, an introductory letter would be mailed with a color photo of the product, a reply card offering a support program, and additional product information. The support programs would be mailed in response to the reply cards, arriving just prior to the launch. A response rate of at least 50% was anticipated based on past direct mail campaigns.

EXHIBIT 5

Sample Niconil logo and packaging

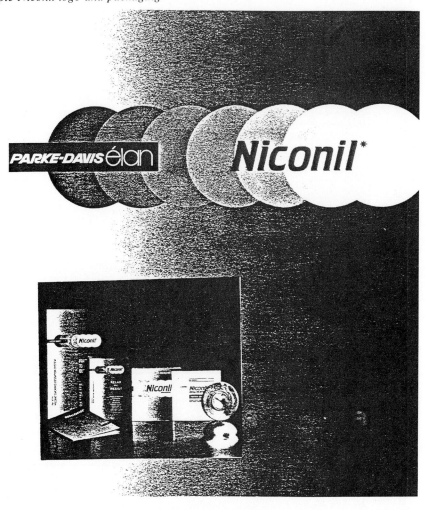

EXHIBIT 6A

Niconil advertising concept (A)

EXHIBIT 6B

Niconil advertising concept (B)

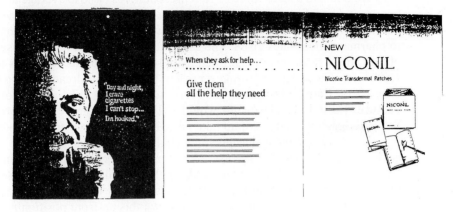

Public Relations

The formal Niconil product announcement was scheduled to occur in Dublin at a professional event that WLI had dubbed the "Smoking Cessation Institute Symposium." The symposium would be chaired by Professor Anthony Clare, the narrator of the Niconil audiotape; Professor Hickey, an expert in preventive cardiology; and Professors Masterson and J. Kelly from Elan Corporation. Open to members of the medical profession and media, the event was intended to focus attention on the dangers of smoking and to highlight Niconil as a groundbreaking product designed to address this health hazard.

WLI had sought endorsements from both the Irish Cancer Society and the Irish Heart Foundation, two national health organizations that actively advocated smoking cessation. Because both nonprofit institutions relied on donations for financing and were concerned that a specific product endorsement would jeopardize their tax-exempt status, they refused to endorse Niconil directly. Representatives from each institution had, however, stated their intention to attend the launch symposium.

In advance of the symposium, a press release and supporting materials would be distributed to the media. Emphasis would be placed on the role that Niconil would play in disease prevention. It would also be noted that Niconil had been developed and manufactured locally and had the potential for worldwide sales. Other planned public relations activities included a roundtable dinner for prominent opinion leaders in the medical community. Publicity in the media was planned to coincide with key "commitment to change" times such as New Year's and Lent.[10]

---

[10] Lent was an annual penitential period during spring of the Roman Catholic religious calendar that was still observed by many of the 95% of the Irish who were Roman Catholic.

Sales Strategy

WLI Ireland had a sales force of 16 representatives, whose average annual salary, bonus, and benefits amounted to £25,000 in 1988. They focused their selling efforts on 1,600 Irish GPs who were most accessible geographically and most amenable to pharmaceutical sales visits. The sales staff was divided into three selling teams of four to six representatives. Each team sold separate product lines to the same 1,600 GPs. The team that would represent Niconil was already selling three other drugs from Elan Corporation that were marketed by WLI as part of their joint venture. These four salespeople would add Niconil to their existing product lines. Sales training on Niconil would take place one month prior to the product launch.

The pharmaceutical salesperson's challenge was to maintain the attention of each GP long enough to discuss each item in his or her product line. Because Niconil was expected to be of greatest interest to GPs, the salespeople were keen to present Niconil first during the sales visit, followed by the less exciting products. Normally, a new product would receive this up-front positioning. However, Dixon argued that Niconil should be presented last during the sales call to maximize the time that a salesperson spent with each GP and to prevent the sales time devoted to the other three Elan products from being cannibalized by Niconil. Based on revenue projections for all four products, salespeople would be instructed to spend no more than 15% of their sales call time on Niconil. On average, each WLI salesperson called on six to seven doctors per day. The goal was for each sales team to call on the 1,600 targeted GPs once every three months. In the case of Niconil, all 16 salespeople would present the new brand during their calls for six weeks after launch.

Critical Decisions

With just three months to go before the launch of Niconil, Dixon felt he had to comply with the international division's suggestion to include a 14-day supply of patches in each Niconil package, but he debated whether to price the product on a par with or at a premium to cigarettes. Equally important, he had to decide which sales forecast was more accurate so that he could plan production capacity. And finally, he needed to make decisions on the communications program: which advertising concept would be the most effective, what other efforts could be made to enhance product acceptance, and whether the current budget was adequate to support Warner-Lambert's first national launch of such an innovative product.

PRODUCT POLICY

NESTLÉ ITALY

Giorgio Baruffa, product manager for Nescafé instant coffee at Nestlé Italy, was considering options for the future marketing strategy of the brand. Nescafé had been marketed in Italy for 30 years but held less than a 1% share of the Italian coffee market. In a recent single city test, Nescafé had experimented with a 14% price decrease with the objective of increasing market share. The price reduction increased short-term sales volume by 25%, but did not have a sustained impact on market share and weakened user and nonuser perceptions of Nescafé's quality and reliability.

Mr. Bechi, marketing director of Nestlé Italy, and Mr. Baruffa called a meeting in March 1989 to discuss Nescafé's strategic options. The group—which included Mr. Mazzei, the chief financial officer, Mr. Giuliani, head of strategic planning, and Mr. Baruffa's brand assistant—had to decide whether Nescafé should aim to penetrate further its current target market or seek out one or more new target groups.

Company Background

Nestlé was founded in Switzerland in 1866 to process dairy products. Nestlé became well known as a manufacturer of infant feeding formulas, developing successful products such as Nestlé powdered milk and condensed milk. The company grew through new-product introductions and acquisitions of other companies, both inside and outside the food industry. By 1988, Nestlé SA generated revenues of $20 billion. It had 160,000 employees working in 200 plants worldwide. Decision-making responsibility was decentralized to ensure that the

This case was prepared by Professor John A. Quelch in association with Michele Costabile, SDA Bocconi, Italy. Copyright © 1992 by the President and Fellows of Harvard College. Harvard Business School case 593-009.

operating unit in each country responded to local market conditions. Nestlé competed worldwide in a variety of product groups including the following:

- Chocolate, with the Gala and Frigor brands.
- Instant coffee, with the Taster's Choice and Nescafé brands.
- Instant beverages, with the Nesquick (or Quik) and Orzoro brands.
- Soups and bouillon cubes, with the Maggi brand.
- Preserves and fruit juices.
- Pharmaceuticals and cosmetics, with the L'Oréal line.

Nestlé was the world's largest buyer of raw coffee beans and a major producer of instant coffee. In the 1930s, when raw coffee supply exceeded demand, Nestlé researchers perfected a dehydration process to preserve coffee in a concentrated and soluble form while maintaining its flavor and aroma. The Nescafé brand of instant coffee was launched in 1938 just before World War II. It was adopted by the armed forces due to its convenience and ease of use. Instant coffee quickly gained worldwide acceptance. By 1988, the world drank more than 170 million cups of Nescafé a day. In 1988, Nestlé's advertising budget to promote Nescafé worldwide was $312 million.

Nestlé Italy, a Milan-based company, sold over 80 products in 10 categories and generated about $1 billion in sales in 1988. Nestlé Italy was the share leader in milk modifiers (with Nesquick) and instant coffee. In Italy, Nescafé was offered in three blends: Nescafé Classic, Nescafé Gran Aroma (a stronger, premium quality coffee), and Nescafé Relax (a decaffeinated coffee). Nescafé contributed 3% of Nestlé Italy revenues and 7% of net profits in 1988. Nescafé accounted for 5% of Nestlé Italy's total advertising expenditures and 2% of total consumer and trade promotion expenditures.

Coffee Consumption in Italy

The Arabs discovered the process of roasting coffee beans at the end of the 14th century. Since then, coffee had been consumed both in the home and in public as a social beverage. From the 18th century, coffeehouses in Europe were patronized by intellectuals who used the stimulus of the aromatic beverage to sustain their poetic or political dissertation. In Italy, coffeehouses were once called "schools of knowledge."

The range of blends, degree of roasting, methods of preparation, and reasons for coffee consumption varied widely across countries. Different consumer segments viewed coffee as a stimulant, as a thirst quencher, or, when mixed with a small amount of water, as an elixir.

In 1988, the highest per capita coffee consumption was in Scandinavia at 12 kg, followed by the Netherlands (9), Germany (7), France (6), the United States (4.6), Italy (4.3), the United Kingdom (2), Greece (2), and Spain (2). The Italian instant coffee market was comparatively underdeveloped. In Italy, instant coffee accounted for 1% of total coffee consumption in 1988 versus 8% in the

Netherlands, 10% in Germany, 30% in France, 34% in the United States, 37% in Spain, 51% in Greece, and over 90% in the United Kingdom and Ireland.

Nestlé executives identified several consumer trends that could affect the consumption and marketing of coffee in Italy. These included:

- An increase in adult women in the work force to over 30% in 1988. This resulted in more food consumption outside the home and increased purchases of ready-to-eat, frozen, and other convenience foods.
- Increased international travel, both into and out of the country, which exposed Italians to the food consumption habits of other cultures.
- Lower birth rates and younger life spans, causing an aging of the population and a reduction in average household size. The number of Italians over 55 years was expected to increase to 31% of the population by 1997. The average disposable income of this group was also rising significantly.
- A greater awareness of health issues in the diet. As a result, there was increased interest in consumption of fresh, authentic products, especially among better-educated young people. For example, fruit and vegetable consumption increased 12% from 1986 to 1988. Similarly, nonalcoholic beverage consumption increased by over 30% between 1983 and 1988, with mineral water up 35%, soft drinks up 32%, and fruit juices up 40%.

Many younger, more health-conscious Italian consumers perceived coffee as an unhealthy beverage. In 1988, the highest level of coffee consumption was among the 45–54 age group, as shown in Table A:

TABLE A

Age	Percentage Who Usually Drink Coffee	Average Annual per Capita Consumption (kg)	Percentage of Total Consumption	Percentage of Italian Population*
15–24	50	3.04	12.4	16.5
25–34	70	4.36	20.5	14.2
34–45	81	4.60	23.0	13.1
45–54	83	4.90	24.0	12.6
55–69	67	3.13	15.1	15.6
70+	60	1.86	5.0	9.7

* NOTE: 18.3% of the population was under 15 years in 1988.

Industry Structure and Competition

The structure of the Italian coffee market is shown in chart form in Exhibit 1. Around 750 firms produced their own blends of roast and ground coffee, buying raw coffee beans either directly from growers or, in the case of the smaller producers, from importers or agents. The coffee roasters sold their blends through retailers to the end consumer (the "family segment") and/or through coffee-houses, restaurants, and other institutional outlets (the "CHR segment"). As

Exhibit 1

The structure of the Italian coffee market

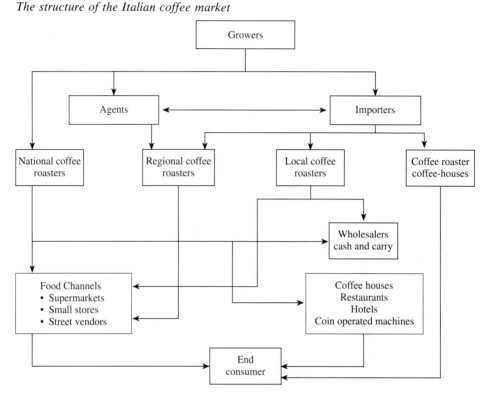

shown in Exhibit 2 on the following page, the CHR segment accounted for 31% of the coffee volume consumed in Italy in 1988 but 80% of the associated consumer expenditures. Consumption of instant and decaffeinated coffee was minimal. The total volume of coffee consumed was expected to grow 2% annually.

Factory sales of coffee in Italy in 1988 approached 1,700 billion lire, as indicated in Exhibit 3 on page 213.[1] Low entry barriers, regional taste preferences, minimal overheads, and entrenched distribution explained the continued survival of many small coffee roasters, each serving a town or a region. However, the combined market share of the national producers was increasing. In 1988, the top four national coffee roasters controlled 42% of the market, while the next four companies accounted for a further 10%. They enjoyed the efficiencies of national advertising and distribution, quantity discounts when purchasing coffee beans on the world market, and greater negotiating power with the trade. They tended to offer more complete product lines than the smaller and medium-sized producers and to initiate packaging innovations such as the vacuum pack. Exhibit 4 (page 213) summarizes the retail penetration by type of channel and number of items stocked per outlet for the major producers. Exhibit 5 (page 214) plots the principal competitors on two strategic maps.

---

[1] In 1988, $1.00 was equivalent to 1,500 lire.

EXHIBIT 2 Italian Coffee Market, 1988 Retail Sales (in Thousands of Tons and Billion Lire)

	Family Segment				CHR Segment				Total			
	Volume (000 Tons)	Percent	Value (Billion Lire)	Percent	Volume (000 Tons)	Percent	Value (Billion Lire)	Percent	Volume (000 Tons)	Percent	Value (Billion Lire)	Percent
Normal	144.9	69%	2,105	20%	65.1	31%	8,267	80%	210.0	97%	10,372	95%
Decaffeinated	2.9	58	48	10	2.2	42	410	90	5.1	2	457	4
Instant	0.7	88	69	49	0.1	12	72	51	0.8	1	141	1
Total	148.5	69%	2,222	20%	67.4	31%	8,749	80%	215.9	100%	10,970	100%

NOTE: "Normal" refers to regular roast and ground coffee. "Instant" includes decaffeinated instant.

EXHIBIT 3 **A. Roast and Ground Coffee: Italian Market Shares of Main Producers by Segment, 1988**

	Family Segment				CHR Segment			
	Quantity (000 Tons)		Factory Prices (Billion Lire)		Quantity (000 Tons)		Factory Prices (Billion Lire)	
Lavazza	42.0	30.7%	405	34.6%	3.0	6.5%	35	6.7%
Procter & Gamble	12.3	9.0	108	9.2	—	—	—	—
Café do Brasil	10.2	7.4	83	7.1	0.5	1.1	4	0.8
Illy Caffé	0.4	0.3	6	0.5	1.5	3.2	30	5.7
Segafredo	4.4	3.2	37	3.2	4.3	9.4	45	8.5
Sao Café	7.0	5.1	58	5.0	—	—	—	—
Total market	137.0		1,170		45.7		520	

B. Instant Coffee: Italian Market Shares of Main Producers, 1988

	Quantity (Tons)	Percent	Value (Billion Lire)	Percent
Nestlé	650	77.7%	35	80.0%
Crippa & Berger	110	13.1	7	15.9
Others	76	9.2	2	4.1
Total market	836	100.0%	44	100.0%

EXHIBIT 4 **Retail Penetration and Average Number of SKUs (Stockkeeping Units) by Channel for Principal Coffee Brands, October 1988**

	Hypermarkets		Supermarkets		Convenience Stores	
Lavazza	100.0%	12.2	100.0%	11.1	95.5%	10.9
Procter & Gamble	100.0	5.9	94.6	5.9	95.5	4.7
Nestlé	100.0	5.7	100.0	7.2	100.0	6.1
Crippa & Berger	100.0	5.5	100.0	5.4	95.5	3.6
Café do Brasil	30.4	2.2	8.9	3.0	25.5	1.5
Illy Caffé	10.5	2.0	15.7	2.0	5.5	1.0
Segafredo	69.6	3.9	60.7	3.9	9.1	2.0
Sao Café	69.6	4.5	70.5	4.5	40.5	3.0

With industry consolidation, advertising expenditures on brands of coffee more than doubled between 1985 and 1988, as indicated in Exhibit 6 on page 215. Likewise, the advertising-to-sales ratios of most major producers rose, as shown in Exhibit 7 (page 215).

The principal competitors in the Italian coffee market were as follows:

• *Lavazza SpA,* a family-owned company based in Turin, held the largest share of the coffee market, and was the 10th largest food company in

EXHIBIT 5

Italian coffee market strategic groups

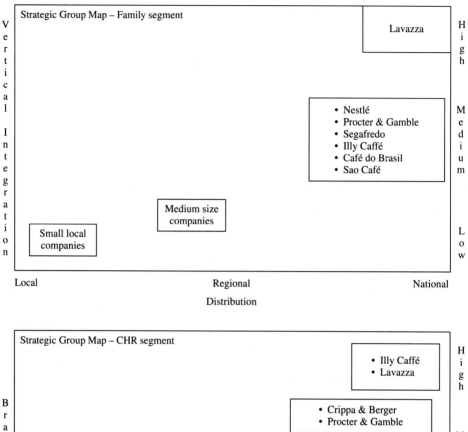

Strategic Group Map – Family segment

Vertical Integration

- Lavazza (High)

- Nestlé
- Procter & Gamble
- Segafredo
- Illy Caffé
- Café do Brasil
- Sao Café
(Medium)

Medium size companies

Small local companies (Low)

Local   Regional   National

Distribution

Strategic Group Map – CHR segment

Brand Image

- Illy Caffé
- Lavazza
(High)

- Crippa & Berger
- Procter & Gamble

- Café do Brasil
- Sao Café
- Segafredo
(Medium)

Small local companies

Medium size companies

Local   Regional   National

Distribution

Italy. Lavazza was the only company to offer a complete line of nationally distributed products. Lavazza offered 11 brands and blends at different price-quality points but all advertised under the Lavazza umbrella. One of these brands was Bourbon roast and ground, which, until 1987,

EXHIBIT 6   Roast and Ground Coffee: Percentages of Total Media Advertising Expenditures in Italy of Major Producers from 1985 to 1988

Company	1985	1986	1987	1988
Lavazza	36%	46%	34%	40%
Procter & Gamble	24	24	27	20
Nestlé	14	12	—	—
Café do Brasil	—	7	11	14
Illy Caffé	3	4	7	6
Segafredo-Zanetti	1	—	5	7
Sao Café	9	3	4	1
Mauro	3	4	5	6
Altri	10	—	6	6
Total	100%	100%	100%	100%
Billions of lire	48	68	85	129

NOTE: Nestlé sold its brand of roast and ground coffee in 1987.
SOURCE: Company records and AGB.

EXHIBIT 7   Coffee: Advertising Expenditures as a Percentage of Sales for Major Italian Coffee Brands, 1986 to 1988

Company	Advertising Investments (Billions of Lire)			Advertising as Percentage of Total Sales		
	1986	1987	1988	1986	1987	1988
Lavazza	40.0	34.0	62.0	6.6%	6.8%	11.8%
Procter & Gamble	16.0	22.6	40.4	10.2	18.3	36.6
Nestlé	16.8	7.4	4.3	17.7	9.1	5.9
Crippa & Berger	6.0	7.6	13.2	9.2	15.2	28.1
Café do Brasil	5.0	9.4	18.0	4.8	10.1	20.0
Illy Caffé	3.0	6.0	7.4	8.4	15.9	16.8
Segafredo	—	4.3	9.5	n.a.*	4.6	9.0
Sao Café	2.0	3.5	1.3	2.3	5.2	2.2
Mauro	3.0	4.3	7.6	6.0	10.5	22.4

NOTE: Data included expenditures in support of decaffeinated and instant coffees as well as roast and ground.
* n.a. = Not available.
SOURCE: Company records and AGB.

Breakdown of Advertising by Product Type for Three Major Producers, 1988

Lavazza	17.4% Decaf
	82.6% Roast and ground
Nestlé	9.5% Decaf
	90.5% Regular and instant
Crippa & Berger	68.7% Decaf (Hag)
	31.3% Roast and ground

was owned by Nestlé. Lavazza accounted for 40% of coffee advertising in Italy. A well-known television advertisement involved a testimonial by an Italian actor which reaffirmed the "Italian" quality of Lavazza coffee and concluded with the selling line "The more you push it down, the more it pulls you up!" The company also sponsored the 1988 World Cup Ski Championships in an effort to present a more youthful image.

- *Segafredo-Zanetti, SpA* of Bologna produced roast and ground coffee and was the first company to introduce a combination pack of two 250-gram vacuum-packed bags of coffee for the family segment. Previously, Segafredo had sold only in the CHR segment, for which it also produced espresso machines sold under the Segafredo name. The company's communications program concentrated on sponsorships of national and international sporting events.

- *Crippa & Berger (C&B)* of Milan was the first company to market decaffeinated coffee in Italy. This company competed directly with Nestlé through its own brand of instant coffee, Faemino. Crippa & Berger's other brands were Gah (low caffeine and low fat) and Hag, which held 65% of the decaffeinated market compared to 27% for Lavazza's decaffeinated brand. C&B invested 28% of sales in advertising in 1988, two-thirds of which was spent on promoting Hag. The advertising was aimed at justifying the premium price of the Hag brand to both the family and the CHR segments. The company did not support Faemino with significant advertising.

- *Procter & Gamble Italia,* a subsidiary of the Cincinnati-based company, marketed the Splendid brand. Distribution penetration was excellent thanks to the coverage achieved by P&G's sales force in marketing the company's broad product line. Splendid was promoted through sponsored television programs with high viewer ratings. In 1988, Splendid Decaffeinato was introduced and allocated an advertising budget of $15 million, more than that for Splendid roast and ground. In 1988, P&G increased its advertising-to-sales ratio to 37% compared with 8.5% for the category as a whole. Splendid Oro and Classic were advertised as the coffees used in the most prestigious restaurants, while Decaffeinato was targeted at large families.

- *Illy Caffé* of Trieste produced a single blend of ground coffee with seven different levels of roasting. Illy Caffé was known for its excellent quality and also marketed a line of decaffeinated and low-caffeine coffees under the Mite brand name. Illy advertising emphasized the brand's comparative superiority. "The best, maestro," was the answer of an American patron in an Italian coffee shop when asked his judgment of Illy coffee.

- *Consorzio Sao Caffé* was a consortium of eight local producers formed in 1973 to pool their resources behind a single brand. The consortium advertised its Sao brand on the basis of the quality implied by its Brazilian-sounding name.

- *Café do Brasil* marketed Café Kimbo, a brand favored in southern Italy. Café Kimbo had gained market share rapidly as a result of competitive pricing and memorable advertising. In its television commercial, a well-known anchorperson tasted the coffee in a roasting plant and emphasized the freshness and rich taste of the Kimbo brand.

Marketing Coffee

Most of the national brands offered the consumer several blends in a variety of packages. Some producers bought instant and/or decaffeinated coffee from other firms to sell under their own brand names.

During most of the 1980s, a worldwide surplus of coffee beans depressed raw material prices. The consequent cost savings enabled producers to offer higher quality blends without increasing retail prices. By 1988, 4 million Italian households made coffee at home with restaurant-style espresso machines, and they were particularly interested in premium-quality blends.

The major brands were distributed through both the family and CHR segments. It was hard for producers to ensure that coffee served in coffeehouses was identified by brand. However, because many consumers believed that coffee made in a coffeehouse was better than that made at home, a strong brand presence in the CHR segment coud help a brand's retail image.

Retailers selected coffees to stock on the basis of brand reputation, margin and turnover, periodic trade discounts, and "three-for-two" consumer promotions. For CHR operators, brand name was less important than consistent quality at a competitive price and, for smaller outlets, the leasing and servicing of espresso machines.

Coffee was sold to the family segment in 200- to 250-gram bags (49% volume share), 400- to 500-gram bags (38%), 500-gram tins (4%) and 1-kg bags (9%). Pliable bags replaced tins in the 1980s as the principal form of packaging. Vacuum-sealed packages with double wrapping were introduced by the leading producers in 1985 to extend the shelf life of ground coffee. Instant coffee including Nescafé was available in small glass jars containing 50 to 125 grams. Research showed that Nescafé's glass jar, large lid, and granular appearance were not associated with "real" coffee.

Details of the cost structures for roast and ground coffee, Nescafé instant coffee, and espresso sold through CHR outlets are presented in Exhibit 8 on the next page. The average producer price of a kilo of roasted coffee in 1988 was 10,400 lire (including a 6% government tax). A kilo of decaffeinated coffee sold for 30,000 lire, and a kilo of instant coffee, which produced four times as many servings as the equivalent weight of roast and ground, cost 51,000 lire.

CHR operators paid producers, on average, 18,000 lire (including government tax) for a kilo of roast and ground. The end consumer paid seven to eight times this cost, or 800–900 lire, for a cup of espresso coffee using 6 grams.

EXHIBIT 8   Cost Structures for Roast and Ground Coffee, Nescafé, and Espresso in 1988 (Lire)

	Roast and Ground *(250 Gram)*	*Nescafé* *(125 Gram)*	*Espresso (CHR)* *(6 Gram)*
Suggested retailer selling price	3,250	7,500	800
Producer selling price	2,600	6,375	111
Cost of goods sold	2,150	3,160	80
Manufacturing	1,490	2,810	56
Distribution	660	350	24
Contribution margin	450	3,215	31
Sales promotion	45	374	0.3
Trade	10	250	0.3
Consumer	35	124	—
Advertising	30	426	0.5
Contribution after marketing expenses	375	2,415	30

Nescafé Marketing in Italy

The flavor of Nescafé in Italy was different from that of Nescafé in other European countries. The roasting and solubilization processes and the raw materials used were specifically adapted to Italian consumer tastes. However, during the 40 years following its launch in Italy in 1938, Nescafé sales grew slowly to only 400 tons by 1978.

Nestlé's main objective when it launched Nescafé was to have the product, although soluble, perceived as "real" coffee. From the outset, Nestlé executives had to combat consumer doubts that a coffee which was easy to prepare could be as good as "real" coffee. Italian consumers aged over 40 perceived Italian espresso as the only "real" coffee flavor and taste, while younger consumers tended to view espresso coffee, like tobacco and alcohol, as "old-fashioned." There was therefore a market opportunity for a lighter, good-tasting, and more aromatic coffee. Nescafé advertising aimed to affirm the good taste and quality of Nescafé compared to other Italian coffee. A typical advertisement in the 1970s was, "Hmm, what is it . . . what's happening . . . I smell coffee . . . Nescafé the best of them all." However, most consumers found this direct comparison to "real" coffee unconvincing. Many consumers continued to believe that Nescafé was "missing something" and was no substitute for "real" coffee. Nescafé was viewed as a backup product for emergency use and best suited for singles and older people.

Image-tracking studies between 1978 and 1988 showed that Nescafé users and nonusers perceived both taste and flavor improvements. However, as indicated in Exhibit 9, Nescafé was often seen as a coffee used by lonely and/or lazy people. From 1979 to 1983, Nescafé tried a more "personal" advertising campaign, which

EXHIBIT 9   Selected Results of Nescafé Image Tracking Study: 1978–1988

	Total Italy				Total Nescafé Users			
	1978	*1981*	*1985*	*1988*	*1978*	*1981*	*1985*	*1988*
Nescafé has:								
A good taste	2.2	2.3	2.5	2.6	2.4	3.1	3.4	3.6
No flavor	3.4	3.6	3.0	3.0	3.3	3.1	2.4	2.2
Nescafé is:								
A sad product	3.2	2.9	2.6	2.7	3.0	2.2	1.9	1.7
Coffee with other ingredients	2.9	2.8	2.6	2.5	3.4	4.1	4.2	4.3
Convenient	3.1	3.1	3.2	3.2	3.4	4.1	4.2	4.3
For lonely people	2.9	2.8	2.9	2.7	3.1	3.4	3.3	3.3
For lazy people	3.5	3.7	3.5	3.6	3.5	3.5	3.3	3.6

KEY: 5 = Agree; 1 = Disagree

did not focus solely on the product but rather showed "typical" people in the work force (e.g., a forest ranger, a dockworker, and a train conductor) enjoying Nescafé. The campaign aimed to show that Nescafé was for anyone who "wants something more out of life" and "gives something more to it." A print advertisement from the campaign is presented in Exhibit 10. The advertising campaign was reinforced with sampling programs and displays at the point of purchase.

Despite this effort, the annual tracking study did not show dramatic improvements in the brand's image. Nescafé continued to be widely viewed as inappropriate for those who wanted "gratification" or "a recharge" from their coffee. Nonetheless, sales exceeded 500 tons by 1983.

From 1984 to 1986, a Nescafé advertisement developed in France was also used in Italy. This execution portrayed an exotic train journey interspersed with images of locations where coffee was grown. The ad supported Nescafé's quality claims by highlighting Nescafé's origins without using direct comparisons to traditional Italian coffee. Nescafé's 1985 image tracking study showed that the brand had gained in perceived quality and reliability. Sales volume increased to 580 tons in 1986 and to 650 tons in 1988.

The results of a 1987 study involving one-on-one interviews with Italian coffee drinkers are reported in Exhibit 11 (page 221). The study showed that Nescafé's share of usage occasions was greatest among older people who were more sensitive to caffeine. Those aged 55 and over represented 80% of Nescafé's consumers, yet their average per capita consumption of Nescafé did not exceed one cup per day. Nescafé was preferred for its ease of preparation during moments of relaxation at home and for its less "aggressive" image. Awareness tracking studies, reported in Exhibit 12, showed Nescafé brand awareness had reached 83% of consumers by 1988. However, despite good distribution, Nescafé's household penetration was only 14%. Nescafé sales were disproportionately high in the larger northern Italian cities, as indicated in Exhibit 13, where consumers preferred sweeter blends. Exhibit 14 summarizes the conclusions of a 1988 focus group which asked consumers to compare Nescafé as a milk modifier with mocha coffee.

EXHIBIT 10

Nescafé print advertisement, 1980

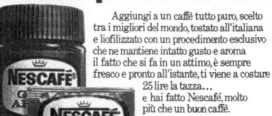

EXHIBIT 11   Results of Coffee Motivation Study, 1987

- A majority of respondents agreed with the following statements:

  "Espresso is true coffee."

  "Nescafé is not as strong as normal coffee."

  "Espresso coffee is strong, flavorful, and aromatic."

  "Nescafé is not a real coffee."

  "Nescafé is easier to handle."

  "Nescafé is used only in 'emergencies.'"

  "Nescafé is for older people."

- Nescafé was regarded as "easy to make," especially by Nescafé users. Nonusers more often agreed that "preparing a pot of coffee is not a waste of time."

- "Coffee, tobacco, and alcohol" were commonly regarded by young people as health risks.

- Two-thirds of Nescafé drinkers preferred to consume it with meals or in the afternoon. The remaining one-third used it primarily as a "milk modifier" in the morning.

- The three different formulations of Nescafé were easily distinguished by users.

- Forty-three percent of consumers considered Nescafé "lighter" than an espresso or "mocha" coffee; 20% considered it equivalent on this dimension; and 37% had no opinion.

EXHIBIT 12   Results of Nescafé Brand Awareness Study, 1978–1988*

	1978	1981	1985	1988
Have heard of Nescafé	73%	71%	74%	83%
Have tried Nescafé	29	33	38	39
Have not tried Nescafé	44	38	36	44
Have tried Nescafé in past three months	9	12	13	14
User Habits Within Past Three Months				
Strong	33%	37%	41%	45%
Average	34	28	24	24
Weak	33	36	35	31

* Base = 100 respondents.

KEY: Strong = Every day or nearly every day

Average = One to three times a week

Weak = Within three months

EXHIBIT 13   Nescafé versus Roast and Ground Coffee Consumption in Major Italian Cities

	Percent of Italian Population	Percent of Total Italian Roast and Ground Consumption	Percent of Total Italian Nescafé Consumption
Rome	7.0%	9.1%	4.2%
Milan	4.0	5.7	29.5
Turin	2.5	3.1	5.1
Naples	3.2	4.2	0.9
Bologna	2.2	2.7	2.4
Florence	1.8	1.9	2.7
Palermo	1.6	1.8	0.7

EXHIBIT 14   Conclusions of 1988 Focus Group Comparing Nescafé as a Milk Modifier with Mocha/Espresso

---

Convenience

Nescafé user: Convenience is one of the most important attributes of Nescafé—it's the easiest way to have milk and coffee.

Nescafé nonuser: Those who drink mocha coffee do not consider it inconvenient to prepare.

Concentration of Coffee Flavor

Nescafé user: Both flavor and taste are excellent; the foamy consistency when mixed with milk is closer to cappuccino than normal milk and coffee.

Nescafé nonuser: Both flavor and taste are good; but why drink Nescafé when one can have mocha and milk?

Caffeine and Stimulating Capability

Nescafé user: Nescafé is less stimulating than espresso, but caffeine is not a priority.

Nescafé nonuser: Espresso drinkers want a level of stimulation from coffee which Nescafé does not provide.

Conclusion

Nescafé needed a revised marketing plan to increase sales. Nescafé already enjoyed excellent distribution penetration and additional manufacturing capacity was available.

At the management meeting, Mr. Baruffa laid out four options for Nescafé:

1. Focus further on older consumers, already heavy users of Nescafé.
2. Broaden Nescafé's positioning to include its use as a milk modifier, particularly use of Nescafé Classic as a morning beverage with milk.
3. Target younger and more "cosmopolitan" professionals, positioning Nescafé (particularly Gran Aroma) as an international coffee beverage.
4. Try to penetrate the CHR segment of the market.

Mr. Baruffa argued that the first option was the least attractive. He believed that per capita coffee consumption among older consumers could not be increased significantly, though demographic trends indicated that the segment would grow as a percentage of the total Italian population.

Mr. Bechi shifted discussion to the second option. He believed that "youngsters should be the target audience for the next five years." He was concerned about positioning Nescafé as a milk modifier due to Nestlé Italy's leadership in that category with Nesquick and Orzoro. He warned the group about cannibalization and the likely concerns of the milk modifier brand managers.

However, Mr. Baruffa emphasized that younger people's more open-minded attitude toward Nescafé was an important opportunity. Could Nescafé be presented to young people as both a milk modifier and a "new, less-caffeinated alternative to regular coffee"?

Mr. Mazzei, the CFO, discouraged further emphasis on the CHR segment. He argued that the trade promotion investment to secure extra distribution would not pay back. He also believed consumers were less likely to switch from espresso or "real" coffee to Nescafé in coffeehouses and restaurants.

Mr. Giuliani argued that Nescafé should be positioned as an international coffee, not as an Italian coffee, to cosmopolitan consumers who populated the larger northern Italian cities. He believed that there was a growing "transnational consumer" segment comprising sophisticated, well-traveled consumers, who were developing "universal" consumption habits and who were attracted to international brands, even in food products.

12 NISSAN MOTOR CO., LTD

Marketing Strategy for the European Market

In February 1989, in anticipation of the European Community (EC) market integration in 1992, Kiyoshi Sekiguchi, general manager, and Shu Gomi, deputy general manager, European sales group of Nissan Motor Co., Ltd., were discussing how to expand Nissan's market penetration in three principal southern European countries: France, Italy, and Spain.

Japanese carmakers had voluntarily limited their total exports to Europe to a ceiling of about 10% of the EC market, which accounted for 90% of the total Western European market. In addition, France, Italy, and Spain had imposed severe restrictions on Japanese imports, resulting in quite small sales of Nissan in these countries. However, because Nissan started to export the Bluebird (equivalent to its Stanza model in the United States), which was manufactured in its UK factory, to the European continent in late 1988, and because the restrictions by individual EC countries on Japanese car imports were likely to be relieved at the advent of EC integration, Nissan believed that full-scale penetration into these three European countries would become possible.

Although Sekiguchi and Gomi needed to develop a marketing strategy for the entire European market in light of the tougher competition expected after 1992, the more immediate decision was how much marketing effort to allocate to two models, the 1800-cc upper-medium-sized Bluebird and a superminicar like the Micra (hereafter New Micra). Nissan manufactured the Bluebird in its UK factory, but it planned to manufacture the New Micra there as well until 1992. Of course, to serve the markets adequately, it needed to market a complete product line of five or six models, including exports from Japan. Among them, the models that were especially important strategically were the Bluebird and the New Micra. Because resources—especially for advertising—that could be allocated to

This case was prepared by Professor Kyoichi Ikeo of Keio University, Japan, in association with Professor John A. Quelch. Copyright © 1989 by the President and Fellows of Harvard College. Harvard Business School case 590-018.

Exhibit 1

Nissan Bluebird and Nissan Micra

France, Italy, and Spain were limited, Sekiguchi and Gomi had to decide which model to emphasize and how to promote both of them in those countries and then recommend their decision to Yoshikazu Kawana, director of the European sales group. Exhibit 1 (previous page) shows the current Bluebird and Micra models.

Company Background

In 1935, Nissan Motor Co., Ltd., which had been established in 1933 by Gisuke Ayukawa, started the mass production of automobiles in Japan with a small 750-cc car. It eventually grew to include a full-sized 3670-cc car in its product line, expanding its production volume and becoming, along with Toyota and Isuzu, one of the leading companies in the Japanese automobile industry. However, due to shortage of material during World War II, Nissan was obliged to focus on truck production and to decrease its car output. The end of the war brought its production to a standstill.

Nissan's growth in truck and car production after World War II was due to the special procurement needs of the Korean War and the increased household penetration of cars in Japan beginning in the late 1950s. In particular, the enormous success of the new small-sized cars in the 1960s, when a major portion of vehicle demand moved from trucks and medium-sized cars for business use to small-sized

EXHIBIT 2   Nonconsolidated Statements of Income: 1984–1988*
(in Millions of Yen)

	1984	1985	1986	1987	1988
Net sales	3,460,124	3,618,076	3,754,172	3,429,317	3,418,671
Cost of sales	(2,811,052)	(2,943,384)	(3,099,243)	(2,948,127)	(2,882,252)
Gross profit	649,071	674,692	654,928	481,190	536,418
Selling, general, and administrative expenses	(572,947)	(585,155)	(584,870)	(475,691)	(470,779)
Operating income	76,124	89,537	70,057	5,499	65,639
Other Income (Expense)					
Interest income	67,559	72,325	70,494	58,989	50,548
Interest expense	(46,012)	(46,190)	(42,237)	(38,428)	(36,594)
Other†	30,377	43,385	10,084	83,652	59,971
	51,925	69,519	38,343	104,214	73,924
Income before income taxes	128,049	159,056	108,400	109,711	139,562
Income taxes	(57,517)	(84,780)	(43,648)	(63,105)	(100,978)
Net income	70,532	74,276	64,752	46,606	38,584

* Years ended March 31, 1984–1988.

† *Other* consists of dividend income, net realized gain on sales of securities, and other sources.

**EXHIBIT 3   Total Sales of Japanese Car Manufacturers: 1983–1988
(in Millions of Yen)**

	1983	1984	1985	1986	1987	1988
Nissan	3,187,722	3,460,124	3,618,076	3,754,172	3,429,317	3,418,671
Toyota	4,892,663	5,472,681	6,064,420	6,304,858	6,024,909	6,691,299
Honda	1,746,919	1,846,028	1,929,519	2,245,743	2,334,597	2,650,077*
Mazda	1,364,229	1,431,815	1,569,553	1,626,187	1,602,293	1,844,300
Mitsubishi	1,061,375	1,173,631	1,408,307	1,578,823	1,558,670	1,752,697
Isuzu	684,624	769,071	1,016,250	1,013,434	909,915	1,023,300
Suzuki	542,319	524,259	580,841	722,336	744,854	759,550
Subaru	580,052	602,735	672,071	768,424	715,717	686,238
Daihatsu	425,909	469,950	515,911	535,645	557,627	445,665†

* Thirteen months, due to alteration of settlement term.
† Nine months, due to alteration of settlement term.
SOURCE: Company records.

cars for business use to small-sized cars for personal use, gave Nissan a firm footing in the Japanese automobile industry.

Exports of Nissan cars started in 1958 and increased from 10,000 units in 1960 to 400,000 in 1970. During the 1970s, partly because of the rise in gasoline prices, high-quality, fuel-efficient Japanese cars dramatically increased their share of the North American market. Nissan exported 1.46 million units in 1980.

By the 1988 fiscal year, Nissan sales totaled 3,400 billion yen. It manufactured 2.16 million units in domestic factories and 0.52 million units in foreign factories, and it exported 1.14 million units from Japan. Exhibit 2 presents Nissan income statements for 1984 to 1988, and Exhibit 3 summarizes total sales, in millions of yen, of Japanese automobile manufacturers for 1983 to 1988.

Penetrating the European Market

Nissan's European market penetration began with exports to Finland in 1959. The company concentrated first on the northern European countries, not entering the EC countries until the late 1960s. Its exports to Europe increased from 3,600 vehicles in 1964 to 163,000 in 1973 and reached 240,000 in 1978.

However, protectionist sentiment against increased car exports from Japan began appearing in several countries in the late 1970s, resulting in the 1981 voluntary ceiling on exports to the United States and various restrictions and surveillances in European countries. Management expected this protectionist atmosphere to continue and decided in 1980 to begin to move local production overseas. In Europe, it acquired Motor Iberica, SA, to make commercial vehicles in Spain and founded Nissan Motor Manufacturing UK, Ltd., to make passenger cars in the United Kingdom. These decisive steps were in stark contrast to Toyota's strategy, which placed much less emphasis on local production.

Nissan Motor Iberica, SA (NMISA)

In 1980 Nissan acquired a 35.85% equity stake in Motor Iberica, the largest commercial vehicle manufacturer in Spain, participated in its administration, and helped make it a more efficient manufacturer. In 1983, it started to manufacture vehicles under its own brand, gradually increasing its share holdings to 68% by 1989.

In 1988, NMISA manufactured 76,000 commercial vehicles, of which 66% were Nissan's and the rest Motor Iberica's. Of all the commercial vehicles NMISA manufactured, 32% were exported, mainly to other European countries. NMISA's performance was favorable, and its cumulative losses were covered by profits in fiscal year 1988.

Nissan Motor Manufacturing UK Ltd. (NMUK)

To manufacture passenger cars, Nissan founded NMUK as a local subsidiary in 1984 and began constructing a factory in Sunderland, near Newcastle, in northeast England. Completed in 1986, the factory produced an upper-medium-sized car called the Bluebird. Because Nissan volunteered to manufacture with 60% value-based local content rising to 80% by 1991, the British government in January 1988 authorized the Bluebird as a UK-made car.[1] The EC Commission supported the UK position. However, the French government insisted that local content had to reach 80% for EC approval and threatened to count UK-built Bluebirds against its 3% Japanese import ceiling until they reached 80% local content. The UK-made Bluebird began to be exported to other EC member countries in late 1988, when it had reached 70% local content. In 1988, the Sunderland factory purchased components from 113 European companies. The French government finally conceded that the Bluebird could be exported to France without any restriction or duty, though the possibility of reducing quotas on car imports from Japan to France remained.

Although it would be some time before NMUK would be operating in the black because of the huge initial investment,[2] production volume grew smoothly: 5,079 in 1986; 28,797 in 1987; and 56,744 in 1988. Nissan planned to expand production even further, to 100,000 a year in 1990, when it would introduce a new version of the Bluebird, and to 200,000 by 1992, when it would add the New Micra. By 1988, NMUK had invested 50 billion yen and planned to invest an additional 80 billion yen before full production was reached in 1992. Although

---

[1] Value-based local content was calculated by subtracting from the factory price of the car the value of components and materials imported from outside the EC. Some protectionists advocated the use of cost-based local content, which took into account the full production cost including all overheads as well as design and engineering costs. However, this approach was much harder to monitor and police. Others demanded local manufacturing of specific components such as engines, transmissions, axles, and electronic components. To achieve 80% local content, it was, however, necessary for either engines or transmissions to be locally sourced.

[2] £125 million of the investment was contributed by the UK government, motivated by the additional employment opportunities the plant would bring to the northeast.

EXHIBIT 4   **Cost Structure of Nissan for Selling in the Netherlands***

	Nissan's UK-Made Cars		*Nissan's Japan-Made Cars (Average)*
	Bluebird†	*New Micra††*	
Retail price	100%	100%	100%
Dealer margin	18	18	18
Distributor selling price	82	82	82
Distributor margin	12	12	12
Nissan selling price	70	70	70
Transportation cost	3.5	4	8
Duty	0	0	10
Labor cost	8	10	12
Parts and material cost	39	40	32
Overhead and selling cost	12	10	3

* Percent of retail price, excluding taxes other than duty.
† 1988 figures.
†† Estimated figures for the year production began.

Nissan's UK cost structure was not publicly available, Exhibit 4, which shows Nissan's cost structure for selling in the Netherlands, can be treated as an approximation.

Market Integration of the EC

A major impact on Nissan's European operations was the planned market integration of the EC in 1992. An integrated EC would liberate the movement of products, services, people, and capital within the Community and consolidate technical standards that hitherto had been determined by individual member countries. Much progress had already been achieved toward harmonization of technical standards for cars. By 1988, 41 of 44 voluntary technical directives proposed in 1970 had been adopted by all EC-member states. The remaining three—on tires, windshields, and towing weights—were expected to be tabled soon by the European Commission, and all were expected to be made mandatory by 1990, permitting single-type approval for the entire EC market.

Thanks to a more efficient allocation of production facilities, and concentration and reduction of inventories, production and logistics costs were expected by industry analysts to decrease as a result of the 1992 program. According to the EC Commission, such cost reductions were valued at 853 billion yen. If all these cost savings were passed through as lower prices, average retail auto prices would be lowered by 5.7%, and consequently the market would expand by more than 6%. Market expansion would be especially strong in countries such as Spain and the United Kingdom where harmonization of value-added taxes and excise taxes on cars would substantially reduce retail prices.

At the same time, market integration was expected by analysts to intensify competition in the automobile industry and thereby to magnify the differences among companies. Therefore, in preparing for 1992, European auto companies made great efforts to expand, modernize, or reallocate their production resources.

Market integration promised to affect import restrictions on Japanese automobiles. Although the voluntary EC-wide ceiling on all Japanese imports was expected to remain, the bilateral import quotas on Japanese cars imposed by France, Italy, and Spain had to cease. French officials, in particular, pressed for maintenance of the EC-wide ceiling on Japanese imports, for an 80% EC-wide local content requirement, and for higher exports of EC-made cars to Japan. They were also sensitive to the possibility of Japanese companies shipping US-made cars to Europe to circumvent the EC-wide quota. Realistic observers foresaw a transition period whereby restrictions on Japanese automobile imports would be phased out gradually to give national producers such as Fiat and Renault time to improve the efficiency of their operations before they had to face open Japanese competition.

In addition, the possibility of cost reductions made local production more attractive for the Japanese. In this respect, Nissan had an advantage over other Japanese companies: a proven record in Spain and the United Kingdom. However, the other Japanese automobile companies, such as Toyota and Mazda, were moving toward local production in Europe. Exhibit 5 summarizes these

EXHIBIT 5   Movements of Major Japanese Automobile Companies toward Local Production in Europe*

Company's Name	Country	Outline
Nissan	Spain	Manufacturing 76,000 commercial vehicles a year (in 1988).
Nissan	United Kingdom	Manufacturing 57,000 upper-medium-sized cars a year (in 1988).
Toyota	West Germany	Planning to manufacture 15,000 small trucks a year (from 1989) in a Volkswagen factory in Hanover.
Toyota	United Kingdom	Planning to manufacture 200,000 upper-medium-sized cars a year (from 1992).
Honda	United Kingdom	Manufacturing 84,000 medium-sized cars a year (in 1987) jointly with the Rover Group.
Mazda	Spain	Considering the manufacture of 25,000 commercial vehicles a year.
Mazda	Undecided	Considering the manufacture of 200,000 upper-medium-sized cars a year (from 1992) in a Ford factory with which Mazda is affiliated.
Isuzu	United Kingdom	Manufacturing 5,400 commercial vehicles a year (in 1987) in a joint venture with General Motors.
Suzuki	Spain	Manufacturing 25,000 small four-wheel-drive off-road vehicles a year (in 1987) jointly with Land Rover Santana.
Subaru	France	Considering the manufacture of 30,000 vehicles a year in northwestern France.

* Excluding knockdown productions.

endeavors. Some executives of European automobile companies worried that Japanese local production would bring overcapacity and price erosion to the European market. But countries with no automotive industry, such as Greece and Ireland, welcomed the Japanese as a means of increasing price competition in their markets. In addition, certain EC countries, particularly the United Kingdom, actively sought additional Japanese investment in car production following the decline of their domestic manufacturers.

Middle-Range Plan for the European Market

Although Japanese automobile sales in Europe were small when compared with domestic or North American counterparts, there was large potential for growth if their plans for local production were put into practice and EC market integration was carried out. In particular, Nissan, which trailed Toyota and was closely followed by Honda in share of the domestic and North American markets, had capitalized on its competitive advantage in the European market, where it had the largest market share among the Japanese companies, thanks in part to its early establishment of local production facilities. Exhibit 6 shows the overall market shares of Japanese and major European companies in the Western European car market.

EXHIBIT 6   Western Europe—Overall Market Share in Car Market, 1983–1988

	1983	1984	1985	1986	1987	1988 (Estimated)
VW group*	13.02%	13.56%	14.37%	14.70%	14.95%	14.44%
Ford Europe	12.47	12.80	11.90	11.67	11.93	11.45
Fiat group†	13.78	14.48	13.74	14.01	14.20	15.35
Peugeot group††	11.71	11.50	11.52	11.38	12.12	12.83
GM Europe§	11.07	11.04	11.36	10.95	10.55	10.29
Renault group	12.63	10.90	10.65	10.61	10.62	10.34
Total Japanese	10.06	10.27	10.77	11.71	11.38	11.00
Nissan	2.79	2.83	2.89	3.00	2.93	2.84
Toyota	2.25	2.24	2.58	2.88	2.81	2.66
Honda	1.02	1.14	1.11	1.17	1.03	1.11
Mazda	2.01	1.97	1.91	2.05	1.90	1.88
Mitsubishi	0.98	1.09	1.10	1.21	1.22	1.10
Suzuki	0.42	0.43	0.47	0.58	0.65	0.66
Subaru	0.29	0.30	0.38	0.44	0.45	0.40
Daihatsu	0.27	0.24	0.28	0.32	0.30	0.25

* VW group consisted of Volkswagen and Audi until 1985. In 1986, SEAT joined the VW group.
† Fiat group consisted of Fiat, Autobianchi, Lancia, and Ferrari until 1986. In 1987, Alfa Romeo joined the Fiat group.
†† Peugeot group includes Peugeot, Citroen, and Talbot.
§ GM Europe includes Opel and Vauxhall.
SOURCE: DRI World Automotive Forecast Report.

Given the importance and rapid growth of the European market (car registrations increased 5% in 1988), Nissan management formulated a plan in the fall of 1988 to strengthen its competitive position until 1992. The main goals to be achieved by 1992 were as follows:

1. Raise Nissan's market share in the European car market to 4.5% by 1992 and increase car production in the United Kingdom to 200,000 and truck production in Spain to 100,000.
2. Improve Nissan's brand image by reinforcing the quality of its sales and service organizations in Europe.
3. Further decentralize Nissan's responsibility for European operations, including product design, production, marketing, and sales.

According to the plan, Nissan's sales increase in Europe would be accomplished mainly through is UK-made cars, because exports from Japan had to contend with trade restrictions, political friction, and a decrease in per unit contribution and price competitiveness due to appreciation of the yen. Reinforcing the sales and service organization and localizing overall European operations were measures to achieve the market penetration needed to justify increased production, achieve further scale economies, and increase productivity.

To coordinate European operations, Nissan established a European Technical Center (NETC) in the United Kingdom in 1988 and planned to start the operation of Nissan Europe NV in the Netherlands in 1990. Whereas Nissan had previously developed all of its products in Japan, NETC would, through the combined efforts of Japanese and European staff, produce new cars to meet European consumer needs. Moreover, because models for local production, which were designed in Japan, often required special orders from European parts suppliers, materials costs increased. NETC's objective was to design cars that incorporated standard parts available in Europe at lower costs—for example, a new Bluebird model to be launched in 1990, the New Micra to be launched by 1992, and any new commercial vehicles that would be manufactured in Spain.

Nissan Europe NV would be responsible for coordinating all development, production, logistics, and marketing in Europe, most of which had been done in Tokyo. And it would formulate overall marketing strategy for Europe, in place of the Europe Sales Group in Tokyo. Distributors in each country would continue to draft national marketing plans that were integrated with the regional plan.

Furthermore, Nissan Europe would play a key role in consolidating logistics under EC integration, which would facilitate the free flow of goods within the EC and unify the technical standards. Nissan's plan was to gather orders from local distributors in each country and to relay them to the United Kingdom, Spain, and Tokyo. Also, Nissan Europe would totally oversee the transportation from each factory to each dealer via the large-scale collection and delivery center and predelivery inspection facility, which were under construction in Amsterdam. Therefore, transportation and inventory functions for cars and commercial vehicles, which had been shared by Nissan and local distributors, would be performed by Nissan Europe and its subsidiary logistics company. The only logistics function left to distributors would be that for parts.

Trends in the European Market

The European car market in 1987 comprised 12.4 million units, one-third of the total world market, and 10 million of these sales were accounted for by five countries: West Germany, the United Kingdom, France, Italy, and Spain. Exhibit 7 shows new-car sales in European countries and other major markets. Exhibits 8 and 9 provide new-car sales data for European countries in 1987 and 1988. Exhibits 10 and 11 provide market segmentation data for each major European country. Exhibit 12 shows profiles of European countries. Exhibit 13 profiles Nissan's distributors.

To catch up to the Japanese, European carmakers needed to improve productivity by one-third; it took Japanese workers 20 hours to assemble a car, whereas the European average was 36 hours and the US 26.5 hours. While local content restrictions were designed to make Japanese assembly in Europe more costly, industry analysts believed that, even with a 90% requirement, Japanese plants in Europe would be more efficient than those run by the European manufacturers.

EXHIBIT 7   New-Car Sales—Overall World Market, 1983–1989 (000s of Units)

	1983	*1984*	*1985*	*1986*	*1987*	*1988 (Est.)*	*1989 (Est.)*
West Germany	2,427	2,394	2,379	2,829	2,916	2,730	2,660
France	2,018	1,758	1,766	1,912	2,105	2,217	2,146
United Kingdom	1,792	1,750	1,832	1,882	2,014	2,195	1,939
Italy	1,581	1,636	1,746	1,825	1,977	2,131	2,002
Spain	547	520	572	686	925	1,039	1,089
Netherlands	459	461	496	561	556	485	550
Belgium	339	352	360	395	406	435	426
Other EC countries	329	342	388	402	353	388	531
EC total	9,492	9,212	9,540	10,492	11,251	11,620	11,343
Sweden	217	231	263	270	316	331	352
Switzerland	274	267	265	300	303	322	327
Other western European countries	486	450	540	572	509	505	599
Western European total	10,494	10,161	10,608	11,635	12,380	12,779	12,622
United States	9,181	10,393	11,043	11,452	10,227	10,699	10,623
Canada	842	964	1,137	1,089	1,057	1,013	1,196
North American total	10,023	11,357	12,180	12,541	11,284	11,711	11,819
Japan	3,136	3,096	3,104	3,146	3,275	3,609	3,497
World total	29,151	30,289	31,821	33,049	32,657	34,277	35,528

SOURCE: DRI World Automotive Forecast Report.

EXHIBIT 8　New-Car Sales in Major European Countries, 1987 (000s of Units)

	West Germany	France	United Kingdom	Italy	Spain	Nether-lands	Belgium	Sweden	Switzerland
Total	2,915.7	2,105.2	2,013.7	1,976.5	924.8	555.7	406.2	316.0	303.3
By manufacturer:									
VW Group	872.2	159.3	116.2	225.8	161.2	63.0	65.6	37.7	50.0
Ford Europe	300.8	143.4	580.1	78.4	142.1	56.0	39.5	34.3	21.2
Fiat Group	132.8	151.8	74.3	1,179.9	69.6	35.3	18.5	8.2	29.5
Peugeot Group	123.3	703.5	147.3	148.8	154.2	65.0	57.3	11.0	25.1
GM Europe	453.3	96.8	270.8	57.3	130.1	88.6	46.8	31.1	37.6
Renault Group	89.6	641.7	78.7	154.2	209.4	22.6	35.3	5.1	16.6
Total Japanese*	441.4	63.1	225.4	13.7	6.8	144.0	83.5	68.5	87.6
Nissan	84.5	17.8	114.2	0.0	2.1	31.3	19.4	18.1	13.7
Toyota	93.3	14.3	38.3	2.0	2.1	31.2	26.8	22.8	26.6
Honda	41.5	10.2	24.7	0.2	0.5	11.9	8.5	4.1	7.6
Mazda	91.0	16.6	18.8	0.0	0.5	24.5	10.6	13.9	8.1
Mitsubishi	68.6	3.3	11.8	0.7	1.0	15.3	9.6	3.6	11.1
Suzuki	27.1	0.9	5.6	9.9	0.4	18.0	3.3	2.4	4.1
Subaru	16.7	0.0	5.0	0.4	0.1	4.7	3.0	1.8	14.3
Daihatsu	13.0	0.0	4.6	0.5	0.0	7.1	2.3	1.7	1.4

* Total Japanese in Italy and Spain exceed the quotas on car imports from Japan, because some parts of commercial vehicles, manufactured by Nissan and Suzuki in Spain and knocked down by Toyota and Mitsubishi in Portugal, are counted as passenger cars. Furthermore, in the case of Italy, indirect imports via other European countries boost the sales of Japanese cars.

SOURCE: DRI World Automotive Forecast Report.

EXHIBIT 9　Estimated New-Car Sales in Major European Countries, 1988 (000s of Units)

	West Germany	France	United Kingdom	Italy	Spain	Nether-lands	Belgium	Sweden	Switzerland
Total	2,730.2	2,216.8	2,195.4	2,030.9	1,039.2	484.8	435.0	331.3	322.1
By Manufacturer									
VW group	797.0	168.8	125.4	220.3	196.5	54.7	70.7	36.8	50.9
Ford Europe	269.9	139.2	582.2	79.6	152.9	50.6	44.5	34.0	21.5
Fiat group	138.9	217.1	86.6	1,211.7	85.4	29.4	16.3	7.6	31.0
Peugeot group	108.4	740.2	187.1	165.1	197.4	60.6	65.6	14.7	23.9
GM Europe	418.4	104.1	302.2	71.6	136.6	69.0	50.4	28.7	38.4
Renault group	84.8	639.4	84.4	148.0	217.7	21.3	38.9	4.7	16.6
Total Japanese	390.0	65.0	247.5	10.7	8.3	127.5	88.4	81.4	100.0
Nissan	71.9	18.7	132.6	0.2	2.8	23.9	20.5	19.8	13.5
Toyota	77.2	14.9	39.2	0.6	2.2	23.3	29.1	25.5	31.0
Honda	45.7	10.6	25.9	0.5	0.6	12.0	9.0	5.5	8.3
Mazda	82.6	17.2	20.4	0.1	0.6	24.5	9.8	18.3	12.3
Mitsubishi	55.0	3.0	12.4	0.8	1.0	13.1	9.4	6.0	13.1
Suzuki	26.7	0.6	5.9	7.8	1.0	18.2	3.8	3.3	4.7
Subaru	13.7	0.0	4.5	0.2	0.1	5.1	3.3	1.6	14.1
Daihatsu	10.7	0.0	3.4	0.5	0.0	7.3	3.2	1.2	1.7

SOURCE: DRI World Automotive Forecast Report.

EXHIBIT 10 New-Car Sales by Segment, 1987 (000s of Units)

	West Germany	France	United Kingdom	Italy	Spain
Total sales	2,915.7	2,105.2	2,013.7	1,976.6	924.8
By Segment					
Utility	2.22%	4.06%	2.30%	18.50%⎫	43.0%*
Supermini	14.46	40.31	25.51	38.94 ⎭	
Lower-Medium	35.62	23.03	34.41	25.37	37.1
Upper-Medium	22.92	22.25	25.48	8.06	13.9
Executive	24.76	10.35	12.31	9.14	6.0†

* Includes Utility and Supermini.
† Includes sports cars such as the Nissan 300ZX. In other countries, sports cars are included in each segment according to vehicle size.

NOTE: Typical models included in each segment are the following:

Utility .... Fiat 126, Renault R4, Suzuki Cervo
Supermini .... Fiat Uno, Ford Fiesta, Nissan New Micra, Peugeot 104, Toyota Starlet, VW Polo
Lower-Medium .... Fiat Tipo, Ford Escort, Honda Civic, Nissan Sunny, Nissan Violet, Toyota Corolla, Toyota Tercel, VW Golf
Upper-Medium .... Audi 80/90, Ford Capri, Honda Accord, Nissan Bluebird, Nissan Prairie, Renault Fuego, Toyota Camry, Toyota Carina
Executive .... Audi 100/200, BMW (all models), Honda Legend, Mazda RX7, Nissan Cedric/Laurel, Nissan 280/300ZX, Nissan Silvia, Toyota Celica, Toyota Crown, Toyota Supra

SOURCE: DRI World Automotive Forecast Report and company records.

EXHIBIT 11 New-Car Sales of Japanese Companies by Segment, 1987 (000s of Units)

	West Germany	France	United Kingdom	Italy
Nissan				
Supermini	21.8	5.1	38.9	0.0
Lower-Medium	31.6	6.2	36.7	0.0
Upper-Medium	25.0	4.8	35.3	0.0
Executive	6.2	1.7	3.3	0.0
Toyota				
Supermini	16.6	0.0	1.2	0.0
Lower-Medium	39.0	7.9	17.1	0.0
Upper-Medium	28.7	3.1	9.8	0.0
Executive	9.0	3.3	10.1	2.0
Honda				
Supermini	0.1	0.0	0.0	0.0
Lower-Medium	19.3	5.2	5.8	0.0
Upper-Medium	21.9	4.8	18.2	0.2
Executive	0.2	0.2	0.8	0.0
Mazda				
Supermini	0.0	0.0	0.0	0.0
Lower-Medium	47.9	9.7	11.9	0.0
Upper-Medium	40.0	5.6	6.2	0.0
Executive	3.0	1.2	0.7	0.0

SOURCE: DRI World Automotive Forecast Report.

EXHIBIT 12   Profiles of Major European Countries, 1987

	West Germany	France	United Kingdom	Italy	Spain	Nether-lands	Belgium	Sweden	Switzerland
Car sales (000)	2,915.7	2,105.2	2,013.7	1,976.5	924.8	555.7	406.2	316.0	303.3
Commercial vehicle sales (000)	113.7	369.4	252.8	163.0	170.0	69.6	28.8	29.5	24.3
Nissan's commercial vehicle sales (000)	2.9	3.1	10.5	4.0	33.7	3.1	1.5	2.8	1.3
Total sales (000)	3,029.4	2,474.6	2,266.5	2,139.5	1,094.8	625.3	435.0	345.5	327.6
Car production (000)	4,374	3,052	1,143	1,713	1,403	125	277	432	0
Car export (000)	2,451	1,681	226	641	707	112	228	340	0
Car import (000)	1,012	760	1,041	780	188	535	n.a.†	226	n.a.
Number of cars per 1,000 people	468	385	360	392	264	340	351	400	423
Car price index* (exclusive of tax)	128	128	144	129	151	122	121	n.a.	n.a.
Car price index* (inclusive of tax)	105	124	129	112	139	135	109	n.a.	n.a.

* The EC market with the lowest price is indexed at 100 in both cases.
† n.a. = Not available.
SOURCE: DRI World Automotive Forecast Report, BEUC Car Report, company records.

EXHIBIT 13   Profiles of Nissan's Distributors in Major European Countries

Country	Name of Distributor	Percent of Shares Held by Nissan	Number of Dealers	Number of Nissan Employees
West Germany	Nissan Motor Deutschland	100%	734	4
France	Richard-Nissan	9.6	203	1
United Kingdom	Nissan UK	0	450	0
Italy	Nissan Italia	64.2	160	2
Spain	Nissan Motor Iberica	68	148	19
Netherlands	Nissan Motor Nederland	100	170	3
Belgium	NV Nissan Belgium	0	345	0
Sweden	Philipson Bil	0	50	0
Switzerland	Nissan Motor Schweiz	100	284	3

SOURCE: Company records.

West Germany

West Germany had the largest car market in Europe, with sales of about 3 million units a year and no restrictions imposed on imports; therefore, Japanese companies were able to achieve considerable car sales. However with highly competitive companies like Volkswagen, the West German market was regarded as having the stiffest competition in Europe. Generally, West German consumers, known as serious readers of car magazines, were knowledgeable about cars and apt to consider numerous data before purchasing. Table A shows the relative importance of product attributes in major European countries. Regarding vehicle size, models larger than the supermini had a large market share, especially when compared with their share in the southern European countries.

TABLE A   Relative Importance of Product Attributes by Country*

	West Germany	United Kingdom	France	Italy	Spain
Performance	*	*			
Fuel economy					*
Price		*	*	*	*
Styling			*		
Quality	*				
Accessories				*	
Maintenance	*				

* An asterisk (*) indicates a particularly important attribute. Its absence does not mean a lack of importance.
SOURCE: Estimate of Mr. Shu Gomi, deputy general manager.

Among Japanese competitors, Mazda focused on West Germany, where it had a relatively high market share, followed by Toyota and then Nissan. Although Nissan hoped to increase its market share in West Germany as production volume in its UK factory increased, it was thought that the market could absorb only a limited quantity.

West Germany took the most liberal view toward Japanese competition in the automobile industry because its car companies dominated other EC car manufacturers in the Japanese market, holding a 2% market share (80,000 units) by 1988. In addition, an open EC car market with the French, Spanish, and Italian bilateral quotas removed would mean that the bulk of imported Japanese cars would no longer be forced on the northern EC countries as was currently the case.

United Kingdom

A unique feature of the UK market was that fleet sales, purchases by companies for use by their employees, accounted for more than half of the total car sales. Because most of the fleet sales were of upper-medium-sized 1,600-cc to 2,000-cc cars, this class held about a 25% unit share of the total car market. The UK-made Bluebird was an upper-medium-sized car suitable for fleet sales.

In addition to the voluntary ceiling on all Japanese imports to EC countries, Japanese car imports in the United Kingdom were limited to 11% of the total market by a gentlemen's agreement between each country's associations of automobile manufacturers. But, because Nissan's sales were so high when this casual agreement was made, it obtained a very favorable import quota, gaining 6% of the market, the largest share of all the Japanese imports, and vying with Volkswagen for fourth position in the market, following Ford, GM, and Peugeot. Owing to the growth of the UK market, Nissan sales reached more than 100,000, representing 35% of its European unit sales. Also, the UK-made Bluebird was sold mostly in the UK market from 1986 to 1988, partly because until 1987 the EC had treated it as a Japanese import.

On January 27, 1989, Toyota announced that it would construct a factory in the United Kingdom to manufacture, beginning in 1992, 200,000 units a year of an upper-medium-sized 1,800-cc car. The local content was set to start at 60% and reach 80% as soon as possible. Local production by Toyota would inevitably make competition more severe because a considerable portion of Toyota's UK-made cars had to be sold in the UK market. Therefore, the extent to which Nissan could depend on the UK market was more circumscribed; when it increased UK production, it needed to depend more heavily on exports to the European continent.

The local distributor was Nissan UK, which was 100% owned by a local businessman and had 450 dealers. Nissan UK was an excellent distributor, as shown by its market share in the United Kingdom; however, Nissan wished to increase its own influence over marketing in the United Kingdom and to coordinate it under a single strategy for Europe, and therefore planned to acquire the distributor. But negotiations between the two had not been successful so far, and it was somewhat uncertain that Nissan could control the marketing and logistics in the United Kingdom as they did in other countries.

France

Although France had a large car market, with about 2.2 million units a year, total imports of Japanese cars were limited to five manufacturers: Toyota, Nissan, Mitsubishi, Honda, and Mazda, which shared 3% of the market. The supermini class was the largest segment, followed by the lower- and upper-medium-sized cars. French consumers were thought to be price conscious and less sensitive to quality than consumers in West Germany and the Netherlands.

The French automobile companies, Peugeot and Renault, held more than a 60% market share, and the total share of imported cars was only one-third. Despite having the largest market share, Peugeot had not achieved productivity as high as had the Japanese manufacturers and therefore attempted to enlarge and modernize its production facilities in preparation for 1992. However, Renault was heavily in debt and lacked the capital to make substantial investments to raise productivity.

Nissan's marketing organization in France was weak because sales had been restricted. The exclusive distributor, Richard-Nissan SA, of which Nissan owned 9.6%, was limited in management and marketing capability. Thus, Nissan was making efforts to strengthen the capability of Richard-Nissan. Richard-Nissan served 203 dealers in France, most of which sold only Japanese-made cars and Nissan's Spanish-made commercial vehicles. However, these dealers were relatively small in size, varying from family-run shops with 3 to 4 employees to companies with about 20 employees.

Italy

The Italian car market, highly restricted since 1957, represented about 2 million units a year; however, in 1988, Japanese car imports were restricted to only 3,300 units, of which 750 were off-road vehicles. Fiat, which was the largest automobile company in Italy, held the highest market share not only in Italy (60%) but in all of Europe (15.5%), due in part to its dominance of the domestic market and the launch of a successful new lower-medium-sized car. However, 54% of its sales were in Italy. Expecting an end to the Italian market's restrictive quota on Japanese imports by 1992, Fiat aggressively increased its investment in production facilities and R&D, shortened the time to develop new products, and improved productivity.

A unique characteristic of the Italian car market was the large market share of the utility-class car. Italian consumers, like the French and Spanish, but unlike the other Europeans, tended to be price rather than quality sensitive.

Nissan sold through 160 dealerships organized under Nissan Italia SpA, a joint venture of Nissan (64.2%) and NMISA (35.8%). However, because the company's car imports had been so restricted, these dealers were experienced mainly in selling Spanish-manufactured commercial vehicles, which accounted for 6,200 units in 1988. Therefore, because the average dealership had fewer than 10 employees and sold other companies' vehicles as well as Nissan's, sales performance was not strong. Nissan Italia planned to recruit or establish larger dealerships that were expected to stock Nissan vehicles only.

Spain

The car market in Spain expanded rapidly from a plateau of 500,000 units in 1985 to more than 1 million units in 1988. However, in 1988, the total Japanese quota was still only 3,200 units, including imports via other EC countries. This quota was slated to increase to about 7,000 in 1990 and, eventually, be integrated into the voluntary ceiling on total Japanese imports into EC countries.

Spanish market characteristics were similar to those in France and Italy; car demand concentrated on utility, supermini, and lower-medium classes, and price tended to be more important than quality.

Although Spain's car market was the fifth largest in Europe in unit sales, it had outstripped the United Kingdom in production to become the fourth largest since 1984 because of heavy investment by foreign companies attracted by lower labor costs and Spain's entry into the EC. However, all Spanish car manufacturers were controlled by foreign companies. Among them, SEAT, an affiliate of Volkswagen, was positioned as a base for manufacturing smaller cars for southern Europe and considered fairly competitive.

Japanese companies had little business presence in passenger cars. However, regarding commercial vehicles, Nissan carried out local production through NMISA and held about a 20% market share in 1987. Also, Suzuki bought 17% of a local commercial vehicle manufacturer. Land-Rover Santana SA, which made a small four-wheel-drive off-road vehicle in Spain.

Although NMISA had 143 dealers for selling its commercial vehicles, it served also as a local distributor of Nissan's passenger cars. With 70 to 80 employees, the dealerships were on average relatively larger than those in other European countries. But, because they handled mostly commercial vehicles, they had very limited experience in selling passenger cars. Recognizing the need to alter the dealerships, Nissan asked them to meet appropriate standards as to space, appearance, capital, organization, and other qualities conducive to selling passenger cars.

Other Countries

In addition to the "Big Five," the Japanese held more than a 30% market share in countries such as Ireland, Denmark, Finland, Norway, and Austria, which had no automobile industry and no restrictions on car imports. Even in other European countries, such as the Netherlands, Belgium, Sweden, and Switzerland, the Japanese held more than a 20% market share, except in Portugal, where quotas were enforced. Consequently, room for raising market share was limited. Also, because individual market sizes were small, Nissan could not depend much on additional sales in these countries as it expanded production in the United Kingdom.

However, the three major southern European markets, France, Italy, and Spain, were large in size and underexploited due to import restrictions. And in Italy and Spain, the UK-made Bluebird was expected to be approved for import as an EC-made car. Even in France, importation was close to being conceded, though some uncertainties remained. Therefore, it was mostly agreed within Nissan that to increase sales in Europe on a large scale, exploiting these three markets would be critical.

Promotion Strategy

Sekiguchi and Gomi consulted with their colleagues on Nissan's marketing strategy for southern Europe. All agreed that the European market was important and that the three southern countries needed to be exploited in order to retain the competitive advantage in Europe. And they agreed to market five or six car models, including the Bluebird and the New Micra, in the three countries. The major issue was how to allocate marketing resources between the two UK-made models, because both the cars were strategically important yet available marketing funds for the three countries were limited.

The most significant constraint was on the advertising budget. Nissan advertising in Europe was placed by Nissan itself, by national distributors, and by local dealers. Nissan's advertising copy was created first in English, translated into the appropriate language, and exposed to all European countries at the same time with the same message. Consequently, it was not that easy to stress a particular model for a particular country.

Advertising by each local distributor was prepared separately, though guided by Nissan's total marketing strategy for Europe. Distributor advertisements were paid for mostly out of their 12% margins and placed mainly in print media. The importance of television advertising was increasing, though its role was still relatively limited compared with that in North America or Japan. Recently, the West German distributor, planning to run a large-scale TV campaign, had asked Nissan to bear some part of the cost. In France, Italy, and Spain the distributors' small sales volumes restricted the level of their advertising budgets. Any mass medium advertising in these markets would therefore have to focus on either the Bluebird or the New Micra, even if Nissan or Nissan Europe provided supplemental funds.

Dealer advertisements, which were placed mostly in print media, were often funded by local distributors—so long as the advertising met certain content criteria—usually up to 50% of their cost. These allowances to dealers reduced correspondingly the size of distributor advertising budgets.

Bluebird versus New Micra

Executives supporting the New Micra pointed to the relatively faster growth in sales of small cars and emphasized that a higher percentage of consumers in the southern European countries purchased smaller cars. They asserted that these markets where more potential demand existed should be targeted. And, to establish strong distribution channels, Nissan needed a rapid sales increase, which was more likely to be accomplished by the New Micra than the Bluebird.

That the New Micra would not face direct competition with other Japanese companies was another important factor in its favor. Nissan felt uneasy about competitors of similar background and image, though it would also have to compete with local European companies. But the only other Japanese car company currently engaged in local production was Honda, which jointly manufactured medium-sized cars with the Rover Group in the United Kingdom. Although Toyota decided to start local production in the United Kingdom in 1992 and needed to exploit the French, Italian, and Spanish markets for the same reasons as Nissan, the model to be manufactured in the Toyota UK factory was an upper-medium-sized car. Moreover, Nissan executives were confident that no other Japanese car company could manufacture in Europe a supermini-class car like the New Micra, at least not before 1992. Therefore, the New Micra would be insulated from direct Japanese competition for a while.

One of the major reasons for supporting the Bluebird was that its profit margin per unit was higher than that for the New Micra. Also, emphasizing the Bluebird would generate further increases in unit profit contribution because of experience curve and scale economy effects in the UK factory. If the New Micra were emphasized, reaching break-even on Bluebird production in the UK factory would be delayed.

Another reason for supporting the Bluebird was the probability that the New Micra would attract more attention among Nissan's European competitors. Major southern European car companies like Fiat, Peugeot, and Renault, which were very influential in automobile-related policy making in their respective countries, focused mainly on the small-sized-car market, especially in southern Europe.

Accordingly, stressing the New Micra meant head-on competition with these companies and, in the long term, could cause further trade friction, which in turn might result in regulations detrimental to Japanese car companies.

Furthermore, Nissan's image in Europe had to be considered. Formerly, European countries had been in advance of Japan in developing the medium- or small-sized car; therefore, Japanese car designers had some yearning for the European car. Then, Japanese car companies became competitive in the North American and European markets by improving production technology and manufacturing efficiencies. However, differing from North America, where the Japanese had earlier faced no direct local competition for medium- or small-sized cars, Europe had had several competitive local manufacturers in those classes of car. Thus, in Europe, the Japanese car had long been regarded as low priced, and higher-priced Japanese cars had tended to sell poorly. But the image of Japanese cars was improving, and they were now regarded as superior in quality to French and Italian cars, though still inferior to the West German.

At the same time, each Japanese company tried to create its own unique image. For example, Toyota featured high performance, Honda emphasized upgraded value-added cars, and Mazda focused on building market share in sophisticated, performance-oriented West Germany, making special efforts to develop cars tailored to the European market. Among these competitors, Nissan was seen as an average Japanese carmaker. Hence, it sometimes happened that Nissan perpetuated the low-priced car image of the Japanese car, and focusing on the New Micra would reinforce this view.

However, in the three southern European countries, Nissan was not a well-known name, except in Spain, thanks to its locally produced commercial vehicles. Because sales were currently low due to import restrictions, Nissan executives believed it would be important to raise awareness immediately upon the lifting of the restrictions in order to obtain a favorable competitive position in these countries. The New Micra, with its broader appeal and promise of higher unit sales volume, seemed to be the model to emphasize.

13

MCDONALD'S
The Greening of the Golden Arches

Go away. We don't want your garbage: we've got no place to put it, and enough pollution problems already so don't think you can just burn it . . .

We don't want companies which kill rain forests to raise cattle.

Sure, your hamburgers might take five minutes to eat, but your packaging will take the earth several centuries to digest.

These were just some of the comments that Peter Oehl, director of environmental affairs for McDonald's Germany, continued to see in the papers with growing frequency since the late 1980s. They came from city councilmen, governmental ministers, and environmental demonstrators alike. He reflected:

The problem of paper litter and waste has been haunting us for almost 20 years. We can't seem to win: we tell people that we don't purchase beef raised on rain forest land, but it doesn't seem to make the slightest bit of difference. We tell them we're doing more about recycling than most other companies, but look at what happens . . . What do they expect us to do?

A "grand opening," as McDonald's employees called it, was always a major event for the company, and everyone involved tried to make certain that all the right local notables, celebrities, and press be present at the opening of the first McDonald's in what had been East Germany. It was to be carried out in the way that McDonald's, the American fast-food giant, knew best—with marching bands, much fanfare, balloons, lights, and the famous "arches." The restaurant staff had also been geared up, ready to handle the eager and curious customers who were expected to stream in on that cold day in December 1990.

This case was prepared by Professor Sandra Vandermerwe and Dr. Marika Taishoff. Copyright © 1991 by the International Institute for Management Development (IMD), Lausanne, Switzerland. Not to be used or reproduced without permission. IMD case 398.

243

Despite the numerous meetings and information exchanges with the authorities, Oehl and his colleagues had had a hard time avoiding a repeat of the East Berlin incident. There the city council had refused to give the company permission to set up a mobile "Big Mac" stand in Alexanderplatz, the historical center of Berlin. The reason? They wanted to limit street vendors and the litter they inevitably created. And so, McDonald's decided to set up its Big Mac store in a smaller city. Although ecologically devastated, the focus of contention in East Germany was around the litter resulting from McDonald's packaging.

McDonald's Formula for Success

From day one, the concept was simple and would be the pivotal feature in what became an American, and an international, symbol of the ease and convenience of the postwar consumer society.

After World War II, Richard and Maurice McDonald were having trouble staffing their San Bernardino, California, carhop restaurant; there was the usual parade of drunks and drifters. "We said," Dick McDonald recalled, "let's get rid of it all. Out went dishes, glasses, and silverware. Out went service, the dishwashers, and the long menu. We decided to serve just hamburgers, drinks, and french fries on paper plates. Everything prepared in advance, everything uniform. All geared to heavy volume in a short amount of time."

When Ray Kroc, a milkshake multimixer salesman, came across the McDonald brothers' diner in 1954, he was astounded: "This little drive-in had people standing in line. The volume was incredible." Together with the two brothers, they began to sell franchises, and in 1955 the first of the Golden Arches opened for business.

McDonald's launched the fast-food industry. Ten years after its creation, the company had sold 3 billion hamburgers from its 1,000+ outlets. During the 1970s, it grew an average of almost 30% annually, a growth rate which was propelled by increasing the number of units by an average annual rate of 15%, extending store hours to include breakfast, expanding the menu and concurrently the check size, and adding new services such as the Drive-Thru window.

In the affluent postwar years, suburbia fanned out and each family had at least one car; people became more mobile and less patient; they hated to wait—especially for fast food. At McDonald's, all a customer had to do was pull up, order, and eat the already prepared food on site or, simpler still, take it away in handy, throwaway cartons and packaging. Individual disposable wrappings soon replaced the large refillable dispensers for ketchup, mustard, dressing, salt, pepper, and sugar.

The tight standards that the company insisted on were expressed by its motto, "QSCV"—quality, service, cleanliness, value. The McDonald's "Hamburger University" was established to ensure that all employees be uniformly trained to apply these quality criteria in all behind-the-counter operations and counter procedures. In addition to quality, the company's strategy focused on quick service at affordable prices. Buns, french fries, and meat patties were delivered in large corrugated containers, salads came prepackaged, and the bulk of the kitchen work was limited to deep frying according to standardized procedures. McDonald's employees did not wait on tables or wash dishes; they flipped hamburgers and worked the checkout counters. Customer waiting time had to be kept to a carefully determined minimum, so the burgers and fries were prepared in advance and kept as warm and moist as possible for peak hour crowds. The art was not just to be able to prepare a burger in 1 minute, but to be able to serve it in no more than 10; afterwards, it had to be thrown away.

Worldwide Growth and Garbage

The company's growth surged throughout the 1970s and 1980s, and McDonald's became as recognizable a feature of America as Disneyland. The hamburger chain, which spent over 6% of its total sales on advertising, was among the most advertised single brands in the world. Almost $1 million a day was spent on television spots. In any given year, 96% of American consumers ate at a McDonald's, and the chain served 7% of the US population every day.

Between 1979 and 1989, the company's systemwide compound annual growth rate was 12%, of which US sales accounted for 10% and international sales 19%; during that same decade, its compound annual growth in net income was 14% and in net income per share 16%; its assets grew by 15% and return on common stock by 25%. It was not long before the arches began to appear on the international landscape as well. In 1985, international sales constituted 20% of total sales; in 1989 they jumped to 30%. Of the 11,500 outlets worldwide, 8,000 were in the United States. By the end of the 1980s, McDonald's was the largest restaurant chain in England, Germany, Canada, Australia, and Japan; it was the most successful American retailer in the international market and the largest owner of retail property in the world.

In 1990, too, despite predictions of a slowdown in the fast-food industry, the company posted record earnings, increasing its worldwide sales to $18.76 billion from $17.33 billion. Although sales per store in the United States diminished somewhat, and quarterly earnings growth was not as dramatic as in the previous decade, this was more than offset by the strong growth in overseas operations. McDonald's was now the largest food service organization in the world.

Although fast-food competitors soon came on the scene, McDonald's stayed ahead with over 30% of the market. During the 80s, the two major competitors, Wendy's and Burger King, each closed about 150 restaurants annually, while McDonald's was opening a new one every 17 hours. The company viewed any establishment that sold food—quick-service eating establishments, mom-and-pop stores, take-outs, pizza parlors, coffee shops, convenience food stores, delis, supermarket freezers, and microwave ovens—as competition.

Despite instructions, which were in place almost from day one of the company's existence, that restaurant crews pick up all paper wrappings, napkins, soda goblets, and other typical fast-food remnants within a one-block radius of each establishment, the litter around the stores quickly accumulated. By the 70s, this situation stoked the anger of conservationists, such leading US consumer advocates as Ralph Nader, and environmental lobbies, which conducted a series of analyses to determine the source of the waste, as well as where and how it was destined to ultimately end up.

When such groups wanted to know "How many trees have to be cut down just to end up as street litter afterwards?" it was a prelude to the debate that would emerge a decade later about McDonald's role in the deforestation of the Brazilian rainforest.

From Paper to Plastic Packaging

In 1976 the company decided to switch to polystyrene packaging, which was more cost effective than paper. Polystyrene, a rigid transparent thermoplastic with excellent electrical and physical insulating properties, was a lightweight material derived from petroleum and natural gas by-products. McDonald's contracted the Stanford Research Institute to perform an environmental impact study in the United States comparing paper packaging with the proposed polystyrene plastic packaging.

The institute analyzed the two packaging alternatives from a variety of aspects, ranging from source to disposal: the amount of energy to manufacture, resource depletion, weight and volume in landfills, and potential for recycling. Based on these criteria, the study concluded:

1. There appears to be no supportable basis for any claim that paper-related products are superior from an environmental standpoint to plastic-related ones, including polystyrene;
2. The weight of existing evidence to date, for which there is no countermanding data, indicates that the favorable true environmental balance, if any, would be in the direction of the plastic-related product.

Based on these findings, beginning in 1977 McDonald's started using polystyrene instead of paper wherever possible, especially for its beverage cups and goblets, sandwich containers, and clamshell hamburger containers. The company believed that it was not only behaving ecologically, but that its customers would also get improved products and service; polystyrene retained heat, moisture, and freshness better, and was "cleaner" than paper since it stopped grease spills. Shortly thereafter, foam plastic accounted for 75% of McDonald's total plastic use; plastic forks, knives, and spoons; cup and salad bowl lid covers; and coffee stirrers accounted for the remaining 25% of plastic used.

During the 80s, the environmental movement began to gather steam. Waste was measured, litter was scrutinized, and fingers continued to point. As the number of hamburgers sold each year at McDonald's increased, so too did the consumer protest over the amount of packaging waste. In the United States the company's marketing people soon had to deal with the bags of letters reproaching the company for its role in garbage production. Schoolchildren began sending boxes of the foam clamshell back to the firm with notes blaming it for littering streets, choking waste bins, and cluttering landfills.

Cost Initiatives and Environmental Repercussions

The accelerating rise in US per capita solid waste generation led to an equally steep drop in available landfill space: In 1975 there were 18,500 landfill sites; less than a decade later only 6,000 remained, and it was estimated that only half of those would be operative by the mid-1990s. In most countries in Europe, the situation was even worse by the end of the 80s, with most landfills closed and recourse to incineration contraindicated due to air pollution effects.

To minimize the use of resources and reduce waste and pollution, McDonald's took several initiatives:

- In 1978, the weight of sandwich wrap was reduced, resulting in a packaging reduction of 3 million pounds a year.
- In 1981, the large fry box was redesigned, lowering packaging weight by 600,000 pounds per year.
- Corrugated dividers were removed from cup packaging, thus saving 2 million pounds of paper.
- In 1983, the heavy paper-foam hot cup was replaced by a light foam-only cup, a packaging reduction of more than a million pounds a year.
- In 1984, the thickness of the foam sandwich container was reduced by 28%, saving 3 million pounds in packaging.
- Shaving the straws by 25% saved 2 million pounds of packaging.
- In 1987, two years before being required by international legislation, McDonald's instructed its suppliers to cease using CFCs as an expansion agent in the manufacture of polystyrene foam cups.
- In 1989, a new Coke distribution system was initiated; rather than shipping the soft drink mix in cartons to all the outlets, the syrup was pumped directly from delivery trucks into tanks in the restaurants, thereby saving two million pounds of packaging.

These measures, together with some others, helped the company in the United States reduce the amount of its packaging waste by over 24 million pounds within the space of a decade. (Refer to Exhibit 1 for US waste stream composition, and Exhibit 2 for a breakdown of waste at a McDonald's outlet in the United States.)

McDonald's became the largest user of recycled paper in the restaurant industry worldwide, spending $60 million a year on recycled paper for its 2 billion tray liners and napkins and for its 500 million "Happy Meal" boxes. The company's 1989 annual report, which focused on the environment, was printed entirely on recycled paper generated from the paper waste of its offices and outlets worldwide.

Extensive advertising budgets were allocated by marketing for communicating these initiatives to customers. A campaign was also launched that categorically denied any responsibility for the destruction of the Brazilian rainforest:

EXHIBIT 1

US waste stream composition (by weight)

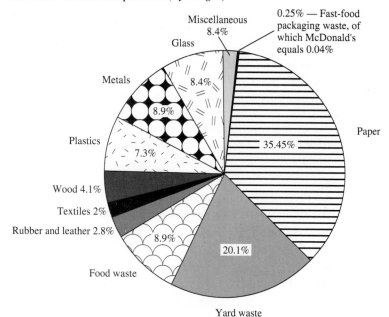

SOURCE: Adapted from Franklin Associates Ltd., 1989. Reprinted in "McDonald's and the Environment" (McDonald's publication, 1990).

EXHIBIT 2

Major sources of waste at McDonald's USA

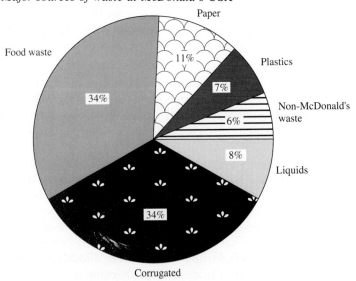

SOURCE: Adapted from *The Wall Street Journal*, April 17, 1991.

Nowhere in the world, consumers were informed, did McDonald's purchase beef which had been raised on rainforest land. Similar campaigns were intended to exonerate the firm from damage to the ozone layer.

The Plastic Dilemma

Plastics continued to be singled out as major culprits in the US landfill shortage problem since, in contrast to yard waste and papers, both organic in nature, plastics were synthetic and were not biodegradable in landfills.

In the United States, 1 billion pounds of polystyrene were produced annually for the food service packaging industry; McDonald's purchased 75 million pounds of it. Once dumped, polystyrene accounted for ¼ of 1 percent of landfill volume. The 4,000 pounds of polystyrene waste generated annually by each fast-food restaurant was equal to ⅐ of 1 percent of total waste.

McDonald's justified its continued use of polystyrene to customers and environmental interest groups through PR, marketing, and advertising campaigns, concentrating on:

- *Recyclability:* Polystyrene was 100% recyclable and could be made into a variety of products such as serving trays, carpet fibers, insulation board, videocassettes, park benches, and garbage bins.
- *Separability:* Wax-coated paper, the suggested alternative to polystyrene, was not a good idea, McDonald's countered, because the wax and the paper would have to be separated before recycling.
- *Biodegradability:* Refuting the biodegradability arguments used by those who supported paper-based packaging, findings at the University of Arizona revealed that paper in a landfill, with no exposure to air, water, and microorganisms, would not readily decompose, and in fact the process could take decades.
- *Energy efficiency:* Paper mills consumed more energy and produced more waste water than foam manufacturing plants did, according to a study by the US Environmental Protection Agency.
- *Sanitation:* A study by the American Public Health Association confirmed that reusable plates, cups, and utensils were much less sanitary than disposable products.
- *Incineration:* Polystyrene foam was safer and less expensive to incinerate than paper since, when incinerated, it produced harmless, nontoxic ash, carbon dioxide, and water.

The fact that polystyrene did not decompose was also considered a positive factor, since, chemically inert, it could not create dangerous toxics in the decomposition process. Also, although foam packaging appeared bulky, 90% was air which compressed easily in a compactor or under the weight of a landfill. Using a study by the German Society for Research into the Packaging Market, the company stated that alternatives to plastic packaging would result in a 404% increase in the weight of waste thrown into landfills, and 256% in the volume of such waste.

Critics still pointed out that the manufacture of plastics depended on nonrenewable resources (i.e., on oil and petroleum), while paper was based on a renewable resource. Moreover, they added, while paper recycling was a well-established practice with a growing market demand, this was not the case for plastics; most plastics were simply being dumped. Plastics were more difficult to recycle; only 1% were being recycled in the United States and 5% in Europe. The comparative figures for paper recycling were 25% in the United States and 45% in Europe.

McDonald's realized that in order to be truly committed to the environment, it would have to do more than just say so. Some firm steps would be needed, but it could not take them all alone, and suppliers would have to become even more involved.

Working with the Suppliers

In 1989, in response to mounting consumer pressure, McDonald's instructed its more than 700 suppliers worldwide that, if they wished to continue to do business with the firm, they would have to adapt their products and packaging to the new and increasingly rigorous environmental standards that the company had now staked its image on and assumed responsibility for.

These suppliers ranged from agricultural, livestock, and dairy producers, to drinks manufacturers, and to paper, corrugated, and plastics suppliers. In the United States, the environmental directives were aimed almost exclusively at packaging suppliers. The new requirements that suppliers had to fulfill ranged from using corrugated boxes with at least 35% recycled content through the directive that the thickness of foam containers be reduced by 29% and the weight of plastic straws and sandwich wrappers be another 20% lighter. The same directives were applied in Europe, where agricultural suppliers were also requested to use fertilizers and pesticides that were environmentally safe.

In late 1989 McDonald's, together with eight leading plastics suppliers—including Amoco, Mobil, and the major polystyrene manufacturer Dow—announced a trial program to begin collecting polystyrene food containers from 450 New England restaurants in the United States. The program, the initial cost of which was $16 million, was intended to eventually become national in scope.

The plastics producers formed a new company that would purchase a recycling facility and build others across the United States; McDonald's subsidized the collection and hauling costs. The goal was to recycle, by 1995, at least 25% of the 1 billion pounds of polystyrene used in food services packaging. In order to make the plan work, restaurant patrons were asked to dispose of their plastic containers separately in specially marked baskets. The separate handling of the plastic packaging and the education of customers was estimated to cost each store $400 a month.

Back to Paper

Despite these initiatives, consumers continued to write letters and complain to the company about its waste, and pressure continued to escalate. Ralph Nader stated blatantly that grassroots environmental groups were not convinced that McDonald's was serious about creating a better environment, and the American conservationist group Friends of the Earth said that if the chain were really serious, it would give customers the choice of eating from a real plate.

In August 1990, in a dramatic move, the company signed an agreement with the Environmental Defense Fund. The EDF, a Washington-based public policy group, established itself as a major lobbying organization representing consumers' environmental concerns in 1972 when it succeeded in banning the insecticide DDT from the American market. Now the EDF and McDonald's would create a joint task force to study the solid waste problem and arrive at mutually acceptable solutions.

The EDF task force members were allowed to analyze purchasing data and were given free access to McDonald's operations and to suppliers' factories. They also had stints as fry cooks and bun flippers.

It took three months for the first recommendation to be drafted by the EDF and accepted by McDonald's. As part of a package of 42 recommendations intended to reduce waste by over 80% at the 11,500 outlets within a few years, polystyrene would, after 15 years of use, be abandoned, and the company would revert to paper packaging.

McDonald's acknowledged that its decision had been open to considerable debate, especially since there was no conclusive scientific evidence to substantiate it. The bottom line, the company explained, for the drive back to paper was that there were still customers who did not understand that plastic was recyclable. The customer, the company underscored, always came first at McDonald's and always *would* come first. Since the customer did not feel happy about plastics, the company would stop using it.

The firm's participation in the polystyrene recycling program was halted, and McDonald's purchasing department now had to look to suppliers who could design and deliver efficient paper-based packaging. Marketing's efforts were geared both at attracting such suppliers and informing the American public of the company's new move.

The directive would be effective immediately in its US stores, with international operations expected to follow. While country managers were allowed some leeway in adapting the new standards to their specific market requirements, it was expected that they would abide by the directive from headquarters unless circumstances were so market specific as to warrant a different approach.

McDonald's Germany

Shortly after city officials throughout Germany began urging McDonald's to switch from disposable to reusable packaging, Peter Oehl received the news from headquarters to revert to paper. He knew he was in trouble. He was stunned by the company's decision to switch from plastic to paper, which had been the cause of so much trouble in the past 15 years. He also knew that he would not only have to justify such a radical switch to the German public, but would also have to find a practical solution about what to do with the paper after its use as packaging. And even if he abided by the US directive, how long would it be until the municipal and consumer pressure again mounted to demand a move to reusables? In any event, the European, and especially the German, situation had always been different from the one in the United States.

In 1970, when McDonald's set up its first European venture in Holland, fast food was effectively unknown in Europe. The very notion of eating out, which had become an almost routine and daily habit for Americans, was still an experience reserved for special occasions and certain lifestyles in the European market, where restaurants were tradition bound—full linen service, waiters, wine stewards, and, of course, multicourse meals. Even "family restaurants" were rare, and middle-class people did not go out to eat casually.

Despite these traditional habits and the absence of suburbia, the uniquely American concepts of quick-service food, drive-ins, and self-service restaurants caught on.

When McDonald's opened its first German restaurant in 1971, it veered away from its standard interiors and menus. It offered chicken and even played with the idea of serving bratwurst. In Germany, hamburgers were associated with natives of Hamburg, but not with meat. Beer was on the menu, too, and the somber wood-paneled interiors resembled German *bierkellers*.

However, that look had discouraged families from going inside, and the beer encouraged motorcycle gangs to loiter outside. Not until the German outlets were located in downtown areas, and standardized in appearance with a menu identical to the one in America, did the chain begin to prosper. Creative and humorous advertising concepts were used to deflect criticism that American eating habits were denigrating German culture. By 1990, McDonald's was the leading restaurant operator in Germany, with 330 outlets, annual sales of over DM 1 billion, and major plans to be the first fast-food operator in the former East Germany.

The Challenge for McDonald's Germany

A lot had been riding on the creation of the post of director of environmental affairs, which the board of directors offered Peter Oehl in 1988. Over 80% of German consumers were willing to pay more for environmentally sound goods, and incidents were frequent where "green" groups, as a protest against needless waste, would rip the packaging off products in supermarkets. (Refer to Exhibit 3 for an illustration of what comprises German household waste.)

Although the Green party in Germany was a political minority, its policies and principles on ecological issues were quickly adopted by all the mainstream parties. Environmental legislation in Germany reflected this popular sentiment. Of all the members of the OECD, the Germans spent the highest percentage of their GDP on environmental protection policies.

EXHIBIT 3

German waste stream composition (by weight)

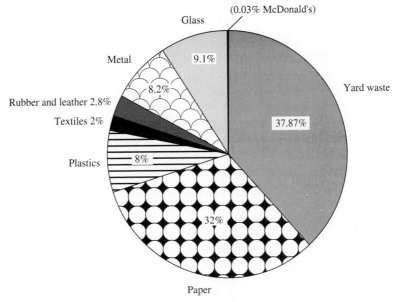

SOURCE: Adapted from Statistisches Bundesamt, 1987. Reprinted in: "Das McDonald's Umweltprogramm: Wertstoffrückgewinnung" (McDonald's Publication, 1990).

Packaging had been a special target of this legislation. By requiring distributors and retailers to be the ones to manage the problems of waste caused by consumer goods packaging, the German government effectively put the cradle-to-grave approach to product management into practice.

The lack of landfill space was common everywhere in Germany, but it was especially acute in some regions, which led to the creation and enforcement of stringent waste management requirements:

- There were 200 German cities that planned to prohibit the use of disposable packaging, in restaurants and for take-out, if the municipality had to deal with the waste that ensued.
- In other cities, the municipal authorities planned to prohibit landfilling outright except when necessary, with the burden of proving such necessity falling on the waste producer. Under such a system, if the big generators of waste—hospitals, train stations, stadiums, airports, hotels, and restaurants—needed to use a landfill, whose costs were expected to more than double by 1992, the authorities would first have to be satisfied that the material in question could not be recycled.
- Other municipal areas threatened to drastically hike—by as much as 1,600%—their fees for separating unseparated trash.

- Some cities simply refused to grant companies such as McDonald's operating licenses unless they could be satisfied beyond any doubt that the company would be able to handle its waste problem on its own, without recourse to municipal landfills or incineration.

On the day Oehl received the directive to move back to paper, he was more convinced than ever that if McDonald's were to switch its image from an "enemy of the earth" to a "caring company," it would have to look well beyond the present situation and take a leap ahead in time to anticipate the consequences, and payoffs, of its current actions. As he gazed out the window at the new "Hamburger University," still under construction at McDonald's Munich-based German headquarters and which was intended, like its American prototype, to imbue all McDonald's employees with the company's standards of quality and operational principles, he thought:

> By the time that building is finished, I'll make certain that all the graduates know more than just what a recyclable plastic is. What I want is for them to understand, and have the courage to apply, the kinds of changes that will be necessary. And this means starting right from the beginning of the process, making sure that our cattle are "happy cows" living under the right conditions, through to the ingredients in our food and the processes we use in the kitchen, all the way to making sure that every bit of waste we create can be used and reused again and again, eventually as biogas to fuel our stores.

Closing the Loop

The leap ahead in time that the German situation required, he knew, meant more than switching from plastic to paper or even from a disposable plate to a reusable one. Ideally, Oehl envisaged that 100% of the material that remained on site after original use—organic, paper, and plastic—should be recyclable, reusable, or convertible into energy: in other words, capable of being transformed into valuable goods.

Forty-four percent of McDonald's waste was kitchen waste, 14% was plastic, and 42% paper. (Refer to Exhibit 4 for a breakdown of waste in McDonald's Germany.) If the company were to achieve the zero waste scenario that Oehl intended, these materials would first have to be collected and separated. Then, through an integrated separation and recycling process, remade and reused, either in their original forms—as packaging, for example—or as a new product—a waste bin, for instance, remanufactured from McDonald's plastic waste, or leftover shortening treated and then reused by the cosmetics industry.

Based on his discussions with specialized waste engineering firms and other experts, a five-step process would be necessary if the amount of waste destined for landfills or incinerators were to be reduced to almost zero:

1. The packaging material used for delivering the buns, meat patties, and condiments to each restaurant, as well as the packaging the restaurant used for its own meals, would have to be standardized.

EXHIBIT 4

Major sources of waste at McDonald's Germany

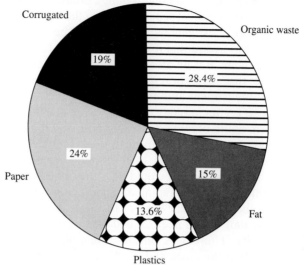

SOURCE: Adapted from "Das McDonald's Umweltprogramm: Wertstoffrückgewinnung" (McDonald's Publication, 1990).

2. Unnecessary packaging, both for in-house and takeaway sales, would have to be reduced.

3. Customers and/or McDonald's employees would have to separate those materials, such as cardboard, plastics, and metal cans, for which existing collecting and recycling systems were available.

4. The remaining waste mixture—primarily paper, small plastic items, and food—would then be treated in an integrated system in which the plastic would be chemically broken down to be recycled, and the paper and organics processed into compost and biogas.

5. Ultimately, these new raw materials could be reused within the restaurant chain itself as a source of construction material, road gravel, and energy sources for stores.

Oehl found two firms that, if they worked together, could make the system feasible: BTA, a small Munich-based waste engineering firm, which had developed a process to separate plastics and other lighter material from paper and organic waste, and then convert that paper and organic waste into compost while effectively creating biogas as an alternative source of energy; and Belland, a Swiss plastics engineering company, which had already spent SF 70 million in an attempt to develop and produce a group of water-soluble plastic polymers.

The fast-food chain had already invested SF 2.4 million in developing a project with Belland to find a plastic with built-in separability and recyclability suitable for use in all consumer packaging. The idea, Oehl reasoned, was to seek out the "chemical fingerprints" in those plastics. The major advantage of the Belland technology was that it built a breaking point into the polymer chain which allowed easy chemical separation from the other materials. If this could be applied to consumer packaging as well, it would be the key to cost-effective recycling.

Oehl was aware that it was much harder to take chemicals apart than it was to combine them. But he also knew that, as the crucial first step in closing the loop on waste, this separation process warranted more than an advertising expense. It required investment and commitment.

The BTA technology was based on the use of microorganisms that could transform liquid organic waste into biogas, which, once purified, could be used as a source of energy—one-third to meet the needs of the process itself, with the remaining two-thirds sold to third-party markets as energy. The solid organic waste, as well as paper, would be transformed into almost heavy-metal-free compost suitable for landscaping and gardening.

For such a circular system to work, a BTA plant with an attached Belland recycling unit would need 20,000 tons of waste annually; McDonald's generated 15,000 tons. There was only one test-plant site in Germany, and, taking into consideration the costs and time involved in the logistics, Oehl reasoned that 15 fully operating plants would have to be constructed throughout the country, within a 50-kilometer radius of each major city, at a total cost of DM 250 million. He began negotiating with other major waste producers, including hospitals, airports, stadiums, hotels, and restaurants.

The average cost to handle one ton of waste in a landfill in 1990 was DM 200; to incinerate a ton would cost DM 250. The cost of hauling a ton of waste to either a municipal landfill or incineration site was DM 130. All these prices were expected to at least double within the next two to four years. The estimated processing cost per ton of waste using the McDonald's/Belland/BTA system was expected to be approximately DM 200. The price of hauling the waste depended heavily on how many plants could be constructed and how their distribution service network could be designed.

It was clear to Oehl, as he reread the memo announcing the move back to paper, that he would have to think things through very carefully before making a recommendation to his management. Simply abiding by the US decision, ignoring it, or looking for other solutions was a question of weighing the various pros and cons:

> After all, the German market is so different from the American one, and we've already spent so much money and effort on environmental R&D in plastics. My solution could be even more cost effective than the existing one if we could involve the other fast-food chains and some other industries, and so create economies of scale.
>
> On the other hand, one of the key factors for our worldwide strength and reputation is the consistency of our products and services everywhere. Would marketing be able to sell the idea to customers who were so antiplastic? What if it costs more? Consumers may say that they'd pay more for "green" products, but would they be willing to pay more for a Big Mac if the new packaging ends up costing more?

There are some people in the company who say we should take a lower profile on the environment. According to them, we've already gotten ourselves into enough trouble without being able to please anyone. McDonald's should just stick to making and selling fast food and avoid any risky ideas, especially since US quarterly earnings figures are down . . .

I *know* that constantly looking for green-friendly packaging alternatives is the kind of halfway measure which can never work in the long term. We must be able to deliver the same kind of uncompromising excellence in the environmental arena as we do with our hamburgers and our in-store service.

Customers have always come first for the company, and making certain that they are happy is a prime corporate objective. Should customers drive the decision on this one? Maybe once and for all we simply have to do the things we believe are right, even if it means that our customers will be unhappy for a while.

And if I decide not to abide by headquarters' decision, how will I be able to explain it to them?

JIFFY

Managing for Customer Orientation

14

"Who really are our customers? To be quite honest, we just don't know." It was a comment Peter Lewis would never forget. One of Jiffy Packaging Company Ltd.'s seasoned old salesmen had uttered it shortly after Lewis's arrival as managing director of the firm in February 1991. The salesman had gone on to say that every single firm in the Winsford Industrial Estate near Manchester, where Jiffy Packaging was located, as well as those in every other industrial park in the United Kingdom, was a potential customer. In fact, every firm, from the giant multinationals to the corner shops, used protective packaging in one form or another. "But, to really find out who they are, you'd probably have to go and ask the distributors," the salesman had concluded.

The comment that had bothered Peter Lewis then was of even greater concern to him now, eight months later. It had been one of the issues that he and his management team had been confronting on a regular basis since his arrival at the firm. Now that the customer survey was completed and ready for discussion, perhaps more light could be shed on what was really happening in the marketplace.

Lewis parked his car and reached for his attaché case, heavy because of the 250-page customer survey. He quickly made his way to the central building. Commissioning the survey had been one of his first actions as managing director of Jiffy; after three months of preparation, it was now time to make decisions. He passed the lorries, still loading up the pallets of protective packaging—everything from large bundles of bubble wrap to rolls of corrugated paper, layers of foam and laminate, and the famous yellow paper-cushioned Jiffy postal bags—from the warehouse to be transported to distributors throughout the United Kingdom.

The three other members of his management team—the director of production and operations, the director of finance, and the sales director—were already

This case was prepared by Professor Sandra Vandermerwe and Dr. Marika Taishoff. Copyright © 1993 by the International Management Development Institute (IMD), Lausanne, Switzerland. Not to be used or reproduced without permission directly from IMD. IMD case 435.

seated when Lewis entered his office, the only one large enough to accommodate them all.

Each of the men had by now studied his copy of the survey. "Well gentlemen," Lewis began, "We have the facts: What our distributors have to say is pretty much in this document. And now it's up to us to decide how to conduct business in the future and with whom. What we can't do any longer is sit back believing everything is OK because we are the UK's number one protective packaging manufacturer." He poured himself a strong cup of black coffee from the thermos flask.

"Well, one thing is sure," Cy Brown, director of operations and production, replied. "Our product still has the best technical quality. The Americans and Japanese can try all they like, but they can't beat us on that score."

"Sure, but they're still making inroads into our market," Lewis replied. "Why? If our products are better and we are flexible on price, I can't see any good reason for distributors to choose them."

"It's easy—they're bucking the system: They're going direct, avoiding distributors on some of the major lines and customers, cutting prices. Even though I sometimes get the impression," Brown glanced at James Stade, Jiffy's sales director, "that our salespeople are virtually giving away most of our products."

"Hold it," Stade interrupted. "This is not the good old days, when we were the only ones making the padded bag and distributors banged down our doors for our products. Today, we've got to negotiate on price; it's the name of the game, especially with the reputation we've got for being a premium pricer."

There was pause, interrupted by Martin Ashe, director of finance. "If our products are top quality, made from the best materials money can buy, we have a right to higher margins. Yet here we are: Distributors are driving prices down, and our market share and ROI is taking a knock."

Lewis rose and walked over to the window which overlooked the road. The lorries were slowly rumbling out of the industrial park, heading off in different directions. He continued: "From what I can tell, if we believe this document, our customers are trying to tell us something and it's not just about the technical product or the price. And, unless we are prepared to seriously take note and do things differently, we can never hope to regain our profitability, let alone lead the industry."

Jiffy's History and Culture

Jiffy Packaging Company Ltd. was established in 1963 following an agreement between the Baldwin Company Ltd. of Manchester and Birmingham in the United Kingdom, and the Jiffy Manufacturing Company based in New Jersey in the United States. The Baldwin Company, which began operations in 1896 as a manufacturer of wood wool, began producing cushion pads after World War II. The 1963 agreement with the American company gave the Baldwin company the exclusive manufacturing rights for the Jiffy Padded Bag in the United Kingdom and Ireland.

Jiffy had always been run as a private family-owned business, with a culture strongly influenced and dominated by the Baldwins: They were the ones who made the decisions that employees were expected to follow to the letter. Tasks were preset and specified, and people were expected to get on with them. Consequently, there was no emphasis on teaming and little formal occasion for upper- or middle-management employees to get together and discuss company strategy or objectives. Not only was there no occasion for such gatherings, there was no physical forum for them: Jiffy's headquarters had no conference room or office large enough for group sessions. Offices were small, separated by walls, flights of stairs, and narrow corridors.

Under the leadership of the two Baldwin brothers, known as Mr. Brian and Mr. Jonathan to employees, turnover and profits grew rapidly over the next quarter-century at the family-owned business. Beginning in 1964, Jiffy began to extend its product range, including the distribution of packaging materials other than wood wool. In 1968, the company began producing the Jiffy range of corrugated, laminated, paper protective packaging materials.

In 1975, Jiffy slowly began phasing out production of wood wool, replacing it in 1982 with the first polyethylene foam plank, known as Jiffycel. Three years later, the company began producing polyethylene bubble packaging, an air-filled plastic material, which it soon utilised in the Mailmiser Jiffy Bag, a lower weight version of the Jiffy Cushioned Postal Bag that was reputedly as strong but much cheaper. In early 1987, Jiffy gave its distribution arm its own identity under the name of Ambassador Packaging Ltd.

Throughout the 80s, supported by strong economic growth, the company's profits grew by 5% a year. The Baldwins' key objective had always been bottom line results, and, by mid-decade, they had stopped making any new capital or equipment investments. By the late 80s, certain regions—especially those around the Manchester area—began to feel the pinch of the recession. Environmental concerns were mounting rapidly, with plastics industries being scrutinized and singled out as environmental offenders by watchdog agencies and by municipal and legislative authorities. Increasingly, it became apparent that major investments would have to made by these industries if the penalties and fines soon to be levied against environmental offenders were to be avoided. Until the sale of the company, no environmental initiatives had been taken by Jiffy's management.

In 1988, turnover was £15 million, having plateaued after eight years of steady increase; its market share also stabilized, though as the recession progressed further, the size of the market began to shrink. That same year, the directors of the Baldwin Group Ltd., who owned all the shares of Jiffy Packaging Company Ltd., sold the company to the Dutch paper, packaging, and printing company Buhrmann Tetterode (BT). The previous management team continued to run the business, although with the Baldwins gone, the once cohesive board began to disintegrate because of infighting and politicking. Between 1989 and 1990, the company's ROI was reduced by almost half—from 27% to 15%—and, with adjustments for inflation, profits were down by 8%.

In June 1990, the entire board of directors resigned, to take effect one year later. At the same time, BT decided that Jiffy and Ambassador would report as two separate companies to the president of Buhrmann Tetterode's Flexible and

Protective Packaging Division. Ambassador had thus become an entirely independent company, allowed to do business with any supplier it wished and no longer locked into Jiffy alone.

Jiffy's Product Line

Jiffy's business was founded on protective packaging, a material used to cushion objects from damage during transport or storage. Objects requiring protection under such conditions were small or large, of high or low value—anything subject to breakage or spoilage when moved, delivered, or sent.

Products made by Jiffy were both paper and plastics based. Prior to the 1988 divestiture, Paper Packaging and Plastic Packaging were two separate divisions of the company, housed in different sectors of the Winsford Industrial Park. Following BT's purchase of the company, the two divisions were replaced by six basic product lines: postal bags (both paper and plastic), plastic bubble wrap, plastic foam, plank, laminates, and corrugated paper products. (For a breakdown of these product lines, together with their general application possibilities, refer to Exhibits 1 and 2.)

The most well-known product by far was the original cushioned Jiffy postal bag; the brand, synonomous with cushioned padded envelopes, had become a generic term—like Hoover, Xerox, and Kleenex. No one else made a paper-cushioned bag in the United Kingdom. As a highly branded product, the Jiffy Bag was unique, with very specific and evident applications. It was also by far the most profitable of the company's offerings. The Mailmiser, an offshoot of the Jiffy padded bag, was based on plastic bubble cushioning. This protective filler, lower in weight and cost than paper padding, was the same that competitors used. However, it had yet to achieve the same degree of branding or market penetration as the original paper-cushioned version.

All of these postal bags were used to send relatively small-sized items that needed protection—engineering supplies, medical instruments, electronic components, computer parts, and so on. The paper and plastic packaging sold in bulk—such as the foams, laminates, plank, bubble wrap, and corrugated paper—were largely perceived in the market to have very similar applications: to cushion large items. Typically, the bubbles and corrugated paper were used as protective wrapping around such items as furniture and office equipment, while the foams and laminates were supports and stabilizers for things like computers and home appliances. Brown paper, cardboard, and boxes were all suitable substitutes for these materials, in particular for the laminates. Bags were more expensive than bulk packaging, and paper was more expensive than plastic because of higher raw material and process costs.

Jiffy highlighted its very wide product range in protective packaging with the slogan "Only Jiffy gives you the choice . . . ," which appeared in many of its promotional materials sent to distributors. Many people at Jiffy felt that the range was too large and that products were simply cannibalizing each other. What Lewis often heard was that they should be looking at more applications rather than merely having more products.

EXHIBIT 1

Jiffy product lines and product map

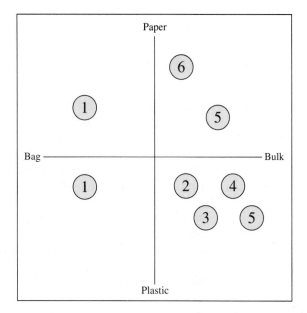

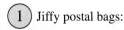 Jiffy postal bags:

Protective paper and/or plastic-based envelopes, used for items that required protection when sent through the mail.
- Padded bag (macerated, recycled newspaper was the chief protective filler)
- Mailmiser (plastic bubble protective filler, lighter weight)
- Utility (less protective filler than padded or mailmiser, lighter weight)

② Jiffy bubble:

Plastic-based protective wrapping material, used to wrap fragile, delicate goods.
- Reels
- Sheet/die cuts
- Perforated
- Pouches

③ Foam (plastic foam packaging):

Plastic-based protective wrapping material, used as form of soft padding, especially for engineering and electric components, medial equipment.
- Jiffy foam
- Jiffy blue foam

④ Low-density polyethylene plastic (LDPE) plank:

A very firm, closed-cell form of foam plastic, used to buttress and support stereos, computers.
- Jiffycel

⑤ Laminates:

Foam with either a paper or plastic sheet laminated to it, provides cushioning and such surface protection as impermeability and heat resistance.
- Foam Kraft Laminate

⑥ Rugated products:

Protective paper packaging, used primarily to wrap around furniture and home appliances.
- Custom wrap
- Kushion Kraft
- Vanguard blankets

EXHIBIT 2

Jiffy product line—general application

Competitors and Market Share

In 1991, the total market for protective packaging in the United Kingdom was estimated to be worth £37 million; Jiffy's 40% share of that market had been relatively constant since 1989–1991. Of the £37 million, £29 million came from the industrial companies which used protective packaging; the remaining £8 million was based on postal bag sales, of which £2.7 million stemmed from commercial and stationery retailers. Jiffy's management sensed that more could be done to expand the postal bag to the general public if only it were presented more creatively and in a wider range of retail outlets. (Refer to Exhibit 3 for market share and competitive position in different product lines.)

Jiffy's padded postal bag had been the first commercialized form of protective packaging. (Refer to Exhibit 4 for illustration and representative advertising.) While competitors began to enter the UK market in all of Jiffy's product lines beginning in the mid to late 80s, becoming especially aggressive in 1987 and 1988, Jiffy maintained the exclusive manufacturing license for the paper-padded bag, deemed a costly investment for competitors to imitate. In Lewis's view—shared by many others—a lot of things could still be done with cushioning material that no one had ever seriously thought about.

EXHIBIT 3

Market for protective packaging and market share

	Postal bag	Bubble	Plank	Rugated	Laminated	Foam
Worth of market	£ 8 mn. of which cushioned = £ 3.2 mn.	£13.2 mn.	£5 mn.	£3.5 mn.	£2.5 mn.	£4.5 mn.
Jiffy % share	70% (100% in cushioned)	19%	36%	43%	49%	50%
Jiffy turnover	£5.62 mn.	£2.55 mn.	£1.82 mn.	£1.53 mn.	£1.23 mn.	£2.25 mn.
Main competitors	Sealed Air Sansetsu Aroful	Sealed Air Sansetsu	Dow BASF BXL	Dependable	Sealed Air Sansetsu	Sealed Air

EXHIBIT 4

Illustration of padded bag

The American company Sealed Air first entered the UK market in the mid-80s with its version of protective packaging, based entirely on bubble plastic rather than paper wrap. With the exception of the paper bag, the company's product range was comparable to Jiffy's in the United Kingdom. Sealed Air had, however, purchased the American operations of Jiffy and sold the Jiffy paper-based bag in the United States under the name *Jiffy By Sealed Air*.

When Sealed Air discovered and commercialized the first CFC-free foam in 1988, the market responded very positively. It was assumed that Jiffy had lost many formerly loyal distributors and end users, although there was no research to substantiate this belief. Overall, though, Jiffy was able to get around the environmental pressures because its paper bag, whose padding was made of recycled newspapers, was perceived by the marketplace as more environmentally oriented than any kind of plastic packaging.

Sealed Air was well known for regularly introducing new products for new uses. In 1991, for instance, it introduced the first microbubble wrap, which rapidly filled the gap in protective packaging for miniaturized components and computer chips. The year before, it had created and introduced a machine specially designed for some of its end users with specific application needs. Rather than providing them with standard or even precut foam sizes and types, this machine let customers cut and slice foam and bubble wraps to their own specific needs. The company intended to expand its sales of machinery, as well as packaging, direct to end users in the years ahead.

The Japanese company Sansetsu had also begun to be a force in the marketplace by the late 80s. Although Sansetsu, which had only a minimal sales force, was still small enough under UK law at the turn of the decade not to have to report its earnings, the firm was known to have grown at an extremely rapid clip thanks to its highly aggressive pricing policies. It was particularly strong in bubble wraps and in bubble-protected postal bags. Bubble itself, as far as Sansetsu was concerned, was a commodity and followed a cost experience curve from which the company benefited. Because of Jiffy's archaic machinery and equipment, high costs of labour, and traditional work processes, its manufacturing costs were high even in the commodity lines when compared with those of the Japanese company or with Sealed Air.

While Sealed Air competed in practically every one of Jiffy's product categories, other smaller companies—such as Arofol, Dependable, BSK, Sentinel, and Sansetsu—competed in select product lines such as envelopes, bubble, and corrugated paper. In contrast to Jiffy, the offerings by Sansetsu and Sealed Air, which were almost entirely plastics based, were much more focused both in terms of products and their applications.

Distributors and the Route to Market

Jiffy had 36 distributor customers, which together served approximately 100 outlets. Ninety percent of its turnover came from the top 10 distributors, of which the top 5 contributed 80%. Ambassador, which prior to the Baldwins' selling out had been Jiffy's distribution arm and had become a separate and independent company since that time, had about a 40% share of that 80%; the company also had about 15% of the total UK market for protective packaging. While Ambassador had approximately 70 suppliers aside from Jiffy, it stocked no products that were in competition with Jiffy's. The other four distributors all carried Jiffy as well as the Sealed Air and Sansetsu lines, and typically had 500–600 customers each, with no specialization in any particular segment. Depending on the product line, the five top distributors accounted for anywhere between 40% and 80% of Jiffy's business. Together, they had over 50% of the total UK market in those lines in which Jiffy did business.

In contrast to its major competitors, Jiffy sold to the market only through distributors. In fact, Jiffy was careful never to deal directly with the final customers. As one Jiffy salesman put it, while he might occasionally meet with end users and even find a suitable potential client for protective packaging, his job "was to do the donkey's work—even if I find the account and convince the client, I would never sign it up directly, but would give it to the distributor." In his own words, the primary role of Jiffy salesmen was to serve distributors and sell packaging, not to build up their business.

The distributor was Jiffy's customer, and the packaging company saw little need or occasion for contact with end users. Distributors were reluctant to share information about customers and, in the past, several distributors had made it clear to Jiffy that they would not welcome any interface between their supplier and their customers. If distributors did ask for special deliveries or technical assistance, Jiffy tried to comply. For instance, Jiffy frequently delivered directly, once an order had been received from the distributor, to engineering and electrical components firms, which purchased packaging in large volumes.

Although it was reputed to maintain good relationships with distributors, Sealed Air had from the outset also dealt directly with certain end users, the most well known being the motor industry. Sansetsu deliberately kept distributors to a minimum, using the smaller ones only to reach certain markets where it was not possible to get the kind of local coverage the company wanted single-handedly.

The only end users Jiffy dealt with directly were the General Post Office (GPO) and the Ministry of Defense (MOD). Its accounts with the GPO, to whom it sold padded envelopes and bubble envelopes, and with the MOD were each worth several hundred thousand pounds. There was no real agreement at Jiffy as to who the other end users were: Everyone at Jiffy had his own version.

Internal estimates, a general knowledge of the market, and gut feel provided by its former distribution arm, Ambassador, gave Jiffy a fairly good guess about the identity of the largest users. The smaller ones were only known to the distributors, and even they were not entirely known, since 30-40% of the distributors sold through subdistributors. Most managers at Jiffy agreed that firms which made engineering and electronic supplies, parts, and components together accounted for just over 50% of the end-user market. Computer supplies, office and furniture products and removal, and cosmetics and toiletries each contributed around 10%. The remainder was estimated to be made up of pharmaceuticals (4%), mail order

(3%), forwarding and aviation (3%), services (3%), cigarettes and tobacco (3%), and other industries (5%).

Prices, Promotion, and Profitability

Plastic and paper were Jiffy's two main raw material costs. While the cost of paper was generally higher, it was also more stable. Resin-based plastic costs fluctuated widely depending on the price of oil. Annually, Jiffy had to buy 3,000 tons of plastic resin, the cost of which within any one year could vary from £400 to £800 a ton. The company's Italian subsidiary, which produced only plastic-based protective packaging, changed its market prices every month depending on resin costs.

Capacity issues also contributed to the company's operating costs. In 1988, under new ownership, the company had drastically reduced its stock. Shortly thereafter, this cutback resulted in having serious undercapacity, and, even though its machines were running seven days a week, the company did not have enough padded bags to meet all the distributors' requests. By early 1989, the company had invested in three major pieces of capital equipment to automate and hasten the production of its Jiffycell, Mailmiser, and bubble wraps, resulting in a 100% increase in productivity for these lines. With the recession, overcapacity in the market was running near 40%.

While the company had always maintained a price premium image in the market, its salesmen frequently negotiated volume-based prices, which could differ widely from list prices. The padded bag, for instance, could be priced differently according to the distributor, and even the same distributor might be quoted several prices on the bag, depending on the size of its customers' requests. Ambassador's volume with Jiffy was twice as large as that of the nearest distributor. Jiffy also ran Ambassador's health and pension schemes free of charge. As Lewis expressed it, "Our distributors are being pushed away from us by our relationship with Ambassador and pushed toward us by our competitors going direct."

All distributors had catalogs indicating the kinds of packaging they supplied. In early 1991, Abbott's, Jiffy's second largest distributor—whose stock was 40% Jiffy products, published a catalog with a price list for all the products it stocked. The price list was designed to hasten and simplify the purchasing process for end users; all they had to do was phone in to Abbott's, give the order number and the volume desired, and the goods were shipped immediately. Abbott's claimed that because ordering had become so much easier, the price catalog significantly increased business. It had also helped the distributor cut expenses, since salesmen no longer had to be out in the field so frequently. To date, no other distributor had included prices in its catalog. (Refer to Exhibit 5 for a representative page from Abbott's catalog.)

Peter Lewis Enters the Scene

Peter Lewis, a calm and soft-spoken 37-year-old, came to Jiffy in February 1991 after having been managing director of several divisions within a firm that supplied plastic cups and utensils to the catering industry. His background was

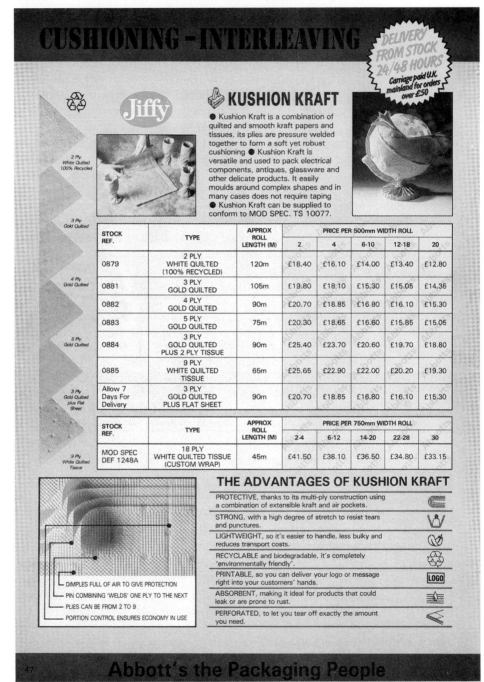

CUSHIONING – INTERLEAVING

DELIVERY FROM STOCK 24/48 HOURS
Carriage paid U.K. mainland for orders over £50

Jiffy

KUSHION KRAFT

● Kushion Kraft is a combination of quilted and smooth kraft papers and tissues, its plies are pressure welded together to form a soft yet robust cushioning ● Kushion Kraft is versatile and used to pack electrical components, antiques, glassware and other delicate products. It easily moulds around complex shapes and in many cases does not require taping ● Kushion Kraft can be supplied to conform to MOD SPEC. TS 10077.

2 Ply White Quilted 100% Recycled

3 Ply Gold Quilted

4 Ply Gold Quilted

5 Ply Gold Quilted

3 Ply Gold Quilted plus Flat Sheet

9 Ply White Quilted Tissue

STOCK REF.	TYPE	APPROX ROLL LENGTH (M)	PRICE PER 500mm WIDTH ROLL				
			2	4	6-10	12-18	20
0879	2 PLY WHITE QUILTED (100% RECYCLED)	120m	£18.40	£16.10	£14.00	£13.40	£12.80
0881	3 PLY GOLD QUILTED	105m	£19.80	£18.10	£15.30	£15.05	£14.35
0882	4 PLY GOLD QUILTED	90m	£20.70	£18.85	£16.80	£16.10	£15.30
0883	5 PLY GOLD QUILTED	75m	£20.30	£18.65	£16.60	£15.85	£15.05
0884	3 PLY GOLD QUILTED PLUS 2 PLY TISSUE	90m	£25.40	£23.70	£20.60	£19.70	£18.80
0885	9 PLY WHITE QUILTED TISSUE	65m	£25.65	£22.90	£22.00	£20.20	£19.30
Allow 7 Days For Delivery	3 PLY GOLD QUILTED PLUS FLAT SHEET	90m	£20.70	£18.85	£16.80	£16.10	£15.30

STOCK REF.	TYPE	APPROX ROLL LENGTH (M)	PRICE PER 750mm WIDTH ROLL				
			2-4	6-12	14-20	22-28	30
MOD SPEC DEF 1248A	18 PLY WHITE QUILTED TISSUE (CUSTOM WRAP)	45m	£41.50	£38.10	£36.50	£34.80	£33.15

THE ADVANTAGES OF KUSHION KRAFT

PROTECTIVE, thanks to its multi-ply construction using a combination of extensible kraft and air pockets.

STRONG, with a high degree of stretch to resist tears and punctures.

LIGHTWEIGHT, so it's easier to handle, less bulky and reduces transport costs.

RECYCLABLE and biodegradable, it's completely 'environmentally friendly'.

PRINTABLE, so you can deliver your logo or message right into your customers' hands.

ABSORBENT, making it ideal for products that could leak or are prone to rust.

PERFORATED, to let you tear off exactly the amount you need.

- DIMPLES FULL OF AIR TO GIVE PROTECTION
- PIN COMBINING 'WELDS' ONE PLY TO THE NEXT
- PLIES CAN BE FROM 2 TO 9
- PORTION CONTROL ENSURES ECONOMY IN USE

47   **Abbott's the Packaging People**

primarily in marketing and sales, but he had also had redundancy program experience. He had never before worked in industrial packaging.

Although his official appointment began on February 1, 1991, all of January had been a sort of induction period—getting to know the company, its employees, and distributors. The day his offical tenure began, he had been given an entirely new management committee, which had been appointed by the previous board of directors. It was composed of Cy Brown, the director of operations and production, who at 38 years old had just been promoted to this position after being with the company for eight years; Martin Ashe, 35 years old, the finance director who had been with Jiffy for a year and half before moving into this managerial position; and James Stade, 45, who had been in sales for several years.

Lewis began his first day as CEO by taking his team offsite for a brainstorming session. The purpose of the two-day meeting was especially to exchange ideas, as well as to become more familiar with one another's aims and work styles and the problems of each function. For Lewis, this was the only way to create the kind of tight working relationship he felt was critical to Jiffy's success. He first explained that he foresaw the same downward trend for the first half of 1991 that had marked the past five years. Yet he would not hand down any tablets of stone, nor did he have a magic wand. "There is no miraculous solution," he told the three men. "We are in this together." But he tried to make it positive by reiterating, "This is the dawn of a new era, and we can decide how to become more market oriented from now on."

Lewis listed the main change forces he saw:

1. *Competitors:* "There are more of them, especially in the past two years."

2. *Environmental pressures on the use of plastics and on CFC production:* "Funds may have to be put aside for capital investments in eco-friendly processes and products, and for waste disposal and recycling techniques."

3. *Rapid emergence of substitutes for traditional protective packaging materials*: "For instance, bubble wrap can be replaced by old newspapers."

4. *Radical and rapid change in distribution patterns:* "Our two lead competitors continue to bypass the traditional dynamics of the market by going directly to end users."

5. *Unabated overcapacity in the marketplace*: "When we introduce a new line, then so do Sealed Air and Sansetsu; the market is just choking up."

6. *End users:* "Improvements in technology have led to more and more value being packed into smaller items. On the one hand, this could mean less packaging; on the other, manufacturers will be more concerned about the quality and efficacy of the packaging."

"This leads me to another point," Lewis concluded. "There's been a change in our distributor customers." He enumerated the transformations occurring among them:

1. *Distributors are developing large national chains:* "While there are fewer of them, they're much bigger and more powerful than ever before."
2. *Costs:* "They are therefore able to push as much of their costs as possible back to us."
3. *Ambassador:* "I think some of the distributors are still unhappy about what they see as the privileged treatment Ambassador is getting from us."
4. *Knowledge:* "They're as well informed about the marketplace as we used to be. They can't be played off against each other. And our competitors are getting stronger every day."

Lewis had already been told that it had been common practice for Jiffy to "police" the marketplace, ensuring that no distributor tried to undercut another on price. Whenever that had happened, the distributor who had been underbid would phone the Baldwins, who would in turn put pressure on the aggressive distributor. Over the past five years, however, that situation had entirely changed, as distributors relied on their customers rather than their supplier to resolve such price wars.

The Customer Survey

For Peter Lewis, it had become abundantly clear that if Jiffy Packaging were to successfully move ahead into the 90s—and all that this entailed in terms of over-coming if not surpassing competitive threats and inroads, handling the new patterns in the distributor market, and riding the recession through—the company would have to take an entirely new tack focused on customers: who they were, what their needs were, and which ones were most important. The first step in delineating a customer-driven strategy was taken in the summer of 1991, when Jiffy commissioned a customer survey.

The key objectives of the survey were finding out who the lead distributors were, what they thought of the company, and how they compared it to the competitors. But Lewis also wanted to know more about end users. How much did they know about Jiffy, and did they know the right things? After several months on the job, he was still getting letters from irate consumers who wanted to know "Why is your company using asbestos in your padded bags when we all know it's dangerous for people's health and the environment?" He had also received some complaints from industrial end users about goods that had been damaged in transport.

Prior to Lewis's arrival, other attempts at customer research had been made at Jiffy. Lewis considered them ineffective and even counterproductive. One such vehicle had been advertising, which constituted 2% of turnover. Some of Jiffy's advertisements—descriptions of the packaging material that had included a response card to be sent directly to the dealers—had been geared to elicit customer inquiries and follow-up visits to end users by distributor representatives. However, distributors soon began complaining to Jiffy: They called the advertising initiative "a wild-goose chase." It had been a waste of time for their salespeople to go to some household in the middle of nowhere only for a sample pack of bubble wrap and perhaps an order for five more. Distributors had stopped responding, and Jiffy had stopped advertising.

The mandate given to the market research firm retained to do the customer survey was to assess the strength of the Jiffy brand name at both the distributor and end-user levels; to identify the perceived differentiating factors recognized by users of Jiffy and of competitive products; to determine customer purchasing criteria; to identify the firm's strengths and weaknesses compared to its major competitors; and to analyze the distributors' requirements so that Jiffy could determine which resources to use to support them.

The 35 largest distributor depots were selected for the survey. Personal interviews of approximately one hour each took place, touching on six different areas:

- Distributor requirements.
- Image of suppliers among distributors.
- Brand awareness and usage among distributors.
- Product image among distributors.
- Brand strength among distributors.
- How can Jiffy improve?—the distributors' view.

On the end-user side, 100 telephone interviews were carried out in order to determine general end-user perceptions of the protective packaging market. In both instances, rank order techniques—together with open-ended questions—were used to elicit their views. (See the appendix for a selection of representative responses.)

By the early fall of 1991, the customer survey had been completed. Peter Lewis had called a meeting of his management team that early September morning to get their feedback, comments, and suggestions. As he viewed it, the research would be a critical exercise for helping the company meet both its current requirements and its future aims. In the short term, it would provide immediate feedback from the marketplace and a quick picture of distributor and some end-user attitudes and needs. In the long term, it would create a framework for the design and implementation of a strategy to see them through the 90s and hopefully even beyond.

APPENDIX
SELECTIVE SURVEY RESULTS REPRESENTATIVE OF RESPONSES

I. Distributor Requirements and Purchasing Criteria

Criteria	Average Score
1. Reliable deliveries	9.53
2. Good relationship with supplier	9.20
3. High-quality product	9.17
4. High margin for distributors	9.10
5. Short delivery lead times	8.67
6. Samples/literature provided	8.53
7. Good field sales support	8.50
8. Wide range of sizes and types	7.90
9. Product has well-known brand name	7.63
10. Good promotional support	7.63
11. End users request the brand	7.37
12. Low price to end user	7.33
13. Effective supplier advertising	7.23
14. Environment-friendly products	7.17
15. Supplier provides good sales leads	7.07

What Are Other Important Considerations?

- "How many distributors have they got or are likely to appoint? I see little point in a manufacturer offering to sell to any packaging distributors; all it does is undermine the market."
- "The flexibility of the supplier to supply as and when required is very important to us."

II. Image of Supplier Among Distributors

Overall Supplier League Table

1. Jiffy Packaging
2. Sealed Air
3. Anglia
4. Sansetsu
5. British Sisalkraft
6. Sentinel

Jiffy Packaging Performance against Purchasing Criteria

Criteria	Jiffy Ranking
1. Reliable deliveries	3rd
2. Good relationship with supplier	1st
3. High-quality product	1st
4. High margin for distributors	4th
5. Samples/literature provided	2nd
6. Short delivery lead times	4th
7. Good field sales support	2nd
8. Wide range of sizes and types	1st
9. Product has well-known brand name	1st
10. Good promotional support	2nd
11. End users request the brand	1st
12. Low price to end user	4th
13. Effective supplier advertising	1st
14. Environment-friendly products	1st
15. Supplier provides goods sales leads	1st

What Improvements Do You Suggest?

- "The strength is the product; very good quality. Support in all fields is good, although sales leads could be better. I feel they don't understand us as a customer, telling me *'I'm the man in the middle'* to fob me off, and tutting at me, forgetting I am the customer. Switchboard could be improved—too much of *'Jiffy, good morning'* then the line goes down until someone answers the extension. It's quick but you don't always get through to who you want to speak to. I'd like them to say *'Who would you like to speak to? Could I have your name'* and then come back to me if there is no reply."

- "Jiffy have got a brand name and an enormous range of products. They're good at what they do. I don't know how good they'd be without the name. In some areas they have too many products. I don't think they promote themselves or their products very well because historically they haven't really needed to, and because it's us who go out and sell their products for them. This survey is to my knowledge the first bit of marketing they have done."

What Is Your General Opinion of Jiffy?

- "Service is dependable. Quality is excellent, well manufactured, well designed, and good quality raw materials are used. Not in touch with today's customer needs. Customers want a flat foam, not the corrugated effect that Jiffy produce. They are market leader, they are following the competition rather than leading it. They will probably have to go for a flat foam in the end."

- "Inflexible. No one will give you a positive answer on when the product will be delivered quickly. Jiffy can't make a snap decision to an unscheduled order. Other suppliers give preference to urgent orders but Jiffy don't. Their only strength is their padded bag—which is 95% of our postal bag sales. It's an established brand name that's been around for years."

- "The actual name. It's like Hoover. It is synonymous with packaging. The product is very good, but service to the distributor lets them down. We receive incomplete orders 35–40% of the time. It affects our customers—a snowball effect. Long lead times with fabrication (i.e., sheets and pouches); delivery times of these are frequently not met. Although the sales office is very helpful.''

- ''A household name. Well known, tried and tested over the years, and good products. Complacency is their weakness, a bit of a smug attitude. They don't pull the stops out to help or service a customer. A *'We'll deliver when we are ready'* attitude.''
- ''They've always had a good reputation—the name Jiffy is important. Relatively competitive but not as competitive as they used to be—they don't seem to want to fight off the opposition—we're not getting support from them pricewise.''

III. Brand Awareness

Why Do You Stock Jiffy?

- ''There's no equivalent to Jiffy Padded. For the amount of Mailmiser I do it's not worth breaking away from the Jiffy range.''
- ''Jiffy Padded is a traditional padded bag there is a demand for. The lighter bags are attractive for lower postal charges. Because we buy foam from Sealed Air, the Mail Lite bags help to make up the volume.''

IV. Product Image

What Is Your Opinion of Jiffy Bags?

- ''A good strong bag. Customers are very price conscious these days; we can no longer sell on the benefits as we used to because of this.''
- ''The protection is good and increases with use; Jiffy are the only ones with this quality.''
- ''It's the premier product [bag]; it's unique, it's green, much stronger than any of the others, the only suitable bag available to send fragile goods away in, it's a 100% quality bag.''

What Is Your Opinion of Custom Wrap?

- ''Has its advantages but they have to be sold to the end user.''
- ''Jiffy are the only ones who do it. It's unique to them; they need to capitalise on that. Should establish a need for it.''
- ''A wide product which performs very well when a suitable application is found but suitable applications are few and far between.''

V. Brand Strength

Do End Users Ask for Protective Envelopes by Brand Name?

	Number of Responses	*Percent of Sample*
Yes	30	100%
No	0	—

Base = 30

Would Customers Specifying Jiffy Protective Envelopes Mind Being Sent Another Make?

	Number of Responses	*Percent of Sample*
Yes	9	30%
No	12	40
Don't know/no answer	9	30

Base = 30

VI. How Can Jiffy Improve?

- "They have a selling company as well as the manufacturing one. Sealed Air only sell through distributors so they are loyal to them. Jiffy are in competition with their distributors—as well as everyone else."

- "They should listen to distributors, to our needs. We are their best customer but we don't get the treatment we deserve."

- "Discuss products more openly. Treat distributors with more respect; we are trying to sell their products! We need support with urgent orders."

- "I'd like to see more of a commercial customer awareness—more moves to satisfy us, the customer. They manufacture and we distribute—the customer is not really the end user; we are the customer to Jiffy and the end user is our customer. We have to react to customer needs in terms of specials or fast orders—Jiffy should respond likewise. We do get what we want, but we do have to push. We need to have the confidence from Jiffy to enable us to be reliable to our customers."

- "Improve the sales leads both in quality and quantity. I'd like to see more market direction in terms of specific uses (new ones) and who is doing what (news items) and could use our products because of what they are doing. Rationalise the paper product range—the whole range should be more readily understandable to the salespeople and the customers. Too many different grades, and the reps don't promote them."

- "Should make their mind up if they're going to be in the protective paper market or not—I feel very strongly about that—they were the brand leaders and they've let them slide and done nothing about it."

- "They could improve on their delivery times; overall they are a very good company. We've recently lost an order due to the fact that they could not deliver on time."

- "We'd like to see an R&D side for new products. Present products are 25–30 years old. There's nothing new. Sit back on their laurels—had the market to themselves for a long time."

- "Do they really have a high support strategy? I get good support when I want it; the rest of the time I'm not aware of any support at all. The marketing support is really not all that good."

- "We really need both; the support is essential, but due to the competition we could do with a lower price. I think we would get more sales if cost were reduced."

- "Today all people are interested in is price coupled with quality, but price tends to take priority."

Importance for end users of various criteria when choosing makes of protective envelope

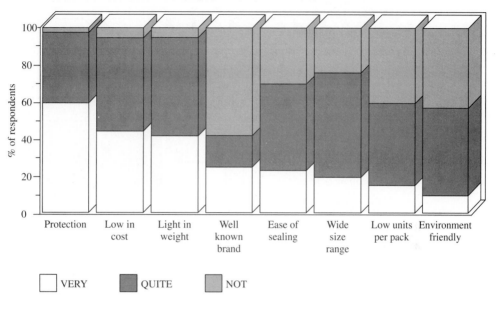

Importance for end users of various criteria when buying foam packaging

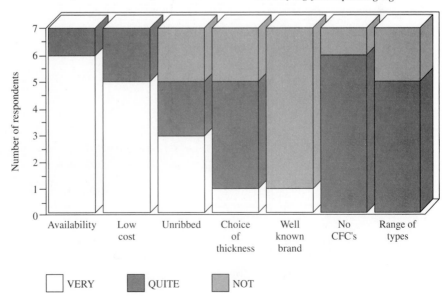

EXHIBIT A-3

Importance for end users of various factors when buying bubble pack

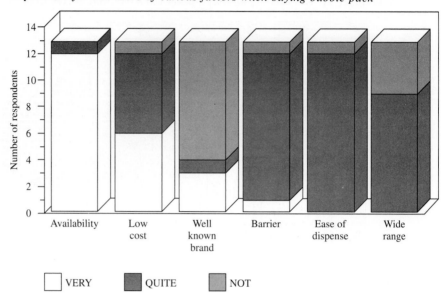

EXHIBIT A-4

Importance for end users of various criteria when purchasing protective paper packaging

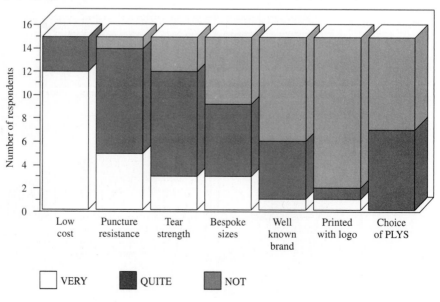

EXHIBIT A-5

Whether end users specify brand when buying protective envelopes

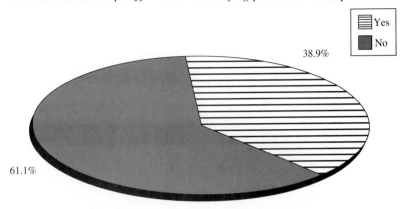

EXHIBIT A-6

Whether end users specify brand when buying bubble pack

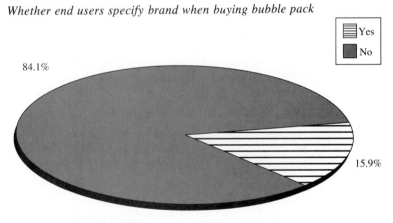

EXHIBIT A-7

Whether end users specify brand when buying foam packaging

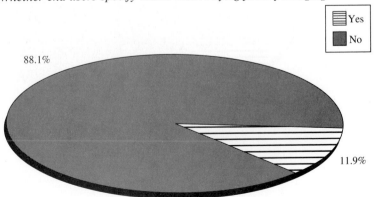

EXHIBIT A-8

Whether end users specify brand when buying protective paper packaging

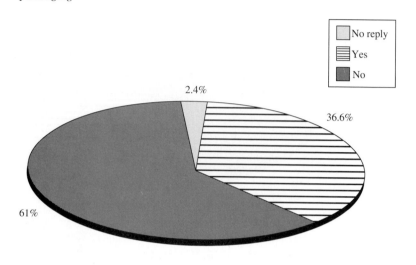

EXHIBIT A-9

Whether end users visited by Jiffy dealer and usefulness of visit

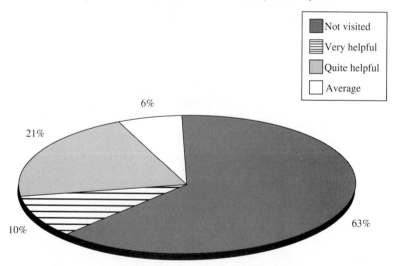

End user opinions of the quality of Jiffy's products

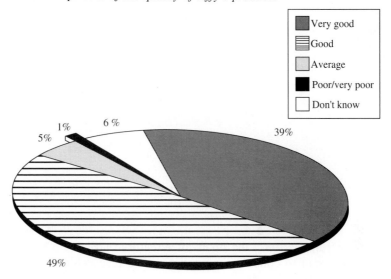

15

BIOKIT SA

On June 1, 1987, the board of directors of Biokit SA, a Spanish biotechnology firm, met to consider its marketing and research and development strategies for the coming decade.

Established in 1973 by IZASA, a diversified supplier of medical equipment, scientific and analytical instrumentation, single-use materials, and reagents, Biokit had grown rapidly. Biokit had developed its R&D, the key to its success, with a broad range of alliances including research associates, business partners, consultants, subcontractors, licensers, and academics holding fellowships. For each of its research projects, which comprised a complex web of subprojects executed in various renowned institutions or in its own premises, Biokit had always managed to secure proprietary control of the key aspects. Francesc Duran, the firm's scientific director, had always maintained that the only way a small European company could excel in biotechnology was by subdividing projects and recruiting the right collaborators for each.

By 1987, Biokit had an extensive product line, but lacked the resources necessary to market it successfully; brand image and corporate identity had yet to be promoted to achieve an image of quality. Management understood that a market orientation was essential if Biokit was to be a significant worldwide competitor. On the other hand, this market orientation had to be achieved without drawing funds away from R&D, on which Biokit spent more than 30% of sales. Exhibit 1 supplies the balance sheet for 1987, and Exhibit 2 the income statement.

This case was prepared by doctoral candidate Jose Luis Nueno under the direction of Professor John A. Quelch. Proprietary data have been disguised. Copyright © 1989 by the President and Fellows of Harvard College. Harvard Business School case 589-113.

Fixed Assets and Long-Term Investments:

Net property, plant, and equipment	200
Goodwill	500
Total R&D	900
Depreciation	(400)
Financial assets	70

Liquid Assets:

Inventories	80
Receivables	350
Cash	90
Total assets	1,290

Equity:

Capital	265
Retained earnings	325

Liabilities:

Short-term	200
Long-term	
Banks	100
R&D support institutions	400
Total equity and liabilities	1,290

NOTE: $1.00 = 117 pesetas.

EXHIBIT 2   **Biokit SA: Income Statement for 1987 (in Millions of Pesetas)**

Sales	807.0	100.0%
Other income*	84.7	10.5
Total income	891.7	110.5
Cost of materials	177.5	22.0
Selling expense	56.4	7.0
Production expense	24.2	3.0
Quality assurance	24.1	3.0
Administrative expense	32.3	4.0
Personnel (without R&D)	217.9	27.0
R&D	242.1	30.0
Depreciation	56.5	7.0
Gross income	60.5	7.5
Net income	40.3	5.0
Cash flow	96.9	12.0

* From research grants.

Company Background

IZASA SL, Biokit's parent, was a subsidiary of a large diversified family-owned holding, with interests in several industries and a total turnover of $1 billion in 1987. To encourage its executives to be entrepreneurial, IZASA pursued an "intrapreneurship" strategy in its new ventures. Most executives' salaries had a fixed and a variable structure, the latter averaging 40% of total compensation and related to achieving previously agreed-on objectives. Through this scheme, the executive identifying an opportunity not directly related to his or her current activity (budget) would have an incentive to bring it to the group and even participate in a profit-sharing scheme of the new activity. Some executives had found interesting projects that led to joint ventures, acquisitions, start-ups, and projects in which the group served as a venture capitalist.

Biokit, started as a company in the chemical-pharmaceutical industry, was a rare example of a fully Spanish-owned company in the field of human laboratory diagnostic reagents.[1] Fully integrated, it covered all the phases of the productive process: research, manufacture, and sale of reagents for the diagnosis of medical conditions such as rheumatism, sexually transmitted diseases, birth abnormalities and pathologies, and viral diseases. Exhibit 3 provides sales forecasts for these reagents by end users.

Biokit's strategy was based on increasing the product line in the above-mentioned areas of medical diagnosis through proprietary skill and technology. For this reason, the company was investing 30% of sales in R&D, compared with an industry average of 10%. According to Jos Manent, Biokit's general manager, competition in the human laboratory diagnostic reagents industry was global because R&D expenses in the product and manufacturing process could not be justified on the basis of a national or even regional market. If research was important, quick worldwide market coverage was critical as soon as a product was available. Because Biokit's products were limited to laboratory analysis and did not require contact with the human body, once developed to the point of delivering a satisfactory performance, they could be marketed. However, introduction of a product required either penetrating an existing market, supplanting another product on the basis of better performance (e.g., quality, price, speed, prediction of results), or creating a market with a reagent that implemented a test with a level of accuracy that was not previously possible.

When considering a potential market, the company set the following criteria:

· Minimum world market of $9 million.
· Minimum yearly growth of 15% in units per year.

---

[1] A reagent was any substance, possibly used in combination with other substances, that performed an analytical diagnostic laboratory procedure. The simplest possible example was the glucose test: to determine the level of glucose in urine, a reagent that changed color when in contact with the glucose was used. This change in color depended on the radicals that attached to the reactive. A simple visual comparison with a predetermined color scale indicated the concentration of glucose in the urine.

EXHIBIT 3   Percentage of Actual and Forecasted US Sales in Dollars by End-User Segment for Selected Immunodiagnostics Techniques

	1986	1990
Viral Diseases		
Corporate laboratories	30%	29%
Hospitals	50	41
Doctors' offices	20	30
Sexually Transmitted Diseases		
Corporate laboratories	10	15
Hospitals	11	15
Doctors' offices and blood banks	79	70

SOURCE: Company records.

- Gross margin of 80% to 85%.
- Maximum product development period of three years.
- Product appeal to major foreign distributors.
- Acquisition of both the antigen[2] and the antibody[3] by Biokit. To make the antibody, an antigen was traditionally supplied to an animal. Recent developments in genetic engineering had resulted in the monoclonal antibody technique, by which a specific antibody was produced "by design," generally by an abnormal plasmatic cell.
- Product focus on sexually transmitted diseases, abnormalities, and the aging process.

In addition to these priorities was the need to keep pace with the latest technological developments, while the average three-year life cycle of the diagnostic products was a constant pressure toward product diversification.

Biokit had 95 employees in 1987. Most managers held MBAs, all R&D personnel held PhDs in biology or chemistry, and the production personnel was also highly qualified. The average age of the management team was 38 years.

Biokit exported to several European countries. The United States and Japan accounted for more than 70% of its sales during the previous five years. The investment requirements for forthcoming R&D projects required not only

---

[2] An antigen was a molecule or a part of a protein molecule that had the capability of producing an immunological response.

[3] An antibody was a protein produced by the plasmatic cells (the cells of the immunological system) as a reaction to specific antigens. The antigen and the antibody were obtained by Biokit if the monoclonal antibody technique was used. They were obtained separately if the antibody was obtained by supplying an antigen to an animal. The monoclonal antibody technique was preferred since it secured the production of the specific antibody to a single antigen, a property that could not be assured if the antibody was supplied by an animal (which may have contracted other diseases aside from the one for which it was inoculated).

increasing the overall sales figure but also maintaining the percentage of sales dedicated to R&D.

Biokit was founded as one of the manufacturing branches of IZASA, which had been importing from the United States the antigen and antibody for the diagnosis of the rheumatoid factor. With an original investment of 2 million pesetas,[4] three technicians were brought in from IZASA to begin to develop the reagent in-house. The reasons for this vertical integration strategy were, first, that the reagent had a substantial market in Spain and, second, that the US manufacturer expressed its intention to establish a wholly owned distribution company in Spain. Such a move could leave IZASA without a source of supply. As a by-product of the R&D effort on the reagent for the rheumatoid factor, Biokit derived the Antigen Estreptolisin O (AEO). To capitalize on this research success was a challenge, because many firms worldwide were manufacturing AEO. AEO was practically the only product Biokit could sell in 1973, and distribution was sought through the Spanish subsidiary-distributor of a Swiss pharmaceutical firm that competed with IZASA. In marketing the AEO that it produced itself through the Swiss subsidiary, Biokit was competing with IZASA, which continued importing the product from its foreign supplier.

The subsidiary-distributor was extremely successful distributing AEO and, when in 1977 Biokit finally derived the reagent for the rheumatoid factor (RRF), was appointed sole and exclusive distributor for the product. Through aggressive pricing, Biokit captured a 15% share of the Spanish market for RRF in its first year.

The Laboratory Reagents Industry[5]

To understand the role of immunological chemistry procedures, one should contemplate its predecessor: the chemistry reagents procedures industry. The growth of both industries was parallel, and most of the pressures that affected one also affected the other.

The science of clinical laboratory medicine was fairly recent. The goal of clinical chemistry reagents, kits, standards, and controls was to aid the physician in providing a specific diagnosis and, in some cases, to predict a possible pathology before the patient demonstrated any symptoms. It was not until 1948, with the introduction of the indirect and direct Coombs tests (also called erythrobastosis fetalis or, more commonly, the Rh factor test), that clinical laboratory medicine became firmly established. Until then, physicians had had to rely on classical medical history and physical examination for diagnosis. A new industry also developed to supply instruments, apparatus, reagents, supplies, disposables, and animals to clinical laboratories. Clinical chemistry machinery and reagents represented the largest dollar shares of clinical laboratory product expenditures.

In the United States, widespread malpractice litigation contributed to dramatic sales growth; risk-averse practitioners were prone to order numerous tests

---

[4] $1 = 117 pesetas.

[5] This section is based on the 1986 Frost and Sullivan report on the clinical reagents industry.

for their patients. Growth was fueled also by the emergence in the early 1970s of automated testing which led to the establishment of large sophisticated laboratories such as National Health Laboratories. Small operations became "collecting stations," subcontracting the testing to major laboratories that could provide a greater range of services at lower prices.

This trend also occurred in Europe. Only large laboratories were able to supply the most sophisticated tests, and the smaller operations became collecting stations. However, increased efficiencies in testing did not mean lower health care costs for the patients because the small operations, physicians, and collecting stations persisted in absorbing the savings as margin. In the United States, as much as 40% of physicians' income was derived from charging exceptionally high (preautomation) margins for the tests that commercial labs billed at reasonable (postautomation) prices.

Another trend that characterized the 1970s was the emergence of disposable laboratory supplies.

In the 1980s many pharmaceutical companies saw the diagnostic products market as a natural extension of their businesses. There were low entry barriers, with the typical entrant being a spin-off of a university research team, sometimes started in humble quarters with very limited financial resources but often with a breakthrough product. The biotechnology market in medical and analytical applications was very fragmented. Companies tended to specialize in groups of products that could be obtained from certain technologies they had mastered. Companies pushed their technological skills to the limit, thereby improving their products and developing new ones. As in the computer industry, it was possible to talk about first-, second-, and third-generation products, with the difference being the degree of advancement of the technologies on which the products were based and their resulting improved performance.

Since the late 1950s, the clinical laboratory diagnostics market had been growing at an estimated 15% per year. By 1986, due to government efforts to control the rise in health costs experienced in the preceding decade and the regulatory and market pressures of government and third-party reimbursement agencies, respectively, this growth had slowed to 8%. In the same year, approximately $670 million was spent in the United States for immunodiagnostics reagents, kits, controls, and standards. Total expenditures in Western Europe, the United States, and Japan approached $1.8 billion. Exhibit 4 presents information on the growth of the various immunodiagnostic techniques for selected diseases; Exhibit 5 and Exhibit 6 break down sales forecasts for the worldwide immunodiagnostic market.

The Biotechnology Industry in the 1990s

Competitive developments in biotechnology in general and in immunodiagnostics in particular were hard to predict. First, the timing and nature of new technology was always uncertain. Second, changing regulations and different national health care systems around the world complicated marketing strategies and precluded standardization.

EXHIBIT 4 **Market Growth for Selected Immunodiagnostic Techniques for Selected Diseases in the United States**

	Volume, 1990 ($ Millions)	Forecast Yearly Growth	Biokit Entry
Viral diseases	$118	10.8%	
Hepatitis B	44	12	1987
Rubella	20	3	1987
Streptococcus A	16	19	1987
Hepatitis A	11	9	1987
Mononucleosis	8	2	1986
Asto O	3	−2	1980
Citomegalovirus	4	20	R&D
Epstein-Barr virus	4	30	R&D
Sexually transmitted diseases	175	10	
AIDS	134	10	R&D
Syphilis	7	5	1980
Chlamydia	9	25	1987
Herpes	4	10	R&D
Neisseria gonorrhea	8	80	R&D
Others	8		

SOURCE: Company records.

EXHIBIT 5 **Market Forecast for all Immunodiagnostic Techniques in Europe* (in Millions of Dollars)**

	1988	1989	1990	1991
France	$130	$154	$185	$225
Italy	296	327	361	389
United Kingdom	64	88	111	135
West Germany	224	265	320	400
All others	183	220	252	284

* Includes: RIO, EP, antisera, serology, pregnancy tests, particle counting, LIA, FIA, EIA, RIA.
SOURCE: Company records.

EXHIBIT 6 **Sales of Immunodiagnostics by Geographic Market, 1986**

	Percent	Millions of Dollars
United States and Canada	40%	$720
Europe:	35	630
West Germany	6	110
France	4	80
Italy	5	100
Japan	15	270
Others	10	180

SOURCE: Company records.

Trends for the 1990s

The trends that experts expected during the late 1980s and early 1990s were the following:

- New diagnostic procedures, such as the increasing use of nonsurgical diagnosis in heart conditions and in vivo (within the patient's body) testing.
- Increased use of computer technology by large laboratories that processed a high volume of tests. Computerization also facilitated the increasing sophistication of some of the test-screening methods.
- Emergence of new therapeutic processes that would require new diagnostic tests, especially in the areas of birth defects and abnormalities and in the control of sexually transmitted diseases.
- Emergence of a "volume" market for blood sample testing in blood banks, due to the risk of intravenous contamination posed by AIDS and hepatitis viruses.
- Growth in the consumer market for self-testing products purchased in local drugstores, a trend that emerged in Europe in the early 1970s with pregnancy and blood/glucose–level tests. Tests for urinary tract infections and sexually transmitted diseases were expected soon in local pharmacies. By the early 1990s, 15 to 20 categories of diagnostic tests were expected to be available as over-the-counter kits.
- The importance of high-technology products based on immunological procedures stemming from recombinant DNA research was expected to increase the possibilities of the field. Recombinant DNA allows the production "by design" of an infinite variety of reagents, enabling scientists to govern a cell's genes. The variety, quantity, and cost of the reagent obtained promised to be much more favorable with this technique.
- Increased participation of the pharmaceutical industry in the clinical diagnostics market. By 1978, pharmaceutical firms started to establish in-house biotechnology R&D programs. By 1982, Du Pont was spending $120 million in biotechnological R&D, Monsanto $62 million, Eli Lilly $60 million, and Hoffman–La Roche $59 million, compared with $9 million and $8 million for large biotechnological firms such as Biogen and Genex, respectively. Regulatory pressures by the national health care systems were both a restriction for the pharmaceutical industry and a cause of growth for the reagents industry. By entering the reagents industry, pharmaceutical firms balanced these regulatory pressures. A portion of their budget devoted to biotechnological R&D would be allocated to externally sponsored R&D. Pharmaceutical firms had a relative advantage over their biotechnological counterparts from their experience in handling large-scale manufacturing and marketing activities.
- Some immunodiagnostics (e.g., radioimmunoessay) were approaching market maturity and encountering severe regulatory restrictions, given

the risks involved in manipulating radioactive materials. Other markets (e.g., chemibioluminiscence) were expected to grow rapidly.[6]

• Because medical practices in France, Germany, and Italy had reached the technical sophistication necessary to warrant the increased use of reagents, these were the markets expected to grow fastest. Some other countries, such as the United Kingdom, had reached the same level of sophistication, but their national health care systems self-supplied reagents that were developed and manufactured by government-owned research laboratories. For this reason, the United Kingdom was a less attractive market in terms of expected growth.

• Acquisitions and mergers were expected to increase in the immunodiagnostics market. Participants were of two types. The first group of firms comprised those founded by or in conjunction with university scientists. Their capabilities lay principally in R&D. The second group comprised pharmaceutical firms with capabilities in and the capital to finance the downstream stages of innovation, process development, manufacturing, product testing, promotion, marketing, and distribution. These stages required not only expertise in conducting them, but also enormous sums of capital. While many pharmaceutical firms sought to develop their own R&D in biotechnology, this complementarity of competitive advantages and the increasing difficulty of raising capital for new start-ups were expected to encourage more joint ventures, mergers, and acquisitions.[7]

Industry Regulation for 1992

Although a common health care policy was one of the European Community's (EC) goals for 1992, the European Commission had worked through seven draft proposals by 1987 without securing agreement by the member states.[8] Industry experts expected the EC to supply general guidelines without identifying the specific classes of products that could or would not be manufactured. Such a move would provide the appearance of a Pan-European policy but be of little help to firms looking to develop Pan-European products.

Each country had its own regulations concerning issues such as the release

---

[6] Traditionally, the antigen/antibody complex and its properties were detected by means of a radioactive "marker" or label. Radioimmunoessay required the use of radioactive isotopes. For this reason, other less risky procedures were being developed based on colorimetric or fluorescent methods.

[7] Gary P. Pisano, Weijan Shan, and David J. Teece, "Joint Ventures and Collaboration in the Biotechnology Industry," in *International Collaborative Ventures in U.S. Manufacturing,* ed. David C. Mowery (Cambridge, MA: Ballinger Publishing Co., 1988), Chapter 6, pp. 183–222.

[8] *The Economist* Intelligence Unit, 1988.

into the environment of new life forms and other genetically engineered materials based on animal embryo research and plant research. Each country also had its own regulations for the research, production, and marketing of such developments. In some cases, these regulations were the same or similar across several countries. For instance, legislative restrictions on radioimmunoessay were similar in all EC countries, based on the restrictions placed on the use and importation of radioactive materials. As far as Pan-European standards or mutual recognition was concerned, the prospects were bleak. Each country required that its own agencies authorize each new-product introduction. This was an extremely time-consuming and costly process in the case of in vivo reagents (those used inside the patient's body) but merely an administrative procedure for in vitro reagents (those used outside the patient's body).

On the other hand, the pharmaceutical industry had developed the European Pharmacopoeia that was accepted throughout the EC. This permitted the same pharmaceutical products to be available in all 12 EC countries. The entry of pharmaceutical firms in the biotechnology industry and the efforts of the European Commission were expected to lead eventually to a similar Pan-European standard for biotechnological products.

Some observers believed that the biotechnology industry might follow trends that were apparent in the pharmaceutical industry. Though there was some agreement among EC countries on pharmaceutical product standards, each country continued to apply its own regulations for advertising, samples, in-store promotions, and the like. This practice advantaged low-cost producing countries like Spain, whose pharmaceutical industry was experiencing booming exports through "gray" marketing. Multinational firms manufacturing in low-cost countries were subject to regulatory price controls which reduced their margins. As a result, there were large differences between the prices charged to consumers in the low-cost and the high-cost countries. These differences allowed local distributors to divert pharmaceuticals produced in low-cost countries to high-cost countries. The EC was not averse to gray marketing, because it was competitive and helped to reduce health care costs. Any similar trend in the reagents industry was likely to be welcomed by local governments and also by the European Commission.

1992 and the Biotechnological Industry

In 1987, the distribution of medical and scientific products in Europe was not consistent from country to country. The leading buyer in most countries was the government because health care was state provided. In France, Italy, and Spain, the health care market was at least 80% financed by government, and in the Netherlands it was almost 90%. Therefore, France tended to buy from companies established in France; Italy, from companies established in Italy; and so on. Some American, Japanese, and European companies had their headquarters in a European country and subsidiaries elsewhere. Many American, Japanese, and

European producers sold to distributors located in different countries. There were no Pan-European companies acting exclusively as distributors, although some manufacturing companies distributed goods from other companies together with their own products. Distribution was very fragmented in countries like West Germany, with hundreds of small distributors, or concentrated in countries like Spain, where a few foreign subsidiaries, IZASA (the leading Spanish distributor), and two or three other Spanish distributors accounted for 80% of sales. The removal of trace barriers in 1992 was expected to promote further industry concentration and increased competition, particularly if important differences among the 12 EC health care systems were also reduced.

Even if the single market program was implemented in 1992, Biokit managers wondered about the extent to which a Spanish manufacturer would be able to sell directly to the French or the Italian government-controlled hospital laboratory systems. In addition, given the specificity of biotechnological products, a close contact between user and seller was necessary. For years Biokit had been selling through distributors, some of whom were worldwide leaders in production and sales of pharmaceuticals and reagents for clinical analysis. Management thought that, by 1988, Biokit would have obtained sufficient market share in several European countries to justify a direct selling organization.

End Users and Decision-Making Processes

The end users of clinical laboratory market reagents were clinical laboratories, both hospital-based and independent. An emerging segment was group practice laboratories that performed tests exclusively for physician outpatient offices and primary care centers. In the United States, 15,500 such laboratories performed 9 billion tests in 1983, generating revenues of $22.6 billion. Most hospitals maintained their own clinical laboratories, although cost reduction pressures were forcing some to share their facilities. In addition, an increasing number of hospitals were contracting out their clinical laboratory operations to commercial laboratories. These contracts usually included an initial up-front payment to the hospital, followed by a percentage override of annual revenues generated through the hospital. The correlation between the number of tests performed and hospital bed size was not precise. Specialty hospitals such as psychiatric institutions did less testing. However, the number of tests performed per patient each year was increasing. Exhibit 7 estimates the number of US hospitals with different test volumes.

In addition there were about 8,500 commercial clinical laboratories in the United States, ranging from small independents to large facilities that were part of national chains. There were also 44,000 laboratories based in physicians' offices and about 4,000 group practice clinical laboratories that performed routine diagnostic procedures for the group's member physicians. Exhibit 8 shows the nonhospital segment breakdown by type of location.

EXHIBIT 7   US Hospital-Based Clinical Laboratories Ranked by Test Volume, 1983*

Annual Test Volume	*Estimated Number of Hospitals*	*Percent of Total*
Up to 49,000	900	12.6%
50,000–99,000	1,940	27.8
100,000–249,000	1,780	25.5
250,000–499,000	1,030	14.8
500,000 or more	1,350	19.3

* To be read: "Nine hundred hospitals (12.6% of the total number of hospitals performing tests in 1983) each performed 49,000 or fewer tests per year."
SOURCE: Company records.

EXHIBIT 8   Nonhospital Commercial Clinical Laboratories by Type of Location in the United States, 1983

	Estimated Number of Labs	*Percent of Total*
Single, one location	6,570	77.3
Multiple locations	1,930	22.7
	8,500	100.0

Nonhospital Commercial Clinical Laboratories Ranked by Test Volume in the United States, 1983

Annual Test Volume	*Number of Labs*	*Percent of Total*
Up to 99,999	6,330	74.5%
100,000–249,999	963	11.3
250,000–499,999	430	5.1
500,000 or more	777	9.1

To be read: "6,330 laboratories (74.5% of the total number of laboratories performing tests in 1983) each performed 99,999 or fewer tests per year."
SOURCE: Company records.

In Europe, the size of the clinical market for immunodiagnostics varied by country, depending partly on the health care reimbursement system. For instance, in France, reimbursement levels had been increasing during the early 1980s, because of the government's socialized health care policy. The number of specialists, general hospitals, and laboratories and the certifications necessary to perform

---

EXHIBIT 9   Characteristics of Three European Reagent Markets

| | | | Hospitals | | | Laboratories | |
| | | | | With | | | |
Country	Reimbursement System	Number of Specialists	Total	Comprehensive Facilities	Number of Pharmacists	Total	Large Labs
France	Allowance levels	30,000	2,500	127	30,000	4,400	880
Italy	Predetermined grants and allowances	9,000	1,900	250	1,200	10,000	2,500
West Germany	Negotiated fee level between insurance company and government intermediary agency	62,000	1,600	n.a.*	28,000	n.a.	300

* n.a. = Not available.
SOURCE: Company records.

immunological tests were the other factors determining market size. Exhibit 9 provides details on the health care systems in several EC countries.

End users cited "product quality," meaning consistency and reliability, as a key dimension driving their buying decisions. Errors resulting from unstable biochemicals could distort interpretation of the test results. Price was not a key concern among end users, but, given equivalent perceived reliability, price could be a tie-breaker. Other factors that played a role in the decision-making process were delivery, technical service, size of the product line, the nature of the interaction with the salesperson, literature citations, recommendations of other professionals, advertising, and appearance of the producer in technical publications. One consistent trend was the increasing sophistication of the buying practices followed by end users. Bidding techniques and centralized group purchasing tended to reduce the importance of distributors who responded by specializing in carrying deep assortments of a particular range of products, or by merging to form larger corporations themselves.

Marketing Opportunities

Manufacturers of immunodiagnostics in the EC were focusing on product and distribution strategies to increase their market penetration. The screening tests with the greatest market growth potential—such as gonorrhea and monoclonal antibodies tests—were widely known and became the focus for many companies' product R&D efforts.

Product bundling was seen as another opportunity for growth. Some competitors were offering to supply instruments free or at low cost in exchange for long-term purchasing arrangements. Others offered multisystem instruments that could be used with a variety of tests.

EXHIBIT 10	**Manufacturers of Tests for Sexually Transmitted Diseases: Worldwide Sales and Market Shares of Principal Industry Participants**

	Sales, 1986 ($ Million)	*Market Share*
Abbott Diagnostics	$53.5	49.3%
Electro Nucleonics	20.0	18.4
BBL-Microbiology	5.6	5.2
Syva	4.2	3.9
Whittaker M.A. Bioproducts	2.1	1.9
Difco Laboratories	1.5	1.4
Behring Diagnostics	0.9	0.8
Others	16.5	15.2

SOURCE: Company records, 1987.

In recent years, manufacturers of clinical laboratory supplies were increasingly selling direct. Traditionally, the role of the distributor had been to identify sales leads and then introduce the manufacturer's representative to the key decision maker in the clinical laboratory. Larger distributors were increasingly emphasizing the specialized knowledge of their salespeople and were therefore able to take a more important role in the closing of the sale. The distributor's role was critical for new manufacturers that lacked the personnel or financial resources needed to go direct. These manufacturers used distributors until they achieved the sales volume necessary to justify going direct.

The alternative to distributors was direct selling through a manufacturer's own sales force. Given the increasing technical sophistication of reagents, several companies had switched to direct selling to ensure that highly technical information was communicated accurately to end users. Others were entering joint ventures with reagent and/or instrument manufacturers for the marketing and/or distribution of their products. Such joint ventures were seen as inevitable, given increasing concentration in the immunodiagnostics industry and the interest of pharmaceutical producers in participating in the industry.

Export Strategies before 1988

The market for human laboratory diagnostic reagents was largely controlled by multinational companies, which, in the early 1980s, were going through a process of concentration. Exhibit 10 presents the market shares of the principal competitors. Western Europe, the United States, and Japan accounted for 90% of world sales. Biokit managers believed that to compete in this "market of giants," they had to emphasize growth and develop both a brand image and international distribution.

Although both assets were intertwined, Biokit focused first on exports of bulk and private-brand product. Bulk product involved the export of only the technological basis of the product and the largest share of its value added, leaving to the importer, generally a distributor, the final steps of the manufacturing process including separating the bulk product into individual doses, packaging, and labeling. Private-brand operations involved full production of the reagent for another manufacturer or distributor that distributed to end users under its own brand name.

This strategy brought Biokit several advantages. First, specializing in bulk production resulted in substantial volume economies in procurement and manufacturing. Second, Biokit was able to increase its market share with a very lean marketing organization and low marketing expenses. Biokit's strategy was product oriented; the key success factor was being able to supply large quantities of product of a consistently high quality. Third, the strategy permitted Biokit to concentrate its limited resources on R&D and manufacturing rather than dilute its initial effort through marketing expenses. Fourth, the need to achieve the quality standards required by multinational manufacturers and distributors that bought Biokit's in-bulk products required that Biokit's manufacturing operations be of the highest standard.

Further, to achieve international recognition, Biokit needed to develop relationships with well-known multinational customers, particularly because Spain was not a recognized source of high-quality medical products. Some Biokit marketing managers maintained that the firm could focus on exporting its products to developing countries instead of the highly industrialized markets that it pursued for in-bulk sales. However, the combined market of these developing countries was quite small, end users were less sophisticated, and payments were often delayed. On the other hand, proponents of the developing countries' alternative maintained that the in-bulk strategy made Biokit dependent on the multinationals. They also claimed that in-bulk and private-label sales commoditized a specialized high-technology product, making delivery and cost the only two bases for competition. Gross margins were lower, yet sales uncertainty was high because customers could drop Biokit as a supplier with minimal notice. Further, given the nature of competition and the percentages of sales that Biokit was dedicating to R&D, reliance on high-volume, low-margin customers could result in slower growth.

By 1983, the firm's top management was becoming more sensitive to overreliance on multinational customers. A barrier to any change in strategy that might result in Biokit's competing with its own multinational customers was that the in-bulk and private-brand operations were at full capacity. To minimize retaliation by current customers, the marketing department suggested distributing a self-contained diagnostic test kit under the Biokit brand. The kit was introduced in West Germany, Italy, and France, where the existing customers did not perceive this new product as directly competitive.

The kit strategy allowed Biokit to sell a product under its own brand in an industry where end user brand loyalty was a key dimension of competition. It also resulted in improved margins, because the bundling of all the elements necessary for the performance of the test permitted Biokit to charge a higher price than those obtained for private-brand and in-bulk sales. The introduction of the kit was a success. As a result, Biokit extended the kit approach to other products. By 1987, it sold such kits in the five most important markets of the world.

In West Germany, Biokit decided to adopt a dual marketing approach, selling both through a distributor, Labor Diagnostica GmbH, and directly to large end users. It was also able to maintain its bulk and private-brand sales. Since the kit sales were fueled by the trend toward self-testing and increased use of disposable materials, virtually no cannibalization of private-brand sales occurred. Biokit was quite satisfied with the relationship with its German distributor.

In France, the dual approach was also followed, but with mixed results. The distributors that Biokit approached were less willing than those in West Germany to make strong commitments to the company, and, partly for that reason, no exclusive agreements were signed. Bulk and private-label sales were equally important. Biokit sold directly to some large end users and signed agreements with three regional distributors. However, sales through the distributors were discouraging; coverage seemed limited to the area surrounding Paris, which accounted for two-thirds of the sales.

The sales breakdown in Italy was similar to that in West Germany. A single distributor, Biomedical Services S.p.a., had been appointed, with mixed results. Sales orders were uneven and unpredictable, causing production scheduling problems. On the other hand, coverage was satisfactory. Additionally, in-bulk and private-brand sales were cannibalized by kit sales because the Italian market had not experienced the disposable and self-testing growth evident in West Germany. However, Biokit had not experienced any direct manufacturer retaliation.

In Japan, Biokit adopted a different strategy, establishing Nipon Biokit Ltd. to sell directly bulk and private-label product. The sales of this subsidiary equaled those of West Germany, Italy, and France combined, encouraging some Biokit executives to favor direct distribution in Europe as a next step. On the other hand, sales of Nippon Biokit were concentrated in the commodity segment, and although the idea of selling under private brand was being explored, the risks of retaliation by manufacturer-customers could be high.

In the United States, Biokit established Biokit USA Inc. Sales to the United States started in 1981, when private-brand sales were initiated with the American Dade division of American Hospital Supply Corporation. Through this client, a 22% market share in syphilis reagents was achieved. Sales in 1987 were principally private-brand and in-bulk, as in Japan. The success of the American Dade relationship made management reluctant to explore the introduction of branded products. On the other hand, the United States was a "showcase" market for biotechnological reagents, and a success in marketing branded products there could facilitate their introduction in other markets.

Reconsidering the Distribution Strategy

Despite these international sales successes, management believed that Biokit lacked sufficient control over its international channels. Reliance on distributors precluded the establishment of a coherent brand policy. Reagent distributors

EXHIBIT 11   Biokit Sales in 1987 by Channel of Distribution *

	Sales (in Millions of Pesetas)	Sales
Bulk	108	23%
OEM	234	49
Branded	133	28

* IZASA not included.
SOURCE: Company records.

EXHIBIT 12   Biokit Sales and Earnings Forecasts, 1988–1992 (Millions of Pesetas)

	1988	1989	1990	1991	1992
Sales	870	980	1,421	2,060	2,987
Earnings	260	294	440	659	985
Earnings/sales	30	30	31	32	33

SOURCE: Company records.

carried too many products to give substantial attention to any one. They paid little attention to Biokit's requests for more sales push and were not specially receptive to Biokit's offers of sales support. Concerned that Biokit might consider selling directly once sales reached the necessary volume, the distributors supplied little information about their markets. Exhibit 11 reviews Biokit's 1987 sales by distribution channel, and Exhibit 12 summarizes Biokit sales forecasts for the period 1988–1992.

Manent was concerned also about the breadth of the product line. By June 1987, it exceeded 30 product items in four high-growth segments of biotechnology: rheumatism reagents; venereal disease diagnostics such as syphilis and gonorrhea; viral disease reagents for toxoplasmosis, mononucleosis, and hepatitis; and fertility. By the end of 1989, two new products were expected to be ready for market: chlamydia and citomegalovirus diagnosis reagents.

Under these circumstances, Manent was contemplating vertical integration in distribution in at least five of Biokit's most important markets: France, West Germany, Italy, Japan, and the United States. He estimated that the extra cost of

EXHIBIT 13   Alliances between European and Non-European High-Technology Companies, June 1987 to September 1988

	Europe–Europe*	EC–USA†	USA–EC††	Japan–EC	Total
Takeovers and mergers	69	74	71	17	231
Joint ventures and alliances other than mergers	134	← 94 →		42	270
Total	203	← 239 →		59	501

* Including alliances involving non-EC companies from Finland, Sweden, and Switzerland, in eight takeovers and 21 joint ventures.
† Alliances initiated by EC companies.
†† Alliances initiated by US companies.
SOURCE: *The Economist* Intelligence Unit, 1988.

such a strategy would be $2 million, $3.2 million, and $3.9 million for the first, second, and third years, respectively. Among the issues to consider in executing this strategy was the type of organization to establish in each country, the degree of participation by Biokit in each venture, the criteria for and eventual choice of partner, and the arrangements that would have to be made with existing distributors and multinational customers.

New Attitude toward Strategic Alliances[9]

Many European companies facing the challenge of a more integrated market after 1992 were considering whether they were large enough to survive. High-technology industries, including biotechnology, were seen by industry experts as ripe for mergers, acquisitions, and other cooperative strategies involving both European and non-European firms. The pace of technology change and short product life cycles, perhaps more so than the prospect of EC integration in 1992, accounted for this trend. Exhibits 13, 14, and 15 summarize the number and pattern of recent strategic alliances involving European high-tech companies. Exhibit 16 reviews the motives for strategic alliances in biotechnology.

The business climate for mergers and joint ventures varied among the EC countries. The United Kingdom, Ireland, and Spain actively encouraged alliances

---

[9] Strategic alliances were formal industrial, commercial, financial, or technological alliances established between two or more firms with such purposes as achieving the size necessary to compete, rationalizing or restructuring their processes, and achieving economies of scale, resources for innovation, or marketing efficiencies.

EXHIBIT 14 Sector Breakdown of Competitive Alliances Involving European High-Technology Companies, June 1987 to September 1988

	Mergers	Other Cooperative Ventures
Biotechnology	14	23
Pharmaceuticals	4	15
Chemicals	11	21
Computer hardware	2	9
Computer software	9	11
Electricals	13	25
Machinery	7	14
Others	9	16
Total	69	134

SOURCE: *The Economist* Intelligence Unit, 1988.

EXHIBIT 15 Joint Venture Activity in Europe by Country of Participating Company, June 1987 to September 1988

Belgium	15	Japan	42
Denmark	12	Netherlands	45
France	53	Portugal	5
Greece	11	Spain	36
Italy	34	United Kingdom	97
West Germany	82	United States	94

SOURCE: *The Economist* Intelligence Unit, 1988.

EXHIBIT 16 Cross-Sectional Comparison of the Motives for Collaboration in Biotechnology

Function	Pharmaceuticals	Diagnostics	Animal Health	Specialty Chemicals
R&D	34%	17%	36%	40%
R&D and marketing	13	10	21	10
Manufacturing	7	10	0	10
Marketing	21	31	36	20
Supply	2	21	0	0
Technology transfer	22	10	7	20
Other	1	0	0	0
	100%	100%	100%	100%

SOURCE: Based on Pisano, Shan, and Teece, "Joint Ventures," pp. 183–222.

involving both European and non-European firms. In France and Italy, a more protective environment, bureaucratic formalities, and tangled ownership structures were major obstacles. In West Germany, the public policy posture was neutral but the capital structure of companies and their dependence on the banking system impeded takeovers, especially if they were unfriendly. Greece was extremely protectionist and differed from the other southern European countries in not viewing the joint venture as an important means to acquiring more advanced technology and more rapid business expansion. Nevertheless, the 1992 program was thought likely to reduce the existing legal restraints on mergers that could be imposed by each country.

There were multiple motives for biotechnology alliances. Joint ventures between large and small firms were caused by the small firms' need to gain access to markets and capital to launch their new products. Unilever, for example, had acquired several small European firms to gain access to biological reagents. Other biotechnology companies used alliances to pursue research links with companies in Japan and the United States. Fisons (United Kingdom) and Novo (Denmark) had been particularly active in Japan and the United States, respectively. L'Oréal (France) had established joint ventures with US and Japanese firms.

The EC and its member countries had launched a number of programs to support technology development and innovation. The EC budget for technology development programs in 1986 was about 1 billion ECU. Most EC or Pan-European support programs could be tapped along with other sources of support at the country or regional level.

Technology alliances had become more prevalent since 1984, when several EC organizations were established to review and fund project proposals. The most important of these frameworks were ESPRIT (European Strategic Program for Research and Development in Information Technology), BRITE (Basic Research in Industrial Technologies for Europe), and RACE (Research and Development in Advanced Communications Technology for Europe). All these programs funded alliances only to develop technology, generally between partners from different EC states. More than 1,000 companies participated in these programs by 1987.

EUREKA in particular was initiated under the leadership of France's president, François Mitterrand. European countries (including non-EC members such as Switzerland, Sweden, Austria, and Norway) agreed to launch an initiative to stimulate innovation in Europe and to strengthen European high-technology industries in competition with Japan and the United States. The focus of EUREKA was development rather than basic research. Each country set up a national EUREKA secretariat to administer the program. To qualify for EUREKA, projects had to be submitted by corporations or institutions from more than one of the EUREKA member countries. This forced cooperation was intended to avoid duplication and boost efficiency.

The Spanish secretariat of EUREKA resided at CDTI, an autonomous institution attached to the Ministry of Industry and Energy. CDTI served as a government venture capital corporation, granting loans for R&D. These loans were paid back through royalties on sales of the resulting products. If an R&D effort failed, CDTI could not claim the return of the money.

Because Biokit had a strong reputation at CDTI after years of successful use of R&D loans, CDTI encouraged Biokit to participate in one EUREKA program. Biokit was at the time negotiating the joint development of a product with A.P. Technologies, a British laboratory. A.P. Technologies performed contract research and, according to Biokit's scientific director, was one of the world leaders in several key technologies involved in developing their proposed new product. Biokit and A.P. Technologies obtained joint funding for this project under the EUREKA program. In Spain, as well as in other EC countries, EUREKA projects received up to 50% of the funds required in the form of either a grant or a loan. In addition to the subsidy, the EUREKA funding brought valuable publicity. Stories on Biokit appeared in *The Wall Street Journal, The Financial Times,* and other leading business publications.

Biokit had been involved in one other strategic alliance in R&D. In 1987, it started a project with a US and an Italian university for the development of testing equipment based on a patent purchased from the Massachusetts Institute of Technology. No strategic alliances had been initiated in distribution, although this was an option that Biokit management contemplated for the future.

Marketing Strategy for the 1990s

Manent reasoned in front of the board of directors that the market for branded reagents was becoming more global and therefore more similar to the markets for in-bulk and private-brand reagents. Regulatory changes pointed toward a progressive normalization of standards and practices in the biotechnological industry. To be successful as a small biotechnological firm researching and manufacturing in Spain and facing the removal of intra-EC trade barriers in 1992, Biokit's perspective had to be global. Particularly important was the decision on Biokit's distribution strategy for the 1990s.

Manent's proposal to the board was to develop further Biokit's own distribution network so that, unless a distributor willing to make the necessary commitments could be found, Biokit would sell directly under its own brand name. Manent thought that, before 1992, he should have distribution points in all the major EC countries. The United States and Japan could be handled by strengthening the current subsidiaries. In spite of 1992, he thought that each major European country would still require an individual approach. Given the limited resources of Biokit, he thought that the best solution would be to establish distribution alliances, as had been done in the R&D area. He was confident that the company could implement a coherent sales program while sharing ownership of the channels.

Manent determined to approach the best distributors of reagents in various countries and convince each of them to establish an independent joint venture to sell Biokit's products. He knew that the success of this strategy depended on Biokit's products maintaining their excellent quality, on the manufacturing system continuing to benefit from the learning curve and lower costs, and on the R&D laboratory maintaining its creativity and high productivity.

16

DAVID DEL CURTO
SA

In June 1989, Lothar Meier, president of David Del Curto SA (DDC), reflected on his company's future in the European Community's (EC) impending integrated market. Headquartered in Chile, DDC was the largest private company in the southern hemisphere dedicated to the export of fresh fruit. Though it exported to more than 35 countries, its products were sold mainly in the northern hemisphere to supply "contraseasonal" (off-season) needs for fresh fruit.

Lothar Meier wondered whether the 1992 EC market integration program represented a threat or an opportunity to DDC. In addition, he pondered the decisions he would have to make about the company's entry strategy in Europe, its marketing organization, distribution channels, and branding and communications policies.

Company Background

In 1949, David Del Curto Libera emigrated from Italy to Chile, where he joined his uncle Antonio in running a small firm in the Aconcagua Valley, about 60 miles north from Santiago. The company exported onions, garlic, melons, almonds, chestnuts, and walnuts to Argentina.

In 1953, David Del Curto founded his own firm in the same business. In 1956, the new company started exporting and added some leguminous crops such as lentils, beans, and peas as well as honey to its product line. During a trip to West Germany, David Del Curto met Lothar Meier, a young German trained in foreign

This case was prepared by Professor Jon I. Martinez of the Universidad Adolfo Ibanez, Santiago, Chile, in association with Professor John A. Quelch. Copyright © 1989 by the President and Fellows of Harvard College. Harvard Business School case 590-016.

trade who worked in the cereals department of a DDC agent. David Del Curto offered Meier a job at DDC to promote cereals, and he arrived in Chile in 1958.

In 1958, DDC entered the fresh fruit business and began to export nectarines, peaches, and plums to the US market. However, the firm's main exports were still grains and brans to West Germany and the United Kingdom, animal feds to Scandinavia, melons to the United States, onions to the United Kingdom, garlic to Brazil, walnuts to Argentina, prunes to Europe, and honey to West Germany. In 1963, DDC became interested in exporting apples and pears and, four years later, bought its first orchard. By then, DDC was the fifth largest Chilean exporter of fresh fruit.

Increases in its apple business prompted DDC to build in 1971 the first private fruit plant in Chile for selecting, standardizing quality of, packing, and precooling fruit to ensure resistance to damage during transportation and distribution. Subsequently, the company built six additional fruit plants—three in the 1970s and three in the 1980s.

In 1971, DDC became the third largest exporter of fresh fruit from Chile, and four years later the first. This rapid growth was due to DDC's leadership in three areas. First, because of David del Curto's knowledge of consumption patterns in foreign markets, the company was able to advise growers on which varieties to plant. It worked with Chilean and foreign agronomists specializing in fruit research to advise growers about plantation planning, soil fumigation, and other modern farming methods.

Second, DDC pioneered in plant engineering. Chilean fruit had not always arrived in good condition in world markets due to improper postharvest storage. David Del Curto persuaded growers that they had to take more responsibility for the appearance and quality of the fruit that they cultivated to combat this problem. Hence, DDC obliged growers to participate in the final outcome of the selling process by accepting their fruit only on consignment, the same system imposed on DDC by its distribution agents.

Third, the company pioneered in opening several new markets for Chilean products, including the Middle East in 1974 and Southeast Asia in 1976. Because DDC understood each country's different consumer preferences and needs, the company was very successful in the European market from the outset.

The Company in 1989

In 1983, David Del Curto died in an air accident. Ownership of the company passed to his family and to Lothar Meier, Manuel Sánchez, and Ramón Guerrero, who had been shareholders since 1978. These executives became president, vice president, and executive director, respectively.

In the 1987–1988 season (from September to August), DDC became the first Chilean firm to break the 10-million-box barrier, exporting a volume of 13.7 million boxes (about 140,000 metric tons) valued at $85.3 million. This volume represented about 15% of Chile's total fresh fruit exports. (Exhibit 1 shows company

---

EXHIBIT 1   Evolution of Company Exports

| Year | Volume | | Value in $000 | Share of Chilean Exports |
	000 Boxes	Tons*		
1980	5,157	1,906	$43,897.6	23.7 %
1981	7,126	515	54,003.6	28.5
1982	6,628	817	54,043.7	24.01
1983	5,871	384	42,899.2	16.48
1984	7,596	927	55,376.9	17.42
1985	8,808	602	61,745.8	16.83
1986	9,346	454	69,113.9	15.74
1987	9,889	442	76,742.7	13.79
1988	13,651	621	85,278.7	15.2

* Some dry fruit, such as walnuts, was exported in bags and therefore measured in tons. This column is *in addition* to boxes of fruit.

SOURCE: Company records.

EXHIBIT 2   Selected Financial Indexes

	1987	*1988*
Liquidity Ratios		
Current ratio	1.02	1.03
Quick ratio	0.78	0.78
Debt Ratios		
Total debt/equity	4.84	4.83
Long-term debt/equity	67.44%	86.62%
Profitability Ratios		
Gross profit margin	11.77%	11.27%
Net profit margin	3.67	2.65
Return on equity	23.03	16.02
Return on assets	3.79	2.67

SOURCE: Company records.

---

exports and share of Chilean exports from 1980 to 1988.) Net profit in 1988 was about $2.5 million, which represented a 16% return on equity. (Exhibit 2 shows selected financial indexes.) Besides exports, DDC's revenues included $3 million in domestic fruit sales and sales of products and services worth about $7 million to growers.

Though its main activity was the export of fresh fruit, DDC defined itself as an "agroindustrial producer and marketer of fresh fruit, dry fruit, and vegetables, with worldwide distribution." Its basic operating cycle consisted of six phases: production, selection, packing, shipping, distribution, and marketing of the fruit.

The staff consisted of about 550 permanent employees and over 2,500 temporary workers due to the high seasonality of operations. DDC maintained some 25 to 30 employees in major ports abroad to supervise product unloading and clearance and to coordinate its distribution.

Only 15% of the fruit the company exported came from its land and land held by the company's owners; the rest was provided by a network of more than 800 independent growers in Chile. DDC maintained one- to five-year contracts with these growers and provided several support services. These services included technical assistance (on fertilization, irrigation, pest and disease control, weed control, growth regulations, pruning, thinning, maturity development, and harvest readiness), delivery scheduling, financing, and a computerized service that kept each grower constantly informed about its fruit's progress and the average prices in overseas markets.

DDC's main products were grapes, which represented about 50% of its exports in US dollars and 53% in volume; stone fruits, 19% and 18%, respectively; apples, 18% and 18%; pears, 6% and 5%; and kiwi fruit, 2% and 2%. Exhibit 3 (next page) illustrates some of the company's main products. The shares of DDC exports accounted for by various destination markets was as follows:

	1986	*1987*	*1988*
United States and Canada	61%	61%	59%
Europe and Scandinavia	22	23	31
Middle East	12	12	7
Far East	4	4	2
South America	1	1	1

More detailed information about DDC's products and markets is presented in Exhibit 4 on page 311.

The Fresh Fruit Industry in Chile

The fresh fruit industry accounted for over 1% of Chile's total GDP. In addition, it was the second most important generator of foreign currency in Chile, after copper mining. In the 1987–1988 season, fruit exports valued at $680 million represented 10% of total Chilean exports that year. More than $800 million in exports was expected in 1988–1989.

Although Chilean fruit represented only 2.3% of all world trade in fruit, its relative importance was higher for selected products: 16% of grapes, 6.1% of apples, and 4.5% of pears. Chile was a major southern hemisphere supplier to the contraseasonal markets of North America and Europe. During winter and spring in the northern hemisphere, Chile accounted for 80% of world trade in grapes, 92% in peaches and nectarines, 31% in apples, and 23% in pears.

EXHIBIT 3

Main products and varieties exported

Exhibit 4 Shipments from May 31, 1988, to May 31, 1989

	Year	US East Coast	US West Coast	Middle East	Far East	Europe	South America	Total Maritime	Air and Truck	Total
Nectarines	1987	270,901	143,398	65,434		52,542	744	533,019	47,450	580,469
	1988	376,989	363,907	28,655		85,221		854,772	54,247	912,019
	1989	357,761	508,930	54,008		97,136		1,017,835	79,300	1,097,135
Plums	1987	343,645	125,181	55,381		31,212	1,896	557,315	37,911	595,226
	1988	376,115	217,712	2,688		75,105		671,620	28,847	700,467
	1989	441,948	507,483	32,755	10,136	104,527		1,096,849	90,833	1,187,682
Peaches	1987	159,971	60,136	4,321			416	224,844	35,632	260,476
	1988	237,624	200,507	4,000		1,242		443,373	32,817	476,190
	1989	278,734	343,614	1,404		19,770		643,522	93,265	738,787
Apples	1987	138,273	65,807	319,175	188,832	944,109	12,458	1,668,654	624	1,669,278
	1988	108,234	47,138	469,251	41,903	1,167,277	15,948	1,849,751		1,849,751
	1989	140,238	150,897	407,310	36,000	1,279,914	23,592	2,037,951		2,037,951
Pears	1987	114,047	44,286	40,480	32,231	257,679	960	489,653	144	489,797
	1988	240,136	44,906	33,368	8,016	363,922		688,348		688,348
	1989	274,454	121,148	26,331	22,848	511,551		956,332	20	956,352
Grapes	1987	2,581,922	1,459,671	361,039	65,287	737,873	7,032	5,212,824	74,729	5,287,553
	1988	3,073,236	2,263,876	194,029	81,757	1,572,658		7,185,556	51,538	7,237,094
	1989	2,255,177	2,827,390	76,628	142,734	1,495,225		6,797,154	102,163	6,899,317
Cherries	1987	336	336					672	32,271	32,943
	1988	10,368	16,848					27,216	53,280	80,496
	1989	11,872	13,050					24,922	64,935	89,857
Apricots	1987	10,544	1,152	3,408				15,104	10,567	25,671
	1988	16,152	11,476	2,848				30,476	12,023	42,499
	1989	21,993	23,047	2,611	1,762			49,440	21,396	70,836
Melons	1987	39,941	12,270	3,890		930		57,031	2,785	59,816
	1988	4,005	1,335			19,071		24,411		24,411
	1989									
Onions	1987	16,218	6,720			55,523		78,461		78,461
	1988	27,646	8,634			128,070		164,950		164,950
	1989	11,280	11,568			129,687		152,535		152,535
Watermelons	1987					332		332		332
	1988									
	1989					1,358		1,358		1,358
Lemons	1987									
	1988									
	1989									
Kiwis	1987					8,517		8,517		8,517
	1988	12,960	17,928			278,199		309,087		309,087
	1989	9,072	5,184			334,337		348,593	9,718	358,311
Garlic	1987					3,228		3,228		3,228
	1988		6,052			3,168		10,120		10,120
	1989		2,112			2,640		4,752		4,752

EXHIBIT 4 *(concluded)*

	Year	US East Coast	US West Coast	Middle East	Far East	Europe	South America	Total Maritime	Air and Truck	Total
Persimmons	1987									
	1988									
	1989					3,963		3,963		3,963
Asparagus	1987									
	1988								28,087	29,087
	1989	100						100	41,210	41,310
Artichokes	1987									
	1988	504						504		504
	1989	80						80		80
Nuts	1987									
	1988									
	1989									
Raisins	1987									
	1988	1,800				6,053		7,853		7,853
	1989	10,800			2,050	20,500		33,350		33,350
Prunes	1987									
	1988					100		100		100
	1989									
Totals	1987	3,675,798	1,918,927	853,128	286,350	2,091,945	23,506	8,849,654	242,113	9,091,767
	1988	4,485,769	1,199,219	734,839	131,676	3,700,686	15,948	12,268,137	263,839	12,531,976
	1989	3,813,509	4,514,450	601,047	215,530	4,000,708	24,592	11,168,836	502,840	13,671,676

The area planted with fruit in Chile had grown almost three times since 1973, while export volumes had increased more than 20 times. Data on the two main crops illustrating this growth are presented in Table A:

TABLE A   Evolution of Planted Surface (in Hectares) and Exports (in Tons)

	1973	1978	1983	1988
Grapes				
Surface	4,150	10,300	24,100	42,200
Exports	13,600	51,100	149,930	359,900
Apples				
Surface	11,290	13,800	18,100	22,500
Exports	24,500	116,100	179,296	347,336

SOURCES: ODEPA and Asociación de Exportadores de Chile AG.

The fruit industry in Chile comprised about 11,000 growers, most of whom sold abroad through nearly 100 exporting firms. Data on the first six, accounting for 57% of exports in volume, are presented in Table B:

TABLE B   **Leading Chilean Fruit Exporters**

	Total Exports*	Percent	Exports to Europe*	Percent
1. David Del Curto SA	13,661	15.2%	3,694	11.5%
2. Standard Trading	11,609	13.5	5,325	16.6
3. United Trading Company	8,050	9.4	2,775	8.6
4. Unifrutti Traders	6,933	8.1	1,799	5.6
5. Frupac Ltda.	5,299	6.2	1,605	5.0
6. Coopefrut Ltda.	3,909	4.5	2,065	6.4

* 1987–1988 season, in 000 boxes (1 ton = 95–100 boxes).
SOURCES: Servicio Agrícola Ganadero and Asociación de Exportadores de Chile AG.

All six leading companies competed worldwide and especially in Europe. DDC's main competitors were the following:

- *Standard Trading* was a wholly owned subsidiary of the American multinational Castle & Cooke, one of the leaders in the world fruit business. It established operations in Chile in the early 1980s. It marketed in Europe under the Dole brand through a branch network that organized distribution.

- *United Trading Company* was owned by an important Arab consortium with several businesses in Chile. New to the fruit business, it began operations in Chile in the early 1980s. It sold in Europe through distribution agents and in the United States through a joint venture with Californian partners.

- *Unifrutti Traders* was owned by an Italian family. It marketed fruit throughout Europe but particularly in Italy. It began operations in Chile in 1983. Its subsidiary, Unifrutti of America, distributed to the US market, while elsewhere it marketed through distribution agents.

- *Frupac* was a Chilean firm owned by several growers who joined together in 1979 to export their own fruit. It was the first Chilean company to establish subsidiaries in the United States and Europe to import and market its own fruit. Frupac's operations were international in scope: It owned plantations in Peru, businesses in Argentina, and also marketed Mexican fruit worldwide.

- *Coopefrut* was a cooperative founded in 1964 by Chilean owners that focused on apples. It used two distribution agents in the United States and several in Europe. It had recently established a branch in Europe to import its own fruit and support the marketing activities of its distribution agents.

The World Market for Fresh Fruit

The world production of fresh fruit was about 210 million tons in 1983–1985. The main producers were Brazil, the United States, Italy, Israel, and Spain in citrus; the Soviet Union, Italy, and the United States in stone fruits; the Soviet Union,

China, France, and Italy in apples and pears; and Brazil, Philippines, India, and Colombia in bananas.

World trade in fresh fruit represented about 10% of world production and almost doubled in volume between 1963 and 1983, as shown in Table C:

TABLE C   **World Trade in Fresh Fruit**

	1963		1973		1983	
	000 Tons	*Percent*	*000 Tons*	*Percent*	*000 Tons*	*Percent*
Bananas	4,088	38.1%	6,603	39.4%	6,762	33.6%
Oranges	2,923	27.3	4,543	27.1	4,994	24.8
Apples	1,588	14.8	2,448	14.6	3,535	17.6
Grapes	720	6.7	896	5.3	1,139	5.7
Other	1,415	13.1	2,310	13.6	3,711	18.3
Total	10,734	100.0%	16,800	100.0%	20,141	100.0%

SOURCE: FAO.

Europe was both the main exporter and importer of fresh fruit in the world. It accounted for 30% of world exports and 54% of world imports. The main exporting countries were Spain, 9%; the United States 8%; Italy, 6%; and Ecuador, 5%, while the United States, 15%; West Germany, 14%; France, 9%; and the United Kingdom, 6% were the main importers.

The European Fresh Fruit Market

Basic Patterns

The per capita consumption of fruit differed markedly across countries in the EC. Table D shows the evolution of consumption (in kilograms per capita) for all fresh fruit except citrus and for apples, the most heavily consumed fruit:

TABLE D   **Evolution of Fresh Fruit Consumption in Europe (Kilograms per Capita)**

	All Fresh Fruit*		Apples	
	1973–1974	*1984–1985*	*1973–1974*	*1984–1985*
Belgium/Luxembourg	55	50	24	20
Denmark	42	38	14	19
France	56	55	17	16
Greece	56	77	21	22
Holland	66	64	36	33
Ireland	28	30	10	18
Italy	68	69	15	20

TABLE D   *(concluded)*

	All Fresh Fruit*		Apples	
	1973–1974	*1984–1985*	*1973–1974*	*1984–1985*
Portugal	n.a.†	37	n.a.	9
Spain	n.a.	67	n.a.	21
United Kingdom	31	38	12	12
West Germany	86	79	22	22
Europe	60	60	18	19

* Not including citrus.
† n.a. = Not available.
SOURCE: Eurostat.

Consumption patterns in each country were rather stable except in Greece where per capita fruit consumption had increased significantly. However, there were great differences among countries. For instance, per capita consumption in West Germany and Greece was more than double that in Ireland and the United Kingdom.

Total EC production of fresh fruit reached 28.3 million tons in 1985, representing 13.5% of world production. Table E shows the production (in thousand tons) by country of all fruits, production of apples alone, and the percentage of fruit consumed in each country that was homegrown:

TABLE E   Fresh Fruit Production in Europe, 1985

	All Fresh Fruits*	Apples	Self-Supply†
Belgium/Luxembourg	353	222	61%
Denmark	73	45	38
France	3,433	1,793	89
Greece	2,265	267	125
Holland	439	300	57
Ireland	15	9	15
Italy	6,802	2,014	128
Portugal	419	95	95
Spain	4,188	1,004	116
United Kingdom	494	301	22
West Germany	2,694	1,383	54
Europe 12	21,175†	7,433	87

* Not including citrus.
† Part of this production was exported or was used for animal feed or in the food-processing industry.
SOURCE: Eurostat.

The countries that consumed the least fruit were those with the lowest self-supply ratios: Ireland, the United Kingdom, and Denmark. The opposite was also true: Italy, Spain, and Greece, with self-supply ratios over 100%, were among the heaviest consumers.

European markets not only differed significantly in consumption per capita, but also in tastes and preferences for varieties, sizes, quality, and color. For instance, UK consumers preferred red apples with intense red color, excellent quality, in all varieties, and in medium to small sizes. Spaniards preferred streaky varieties, with little color, medium quality, but large in size. For Italians, variety and color were not important features, but they insisted on big apples. Finally, Germans preferred small size, medium color, and were not as exacting on quality. In general, consumers in Mediterranean countries had stronger preferences regarding size and quality because these countries produced excellent fruit; conversely, consumers in northern Europe were not so demanding since they produced less.

EC imports of all fresh fruit, except citrus, and of apples were as follows (in thousands of tons):

	1983	1984	1985	1986
All fresh fruits*	1,393	1,573	1,642	1,517
Apples	419	504	475	508

* Not including citrus.
SOURCE: Eurostat.

Almost all the fruit imported into the EC during winter and spring came from the southern hemisphere. The main suppliers to the EC in 1986 are listed in Table F:

TABLE F   Sources of EC Fruit Imports, 1986 (in Thousands of Tons)

	Deciduous	Citrus	Subtropical	Other	Total
South Africa	250	299	20	5	504
Chile	205	2	—	—	210
New Zealand	98	—	1	40	139
Argentina	50	86	—	—	136
Brazil	1	73	5	4	83
Uruguay	—	39	—	1	40
Australia	18	3	—	1	22
Total Southern Hemisphere	622	432	26	54	1,134

SOURCE: Eurofruit.

Key Markets

In 1988, The Marketing Unit, Saatchi & Saatchi affiliate, performed a study for the Chilean Association of Fruit Exporters. The study focused on the three main markets for Chilean fruit: West Germany, France, and the United Kingdom.

West Germany was the largest European fruit market, with an annual consumption of about 5 million tons. It was a stable and mature market, increasing in value but static in volume. Due to its high per capita consumption (the highest in Europe) and its relatively low self-supply ratio average (54%), West Germany was the largest market for imports, with a well-developed contraseasonal market (approximately 30% of all apples). Its principal contraseasonal sources were Chile 11%, South Africa 9%, New Zealand 7%, and Argentina 3%.

The trade structure was very decentralized. There were many independent stores (125,000); local and regional (rather than national) chains and department stores (about 30,000); purchasing co-ops; and "symbol groups," which bought on behalf of individually owned stores. Exhibit 5 diagrams the distribution system for fresh fruit in West Germany.

EXHIBIT 5

Channels of distribution of fresh fruit in West Germany

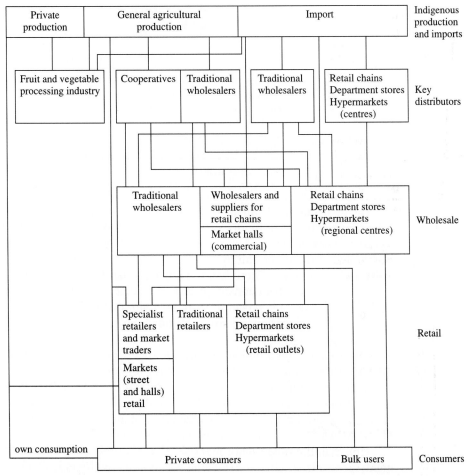

SOURCE: The Marketing Unit.

Both the independents and chains tended to be conservative. The worldwide trend toward retail concentration was developing fairly slowly in West Germany. There were also many regional differences with suppliers operating for the most part on a regional basis. Hence, a great number of primary wholesalers was needed to supply the West German market.

France was a mature market with an annual consumption of about three million tons. Due to its high self-supply ratio and per capita consumption a little under the EC average, its import volume was modest, but exports were high. The contraseasonal fruit market was still underdeveloped but growing, while the seasonal market was in slow decline. The apple market was dominated by the home-grown Golden Delicious variety; contraseasonal apple imports accounted for about 15% of consumption. The key contraseasonal suppliers were Chile, 35%; Italy, 20%; New Zealand, 12%; and South Africa, 11%.

The trade structure was rather fragmented, as indicated in Table G:

TABLE G   Retail Channels for Fresh Fruit in France

	Number	Fruit Share
Markets	9,000	29.4%
Supermarkets	11,000	22.7
General stores	29,500	14.1
Greengrocers	5,000	11.4
Hypermarkets	550	9.9
Other	n.a.*	12.5

* n.a. = Not available.

The distribution channels for fresh fruit in France are diagrammed in Exhibit 6. France had the most rigidly structured distribution system of any of the key EC markets. It was dominated at one end by a few large chains (hypermarkets/super-stores) and at the other end by a very large number of small independents selling fruits and vegetables. There were major regional differences between north and south in patterns of fruit consumption and channel structure. There was a gradual shift of share and trade power toward the major chains in the north. However, the rural south was more conservative, dominated by markets and small shopkeepers, and loath to accept imports.

The *United Kingdom* had one of the lowest per capita consumption levels in the EC. Like France and West Germany, it was a stable, mature market with declining consumption year to year, but increasing in value. With a low self-supply ratio, the contraseasonal fruit market in the United Kingdom was still developing, driven by the major chains. Its main contraseasonal suppliers were South Africa, 25%; New Zealand, 11%; and Chile, 7%.

Unlike in the other major markets, the UK trade structure for fresh fruit was highly centralized. Grocery retailing was dominated by only 10 chains. The retail channels for fresh fruit were as follows:

	Number	*Fruit Share*
Chains	> 30,000	> 45%
Greengrocers	> 15,000	> 30
Independents	> 70,000	> 20

All retailers bought through wholesalers/importers. Innovations were initiated and driven by the chains. The distribution system for fresh fruit in the United Kingdom is diagrammed in Exhibit 7 on the following page.

Consumer Attitudes, Habits, and Trends

According to The Marketing Unit survey, consumer attitudes were basically similar in all three major markets. Consumers bought primarily on the basis of visual appearance. The fruit's country of origin, like Chile or South Africa, was not usually advertised at the point of sale, and consumers did not generally ask for this information.

The main factors that seemed to determine fruit purchasing were price, quality, varieties, visual appeal, trust in the retail outlet, seasonal habits, and fashion

EXHIBIT 6

Channels of distribution of fresh fruit in France

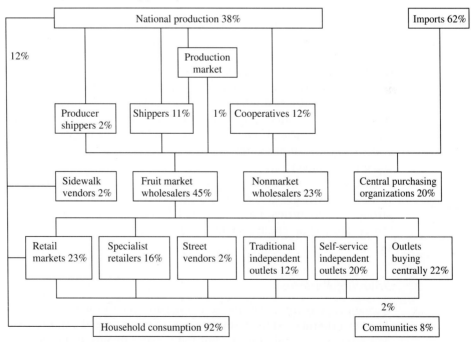

NOTE: These descriptions are the standard ones used for the French retail/wholesale markets.
SOURCE: The Marketing Unit.

EXHIBIT 7

Channels of distribution of fresh fruit in the United Kingdom

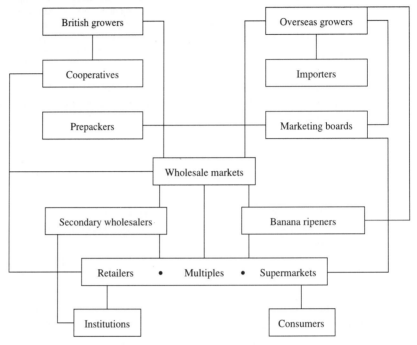

SOURCE: The Marketing Unit.

(as in the case of kiwi fruit). In some markets, like the United Kingdom, consumers tended to buy with their eyes and had a very low brand awareness of fruit. Branding of fruit was often precluded by the risk of bruising, especially in the case of soft fruit. Consumer recall of brands of fruit was low, though some brands like Cape (South Africa's brand) did have significant consumer awareness. Some analysts believed that branding had a greater benefit in marketing to the trade than to the end consumer.

Recently, consumers were showing more interest in exotic fruits, such as kiwi fruit, and better quality and new varieties of staple fruit. This upmarket trend was stronger in countries like the United Kingdom with a more concentrated trade where the major chains sought to boost their margins on a stable volume of demand.

Sourcing Patterns

Consumers did not determine sourcing patterns. These were decided by the trade. The key criteria used to select the country of origin and exporter were availability, consistency of supply throughout the season, quality of produce, price (adjusted for the exchange rate), and service.

Chilean Fruit Positioning in the EC Market

Chile's share of the EC contraseasonal fruit market grew significantly in the 1980s. It was the leader in West Germany and France with 11% and 35% market shares, respectively, and third after South Africa and New Zealand (its main competitors) in the United Kingdom. Table H shows the mix of Chilean products in these three key markets:

TABLE H   Mix of Chilean Fruits by Volume and Value in Three EC Markets

	Germany		France		United Kingdom	
	Percent Volume	*Percent Value*	*Percent Volume*	*Percent Value*	*Percent Volume*	*Percent Value*
Apples	81%	72%	69%	56%	58%	41%
Pears	7	8	15	13	4	3
Grapes	6	12	12	20	27	42
Plums	—	—	1	2	1	2
Peaches	—	1	2	5	1	2
Other	5	7	2	5	10	11

According to market observers, the key sources of competitive advantage for Chile were (1) a relatively neutral political profile compared to South Africa; (2) recent rapid increases in overall fruit quality; (3) a longer harvesting season; (4) a speed of delivery which rivaled that of South Africa; and (5) a broad and competitive range of deciduous fruits.

Image

Retail and wholesale perceptions of Chilean fruit quality varied across markets. West German and French distributors considered Chilean products to be of very good quality. Germans tended to believe the Chilean fruit had "little or no chemical treatment." Chilean exporters were viewed as responsive, particularly by French importers. In the United Kingdom, Chilean fruit was seen as fairly good in quality, but not as good as that from South Africa or New Zealand.

The main criticisms made by the trade about Chilean fruit concerned consistency of quality and consistency of supply. Other problems mentioned by the trade in Europe were the lack of consumer awareness of fruit originating from Chile, the lack of overall coordination among Chilean exporters which led to missed marketing opportunities, and the lack of standardization in packaging.

Trade Relations and Marketing

Both South Africa and New Zealand had marketing organizations in West Germany, France, and the United Kingdom. These government-controlled organizations were called "marketing boards" ("UNIFRUCO" and A.P.M.B., respectively). The mission of these organizations was to coordinate harvesting, shipping, importing, and marketing. The marketing boards distributed the fruit through a "panel" system. Panel appointments were franchises granted to wholesalers by producers to sell fruit on their behalf. Panelists were selected by the marketing boards and were reviewed on a yearly basis. They sold to retail customers on a fixed commission basis which ranged from 5 to 8 percent. The price at which the fruit was sold was set by the central marketing board. Panelists meant that the producers did not have to trade directly.

The marketing board was also in charge of all marketing activities. The main activities were advertising, promotion, and branding. For instance, South Africa's board UNIFRUCO created awareness for its brands "Cape" and "Outspan" through advertising (mainly on radio) and promotional material for the point of sale (posters, educational leaflets describing the fruit's nutritional value, mobiles, brand logos, brochures, carrier bags, and sometimes badges and T-shirts). In addition, UNIFRUCO advertised in trade magazines. It was estimated that UNIFRUCO spent in 1987 about $2.1 million on its communications program for the Cape brand in the United Kingdom, West Germany, and France.

Chile did not use a marketing board or panelists and operated in an "uncoordinated" way through distribution agents and importers in all three countries. Chile performed almost no marketing activities and had very little direct contact with the major retailers. Except for Standard Trading's Dole brand, Chilean fruit was usually unbranded. Finally, Chilean exporters had never attempted to promote their fruit generically in Europe; only a few individual exporters advertised in trade magazines.

Implications of 1992 for the Fresh Fruit Market

Although the impact of the 1992 market integration program on the fresh fruit market was not yet clear, some changes were expected. The EC Commission was expected to decrease agricultural subsidies because of the enormous cost of the Common Agricultural Policy (CAP). EC authorities were concerned about the continuing rapid growth of the CAP budget, caused by consistent excess production and large stockpiles of certain food products. In 1988, CAP net expenses reached 25.2 billion ECUs,[1] accounting for 65% of the EC's general budget. About 7% of these expenses subsidized fruit and vegetables.

However, analysts believed that, even if agricultural subsidies were reduced, some measures would have to be taken to protect agriculture, a sector that employed 8.8% of EC workers. There was growing pressure on the Commission from COPA (the European growers association) to restrict imports from southern hemisphere suppliers. The reasons were overproduction of apples (primarily in France and Italy) and the support of other growers of peaches, nectarines, and strawberries. Balanced against this pressure was the Commission's awareness that it had to ensure competitive prices for EC consumers.

---

[1] In 1988, one ECU was between $1.10 and $1.20.

These pressures had led to restrictions being imposed on southern hemisphere suppliers in the fresh fruit market, first on apples and then on grapes. The restriction on apples, applied in 1988, consisted of quotas on imports that, as shown in Table I, had grown significantly since 1984:

TABLE I   EC Imports of Apples, 1984–1989 (in Thousands of Tons)

	1984	*1985*	*1986*	*1987*	*1988**	*1989**
South Africa	157	147	164	170	195	188
Chile	98	87	151	161	142	168
New Zealand	77	96	97	105	128	135
Argentina	53	64	32	53	79	78
Australia	2	10	6	8	6	11
Total	388	405	451	497	550	580

* Quotas.
SOURCE: Eurostat.

The producing country most damaged by the quotas was Chile, which until 1987 had exhibited the greatest growth. Whereas South Africa was assigned a quota of 165,000 tons, Chile's quota was only 130,000; its capacity was 190,000. Finally, South Africa was actually allowed to supply 195,000 tons, but Chilean imports were halted at 142,130. Thousands of tons of product en route to Europe had to be thrown away. Chile had recourse to the General Agreement on Tariffs and Trade (GATT), and one year later the GATT Group of Experts passed judgment favorable to Chile in an unprecedented verdict. For 1989, the EC assigned 188,000 tons to South Africa, and Chile negotiated a voluntary agreement for 168,000.

Fruit imported from outside the EC was charged a standard tariff that ranged between 5% and 22% for all EC countries, depending on type of fruit and variety. Also, tariffs were higher at the beginning and end of the season to protect the sale of EC-grown fruit. For example, tariffs for apples were 8% from January 1 to March 31, 6% from April 1 to July 31, and 14% from August 1 to December 31. It was thought that these tariffs would not be higher, but would remain steady or even go lower. Besides tariffs, other restrictions included quotas, minimum prices, licenses to import some types of fruit, and sanitary regulations. The general trend, even before 1992, was to harmonize and standardize all sanitary regulations in the EC countries. Although these regulations varied from country to country, especially in Italy, the fruit that had passed the tests in whatever European port it had entered was allowed to move to other countries without further controls. Therefore, there already was a free movement of fruit across EC markets.

Consumer preferences after 1992 were difficult to predict. Despite the deep differences in tastes, habits, and patterns of consumption, experts forecast a slow but continuous homogenization of European markets. The free movement of workers, easier travel across countries without border controls, development of

Pan-European television and other media, and an increasing concentration of distribution were among the factors that argued for further similarities among European consumers.

DDC Operations in Europe

Markets and Products

DDC sold in all of Western Europe except Portugal. It could not sell in Eastern Europe because of a boycott on Chilean products since the overthrow of Allende's socialist government in 1973. DDC's European sales in 1988 were $17.83 million, which represented 20.9% of total company exports. The 3.7 million boxes exported to Europe in 1988, which accounted for 27.1% of company export sales by volume, had the following initial destination:

Holland and Belgium	22%
United Kingdom	20
West Germany	17
France	13
Italy	12
Sweden, Finland, Denmark, and Norway	11
Other	5

DDC did not know where its fruit was finally consumed. Actual consumption in Holland and Belgium was only 5% of the shipments. The main markets for DDC's fruit were West Germany, the United Kingdom, France, Italy, and Scandinavian countries.

The types of fruit DDC exported to Europe in 1988 were grapes (43% of volume), apples (32%), pears (10%), kiwi fruit (8%), and stone fruits (4%).

Distribution

The company used different distribution arrangements in each EC market:

Holland, Belgium, Switzerland, Austria	Distribution Agent 1
United Kingdom and Ireland	Distribution Agent 2
West Germany	Distribution Agent 3 and Central Purchasing Org. 1
France	Distribution Agent 4
Italy and Greece	Distribution Agent 5
Sweden, Finland, Norway, Denmark	Central Purchasing Org. 2
Spain	Importers

For most of the EC markets, DDC used five distribution agents to sell and market its products. They were independent agents paid by commission who sold to various wholesalers and retailers, including most supermarket and hypermarket chains. Additionally, the company sold directly to two central purchasing organizations. One belonged to a West German supermarket chain and the other to the Union of Scandinavian Consumer Cooperatives. Finally, DCC's clients in Spain were three importers and producers of fruit.

The distribution agents worked exclusively for DDC during the contraseason but represented other firms from Europe and other countries during the rest of the year.

DDC executives met each distribution agent personally twice a season to discuss the distribution strategy and prepare annual orders based on historical trends and expected changes during the next season. In these meetings they also analyzed the total supply situation in Europe: new varieties, countries of origin, qualities, types of packing, new transportation technologies, forecasted prices and volumes, and the mix of varieties to include in future shipments. Distribution agents also sent weekly market reports by telex or fax which commented on volume sold that week, estimated prices, the general market situation, and future prospects.

Pricing

Due to fruit's perishable nature, its uncertain condition after transportation, and changing consumer tastes, fruit prices were highly volatile both seasonally and from year to year. However, early contraseasonal prices were typically much higher because of the insufficient supply at the beginning of the winter, but then fell quickly. Thanks to the quality of its fruit, its prestige as the largest and oldest Chilean supplier, and dependable supply throughout the contraseason, DDC usually obtained prices a little higher than average in the market.

DDC used three methods to sell fruit: firm price, minimum guarantee, and free consignment. DDC employed the first method with Spanish importers, the second with German and Scandinavian central purchasing organizations, and the third with distribution agents. Under free consignment, the exporter delivered the fruit to the destination port distribution agent, who sold it to wholesalers and retailers at the highest possible price. After the sale, the distribution agent presented a "sales account" which detailed sales revenues for each product minus customs fees, duties, handling of fruit in the port, cold storage, internal transportation, and other expenses.

Agents' commissions were normally 8% of the selling price. DDC's sales to wholesalers and retailers worldwide in 1988 totaled about $150 million. However, its net revenues were only $85.3 million. The difference, about $65 million, was used by distribution agents to pay their commissions (8% of $150 million), distribution expenses, port expenses, duties, and freight and insurance. From net revenues, DDC deducted a commission of 8%, which was standard among Chilean exporters. Other DDC income came from all services and products provided to

---

EXHIBIT 8   Cost Breakdown of a Typical Export of Apples and Grapes to Europe*

		Apples	Grapes
	Selling price to wholesalers or retailers in Europe	100%	100%
Minus:	Distribution agent's commission (over selling price)	8	8
	Expenses in Europe (discounted by the distribution agent):		
	• Port and distribution expenses (discharge, handling, trucking, storage, etc.)	7–8	5–6
	• Duties	5–6	11–13
	• Freight and insurance	34–37	17–20
Equal:	FOB Chile	41–46	53–59
Minus:	Exporter's commission (8% over FOB price)	3–4	4–5
	Expenses in Chile (discounted by the exporter):		
	• Port expenses	0.9	1.3
	• Domestic freight	2.0	1.6
	• Cooling	2.1	2.8
	• Packing service	3.5	6.7
	• Packing materials	13.4	12.5
Equal:	Grower's revenue	15–21	23–30

* Data from 1987–88 season for Granny Smith apples and Ribier and Thomson Seedless grapes, the varieties most exported to Europe. Costs have been estimated over the following average prices per box: apples $13.5–$14.5 (18.2 kilograms) and grapes $8.5–$9.5 (5 kilograms).

SOURCE: Casewriter estimates based on information given by several fresh fruit exporters.

EXHIBIT 9

Organization chart of the commercial area

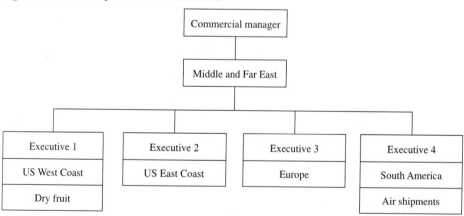

growers. Exhibit 8 shows a typical cost breakdown on fruit exported to Europe from Chile.

Organization and control

The company's commercial department consisted of a manager and four executives, as shown in Exhibit 9. Basically, it was structured according to geography.

One executive was in charge of the US West Coast market and dry fruit exports; another was responsible for the US East Coast market; the third coordinated the European markets; and the fourth was in charge of South America and air shipments. Apart from managing the whole department, the commercial manager oversaw the Middle and Far East markets.

The executive in charge of the European markets was Rodrigo Falcone, who described his task in this way:

> My objective is to maximize the revenues for the boxes sent to Europe. To accomplish this task, I have to be in close and permanent contact with each distribution agent so as to move the fruit toward the highest priced markets.

Rodrigo Falcone's mission was to coordinate and control all shipments to Europe in order to secure the maximum possible price for the fruit delivered on consignment to distribution agents. First, the fruit was allocated to distribution agents from Chile, and then Rodrigo Falcone reallocated it to agents whose markets offered better prices at any time. This task required almost instantaneous decisions by phone, telex, or fax.

Rodrigo Falcone had no established travel plan; every year was different due to changing market conditions. However, he usually worked in Europe from March to August and in Chile the rest of the year. While in Europe, he worked in different markets, but resided in Hamburg, West Germany. His operations base was the Central Representation Office for Europe. The company did not own this organization, but used it exclusively during the contraseason. Like distribution agents, the organization worked with both European fruit and products from tropical countries. It had a permanent staff of six or seven people, all West Germans. Its functions were (*a*) to coordinate the logistics (regular shipments, charters, and the reallocation of fruit to different markets); (*b*) to serve as the communications center (telex, fax, and mail); and (*c*) to supervise the financial and administrative activities of DDC's European business (payments, collection, credit lines for ships, and handling of all kinds of formalities, documents, and other papers). In sum, the organization focused not on the marketing of the fruit but on the coordination of operations.

Finally, DDC employed a full-time agronomist engineer in Rotterdam, the main port of entry for its fruit in Europe. Other agronomists and technicians traveled from Chile to inspect the fruit's condition on its arrival in Europe. They ensured quality control and monitored the effectiveness of different experimental packing techniques.

Branding and Communications

DDC's fruit in Europe neither carried its own brand nor that of any distribution agent. Only a few supermarket chains used displays that included boxes with the logo "Del Curto–Chile"; normally these retailers did not brand their fruit. Merchandising activities were performed by neither DDC nor distribution agents. From time to time, chains offered special promotions of DDC products.

The company did not advertise its products to the final consumer; however, it did place some full-color institutional or image advertisements targeted at the trade in specialized magazines such as *Fruchthandel* from West Germany and *Eurofruit* from the United Kingdom. These were bimonthly publications sold by subscription to importers, distributors, wholesalers, supermarket chains, and exporters throughout the world. The distribution agents neither advertised nor promoted DDC's fruit, but only advertised their own firms' capabilities.

Reviewing the European Strategy

In mid-June 1989, Lothar Meier wondered whether the trends and expected changes in the EC fresh fruit market would necessitate modifying his company's strategy.

Organization

His first concern was the suitability of DDC's organization and distribution in Europe. There were at least three alternatives: first, to continue with the current way of doing business in Europe; second, to create a subsidiary that could import, distribute, and market its own fruit; and third, to foster the creation of a marketing board for all Chilean fruit, like the ones run by South Africa, New Zealand, and Israel. This last alternative was not considered by Lothar Meier, but was a possibility suggested by some market observers.

Of the six main Chilean exporters, four had European sales subsidiaries or operated through their parent companies' European networks. DDC had previously rejected the idea of a sales office to import, distribute, or market its fruit in Europe. Lothar Meier concurred with the opinion of Rodrigo Falcone, the executive in charge in Europe:

> If we had a sales branch in Europe, we would need at least 15 employees to manage our current volume, and this would reduce our flexibility. For instance, if the dollar goes up much, if there is a significant fall in demand, or the export of some product into the EC market is suddenly forbidden, we can divert our fruit to the USA and deliver less in Europe. If we did do this, we couldn't justify the fixed expenses of a subsidiary in Europe. Instead, by being the major private exporter from the southern hemisphere, DDC has the capacity to work with the best distribution agents in each country. After almost 30 years in this business, the company knows all the distribution agents in Europe and works with the best ones. That our main competitors constantly offer them opportunities to join their organizations demonstrates their quality.

Lothar Meier added:

> Besides being a matter of flexibility, it's a matter of cost. If we operate in the European market for just six months a year, we cannot absorb the overhead expenses for the whole year. With our current organization and distribution system we keep our costs low.

Asked about running the sales office all year long and handling fruit of the northern hemisphere in the seasonal market, Lothar Meier stated that instead of continuing to grow in volume and embarking on new ventures, the company should consolidate its current activities.

The third alternative—to promote the creation of a marketing board with other Chilean exporters to coordinate the harvesting, shipping, importing, distribution, and marketing of Chilean fruit in the EC market— was suggested by The Marketing Unit to the Chilean Association of Fruit Exporters as a result of its study (see Exhibit 10).

EXHIBIT 10   Excerpts from marketing unit report

Chile has no marketing organization on site in Europe:
- For Chile, the importers are the trade interface.
- Therefore, there is negligible coordination.
- Activities in Europe are fragmented, opportunistic.

This flexibility and opportunism has served Chile well:
- It has been an appropriate strategy during periods of open access to EC markets and buoyant EC economies.
- Chilean exports to Europe have grown dramatically, due to:
  — Increases in availability.
  — Incentives to importers including dating.
  — Exchange rates favorable to European currencies.

But are flexibility and opportunism right for the new climate?

The New Climate in Europe
1. The EC is closing ranks (and frontiers) against southern hemisphere fruit suppliers. Chile has been singled out for close attention. Chile must expect rigidly applied limitations in the future.
2. Exchange rates expected to continue to move in favor of European currencies at least until the end of 1989.
3. The scope for further cost-effective direct incentives to importers is limited. Investment in marketplace impacts at the point-of-sale is likely to represent the most profitable use of support funds.

The Market Now Demands a Strategic Rather Than a Tactical Approach
Such strategy requires:
- Systematic marketing planning for each major outlet.
- Development of close trade relationships.
- Ability to guarantee supply.
- Point-of-sale merchandising support.

A Marketing Board could perform these tasks.

Organization
Improved organization could improve dramatically the way in which Chile:
- Services the importers.
- Services the retail trade.
- Coordinates supply and demand.
- Demonstrates size, stature, importance.
- Maximizes visibility and *presence* in each market.

A new *organization* should have the following capabilities/functions:
- Tightly knit, *dedicated* resource for *Chilean* fruit.
- Ongoing Pan-European coverage.
- EC liaison capability.
- Handling importer and major trade relations directly.
- Using outside consulting resources for Marketing Services and for Marketing Communications.

SOURCE: Adapted from "Chilean Winter Fruit. A Marketing Plan for 1988/1989 and Beyond, Covering: West Germany, France and the United Kingdom," by The Marketing Unit, February 1988.

Some of the large Chilean exporters were opposed to the marketing board idea. They believed that the central planning and coordination provided by such a board could not compensate for the flexibility and rapid response time that they enjoyed as independent entrepreneurs. To some, the faster growth of Chilean exports compared with those from South Africa and New Zealand proved the superiority of the independent or uncoordinated approach. Lothar Meier agreed with this position. He believed that marketing boards had often failed because of inefficiency and the high costs of production and transportation.

Distribution

As previously mentioned, DDC operated directly with the central purchasing organization of two major supermarket or cooperative chains in West Germany and Sweden. Asked about extending these arrangements to other large chains in Europe and forming joint ventures or strategic alliances, Lothar Meier answered:

> We can't do so much. Our company receives many proposals from important chains. As they are big retailers they want to buy in the country of origin, to have a link there. Currently, we reach all important chains across Europe through our distribution agents. To serve the chains directly, we would need a huge staff. We can't do all the business in the world. We are specialists in a part of the distribution channel.

Branding and Promotion

Finally, Lothar Meier wondered about making a greater marketing effort to increase consumer awareness and loyalty toward Chilean fruit and, in particular, toward DDC's fruit. Two crucial subjects were branding and communications.

On these issues, Lothar Meier commented:

> Advertising to create awareness and loyalty in this business is expensive and ineffective, because it is directed toward the consumer who doesn't see the brand; he sees only apples and grapes. Building a brand in the international fruit market is very costly, and large volumes are needed to absorb those expenses. Chiquita, the famous brand of bananas, sells more than 120 million boxes all over the world. However, this is a brand for just one product shipped by one producer. No Chilean exporter has the volume to warrant such a huge investment.

THE MARKETING PROCESS

MARKETING
ORIENTATION

SKF BEARINGS—MARKET ORIENTATION THROUGH SERVICES

Restructuring the Before and After Market

In the spring of 1987, Mauritz Sahlin, CEO of SKF, the world's largest bearing company, took a bold step. The time had come to do whatever was necessary to improve profitability and return on assets. He knew that his plan would require a complex reorganization of SKF with far-reaching consequences, but he had no other options.

Production had already been rationalized and was fully automated, leaving little room for real savings. The company could not pull back on R&D expenditures, as they were essential to having technological prowess and quality standards. Cutting back on staff would upset the unions and provoke costly work stoppages.

He was convinced that the only viable long-term solution was to change the strategic orientation of SKF from the production line to the market. Amid great uncertainty and speculation, he called together the senior bearing managers from around the world to Saltsjobaden, Sweden, to announce his intention to split the company into three new areas.

"It is essential," he said, "that we optimize by structuring around our market relationships instead of our manufacturing capacity. If we want to remain the industry leader in bearings, we must be prepared to give customers what they want rather than merely sell them what we make."

He knew that the traditional sluggish culture of the company had to be altered. Questions would have to be answered that were not yet part of the

This case was prepared by Professor Sandra Vandermerwe and Dr. Marika Taishoff. Copyright © 1990 by the International Institute for Management Development (IMD), Lausanne, Switzerland. Not to be used or reproduced without permission. IMD case 383.

existing SKF vocabulary. He expected criticism, resistance, and conflict among the divisions—even confusion for a while. He was prepared to take the risks.

The Beginnings and Background

As in many industrial success stories, the formation of SKF happened by chance. At the turn of the century, Sven Wingquist, a young Swedish maintenance engineer, was fed up with the poor quality of bearings, with frequent stoppages and replacements that were not only expensive but took weeks for suppliers to deliver. The frustrated Wingquist got his employer's blessing to begin work on a new bearing in 1905 and soon perfected a product that was more effective and longer lasting than competitors' models. By 1907 Svenska Kullager Fabriken (SKF), the new company set up to produce and market the technological innovation, was in business.

The ball bearing, a device which allows rotation around a shaft or axle with minimal friction, is an essential part of any motion-dependent product, be it car, machine, truck, or train. As a result, high-quality bearings soon became an indispensable item for all major industrial sectors, ranging from electrical and heavy industries to transportation. Over the next six decades, SKF grew in tandem with industrial growth and became the world leader in bearing technology and applications.

Up through the mid-1960s, SKF was highly centralized; all aspects of the business such as logistics, global sales, application engineering, and public relations were handled by the parent company in Göteborg. Five European plants produced a wide range of products geared to their own large local customer base. These regional units concentrated exclusively on the manufacturing process, particularly on maintaining cost effectiveness. Countries did not export to one another or operate internationally except rarely—when the initiative came from Göteborg.

The company's underlying drive was mass production and having high quality standards. In the words of one executive, "Big was beautiful." The plants were given significant capital budget allocations. Large economies of scale meant that huge quantities of bearings could be sold at competitive prices on the world market. Operations were integrated as much as possible both horizontally and vertically. A tools division was acquired in order to expand into the manufacture of engineering products and machine tools. Manufacturing machinery was designed in-house so that material flow systems and production techniques could be perfected and capacity increased.

R&D contributed greatly to SKF's strength. Since most bearings had an average life of five years, there was a continuous need to develop new products. About 200 people in the Netherlands were involved in product development and in improving the engineering and performance standards for the product lines. Input was received from the various plants where R&D had a close relationship. As a general rule, SKF preferred to overdesign its products to ensure that the needs and specifications of the plant managers were met.

The 70s and 80s: Japanese and European Competition

In the early 70s the Japanese, already strong in Asia, entered the European bearings market. As a result, SKF management was forced to cut costs further "by whatever means" as well as begin exporting outside their traditional markets. To reach this goal while developing scale economies, production facilities were rationalized along the lines of the Japanese model; that is, each factory became responsible for making and exporting a specific bearing type for world consumption.

The rise in oil prices in the early 80s, causing a drop in real wealth and in demand for capital goods and consumer durables, put additional pressure on margins. "Production Concept 80," aimed at stimulating effective production, at cutting staff, and at underscoring the manufacturing process in company investment policy, was SKF's response to economic conditions as well as to competitive threats.

This concept, along with the continued emphasis on top quality standards, allowed SKF to remain the number one bearings producer. By the late 80s the company had 20% of the world bearings market share, nearly twice that of its closest competitor, Nippon Seiko of Japan. Another Japanese bearings producer, NTN, had 10%, followed by Germany's F.A.G. and Timken of the United States with 8.5% each, and the Japanese firm Koyo with 6% of the world market.

Bearings producers were not the only competitors on the world scene. Automobile manufacturers, including Ford, Honda, and Mercedes, through their spare parts divisions, were both competitors to and customers of SKF. This was also the case for some specific manufacturers of automobile parts, such as the United Kingdom's Quinton Hazel, which would typically purchase SKF bearings and sell them under its own brand name to distributors, thereby cutting into a segment of SKF's traditional customer base.

SKF's position had always been strongest in Europe and Latin America, with 35% and 30% of these markets, respectively. In the United States, SKF was in third position, with 12%. On average, Europe accounted for almost 60% of SKF's business; North America for 20%; Sweden, 5%; and the rest of the world, 15%. Despite this comparatively strong market share, worldwide economic and industrial conditions continued to squeeze margins during the first half of the decade. This situation came to a head in 1985 when SKF's volume in the United States, susceptible to economic changes and often indicative of what could happen in other regions, plunged 15%. The company was obliged to embark on a substantial restructuring program in the United States.

1986: A Financial Ebb

By 1986, SKF had 48 factories in 13 countries operating at near or full capacity to produce 2 million bearings a day. SKF vigorously promoted its products through 35,000 local dealer and distributor (d/d) outlets worldwide, as well as a direct sales force of 600 throughout 130 countries. Dealers and distributors carried large

EXHIBIT 1   SKF: Financial Profile for 1982–1986 (Consolidated in Billions of Swedish Kronor)

	1982	*1983*	*1984*	*1985*	*1986*
Net sales	14.4	16.2	17.8	20.0	20.1
Operating expenses	13.0	14.9	15.9	17.9	18.0
Income after financial income and expense	.657	.604	1.3	1.4	1.5
Total assets	18.8	18.6	21.8	22.0	22.8
Shareholder equity	5.4	5.2	6.8	6.7	7.3
Return on total assets	8.0	7.4	9.8	9.5	9.3
Price per share	29.2	42.0	43.0	75.0	84.0
Bearings:					
As percentage of total sales	80	82	80	76	77
As percentage of total profits	90	95	80	78	75

SOURCE: Annual reports.

stocks of limited-range high-turnover bearings for SKF, along with competitive bearings and complementary materials and tools.

When Sahlin took the helm as CEO in 1985, SKF was operating at the crest of what amounted to a roller bearing boom. Nevertheless, economic conditions and competitive pressure made it a buyers' market. Bottom-line results began to turn flat at SKF that year, when sales slackened and margins narrowed. (The financial profile for the years 1982 through 1986 is shown in Exhibit 1.)

Segmenting the Bearings Market

With increasing competition, SKF found it more and more difficult to differentiate its product from the others. It had always applied one strategy and organization for all bearing customers. High-quality products were sold in large quantities at competitive prices. Sahlin questioned this approach and, late in 1986, commissioned research to examine the bearings market in detail. He wanted to establish whether the market could be segmented along any natural split among the product lines according to specific customer needs.

Consumers were grouped into three categories:

1. *Automotive Original Equipment Manufacturers (OEM)* (cars, trucks, electrical), with 32% of SKF bearings sales in Swedish Kronor (Skr).
2. *Machinery OEM* (heavy industry, railway, general machinery), with 27% of SKF bearings sales in Skr.
3. *Aftermarket* (vehicles and industrial), with 41% of SKF bearings sales in Skr.

Whereas bearings were regarded as vital components in the OEM market, in the aftermarket they were seen merely as spare parts. Large OEM sales were handled directly by the company's global sales arm. Contracts were substantial and steady. "Large orders were signed and executed in a routine way."

The aftermarket sales were made to distributors and dealers, who in turn served end users. Relationships were entirely different for these markets, as were the services demanded. Delivery requirements, lead times, and quantities, along with type and range of bearings needed, also varied considerably.

There were more than twice as many OEM than aftermarket customers, although fewer in the vehicle business than in machinery. Automotive OEM customers were large and tended to operate centrally on a European, if not global, scale. By contrast, machinery OEM users were smaller; their particular strengths tended to be in specific industries and geographic locations. Large OEM customers made up roughly 40% of the total SKF bearings sales in kronor. Lead times were stable and predictable, making forecasting straightforward. Profit margins were low in the OEM sector. The larger OEM customers, who often set their own prices on substantial, long-term contracts, were particularly cost conscious since "every cent saved was money in the bank." SKF was thus under constant competitive pressure to keep price increases at or below the inflation rate.

OEM customers were considered the glamorous end of the business, always given priority by the SKF factories. High volume production and sales standards set for the large OEM customers were applied throughout the rest of the organization. OEMs were not only allocated most of the new-product funding, but also attracted SKF's best talent. Some of the reasons for this situation were:

- OEMs would typically deal with big-name customers like Volkswagen or Ford, and would be involved in negotiations at a senior managerial level.
- Technical developments for OEMs were more challenging than for the aftermarket because they tended to be more complex and state of the art.
- Orders for the OEM were larger, steadier, and more consistent, with lead times that made well-defined production schedules possible.

By contrast, the aftermarket tended to concentrate on single sale deals for motor dealers and factories. Although price was important, these clients, for whom speed, availability, and assistance were essential, were prepared to pay more than the OEM customers. In fact, the higher prices in the aftermarket enabled SKF to do OEM business that otherwise may not have been justified. It had long been suspected that, despite being largely limited to single sales, the aftermarket was the most profitable part of the business. However, since operating results for all the markets were consolidated, this impression was never really confirmed.

The aftermarket was subdivided into two separate categories:

1. *The industrial aftermarket* (factory owners and plant managers), with 66% of SKF aftermarket sales in Skr.
2. *The vehicle aftermarket* (fleet owners and repair shops), with 34% of SKF aftermarket sales in Skr.

In their *industrial* aftermarket business, which contributed two-thirds to the overall aftermarket sales, SKF had concentrated mainly on steel and paper mills. Mines and railways were also a part of this business. These customers had the same basic needs wherever they were geographically situated. The distributor network accounted for 80% of the sales.

For industrial users, the cost of the bearing was "peanuts compared to the cost of standstill." They sought to minimize downtime and maximize the recovery speed. Customers spent 75% of downtime locating the proper equipment and people, and only 25% on actually repairing the machine.

The lifetime of a bearing played a fundamental role in the success of these customers' production activities. Longevity was affected by (1) the quality of the product, (2) how it was installed, (3) protecting the bearing from the environment, and (4) the quality of maintenance management at the factory. The last three factors depended on the users. Most bearings failed because of incorrect installation, inadequate or improper lubrication, or environmental contamination.

The *vehicle* aftermarket accounted for one-third of total aftermarket sales. Despite the fact that the automobile and truck sectors contributed 24% of SKF's OEM sales, the aftermarket had been relatively ignored. This neglect stemmed from the basic principle "If we made it, we sold it." And since SKF made a limited range of bearings compared to the great variety of autos, the aftermarket had never been considered a priority.

Dealers for automotive OEMs and independent distributors channeled spare parts through to the car and truck market. Because of the better service they were receiving, garage and fleet owners were increasingly shifting their business to the independents. Bearings comprised only 3–4% of distributor and retailer sales, compared to between 30% and 70% in the industrial aftermarket. The distance from the bearing manufacturer to the final user was much longer in the vehicle aftermarket, with the channel consisting of wholesalers, large retailers, and garages. Since cross-referencing of bearing components was not consistent in the industry, it was difficult to ascertain which manufacturer's part was being replaced.

Vehicle dealers and repair shops wanted a bearing quickly because car owners expected vehicles back within a couple of hours. They also needed the right bearing for that particular vehicle. Replacing a bearing presented three problems for the bearing installer: (1) where to find the correct bearing, (2) how to mount and install it, and (3) how to obtain the various accessories to get the job done.

SKF had always regarded distributors as customers rather than as part of the channel to the end user. Bearings were sold *to* them instead of *through* them. Relationships with end users were left in the distributors' hands. Salespeople loaded up the distributors' shelves and devised all sorts of deals to gain volume, even if items had to be taken back unsold. The distributor network gave Bearing Services the necessary local presence and coverage, and it was often more cost effective than using a direct sales force to get the bearings to the customer. There was, however, no guaranteed preference for the SKF brand.

Splitting the Organization

Research showed that the market for bearings was far from homogeneous. This information confirmed Sahlin's instincts that different target segments had to have their own market strategies and organizations.

No one knew what to expect when Sahlin convened an urgent meeting in Saltsjobaden. As one manager described it, "Phone calls had been made back and forth to try to find out what was going on and who had been invited. Most of us only found out the next day when it made *The Financial Times*." At the meeting, Sahlin announced that, as of September 1, the bearings group would be officially reorganized into three new areas.

1. *Bearing Industries* would include all the manufacturing plants producing "standard" bearings for OEM, both machinery and automotive. The selling would be done by its own sales force in countries where SKF had factories, such as Germany, France, the United Kingdom, the United States, Sweden, Brazil, Argentina, Mexico, and Italy. In other countries, such as Switzerland, Belgium, and Holland, Bearing Services would do the selling.

2. *Bearing Services,* carved out of the global sales organization, would handle the entire vehicle and industrial aftermarket as well as some of the smaller OEM clients with whom the aftermarket distributors did business.

3. *Specialty Bearings* would handle products outside the standard line which needed highly specialized skills. This division would have its own factories and would utilize Bearing Industries' and Bearing Services' sales force in most countries. Customers included the aerospace industry, medical equipment suppliers, large machine tool producers, and satellite manufacturers which required custom-designed products for highly specialized applications.

Each business area would have its own CEO and separate worldwide profit responsibility. Efforts would be made to keep these autonomous, thus minimizing the need for coordination. Sahlin believed the new structure would allow each business unit to be more flexible, to target and get close to its own customers, thereby commanding better margins. (For the old and new group organization structures, see Exhibit 2.)

The research confirmed Sahlin's earlier instinct that the aftermarket was indeed the profitable end of the business. He had long believed that this market had not been given enough attention, but nothing had been done because it was not clear what to do and the financial significance of the aftermarket had never been established. Sahlin was convinced that the key to future profits and customer loyalty was in offering the aftermarket SKF know-how and expertise. Bearing Services, he decided, would be a major focus for the company in the future.

The sales management teams that had been dealing with the aftermarket had previously reported to the manufacturing companies. Now, in the newly formed

EXHIBIT 2

Old and new organizational structures

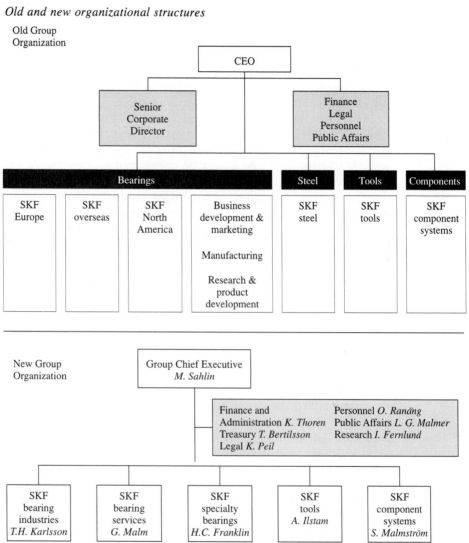

Old Group
Organization

Bearing Services, they were elevated to the same status as that of their former bosses. Sales and marketing directors in various countries became managing directors (MDs).

Transforming the Change Process

Previously, all changes at SKF had been very structured. Typically, before any decision could be made, numerous studies were undertaken and proposals scrutinized in order to minimize risk. A kind of "bible" was then written stating exactly how the change would take place—what had to be done, by when, and by whom. As little as possible was left to chance. Sales budgets, production budgets, and action plans were put in place before the new process began.

It was clear to Sahlin that SKF not only had to become a market-focused company, but the process of change itself had to be transformed. Although the ultimate goal of improving profits was straightforward, exactly how it would evolve was not 100% clear. The company would have to learn by doing, by feeling out the market and being as flexible as possible.

One thing was obvious: The entire culture of the company needed a jolt. The manufacturing functions had always had the clout, but they would have to give up some of that power. The financial approach to the market would have to change as well. Marketing could no longer be considered an expense or cost center, but would have to be handled like any other capital investment.

Sahlin knew it would be impossible to move the whole company at once. He expected Bearing Services to be a springboard to a new SKF market culture. Once they began making positive inroads into the market, he was convinced that the rest of the organization would follow. The goal was not to push for sudden and monumental changes but rather to let things take shape as they moved along. Small positive steps had to be taken to influence people and convince them about the new SKF way. He drafted a rough outline of how the organization would look and some guidelines for implementation. He wanted that the company's technical expertise be used to serve customers more fully, thus giving SKF a significant competitive edge. A new CEO would be appointed to each of the three areas and left to formulate his own plan.

Göran Malm, a sales and marketing specialist with a financial background, had been the European marketing and sales manager for SKF. He had been Singapore area manager for less than a year when Sahlin called and asked him to head Bearing Services. Malm, who had been pushing for change at SKF for some time, had initiated and set up maintenance support centers in Sweden to provide services for the aftermarket there. He was, Sahlin believed, the ideal candidate for the job. At first Malm was reluctant; he'd only just begun to develop a network in Singapore. Sahlin remained adamant: "I decide on the priorities, Göran," came his voice late one night. "I need you back here. You understand the aftermarket and what the customers want. Let me have your decision soon, Göran."

Malm had smiled as he put down the phone. He knew the job would be tough, but he also knew he couldn't resist the offer to lead Bearing Services.

Some Reactions to the Restructuring

- Most aftermarket salespeople liked the idea of the split; they would finally be elevated from the second-class status to which they felt they had been relegated. As one marketing director expressed it, "Suddenly we felt that we were as important as the guys in manufacturing. It was incredible. We knew then that Sahlin was serious about becoming customer oriented. There had been lots of jokes about the d/d club or, as some called it, the dinner/dance club. That's the way those of us in the aftermarket were seen—wining and dining customers without doing any real work. We were happy that at last someone was listening to us and we could concentrate on customers' needs.''

· Some of the more traditional administration, engineering, and financial executives lacked enthusiasm. They couldn't quite see the point. "It will simply add extra costs we don't want or need in our business" was the typical remark.

· Another reservation was whether to take the restructuring seriously. "This is just another reorganization. We've had so many; how long will this one last?" was the refrain.

· Several thought that too many questions had been left unanswered and that the ultimate objectives were still too vague. It wasn't that they necessarily disagreed with the overall plan; they wanted more data and details so they could "proceed in an orderly SKF fashion."

· Others felt that such a novel approach would simply not be feasible in an institution as bureaucratic as SKF. The stringent reporting requirements to head office and rigid structural barriers were just some of the many obstacles which would have to be overcome. These executives were not convinced that the new structure could fit the managerial techniques and tools that they knew worked.

· The MDs who had previously controlled both sales and aftermarket did not all react positively when they heard Sahlin's reorganization plan. Some resented the sudden change in status of the people who had previously been working for them, and who would be taking away a chunk of their business and their profits. "Some executives tried to get around it by saying yes, but then delayed implementation."

When challenged about these concerns, Sahlin stated repeatedly that he understood the difficulties ahead but was prepared to take whatever risks were necessary.

18

SCANDINAVIAN AIRLINES SYSTEM (SAS) REVISITED (A)

Customer Relationships through Services in the 80s

The oil price crises of the 1970s and a worldwide recession at the end of the decade had cut deeply into the airline industry. Most airlines had experienced a deficit, and many carriers had had to resort to dramatic survival tactics to stay in business. IATA, the International Air Transport Association cartel, had accumulated losses of $5 billion during these years. As individual airlines devised strategies to recover from disastrous lows, the first wave of US airline deregulation started being felt in Europe. There was price competition on the transatlantic routes from upstart new carriers with cutthroat tariffs. At the same time, new lower-cost Asian competitors appeared in the skies.

Scandinavian Airlines System (SAS), the national carrier of Denmark, Norway, and Sweden, had not been spared during the crisis years. Despite 17 consecutive years of profitable business, by 1981 SAS was struggling with a severe downturn in business and an accumulated two-year deficit of £30 (Skr 150) million. SAS's multinational board of directors was understandably concerned.

After the company president, Knut Hagrup, resigned in 1978, he was replaced by Carl-Olov Munkberg. Munkberg tried to correct the situation with drastic cost cutting, which included the elimination of 1,300 jobs through attrition. Spending was reduced, but morale suffered and so did SAS's reputation. Then Curt Nicolin, an SAS director and chairman of ASEA, Sweden's huge electrical equipment manufacturer, persuaded the board to bring in Jan Carlzon. Young and energetic, Carlzon had a flair for marketing which had made him a public figure in Scandinavia, where his views on business and government financing had been sought by press and television.

This case series was prepared by Professor Sandra Vandermerwe. Copyright © 1992 by the International Institute for Management Development (IMD), Lausanne, Switzerland. Not to be used or reproduced without permission. IMD case 416.

His philosophy that the public would respond to creative and positive solutions, and less bureaucracy, had struck a popular chord. In fact, he had two success stories behind him to prove it. In his first year as head of Vigressor, a wholly owned tourist subsidiary of SAS, Carlzon had turned the company's results from deficits to profits. During the four years of his tenure, he had expanded retail outlets throughout Sweden and Norway, added a hotel division, and created holiday areas in 20 countries.

The Carlzon Philosophy: We Fly People, Not Planes

Carlzon believed that SAS had become an "introverted" organisation which had lost its awareness of the customers' needs. He felt that management had been putting most of its attention on the mundane aspects of flying airplanes and not enough on the quality of its customers' experience. In his words, "They had focused on machines instead of people—both employees and customers." In contrast to the conservative and stately Scandinavian tradition, he wanted to change their airline from a technical and production-oriented company to a market-focused one, by making all personnel obsessively aware of customer service. He believed he could force attitudinal and structural changes in SAS that would bring the delivery system into harmony with the customers' needs. This approach, he reasoned, would convince the market that SAS was significantly different from all other airline choices.

A service company, he argued, needed a different approach to the customer from manufacturers of tangible products, where the quality could be measured before leaving the factory. "SAS," he pointed out, "is not the airline, or head office, or an overhaul station: It is nothing tangible. It is the contact between one customer in the market and one SAS employee in the front line." He referred to this concept as "the moment of truth," that is, any episode where a customer would come into contact with some aspect of the company, however remote, and thereby have an opportunity to form an impression. Employees had avoided this kind of contact in the past. No one had wanted to deal with customers, as such interruptions were considered to be a nuisance in their daily routines. "SAS," he declared, "had 50,000 moments of truth out in the market every day." That meant 50,000 opportunities to satisfy or dissatisfy customers.

Executives had regarded the buying of even larger and faster airplanes as their most important responsibility. Carlzon frequently commented on this outlook in communication sessions with staff:

> We used to think our biggest assets were aircraft, overhaul stations, and technical resources. But we have only one real asset, and that is a satisfied customer prepared to come back to SAS and pay for our costs once more. That's why the assets on our balance sheet should show the number of satisfied customers who have flown with SAS during the year rather than the number of airplanes, which are not worth one single cent as long as there is no second-hand market in the world for used aircraft, and nobody wants to pay for a flight on those airplanes. So it's really fooling the banks to call them the assets.

The Project Team Approach: Parallel Managing

Carlzon's immediate priority early in 1981 was to find a way to change the SAS situation in the shortest possible time. He took a different approach from his days at Linjeflyg, where he had planned and executed the turnaround within the existing line organisation. This time, he decided to arrange the process of change from outside the formal SAS culture and structure by creating, for a five-month period, a parallel management system.

He delegated total responsibility for the daily operation of the airline to one of his managers, Helge Lindberg. Thus, he was free to head up a small project team of handpicked people: a few trusted executives and new recruits who would become key players once implementation began, and a group of individuals from an outside consulting company and the advertising agency.

The project team's task was to analyse the historical background outside and inside the company, and the organisational climate and functioning of SAS. It took a week for them to isolate the major characteristics of the business and its main weaknesses, and to come up with the direction the change should take. Then, they defined the goals and formal strategies. This process lasted from December 1, 1980, to March 2, 1981, followed by a few months of discussion and refining, before the full plan was presented to the board in June 1981. Carlzon recalled:

> In the beginning, we had to decide what part of the market SAS should do business with, so that all our services could be designed to meet those specific market needs and no other. This included reducing the costs this market was not prepared to pay and eventually eliminating them, so that every resource of expense was profitable. In the past, we had hurt ourselves a little more every year by cutting away at services that customers were prepared to pay for. And we got stuck with administration overheads that they were unprepared to support.

The plan was that the project team would eventually spearhead the implementation of the various tasks. Executives would either create new departments or take over old ones in the new mode, as strategies came on stream in a kind of feeder system. Carlzon felt that the new concept would require radical redirection in thinking and energy and that, if handled in the traditional way, it would take too long to diffuse down through the organisation.

The Businessman's Strategy: Managing the Focus

While competitors were cutting back on new product development and promotions, SAS invested heavily in the Businessman's Airline Programme. By positioning SAS as the "businessman's airline," Carlzon hoped to steal passengers from such other carriers as Air France and British Airways, which were upgrading their service but charging for it. Air France, which was selling *classe d'affaires* at a 17% surcharge, demanded that SAS change its strategy and do likewise. When Carlzon refused, Air France retaliated by stopping sales of SAS tickets through their travel agents. Finally, resolution of the conflict reached the government level, and Air France had to match the SAS price.

Research was conducted to establish what aspects of a travel experience businessmen regarded as important both before, during, and after flying. Safety and punctuality came out on top. Carlzon asked management to find ideas to deliver new improved services for business travelers. They came back with recommendations for 150 projects, requiring an estimated investment cost of about $40 million and another $10 million annually for operating costs. These proposals were followed, in rapid succession, by the development and introduction of a series of new services. The projects chosen were to accomplish one of two objectives: to improve the experience of the frequent traveler or to save his time.

Since the business traveler's most important consideration was *arriving* rather than leaving on time, Carlzon instituted a "leave-on-time punctuality drive," which he largely supervised himself. A viewing screen was installed in his office to give him details about all flights, their departure and arrival times, and delays. Sometimes, when a flight was late, he would phone the pilot directly to find out what was wrong. A special function was established in Copenhagen to monitor and analyze the punctuality of flights worldwide.

In the rush to reduce costs per seat mile, many of the world's airlines acquired large, wide-bodied aircraft. These Boeing 747s and McDonnell DC-10s performed well, but airlines found that when seats could not be filled, their costs per passenger seat mile often produced higher-than-expected expenses. Since business travelers, who dominated the world's air traffic, demanded accurate departure times and frequent flights, using these wide-bodied aircraft effectively worked against the strategy of increasing traffic. Carlzon reckoned that SAS would sell even more seats if it ceased trying to fly unsuitable aircraft that inhibited offering more nonstop flights. The DC-9s were stopping at the airline's hub in Copenhagen just to funnel passengers onto the giant airbuses; airbuses were therefore grounded or relegated to charter work.

Carlzon's vision was a craft that he called the "passenger-pleasing plane." Its design would be unorthodox, with 75–80% of the fuselage allocated to passenger comfort and in-cabin baggage storage, instead of the usual 35%. He said, "For the 1990s, our starting point is that we need an aircraft which the passenger wants. Then we can add on engines and the cockpit, not the other way round. He tried to persuade the manufacturers to look beyond what was being built now or was on the drawing board for the business traveler, and to generate their interest in building a passenger-pleasing plane. But he had little success.

In a news conference after an address to Scandinavian businessmen, he picked up a model of a narrow-bodied plane, turned it on its side and said:

> This is what I see. The floor is lower: the roof higher. Seating would be no more than two seats abreast with an aisle. Belly space for the baggage would be reduced because there would be wardrobes for the traveler; businessmen don't want to wait for luggage.

Marginal sales were also regarded as significant to the airline. Since business travel had a pattern, with seasonal variations and preferred departure times and days, it was expected that there would be excess aircraft capacity and crews at other times. A marginal strategy was designed, therefore, to sell to the leisure travel market whatever capacity the business traveler could not use. As one executive put it, "We in services cannot build up stocks to be sold later as other manufacturers do—once the aircraft has left, our production is gone forever." The major thrust of this effort was geared to price differential, low-fair tickets on scheduled flights departing at times not favoured by businessmen. SAS wanted, however, to avoid marginal sales reaching a level where an increase in resources would be needed or where low-fare tickets would compete with full-fare sales.

The business traveler and the leisure traveler could often be the same person in different guises and, depending on his or her role at the time, demands and expectations would vary. Also, the pattern for leisure travel was different. Business travel usually followed general economic trends; that is, the frequency of travel would decline during a recession and price sensitivity would increase. For the business traveler, travel was frequently part of the job. Such travel was the best way to create and maintain contacts, survey new markets, pick up new business ideas, and carry out and finalize deals. Trips were an investment in present and future business.

For the leisure traveler, travel was nearly always associated with recreation and escape from everyday life—a chance to see new places and make new acquaintances. The trip itself was part of the pleasure. In contrast to business trips, vacations were planned far in advance and were seldom changed. For the tourist, price was a very important factor. The pattern of leisure travel was somewhat different, too. Demand could often rise during a recession, possibly because households would reduce investments in capital goods and, instead, spend their money on leisure pursuits. Business and tourist travel patterns showed wide seasonal variations by month, week, and day.

The Culture Revolution: Inverting the Pyramid

Carlzon's "little red book," as it came to be known, was the first step toward involving all SAS employees in the new wave of thinking. He wanted to find a way to communicate to all levels in the organisation that the company was in a serious crisis, fighting for its life, and make them understand what he wanted to do about it. The company's advertising agency was asked to put the strategic plan in more creative terms. They created a booklet in cartoon form called "Let's Get In There and Fight" that detailed the airline's financial condition, the vision of the future, and the plan for delegating responsibility to frontline employees.

At the beginning, people were somewhat surprised by this unusual form of communication, but they got used to it in time and even came to expect it. Resistance came mainly from the technical side of the operation, especially from the older pilots. It became clear early on that, culturally, many Scandinavians regarded the service concept as "not professional." The idea of differentiating service for different customers was particularly foreign to their *jamlikhet*—feelings of egalitarianism. But anxieties were lifted by internal marketing, and morale steadily improved. In fact, employees became excited by the new strategy and all the attention it was getting in the press.

Carlzon and his team personally visited frontliners throughout the SAS system. A training company was hired to put 20,000 managers and employees through a two-day training programme designed to give them a sense of the organisation's purpose and their role in the new concept of customer service. Before launching the mass training phase, Carlzon had hosted an intensive three-week gathering of his top 120 executives and 30 of the senior union representatives. Training for middle managers proceeded more or less in tandem with the frontliner programme, with supervisors joining at large sessions of over 100 people.

In the organisation structure introduced in August 1981, Carlzon erased the pyramid and redrew his concept of the new organisation as a kind of wheel with the CEO at the hub and operating departments revolving around him. Whereas frontline workers with the most customer contact had formerly been at the bottom of the chart, Carlzon put them on top. It became everyone else's responsibility, including his, to "serve" those who directly served the customer. In the new organisation, strong emphasis was given to delegating responsibility down the line, where Carlzon believed competent result-oriented managers should be well-informed personnel who could work without supervision. In his own words, he wanted to "put workers in charge and have management serve as consultants to the organisation." An internal consulting group was set up and asked to work directly with management throughout the company to help overcome obstacles and keep the various projects moving ahead.

The company was divided into various profit centers, varying in size from the airline division all the way down to a particular route. At this level, the route manager as entrepreneur was free to decide the time and number of flights between two cities, contingent on the approval of the governments involved, and he could lease airplanes and flight crews from other divisions.

Carlzon actively tried to encourage initiative on the part of staff to think outwardly about customers instead of inwardly about the head office. He knew that a badly handled "moment of truth" had a terrible effect on customers. For example, according to one story, he applauded a pilot whose plane was grounded by a sit-down strike on the Copenhagen runway, and who responded by opening the bar, taking the passengers on a guided tour of the airport perimeter and pointing out interesting sights. On another occasion, he praised an air hostess for buying sandwiches and coffee for passengers who were delayed. This kind of initiative, he believed, could never happen by simply giving instructions. He declared:

> Telling people what to do only succeeds in putting limitations on them. Information, on the other hand, permits them to know their opportunities and possibilities . . . To free someone from the rigorous control of instructions, policies, and orders, and to give that person freedom to take responsibility for his ideas, decisions, and actions, is to release hidden resources which would otherwise remain inaccessible to both the individual and the company . . . A person who has information cannot avoid taking responsibility.

By the end of 1982, SAS had achieved a totally changed image. It had become the most punctual airline in Europe as well as the number one choice for Scandinavian businessmen. The financial picture had also changed unrecognisably. Corporate overheads had been reduced by 25%, and, from a $10 million loss, the company had achieved a $76 million profit.

SCANDINAVIAN AIRLINES SYSTEM (SAS) REVISITED (B)

Customer Relationships through Services in the 90s

After the turnaround, SAS entered a period of consolidation followed by several years of steady growth and profitability. But after six consecutive years of good, solid bottom-line results, the company was being constantly challenged on all sides. Near the end of the 80s, US deregulation freed the large richer US airlines from their previous restrictions, with the result that cheaper competition loomed threateningly across the Atlantic to the continent of Europe.

Jan Carlzon was acutely aware of the trends in air travel, and of the threats and opportunities that existed for his airline. He had been saying since the early 80s that only a few airlines in Europe could survive deregulation. The ensuing price war that raged over the Atlantic routes had begun to affect the European airlines in a big way. Some American airlines took a much more aggressive stand than what had been anticipated for the 90s, setting up their own feeder systems and actively looking for market share.

European airline executives remembered the rise and fall of Freddie Laker with a mixture of horror and amusement. Laker had launched his low-priced, no-frills flights from the United Kingdom to the United States at the end of the 70s with a lot of show, using highly leveraged DC-10s. When he tried to increase his business by adding very cheap flights to Europe, he was rapidly squeezed out by British Airways and British Caledonian—and went bankrupt. No one wanted to follow that path.

But Scandinavia's high labour cost structure made the airline's personnel expenses twice as high as Asian carriers—where service quality was already giving stiff competition—and a third as high as those costs in the United States. The remote northern location of the region, with its huge sparsely populated countries, presented additional strategic disadvantages for the airline. The three countries of Scandinavia comprised fewer than 18 million people, a base for SAS that many felt was too small to support is own international traffic system.

To stay in business, SAS needed a strategy that would work successfully through the 90s, a period that was likely to be volatile for all, to say the least. Carlzon wanted to position the airline securely in what was going to be a highly competitive and much altered world air travel market. At the new SAS head office in Stockholm, Jan Carlzon met frequently with his management team to consider the various alternatives open to them.

There had been a consensus on the need to act fast in the face of rapidly moving competition, but considerable debate had taken place about how far SAS could go. Some strategic alliances had been forged with other airlines in order to increase the SAS network worldwide. However, a potential agreement with Sabena had failed amid a splurge of bad publicity, and the chance to purchase part of British Caledonian had recently collapsed when British Airways bought the whole airline right out from under SAS. The failure of these two potential partnerships was a bitter disappointment for Jan Carlzon, a setback to his vision to build one integrated airline service worldwide.

Carlzon's Global Vision: Finding Partners

"If your customers are global travelers, your services must be global, too," Carlzon had declared at a management meeting one day early in 1986. Typical of the culture, there had been vigorous discussions, as well as disagreements. Carlzon believed they had no option. He had spent many hours convincing the management and board of directors that it was vital to introduce new global marketing strategies and make whatever acquisitions were necessary to develop the company's services into a total "seamless" travel chain across the world. He believed that all travelers needed somewhere to sleep; transportation to and from the airport; and a way to pay bills, work in comfort, and take a leisure trip once a year. Being nice to customers was not enough; it was essential to offer a horizontal chain of activities representing the totality of service.

Having a global traffic system was the most important component in the scheme, but it was only the beginning. Carlzon's goal was to find partnerships so that SAS could offer a fuller, more global range of services of equal standard for customers at all times—in an airport, on board, in a limousine, in a hotel room, at an automatic teller machine, and so on. He had tried a partnering arrangement with American Airlines some years previously, but it had failed because the two companies had not understood each other. Therefore, he was adamant that SAS should find partners who agreed on the basic strategy: the importance of the customer and how to serve his needs. Carlzon believed that if they shared these common denominators as a goal to work for, the rest would be easy.

When the chance to acquire part of a prestigious hotel chain came along, Carlzon pursued it personally, lobbying with members of his board and raising the vast sum of money needed. He believed this opportunity offered SAS a way to begin implementation of his global vision as well as providing a welcome boost to the company's image, which had suffered badly after the Sabena and British Caledonian deals collapsed. These failures had not only held strategic implications for SAS, but internal implications as well. Putting the customer first and implementing the systems needed to deliver exemplary service had become institutionalized at SAS since the turnaround. However, SAS management and staff had become accustomed to the regular stream of new products and ideas from Jan Carlzon. Sustaining the level of energy and excitement of his teams was a constant challenge for him.

Buying Intercontinental Hotels increased SAS's hotel network from 24 to 127 establishments in 54 countries, thereby forming the basis of a solid worldwide total travel package service concept. For example, following the SAS philosophy to save the customer time, special kiosks at hotels would arrange for boarding the baggage and provide other services to business travelers. To ensure the strategy's success, it was crucial that all activities move smoothly, linking one part of the chain to the next. One example was to provide hotel check-ins at the airport and airport check-ins at the hotels.

A joint agreement with Thai Airlines enabled SAS to offer 13 direct flights to Bangkok. Similar arrangements were made with Varig. Likewise, links were made with all Nippon Airways—Japan's largest airline—and with Canadian Airlines International. SAS purchased 16.8% of Continental Airline Holdings in the United States and 24.9% of the airlines of British Holdings in the United Kingdom, a fierce rival of British Airways which owned four airlines—including British Midland, the second largest carrier flying out of Heathrow airport. Similar transactions were made with Loganair and Manx Airlines. Together, these carriers comprised a well-developed network in the United Kingdom, SAS's largest market.

The purchase of Continental had not been without complications, created in part by the reputation of its owner, as well as by the airline union. Furthermore, the alliance was criticized from both inside and outside SAS because the level of Continental's quality and service was considered inferior. However, Jan Carlzon argued that, with the Continental deal, SAS could offer 60 destinations in the United States via Newark, NJ (just outside New York City), rather than use JFK airport in New York, which was more convenient for customers with connections. Also, he believed that having access to Continental provided an opportunity to add value, as SAS could transfer this learning to establish a formula for frontline service.

An alliance with Swissair meant being able to share aircraft, pilots, air hostesses, training programmes, and facilities. The idea was to merge the travel timetable, that is, create a joint traffic system, thereby giving customers a better deal and reducing overheads. These goals had also not been easy to accomplish. While Swissair valued long-haul customers, SAS was more interested in clients who frequently took short trips. In general, SAS wanted to go further in creating one integrated service and system than most of its partners—such as Finnair, Swissair, and Austrian Airlines. Finnair decided to withdraw, being afraid that its identity would be lost. Swissair was not in favour of going the whole way. For example, it did not want to merge the sales offices, even though the service centers had been integrated.

Carlzon was adamant that there was no option except cooperation. In order to survive, there had to be a critical mass, and none of the smaller countries could accomplish that alone. SAS wished that a number of other companies would realize that they not only had to face competition from domestic lines inside their own borders, but also from outside competition—within Europe as well as the rest of the world. The solution was to choose airlines that dominated in certain hubs and join these hubs together in one strong network. Prestige, Carlzon declared, was a bad reason to form an alliance; the raison d'être must be this: working together to support customers in their worldwide travel experience.

By 1991 he had succeeded in building a large global traffic system. The number of destinations with one-stop service from the Scandinavian capitals had doubled many times over. Through partnerships, customers could travel to 275 places without having to deplane or change flights. Without these partners, SAS could have provided less than half this number of through flights. Since the concept depended on high-quality service, Carlzon wanted to influence the quality of delivery, product development, and marketing. He therefore preferred to acquire ownership stakes in partnering companies.

Pushing On: Avoiding a Mental Hangover

Carlzon's management team concentrated on perfecting the system and having standards in the company after the turnaround. However, many found it difficult to keep the momentum going—Carlzon was no longer so visible, and the staff had become a bit slack. Some senior managers had become skeptical of Carlzon's global initiatives. They first wanted to consolidate their efforts so that everything was right internally. They preferred to become a feeder for Scandinavia rather than enter into a massive global strategy. On paper, this approach looked much more profitable and easier to manage.

Senior management found themselves in intricate and unanticipated new projects with partners that had previously been fierce competitors. How were they to compete and cooperate at the same time? One thing they had discovered was that creating a global network could not be achieved through control. Creative ways had to be found to ensure that both SAS and its partners could win. For example, successfully redesigning the route system with Swissair meant having to find a form of reciprocity where both would gain. Only then could the process of working together actually begin. Another twist was that SAS's partners sometimes also had agreements with other companies as well. Swissair, for example, had a partnership with Delta, a company that SAS believed would prove to be a giant competitor to SAS and its partners.

Carlzon spent most of his time during the late 80s implementing his global vision. To have one integrated chain of services across several companies—airlines as well as others—meant finding several partners, then ensuring that the idea of one seamless service chain was understood and implemented on a worldwide scale. He felt responsible for establishing stability within SAS's operating systems and for promoting constant change and innovation. Carlzon explained:

I didn't want SAS to lose the tempo or fall into a mental hangover. When we were in a crisis, everyone had been motivated. But, then people began to slip back into the old patterns. They sighed and said . . . *"Look, we changed. See what we achieved."* But, it's never over. Satisfying customers is a moving target.

The Carnival Is Over: It's Time to Wake Up

Starting in October 1990, the market dropped dramatically. In the aftermath of the Gulf war, 1991 was a lost year for the entire travel industry. Sweden experienced the worst recession in living memory. Airline business dropped 60%; never before had the industry had to deal with this sort of crisis. By early 1992, the drop had stabilized to around 17% in Sweden and about 5% worldwide. Every class of seat was affected. SAS's excessively high costs, compared to other carriers, put the company at a disadvantage.

As soon as the bad times hit SAS, some people wanted to resume the old ways of the 60s and 70s—concentrating on costs and productivity. They felt that, since the market had disappeared anyway, less effort and money should be spent on customer-related activities. Carlzon disagreed. He claimed that the situation in the 90s was different from that of the 60s and 70s, or even the 80s. In the past, the airline had focused on machines, but this approach could not be allowed to reoccur. During the 80s, the company had achieved a market orientation and had improved the service standards of the whole European airline industry. Now, SAS had to achieve even greater heights in service quality. At this point, the only option was to take the company's market orientation one step further—find the individual in each customer and cater to this individual in a personalized way.

Carlzon realized that people—even businessmen—were not all the same. But by using a database and information system, ground and in-flight staff would be able to identify individuals and cater to their special needs. He shared his feelings with the management:

> Why must I go to the same hotel I've been to 15 times before and get asked the same questions, feel the same anxieties, and have to fill out the same forms? This kills the whole experience before I've even gotten to my room. Why can't this be done beforehand so that all I have to do is sign? We can use our data to get closer to customers, learn things from previous visits, and recommend ways to improve their stay and travel experience . . . because we know them. There are a million ways of showing customers that they are individuals and not just an anonymous number.

Emphasis during the 80s had been on increasing revenues. In the 90s, SAS would have to become even better at serving customers, as well as more productive. Management needed to take what they had learned during the production years and apply it at an even higher level. Waste would not be permissible in the 90s. It would be unethical, Carlzon declared, to spend any money that did not directly lead to the customer's satisfaction.

How to achieve this goal was the challenge that senior management faced as they entered the new year in 1991. They met at Christmastime and concluded that they could not bring back the market for the time being; for whatever reason, it had slipped away. Since the price on every route was fixed by competitive conditions and the level of service was not negotiable, only costs could be adjusted.

The airline's costs on each route should be only what prices could support. If SAS could not provide the right quality, the company must find it outside. Management must look for ways to gain customers and simultaneously cut costs. In other words, they must eliminate expenses that did not benefit customers directly and find ways to save time and be more efficient wherever customers would gain.

Some solutions were proposed and/or put in place. Hardware capacity levels were reduced to be more in line with demand. A goal was set to reduce costs by Skr 3 billion by the end of 1992 and to have 20% increased productivity by the beginning of 1993. Management knew that customers did not care how SAS was administered, so these costs were immediately cut by 50%. In addition to increasing productivity by 20% in the two years 1991–1993, they set a target of gaining 20% every five years thereafter.

People were expected to find ways to work more intelligently. The message was, The 80s are over, times have changed, and we have to work differently. Idle time—found to be as high as 50% in some areas—was no longer acceptable. Management had thought that allowing the staff to chat and have some free time would make them more motivated. Now, however, new work procedures and systems were set up to avoid wasted time, and routine activities in jobs were automated wherever possible.

For instance, the baggage ticket process—which had taken between 10–15 seconds before—was speeded up to 7 seconds, thereby eliminating the need for several people. Five alternative ways to board, including a phone service and automatic boarding machines at the airport and in key customer premises, were offered so that customers would not have to be at the airport early or stand in queues. Tickets—which had not changed since the 40s—were modified; the boarding pass and ticket were combined and automated, so that passengers need not check in in the normal way. This step, however, was only a beginning; the aim was to enable passengers to board the aircraft in the same way as in a bus, using a card with an electronic device.

SAS had to negotiate with 33 unions before all its various employees would accept no increase in pay and longer working hours. For example, a crew working the route from Copenhagen to New York typically would have been passengers between Austria and Copenhagen and not begun their flight duties to the States until Copenhagen. This policy had to change; they would have to work on both flights. Throughout the 80s, pilots had flown 460 hours a year and worn their uniforms eight hours a day, with only four hours spent actually flying. Now, management wanted them to work 560 hours a year and five hours a day. Many other ways were found to save time and money. For instance, having the pilots and crew eat on the plane rather than stop for meals changed the whole scheduling and productivity picture.

The new intensive training programs for frontliners differed from the customer service workshops of the 80s in three ways: each course included top management so that everyone would learn together; emphasis was on ways to give better service without adding to expenses; and employees learned new skills to help them with problem-solving and to make their own decisions when encountering a customer's individual needs.

Everyone was given special training on problem-solving. In the past, many decisions were based on the rules: A missed Apex flight meant a customer had to pay extra. This policy was often the easiest way out for frontliners; the answer was simple and never wrong. Now they were expected to use their own judgment as they helped customers, deciding when and how to bend the rules. When a customer with an Apex ticket was late, the frontliner could decide whether or not to send him free of charge on the next flight. Such a decision would be as correct as the other, depending on the circumstances.

Comprehensive research that had been carried out since the late 80s confirmed that SAS was number one on staff service both in the air and on the ground, in Europe and on intercontinental routes. On a scale of 100, SAS was consistently in the 90 range. But on other services—such as in-flight entertainment, reading material, and duty-free shopping, the airline consistently had low scores compared to its competition—somewhere in the 30 range. The research also showed that the company's rating on meals was slightly above average—in the 70 score bracket.

A number of new-product innovations were proposed. For instance, individualized entertainment on board was being provided by almost every other carrier. But SAS decided to use mobile equipment, which could be requested and brought to a customer on board. This approach was cheaper and more flexible than the fixed systems, both for the company and the customer. "Euro-Sleepers," a first for aviation, were put into business class for intercontinental flights. Passengers could choose whether or not to have this fully reclining seat for a premium of a few hundred dollars. These seats could be prepared before takeoff by modifying the seats and blocking the ones behind.

Learning to Learn: Catching the Headwind

The difference between SAS's new strategy and the 80s turnaround was largely in the emphasis: The object then had mainly been to satisfy customers. Now the idea was to consider them as future investments, to be held as long as possible, with more time spent on attending to their individual needs. In dealing with customers, therefore, the aim was to make them into loyal SAS fliers rather than merely satisfied with the service. Since customers were to be treated as individuals, they must be free to choose the particular options that they wanted. Therefore, rather than sell a whole package, the airline was now offering a comprehensive selection of quality services, thus enabling business travelers to put together an individually designed travel package for each trip.

Efficiency was not a new theme for SAS. But, during the 80s it had somehow not received the attention it deserved. Carlzon reflected:

> I talked about efficiency in 1986 and we set a target of 5% improvement a year, but no urgency was ever felt. It's like a ketchup bottle—you have to push and push and push,

and then suddenly it all starts happening. Now, it's started happening. We had no choice . . . we had to do something. Our productivity is already up by 15% and we've still got a year to go. During the last six months, our market share has gone up by 2% on international flights. We're breaking through.

Carlzon and his team were convinced that their vision and strategy for the 80s had been correct. But they also realized that they had to adapt their strategy to suit the times. Some financial decisions had had to be reversed. Owning all the assets in the network had proved to be unnecessary. For example, some of the less strategic investments had been sold off. AMADEUS—the reservation system created together with Lufthansa, Air France, and Iberia—was sold because it became obvious that it would not lead to any particular competitive advantage. Some of the less important routes were also dropped. Sitting at his round desk on the top floor at company headquarters—a building designed for informality— Carlzon put it this way:

> The decisions taken in the 80s were not wrong. The situation changed. We had to learn from experience. We would have been real fools to stick to our strategy without adapting to the changes going on around us. The 80s taught us how important it is to be flexible enough to know how and when to change. We developed a learning culture to help us manage through both good times and bad.

MARKETING STRATEGY FORMULATION

20 GIOVANNI BUTON

International Marketing Strategy

In September 1989 Nigel Brown, export director and head of international strategic development for Giovanni Buton, was preparing for a meeting with the company's senior management. Brown had scheduled the meeting in order to discuss Buton's international marketing strategy during the next three to five years. He had been in his post only since May, when he returned from the 12-week Program for Management Development at the Harvard Business School. Previously, Brown had spent eight years with United Distillers Corporation, most recently as country director for Italy. After four months on the job, Brown had completed a review of Buton's situation and of recent developments in the European distilled spirits market. Based on this review, he had formed some tentative ideas on directions for Buton's future strategy. Many questions remained, however, and Brown was also attempting to design a program of consumer research in several European countries to provide guidance for decisions about Buton's selection of target markets and segments, product line, and advertising approaches.

Company Background

Giovanni Buton was founded in 1820 by Marquis Filippo Sassoli, a direct descendant of the Medici family, and Giovanni Buton, a master distiller and expert in spirits. They reestablished the long tradition of distilling that had been part of the heritage of the Medicis since the 13th century.

By the late 1980s Giovanni Buton had become Italy's largest spirits producer. The company's principal product, Vecchia Romagna brandy, was Italy's leading spirit brand. In 1987 the Buton Group earned a net income of 5.2 billion lire ($4.8 million) on sales of 151.6 billion lire ($110 million). (See Exhibits 1 and 2.)

This case was prepared by Professor Robert D. Buzzell and Research Assistant Geoffrey Smith. Copyright © 1990 by the President and Fellows of Harvard College. Harvard Business School case 591-023.

EXHIBIT 1 Giovanni Buton: Simplified Balance Sheets, 1984–1987 (Millions of Lire)

	1987	1986	1985	1984
Current Assets				
Cash	8,940	9,232	11,965	8,047
Receivables, net	70,002	68,052	67,026	69,972
Inventories	23,033	21,982	22,103	28,116
Other	2,480	3,888	2,725	3,682
	104,455	103,154	103,819	109,817
Noncurrent Assets				
Property and equipment, net	40,342	40,672	38,585	43,782
Equity in nonconsolidated subsidiaries	10,924	9,627	8,759	5,101
Goodwill	727	872	1,017	1,017
Other	577	1,115	1,351	1,473
	52,570	52,396	49,751	51,650
Total assets	157,025	155,550	153,570	161,467
Current liabilities	66,925	64,072	63,020	72,317
Medium and long-term liabilities	10,998	13,906	14,552	19,508
Total liabilities	77,923	77,978	77,572	92,142
Stockholders' equity	79,102	77,572	75,998	69,325
Total liabilities and equity	157,025	155,550	153,570	161,467

EXHIBIT 2 Giovanni Buton: Simplified Income Statements, 1984–1987 (Millions of Lire)

	1987	1986	1985	1984
Net sales	151,605	150,809	151,205	174,776
Cost of materials	58,918	61,430	62,378	77,725
Operating Expenses				
Production	11,177	11,177	13,420	17,887
Selling, general, and administration	66,650	64,793	59,959	62,948
Other	2,922	3,120	2,848	3,257
	139,667	140,520	138,605	161,817
Operating income	11,938	10,289	12,600	12,959
Nonoperating expenses, net	1,225	1,232	(2,101)	(2,255)
Income before taxes and extraordinary items	13,163	11,521	10,449	10,704
Income taxes	(6,956)	(6,123)	(5,403)	(5,653)
Extraordinary items	(1,000)	—	1,393	735
Net income	5,207	5,398	6,439	5,786

The company's main activity was the production of Vecchia Romagna and a range of other Italian spirit brands. These brands were distributed through a sales organization comprised of 15 Buton area managers and 130 self-employed salesmen who were largely dependent on Buton for their income. The sales organization directly covered approximately 35,000 of the 300,000 spirits outlets in Italy. This coverage was among the highest of any liquor distributor in Italy.

During the 1980s, Buton had also acquired two independent spirits distributors, Italwell, srl, and Rinaldi, SpA. These distributors mainly handled specialty imported spirits with low volumes but high margins. (See Exhibit 3.) Both organizations serviced a customer base of 5,000–10,000 top restaurants, nightclubs, and bars. Italwell and Rinaldi distributed competing portfolios of spirits. Each had fewer than 10 area managers and 120 independent sales representatives who included these companies' products among the many lines they carried.

In 1988, Buton acquired a specialty food distributor, Berselli SpA., that distributed a wide range of specialty Italian and foreign foods to small high-quality food shops and restaurants. Berselli had a direct customer base of approximately 12,000 outlets.

EXHIBIT 3   Brands Distributed by Buton and Subsidiaries

Product	Buton	Rinaldi	Italwell
Brandy	Vecchia Romagna		Bardinet
Whiskey	Glenesk	Cutty Sark	Bell's
	Saltyre	Antiquary	
	W5	Bruichladdich	
Marc	Grappa Libarna	Vieux Marc	Grappa Di
		V. Dalta Cia	Brunello
Dry sparkling	Maximilian I	Monopoles	Cesarini
wine	Equipe 5	Alfred	Sforza
	Corteggio	Rothschild	
Apertif	Rosso Antico		
Bitter	Amaro Gambarotta		
	Petrus Boonekamp		
	Don Bairo		
Vermouth	Gambarotta		
Liqueur	Batida and Buton's	Benedictine	
	line	B & B	
Gin	Todd's	Christie's	
Long drink	Pingo de Pinga		
Vodka		Wodka	
		Wyborowa	Stolichnaya
Port		Taylor's	
Wine		Rinaldi's line	Italwell's line
Beer		Löwenbräu	Oranjeboom
Armagnac		Marquis de	
		Montesquiou	
Rum			Negrita
Cognac			De Luze

Giovanni Buton's Management

The general manager of Giovanni Buton was Filippo Sassoli. Sassoli had been at Buton for 30 years and had extensive administrative experience.

Lorenzo Sassoli was Buton's commercial director and corporate strategy director. Lorenzo Sassoli had begun his career as a doctor. In 1986 he joined Buton; two years later he assumed his present position. He was known as a dynamic and open leader who had a talent for strategic planning.

Filiberto Serpieri managed Buton's production and finances. A veteran of 20 years at Buton, Serpieri had taken over as head of production in 1988.

The domestic marketing operation was managed by Nicoletta D'Alesio. D'Alesio had a strong sales and marketing background, having single-handedly built the Italwell distribution subsidiary. She was viewed as an entrepreneur with a lot of drive.

As export director and director of international strategic development, Nigel Brown managed a 10-person administrative and sales staff and two marketing professionals. Two key staff members for Brown to work with were Erik Kooijmans and Giorgio Pascerini. Kooijmans, age 33, had two years of experience at Rowntree Mackintosh as an assistant product manager, two years with Buton on the domestic marketing side, and one year in export marketing. Pascerini, age 46, was the head of the sales administration department. Pascerini had extensive overseas experience and was a capable and experienced administrator. The exact structure of the export organization was not firmly set, and one task that faced

EXHIBIT 4

Corporate organization

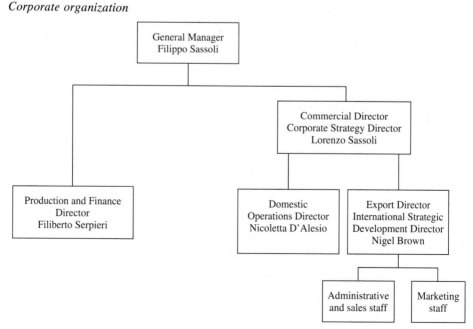

Brown was developing the organization to fit his management style. (Refer to Exhibit 4 on the previous page.)

The Italian Spirits Market

Wine dominated Italian beverage production. In 1986, almost 7.6 billion liters of wine were produced. In comparison, only 1.1 billion liters of spirits (brandy, grappa, etc.) were produced.

Per capita consumption of all alcoholic beverages in Italy had declined steadily during the 1980s. Domestic spirits had lost ground to international categories such as Scotch whiskey, gin, run, and vodka. The domestic brandy market was particularly hard hit by the slump. Thus, while Buton managed to increase its overall market share, its leading spirit brand, a brandy, had declined in sales. Vecchia Romagna accounted for 55% of Buton's total volume in Italy in 1988.

Vecchia Romagna Brandy

"Brandies" were alcoholic beverages produced by distilling wine or fermented juices of fruits other than grapes such as apples, plums, and so on. Brandies varied widely in terms of color, taste, and texture, depending on the types of grapes used and the method of distillation. Consequently, the qualities and prices of different types of brandy varied widely. One type of brandy, cognac, had a special reputation for high quality and a cosmopolitan image among consumers worldwide. Cognac was produced only in a strictly delimited region in France, within which an even smaller area was designated as the source of "fine champagne" cognac. According to Nigel brown, the producers of cognac had successfully "built a myth" about their products by limiting production and by adhering to strict rules regarding production methods and quality designations. In contrast, he pointed out, Vecchia Romagna had no competitors in its region (Romagna) with which it could form a similar association.

Vecchia Romagna was distilled via the "discontinuous" processing method, using traditional stills and extensive aging in dark, cool storage sheds. Two different quality levels were produced: Etichetta Nera (black label), aged at least three years; and Etichetta Oro (gold label), aged at least seven years. A third, superpremium version, aged at least 15 years, was to be introduced in 1990. It would be designated as "Riserva Rara."

Vecchia Romagna was the leading brand in the 2.9 million case Italian brandy market, with a 30% market share in 1988. In contrast, the market shares of other spirits distributed by Buton ranged from 2% (aperitifs) to 6% (dry sparkling wines). Buton supported Vecchia Romagna with a reported advertising budget of 11.6 billion lire in 1987; this represented 75% of total advertising for all brandies. Vecchia Romagna's advertising expenditures ranked ninth among all distilled spirits; Cinzano vermouth was the leader, with outlays of 22.4 billion lire. Only two imported spirits brands, Glen Grant and Chivas (both Scotch whiskeys), outspent Vecchia Romagna.[1]

The International Spirits Market

The international spirits market began to undergo a dramatic change in the late 1980s. Historically, the market had been highly fragmented. While several relatively large concerns existed (Distillers Co., Hiram Walker, Seagram's, and I.D.V.), all the companies were under fairly traditional, conservative management. With the exception of Seagram's, no attempt had been made to vertically integrate into distribution or to acquire additional brands. In April 1986, though, Guinness took over Distillers Co. This action set off a scramble by the four major spirits companies to gain control over their own distribution either through joint ventures or acquisitions. As a result of this consolidation, major brands were withdrawn from many independent distributors.

The Guinness Group in Europe, for example, moved its key brands in Germany and Spain to a joint venture company set up in conjunction with Bacardi. Two other joint ventures were set up to distribute its remaining brands. In France, Guinness moved its major brands into two joint ventures with Moët-Hennessy. In Italy, it rationalized its major distribution system from 22 distributors to 4, acquiring its major distributor along the way. Consolidation of the distribution network also took place in Holland, Belgium, and Denmark.

In addition to becoming more vertically integrated, the spirits industry experienced consolidation through mergers and acquisitions among producers. I.D.V. became part of Grand Metropolitan; Hiram Walker was purchased by Allied-Lyons; Martell was taken over by Seagram's; Guiness took a major stake in Moët-Hennessy; Irish Distillers was acquired by Pernod Richard. The only significant companies left independent were those where the controlling family remained reasonably united and maintained control of the majority of shares, or where the product was either not large enough or international enough to have attracted the major players' interest.

Exhibit 5 gives profiles of the world's five largest distilled spirits producers. All of these companies had made acquisitions during the 1980s, thus broadening their product lines considerably. All of them also marketed "agency brands"— that is, liquors or wines produced by others, for which the major companies acted as importers/national distributors in specific countries. The consolidation of the

---

[1] The advertising expenditure figures cited herein are those reported by a commercial research firm, based on the amounts of broadcast time and print media space used by each brand. Time and space were valued at "list prices" published by the networks and publishers. According to Nigel Brown, the *actual* expenditures for each brand were 35–40% less than the published figures on account of widespread discounting by the media.

EXHIBIT 5   **Profiles of Selected Major Liquor Companies, 1988–89 (Sales in Millions of Cases)**

Company	Home Country	Sales by Product Type					Sales by Region			Major Brands
		Spirits	Wines	Agency Brands	Other	Total	North America	Europe	Other	
IDV/Grand Metropolitan	United Kingdom	44.4	32.6	14.2	—	91.2	50.0	23.1	18.1	Smirnoff, J&B, Gilbey's, Metaxa, Bailey's Irish Cream, Almaden wines
Seagram	Canada	40.3	14.4	5.9	19.0	79.6	49.3	16.4	13.9	Seagram's (VO, 7 Crown, gin), Wolfschmidt, B&G wines
Pernod Richard	France	18.0*	37.0	1.6	—	56.6	2.1	45.2	9.3	Pernod, Richard, Bisquit, Wild Turkey, Dubonnet
Hiram Walker/ Allied Vintners	United Kingdom	28.2	17.0†	6.4	—	51.6	22.1	26.0	3.5	Ballantine's, Teacher's, Canadian Club, Tia Maria
United Distillers/Guiness	United Kingdom	42.1	—	2.9		45.0	17.8	16.0	11.2	Dewar's, Haig, White Horse, I.W. Harper, Schenley's

* Approximately two-thirds of this being anise spirits.
† Including sales of 50–50 joint venture.
SOURCE: *International Drinks Bulletin* (Italy).

industry in the 1980s was in response to two trends that characterized almost all industrialized countries:

- Declining consumption of alcoholic beverages in general, and distilled spirits in particular. In the United States, for example, total consumption of distilled spirits fell by 14% between 1980 and 1987, while consumption per adult declined from 2.9 gallons to 2.3. At the same time, consumers had been switching from the traditional "brown goods" (mostly whiskeys) to spirits that were perceived as being "lighter," especially vodkas, rums, and tequilas.
- The growth in popularity of "international" brands, which were perhaps seen as more cosmopolitan or sophisticated than traditional local spirits. (In the United States, for example, consumption of imported whiskeys—mostly Scotches—grew slightly from 1977 to 1987, while domestic whiskey sales declined by 33%.)

The consolidation of the spirits industry paralleled a similar trend among food producers. Large, diversified multinationals such as Nestlé and BSN had been aggressively pursuing acquisition strategies during the 1980s. One of the most recent large acquisitions was Grand Metropolitan's takeover of Pillsbury.

In Europe, spirits retailing also experienced rapid change. The number of retail outlets in Europe declined at a dramatic rate during the 1980s, because of the growth of major supermarket chains. Throughout Western Europe, small food stores were being displaced by large supermarkets and still larger "hyper-markets." The percentage of total food store sales accounted for by these large stores in 1987 was estimated at 68% in France, over 50% in West Germany and Great Britain, 33% in Spain, and 27% in Italy. By 1992, it was predicted, sales of supermarkets and hypermarkets would exceed 40% of the total in Italy and a much larger share of the more prosperous Northern region.

Retail concentration in Europe resulted in the decline of smaller brands due to the following:

- The need for increased efficiency in the use of shelf space.
- The growth of private-label brands in almost all sectors, thus reducing branded goods' sales.
- The rise in cost of product introductions as major retailers demanded listing fees and evidence of significant consumer advertising before providing shelf space.
- A polarization of the market between major brands with lower margins high volumes and blanket distribution; and smaller, high-margin specialty brands not distributed in the supermarket chains or in airport duty-free outlets.

In contrast to Western Europe, where most spirits sales were made by food stores, spirits distribution in the United States remained largely in the hands of small, specialized independent stores or, in states such as Virginia and

Pennsylvania, state-operated retail outlets. A patchwork of state regulations prevented (with a few exceptions) the sale of alcoholic beverages by food supermarkets and/or the development of large, specialized retail wine and liquor chains.

Prospects for Expanding Buton's Sales in Europe

As Buton's head of international strategic development, Nigel Brown was responsible for developing markets for the company's products outside Italy. In 1988, Buton's sales outside Italy represented only 10% of the company's turnover. Only $2 million of this was Vecchia Romagna, with much of the remainder being bulk sales for bottling under private labels. While North America and Japan were interesting possibilities, Brown was more concerned—at least for the present—with market development in Western Europe. One reason for this was the impending integration of the 12 European Community (EC) countries into a single marketplace. Since 1985, the EC countries had been engaged in a process of harmonizing their product standards and eliminating or simplifying customers and other regulations that inhibited (or added costs to) the free movement of goods, services, capital, and people among the 12 nations. The market integration program, which was scheduled to be complete by the end of 1992, was designed to improve efficiency and stimulate growth in the EC. In addition to reducing the costs of intra-EC trade by eliminating border crossing inspections, the "1992" program was meant to encourage EC-based companies to achieve greater scale economies, thus becoming more competitive with US and Japanese rivals. Responding to this prospect, some large European firms had already merged or formed new "strategic alliances" in order to be prepared for the new, more competitive situation.[2]

The wave of mergers and acquisitions in the European alcoholic beverages industry during the 1980s was, according to industry observers, motivated in part by the prospect of EC market integration. Thus, it appeared likely that fewer, larger beverage producers—each offering a broad range of products—would control an increasing share of total EC sales.

In the early stages of discussion about the 1992 reforms, it had been proposed that rates of taxation on alcoholic beverages be "harmonized" among the EC countries. Harmonization would mean substantial increases in taxes on spirits in some countries (such as Italy) and/or substantial reductions in others (such as the United Kingdom). By mid-1989, however, it appeared that the European Commission had given up on the idea of harmonizing rates of taxation on spirits. The taxes were collected at the retail level so that differences in *wholesale* prices among countries were not great. Differences in retail prices would, after 1992, encourage consumers to buy spirits in low-tax countries for consumption elsewhere. This kind of "transshipping" was not, however, expected to cause major disruptions in

---

[2] See John A. Quelch and Robert D. Buzzell, "Marketing Moves through EC Crossroads," *Sloan Management Review*, Fall 1989, pp. 63–74.

trade flows. There were differences in the tax rates on alcoholic beverages and cigarettes among the various states in the United States; this created incentives for out-of-state purchases by consumers and some small-scale "smuggling." But the extent of the cross-border shopping was believed to be relatively modest.

Brown had reviewed recent trends in spirits consumption, distribution, and marketing in all 12 of the EC countries. Based on this preliminary review, he had decided to focus his attention on three countries—West Germany, Spain, and Greece. Estimates of spirits consumption and imports for these three countries are summarized in Exhibit 6.

• *West Germany:* West Germany's large brandy market and substantial Italian population made it an important area for Buton to examine. The West German spirits market was, however, depressed by a significant increase in the excise duty on liquor beginning in 1982. A national anti-alcohol campaign also served to restrain sales. Despite these problems, demand for certain products, including fruit-based brandy and liqueur, remained strong. Imported brands experienced particularly buoyant growth.

Germany was Buton's largest export market, with sales of Vecchia Romagna brandy in 1988 amounting to 50,000 cases (1 case = 9 liters).

• *Spain:* In Spain, the economy had been expanding rapidly since the country joined the EC. In contrast to the situation in Germany, spirits consumption in Spain was growing, with imports showing especially strong growth from a small base.

EXHIBIT 6   Estimated Consumption and Imports of Spirits (Millions of Cases of 9 Liters Each)

	West Germany	*Spain*	*Greece*
Total Spirits			
1987	41.25	40.84	5.64
1982	46.50	35.50	4.88
Percent change	−11%	+15%	+16%
Brandy			
Domestic			
1987	8.12	10.33	0.75–0.80
1982	9.62	11.77	0.75–0.80
Cognac/Armagnac			
1987	0.78	—	—
1982	0.92	—	—
Other imports			
1987	1.38	0.11*	0.01*
1982	1.27	0.05*	0.007*
Population (millions), 1987	60.9	38.8	9.9
Spirits consumption per capita (liters)	6.2	7.6	4.7

* Includes cognac and Armagnac.

SOURCES: *World Alcohol* (Company Watch Ltd.); *Jobson's Liquor Handbook* (Jobson Publishing Co., 1990).

• *Greece:* Spirits consumption, especially of imported brands, was also increasing in Greece despite high tariff and tax rates. Following a transitional period prior to full membership in the EC, Greek tariffs and nontariff barriers to imports were scheduled to be eliminated by 1990. There appeared to be an opportunity for producers in other EC countries to displace ouzo and domestic brandy consumption.

Nigel Brown believed that it would be necessary, in order to establish Vecchia Romagna as a significant spirits brand in any of the three countries, to invest heavily in advertising and promotion. He estimated that the annual levels of expenditure required (stated in millions of US dollars) would be:

Country	Advertising	Promotion	Listing Fees
Germany	$3.0	$1.0	$1.0
Spain	3.5	0.5	2.5
Greece	4.0	1.0	0.5

Whether investing any of these amounts offered a reasonable prospect of paying off would depend, of course, on whether a viable "positioning" could be achieved for Vecchia Romagna. Brown acknowledged that he lacked adequate information about consumers in any of the three countries. He and his colleagues believed that brandy consumers were predominantly male, aged 35 years or more, and concentrated in rural areas. (Cognac drinkers, however, tended to be younger and to come from higher income groups.)

To get additional information about consumers, Brown planned to retain research firms to conduct focus group interviews in all three countries during September. He also planned to have some questions about spirits consumption, brand preferences, and attitudes included in large-scale "omnibus" consumer surveys. An issue for immediate attention was, What information would be most useful to get from the consumer research?

As Nigel Brown pondered Buton's future, he knew that the company had already come to the firm conclusion that the way forward was to develop the company into an international concern. In particular, three factors were pushing Buton into the international marketplace. The spirits market was increasingly becoming a world of international brands. In almost every market in the world, domestic brands were declining as international brands surged. The approach of 1992 lent even greater momentum to the trend toward an international market. The Italian spirits market was declining at a particularly rapid rate and few opportunities for acquisition existed with Italy.

1. *Market selection:* Possible criteria for selecting markets were as follows: (*a*) size of national brandy market; (*b*) size of imported brandy market; (*c*) availability of distributors; (*d*) level of concentration of retail trade; (*e*) overall cost of entry; and (*f*) distance of market from Italy. While it seemed obvious to focus efforts on markets that were already partially developed, there was no guarantee that these markets offered the best potential for development.

2. *Market segment selection:* Because of the increased polarization between the large volume market and the specialty market, a strategic choice needed to be made as to where to market Buton's existing brands. The choice was whether to go into direct competition with the major domestic products in the volume market or to limit distribution of the brand to traditional "Italian" channels—Italian restaurants and specialty food outlets. This choice would influence the choice of a distributor, the investment levels required, and the long-term production volume expectations.

3. *Acquisition of distribution channels:* The trend toward companies acquiring their own distributors made purchasing a distributor at anything above net asset value an increasingly risky move. The situation was further complicated by the fact that when a change of ownership took place any previous agreements with the brand-owning principals were almost always invalidated.

4. *Create joint venture partnerships with other brand-producing companies:* Buton's main joint venture opportunities seemed to be with companies that had a strong domestic brand that they wished to develop internationally. The agreement could take the form of a cross-shareholding in the distribution companies.

5. *Acquire new brands:* New brands could be acquired either at the international level or the national level. Criteria for acquisition included (*a*) strong brand in its own market; (*b*) strong brand in the international market; (*c*) brand that had potential in the Italian market; (*d*) brand that could use plant, equipment, or spirit that Buton already produced; and (*e*) high potential growth market.

6. *Launch new brands:* In the past Buton had successfully developed new products for the Italian market. How could the company now use these talents for development of international products? Criteria for developing new products included (*a*) first in category; (*b*) sustainable long-term competitive advantage; (*c*) fit with existing production capabilities and distribution channels; and (*d*) potential growth category.

NOKIA-MOBIRA OY
Mobile Telecommunications in Europe

Executives of Nokia-Mobira Oy met at company headquarters in Helsinki, Finland, in December 1988 to review their European marketing strategies. Nokia-Mobira was currently the world leader in the production of mobile phones but was facing increasingly stiff competition from Japanese and American manufacturers.

The European marketing strategy had to be considered in light of the European Community (EC) program to remove internal trade barriers by 1992. Between 1978 and 1986, the worldwide telecommunications industry grew rapidly, but the EC share of world exports declined from 40% to 20%. Analysts attributed the decline to the fragmentation of European production which resulted from the continued application of different national equipment standards and type-approval policies. The market dominance of publicly owned telecommunications monopolies (PTTs) resulted in duplication of R&D efforts and increased costs. Between 1979 and 1989, telecommunications equipment was 80–100% more expensive in Europe than in the United States.

Through EC-funded research programs and the harmonization of national technical standards, the EC hoped to rejuvenate its telecommunications industry. As a company headquartered within Europe but outside the EC, Nokia-Mobira was concerned about the marketing opportunities and challenges these developments presented.

The Evolution of Mobile Telecommunications

Between 1920 and 1970, mobile telecommunications technology changed little except that the size of the equipment decreased significantly. Products consisted primarily of closed radiophone systems ("walkie-talkies") and car radiotelephones.

This case was written by Research Associate Ilkka Lipasti and Professor Martii M. Kaila, both of the Helsinki University of Technology, in association with Professor John A. Quelch. Copyright © 1989 by the President and Fellows of Harvard College. Harvard Business School case 589-112.

The limited number of free radio frequencies restricted the growth of the industry until the introduction of citizens band radios (CBs), which allowed a large number of users to communicate in a limited frequency and within a limited geographical area. To some extent, the CB replaced the public mobile phone in countries like the United States that did not have a wide network of radio stations for car phones. However, CBs, like mobile phones, were not connected to any telephone network, nor did they allow much privacy.

In the late 1970s, the industry changed dramatically. Paging and public mobile radio technologies were introduced, and cellular technology and closed cordless telephone systems soon followed. In addition, as indicated in Exhibits 1 and 2, through the adaptation of digital technology, several of the many new services facilitated by these technologies could be integrated. Along with technological innovation came a restructuring of the industry. These new products and services were not introduced by the large traditional telecommunications firms but by entrepreneurial firms in the semiconductor and the office automation industries. Learning curve effects had been rapid, and consequently prices had dropped significantly, especially in countries with deregulated distribution of equipment and air time.[1]

Cellular Radio

A cellular system consisted of a central computerized telephone exchange that controlled several base stations, which in turn connected to the user's mobile telephone. The system had evolved from computer technology that allowed a more economical use of frequencies. Instead of each available frequency being

EXHIBIT 1

Timing of innovations in telecommunications services

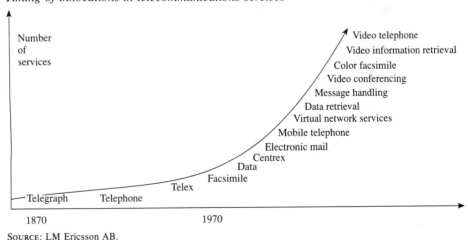

SOURCE: LM Ericsson AB.

---

[1] European Mobile Communications, *Quarterly Report,* Issue 5, 1988.

EXHIBIT 2

The evolution of telecommunications services

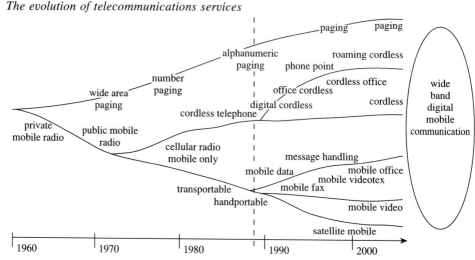

SOURCE: Nokia-Mobira Oy and Consortium British Teleconsult/Consultel/Delecon et al.

restricted to one caller at a time, the new technology, which originated in Japan and in the Nordic countries in the late 1970s, allowed many callers to use the same frequency simultaneously. Appendix 1 describes cellular technology in more detail.

In 1984, the United States introduced the AMPS cellular system; the Nordic countries introduced the NMT system; and the Japanese, the NTT system. The United Kingdom launched the TACS system in 1985. Between 1985 and 1988, the number of nations with operational cellular networks grew to 53, with the AMPS, NMT, and TACS systems claiming the largest bulk of subscribers.

Although the market was fragmented, the Nordic countries offered a geographical area with a common cellular system that allowed transfer of calls across national boundaries. Due to deregulation in the United States and the United Kingdom, the subscriber growth rate in these countries was the most rapid; the United States accounted for 55% of the 3.2 million subscribers worldwide, as opposed to Europe's 36%. However, the Nordic countries still recorded the highest cellular penetration.[2] Because of overcrowding of the systems, analysts expected digitalization to be the next technological advance to be tested in early 1990. Cellular telephone and paging were currently the fastest growing sectors in the telecommunications industry.[3]

In 1989, there were three main product applications for cellular radios: mobile, transportable, and handportable phones. The segment sizes varied widely by country depending on the system capacities available and also on the timing of each product's introduction. (See Exhibit 3.) For example, the handportable

---

[2] "The Benefits of Completing the Internal Market for Telecommunication," Commission of the European Communities Report, 1988.

[3] European Mobile Communications, *Quarterly Report.*

EXHIBIT 3

Cellular product segments in major market areas, 1988

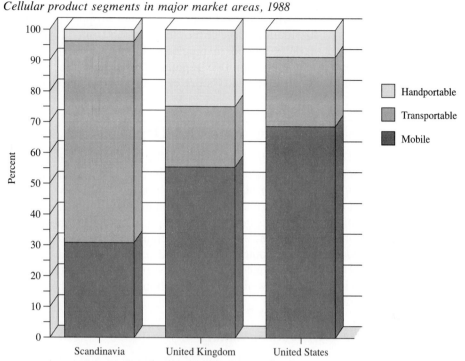

SOURCE: Nokia-Mobira and European Mobile Communications, EMC.

phone segment in the United States was small compared to that of the United Kingdom, due to differences in system capacity and, consequently, in price. In Scandinavia, the handportable segment was also very small, but this was due to the late introduction of the NMT-900 system.[4]

Most of the companies involved in the cellular industry also had expertise in either telecommunications, radio communication, office automation, or consumer electronics. Like all telecommunications industries, the cellular business was regulated to some extent by international and national standards. Three regions of the world—North America, Europe, Southeast Asia—each had their own central standards organization, which usually included representatives from the relevant PTTs. Internationally, the standards-setting process was regulated to a modest degree by the CCITT organization in the International Telecommunications Union.

In most countries, the cellular radio end user was typically a senior executive or a small business owner. Because of this upmarket bias, prices were generally high, and the market sizes small. However, in the United Kingdom and Scandinavia, the markets were considerably different—much larger and characterized by lower prices and a greater variety of business customers. In 1987, the market share accounted for by corporate purchases in Britain was estimated at 37%,

---

[4] European Mobile Communications, *Quarterly Report*.

while small business owners and self-employed people accounted for a 57% portion.[5] Consumers, at 2–3%, still represented a small portion of the market, but this market segment was expected to grow as prices dropped and networks improved. In terms of distribution, large corporations in the United Kingdom and other more developed markets tended to purchase directly from the manufacturer or the importer, while the other two segments purchased the product either from a telecommunications specialty store or from a consumer electronics outlet.

Company Background and Organization

Nokia Oy was established in Finland in 1865 as a manufacturer of paper and rubber products. In the mid-1970s, the firm began to expand internationally and to develop a business in high-technology products. By 1987, Nokia was Finland's largest company in terms of market capitalization and had sales of $3.4 billion. Its electronic division was both the fastest-growing and the most profitable of its four divisions—electronics, cables and machinery, paper and chemicals, and rubber and floorings. Electronics sales totaled $1.6 billion, and profit, $170 million in 1987. Half of Nokia's electronics sales were made by companies it had acquired in West Germany and Sweden, which continued to market their products under their own trademarks.

Mobile Telephones Subsidiary

Nokia-Mobira Oy, a wholly owned subsidiary of Nokia Oy, designed, manufactured, and marketed mobile telephones and wide-area paging equipment, as well as cordless telephones and terminals for mobile data transmission. Nokia-Mobira limited itself strictly to end-user equipment, leaving the system infrastructure to Nokia Cellular Systems, another subsidiary of Nokia Oy.

When Nokia Oy acquired the first Finnish radiophone company, Televa, in 1925, the business that would later become Nokia-Mobira began operations. It produced its first radiophones in 1963, distributing them to the Finnish Army. In 1971, it introduced the public mobile phone. In 1979, the Mobira company was established as a joint venture between Nokia and Salora. By 1980, sales in Finland and Sweden totaled $12 million. In 1981, Mobira established a Swedish subsidiary and began distribution in seven other European countries. In 1982, Salora sold its share in Mobira to Nokia, and the company then became Nokia-Mobira.

In 1987, Nokia-Mobira's sales were $270 million. Sales for 1988 were expected to be over $320 million, of which one-quarter would be domestic sales. Nokia-Mobira employed about 2,400 people and claimed a 14% world market share. Moreover, in important product markets such as the AMPS system and the NMT system, Nokia was the market leader.

When the US market began to develop, Mobira needed an American business partner with an existing distributor network. In 1984, Mobira made an agreement with Tandy Corporation to set up a joint venture manufacturing plant in South

---

[5] Business Decisions Limited report, 1987.

Korea and to distribute phones through Tandy's Radio Shack outlets under the Radio Shack brand name. By 1988, Mobira had subsidiaries in the United Kingdom, the Federal Republic of Germany, Sweden, Norway, Denmark, the United States, and Canada; it also had joint ventures in South Korea and France.

Company Organization 1980–1988

In 1980, Nokia-Mobira had two factories. One produced mobile phones and pagers, while the second concentrated on support stations for dedicated networks and on standard radiophones. However, by late 1982, the growth expectations for NMT cellular radios and the introduction of new cellular systems in Germany, The United Kingdom, and France prompted Nokia to add independent production plants for each system. The organization is depicted in Exhibit 4. The fragmentation of

EXHIBIT 4

Nokia-Mobira organization chart, 1987

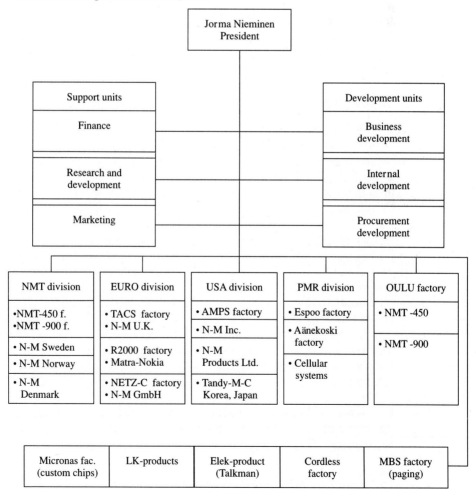

production into a large number of fairly small units provided the company with flexibility as well as the motivation that came from decentralization. However, it also meant duplication of product costs. It became clear by early 1988 that the company could not compete with the cost structures of its main competitors.

Under a new president, Timo Louhenkilpi, the firm continued to refine its organizational structure to achieve greater cost effectiveness. Louhenkilpi counseled, ''We must learn more from others' experiences and increase interrelationships in the company.'' Exhibit 5 shows the organization established in 1988. The

EXHIBIT 5

Nokia-Mobira organization chart, 1988

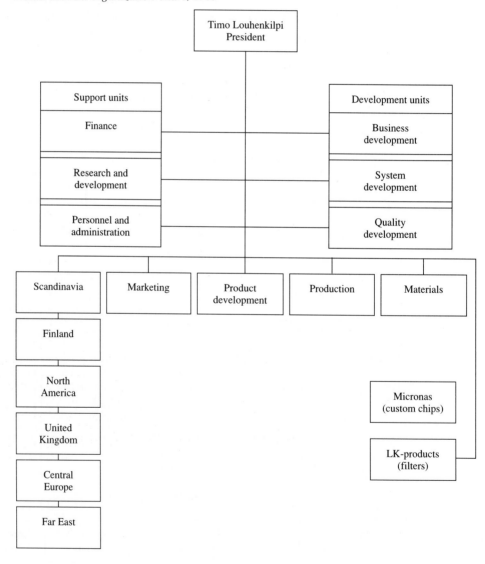

newly formed management team looked for synergies between the various Nokia divisions. Nokia Cellular systems was established as an independent company with exclusive control of the cellular systems product line.

Cellular Market Development in Europe

European Cellular Networks

In 1988, there were 18 cellular networks in Europe, which served over a million subscribers.[6] There were six different types of systems in operation—NMT, TACS, Radiocom 2000, C-450, RTMS, and Comvik—described in more detail in Appendix 2. Not only were these systems largely incompatible, but networks that operated under the same system were also not always compatible. For example, the NMT-450, the predominant system in terms of subscriber volume, was not produced to uniform specifications, and therefore its own network components were not always compatible with one another.

There were three main groups of countries within which networks could be connected across national boundaries: Scandinavia, The Benelux Countries, and the United Kingdom and Ireland. As indicated in Exhibit 6, the two major systems

EXHIBIT 6

European cellular systems subscriber bases, 1981–88

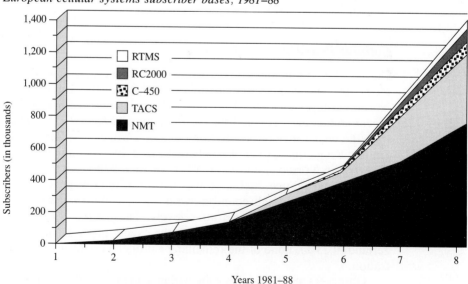

SOURCE: European Mobile Communication, *Quarterly Report,* Issue 5, 1988.

---

[6] Most of this section is based on Europe Mobile Communications, *Quarterly Report,* Issue 5, 1988.

EXHIBIT 7

Speed of market penetration by country

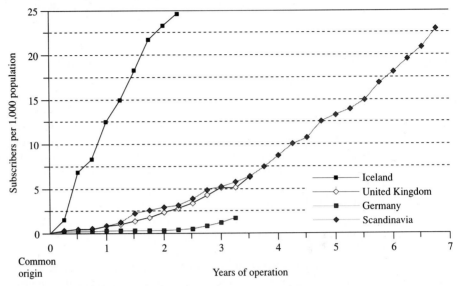

SOURCE: European Mobile Communications, *Quarterly Report,* Issue 5, 1988.

used throughout Europe were NMT and TACS; NMT was losing share to TACS. The other four system types had not thus far succeeded in establishing a significant share of subscriber volume.

Cellular Penetration by Country

During 1988, the number of European subscribers grew at about 6% each month. However, the main sources of this growth were the United Kingdom and the Nordic countries, with the United Kingdom responsible for about 45% of the most recent annual increase, and the Nordic countries for 27%. Exhibits 7 and 8 illustrate the wide range of penetration rates in European countries. For example the United Kingdom market was characterized by medium penetration and high growth; the Nordic countries' market, by high penetration and medium growth; Germany and France, by both low penetration and low growth. In terms of penetration, Norway led all countries with 3.3%, while the Scandinavian countries generally enjoyed high penetration levels. The United Kingdom followed some distance behind with 0.65%, and with the exception of Austria (0.41%) and Switzerland (0.23%), none of the remaining European countries exceeded 0.2% penetration.

Observers attributed this wide variance in market penetration from country to country to the age of the systems and the different degrees of deregulation, competition, and marketing efforts, as well as to the type of network being implemented. For example, the slow growth in Germany was attributed to the technical complexity of Germany's national network and to the resulting poor connection

Exhibit 8

Cellular penetration by country, 1988

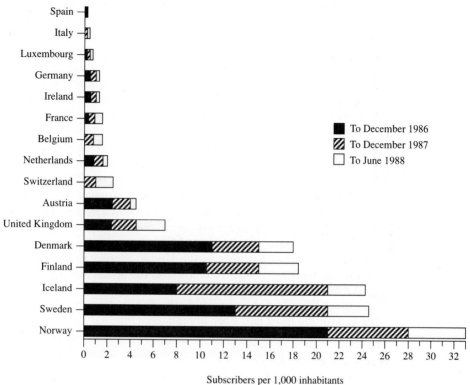

Subscribers per 1,000 inhabitants

Source: European Mobile Communications, *Quarterly Report,* Issue 5, 1988.

quality and high tariffs. On the other hand, analysts credited Iceland's high growth to a delayed adoption of an already-proven system, NMT, which served well the needs of its fishing fleet. Scandinavia's high-growth rates may have been encouraged by the sparseness of population and by the PTTs' early market orientation.[7] In the United Kingdom, growth was mainly spurred by the competition; two competing networks ensured aggressive marketing and more rapid market penetration.

Competition

Network Operations.   As of 1988, among 16 European countries, only the United Kingdom and Sweden had competing networks within their boundaries. In Sweden, Televerket, the public telephone company, competed with a small network

---

[7] "Survey on Mobile Communications," *Financial Times,* September 12, 1988.

run by Comvik. Comvik's subscribers numbered only 14,000 versus the PTT's 193,000. In the United Kingdom, strong competition existed between two privately owned cellular networks, Cellnet and Vodafone. The privatized British Telecom owned 60% of Cellnet while Securicor owned 40%; Racal owned Vodafone 100%. The British distribution system was also unique. British network operators did not sell air time directly to end users. Instead, independent service providers sold air time, either directly or through a dealer network. The British approach to distribution was expected to become more widespread in Europe.[8] Appendix 3 describes the British marketing system for cellular in more detail.

In 1987, France joined Britain and Scandinavia in allowing domestic competition in cellular networks. Its second system was expected to begin operations in 1989, at which point the PTT, France Telecom, with its Matra-designed Radiocom 2000 system, would begin to lose its monopoly position. However, all other cellular networks in Europe were still monopolies as of 1989.

Competition was believed to have had a stronger impact on cellular equipment prices than on air-time rates. In the United Kingdom this may have been because networks competed more on coverage than in tariffs. As shown in Exhibit 9, the equipment prices in the United Kingdom were by far the lowest in Europe in 1988—almost as low as those in the United States. British air-time rates, on the other hand, were only slightly below the European average.

Equipment Distribution.   By 1988, the distribution of cellular equipment in Europe had for the most part been liberalized. Only Italy and the Netherlands limited the distribution of equipment to their PTTs. However, the degree of liberalization in the equipment markets varied considerably among European countries. With

Exhibit 9

World price levels, 1988 (Equipment prices and air-time rates in Europe, in GBP)

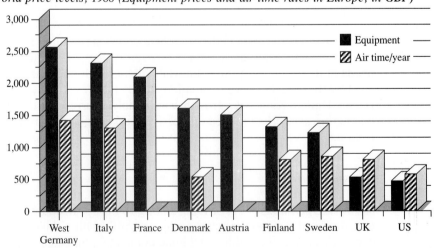

Source: European Mobile Communications, EMC.

---

[8] Juha Pinomaa, "A Study of Distribution Strategies for Cellular Equipment in the United Kingdom," Helsinki University of Technology, 1988.

the exception of the United Kingdom, European distribution channels consisted of national network operators, telecommunications specialty stores, and importers. Yet, despite the similarity in distribution systems, almost all countries had unique type-approval standards and other technical entry barriers that effectively blocked the use of standard products. In addition, domestic producers were emerging in most countries. Particularly in Germany, continuously changing specification represented a serious barrier to entry.

Substitutes for Cellular

The major substitutes for cellular radio were amateur and citizens band radios, radio paging, cordless phone, and private mobile radios. Exhibit 10 provides data

EXHIBIT 10

A. Cellular substitutes in the United Kingdom

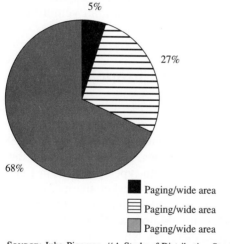

The UK mobile communication market in 1988

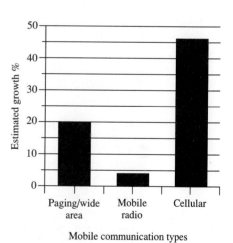

Mobile communication growth rates in the UK in 1988

■ Paging/wide area
▤ Paging/wide area
▨ Paging/wide area

SOURCE: Juha Pinomaa, "A Study of Distribution Strategies in the United Kingdom."

B. Rating the options for mobile communication

	Payphone	Telepoint (CT2)	Car Cellular	Portable Cellular
Unit costs ($)	$0	$180–$360	$900–$1,080	$1,440–$2,700
Call cost (above PSTN*)	25¢	18¢ per minute	45¢ per minute	45¢ per minute
Call type	Outgoing only	Outgoing only	Two-way	Two-way
Convenience				
Handset Needs	None	One person	In car	One person
Call Location	Fixed	Fixed	Mobile	Mobile

* Rates for public switched telephone network.
SOURCE: Logica pls and Nokia Cellular Systems.

on these substitutes. New forms of electronic data communications, such as facsimile and electronic mail, tended to complement rather than substitute for cellular. Mobile radios were not a major threat to cellular radio because they were primarily used when a closed system was appropriate. Only cordless phones were in direct competition with cellular. Because they were cheaper and provided access to the public telephone network, the first generation of cordless phones also replaced some in-company mobile radio systems.

Using a special radio network similar to that of the cellular network, the second generation of cordless phones could operate outside of an office, making them a serious threat to the handportable cellular radio. The other advantages of the second generation cordless, also known as CT2, were its relatively low equipment and usage costs, its small size, and its light weight. However, it also had disadvantages: It required a separate radio pager to receive messages; and there was only a limited number of ''phonepoints'' where this type of phone was operable. Nevertheless, the CT2 was being marketed in the United Kingdom where it was developed. Because its standards had been approved by the member states of the EC in 1989, it was expected to be adopted in other EC countries as well. Three major equipment manufacturers—Philips, Motorola, and Nokia-Mobira—had become involved in system development in the United Kingdom. Nokia had participated in the design of the new system through a joint venture with Shaye Communications, Ltd.

Equipment Manufacturers in Europe

Competitor Strategies

There were 31 cellular equipment manufacturers in Europe in 1988. With representation in 14 out of 16 European countries, Nokia-Mobira had the widest coverage. Exhibit 11 lists the manufacturers with type approvals in Europe as of 1988. Exhibit 12 shows worldwide and European market shares for cellular equipment as of 1988. Only 6 of the 31 cellular manufacturers operating in Europe were also major global players: Nokia-Mobira, Motorola, NEC, Panasonic, Novatel, and Mitsubishi. The European manufacturers whose markets were limited to Europe—Philips, Siemens, Ericsson, and Technophone—were almost invisible in markets beyond Europe (for example, in the United States). On the other hand, the European markets were not dominated by the Japanese manufacturers, as were most of the other world markets. NEC, Panasonic, and Mitsubishi together held almost half of the world market, while in Europe, they had a combined market share of only 28%. Companies with significant shares of the US market that had not yet entered the European market, such as OKI and Toshiba, were expected to do so as the market developed further.

In Europe, the clear market leader was Motorola, the American semiconductor company that had entered the EC market through the purchase of Storno, a Danish cellular firm. Relative to Motorola, Nokia was weak in the UK market but still the market leader in Scandinavia.

EXHIBIT 11 Cellular Manufacturers in Europe*

Manufacturer	Number	Note	Scandinavia					UK	IR	Benelux			F	D	E	A	I	CH
			S	DK	IS	N	SF			B	NL	LX						
AEG	1													X				
AT&T/Hitachi	1							X										
Autophon	1												X					
Bosch	1	1											X					
Cetelco	5	2	X	X		X	X											X
Dancall	9	3	X	X	X	X	X	X		X						X		X
Ericsson	9		X	X	X	X	X								X	X		X
Hitachi	1	4						X										
Italtel	1	5															X	
JRC/Cleartone	2							X	X									
Kokusai	7		X	X		X	X	X								X		X
Matra	1	6											X					
Mitsubishi	9		X	X	X	X	X	X	X					X				X
Mobira	14		X	X	X	X	X	X	X	X	X	X	X			X		X
Motorola	10		X	X	X	X	X	X	X	X						X		X
NEC	8		X	X	X	X	X	X	X									X
Novatel/Astec	2							X	X									
OTE	1	5															X	
Panasonic	8		X	X	X	X	X	X	X									X
Philips AP	12		X	X	X	X	X	X		X	X	X			X	X		X
Philips PKI	1													X				
Racal-Orbitel	1	7						X										
Radiotel	1												X					
Siemens	10		X	X		X	X			X	X	X		X		X		X
Simonsen	6		X	X	X	X	X											X
Storno	10		X	X	X	X	X			X			X	X		X		X
Talco	1												X					
Technophone	7	8	X					X	X				X	X		X		X
Telettra	1	5															X	
Toyocom	2	9	X					X										
Number/country			15	12	10	13	13	15	8	6	3	3	7	4	3	9	3	14

* Table does *not* include products supplied on a "badge engineered basis."

NOTES:
1. Bosch is present as a distributor of cellular phones in several countries, but has own products only in France. It is developing its own product for C-450 in Germany.
2. Only NMT-450, NMT-900 in planning stage.
3. Dancall markets through Autophon in Austria and plans to do the same in France.
4. Hitachi has made two entries into the United Kingdom. First, indirectly as a supplier of the radio side of the Racal marketed AT&T VIP product, and second, with a handportable through British Telecom.
5. There are three national manufacturers for Italy's RTMS-450 network: Italtel, OTE, and Telettra.
6. Matra's entry to equipment markets was heavily supported by Nokia-Mobira technology.
7. Racal's Citifone handportable was designed in collaboration with E.F. Johnsen.
8. The UK-manufactured technophone is marketed by Comvik in Sweden, BBC in Switzerland, ATR in France, SEL in Germany (SEL financed the development costs), and by Alcatel and Elin in Austria.
9. Toyocom products are marketed by STC in the United Kingdom and Comvik in Sweden.

EXHIBIT 12   **Worldwide and European Equipment Market Shares, 1988**

	World	*European*
Nokia-Mobira	13.8%	12.2%
Motorola	13.4	19.4
NEC	11.9	14.4
Panasonic	9.4	10.1
Toshiba	8.2	
Mitsubishi	8.1	3.1
OKI	5.9	
Novatel	5.9	4.7
Uniden	3.4	
Ericsson	2.8	7.2
Philips	2.5	6.4
Siemens	2.4	6.2
Other	12.4	16.3

Nokia-Mobira's principal competitors in Europe were Motorola, NEC, Panasonic, Technophone, Mitsubishi, Novatel, Philips, and Ericsson.[9] In 1987, NEC, Panasonic, Philips, and Mitsubishi had on average triple the resources invested in communications technology that Nokia had. They were on average five times bigger than Nokia in sales, and they all had extensive experience in other information-related technologies such as telefax machines, copiers, and computers. Motorola and Ericsson were similar to Nokia in terms of sales and communications technology resources, although Motorola's know-how in integrated circuits was superior to Nokia's. All of these firms, particularly Philips and Motorola, increasingly pursued joint ventures and strategic alliances with other telecommunications companies in order to share development risks and costs, and to develop more varied products. Nokia's two smaller, nonconglomerate competitors, Novatel and Technophone, had less than half Nokia's sales, but they focused on only cellular radios. Moreover, Technophone had specifically targeted the handportable segment.

Various of Nokia-Mobira's major competitors employed the generic strategies of cost leadership, differentiation, and focus, as indicated in Exhibit 13. Companies like Motorola and NEC, with products in the low-price segment of the market pursued a cost-leadership strategy; Nokia, Panasonic, Philips, and Mitsubishi, which produced high- and middle-priced products, followed a strategy of differentiation; and Novatel and Technophone, operating in only one product/market segment, implemented a focus strategy.

Companies pursuing cost leadership tended to command higher market shares. Those pursuing differentiation seemed to have enjoyed higher profits,

---

[9] Technophone and Mitsubishi marketed handportables only.

EXHIBIT 13

European strategies of major cellular manufacturers

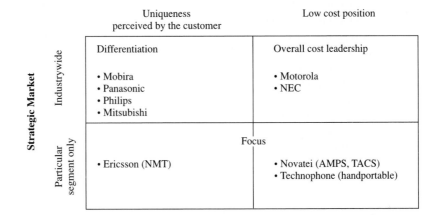

Strategic Advantage

	Uniqueness perceived by the customer	Low cost position
Industrywide	Differentiation • Mobira • Panasonic • Philips • Mitsubishi	Overall cost leadership • Motorola • NEC
Particular segment only	Focus • Ericsson (NMT)	• Novatei (AMPS, TACS) • Technophone (handportable)

*(Left axis label: **Strategic Market**)*

Product-Market Strategies of Major Manufacturers in 1988

Product Scope

Systems Scope	Wide	Focus
Wide (all)	• Mobira • Motorola • Philips	• Technophone
Wide (major)	• NEC • Panasonic • Mitsubishi	
Focus (1-2)	• Ericsson • Novatel	

SOURCE: European Mobile Communications, EMC, and Nokia-Mobira, among others.

although consumers were not always willing to pay more for extra features. This was especially true in the United Kingdom and in other more developed markets.

Each manufacturer coordinated the range of products and systems it made according to its generic strategy. For example, those that pursued cost leadership manufactured for a broad range of systems. The majority of Nokia-Mobira's key competitors marketed equipment for multiple systems and product-market segments, although only Nokia-Mobira, Motorola, Technophone, and Philips had equipment for every cellular system in operation. Novatel and Ericsson were the only major players to focus on only one or two systems.

Brand Choice Criteria

Through dealer surveys, Nokia mapped the most important end-user purchase criteria, both for the mobile and for the handportable cellular radio. Research results indicated that, for the mobile radio, price, reliability, reception, design, and brand were considered especially important. In the case of handportables, battery life, size, and reception were the most important product features to end users. According to two consumer surveys, summarized in Exhibit 14, Finnish end users considered reliability and brand image to be the most important product features, and British users were more concerned with price and design. These variations reflected not only differences in user preferences but also differences in industry structure and market maturity.

Another survey, summarized in Exhibit 15, measured the ability of European manufacturers to meet user criteria. While Nokia outperformed some of its major competitors in reliability, reception, and brand image, the firm was less competitive on price and on design. The lack of a "hands free" feature was another serious drawback to Nokia's product offering, although Nokia outperformed all major competitors in battery life and reception. Nokia was also constrained by its cost structure and the fact that its brand name was relatively unknown outside of Scandinavia.

EXHIBIT 14

Brand choice criteria in the United Kingdom and Finland

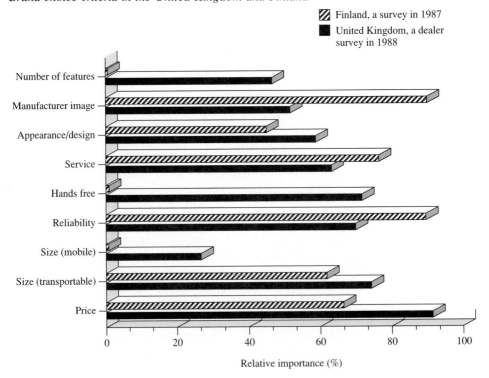

Relative importance (%)

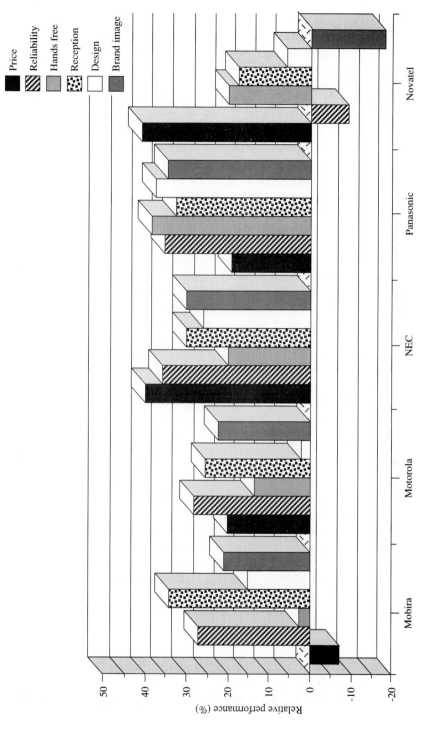

EXHIBIT 15

Relative customer perceptions of major European manufacturers

389

Distribution

The major cellular radio manufacturers followed varied market entry, distribution, and brand strategies both within and across geographical markets, as indicated in Exhibit 16. Philips, the European consumer electronics giant, almost always used direct distribution as a market entry mode, whereas Technophone, a relatively small company, invariably distributed through importers, OEM agreements, and joint ventures. The big Japanese companies—NEC, Panasonic, and Mitsubishi—usually entered a new international market via an OEM agreement or an importer, and later introduced their own brands and direct distribution. In contrast, Novatel supplied both the British and the American market under various brand names through a single distributor, the Carphone Group, whose network included Volvo and Ford dealers.

The distribution penetration and brand awareness level of both Ericsson and Nokia-Mobira were very good in the Nordic countries and satisfactory in other markets. However, their cost positions were poor, particularly that of Nokia-Mobira in the United Kingdom. Both Nokia-Mobira and Ericsson had been relatively successful in penetrating regulated markets, either through joint venture with cellular system developers or through the local public telephone companies. Philips and Siemens had also enjoyed some success through joint ventures— Siemens in Austria, and Philips and Siemens in Switzerland. In contrast, Motorola had a very good cost position and intensive distribution but relatively poor channel control. NEC in pursuing a cost leadership strategy, had introduced several brands distributed through multiple channels. Panasonic based its differentiation strategy on high product quality but distributed its products broadly through importers and wholesalers. Hence, its channel control was poor, though its market coverage was good. Novatel gained good market share through the use of exclusive, well-selected importers.

Most competitors marketed under their own brand names in the more highly developed markets, such as the United Kingdom and Scandinavia, but used joint ventures or OEM manufacturers in closed or regulated markets such as France. As might be expected, companies pursuing a differentiation strategy used their own brand names and direct distribution to ensure tight control. On the other hand, companies pursuing a cost leadership strategy were more interested in wide coverage and efficient distribution, typically using several brands and distributors. Philips, Nokia-Mobira, Motorola, and Technophone had begun to supply air time in order to assist their dealers in promoting their products.

Market Communications

Almost all manufacturers using direct distribution invested heavily in promotion to support their dealer networks. Manufacturers such as NEC employing a cost leadership strategy pursued intensive distribution and were among the heavier advertisers. Motorola and Philips emphasized sales promotion instead of advertising because their brand awareness was already high, whereas Nokia-Mobira and Ericsson (and Technophone in the United Kingdom) did use advertising to create

EXHIBIT 16

Market entry strategies by manufacturers in six European markets

Manufacturers	Austria — Direct operation	Austria — Importer/OEM agreements	Austria — Joint-venture/License	Austria — Own brand	Austria — Local brand(s)	Austria — Market share %	France — Direct operation	France — Importer/OEM agreements	France — Joint-venture/License	France — Own brand	France — Local brand(s)	France — Market share %	Germany — Direct operation	Germany — Importer/OEM agreements	Germany — Joint-venture/License	Germany — Own brand	Germany — Local brand(s)	Germany — Market share %	Scandinavia — Direct operation	Scandinavia — Importer/OEM agreements	Scandinavia — Joint-venture/License	Scandinavia — Own brand	Scandinavia — Local brand(s)	Scandinavia — Market share %	Switzerland — Direct operation	Switzerland — Importer/OEM agreements	Switzerland — Joint-venture/License	Switzerland — Own brand	Switzerland — Local brand(s)	Switzerland — Market share %	UK — Direct operation	UK — Importer/OEM agreements	UK — Joint-venture/License	UK — Air-time sales	UK — Own brand	UK — Local brand(s)	UK — Market share %
Subscribers (June 1988)						34,408						68,870						70,290						522,964						13,970							366,000
Mobira	—	•	—	•	•	27	•	•	—	•→	•	25?	•	—	—	•	—	new	•	—	—	•	—	20	—	•	—	•	—	?	•	•	—	•	•	—	6
Motorola	—	•	—	•	—	2-4	—	•	—	•	—	?	•	—	—	•	•	>20	—	—	—	•	—	17	•	—	—	•	—	?	•	•	—	—	•	—	33
NEC	—	—	—	—	—	—	—	—	—	—	—	—	—	—	—	—	—	—	•	—	—	•	—	5	•	•	—	•	—	?	—	•	—	—	•→	•	25
Panasonic	—	—	—	—	—	—	—	—	—	—	—	—	—	—	—	—	—	—	•	—	—	•	—	7	—	•	—	•	•	?	—	•	—	—	•	—	10
Technophone	—	•	—	•	—	new	—	•	—	—	•	?	—	—	—	•	•	new	—	—	—	—	—	—	—	•	—	•	•	?	•	•	—	•	•→	•	(23)
Mitsubishi	—	—	—	—	—	—	—	—	—	—	—	—	—	—	—	—	—	—	—	•	—	•	—	7	—	•	—	•	—	?	—	•	—	—	•→	—	3
Novatel	—	—	—	—	—	—	—	—	—	—	—	—	—	—	—	—	—	—	—	—	—	—	—	—	—	—	—	—	—	—	—	•	—	—	•	—	10
Philips	•	—	—	•	—	20	—	—	—	—	—	—	—	—	—	•	•	>20	•	—	—	•	—	9	—	•	—	•	—	?	—	•	—	—	•	—	0,1
Ericsson	—	•	—	•	•	14	—	—	—	—	—	—	—	—	—	—	—	—	•	—	—	•	—	15	—	—	—	•	—	?	—	—	—	—	—	—	—
Large, local competitor	Siemens (assembly j – v)					23	Radiotel and Talco					?	AEG and Siemens					>40													JRC, licensed to Cleartone						8

NOTE: Arrows indicate direction of development; market leaders are indicated with a grey tone.

brand awareness. On the other hand, NEC, Panasonic, and Mitsubishi tended to rely instead on wholesalers and importers to handle their product advertising. Novatel and all manufacturers using OEM agreements—Hitachi, Technophone outside the United Kingdom, and others—delegated promotion to their importers and wholesalers. With the exception of Novatel, the result was often poor promotion.

Summary

Analysts believed that the European markets were at varying stages of the product life cycle. The lesser-developed markets—Italy, Germany, and France—were still in the introduction stage. In these countries, cellular radio had an upmarket image. Marketing channels, primarily specialty stores and manufacturer's representatives, emphasized customer service and high prices. The United Kingdom and Scandinavian markets were in the growth stage, perhaps in the late growth stage in the case of some subcategories such as transportable phones. Prices in these markets were low or falling, as in Scandinavia.

The Impact of 1992

Toward a Competitive EC Telecommunications market

On June 30, 1987, the Commission of the EC submitted a Green Paper that focused on the development of telecommunications services and equipment. The Commission listed the following objectives:

- Phase opening of the terminal market.
- Competition in all value-added services.
- Communitywide interoperability.
- Opening of public network procurement.
- Separation of regulatory and operational activities of PTTs.
- Continuous review of the activities of PTTs and private providers.
- Cooperation at all levels.
- Consensus in technical standards, frequencies, and tariffs.
- Establishment of the European Telecommunications Standards Institute by April 1988.

Two overarching ideas in the Green Paper were interoperability and a consensus on tariffs. From the cellular equipment manufacturer's point of view, the Green Paper offered several promising opportunities. First, the opening of public procurement would eventually end the PTTs' favoritism of local manufacturers. Second, mutual recognition of each country's type-approval criteria for terminal equipment, scheduled for December 1990, would remove entry barriers to new equipment from non-national suppliers. Third, analysts expected cost-based tariffs and full competition in value-added services to lead to a price-competitive market structure similar to that in the United Kingdom, and hence to increase demand for cellular phones.

Groupe Special Mobile (GSM)

CEPT, a cooperative organization of European PTTs, formed GSM to ensure Europe's competitiveness in cellular technology, particularly against Asian competition. GSM's major objective was to create and implement standards and specifications for a Pan-European digital cellular system. A time line was set for the coordinated implementation of a digital cellular network. By the end of 1988, several operators in Europe had begun to award letters of intent to successful bidders for digital systems. The first systems were slated to start operation in June 1991. The new digital system had several important characteristics.

• *Pan-European roaming*: The system enabled an individual in any European country that had adopted the GSM system to receive and transmit calls throughout the system. To reach this goal, several billing-related problems had to be solved. However, the Green Paper emphasized that the GSM operation should not be given to a monopoly. Difficulties to be resolved included determining what the caller's choice should be in a border area where networks of more than one country could operate, and how the caller would be billed.

• *Call-handling capacity*: Analysts estimated that the analog networks in Europe could handle about 4.35 million subscribers, while the digital network could handle over 6 million subscribers in one country alone. This added capacity was important because, by 1989, the existing analog cellular networks in some EC countries had already become quite congested.

• *Special services*: The aim of the GSM working group was to design a state-of-the-art system that would offer transfer of data, picture, and voice all through the same channel. Some manufacturers had complained that the system was too elaborate, that services such as the transmission of text data were not really necessary, and that the system would be costly to implement. Several surveys indicated that speech would remain the most important form of data transmission in cellular systems for the next several years.

Nokia-Mobira was developing both systems and equipment for GSM in a joint venture with AEG and Alcatel. Most of the other key European suppliers—Bosch, Ericsson, Matra, and Philips—were similarly involved in system development through different joint ventures. Motorola was also heavily involved in research and development work and had submitted competitive bids in Scandinavia, the United Kingdom, and Spain. Nokia-Mobira had also formed an alliance with AT&T to develop the semiconductors that were critical to successful GSM equipment. Motorola and the major Japanese competitors—NEC, Toshiba, and Mitsubishi—had highly developed semiconductor technology. One-third of the manufacturing costs for cellular radio was in the special integrated circuits needed for digitalization. Moreover, the need to incorporate the new technology and special features of the system into small and lightweight handportables made the task even more challenging.

Cellular Equipment Demand in 1992

Analysts believed that the key factors that would determine the demand for digital cellular systems were the following: the increasing congestion in existing analog cellular services, competitive network operations, attractiveness of the equipment, and special features of the system. Although demand estimates varied widely, some analysts forecast 5 million systems would be required by 1996. Other more skeptical analysts wondered whether European bureaucrats had "shot themselves in the foot" while trying to ensure European competitiveness by specifying an overly complex system. Based on a comparison of European digital cellular system development with that of the United States, they predicted that 1996 demand would only amount to 2 million systems.

In Europe the PTTs or manufacturers provided the specifications for each new system, but in the United States open competition determined the most widely used system. The result in the United States was a more effective and simpler system than in Europe. Though the US market was more open to foreign competition, this ensured lower costs and competitive prices. Some skeptical analysts believed that digital cellular radio in Europe would not be able to compete effectively against the analog networks, particularly the NMT-900 system in Scandinavia and possibly the new French and German systems. A key question was whether the new French and German systems would ever be compatible with the current Scandinavian system—and possibly the future Swiss, Dutch, and Belgian NMT-900 systems—thereby facilitating Pan-European roaming.

Another factor that could limit the growth of the digital cellular market in Europe was the development of both Europe-wide radio paging, ERMES, and the second-generation cordless, CT2. Market demand would be further limited if the prices for digital cellular equipment did not drop and if the size of the equipment could not be adequately miniaturized. On the other hand, demand for Pan-European cellular radio would probably be enhanced by the increased travel within the EC following the removal of border controls and by cost reductions due to learning curve effects in analog cellular equipment manufacturing, as had occurred in the United States and the United Kingdom. Moreover, competition at the service provider level could accelerate the building of network coverage. New user groups could include ships and boats in the Mediterranean; trucks and vans on the continent; and businesspeople calling from planes, airports, and private cars. A 1988 survey established that 2 million out of the 4 million car owners who crossed EC borders regularly were interested in cellular services. In addition, one-third of the EC's 9 million farmers used private mobile radio systems, and many could be attracted to cellular radio. As suggested in Exhibit 17, there could be over 8 million subscribers in the EC in 1992 versus the 1.4 million in 1988, assuming that the penetration reached in Scandinavia in 1988 would be the 1992 European penetration level. Most of the growth would probably take place outside Scandinavia, particularly in Germany, France, Belgium, and the United Kingdom.

Price.   Analysts expected price competition to intensify in Europe as 1992 approached, thanks to the emergence of competing network operators and the opening of the terminal markets. Moreover, market expansion was likely to occur in

EXHIBIT 17

Cellular demand forecast for Europe

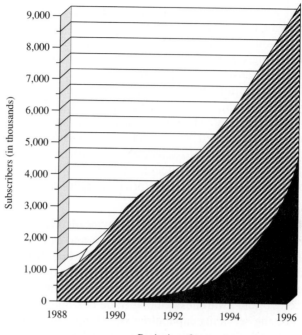

SOURCE: European Mobile Communications, BisMacintosh, and Nokia-Mobira Oy.

response to progressively lower prices, and premium-priced products were expected to hold a decreasing market share.

Distribution.   Competition among distributors might increase the demand for cellular radio. However, analysts saw distribution primarily as a result rather than as a determinant of demand. The introduction of cellular radio would not in itself cause any dramatic changes in distribution methods or channels. More likely, the distribution of digital equipment would follow the pattern for analog cellular equipment.

Many thought that the handportable phone would open a broader range of distribution channels for cellular phones. Because they did not require any installation or special services, these phones could be mass-marketed. For example, in the United States, they were already being sold by mail order. In Hong Kong, specialty stores distributed them as "hot phones," registered and ready for immediate use. Prices and margins were expected to decrease as distribution expanded.

Specialty outlets were expected to lose their position as the principal channel by 1992, while direct business-to-business operations were expected to continue their strong growth. Consumer electronics outlets were thought likely to concentrate on selling lower-priced equipment. Products were expected to become more differentiated as technologies converged. Standard equipment would be mass-marketed, while specialty phones would be sold through more focused outlets. Overall, however, standard phones were expected to dominate the market for the next several years and to be offered increasingly as optional or even standard equipment in new automobiles.

Another factor transforming the distribution system was the emergence of increasingly powerful chains of consumer electronics outlets in Europe. Lower inventory costs, increased bargaining power and the promise of free movement of labor and capital in 1992 had already prompted several hypermarkets in France, Spain, Belgium, and the Netherlands to form cross-border chains. These chains were likely to introduce their own brands and press for lower prices, as they had done in the United States and the United Kingdom. Such a trend would force European suppliers to select clearly either a differentiation or a cost leadership strategy. Suppliers that decided to sell only through OEM agreements would have to be prepared for intensive price competition.

Marketing Communications.   Growing demand, changing distribution patterns, and the proliferation of new broadcast and print media presented new opportunities for marketing communications in Europe as 1992 approached. The increasing emphasis on business-to-business selling required larger direct sales forces and better brand awareness. Selling through consumer electronics outlets required strong brand awareness among trade customers and good product quality control (since the servicing capabilities of selling outlets would be limited) and the use of proven sales promotion methods. Since the likely end user was a frequent traveler within Europe, there would be an opportunity for Pan-European advertising and sales campaigns. To create a new Pan-European brand would require substantial advertising. Existing, well-known brands could more readily support such communications programs.

Conclusion

Industry experts agreed that the major marketing impacts of the 1992 program on the cellular industry would be in the areas of market demand, price, distribution, and marketing communications. Demand was expected to grow substantially. Price competition would intensify, and a standard product would probably dominate the market for a few years. Subsequently, as technologies converged, other features would be bolted onto cellular phones and product differentiation would resurface. New distribution channels would emerge, primarily as a result of the handportable phone. Mass marketing through consumer electronics outlets and direct business-to-business selling would be the dominant forms of distribution by 1992. Finally, the promotion costs to develop Pan-European brands were expected to be high. An eventual industry shakeout of less-well-known manufacturers was predicted. Given all of these trends and expectations, Nokia-Mobira management had to determine the likely impact of the European market integration program and to decide how to compete most effectively in the years preceding and following 1992.

APPENDIX 1
STRUCTURE OF THE CELLULAR SYSTEM

The Cellular System

Cellular technology, developed initially in the 1950s, enables duplex communication (simultaneous receiving and sending) from a mobile radio terminal to the public telephone service. The figure on the following page shows the structure of the cellular system. The system requires the use of modern computer technology, and it is made up of the following component parts:

Mobile Telephone Exchange (MTX)

MTX is the brain of the system and is technically the most complicated part. The cellular system is divided into a number of traffic areas. Each traffic area belongs to a single MTX. The exchange forms the interface between the cellular network and the fixed telephone network. It also switches the calls within the cellular network and controls the operation of the base stations.

Base Station

The base stations are intermediary links without a switching function between the wire and radio transmission. They consist of a low-powered transmitter with computer controller so that more calls can be handled in the same frequency band. In a traffic area, there are a number of base stations spaced about between 8 and 80 km apart. All base stations in the area are connected to the MTX of the traffic area, and all traffic in the area is channeled through it.

Mobile Station

The mobile stations (i.e., the subscriber equipment) come in various forms; they can be handportable, vehicle-borne, or a coin-box type. Each mobile station is registered in a so-called home MTX, usually the MTX controlling the traffic area in which the subscriber normally resides.

A call from an ordinary telephone subscriber is connected on the basis of the first digits of the mobile subscriber's number to his home MTX. The latter stores data on the caller's present location and transmits a call signal over all base stations in that traffic area. The mobile station answers automatically with a call acknowledgement, and the MTX then assigns the mobile station a traffic channel. The call is set up. If the mobile subscriber is in a traffic area of some other MTX, the home MTX hands over the call to the MTX in the visited area. The system enables the mobile station to move between several base stations and even traffic areas without any interruptions in the conversation.

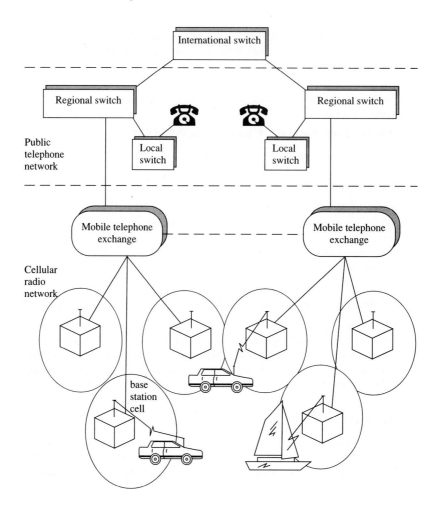

APPENDIX 2
EUROPEAN CELLULAR SYSTEMS

NMT-450 and NMT 900

NMT, Nordic Mobile Telephone, was currently the only analog European cellular system offering multinational compatibility and international roaming. The system had been introduced and developed by the Scandinavian PTTs and by radiophone companies in the late 1970s. There was also an international roaming capability between the Scandinavian Countries and Switzerland's NMT-900 network, which had opened in 1988.

Another region offering compatibility was the Belgian, Luxembourg and the Netherlands NMT-450 network. However, other NMT-450 networks, like the Austrian and Spanish ones, were not operationally compatible with other NMT systems. The operating NMT networks in 1988 were these:

NMT-450	*NMT-900*
Denmark, Finland, Norway, and Sweden	Denmark, Finland, Norway, and Sweden
Iceland	Switzerland
Belgium, Luxembourg, and the Netherlands	
Faeroes	

TACS

TACS (Total Access Communication System) was a refinement of the American 800 Mhz AMPS system. It operated in the 900 MHz region and had been used in the United Kingdom and in Ireland since 1985. International roaming was expected to be possible between Ireland and the United Kingdom in 1989.

Soon after the airwaves began to become congested in 1988, an E-TACS system, operating in two new frequencies, was introduced in central London. E-TACS users could operate in a TACS network, but not the vice versa. The higher filtering requirements of E-TACS made the design of handportables more difficult than for TACS.

Radiocom 2000

Developed by Matra Company in 1985, this "noncellular" system was used only in France. It operated at both 200 MHz and 20 MHz.

C-450

Siemens developed the system in 1985 in Germany. It was also being implemented in Portugal.

RTMS

The RTMS-450 network was developed independently in Italy in 1985. Only Italian suppliers were involved in it. A 900 MHz network was under development in 1988.

Comvik

Comvik was a simpler cellular system to that of NMT, and it was used under the Comvik network in Sweden. It was about $1/12$ of the size of the competing NMT network.

Appendix 3
Cellular Market Structure in the United Kingdom

In the United Kingdom, competition existed at each level in the cellular industry. The two networks, Cellnet and Vodafone, were prohibited by their licenses from selling either services or telephones directly to the end user. Hence, both operators had invested over £200,000 in their networks of service providers. These air-time retailers billed end users for their calls. In 1988 there were over 50 service providers, and many were subsidiaries of companies involved in the telecommunications industry. Some were equipment manufacturers, and some were more service based, like the Automobile Association. Competition among the service providers centered on intensity of distribution and brand recognition. Their profits came mostly from air-time rather than equipment sales.

To gain market share rapidly, the service providers signed up dealers to sell both air time and the equipment. The service providers competed mainly through commissions, dealer bonus schemes, low equipment prices, attractive billing methods, and efficient connection service. In 1988 there were over 2,000 dealers in the United Kingdom. The dealers fell into two main categories: traditional telecommunications and service-oriented dealers, and discount operations. The first group of dealers relied on good after-sale service and tried to make profits from equipment sales. The second group sold equipment at a discount and made their profits from air-time commissions, thus pushing the equipment prices down. The market structure in the United Kingdom is illustrated in the figure. Over 75% of the equipment was wholesaled through service providers and dealers, the rest being sold directly through service provider/manufacturer sales forces.

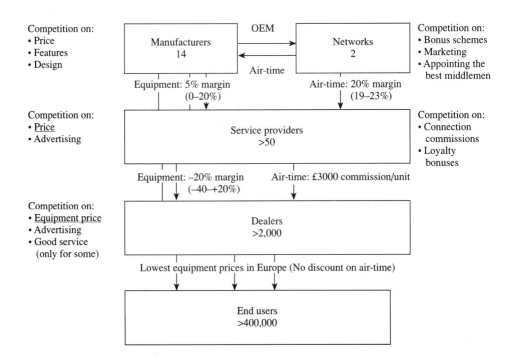

22

NOKIA DATA

Early in 1989, the top management of Nokia Data was mapping the key elements of the firm's strategy for growth and international expansion through the mid-1990s. In the previous year, the Finnish computer company had acquired the Data Systems Division of Sweden's LM Ericsson as a first step toward becoming a major player in the European market for information technology. However, despite the acquisition, less than a quarter of Nokia Data's $1.2 billion sales were generated outside the Nordic market,[1] where it now held the leading position. Management intended to improve the company's spotty international presence by aggressively expanding into the large but also highly competitive markets in the rest of Europe.

A cornerstone of Nokia Data's European growth strategy was what management referred to as a "multidomestic" approach. Management believed that in the fast maturing European market for computers, the key to competitive advantage lay in customer orientation achieved through a strong local identity and domestically tailored marketing programs in each European country. Thus, local hardware and software customization, local branding, local marketing, and local sales and support services constituted the main elements of Nokia Data's multidomestic approach.

Top executives were keenly aware that their planned approach went counter to industry practices, which were increasingly emphasizing Pan-European integration and marketing. In fact, some Nokia managers had expressed doubts regarding the wisdom of the multidomestic approach.

This case was prepared by Research Associate Robert C. Howard under the direction of Professor Kamran Kashani. Copyright © 1989 by IMEDE, Lausanne, Switzerland. Not to be used or reproduced without permission. IMD case 363.

[1] The Nordic market consisted of the three Scandinavian countries (Sweden, Norway, and Denmark) plus Finland.

According to Kalle Isokallio, president of Nokia Data:

We have a different view of the industry than what one reads in the papers. Our industry is no longer high growth or high tech. Both sales and technology are maturing. In this competitive market, we can't compete with majors like IBM or Siemens in volume or new technology. We don't have the resources. Where we can outperform them is by being closer to the computer buyer who prefers to buy from a domestic supplier. In every country where we compete, therefore, we want to be considered as one of the top domestic vendors. Pan-European identity and integration doesn't make sense for us. We are too small for that.

The Nokia Group

Nokia was founded in 1865 in the village of Nokia, Finland, as a timber and paper company. In the subsequent 100 years, Nokia grew and diversified into tires, power transmission, radio, telecommunications, electronics and computer technology. In 1988, the Nokia Group of companies had sales of $5,500 million, earned a net profit of $215 million, and spent 5% of net sales on research and development. With its 44,000 employees, Nokia conducted operations in 32 countries, 17 of which had manufacturing facilities. By 1988, the Nokia Group of companies was Finland's largest publicly traded industrial enterprise. In addition to Helsinki,

EXHIBIT 1   The Nokia Group of Companies
Group Sales (in $ Millions)

Industry Segment	1988	1987	1986
Electronics			
Information systems	1,170*	459	336
Telecommunications	359	364	197
Mobile telephones	271	214	178
Consumer electronics	1,432	678	441
Cables and Machinery			
Cables	557	529	438
Machinery	255	188	163
Electrical wholesaling	245	180	75
Paper, Power, and Chemicals			
Paper	628	589	447
Chemicals	130	110	81
Rubber and Floorings			
Rubber products	342	337	271
Floorings	75	64	51
Group total	5,237	3,500	2,519

* Less Interdivision sales and sales between industry segments.
SOURCE: Company records.

Nokia shares were listed on the stock exchanges in Stockholm, London, Paris, and Frankfurt. (Refer to Exhibit 1 for information on the Nokia Group of companies.)

Nokia Information Systems (NIS)

Nokia's experience with computers dated from 1962, the year when Nokia Electronics was formed to capitalize on the company's recent purchase of its first mainframe. At this time, Nokia implemented a timesharing system with outside companies to handle bookkeeping and other data processing activities. In the late 1960s, Nokia began serving as a sales agent for Honeywell, marketing its complete product line of mainframes, terminals, and printers to the Finnish market. During this period, Nokia management combined their increasing knowledge of hardware with their data processing know-how from timesharing. In the early 1970s, Nokia developed, manufactured, and sold its own minicomputer.

Throughout the 1970s, the Honeywell product line represented a main source of revenue at Nokia Electronics. However, in 1977, prompted by the growth of its customer base in the banking and retailing sectors, Nokia formed a separate department for its own products. In 1981, Nokia expanded its product offering further with its first personal computer, the Mikro Mikko 1. In 1985, Nokia Electronics was split into four divisions: Information Systems, Telecommunications, Mobile Telephones, and Consumer Electronics.

As of 1987, the Honeywell line accounted for 40% of Nokia Information System's revenues in Finland. Honeywell's role was limited to manufacturing performed in the United States, Italy, or Scotland, and to providing operating system software. Aside from adding its own terminals to Honeywell's computers, Nokia was responsible for all applications software, and postsales services. In 1987, Nokia Information Systems enjoyed the leading market share in Finland, where it generated 75% of its total sales.

Nokia Data

With limited growth opportunities in the small Finnish market, Nokia management began searching for an acquisition candidate within the Nordic countries. In 1988, Nokia Information Systems purchased the Data Systems unit of the Ericsson Group in Stockholm and merged the two operations to form Nokia Data. Data Systems produced and marketed a range of minicomputers, personal computers, telephone exchanges, and printers throughout Europe in addition to Hong Kong and Australia. Aside from keeping sales offices in North America and other overseas markets, the Ericsson Group retained a 20% share ownership in Nokia Data. Nokia, on the other hand, was able to strengthen its share of the Nordic countries market and gained the opportunity to expand into Germany, France, Britain, and a number of other European markets. Management believed that increased geographic coverage translated into greater credibility among Nokia's customers and helped ensure the company's survival in the Nordic countries at a time of industry consolidation. By the end of 1988, with sales of $1.2 billion, Nokia Data was the

EXHIBIT 2

Nokia Data: Partial organization chart

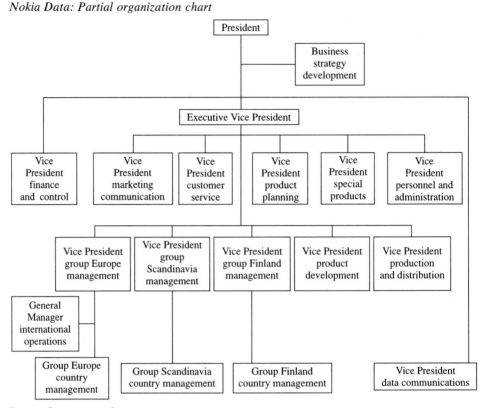

SOURCE: Company records.

largest computer company in the Nordic countries. The firm employed 8,500 employees, had subsidiaries in 10 European countries, and a European installed base of over 700,000 terminals and personal computers. (See Exhibit 2 for the Nokia Data reporting structure.)

The Information Technology Industry

In its broadest sense, information technology (IT) was defined as the industry that combined the data processing and storage power of computers with the distance-transmission capabilities of telecommunications. The industry included all types of computers, word processors, printers, plotters, disk drives, telephones, telephone networks, public databases, and related software. Virtually all organizations used these products. In Western Europe, the manufacturing, finance, retail, and public sectors accounted for the largest expenditures. In 1987, the worldwide market for IT was valued at $407 billion with volume distributed heavily among three geographic markets: North America, 38%; Europe, 26%; and Japan, 30%. For 1989, total industry sales were forecast to reach $505 billion.

Nokia's Data Business

In the vast information technology field, Nokia Data management defined its core business as the sector of the computer industry that focused on terminals, personal computers, and related networks. While the total European computer industry in 1987 was valued at $86 billion, management estimated its industry sector accounted for $20–$22 billion.

Nokia Data's product offering included terminals, personal computers, minicomputers, local area networks (hardware connected to share and exchange information among a group of users), and the related communication links for connecting different brands and classes of computers. In addition to hardware, Nokia Data provided application software and services tailored to meet the needs of its five primary customer segments—in retailing, banking and insurance, manufacturing, government, and general business. Typical examples of general business applications included materials administration, purchasing, order handling, invoicing, database management, word processing, graphics, and spreadsheets. Across Europe, the five segments in which Nokia Data competed were forecast to grow between 7% and 10% per year through the early 1990s.

Markets and Competition

In Europe, Nokia Data competed directly and indirectly with a large number of firms. Exhibit 3 on page 406 shows the top 25 manufacturers in the European data processing market, ranked by their total volume of business in the region. Nokia Data's management believed that such rankings were misleading because not all firms competed in the market sector defined as terminals, personal computers, networks, and related products and services. Instead, to delineate the competition, management used the diagram shown in Exhibit 4, which clustered industry participants around four product/system zones: terminals, personal computers, local area networks, and systems. The four zones differed in their volume potential and product/system configuration. (See Exhibit 5 on page 408 for a summary of Nokia Data's key competitors and their product offerings along the four zones.)

Terminals.   The European terminal market, consisting of keyboards and screens, represented approximately 6% of the European sector in which Nokia Data competed and was valued at $2.2 billion. Terminals had no data processing power of their own and hence had to be connected to a host computer. Sales were divided between add-on terminals (90–95%), where customers expanded an existing system by adding new terminals, and upgrades (5–10%), where customers substituted new terminals for old. The terminal market was contested for by mainframe and minicomputer suppliers, such as IBM and DEC, which were able to sell their own terminals on the strength of their computers and by a large number of component suppliers. Among these were Memorex Telex of US origin and SEl of Germany, which made terminals compatible with existing computers as well as disk drives, cassettes, and other computer accessories. Across Europe, Nokia Data management considered IBM, Memorex Telex, and Olivetti as their primary competitors in the terminal market.

EXHIBIT 3   The 25 Largest Computer Companies Competing in Europe

1987 Rank	Company	Origin	Total Revenue ($ Million, 1987)	European Revenue ($ Million, 1987)	Europe As Percent of Total	Estimated Revenues from Nokia Data's Industry Sector*	Major European Markets‡
1	IBM	United States	$50,485.7	$18,332.5	36%	3,520	F, D, I, UK
2	Siemens	Germany	5,703.0	4,961.6	87	357	D
3	Olivetti	Italy	4,637.2	3,802.5	82	1,041	I, D, F
4	Digital (DEC)	United States	10,391.3	3,533.0	34	73	F, D, I, UK
5	Nixdorf	Germany	2,821.5	2,652.2	94	266	D, F, UK
6	Groupe Bull	France	3,007.5	2,345.8	78	30	F, E, UK
7	Unisys	United States	8,742.0	2,272.9	26	28	F, CH
8	Philips	Netherlands	2,601.6	2,055.2	79	271	NL, D, B, L
9	Hewlett-Packard	United States	5,000.0	1,800.0	36	0	F, D, I, UK
10	STC	United Kingdom	2,123.9	1,720.4	81	40	UK
11	NCR Corp.	United States	5,075.7	1,583.6	31	144	D, F, UK, NL
12	IM Ericsson†	Sweden	1,511.6	1,284.9	85	—	S, D, DK
13	Alcatel NV	France	2,052.1	1,272.3	62	229	F
14	Inspectorate	Switzerland	1,225.0	1,033.0	84	0	CH
15	Société Générale	France	970.1	970.1	100%	0	F
16	Atlantic Computers	United Kingdom	959.7	892.7	93	0	UK
17	Honeywell Bull	United States	2,059.0	885.4	43	21	F, E, I, UK
18	Memorex Intl	Netherlands	1,041.1	832.9	80	54	D, NL
19	Wang Laboratories	United States	3,045.7	822.3	27	49	F, D, I, UK
20	Mannesmann AG	Germany	686.0	617.0	90	90	D
21	Apple Computer	United States	3,041.2	547.4	18	204	F, S
22	Cap Gemini Sogeti	France	682.3	545.8	80	0	F
23	Econocon Intl	Netherlands	674.3	525.9	78	0	NL
24	Amstrad plc	United Kingdom	533.0	501.0	94	250	UK, F, E
25	Amdahl Corp.	United States	1,505.2	493.1	33	0	F, D, I, UK

* Nokia Data's industry sector is defined as terminals, personal computers, LANs, and vertical systems installed in the company's five end-user segments.
† Figures are for year-end 1987, prior to Nokia Information System's acquisition of the Ericsson Data Systems Division. Following the acquisition by Nokia Data in 1988, parts of the company were sold off.
‡ Country codes:

F = France	I = Italy	E = Spain	DK = Denmark	L = Luxembourg
D = Germany	UK = United Kingdom	CH = Switzerland	B = Belgium	NL = the Netherlands

SOURCE: Datamation, company records.

EXHIBIT 4

Nokia Data's industry sector: Product/service zones

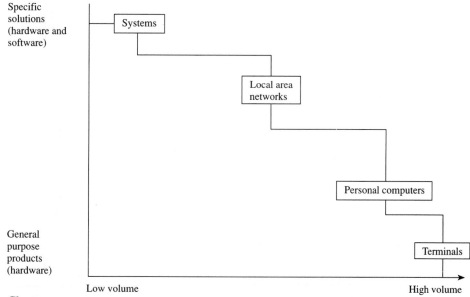

Specific
solutions
(hardware and
software)

General
purpose
products
(hardware)

Low volume   High volume

Glossary:

All terminals and personal computers contained a keyboard plus a video screen.

Terminals had no data processing ability of their own; were connected to a host computer, either a
  minicomputer or a mainframe; and used primarily for entering, retrieving, or manipulating data.

Personal computers had their own data processing capabilities and were used primarily on a
  stand-alone basis, but could also be connected to other computers.

A local area network (LAN) was a connection of terminals and/or personal computers that allowed
  communication among users in the same "network."

A system was a set of hardware to which tailor-made software had been added.

   SOURCE: Company records.

Typical customers for terminals included large organizations, such as banks
and insurance agencies, that processed data with a large central computer and a
score of dispersed terminals. Customers purchasing terminals from component
suppliers, instead of the large computer companies, cited price as an important
factor. More recently, ergonomics had become a criterion as it was believed to
contribute to improved employee comfort and productivity. Since the terminal
market was primarily an add-on market, functions performed for the customer
were installation and, when necessary, after-sales repair.

According to Nokia Data management, keys to success in the terminal market
were compatibility with hardware from the major computer companies, competitive pricing, and credibility as a terminal supplier. Credibility, a sales manager
clarified, meant a supplier was known for dependable products and was large
enough to survive any industry shakeout.

In unit sales, the terminal market was projected to remain stagnant through
the early 1990s and decline thereafter. In 1989 the market was becoming

EXHIBIT 5   **Nokia Data's Main Competitors**

Company/Product	Systems*	Local Area Networks	Personal Computers	Terminals
IBM	All	X	X	X
Siemens	M, G, GB, I	X	X	X
Olivetti	B, R, GB,	X	X	X
Digital (DEC)		X		X
Nixdorf	All	X		X
Bull	GB, M	X	X	X
Unisys	GB, M	X	X	X
Philips	B, I, M, GB	X	X	X
STC	GB, M	X		X
NCR	B, R	X	X	X
Alcatel				X
Memorex				X
Wang	GB	X	X	X
Mannesmann	All	X	X	
Apple	GB	X	X	
Amstrad				
Compaq		X	X	
Commodore			X	

* Nokia Data management defined systems competitors as those offering "solutions" in the company's five
end-user segments. Yet, because the management viewed the competition in terms of industry standards,
proprietary systems, and horizontal product offering, a number of the companies listed in Exhibit 3 were not
seen as direct competitors.
Systems code:
B   = Banking
I   = Insurance
R   = Retail
M = Manufacturing
G   = Government
GB = General Business

increasingly competitive. The average terminal prices in Europe had declined by
about 8% in recent months.

Personal Computers.   In 1988, the European personal computer market was valued at $11 billion and expected to reach $18 billion by 1993. Competitors in this
zone were well-known personal computer manufacturers such as IBM, Olivetti,
Siemens, Amstrad, Apple and Compaq. These firms were further classified by
Nokia Data management according to their origin and historic customer base.
More specifically, IBM, Siemens and Olivetti, for example, had begun with and
enjoyed established reputations in the business community, and were described
by Nokia Data management as having an "institutional" market background. On
the other hand, Amstrad, Apple and Compaq, a few among a large number of
companies, were originally associated with the mass market and said by management to have a "consumer" background.

From 1984 to 1987, the share of all personal computers sold by the institutional group in Europe had declined from 45% to 35%, with the balance of sales

accounted for by the consumer group. Nokia Data considered that it had a more institutional than consumer background.

Regardless of their original customer base, by the late 1980s, competitors from both groups offered stand-alone personal computers direct to large accounts and via retail outlets to the medium-sized and small business and consumer markets. Typically, larger accounts relied on the manufacturer for installation and after-sales services. Smaller accounts as well as individual buyers relied on the manufacturer's dealer or repair network for help, a process that was considered less reliable.

According to Goran Hermannson, a marketing manager in Sweden, in order to succeed in marketing personal computers to large accounts, a hardware supplier had to be known for reliable products and perceived by the customer as large enough to survive the computer industry's eventual consolidation. Companies from the institutional group had an advantage because they already enjoyed a reputation as suppliers of mainframes and minicomputers. More recently, compatibility with hardware from multiple vendors had become an important factor for supplying personal computers to large accounts. Major institutional companies such as IBM, which had traditionally employed its own proprietary systems, were now facing increasing pressure to abandon these in favor of industry standards and multiple vendor compatibility.

Nokia Data management believed that to succeed in the mass market, on the other hand, a supplier needed low manufacturing cost, extensive retail distribution, and a favorable price/performance image in the eyes of the customer. Examples of such companies included Amstrad, Commodore, and Compaq.

Local Area Networks (LANs).   LANs were a collection of computers, printers, cables, and other communications links that allowed a network of users to process data and communicate with one another.

In addition to hardware, LANs were equipped with operating systems software, applications software, and sophisticated LAN management software that allocated data processing among the computers in a network. As a concept in computing, LANs were relatively new to the industry, represented $670 million of the $20–$22 billion segment in which Nokia Data competed, and were expected to grow 20–30% per annum through the middle 1990s. Although LANs could include mainframes and minicomputers, they were built primarily using personal computers. One advantage of LANs was their attractive cost-performance ratio. An independent estimate showed that it cost less than $10,000 per employee to set up a network of personal computers, versus $12,000 for a seat at a minicomputer and $14,000 at a mainframe. In addition to lower hardware costs, networks eliminated the inefficiencies of multiple training staffs, multiple software packages, and data transmission costs.

Typical customers in the LAN segment, according to Goran Hermansson, were companies or departments with fewer than 100 personal computer users. He explained that it was technically easier to implement LAN solutions in smaller companies than in ones with hundreds of personal computers. In addition, he believed that the LAN technology was less popular with central data processing management in larger companies because it allowed individual departments to decide on their own systems independently.

Due to the complexity associated with the design, installation, and maintenance of a LAN, services accounted for a large portion of the purchase price. In addition, customers were keenly aware of the importance of vendor support in the early phases of a LAN's installation. In the words of one Nokia Data customer, it was important to have "someone to shoot" if something went wrong.

According to Nokia Data management, to be successful as a LAN supplier, a company had to enjoy the same qualifications as a personal computer vendor—namely, reliable products, hardware compatibility in a multivendor environment, and customer-perceived longevity. In addition, it had to have the technical know-how to act as a systems integrator, connecting products from one or many vendors. Most important, a LAN supplier had to be willing to service a network that contained products from vendors other than itself and guarantee against a network failure.

Because LANs were built primarily with personal computers, competitors came from both the institutional and the consumer groups. In the institutional group, Nokia Data's largest competitor in Europe was IBM, although companies such as Olivetti and Philips were strong in their local markets. The largest competitor in the consumer group was Compaq.

Systems.   At Nokia Data, a system was defined as a set of hardware and software products tailored to meet a specific need within an industry or industry segment. A system could consist of terminals sold with tailor-made software utilizing a client's existing mainframe or minicomputer. Alternatively, a system could be based on LAN products, complemented by customized software. In 1988, the European systems business was estimated to be $7 billion and projected to grow 10–15% annually through the early 1990s.

As with the personal computer market, systems competitors were categorized by Nokia Data management into institutional and consumer groups. The distinguishing feature between these groups, according to a Nokia Data sales executive, was knowledge about their customers' industries. He explained that companies like IBM and Siemens had accumulated a vast base of experience in industries such as insurance, banking, and manufacturing where centralized data processing, using mainframes and terminals, had been practiced for over two decades. On the other hand, newcomers such as Compaq and Amstrad, with a consumer background, relied more on the industry knowledge of third parties, including value-added resellers (VARs) to compete in the systems market. (See page 412 for more details on VARs.)

Systems customers were typically large organizations which sought to decentralize their data processing activities to a department or work group level. Decentralized data processing was attractive, as it eliminated the users' dependence on a single computer, particularly important in organizations such as banks where a computer breakdown might force shutdown of operations.

Leif Lindfors, a sales manager for Sweden, believed that, as in the LAN market, success in systems required reliable hardware and software. However, he explained, the most important requirement for success in systems was to have a sales force with industry-specific knowledge, assisted by a technical support staff capable of developing customized software. Nokia Data management identified its primary systems competitor as IBM, followed by other institutional companies such as Unisys, Siemens, Olivetti, Nixdorf, and Philips.

Industry Trends

Industry observers, as well as Nokia Data executives, believed several trends were influencing the level and nature of competition in the European data processing market. Among these trends were slowing growth, improved price–performance ratio of hardware, growth of decentralized computing, emergence of industry standards, proliferation of VARs, and the anticipated European integration toward a single market after 1992.

Slowing Growth.   In the late 1980s, the overall growth in the European computer industry was slowing down to single digits. As of 1988, annual growth had declined for the first time below 10%, and some analysts were predicting only 6% yearly growth through 1992. Mainframes and minicomputers had experienced the biggest decline in growth rates as customers shifted to lower-cost computing alternatives such as personal computers and LANs. In fact, analysts expected mainframe and minicomputer sales to grow at only 8% and 3%, respectively, into the early 1990s. Demand for personal computers, however, was expected to remain strong, with 10% growth forecast through 1992.

Price–Performance Ratio.   Advances in computer chip technology had substantially reduced the cost of computing power during the 1980s, a trend that was expected to continue into the 1990s. For example, in 1981, a mainframe capable of processing 1 million instructions per second cost over $400,000; by the early 1990s, the hardware with similar performance was expected to be priced around $50,000. More important, the computing power associated with some earlier mainframes was, by 1988, available in a desktop computer at a fraction of the cost, a trend referred to in the industry as "downsizing." Furthermore, as more and more processing power was provided to end users, analysts believed that powerful personal computers would replace terminals connected to mainframes and minicomputers.

Decentralized Computing.   In the early days of computing, companies needed a mainframe and a multitude of dumb terminals to perform all data processing centrally. The first step toward decentralization occurred with minicomputers, allowing users to process up to 95% of their data within their own departments. The next step in decentralization came with the personal computer, placing data processing capability directly on the end user's desk. Personal computers were, however, limited in their computing capacity and, as stand-alone hardware, did not allow communication among users.

The recent arrival of LAN technology provided an alternative means to decentralize computing by distributing data processing among a work group's or a department's interconnected computers. The use of personal computers in a network gave LANs a computing capacity similar to minicomputers at a fraction of the cost. In the opinion of many analysts, downsizing and distributed processing together were substantially changing the way companies competed in the computer industry. One analyst believed that decentralization was providing end users with more say in computer purchase decisions, leading to an increasing number of specialized narrow segments. The net result, according to another observer, was that the more expensive minicomputer and mainframes would lose sales to the less costly personal computer-based LANs.

Industry Standards.   Throughout the 1980s, minicomputer and mainframe manufacturers such as IBM, DEC, and Siemens, sold their hardware with proprietary software, thus locking customers in to a specific data-handling method. Having made a substantial investment in hardware and software, few customers were willing to purchase new systems from other manufacturers, a decision that could entail difficult and expensive tasks of rewriting old programs.

In contrast to proprietary systems, US-based AT&T developed and licensed UNIX, a nonproprietary operating system that allowed different brands of computers to communicate with one another. Preferred by an increasing number of computer buyers, the use of UNIX-based hardware and software was on the rise worldwide. Industry observers believed that interconnectivity would become an important buying criterion in the 1990s.

Proliferation of VARs.   During the 1980s, the focus of competition in the computer industry had shifted away from hardware toward software and services. Staffan Simberg, vice president of Group Europe, attributed this trend to the "commoditization" of computers, where substantive technological differences in hardware were narrowing among different manufacturers. Another factor was what many in Nokia Data management referred to as the "declining technical sophistication of the average buyer." Increasingly, computer decisions in small to medium-sized companies were being made by noncomputer people who were more concerned with the quality of "solutions" than the technicalities of the "black box."

The two trends combined had given rise to value-added resellers (VARs), independent companies who filled a gap between manufacturers and small to medium-sized clients. VARs bought hardware from a variety of producers, adding customized software and services for narrow vertical user segments such as the legal and medical professions, specialized retailers, plumbing, and farming. VARs competed among themselves and with computer manufacturers in the LANs and systems markets. From modest levels in the 1970s, the number of VARs in Europe had grown in recent years to several hundred. Together they accounted for an estimated $3 billion in industry sales.

To use a VAR for competitive advantage, explained one Nokia Data sales executive, a company had to provide hardware with an attractive price and encourage the resellers to develop applications in their special end-user segments. In an average installation, 65% of the price paid by a customer was accounted for by the cost of hardware to the reseller; the rest went to cover expenses, including costs associated with application development, and margins.

European Integration.   The European Community (EC) had chosen 1992 as the date to integrate its internal market by liberalizing trade and removing barriers among its 12 member states. Increased competition among manufacturers in an open market implied that government procurement could no longer favor a local vendor over another vendor from the EC. Hence, 1992 posed a serious challenge to national computer companies where 50% of sales was to the local government. Increased competition was also expected to lead to concentration in the industry, as companies strove to achieve critical mass and economies of scale. Recent examples of such activities included Alcatel, formed though the merger of ITT's European business and the French CGE group; and Memorex Telex, formed by the merger of Memorex International and the US Telex organization.

Also, in anticipation of 1992, companies such as Apple, IBM, Siemens, and Olivetti were integrating regional operations toward a "European" posture and identity. In the case of Apple, its management had recently created a European research and development center in Paris. "We want to form a strong European identity so that we are able to be part of the European economy."[2] By adopting a regional profile, both European and non-European companies wanted to be better positioned to compete for local government bids after 1992, when procurement policies were no longer biased toward domestic suppliers. In this respect, Olivetti's executive vice president, Elserino Piol, maintained, "The European companies that remain 'national champions' are going to suffer after 1992." The same article concluded, "Europe's computer makers have all opted for the same survival strategy. Each is scrambling to go Pan-European as fast as possible."[3]

Nokia Data's European Strategy

Current Position

At the end of 1988, Nokia Data manufactured its products in Sweden and Finland, and operated wholly owned sales and service branches in all four Nordic countries (Sweden, Norway, Denmark, Finland) in addition to Germany, the Netherlands, Spain, the United Kingdom, France, and Switzerland. In Germany, Nokia Data's largest non-Nordic-countries operation, the company employed a total of 450 in sales and service. Nokia Data also used sales agents, who had previously sold Nokia Information System or Ericsson Data System products, in Finland, Sweden, Belgium, Austria, Italy, Portugal, Hong Kong, and Australia.

---

[2] *Business Marketing,* September 1988.
[3] *Business Week International,* September 12, 1988.

The company assembled most of its products in its own facilities; a minor share of total production was subcontracted to third parties in Nordic countries as well as the Far East. Management saw definite advantages to sourcing internationally and using its own facilities for assembly. Currently, components purchased as far away as the United States and the Far East accounted for 70% of the total cost of production; the rest of the cost was divided equally between labor and plant overhead. Efficient sourcing and materials management were considered critical to overall cost performance. A recent estimate indicated that well-run procurement and manufacturing operations, including rationalized purchasing and investment in modern assembly, could potentially save the company as much as 40% on the production costs of terminals and PCs. One-half of the projected savings would have come from reduced materials cost. Some Nokia Data executives believed that while potential for savings existed, it probably was less than the estimated 40%.

Nokia Data marketed what management called its "horizontal products"— terminals, personal computers, and LAN-based hardware—in all markets. With minor exceptions, these products were based on nonproprietary technologies. "Vertical systems," as management called them, were sales of hardware and software to target segments in banking/insurance, retailing, manufacturing, government, and general business. Nokia Data did not use VARs in a market until management believed the company had a strong local presence. Hence, as of 1988, VARs were only used in Finland and Sweden. Less than 3% of the company's sales were generated through sales agents or VARs.

In Finland, Nokia Data used the Mikko brand for its entire line. In all other markets, Nokia Data used the Alfaskop brand name acquired from Ericsson Data Systems.

Although its products were sold as far away as Hong Kong and Australia, 95% of Nokia Data's sales were concentrated in Europe with Finland, Sweden, and Germany representing 40%, 25%, and 11% of total sales, respectively. (Refer to Exhibits 6, 7, and 8 for a summary of Nokia Data's sales by country, segment, and product.)

Senior managers thought of their company as a sales-driven organization. Although major strategic decisions were made by product groups at headquarters, the regions and country management in larger markets wielded significant influence on short-term policies and sales action. For example, although product design was a headquarters decision, a local sales operation could ask for the development of a special terminal and keyboard for a large order. Local managers in new and "strategic" markets such as Germany, France, and Spain were measured and rewarded based on sales performance. In the more established markets, such as Finland and Sweden, both sales and profitability were considered in performance evaluation.

Competitive Standing

Top management at Nokia Data believed that they enjoyed a number of competitive advantages in their sector of the computer industry. In particular, they

EXHIBIT 6   Nokia Data Sales Summary by Segment ($ Million, 1988)

	Country*									Total	Percent of Total
	SF	*S*	*DK*	*N*	*D*	*NL*	*E*	*UK*	*Others*	*Total*	*of Total*
Retail	34.4	12.1	21.1	2.7	3.0	0	8.3	0	0	81.6	7
Banking/insurance	199.8	144.3	4.5	14.5	23.5	2.7	19.4	0.7	6.0	415.4	35
Manufacturing	75.4	92.3	9.7	11.0	25.0	15.9	13.6	24.5	9.4	276.8	24
Government	88.1	50.4	23.7	6.8	74.5	17.2	7.7	0.6	1.5	270.5	23
General business	106.0	3.3	4.3	4.1	5.3	1.2	1.5	0	0	125.7	11
Total	503.7	302.4	63.3	39.1	131.3	37.0	50.5	25.8	16.9	1,170.0	100
Percent of total	43%	26%	5%	3%	11%	3%	4%	2%	2%	100%	

* Country codes:

SF = Finland   NL = Netherlands
S = Sweden   E = Spain
DK = Denmark   CH = Switzerland
N = Norway
D = Germany   Others = Belgium, Italy, Austria, Portugal, Hong Kong, Australia

SOURCE: Company records.

believed that the large institutional competitors had been slow to respond to the growing customer demand for multivendor connectivity and were consequently up to one year behind Nokia Data in developing the necessary LAN expertise. Companies from the consumer group, on the other hand, were believed to be even further behind in developing networking expertise and, in addition, lacked the industry knowledge of the institutional companies, including Nokia Data. One executive commented that the company's two decades of experience in the banking and retail sectors, combined with its ability to design solutions around hardware from other vendors, were important factors in achieving the 35% and 25% market shares in the Nordic countries' banking and retail segments, respectively.

Nokia Data's other competitive strengths were believed to include the financial backing of a large parent, the Nokia Corporation; the company's small size; and its industry reputation as an ergonomic trendsetter. Because of its smaller size, the company was thought to be more able to keep pace with the evolving industry trends than its larger competitors such as IBM. Furthermore, ergonomics, translated into improved user comfort and productivity, was proving to be a distinct advantage against the smaller manufacturers as well as larger competitors from the institutional group. As an example, Goran Hermansson pointed to the fact that Ericsson, although not a technological forerunner, pioneered the separate keyboard and the tilt-and-swivel screen on personal computers. A more recent innovation was Nokia Data's positive display screen with sharp black characters on a paper-white background designed to reduce eye strain.

Despite these advantages, Yrjänä Ahto, vice president of marketing communication, believed Nokia Data was not sufficiently known outside the Nordic countries, a fact that caused some customers to consider the company "a risky" one to do business with. Furthermore, although top management considered

EXHIBIT 7   Nokia Data Sales Summary by Product and Service Category ($ Million, 1988)

	Country*												
	SF	S	DK	N	D	NL	E	UK	F	CH	Others	Total	Percent of Total
Terminals	56.3	103.6	34.8	10.2	67.0	13.9	24.1	8.6	5.2	10.4	15.5	349.6	29.9
Personal computers	117.2	137.3	14.2	18.8	54.5	18.0	12.1	6.7	9.0	5.3	7.9	401.0	34.3
Peripherals	8.4	10.2	0.2	1.1	0	0.6	4.0	0	0	0	0	24.5	2.1
Minicomputers	56.0	30.2	8.6	7.5	2.1	2.2	5.8	8.6	2.2	0.3	2.9	126.4	10.8
LANs	10.7	13.7	2.9	0.6	3.5	0.9	1.2	0.9	0.2	0	0	34.6	2.9
Service and miscellaneous	226.2	1.5	1.2	0.3	1.2	0.9	2.4	0.2	0	0	0	233.9	20.0
Total	474.8	296.5	61.9	38.5	128.3	36.5	49.6	25.0	16.6	16.0	26.3	1,170.0	100
Percent of total	40.6%	25.4%	5.3%	3.3%	11.0%	3.1%	4.2%	2.1%	1.4%	1.4%	2.2%	100%	

NOTES:
1. The service and miscellaneous figure for Finland includes sales of a large number of turn-key systems projects estimated at around $200 million in total.
2. Peripherals included specialized banking printers, plotters, and personal identification number (PIN) keyboards.
* Country codes:

SF = Finland
S = Sweden
DK = Denmark
N = Norway
D = Germany
NL = Netherlands

E = Spain
UK = United Kingdom
F = France
CH = Switzerland
Others = Belgium, Italy, Austria, Portugal, Hong Kong, Australia

SOURCE: Company records.

EXHIBIT 8   Nokia Data Sales by Products Category, 1988

	Sales ($ Million)	Units	Average Price ($)
Terminals	$349.6	161,106	$ 2,170
Personal computers	401.0	125,312	3,200
Peripherals	24.5	21,993	1,114
Minicomputers	126.4	1,973	64,065
LANs	34.6	245	141,224*

* Includes related terminals, central processing equipment, and connections.

Nokia Data's size to be an asset, some European country managers believed the company was too small, lacking the critical mass and resources necessary to compete with big players like IBM.[4]

Future Strategy

Nokia Data's top management aimed to make their company a leading supplier of terminals, personal computers, LANs, and systems for the European business community. The management wanted to achieve this goal within the next five years and without acquisitions. The targeted turnover for 1993 was set at $2.5 billion, equally distributed between the Nordic countries and the rest of Europe. The targeted revenues represented an annual growth rate of 6% in Nordic countries and 35% outside.

For the next three years, the company planned to concentrate on non-Nordic markets where it operated wholly owned subsidiaries. With the exception of minicomputers, Nokia Data planned to sell its full line in each market. Management believed that its own minicomputer, based on a proprietary operating system, was not competitive in a market that increasingly demanded multivendor connectivity.

Outside the Nordic countries, management also aimed to increase Nokia Data's presence in its five target segments by following the product pathway shown in Exhibit 4, starting with the sale of terminals. Company executives believed that purchases from Nokia Data had to build on a client's existing systems, because customers had already made substantial investments with other companies in hardware, software, and training. Also, because Nokia Data was not well known outside the Nordic countries, management believed that the first step must be to be perceived by the customer as having little, if any, risk. "Consequently," explained Yrjänä Ahto, "terminals were the logical entry point with new clients, as they were far less complex than a LAN or a system and considered less risky. Thereafter, as the company becomes better known and as customers

---

[4] IBM Europe's operations included 15 plants in six countries in addition to nine R&D facilities, seven scientific centers, and sales and service units in all markets. The company claimed a high degree of European content (92%) in its products and integrated manufacturing across the continent.

upgrade terminals to personal computers and LANs, Nokia Data can move up the product line, growing in size and perceived ability to deliver at the upper end.''

Within its five end-user segments, management planned to target the larger organizations within over 500 terminals tied to minicomputers or mainframes but with few personal computers. According to management, sales to large customers were the fastest way to generate volume and to build Nokia Data's image as a reliable supplier of computer products and services, especially when the client was a public organization, such as a local PTT, for example.

Since 1988, the company had undertaken an extensive European advertising campaign in both local and international media to improve its awareness level and consolidate its corporate image. In 1988, $14 million worth of press advertisements promoted the company's products as ''built by Europeans for Europeans.'' Headlined ''For the European Generation,'' the standardized series of color advertisements promoted the company's Alfaskop brand. They appeared in the international edition of such magazines as *The Economist, Time, Newsweek* and *Fortune*. (Refer to Exhibit 9 for sample advertisements.)

Multidomestic Implementation

Nokia Data's senior management believed that a strong local identity and presence in each major European country was crucial to achieving the company's ambitious strategic goals. More specifically, top management aimed to decentralize decision making by adopting what they referred to as a ''multidomestic'' approach. This approach contrasted with Pan-European integration and implied a strong country management voice in local activities.

According to senior managers, a multidomestic implementation of the company's expansion strategy would affect many aspects of its operations. For example, activities such as product development, production, and marketing were to be delegated to the local organizations that had reached a minimum size. Local branding, in particular, was believed essential for a favorable local identity. Management believed that companies which used the same brand in every market did so to their detriment. ''A local image,'' commented Ahto, ''is simply not possible without a local brand—even for companies like IBM which manufacture in almost every European country.'' Similarly, local manufacturing allowed a company to differentiate itself from the competition by reflecting local tastes more closely. As one top executive commented, ''Ultimately, I only care about what the customer wants, even if it's only a red terminal or a blue keyboard.'' (The main elements of the multidomestic approach are highlighted in the appendix and summarized in Exhibit 10 on page 424.)

Nokia Data's multidomestic approach went counter to strategies adopted by others in the industry. In 1988, for example, Apple Computer began to integrate its European operations under the control of a stronger Paris headquarters. According to the company, Apple's national subsidiaries would continue to take care of their own local markets while Paris looked for Pan-European customers and ways to transfer effective strategies regionwide. In the words of an Apple executive, ''When one Apple company comes up with an excellent marketing scheme,

EXHIBIT 9

Sample advertisements for Nokia Data, 1988

Alfaskop 386.
For the European Generation.

You know that 386 in the computer world means the same as a 3.8 litre engine in a 2.0 litre auto world.

You are a European business professional who has outgrown the standard PCs and is looking for the superior processing power and speed that only a 386 work-station can provide.

Alfaskop TT/386 and Alfaskop WS/386 are two new Scandinavian entries in the turbo class. Both of them super-fast PCs and powerful workstations in Local Area Networks.

Alfaskop workstations. Built by Europeans for Europeans.

Knowing the facts today will determine the direction of European development far into the next century.

The ambitious curiosity of the increasingly well-educated young Europeans will change the world.

For the business professional, it is the opportunity to access and process the facts with a speed that can't be overestimated.

NOKIA DATA

Nokia Data is a Scandinavian information technology group specializing in business computers, word-stations and networks for the European business community. With more than 600.000 workstations already installed we rank among the biggest suppliers in Europe.

EXHIBIT 9 *(continued)*

420

EXHIBIT 9 *(continued)*

Alfaskop Thinking.
For the European Generation.

Their thoughts about the future are of vital importance. And they will demand more power and influence than ever in the fulfilment of their ambitions.

You are an important individual.

You need a workstation that makes your job simpler, faster and more fun.

Alfaskop ergonomics.

And you need a workstation that can communicate with the other workstations in your company.

Alfaskop networking.

Alfaskop thinking is that ergonomics and networking is the best way to stimulate your individual creativity and ambitions.

The European solution for the European generation.

You'll be making result-oriented teams where individuality provides the motivation force.

What is happening is that today's personalities are already outpacing yesterday's professionals.

NOKIA DATA

Nokia Data is a Scandinavian information technology group specialising in business computers, workstations and networks for the European business community. With more than 600,000 workstations already installed we rank among the biggest suppliers in Europe.

EXHIBIT 9 *(continued)*

Alfaskop Workstations.
For the European Generation.

They come in all sizes, shapes and ages. Ambitious, creative, demanding.

Released individuality can be an elevating force in any business organization.

Give them workstations perfectly adapted to their taste, needs and demands. And wonderful things will happen.

Don't accept dull conformity! The result of your work depends on your competence, fantasy, creativity, individuality and ambition.

Your workstation is your workmate.

It should make everything easier, faster and more fun.

Alfaskop workstations are built by Europeans for Europeans.

There is one for every system environment and every individual need.

There is one for you.

NOKIA DATA

Nokia Data is a Scandinavian information technology group specializing in business computers, workstations and networks for the European business community. With more than 600.000 workstations already installed we rank among the biggest suppliers in Europe.

EXHIBIT 9 *(concluded)*

423

**EXHIBIT 10   Areas of Primary Management
Responsibility: A Multidomestic
Approach***

	Central	*Local*
R&D		
Basic product design	X	
Applications software		X
Production		
Procurement	Coordination	Purchasing
Manufacturing		X
Marketing		
Advertising:		
General framework	X	
Execution		X
Branding		X
Segmentation		X
Sales force		X
Distribution		X
Pricing (end-user price)		X
Servicing		X

* This chart refers to future division of responsibilities under a
multidomestic approach.
SOURCE: Company records.

Paris headquarters will be responsible for trying to introduce it into other EC countries."[5]

Siemens also had recently restructured its operations to improve competitiveness outside its home market, Germany. Aiming to become a "truly global player," one member of top management was quoted as saying, "In five years, Siemens will be a completely different company. Among Europeans, we will be one of the most aggressive."[6] In recent advertisements (shown in Exhibit 11), the company had billed itself as "the top European computer company in the world market." On another front, IBM was recently capitalizing on the 1992 European integration issue by promoting the concept of integrated operations for a single European market. In a company-sponsored publication called "1992 Now," IBM Europe's president was quoted as saying ". . . in IBM, we manage our European manufacturing activities as if it were 1992."

Nokia Data's outspoken president, Kalle Isokallio, believed that a Pan-European approach was "nonsense," as it assumed homogeneous European markets. He thought that the 1992-related harmonization might bring uniform technical standards, but buyer behavior would still be nationally oriented. To illustrate, Isokallio described a typical German customer as someone "who never buys a

---

[5] *Business Marketing,* September 1988.
[6] *Business Week International,* February 20, 1989.

EXHIBIT 11

Recent ad for Siemens

SIEMENS

prototype and signs nothing but a lengthy and detailed contract.'' In sharp contrast, he pointed to a typical French customer, ''who is willing to try new innovative products and sign a contract on the back of a Gauloise cigarette pack.'' Kalle
Isokallio explained that in a nonhomogeneous EC, characterized by trends toward
decentralized computing and narrow market segments, manufacturers had to get

close to their customers. Therefore, he emphasized, "local density" was the key, with a minimum level of local production, some local development, and strong local brands.

As of early 1989, the company's local presence varied among markets. In Finland and Sweden, for example, management believed they were rightfully a "domestic" company because of local production, local development, and, most important, local brands. "Yet," explained Ahto, "before we can claim to be domestic in non-Nordic countries, we must reach a minimum size. After that, we can start local production and introduce a local brand. But, before we reach that critical mass, we will try to be 'European.'"

Management Discussions

Although Nokia Data management at all levels agreed with the strategic goal of long-term viability through rapid growth, there was less consensus on the specifics of how that might be achieved. For example, concern was expressed at both the headquarters and country organizations about whether the company would be able in the near future to take advantage of the growth in LANs and vertical systems. For one thing, some argued, the company did not enjoy the needed name recognition in most European markets to be considered a credible supplier of highly technical LANs or sophisticated vertical systems. Furthermore, others argued that even where the company had an established reputation, as in most of the Nordic countries, it was for terminals and personal computers rather than the most advanced LANs and systems. "We have too much of an ordinary hardware supplier image," complained Nils Wilborg, head of the Information Department in the Swedish country organization. On a related point, Ingvar Persson, vice president of product planning, explained that while competition centered around hardware in the 1970s and around software in the 1980s, the distinguishing feature in the future would be in services. "Yet," he emphasized, "the market views us as a hardware vendor, not a service provider."

Doubts were also expressed regarding the practicality of and the rationale behind the multidomestic approach. Jürgen Olschewski, the German managing director, believed that Nokia Data's small size in his country was a big obstacle to becoming a full-fledged manufacturing, marketing, and service operation. Nevertheless, he agreed with top management that a strong Germany identity would be an asset in competing against firms such as IBM or Compaq with no local image. A few others wondered, on the other hand, if a multidomestic approach might not fragment the company too much to compete effectively against the larger and more integrated competitors.

Conclusion

Nokia Data's top management knew that some of their colleagues were concerned about the company's future direction. Yet they believed that Nokia Data's fortunes in a maturing industry depended on innovative thinking and quick action close to customers—elements that they thought were inherent in their overall strategy for growth and in their multidomestic approach. Explained Ahto, "Our plans for the future are in line with the corporate culture that we want to establish within Nokia Data—a culture which emphasizes profit performance, business orientation, speedy decision making, and fast action. Doing business under tough conditions has always been fun at Nokia. We want to continue having fun in the future."

APPENDIX
ELEMENTS OF NOKIA DATA'S MULTIDOMESTIC APPROACH

Research and Development

As Nokia Data implemented its multidomestic approach across Europe, management planned to consolidate basic product development such as video display and keyboards in Sweden. Market-specific development, such as language translation and application software, however, would all be performed locally.

Production

The management believed local manufacturing was one of the conditions needed for a local identity. Hence, Nokia Data planned to set up production facilities in each market, once an economically viable minimum sales volume, estimated at around 50,000 personal computers or terminals annually, was achieved. Sourcing of components was to be centralized in Sweden.

Segmentation

As of 1989, Nokia Data's penetration in each of its five primary segments varied considerably across different national markets. As part of *local,* say in local strategies, country management would decide which of the five segments to concentrate on. Local management could also decide to develop a share of its business in segments not considered primary by Stockholm.

Branding

Management believed that the Mikko name in Finland and the Alfaskop name in Norway, Sweden, and Denmark were viewed by those markets as local brands with local image. Outside Scandinavia, management planned to introduce local brands but not until Nokia Data's local brands were perceived to offer Nokia Data a decided advantage especially over nonlocal international brands.

Communication

At the end of 1988, Nokia Data's subsidiaries used the same pictures, advertisements, and brochures, localized only through text translation. In the future, however, each subsidiary would work from a general framework defined in Stockholm, taking responsibility for local execution. Aside from local campaigns designed to promote local brands, Nokia Data headquarters would continue a European-wide English-language corporate advertising campaign in international publications.

Distribution

Currently, decisions regarding the use of VARs or sales agents and the extent of their contribution to local marketing were headquarters decisions. In the future, as sales through such channels increased, local organizations would play a primary role in such decisions.

Pricing

As in the past, future pricing decisions at Nokia Data would be the responsibility of country managers. Aside from pricing in accordance with market conditions, local organizations were to pay Stockholm a transfer price set at their market price, less the local margin of 30–40%. However, no central control on local pricing was foreseen.

Customer Service

In the past, Nokia had maintained more service points than sales offices in a local market, a factor which management believed helped to reassure customers of speedy availability of help when needed. In the future, that policy would not change. But, under local management, the customer services concept was to be broadened to incorporate "Careware," a comprehensive package designed to meet the total needs of most clients.

The Careware concept, formulated in Stockholm for implementation in local organizations, went beyond normal after-sales service and included presales consulting, planning and testing, installation, and technical and educational services. Careware was divided into six groups of "Customer Service Products." The following list represents the content of Careware Services.

Nokia Data's Customer Careware

Operational Services
  Education and Training
  Systems Evaluation
  Network Services
  On-Site Service Representative
  Total Customer Service Responsibility
  System Security Services
  Standby Customer Service
  Safety Tests and Checkups
  Terminal Cleaning

Installation Services
  Project Management and Administration
  Cabling
  Product Installation
  Customizing

Nokia On-Site/Remote Services
Customer Carry-In Services
Nokia Software Services
Nokia Time and Material Service

23 | CIGNA WORLDWIDE

On a gray day in Frankfurt, Germany, in November 1988, Bruce Howson, president of CIGNA Worldwide, Inc. (CWW), convened a strategy meeting of the company's European country directors and key functional managers to discuss how CWW should respond to the European Community's (EC)[1] plan to remove existing internal barriers and restrictions to the free flow of goods and services in 1992.

At this meeting, Howson announced the establishment of a 1992 task force to define the opportunities, threats, and critical issues posed by the 1992 program, and to identify its implications for CWW's European marketing strategy and organization. The task force would report its findings to the Philadelphia home office by December 15, 1988. Exhibit 1 summarizes the CWW organization and lists the 1992 task force members.

Herman Nieuwenhuizen, senior vice president for the Northern European area, was appointed director of the task force. He believed that it should first ask each CWW country manager to assess his or her nation's insurance market and the anticipated impact of the 1992 measures. CWW concentrated on selling commercial property and casualty (P&C) insurance, which represented over 85% of the premiums generated by CWW in Europe in 1987. The task force would use the country managers' appraisals to develop an overall marketing strategy for CWW's European division.

This case was prepared by Jonathan D. Hibbard under the direction of Professor John A Quelch. Copyright © 1989 by the President and Fellows of Harvard College. Harvard Business School case 589-098 (Revised 1992).

[1] The EC comprised 12 member states: Belgium, Denmark, France, Greece, Ireland, Italy, Luxembourg, the Netherlands, Portugal, Spain, the United Kingdom, and West Germany.

EXHIBIT 1

Organization chart

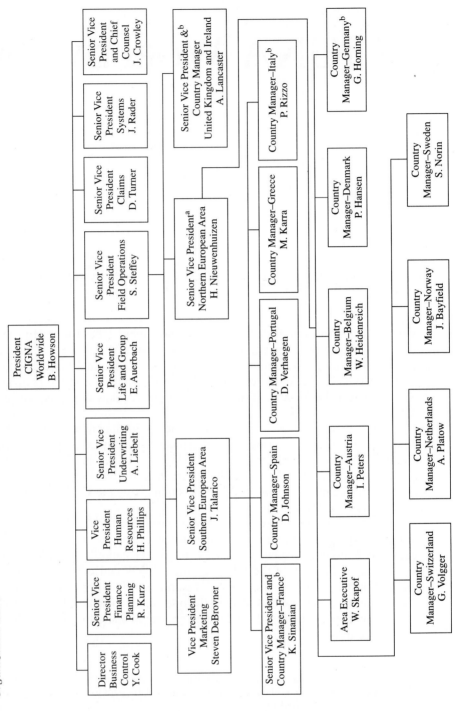

^a Task force chairperson

^b Task force member

The Insurance Market

An insurance policy was a contract that bound the insurer, for a paid premium, to indemnify an insured party against a specified loss. The insurance industry sold three types of insurance: reinsurance, life, and nonlife insurance. Reinsurance and coinsurance were financial agreements between two or more insurance carriers to share the risks of particular policies; premium income was likewise shared. Life insurance covered the financial risks associated with a policyholder's death. Non-life insurance, also known as property and casualty (P&C) insurance, included coverages for individual consumers, known as mass risk insurance (car, home, and liability policies) and coverages for companies, known as large risk insurance (workers' compensation, fire, and business interruption policies).

In 1986 the EC was the second largest insurance market worldwide, account-ing for 22% of total world premiums. Exhibit 2 summarizes selected insurance market and economic data for the countries of the EC, the United States, and Japan.

The major participants in the European insurance industry were insurance carriers, brokers and agents, and customers.

Insurance Carriers

Primary insurance carriers underwrote policies, assuming an insuree's liability in the case of a specified financial loss. Some insurers specialized in one type of insurance, while others handled multiple categories. An insurer gained profits by (1) earning premiums in excess of its losses, (2) earning investment income on the premiums it received, and (3) controlling its operating expenses, which included sales, marketing, commissions, claims adjustments, and backroom operations. While all three elements contributed to a firm's financial performance, most indus-try experts agreed that the overall long-term viability of a company depended on its underwriting success. Since the early 1980s, however, insurance firms had derived the bulk of their profits from investment income. Smart investing of premium income, rather than income sharing with reinsurers, could cushion un-derwriting losses.

The industry applied two performance measures when writing P&C business: the expense ratio and the loss ratio. The expense ratio divided all expenses by net written premiums (NWP).[2] The loss ratio summed all claim losses, claim reserves, and associated administrative costs and divided this sum by net earned premi-ums.[3] The combined ratio (Expense ratio + Loss ratio) represented the total cost of underwriting as a percentage of premiums generated. A combined ratio of less than 100% indicated that underwriting efforts were profitable.

---

[2] NWP equaled the total premiums earned (GWP) minus the portion of GWP reinsured.

[3] Net earned premiums were net written premiums amortized over the policy's life. For exam-ple, a 12-month policy commencing in January 1988 would have a net earned premium equal to 50% of its NWP by July 1988.

EXHIBIT 2 Selected Insurance Information for 1986

	Population (MM)	Insurance per Capita	Total Premiums ($ Billion)*	Premiums as percent of GNP	Nonlife Premiums ($ Billion)	Percent of Nonlife Premiums of Total	Nonlife World Share	Nonlife EC Share	Number of Operating Companies
West Germany	61	$ 978	$ 60	6%	$34.4	57%	7.7%	32.5%	516
United Kingdom	56	807	46	8	18.6	40	4.2	17.6	712
France	55	658	36	5	22.3	62	5.0	21.1	462
Italy	57	253	15	2	11.8	79	2.6	11.2	207
Netherlands	15	788	11	6	6.2	56	1.4	5.9	439
Spain	38	138	5	2	4.3	86	1.0	4.1	520
Belgium and Luxembourg	10	510	5	4	3.7	74	.8	3.5	302
Denmark	5	743	4	5	2.2	55	.5	2.1	235
Ireland	4	616	2	8	.9	45	.2	.9	63
Portugal	10	76	1	3	.7	70	.2	.7	231
Greece	10	46	1	2	.3	30	.07	.3	154
European Community	325	468	186	5					
United States	226	1,746	395	9					
Japan	121	1,399	170	8					

* Premium income was an imperfect indicator of size of a nation's insurance market because, to varying degrees, national governments helped to satisfy insurance requirements through social security benefits. Such benefits were not reported in market estimates of premium income. In addition, many national governments set premium prices, thereby helping to determine the structure of each country's insurance market.
SOURCE: Swiss Reinsurance Company and EC Commission.

Sales and marketing, along with claims adjustments, were the two largest cost factors for an insurance carrier. Sales and marketing were performed through a number of channels, including dedicated agents, independent brokers, and direct marketing to customers. Claims adjustment departments handled customer claims; they had to maintain good client relations while tightly controlling claims costs.

Underwriting and claims processing were both considered backroom operations expenses. Underwriters evaluated the risks customers wished to have covered and often specialized in a particular insurance category and/or specific industry or geographic region. Claims processing was technology intensive and was the one cost area that could benefit from scale economies.

Insurance Brokers and Agents

Insurance brokers and agents were intermediaries between insurance carriers and insurance buyers. They accounted for 80% of the P&C business placed in Europe. Most agents were involved full time in the insurance business and usually represented one carrier's product line.

Unlike agents, brokers were insurance specialists who represented several different carriers. They offered their clients impartial advice in arranging the best insurance terms possible. Brokers often relieved the carriers of such administrative tasks as premium collection and claims handling. Brokers earned commissions of 15–20% of the GWP; agents averaged 10–15% commission. In evaluating insurance companies, brokers scrutinized both claims service and price.

Because they did not have ties to particular carriers, brokers could recommend to their customers that policies be moved to other carriers. Broker power varied by country. In the United Kingdom brokers wrote over 70% of the total P&C business, whereas in France, Italy, and Germany they wrote, respectively, 50%, 45%, and 25%. In most EC countries, the larger brokers did not aggressively seek to switch one another's principal customers.

Industry analysts identified three tiers of brokers. The first tier included international network brokers, such as Marsh & McLennan and Johnson & Higgins. Most European brokerage revenues were concentrated in this top tier. The second tier included large national and regional brokers, while the third tier comprised small local brokers and large insurers with their own exclusive agent networks.

European brokers generated income from three basic sources: commissions, fixed fees, and investment income. Brokers received commissions on policy premiums they wrote for each carrier. They also received an annual profit-sharing commission from these insurers. Brokers sometimes received negotiated fixed fees from larger clients in lieu of commissions from carriers. Investment income was earned when brokers collected policy premiums from clients and earned interest while holding this money for 90 days or more before remitting it to the carrier. Over half of a typical broker's operating expense were salaries and benefits.

Insurance Buyers

Most large companies employed risk managers to place their insurance. When a company shopped for a carrier or broker, a reputation for prompt claims service was especially important. As one risk manager stated, "The capability of an insurer to provide local claims handling service is critical to my carrier decision, especially with multiple sites and multiple languages in my business." Because of the large numbers of brokers and agents, insurance buyers were accustomed to a high level of personal contact.

Once established, the relationship among client, broker, and carrier was fairly stable. The size and complexity of the P&C relationship made it difficult for a client to change carriers. In a typical year, analysts estimated that 10% of the total P&C policies in Europe might change hands. Companies sometimes relied on several carriers for different insurance products but usually kept a particular type of coverage with a single carrier.

Marketing Impact of 1992

Recognizing the economic value of facilitating free flows of people, goods, services, and capital, the governments of the EC member countries agreed to remove their internal trade barriers by December 31, 1992. Many believed that these barriers made European firms less competitive than their US and Japanese counterparts, which benefited from serving much larger domestic markets than those available in any single European nation. The economic integration of the EC, which accounted for 20% of all world trade flows, would create a single market of 325 million consumers, surpassing the United States' 226 million and Japan's 121 million consumers.

The EC believed that, in many industries, market integration would also create economies of scale, leading to lower prices, greater investment, and faster economic growth. Less efficient companies would be driven to increase productivity, merge, or go out of business. However, leaders of some nations outside the EC were disturbed by the prospect of an increasingly protectionist "fortress Europe." The United States and Japan, the largest trading partners of the EC, exported over $110 billion in goods and services to the EC in 1987.

Background to the 1992 Program

The European Community, often called the Common Market, was created in 1957 by the Treaty of Rome as a devastated Europe sought to rebuild its economy after World War II. Initially the EC made progress in eliminating customs duties in trade between member states, but progress slowed because of the economic recession in the mid-1970s.

Following this slow-growth period, the prime ministers of the EC countries pledged to complete the common market at an EC meeting in 1982. A White Paper, published in June 1985, delineated a plan for achieving a single market.

This plan was approved by the member nations and ratified in the Single European Act of 1986, which amended the original Treaty of Rome.

The Single European Act became effective on July 1, 1987. After the date, member states began considering regulations developed at the EC headquarters to remove the physical, technical, and fiscal barriers to a unified market. Exhibit 3 lists the barriers and proposed legislation. Quicker agreement was now expected because majority voting of member nations had replaced a previous requirement for unanimity. Many EC experts, however, believed that there still remained major obstacles to realizing the 1992 program; these hurdles included difficulties in harmonizing technical standards, regulations, and the value-added tax (VAT) rate.

By November 1988, one-third of the 285 legislative reforms detailed in the 1985 White Paper had been adopted by the EC, and over 100 others had been sent to the Council of Ministers for approval. About 90% of the measures were expected to be ready for adoption by the end of 1988. Directives already adopted included common toy safety regulations, a single document for border crossings, abolition of customs formalities, mutual recognition of higher education diplomas, and permission to sell P&C insurance across borders.

EXHIBIT 3   Selected Trade Barriers, Proposals, and Intended Results of the EC 1992 Program

Barriers	*Proposal*	*Intended Result*
Physical	Eliminate:	• Reduce salary costs, administration, and wasted time
• Restrictions on free movement of labor and goods	• Customs posts	
	• Frontier control	• Increase industry efficiency through lower transportation costs and free movement of labor
	• Immigration checkpoints	
Technical	• Mutual recognition: any product legally salable in one member country could be sold throughout the EC	• Reduce costly modifications
• Preventing goods and services legally manufactured and sold in one member state from competing in another state, due to disparate national technical standards on product, health, and environmental regulations		• Increase length of production runs
		• Decrease manufacturing costs
		• Reduce prices
Fiscal	• Two-rate value-added tax system for EC (politically impossible to agree on one rate for all goods)	• Reduce price variations across markets
• Restrictions on capital movements		
• Disparities in value-added tax levels and excise duties		

Effects of the 1992 Program on the European Insurance Market

Although the Treaty of Rome called for the progressive elimination of national regulations that impeded cross-border trade in insurance services, such barriers only fell in the reinsurance market. Lack of progress prompted the nonlife establishment directive of 1973, which provided *freedom of establishment* rights and thus allowed insurance companies based in any single EC country to set up agencies or branches in other EC states. It also set common EC standards for granting operating licenses and calculating minimum solvency margins required for insurers.[4] A UK insurer, for example, was thus entitled to establish a Paris branch, provided that its operations complied with local French insurance regulations.

Freedom of services, however, had not been realized. Freedom of services permitted an insurance company to market a full range of products throughout the EC even if only located in one EC member country. Hence, a UK insurer could directly service a French client without the need for an authorized French branch or agency. Many EC countries including France and Germany did not permit freedom of services. This prompted the EC to issue the second nonlife insurance directive of 1988, allowing insurance firms to market P&C policies freely to large risk customers beginning January 1, 1990. Qualifying customers had to meet two of the following three criteria: 500 or more employees, $29 million minimum in annual revenues, or $14 million minimum in assets. Industry experts estimated that this directive would apply to 70% of the commercial and industrial insurance written in the United Kingdom and 50% of that written in Germany, France, and Italy.

Most analysts predicted that the scope of freedom of services would not be broadened to cover other types of insurable risks, such as life insurance, until the mid-1990s.

In 1992, freedom of services would also apply to independent brokers. Any intermediary based in one EC country would be able to sell policies to clients throughout the EC without having to hold a license in other EC nations.

Opportunities in the European Insurance Method

The gradual breakdown of barriers to selling insurance across national boundaries was expected to intensify the marketing of P&C insurance. In addition, cross-border trade, stimulated by the removal of trade barriers, was expected to increase dramatically and expand demand for insurance services. New insurance product lines would be needed as a result. As one marketing director noted, ''Client companies will want consolidated insurance packages for their subsidiaries throughout Europe.''

---

[4] Solvency margins helped ensure that an insurance company could meet its future obligations toward the insured; these requirements varied by country. Under the 1973 directive, the solvency margin could be maintained only at the head office; branches and agencies needed only to possess sufficient assets to cover liabilities arising out of their own activities.

Many analysts predicted that the second nonlife directive would intensify competition, encourage insurance buyers to shop around, and lead to both lower overheads for insurers and lower premiums for policyholders. One industry executive explained, ''Companies must become more efficient and cost effective; premium margins will become razor-thin in some nations, with only the strong surviving.'' High service expectations by customers, however, could restrict the ability of insurance companies to write commercial insurance policies across borders. Only international insurance companies having their own operations within a country, or being closely associated with local brokers, could provide the necessary service on policies providing international coverage.

The sizes of the nonlife insurance markets in EC member countries are presented in Exhibit 2 (refer to page 432). Premium growth potential was considered greatest in Italy, Spain, and Portugal, where per capita premium levels were very low. Exhibit 4 summarizes the growth rates of nonlife insurance within the EC. Exhibit 5 highlights the variation in insurance prices found between countries.

EXHIBIT 4   EC Insurance Premium Growth Rates
Growth in Premium Income*

	Total Business		Nonlife Insurance	
	1985–1986	*1984–1985*	*1985–1986*	*1984–1985*
West Germany	6.4%	4.2%	4.0%	4.2%
United Kingdom	19.4	6.3	20.6	7.4
France	11.0	6.1	3.3	−0.6
Italy	11.2	7.8	7.6	5.4
Netherlands	8.7	3.3	11.2	0.2
Spain	22.0	4.7	14.0	3.3
Belgium	10.1	1.3	10.3	1.2
Luxembourg	10.6	7.4	10.6	6.8
Denmark	−2.7	21.8	7.6	6.2
Ireland	4.9	−6.9	17.3	10.3
Portugal	12.1	1.8	12.5	0.1
Greece	n.a.†	n.a.	n.a.	n.a.

* Growth has been adjusted for inflation.
† n.a. = Not available.

Forecast of Nonlife Premium Income Growth (Index 1987 = 100)

	1987	*1988*	*1989*	*1990*	*1991*	*1992*
West Germany	100	104	109	113	118	124
United Kingdom	100	110	118	126	134	142
France	100	105	112	118	125	133
Italy	100	110	118	127	137	148

SOURCE: Swiss Reinsurance Company.

EXHIBIT 5   **Insurance Price Comparisons**
Percentage Differences in Prices of Standard Insurance Products
Compared with the Average of the Four Lowest National Prices in 1986

	Home*	Motor†	Commercial Fire, Theft‡	Public Liability§
West Germany	+3	+15	+43	+47
United Kingdom	+90	−17	+27	−7
France	+39	+9	+153	+117
Italy	+81	+148	+245	+77
Netherlands	+17	−7	−1	−16
Spain	−4	+100	+24	+60
Belgium	−16	+30	−9	+13

* Home insurance—Annual cost of fire and theft coverage for a house valued at 70,000 ECU. Contents were valued at 28,000 ECU.
† Motor insurance—Annual cost of comprehensive insurance for a 1.6-liter car. Driver had 10 years experience.
‡ Commercial fire and theft—Annual coverage for premises valued at 387,000 ECU and stock valued at 232,000 ECU.
§ Public liability—Annual premium for engineering company with 20 employees and an annual turnover of 1.29 million ECU.
SOURCE: EC Commission Study.

Because of their open and competitively priced markets, insurers in the United Kingdom and the Netherlands were expected to be better prepared for the 1992 plan. However, in 1988, insurers in these two nations received only 10% of their insurance business from the rest of the EC. Insurers in the tightly regulated markets of West Germany and Italy, together with France, a country burdened with high premium taxes, were thought likely to lose business in the face of more open competition.

Increasing industry regulation at the state level during the 1960s and 1970s had made it more difficult for non-EC insurance companies to operate throughout Europe; consequently, the number of non-EC insurance firms had declined. In addition, many analysts believed that EC subsidiaries of foreign insurers were currently at a competitive disadvantage because they were obliged to meet the solvency margin requirements of each country with local assets rather than corporate assets. Many insurance companies, however, were now expected to enhance their European operations to take advantage of the more open EC insurance market.

A swiss insurance executive offered the following options for US insurers: "US carriers can either make an outright acquisition, or they can set up a strategic alliance with an EC-based insurance company. Acquisitions are more difficult and expensive to carry out than they were in past years because Europeans are snapping up most available takeover targets. A strategic alliance will enable a US company to obtain help from its EC partner in adjusting its products to ensure that they meet local needs."

Many analysts believed several large insurance companies would dominate the newly integrated EC market. One industry CEO stated, "After 1992 all

European insurance companies will feel additional pressure with respect to premiums and commissions. As a result, economies of scale will become decisive. Mergers and acquisitions will therefore increase." The CEO of a British insurer noted, "In 10 years, we will see a concentration of 10–15 large European insurers. The rest will be niche players." According to one European insurance association, EC insurers were involved in 121 mergers and acquisitions between June 1984 and September 1988.

Brokers, like insurers, had to consider the impacts of the 1992 program on their businesses. "The opportunities in the large risk market must first be exploited by brokers," commented an executive of the EC's Insurance Directorate. "If national habits are going to be broken down, brokers will do the job." A Belgian broker stated, "To take advantage of 1992 opportunities, brokers will need to be more informed about conditions, prices, and regulations in other member states, so they can better advise their clients. To properly serve multinational accounts, brokers will need to import favorable foreign rates and conditions and export home advantages to foreign clients." Another broker noted, "Our clients will look for Japanese-style, zero-defect service. Price will not be the driving issue; it will be taken for granted. The business will go to the broker who gets the right price, issues documentation instantly, and, above all, obtains timely payment of claims."

Company Background

CIGNA, Inc., the parent company of CWW, was one of the largest publicly owned financial services companies in the world. Its subsidiaries were leading providers of insurance, health care, employee benefits, and financial services to businesses and individuals worldwide. CIGNA was formed in March 1982, by the merger of Connecticut General Life Insurance Company and INA Corp. Innovation and new products were the hallmark of both predecessor companies. Connecticut General was a pioneer in group life insurance and offered the first major group medical coverage. INA sold the first automobile fire and theft policy and developed the first homeowner's package insurance policy.

CIGNA's International Operations

Connecticut General entered the international market through its acquisition of Aetna Insurance Company in 1962. Aetna was a member of the American Foreign Insurance Association (AFIA), a consortium of insurance carriers based in the United States and doing business overseas. CIGNA acquired AFIA in 1984 for $215 million and merged it into its own international business to form CWW, one of the largest international insurance operations headquartered in the United States.

Before the acquisition, AFIA and CIGNA both maintained area offices in Belgium and had established operations throughout most of the EC. After acquiring AFIA, CIGNA consolidated the two insurance portfolios and personnel into

EXHIBIT 6   Selected Information on CIGNA/AFIA Merger

	1983 Headcount			1983 Net Written Premiums ($ Millions)			1988 CIGNA Europe	
								Net Written Premiums
	CIGNA	AFIA	Combined	CIGNA	AFIA	Combined	Headcount	($ Millions)
West Germany	57	81	138	$ 8.9	$ 19.1	$ 28.0	113	$ 48.1
United Kingdom	355	363	718	129.7	96.4	226.1	575	267.0
France	105	339	444	35.0	54.8	89.8	360	123.7
Italy	81	248	329	9.1	26.4	35.5	254	53.2
Netherlands	68	59	127	17.8	27.8	45.6	81	49.7
Spain	34	104	138	1.7	5.8	7.5	89	22.3
Belgium and Luxembourg	93	86	179	4.6	9.7	14.3	80	25.7
Denmark	17	16	33	1.4	3.6	5.0	13	6.8
Ireland	9	34	43	5.9	11.0	16.9	42	16.5
Portugal	0	0	0	0.0	0.0	0.0	5	0.1
Greece	1	42	43	0.2	4.0	4.2	23	3.3
Total	820	1,372	2,192	$214.3	$258.6	$472.9	1,632	$616.4

EXHIBIT 7   CIGNA Europe: Selected Financial Information*

	West Germany		United Kingdom		France		Italy		Netherlands	
	1987	1985	1987	1985	1987	1985	1987	1985	1987	1985
Premiums Written										
Gross written premiums	81.1	88.8	454.6	582.1	166.5	160.6	72.5	89.2	65.1	102.9
Net written premiums	47.1	32.9	267.0	227.6	123.7	106.5	52.2	60.2	48.7	58.4
Earned premiums (EP)	48.7	32.5	270.2	234.4	125.4	109.7	53.4	60.3	56.0	55.6
Losses incurred	31.1	12.1	217.3	177.2	74.5	84.0	26.2	50.2	57.5	49.8
Commissions (Comm)†	8.5	2.4	48.3	30.7	22.5	13.9	9.7	11.6	10.5	7.3
Taxes	0.8	1.7	0.9	2.5	2.4	5.5	2.7	3.4	0.4	0.5
Local overhead	5.9	6.5	24.3	32.8	17.9	18.7	7.1	10.9	4.4	6.9
Underwriting results	2.4	9.8	(20.6)	(8.8)	8.1	(12.4)	7.7	(15.8)	(16.8)	(8.9)
Investment income (IIN)	5.8	3.5	29.8	24.6	14.7	11.2	13.9	6.3	1.4	6.1
Operating profit	8.2	13.3	9.2	15.8	22.8	(1.2)	21.6	(9.5)	(15.4)	(2.8)
Share of EC profit (%)	15.3%	172.7%	17.2%	205.2%	42.6%	−15.6%	40.4%	−123.4%	−28.8%	−36.4%
Loss ratio (losses/EP)	63.9	37.2	80.4	75.6	59.4	76.6	49.1	83.3	102.7	89.6
Commission ratio (Comm/NWP)	18.0	7.3	18.1	13.5	18.2	13.1	18.6	19.3	21.6	12.5
Expenses + taxes ratio (Expenses + taxes/NWP)	14.2	24.9	9.4	15.5	16.4	22.7	18.8	23.8	9.9	12.7
Combined ratio	96.1	69.4	107.9	104.6	94.0	112.3	86.4	126.3	134.1	114.7
Retention rate (NWP/GWP)	58.1	37.0	58.7	39.1	74.3	66.3	72.0	67.5	74.8	56.8
Expense ratio (Expenses + taxes Comm/NWP)	32.2	32.2	27.5	29.0	34.6	35.8	37.4	43.0	31.4	25.2
Investment ratio (IIN/NWP)	12.3	10.6	11.2	10.8	11.9	10.5	26.6	10.5	2.9	10.4

* CIGNA Europe's recent financial growth was partially due to devaluation of the U.S. dollar and CWW's retention of a higher percentage of its own policies.

† Commissions included fees paid to brokers and agents, as well as commissions received from other insurance companies as part of reinsurance agreements.

one office in Brussels. The acquisition increased the percentage of CIGNA revenues derived from multinational corporations from 6% in 1984 to 12% in 1987. Exhibit 6 summarizes information from the CIGNA/AFIA merger.

CIGNA Insurance company of Europe (CIGNA Europe) was a CIGNA, Inc., subsidiary and part of the CWW organization. In 1987 CWW's sales comprised 10% of CIGNA, Inc.'s total revenues (13% of CIGNA, Inc.'s total revenue and 7% of its operating income was foreign based). CIGNA Europe's revenues, in turn, represented 54% of CWW's total revenue in 1987. Within the EC, the United Kingdom and France accounted for 64% of CIGNA Europe's net premiums. Recent financial results and information for CIGNA Europe and CWW are summarized in Exhibit 7 and Exhibit 8, respectively. Product mix information for CIGNA Europe is summarized in Exhibit 9 on page 443.

Hoping to keep more of its business in-house, CWW was reinsuring fewer policies with other carriers than previously. This increased CIGNA's risk exposure but also enlarged its upside profit potential. As a result, CWW's net premiums were growing faster than gross premiums.

Over 75% of the CWW premiums in each nation were derived from business closely associated with the country in which they were written. The broker and agent system accounted for 95% of CIGNA Europe's premiums, compared to an

Spain		Belgium/Luxembourg		Denmark		Ireland		Portugal		Greece		Total	
1987	*1985*	*1987*	*1985*	*1987*	*1985*	*1987*	*1985*	*1987*	*1985*	*1987*	*1985*	*1987*	*1985*
33.5	35.5	37.0	53.8	8.8	10.2	20.3	20.8	0.2	0.0	7.7	3.0	947.3	1,146.9
21.3	19.7	25.7	28.0	6.2	3.5	15.5	8.6	0.1	0.0	3.3	1.5	610.8	546.9
18.9	19.9	25.8	26.2	6.3	3.0	13.6	7.8	0.1	0.0	3.0	0.7	621.4	550.1
14.2	25.3	17.2	19.5	2.7	2.1	9.9	5.1	0.0	0.0	1.4	0.9	452.0	426.2
3.4	3.1	4.5	3.7	1.3	0.1	2.2	0.3	0.0	0.0	0.9	0.5	112.0	73.0
0.8	0.7	0.8	0.9	0.0	0.0	0.1	0.1	0.0	0.0	0.1	0.1	9.0	15.4
2.9	3.1	3.1	4.1	1.4	1.0	1.6	1.7	0.4	0.1	0.4	0.2	69.2	86.0
(2.4)	(12.3)	0.2	(2.0)	0.9	(0.2)	(0.2)	1.2	(0.3)	(0.1)	0.2	(1.0)	(20.8)	(50.5)
2.3	2.1	2.9	2.9	0.4	0.4	2.7	0.9	0.0	0.0	0.4	0.2	74.3	58.1
(0.1)	(10.2)	3.1	0.9	1.3	0.2	2.5	2.1	(0.3)	(0.1)	0.6	(0.8)	53.5	7.7
−0.2%	−132.5%	5.8%	11.7%	2.4%	2.6%	4.7%	27.3%	−0.6%	−1.3%	1.1%	−10.4%	100.0%	100.0%
75.1	127.1	66.7	74.4	42.9	70.0	72.8	65.4	0.0	0.0	46.7	128.6	72.7	77.5
16.0	15.7	17.5	13.2	21.0	2.9	14.2	3.5	0.0	0.0	27.3	33.3	18.3	13.3
17.4	19.3	15.2	17.9	22.6	28.6	11.0	20.9	400.0	0.0	15.2	20.0	12.8	18.5
108.5	162.2	99.4	105.5	86.4	101.4	98.0	82.8	400.0	0.0	89.1	181.9	103.9	109.4
63.6	55.5	69.5	52.0	70.5	34.3	76.4	41.3	50.0	0.0	42.9	50.0	64.5	47.7
33.3	35.0	32.7	31.1	43.5	31.4	25.2	17.4	400.0	0.0	45.4	53.3	31.1	31.9
10.8	10.7	11.3	10.4	6.5	11.4	17.4	10.5	0.0	0.0	12.1	13.3	12.2	10.6

**EXHIBIT 8   Selected Financial Information for CWW Consolidated Results for
Years Ended December 31, 1985–87 ($ 000)**

	1985	1986	1987
Property and Casualty			
Gross written premiums	$1,730,871	$1,623,586	$1,603,734
Net written premiums	948,896	1,052,194	1,081,604
Net earned premiums	955,657	1,022,543	1,110,307
Losses and expenses	1,061,820	1,088,183	1,164,799
Underwriting results	(106,163)	(65,640)	(54,492)
Investment and other income	99,395	101,298	106,900
Life			
Premiums	143,067	213,772	311,937
Earned premiums	139,289	209,435	300,268
Investment and other income	69,414	129,799	183,035
Benefits and expenses	202,636	328,646	473,869
Operating income	6,057	10,588	9,434
Combined operating income (loss) before noninsurance expenses and income taxes	(701)	46,246	61,800
Property and Casualty Statutory Ratios			
Loss	71.7%	66.6%	65.5%
Expense	39.4	39.8	39.4
Combined	111.1	106.4	104.9

80% average for other European carriers. CWW worked almost exclusively with
the largest brokers, writing policies for multinationals and large risk companies.
The top 10 brokerage firms in Europe wrote 80% of CIGNA Europe's policies.

Corporate customers could be segmented according to size. A major multinational would typically generate over $5 million in annual P&C insurance premiums. Large-, medium-, and small-sized companies would generate $1 million,
$500,000, and $100,000, respectively.

CIGNA Europe competed with the major European insurers, several of which
were expanding their presence in the US market. In 1987 the largest European
insurers were Allianz (Germany), with $10.1 billion in net written premiums;
Generali (Italy), $6.3; Zurich (Switzerland), $6.2; Royal (United Kingdom), $5.8;
and Prudential Corp. (United Kingdom), $5.6. Allianz had the largest dedicated
agent sales force in the European insurance industry and was acquiring and/or
building strategic alliances with insurance companies throughout Europe. Analysts expected that these factors would give the firm a distinct competitive edge
within a barrier-free EC market.

Among CWW's principal competitors in Europe was the New York-based
American International Group (AIG). In 1988, AIG announced that it would
merge most of its European operations into a single company based in Paris,
replacing 13 different national companies that had used six separate computer

EXHIBIT 9   **Selected Information for Product Mix, Product Growth, and Staffing in 1985 and 1988 for CIGNA Europe**

	Property	Casualty	Marine	Health and Accident
1985 Product Mix*				
West Germany	48.3%	15.7%	24.6%	11.4%
United Kingdom	24.2	12.6	45.9	17.2
France	53.4	21.2	7.1	18.4
Italy	38.3	15.9	14.8	31.0
Netherlands	61.3	11.5	23.6	4.0
Spain	44.8	26.7	13.7	15.0
Belgium/				
Luxembourg	58.7	15.9	17.2	8.2
Denmark	53.3	11.1	15.4	20.2
Ireland	47.1	31.2	1.0	20.8
Portugal	0.0	0.0	0.0	0.0
Greece	43.7	32.5	22.0	1.8
Total	37.3%	15.1%	30.5%	17.1%
1988 Product Mix*				
West Germany	64.6%	7.7%	12.5%	18.0%
United Kingdom	50.7	4.1	31.4	13.8
France	59.0	15.1	5.4	20.5
Italy	46.8	15.8	13.1	24.3
Netherlands	49.3	8.1	36.5	6.2
Spain	56.6	8.5	13.1	21.8
Belgium/				
Luxembourg	65.0	14.5	10.6	9.9
Denmark	42.1	3.5	3.5	50.9
Ireland	54.9	23.2	0.4	21.5
Portugal	96.0	0.8	1.1	2.1
Greece	62.4	22.1	15.0	0.5
Total	54.1%	10.3%	18.6%	16.8%

* Product mix represents each line of business as a percentage of net written premiums.

centers, with no central cash control and no corporate identity.[5] AIG had recently announced plans to invest $200 million in its European operations by 1992. AIG had a stronger reputation than CIGNA as a product innovator, particularly in P&C insurance.

Most CWW employees were nationals of the country in which they worked, and were therefore well versed in the local languages and customs, familiar with local laws governing contracts, and attuned to the needs of the local insurance

---

[5] "Who's That Knocking on Foreign Doors? U.S. Insurance Salesmen," *Business Week,* March 6, 1989, pp. 84–85.

community. CWW supported its salespeople with direct marketing (13 million pieces mailed in 1987 versus 9 million in 1985) to generate leads.

CWW's international marketing programs were sometimes tailored to meet local insurance needs. With strong support from the home office in Philadelphia, CWW tried to delegate as much authority as possible at the point of sale by giving country managers the final say in writing a policy. Most country offices were self-sufficient with their own underwriters, clerical staff, and data processing operations. However, local underwriters often contacted the home office for assistance when writing complex commercial and industrial policies.

CWW's 1992 Challenge

CWW executives believed their company was already well placed to meet the 1992 challenge. As Steve DeBrovner, senior vice president of marketing, pointed out, "We're much better positioned than are companies that are not yet even in the EC. Because of our experience with the 1984 CIGNA/AFIA merger, we know how long it takes for a company to become fully operational after an acquisition. The merging of two insurance sales networks can create many more problems than solutions. How to reconcile computer systems, design new policies, and deal with overlapping sales agents are among the problems that arise. Many competent people will be 'on the street' after some of these mergers, and we hope to add some of these quality producers to our staff."

According to analysts, other major US insurers were poorly positioned to take advantage of the 1992 plan. In the past many of them had participated in international insurance through the AFIA insurance pool, which had been acquired by CIGNA. Bruce Howson, president of CWW noted, "Most US insurers without international penetration will have difficulty if they begin now to try to take advantage of developments in the EC. It would mean the investment of millions of dollars and a 10-year process to deal with licensing requirements."

Many CWW executives believed the company's main strength was the large volume of business CWW transacted throughout Europe and the fact that it had fully staffed offices in every EC nation. Other strengths included CWW's capacity to write large risks, good name recognition, and a strong reputation for claims service among company risk managers. One country manager stated, "We know that our local service and our tailored products are of utmost importance to our present customers." CWW spread the word about its large capacity through an advertising campaign built around the message "Size has its advantages." Exhibit 10 shows a recent advertisement that CIGNA Europe ran in selected print media.

CWW had excellent relationships with major US insurance brokers. As a result, CIGNA Europe could rely upon its US-based brokers to provide high-quality insurance packages for its customers needing insurance coverage within the EC. CWW was also expert in writing large policies (especially for P&C coverage) designed for the international market. A CWW country manager pointed out, "We are the only US carrier with an established European flagship, backed by the resources of a large parent company." According to many analysts, European

EXHIBIT 10

CIGNA Europe—recent print advertisement

SIZE DOES HAVE ITS ADVANTAGES.

When you're navigating the unsure waters of today's insurance market, you need stability.

You need a provider backed by the resources of a worldwide company. One with experience to match. As Insurance Company of North America and former AFIA-member companies, we accumulated nearly a century of experience in the property and casualty market in Europe. Now that we've become *CIGNA Insurance Company of Europe S.A.-N.V.*, we also have all the resources you're likely to need. Of course, we've always had an extensive range of services.

Our Marine and Aviation Divisions lead the industry with innovative products and a unique underwriting capability.

At CIGNA, we can meet the needs of all kinds of businesses by offering specialized property and marine coverages as well as comprehensive commercial casualty products. We specialize in developing worldwide insurance programs.

Clearly, we're not just bigger. We're better. And you can learn how much better we are by writing to CIGNA Insurance Company of Europe, S.A.-N.V., CIGNA House, 8 Lime St., London EC3M 7NA, England or to the CIGNA office in your country (listed below).

An insurer with the ability *and* stability you're looking for. It's one more example of CIGNA's commitment to personalized service to business.

Vienna, Austria • Brussels, Belgium • Copenhagen, Denmark • Paris, France • Frankfurt, Federal Republic of Germany • Athens, Greece • Dublin, Ireland • Rome, Italy Rotterdam, The Netherlands • Oslo, Norway • Lisbon, Portugal • Madrid, Spain • Stockholm, Sweden • Zurich, Switzerland • Istanbul, Turkey • London, United Kingdom

markets were nationalistic, and US insurance firms had a reputation for entering and exiting markets at "the drop of a hat" because of the cyclical nature of the business. CWW did not have this reputation, at least in its P&C business. Most brokers and risk managers considered CWW to be a "national" company in each country in which it operated.

CWW executives believed the company's strengths outweighed its weaknesses. However, they knew improvements were needed in order for CWW to remain competitive. CIGNA's different computer systems in EC countries were not compatible, and, of course, outputs were in different national languages. CWW country managers operated as independent businesspeople and shared little information about product revenues, expenses, successes, and failures; any communication among them was purely informal. One country manager commented, "The ability to exchange product, research and development, and financial information will become critical as 1992 approaches. We need a marketing information system that will allow us to do that. Also, we don't have enough intelligence on our leading competitors."

P&C insurance comprised a proportionately greater share of CIGNA Europe's total business (60%) compared to CIGNA, Inc. (40%). CWW executives estimated that 50% of its P&C business would be opened to new competitors by the 1988 nonlife directive. P&C policies were relatively easy for competition to pursue because of the large volume written and rewritten each year. Some CIGNA Europe managers felt that CWW was perhaps too focused on large accounts, while many of its competitors had systems in place to service medium-sized P&C accounts. CWW's EC managers also maintained that the CWW management team was conservative and slow to implement change. One of the managers noted, "CWW's organizational reporting structure is not flexible enough to allow for the quick decisions needed to take advantage of country-level opportunities."

Although CWW was already highly regarded by other European insurers, CWW wanted to develop a corporate identity with brokers, agents, and clients in Europe as strong as that which it enjoyed in the United States. In a recent survey focusing on CIGNA's US image, 63% of risk managers and 79% of brokers indicated that CIGNA provided "high-quality service." CWW also wanted to emulate the cost structure of its parent, CIGNA, Inc., because the expense side of the financial statement was critical to increasing CWW's competitiveness in Europe. As Howson stated, "Currently we have too many cooks and clerks supporting our salespeople."

Commenting on the fact that only 200 out of 1,700 CWW employees were underwriters, Howson noted, "CIGNA Europe's expense ratio is running at 40%, but our European competitors have 35% expense ratios. Some German and French insurance firms are even showing expense ratios of 27%–30%. If we can't remedy this five-point (or more) cost differential, we'll be at a disadvantage as insurance product prices fall in 1990. However, we need to decide what our goals are before we start cutting heads to lower expenses. Our 66% loss ratio for CWW is a great loss ratio and we can't expect to improve on it by much, but we need to focus on other key performance ratios." Table A summarizes key performance ratios for CIGNA Europe:

TABLE A   CIGNA Europe Performance Ratios

	1988	Objective for January 1, 1993
Underwriting ratio*	14.0%	9.0%
Commission ratio†	18.0	19.0
Area office expense ratio‡	3.2	2.0
Home office expense ratio§	5.0	2.5
Total expense ratio	40.2%	32.5%

* Underwriting expenses as a percent of sales.
† Commissions paid as a percent of sales.
‡ Allocated EC area office expenses as a percent of sales.
§ Allocated US home office expenses as a percent of sales.

Howson continued, "It is up to the country managers to grow the business and bring these ratios into line. Our responsibility as European managers is to get on with our 1992 changes now and not wait until 1992, or even until 1990. We can't wait for directives from the home office on these issues."

CWW executives understood the need for coordinated effort in Europe. However, they also realized there were vast differences among the insurance markets of the EC countries. As one CWW European country manager stated, "Some companies will make the mistake of looking at the EC as a whole, offering 'Euro-insurance' products when there are still tremendous differences among nations. If these disparities are not recognized through niche product offerings, these companies might fail to satisfy any of the 325 million consumers in the EC. The key is to continue to think globally but to act in a manner that addresses local needs."

The Task Force Meeting

Nieuwenhuizen opened the task force meeting by outlining some key questions for his country managers: "How should CWW react to the changes occurring in its environment? What changes in market structure and competition are likely? What will happen to distribution channels? What countries will be most affected by the transformation? What are CWW's marketing options, and how can CWW exploit its strengths to better position itself for 1992?"

After six hours of discussion, the task force emerged with an outline of the critical issues, opportunities, and threats that the 1992 integration program posed for CIGNA Europe. The country managers felt the important issues for CWW in Europe were its sales effectiveness (marketing, distribution, and product mix) and cost effectiveness (cost containment, economies of scale, and technology).

At least four strategic options, not necessarily mutually exclusive, had been discussed at the meeting.

1. *Focus on large multinational accounts*: CWW could take advantage of its size, global reach, and industry expertise to develop and sell complex, customized products to this relatively narrow target market. Although the value of each policy would be high and servicing costs as a percent of net written premiums would be low, profit margins would be under pressure. Most multinationals were price sensitive, and many insurance carriers were competing for their business.

2. *Focus on profitable insurance products*: Most CWW revenues in Europe came from sales to national rather than multinational companies. Some CWW executives argued that the national subsidiaries should focus more tightly on profitable lines of business rather than trying to be all things to all people in order to grow their national revenues to cover overhead. In addition, to control the expense ratio, they argued for focusing on writing larger policies for larger companies which could also serve as useful references when Cigna pitched other prospects. However, the "opening" of the large-risk market to competition and government subsidies to state-owned insurance companies both meant that prices and profit margins would remain low.

3. *Focus on second-tier companies*: While most insurance carriers pursued the largest accounts, few specialized products had been developed for medium-sized businesses, which were often underinsured. Price sensitivity and service needs were lower, although claims processing costs as a percentage of net written premiums might be higher than for the larger companies. Some CWW executives thought they could leverage industry-specific insurance products throughout their European network; for example, a property and casualty insurance policy developed for wineries in France could also be offered in Spain and Italy. In addition, in some cases, CWW could efficiently target multiple companies through their common industry or trade associations. Banks were increasingly targeting medium-sized companies with insurance products, but they focused on personal insurance products more than property and casualty policies.

4. *Explore direct marketing*: Though attempting to bypass brokers risked retaliation, direct marketing was becoming increasingly important in the selling of personal insurance products. One reason was that the insurer's financial exposure was more predictable for personal insurance products (with the benefit of actuarial tables) than for property and casualty policies. Because servicing costs as a percentage of net premiums written were higher for personal insurance products, the direct marketer's profitability depended on achieving a high volume of sales over which these servicing costs could be spread.

Many managers thought product research and development could play a vital role in driving CIGNA Europe's future market share and revenue. One manager stated, "We need to develop new products to meet this fast-changing market. We need to look at what is changing technologically within various industries and then target products and services to meet the needs of a specific segment. In this way we can build our business."

The challenges posed by the 1992 program stemmed from the probability of intense price competition and the possibility of delay in reducing the expense ratio handicap. Another threat was voiced by one country manager as follows: "If the EC changes the definition of 'capital' in a future insurance directive, CWW might have to maintain dramatically increased monetary reserves in each country. Such a situation would put a real kink into our 1992 plans.''

As they left the task force meeting, CWW executives could not be sure how broad the EC's future insurance directives would be or how these directives would influence the way CWW did business. One executive commented, ''The firms that will do well in the EC will be those with enough patience and capital to stay in for the long haul.'' The managers were certain, however, that 1990 would be an important year for insurance services and an opportunity for WW to gain a stronger foothold in the European insurance marketplace.

CIBA-GEIGY ALLCOMM—MAKING INTERNAL SERVICES MARKET DRIVEN (A)

Taking the Helm

Nowhere was the move to get internal services closer to customers more strongly felt than among the 150 employees at Ciba-Geigy's communications unit. Allcomm was the first and, for the moment, only unit to actually become a freestanding profit center. It had been an obvious c..oice: It was physically removed from Ciba-Geigy, covered 95% of its overhead in charging, and had already begun to establish a reputation in the outside world, earning 2% of its billings from external chemical clients. Now totally autonomous, it was free to pick and choose its customers and charge for its services at market prices.

It was that simple . . . or was it?

Other internal services—or "central functions" as they had been known for generations at Ciba-Geigy, the Swiss-based global giant—did not become as autonomous as Allcomm in the restructuring that took place in July 1990. The change was part of a radical move to transform the top-heavy, lumbering "super-tanker"—in the words of the chairman—into "a fleet of leaner, faster, more maneuverable and market-efficient ships." In other words, these internal services had to learn how to get closer to their users and respond more competitively.

The need for change had been understood for years at Ciba-Geigy; it was the timing of that change that was critical. In mid-1989 the correct moment came, as new and younger leadership actually began to take over. And, although short-term results for that year had been good, top management sensed that the 1990 figures would be below par and that their achievements could not continue indefinitely unless some fundamental transformations occurred. A small handpicked task force headed by the new CEO at Ciba-Geigy was formed. After three months of deliberation, they presented their proposal. Six months later, in July 1990, quietly and without much fanfare, the new structure came into effect.

This case was prepared by Professor Sandra Vandermerwe and Dr. Marika Taishoff. Copyright © 1992 by the International Institute for Management Development (IMD), Lausanne, Switzerland. Not to be used or reproduced without permission. IMD case 433.

The first priority was to dismantle the formidable head office "central functions," which had virtually controlled internal activities up to that point. By transferring decision-making power from service providers to users, internal services like R&D, management information systems, purchasing, personnel, finance, and communications were expected to become more market focused. If Ciba-Geigy were to remain profitable into the 21st century, top management reasoned that the operating divisions and the departments within them had to have more direct control over product-market decisions and costs. Services offered inside the company would have to behave more like third-party suppliers competing for Ciba-Geigy business.

Jurg Chresta, an energetic and athletic-looking 49-year-old, had learned a lot about the chemical business in his 24 years with Ciba-Geigy and as head of advertising of the Switzerland-based communications central function. In July 1990, he had been given the helm of what would, by the end of the year, become the newly and fully independent communications unit. His mission would be to lead what the chemical giant hoped would become the flagship for the rest of the company. Now, as CEO of the new venture, it was his responsibility to make the transition from a "captive" to a "competitive" market-driven culture.

Although he was excited about the opportunities, he was nevertheless cautious about moving too fast. Several dilemmas had to be resolved and deliberate steps taken to shake off the old Ciba-Geigy ways. Chresta reflected on this situation late one snowy night in December 1990:

> Some people feel that our job is the easiest one; they say we're totally free to pick our customers, price our products, and actually refuse jobs we don't want to do while still riding on the Ciba-Geigy image. This is all true, and, not only that, there's a lot of money to be made if only we can use our expertise to win new outside customers.
>
> But, paradoxically, ours is also the most difficult task. We're no longer protected by the Ciba-Geigy umbrella. Our colleagues are increasingly demanding, and we can't suddenly hike up our prices without losing business. Even though we've built up a name in the business, the rest of the world isn't exactly queuing up, waiting for us.
>
> We have a super bunch of people, many of whom have given their whole lives to the company. That gives us stability and continuity, and fantastic leverage inside the company. On the other hand, it's very different waiting for a colleague who doesn't really care about cost to phone in with a request, and to have to sell our services competitively. Our people are accustomed to taking orders. They used to have a job to do, now they have a job to *sell*. They have to learn to behave differently so they can compete for Ciba-Geigy business, not just take it for granted.

Ciba-Geigy's Worldwide Structure

One of the leading pharmaceutical companies in the world and the largest in Switzerland, the company was formed in 1970 by the merger of two Basel-based chemical firms, CIBA, Ltd., and J.R. Geigy, SA. Ever since those early days, the company had been structured around a three-dimensional matrix: *business divisions* (product lines), *regional centers* (geographic locations), and *central functions* (centralized internal service units located at the head office). (Refer to Exhibit 1 for this matrix.)

The eight *business divisions* made up Ciba-Geigy's core business lines and included: Pharmaceuticals—the largest division (30%); Agriculture (21%); Dyestuffs and Chemicals (15%); Additives (9%); Plastics (9%); and Pigments, Electronics, and Ciba Vision (less than 5%). Staff reporting to the head office were assigned to these product divisions to provide R&D, production, marketing, and planning information and control services.

The company had *regional centers* in Europe, North and South America, Asia, Africa, and the Pacific. The service providers for these regions—for instance, R&D for Pharmaceuticals in Spain, or Agriculture in Hong Kong—resided in the regions but were sent by, and reported to, the central function in Basel.

The 11 *central functions*, which formed the third part of the matrix structure, were located in Basel and reported directly to the board. They were: R&D, Factories, Production Technology, Product Safety, Finance, Control and

EXHIBIT 1

Matrix showing Ciba-Geigy's worldwide structure (simplified)

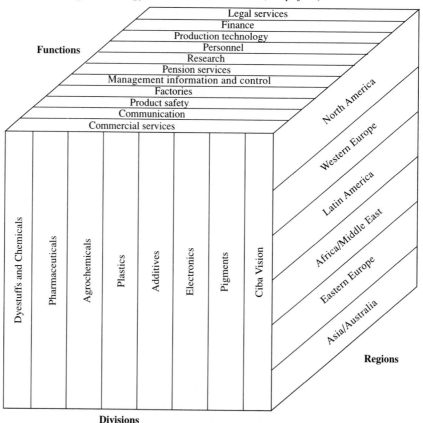

NOTE: The authors have adapted the terminology for ease of discussion.

Management Information Systems, Commercial Services, Communication, Legal, Personnel, and Pension Services. (See Exhibit 2 for an organigram.)

Internal Services before the Change

Before the change, the divisions and regions had no choice; they had to take whatever services and people were sent from these central functions. According to one person:

> It was almost like living in a centralized economy; things being dictated to you—like what you had to buy, how much, and at what price. The only way to influence cost was to reduce the quantity of the service. Quality was a given. And then the service was bad; there were delays and a lot of what we were being told to buy we really didn't need, want, or understand. The technical side of the service was usually OK, but it was often not relevant for our product lines or circumstances. For instance, a division's new product decisions depended on technological decisions made by the central function rather than our own feelings about market needs. We were frequently force-fed information we couldn't use. Instead of supporting us, the services we got often held us up.

A barrage of paper and administration existed between the internal service providers and their users, and a lot of time was spent filling out forms for the head office. Technicians and specialists were assigned as support to core business lines, but these project teams seldom met with users beforehand. New ideas had problems penetrating the bureaucracy. As one executive put it: "Even if you had the best idea in the world, by the time it got through all the layers of signing off—if it actually did—it had been diluted down to nothing and people just lost their nerve."

Divisions were allocated the direct expenses of the services provided by these central functions as well as a percentage of the overhead. Irrespective of whether or not the service had been requested or used, everyone paid a percentage of the overhead, which was determined according to a variety of formulas—ranging from the number of people in a division (e.g., personnel services), the bulk weight of production (e.g., purchasing or information systems services), or time (e.g., legal services). In some cases, people were assigned to divisions by the central functions, but they were responsible to and paid by the functions in Basel.

Internal Services after the Change

In July 1990, the three-dimensional matrix was replaced by a new system in which, depending on the circumstances, the old central functions were split into internal services categories[1] along a spectrum ranging from *still centralized,* through *totally decentralized* and *partly independent,* to *fully independent.* (Refer to Exhibit 3 on page 457 for the new structure.)

---

[1] The authors have adapted the terminology for ease of discussion.

EXHIBIT 2

Organigram showing Ciba-Geigy's worldwide structure (simplified)

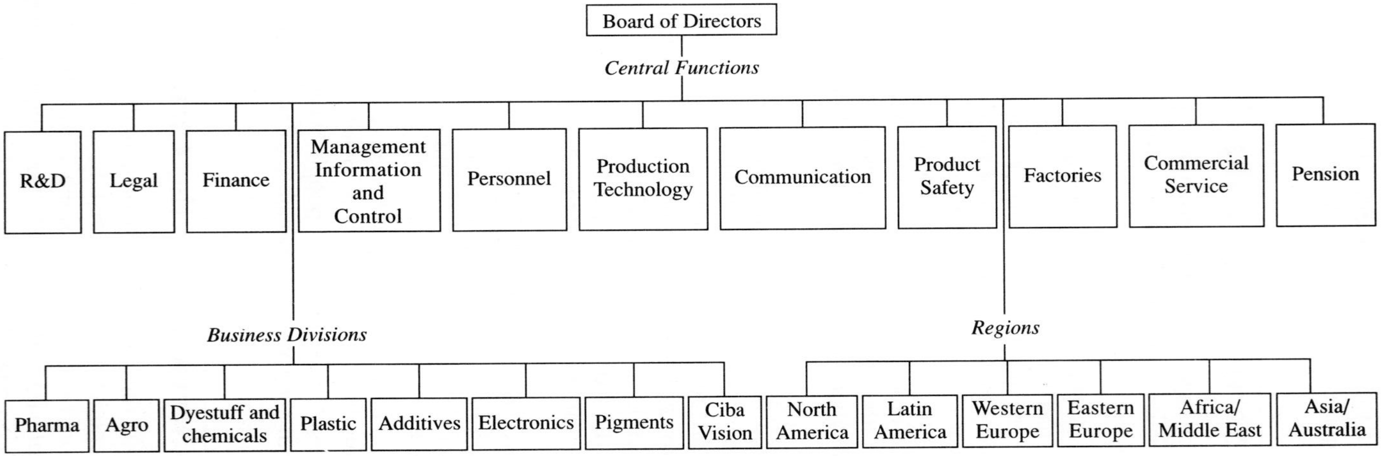

Board of Directors

Central Functions

| R&D | Legal | Finance | Management Information and Control | Personnel | Production Technology | Communication | Product Safety | Factories | Commercial Service | Pension |

Business Divisions

| Pharma | Agro | Dyestuff and chemicals | Plastic | Additives | Electronics | Pigments | Ciba Vision |

Regions

| North America | Latin America | Western Europe | Eastern Europe | Africa/ Middle East | Asia/ Australia |

NOTE: The authors have adapted the terminology for ease of discussion.

EXHIBIT 3

Organigram showing simplified version of Ciba-Geigy's new structure

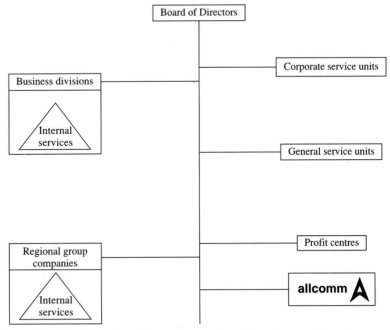

NOTE: The authors have adapted the organigram and terminology for ease of discussion.

Corporate Service Units (Still Centralized)

Seen as essential for global corporate strategy, these units were kept as centralized as possible. They were the services that top management believed needed to serve the board and the company as a whole on a worldwide basis. Divisions and departments were obliged to accept these services and the associated costs. These services were:

Research and development: Research projects in chemistry, biology, physics, and analytics for new technologies and markets.

Finance and control: Responsible for the group corporate treasury and corporate control, countertrading, and accounting for Switzerland.

Human resources: Management development planning and coordination, management training, corporate group personnel, and executive hirings and rankings for Switzerland.

Legal: Group corporate legal services.

Product safety and environment: In-house safety procedures including explosion prevention technologies, biochemical safety procedures, and corporate environmental standards.

Information technology: EDP architecture and security, in-house computer counseling and training, and coordination of technology transfer projects.

The percentage of employees worldwide working for central functions in Basel before the change had been 20%. After the change, less than 5% worked in these corporate service units. Responsible for setting overall policy, they no longer had authority over the divisions, and they reported directly to the board. Costs were allocated in the same way as before, but rather than simply charging a lump sum to a division or department at the end of a given year, costs were supposed to become more transparent.

Divisional and Regional Services (Totally Decentralized)

Services needed by the divisions in Basel and the regional companies abroad in order to accomplish their strategies were decentralized into these operating areas. Employees were sent to the respective service departments within the divisions and countries, and reported directly to them. The number of employees working inside the divisions grew from 58% before the change to 73% afterward. Costs of these services were absorbed into the divisions' overheads.

General Service Units (Partly Independent)

In order to create a spirit of competition, 11 services became "general service units." In principle, users were not obliged to use these services; if they preferred, they could go to third parties. Similarly, some of these services were allowed to compete on the open market as well. The services in this category were:

Four factories: Infrastructure and services for manufacturing the operating units' product lines.

Engineering and process technology: Investment projects, environmental protection process technology, and materials technology.

Research services: Scientific information on analytics, physics, catalysis/synthesis, and patent requirements for various countries.

Information services: Systems development and maintenance, mathematics and operations research, communications systems, and a computing center.

Personnel (Switzerland): Recruitment, training, and development for Swiss operations.

Administration of pension funds and investment in real estate: Advice and information on corporate policies and practices.

Purchasing services: Purchasing of chemicals, nonchemicals, and general office supplies; transportation.

Communications: Advertising, media, audiovision, exhibition stands, and print production and distribution.

Freedom to buy from third parties was limited by circumstances: If labeled *requested,* users were entitled to take or leave them. But a *required* service was one that the board felt was of strategic value to the company, one that entailed immense investment—the factories' fire brigades, for example—and therefore justified tight control and distributing of the costs throughout the organization.

General service units were expected to break even. The plan was to offer more of these services to the outside market as time progressed and eventually convert some of them into profit centers, as had been done with Allcomm.

Some services fell into more than one category. For instance, the basic chemical research in R&D was kept central, while the other aspects were distributed into the individual operating units. At the same time, some specific R&D services such as toxicology could be bought from, and sold to, the outside. The idea was to try and let competitive conditions prevail as much as possible internally so that Ciba-Geigy could become more competitive externally.

Information services fell into three categories. The centralized corporate service information unit supplied the board with data, handled network information systems, and designed EDP architecture on a worldwide basis. Each division had information specialists who could make software decisions and put together project teams to handle their own specific problems. There was also a general information service unit offering the various divisions special information projects that required specialized hardware or know-how.

The agriculture division took a major step in the information domain. It decided to operate an information agency that, in contrast to the other services dedicated to a division, also competed with the general service unit and planned ultimately to break even. This was an experiment to see if divisional services could be attached to specific product-markets and, at the same time, build up the know-how to attract other users, even from outside.

Profit Centres (Fully Independent)

Making general service units into autonomous profit centres was a longer-term goal that top management considered during the planning phase between September and December 1989. These services would compete for business from both Ciba-Geigy and other customers. They would have to learn to design and deliver services that were not only of the highest caliber, but also customized to the needs of the marketplace.

They looked for a central function where the risks of failure were minimal and which could be used as a role model for an independent profit center. Before long, the right candidate became apparent—the communications services unit.

Allcomm Becomes the Role Model

Ciba-Geigy's communications unit had always been referred to as Allschwil, the name of the small suburb—20 minutes from central Basel—where it was located. The unit had never been part of the sprawling Ciba-Geigy physical headquarters.

After the restructuring in July 1990, it became a general service unit, remaining in Allschwil on premises owned by Ciba-Geigy and for which the communications unit, now called Allcomm, paid market rates.

The group had acquired a unique know-how in chemical and pharmaceutical communications, an area where very few European advertising agencies had expertise. Although most of its billings were in-house, it did have some small outside clients in specialty chemicals who did not compete directly with Ciba-Geigy's product lines.

In 1981, when Ciba-Geigy's return on investment was down by 3–4%, a debate ensued on where to cut costs. Some top management felt that advertising services should be abolished, cut down, or spun off as an independent company. A decision was made to downsize. In 1983, advertising became a cost center and began to charge for its services. Users were not given quotes, and charges were based only on the direct salary costs. Overheads were absorbed by Ciba-Geigy. Charges for services which had to be bought from third-party suppliers had no profit margin. An executive recalled:

> Internal communication service charges were considered "free" by users, so it was really like monopoly money: from one pocket to another. Many didn't actually understand or care what a job really cost since it was being subsidized from the top anyway. Often they were getting jobs done much more cheaply than if they went outside, but they didn't always appreciate that fact. We had the equipment and delivered technical quality that they never could have found elsewhere at the same price. Some product managers never even knew what they were paying. The cost of our time for, say, advertising or exhibition work was charged in one lump sum to the division.

A price list, which was basically a standardized hourly rate sheet, was established for the services offered. Prices, however, were rarely discussed with customers. They were essentially calculated according to the amount of time a job would take, plus the kinds of materials—film, video, cardboard, and so on—it would require. Thus, it was a budgetary tool rather than a quoting instrument for customers.

The communications group was assessed by the Ciba-Geigy management committee every four years to determine if its prices were in line with those of outside suppliers and vendors. This exercise was done to verify that the group's cost budget was being satisfactorily met and to ascertain the amount of volume needed in the different areas in order to cover costs. However, as frontline business began to have more experience with outside agencies, they grew more money conscious, which in turn forced the communications staff to begin revising its own pricing standards.

Employees responsible for customer liaisons—who comprised approximately 10% of the 150 total—typically handled user requests in a uniform manner. Whenever internal users had requests, they would mark the appropriate spaces on the "communication service request forms" and return them to the unit. Chresta recalled that the employees responsible for account management were basically "letterboxes." The assignments given by customers were rarely defined with clarity or precision. Typically, they would ask for the same service as the year before, which could range from 10 stands for an agrochemical convention, to a print campaign to hire apprentices. The other 90% of the work was in administrative, design, graphic, and staff functions. Staff were not expected to deal with customers, and, if they did, it was typically because of a problem.

No matter what his or her job, if someone were selected by the unit's management for a promotion, the Assessment Board would first have to be contacted. This board, made up of Ciba-Geigy top management, would review and pass judgment on the promotion request, based on whether or not the nominee had met two preset criteria: deadlines and budgets. The aim was to ensure that a parity existed in Ciba-Geigy salaries, which were comparatively high for Switzerland. This parity was based on the individual's general qualifications and number of years with the company rather than the kind of activity he had performed. A lab assistant in the pharmaceutical division, for instance, was expected to earn a salary similar to that of a young graphic designer in the communications unit.

First Reactions to the Change

Six months after it became a general service unit, communications was made into an independent profit center, wholly owned by Ciba-Geigy. Organizationally, it was divided into seven sections and controlled by an operational management committee composed of the directors of each of the seven sections, as well as Jurg Chresta. None of the members of this management committee had had previous managerial experience. Long-term strategic and personnel issues were handled by four members of the committee together with Chresta. (Refer to Exhibit 4 for an organigram.) Allcomm had the right to refuse work, charge market prices, hire and fire new people, and go outside for new business. An agreement was reached by which Ciba-Geigy had first call in the event of a conflict of interest or shortage

EXHIBIT 4

Organigram showing Allcomm's new structure

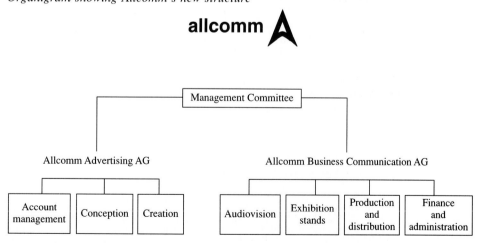

NOTE: The authors have adapted the terminology for ease of discussion.

of resources. In return, the company guaranteed to cover 100% of the profit center's gross 1990 income for the first year, 90% for the next year, and 80% for the third year. Chresta recalled:

> At first people were shocked. We provided them with a "question box" and got over 200 responses. Job security and other personal issues came up first. People wanted guarantees that for at least the next three years they would not be worse off than before the change. We had to constantly reassure them and agreed to honour all Ciba-Geigy contracts, and to stick to the cost-of-living salary index and pension scheme.
>
> Some people felt abandoned, as though they had been deserted by their family. They took it personally when people with whom they had worked for years began to look elsewhere for their ad campaigns. Before, they had been on an equal footing with their colleagues. Now, those same people were calling the shots!
>
> For others, it was an emotional issue. They didn't want to cut the umbilical cord with a large, secure, and socially prominent corporation for which many had worked for over a quarter of a century, if not longer. Ciba-Geigy's top management had hired them and posted them to the communications unit, and they felt accountable to the company. "We came to Ciba-Geigy for a good reason and that's where we want to stay," was a typical remark. "Why should we be forced to leave?" In addition to everything else, for the first six months after the announcement, we didn't even have our new name. "Who are we?" many wanted to know.
>
> About 10% wanted to leave and we let them. We didn't want to keep the nonperformers. We also tried an early retirement scheme. We had lots of meetings so that they could talk, and invariably morale went up after a meeting. Reactions varied from one individual to another.
>
> The younger entrepreneurs, about 10% of the staff, couldn't wait to get started. Self-driven and impatient to make their mark, they didn't care about the details. I remember one day someone saying "to be free, feel free, is the best feeling in the world."
>
> About 30% were quite flexible and happy to get going, provided they were able to do the kind of work they liked and their status remained intact. They wanted to make the change and to become creators rather than administrators and bureaucrats.
>
> About 40% were resistant. They were afraid of taking decisions and making mistakes. "Will we make it?" was their main worry. They were scared that if we failed they would be out on the street looking for a job. They worked with dedication but not real conviction. For them, seeing was believing, so I kept talking to them—days, nights, and weekends—about our new successes as well as our mistakes, so they wouldn't be afraid to learn.
>
> A small lead group of about 10% were outright against it. They were in near revolt in the beginning and demanded constant personal attention.

Challenges on the Horizon

Just a week before Christmas, as he sat in his office, Chresta remembered the first day he had been summoned into the CEO's office. Although he had been given 24 hours to decide if he wanted to accept the job of CEO of the new profit center, his answer had been an instantaneous yes. Despite his enthusiasm, he had anticipated that the job would be tough. Before, he had had to make sure that requests were handled within a reasonable time period and with a minimum budget. Now, he had to create an entirely new organization. "It reminds me of what's going on in reunified Germany," he said. "One day people in the East simply had jobs and took orders, and then, suddenly, they had to be part of a free market mentality."

Chresta and the management committee had agreed with the board on All-comm's financial objectives, although one or two of his top team were doubtful that it could be achieved. The intention was to fully break even by year two—at the end of 1992, which would probably mean adding another million and a half Swiss francs in turnover to their SF 19 million in charges.

Despite the guarantees of the agreement, Chresta wanted to prove to his staff that they could compete in a truly market-driven manner right from the start. He had to carefully consider his options and get the change process moving:

- He could aim exclusively at Ciba-Geigy for the first few years and try to get a large proportion of its business. This would mean treating Ciba-Geigy users as customers rather than colleagues. These users were already familiar to Allcomm, and it would give his staff some time to learn new behaviours before venturing into the "real" world.
- He could try to get some outside business immediately. If so, the question was whom to target and how to position the agency. Allcomm was relatively well known in the chemical industry and in Switzerland. Should he aim for other industries? Should he stay in Switzerland or try to get an international group of clients? Were any customers really domestic anymore? Should they go for many small accounts, or for the medium and larger ones?

Chresta also had to make a decision on the portfolio of services that Allcomm would provide in the future. Ciba-Geigy may have always referred to them as the advertising unit, but advertising was but one small part of a client's needs, he felt. He personally saw Allcomm as a total communications factory with a head (the thinkers), hands (production), and feet (account management). And, if they could develop the right kinds of new services, they could get into the minds and hearts of their customers early on as they developed their marketing strategies, and thereby provide them with a total communications solution.

The prices for these services also had to be addressed. Chresta was certain that Ciba-Geigy users would pay market prices. They would soon realize that, if they went outside, it would take months or even years for a new agency to get to know the business the way Ciba-Geigy did. And they would be prepared to pay for that expertise. On the other hand, Chresta had learned that if people had to pay, their need for things suddenly would diminish! With their newfound freedom, Ciba-Geigy users had already become more discretionary about what they wanted and more demanding in what they expected. Divisions asked for quotes, alternatives, and details about delivery time. They requested itemized costs and reassurance that budgets and timing would be honoured. Indeed, no longer was it just the advert or the point-of-sale material they wanted; now they wanted results, and they wanted them quickly.

Allcomm would have to learn to use resources more carefully. In the past, a Swiss camera crew would have been sent to do a project, say in Hungary, even though a local Hungarian crew could have done it just as well. That had to stop. And this raised another issue: Which services should Allcomm itself offer, and which could be bought from outside? Ideally, by the third year (i.e., in 1993), Chresta thought that Allcomm should be profitable and earning 20% of its revenues from outside clients. "After that, we should be entirely independent and capable of capturing 50% of our business from the outside."

"There's no doubt," he mused as he looked down at the colorful new recruitment campaign for young apprentices, which was scheduled for presentation to the personnel department next day, "people are the real challenge in this business—what else have we got?" Since he could not simply release Ciba-Geigy people, Chresta would have to motivate them to change their behaviour. How to get them to use their initiative and become more adventurous was something that had persistently preoccupied him over the past few months. He could hire new blood, but that would cost a great deal and, if he acted too quickly, a generation gap might result. On the other hand, how long could he afford to wait? "Just look at this ad," he exclaimed. "We *can* innovate if we want to. It reminds me of the posters for the movie *Saturday Night Fever*. So different from those we made in the good old days, when all that kids wanted from a job was lifelong employment and security with the firm."

With their collective expertise in chemicals and pharmaceuticals, it would be foolish to discard the Ciba-Geigy relationship. But, as long as that company remained the predominant client, he knew that it would be difficult to change people and bring out their innate talents. He sighed wearily as he looked at his watch. There was a lot to be done. But now it was time to go home to his family. One thing was certain, he thought, as he picked up his briefcase heavy with Christmas gifts for his wife and children: He had been made captain of a ship thrust onto an entirely new sea, with no maps or compass for guidance. And his crew was far from unanimous about setting out to sail, or winning the race.

CIBA-GEIGY ALLCOMM—MAKING INTERNAL SERVICES MARKET DRIVEN (B)

Setting Sail

Any firm would have been thrilled at getting the new Ciba visual identity campaign to publicize worldwide the change in the corporation's name from Ciba-Geigy to Ciba. (See Exhibit 1 on the following page for the old and new logos.) But none more so than Allcomm. "Who would have thought," Jurg Chresta declared on that early morning in September 1992, "that we would have had to fight so hard for a job—from the one customer we once held captive?" It was a warm Indian summer day, and the sun shone brightly into his office. He took his jacket off, rolled up his sleeves, and turned to Fred Wagner, recently appointed as head of finance and administration. The two were preparing for a management committee meeting later that day.

Wagner, who had spent over 10 years in Ciba-Geigy's legal department before coming to Allcomm in July 1992, looked at Chresta thoughtfully before responding, and then said, "You mean to tell me that you actually worked harder for this account than for the Amnesty International deal?"

Chresta laughed and then went on to explain: "Are you kidding? Winning Amnesty was like falling off a log compared to getting the Ciba deal. Maybe I'm exaggerating a little. But seriously, Fred, you've got no idea how we had to fight for that deal. The 'experimental group' moved right in and convinced Amnesty that we had what it took to make their campaign work. But with Ciba we had to get around the politics as well, and that was a completely different story. Let me tell you, the new guy in charge at corporate didn't even want to speak to us at the beginning. In fact, he told me, 'If I want to change Ciba-Geigy's communications, I can't use anyone who's worked for us in the past.'"

"How did you get around that attitude?" Wagner asked, now thoroughly intrigued.

This case was prepared by Professor Sandra Vandermerwe and Dr. Marika Taishoff. Copyright © 1992 by the International Institute for Management Development (IMD), Lausanne, Switzerland. Not to be used or reproduced without permission. IMD case 434.

"I had to get some help from the top," Chresta replied. "And we got the business unit managers involved. They ended up persuading Basel that we were the best people for the job. And we are, I can assure you."

True to its word, Ciba-Geigy had financially supported the fledgling group during its first full year and a half of independence. It had guaranteed that Allcomm would have the same amount of turnover, SF 20.5 million, as in 1990. The volume of Ciba-Geigy business—which was mostly routine and small jobs—did, in fact, drop due to the chemical company's own restructuring plans and cost-cutting program. This shortfall, however, was covered by Ciba-Geigy's turnover guarantee provision.

Chresta was proud of Allcomm's accomplishments in the just under two years of its existence. The Ciba logo deal was proof enough that dramatic strides had been made in the firm's customer-satisfying capabilities. The Swiss advertising campaign for Amnesty International, the nongovernmental worldwide humanitarian organization—together with new deals from a Swiss fashion company, Feldpausch, which operated in the German part of the country, and the Swiss brewery Warteck—was testimony to the fact that headway had also been made in the larger outside market. "And right now," Chresta went on, "we're all waiting anxiously to see if we got the auto account. Now that will be a big coup." He checked his watch. It was 10:45. "We had better get going; we don't want to be late for your first management meeting." He rose, leading the way. "So you see, Fred, we're OK . . . and if we continue moving at this pace, we might even strike it rich!"

They walked up a flight of stairs and along a series of spotless corridors. The offices were immaculate, all identically modern to the point of being spartan. Then they passed through the area that belonged to the experimental group. Drawings, sketches, and papier-mâché models, which changed almost every day, lined the corridors. Each of the six offices was different. Some offices had wood floors, some had concrete; some were painted in colourful patterns, some had stark black-and-white tiles. Layout models were strewn on the floors; others were suspended from the ceilings.

EXHIBIT 1

Old and new logos reflecting change in corporation's name

"They are really something different," Wagner remarked with amusement, noting also all the crumpled wads of paper which spilled out of the bins, onto the floors, and into the hallways. "Yeah," Chresta said, "they certainly are." Finally, the two men reached the conference room and entered.

Allcomm after Two Years

The other six committee members were already present. Allcomm was now composed of eight divisions, having added, at the beginning of 1992, a new one called Marketing Communication to handle market research, as well as a unique, technologically based expert market intelligence system. These divisions fell under either one of the two operating areas, Advertising or Business Communications. (See Exhibit 2 for the structure.)

Chresta opened the discussion by announcing that the Ciba visual identity campaign had been won. There was spontaneous applause. Then one of the members asked, "Don't tell me the 'chaos group' actually got into Basel?"

"No," Chresta answered with a grin. "As a matter of fact, we oldtimers were the ones who did it. And I'm pleased to say that the 'chaos group,' as you call them, has just won the Amnesty International campaign." More applause.

Chresta had created the experimental group in February 1992. He had personally gone looking for people who were more innovative and less tradition-bound. He found six individuals with these traits: Three—including a lawyer—came from outside agencies; of the remaining three, one was a talented artist, one a

Exhibit 2

Allcomm's new organization structure

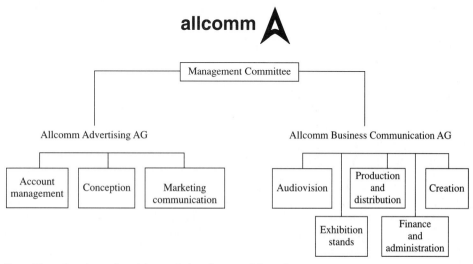

NOTE: The authors have adapted the terminology for ease of discussion.

secretary, and the sixth was a former communications unit misfit who had been looking for something else to do. All of these group members shared the characteristics he had been looking for: They were excellent team players and did anything and everything necessary—working days, nights, and weekends—to get the customer's job done. They were also willing to take risks. "I want you to be a self-managed team," Chresta had told them. "Show the world that you can get the business and satisfy our market. No one will interfere with you if you deliver the goods."

Within seven months, they had signed up Amnesty International, the Feldpausch Fashion House, Warteck Beer, and several other smaller projects. Now they were waiting with bated breath for the outcome of the Swiss car dealership campaign. They were convinced that their chances of winning it were rather good. Chresta had encouraged them to try to transfer the learning from one account to another. In this way, he hoped that they could build "economies of know-how" as well as cut the costs of material development. In this instance, an idea for a multimedia project they had originally developed for Swatch was taken up and adapted for the Swiss car dealership. The underlying concept was new to Allcomm and the trade. It involved a promotional program for retailers that allowed them, via interactive systems technologies, instant access to constantly updated information stored on digitalized systems.

The experimental group—or chaos group, as everyone at Allcomm and at Ciba referred to it—had actually chosen its own name, Allcomm 2, which was emblazoned on all its brochures and promotional material. The group had initially opted for the name A2, but Chresta had vetoed that idea. On two other occasions, Chresta had had to step in and interfere: He had banned bringing mountain bikes and dogs into the office and had halted the distribution of the group's prospectus—because their humourous version of the corporate organigram offended many of the other Allcomm employees and the board of Ciba-Geigy.

Chresta remarked that some of his employees liked to complain that they were not given the same freedom as members of the experimental group. But he would always retort, "No one ever told you you couldn't be like them."

Courting the Customer

By September 1992, Allcomm had approximately 3,800 customers. Of these, 10% were non-Ciba-Geigy clients who contributed about 15% to the total turnover. Some of these outside clients were Ciba-Geigy competitors in nonstrategic product/markets. Approximately 90% of all customers selected just a few bits and pieces of the 450 different Allcomm services offered. The remaining 10% had bought a complete communications strategy.

Chresta had begun reducing the number of accounts to be serviced by Ciba-Geigy. He had found that many customers were not only too expensive to maintain, but that they could not provide the kind of long-term relationship he was now pursuing. Many of Ciba's longstanding customers simply used its services for the sake of convenience. Chresta decided that this kind of business must be discontinued.

> If you ask people around here how many customers we have, they'll say 3,800. And they say that 380 people outside of Ciba deal with us. But, they forget that almost all of these customers just do an ad here, and a leaflet there, with us. Our real challenge is to have fewer customers doing more things with us and make them more profitable.

The advertising department segmented its market into health and nutrition, agriculture, industrial, environment, and public/not-for-profit. As for business communications, Chresta's aim was to provide a full communications offering—from strategic planning through to execution, and so he targeted companies that needed more than one kind of communication service. He was less concerned about the industries in which these firms operated than about Allcomm's ability to fulfill their requirements. The potential market in Switzerland totaled 200 businesses, essentially industrial corporations in need of business-to-business communications. Chresta also figured that there were 50 companies worth targeting in some of the other major geographic markets: France, Germany, Spain, the Benelux, and Scandinavia (primarily Sweden and Denmark). Here, he used the same potential customer criteria as he did for Swiss firms.

Chresta believed that the relationship between Allcomm and its customers needed to begin early on, so that their marketing strategies could be developed together and then seen through from the inception of the campaign to implementation. The Ciba campaign was a prototype of the kind of setup now being sought: putting people together with customers and working with them from the beginning until the very end. This arrangement, Chresta reckoned, put Allcomm in the driver's seat and kept competitors out.

One of the dilemmas still facing Chresta was deciding which services to offer, which to eliminate, and what new ones to introduce. As criteria, he considered whether a service was necessary for having an innovative communications strategy and could be profitably executed. For instance, a new, expert-system-based market research service had been added. The service was able to assess how well a given advertising campaign was likely to do under a variety of market conditions. A number of consumer firms used this service, which Chresta believed would in turn create an entrée for providing still more services to such firms. While he agreed that, from a consulting standpoint, Allcomm should offer everything, he knew that, from a production standpoint, this was not always possible. Allcomm had to cut down on services and buy them from others who could do them more efficiently.

Another factor to be considered was that customers increasingly were demanding the globalization of services. It seemed that Allcomm had no option but to begin building a global network to meet such needs. One of Allcomm's Swiss health customers, for instance, was expanding in the United States and asked Allcomm to be its agent there. Anticipating this trend, Chresta had already entered into two cooperative arrangements in Brussels and two in New York. He had also arranged partnering agreements with suppliers in Switzerland to ensure that Allcomm would have capacity when needed.

Organizing to Work with the Customer

In the two years of its existence, the number of people at Allcomm had remained relatively constant at 140. The personnel turnover of about 12% was considered normal in the communications field. Most of that turnover was among the younger staff members, some of whom went on to form their own businesses. For example, two individuals—after their initial training with Allcomm—successfully opened a graphic design office in the United States, which was reported to be doing well.

Just over 40% of the employees now dealt directly with customers, thus fulfilling Chresta's objective of maximizing exposure to customers as an opportunity to cement relationships. This rule applied as much to the administrative as to the frontline people. For example, some administrative staff who had never given customers any thought were now involved in the account management process. The account manager, for instance, had to make certain that customers understood all the details of the contract prior to signing and that each fine print clause of the billing and payment agreements was clear and acceptable to them.

Chresta was equally adamant that all employees, no matter what their job, be involved in quality measures to ensure that the customer's expectations could be managed and met. What customers expected was discussed in detail before finalizing an order. The briefing sessions he had with employees were thorough, so that both time and energy would not be wasted later. The agreed-upon terms were then defined in writing. Although, at present, this process could only take place with large clients, Chresta intended to follow the same procedure with all customers before long.

Chresta admitted that he felt it was vitally important to spend time, and have a mutual dialogue and discussion, with customers:

> Before, whenever staff had to deal with a customer, the mood was either one of indifference or confrontation. You never discussed needs. Now, we recognize that the business we're really in is a people business. And that means we've got to get our customers to talk to us; we have to find ways for them to feel that they can discuss their needs and objectives with us. They've got to trust us. And that takes not only talent but time.

Relationships had to be built where they had never before existed. They also had to be maintained. There was one case that Chresta particularly liked to recount about a longstanding Ciba client. The account was the standard kind, with print campaigns run at specified and predetermined times of the year. The relationship had endured for years, and there was little reason to believe that it could ever be jeopardized. Then, when it was time to receive the next order, it never came; the client had decided to do business elsewhere. Over the next three booking periods, Allcomm phoned and made a bid for the order, but each time Allcomm's bid was refused. Then Chresta recommended that the account manager and his team visit the client and talk. They learned that the client had indeed been very happy with Allcomm, but there was a particular freelance designer from a competing agency that the client wanted to use. Allcomm immediately arranged to hire the designer for the job. The account was saved. Chresta said, "We just have to learn to be flexible and do whatever's necessary to make customers happy, even if it includes using a competing agency. We don't have to do everything ourselves, as long as we are calling the shots."

Teaming at Allcomm

Chresta tried to strike a balance between two seemingly contradictory imperatives. He wanted to instill in his people an entrepreneurial spirit so that they would take risks and push their creative talents, but at the same time—as he frequently reminded them—they had to make a profit. "It was like a pendulum swing," Chresta remarked. "On the one hand, we have to make money as quickly as possible, while, on the other, we have to cultivate long-term customer relationships." Looking for ways to achieve economies of know-how, he tried to motivate staff to build on previous ideas and to work and learn so that they could execute projects more creatively, more quickly, and more productively. Teaming was a way to achieve this goal.

Chresta's approach to teaming was to get people together from different specializations and turn them loose on a project. He had taken this approach with the experimental group, and that was the model he wanted others to emulate. As he saw it, there was no other option: First of all, he believed that teaming was the most appropriate way to sell communication strategies, and, second, he was convinced that it was the only way to motivate his people—whose energy, creativity, and abilities to blend their skills was ultimately, in fact, Allcomm's only real product.

It was Chresta's practice to personally interview all candidates in the process of being hired. A person's ability to be a team player was rarely apparent on the first interview. It would usually require a second round, on "neutral" territory such as a restaurant. Even after that, Chresta had learned that it was safer to have candidates work for a while on a freelance basis with the team before signing them up permanently.

For Chresta, it was clear that everyone on a team would, at one time or another, have to be a leader; such was the nature of teaming in a know-how-oriented environment. He therefore embarked on a series of "team building and leadership" courses at Allcomm, which he insisted everyone attend. The skills and know-how taught in these courses resulted in the development of a new program for 7,000 Ciba managers.

From the very beginning, Chresta had decided to drop all hierarchical titles. Instead of being identified by rank, people were designated by the activities they performed. The martial labels—director, vice director, assistant vice director, and so on, which had little meaning to anyone outside the company—were replaced by professional differentiators like photographer, graphic designer, market analyst, and account manager. Chresta believed that customers were not interested in formal titles; what they wanted to know was what the person could do for them. There was a limit, however, as to how far this attitude toward titles could be taken; Chresta himself liked to joke, "Otherwise, window cleaners might end up being known as 'clear view managers'!"

Many of the oldtimers at Allcomm had difficulty with this policy, especially those who had been waiting years and years for promotions and suddenly found that titles—no longer significant—were being dropped. Chresta explained that the traditional formal titles had been more an internal than an external motivational tool. They got in the way of effectively designing and negotiating business communication strategy packages. In any case, he argued, team contact would have to be made at numerous levels within the potential client company. Hierarchical designations had little relevance in such meetings, he insisted, and were even known to obstruct their efficacy.

Chresta worked to get the teams identified and recognized, even though he knew that this approach radically differed from the typical Swiss culture, where emphasis was on the individual. But he firmly believed that everything had to be done to make the team, rather than any single person, the hero. He had different teams working separately on the same project, so as to instill a sense of competition and boost profitability. All team achievements were publicized in-house as a form of public recognition. If a team did well, its members were given a spontaneous reward. He fervently believed that money motivated people only up to a point. Some employees, for instance, were more enthused by the possibility of traveling to faraway places than by an extra financial incentive. And, in order to keep employees interested and motivated, he went to great pains to understand what individuals valued and to find ways to gear the incentives accordingly.

Employee and Customer Satisfaction Surveys

Both an employee and a customer survey had been completed during 1992. The same outside professional firm, together with Ciba-Geigy's corporate planning function, had been retained to do both surveys. The employee survey was based on a questionnaire that had been sent out during the spring holidays; it was returned within 14 days by 80% of the employees. The customer survey was a combination of standardized written responses and qualitative interviews. The first part had been sent to 95 customers, both within Ciba-Geigy and outside. Thirty-five customers responded. Sixteen face-to-face interviews were also conducted, with 10 Ciba-Geigy customers and 6 external customers. (See Exhibit 3 for results of the employee survey.)

While the sample for the customer survey was small, Allcomm did seem to be on the right track. Chresta was particularly proud of these responses, which came out of semantic differentials:

- "Allcomm comes close to being the ideal communications company." (78%)
- "I would recommend Allcomm to other businesses." (9 out of 10 interviewed)

Selective responses from Employee Satisfaction Survey

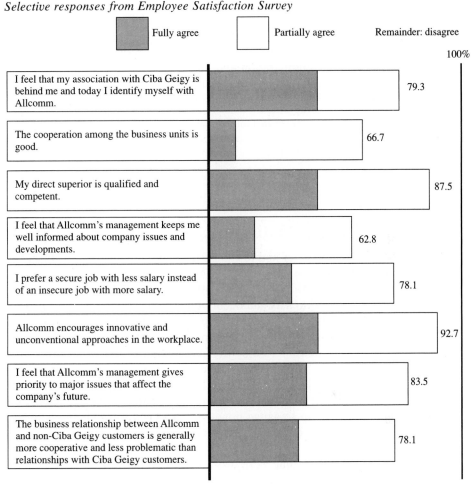

Some of the reasons given by the 22% of the customers who felt that Allcomm still had to improve included:

- "Allcomm should do more publicity: the company is not well enough known." (30%)
- "Allcomm should try to improve its innovative and creative potential." (35%)
- "The firm should try to focus on certain products and services, not be so widespread." (40%)
- "Allcomm is a reliable company, but too traditional." (50%)
- "Allcomm is not emotional, not flippant enough." (50%)
- "There's still too much of a Ciba-Geigy culture at Allcomm." (60%)

Chresta considered the experimental group a great success. He intended to extend the way they operated to the entire Advertising Group, thereby diffusing still further the unique culture they had created. The result would mean that close to 20% of all Allcomm employees would be working according to a more market-driven mentality. But, because they had been great at getting business and "lousy" at administration and finance, he decided to strengthen that part of the group's infrastructure in his plan. What Chresta wanted to avoid, though, was changing the whole organization simultaneously:

> That would cause instability. I want people to feel secure, not afraid and uncertain. The object is to build a culture of continuous improvement, not to cause chaos. I want people to come to expect change and accept it as a perfectly natural feature of their lives.

Measuring, Motivating, and Rewarding Staff

Allcomm no longer had to call in the Assessment Board for promotional approval, as it had done in the past. It now designed and applied its own measuring rods, which were both quantitative and qualitative. The former was based on whether bottom-line forecasts had been satisfactorily met. This was new for many employees, who were now directly responsible for managing their part of the business. The latter—qualitative performance measures—were jointly designed for the upcoming 12-month period by the individual together with his/her coach. At the end of that period, both parties would try to reach a mutual agreement as to how well the employee performed, where improvement was needed, and how to achieve it. From time to time, lead customers participated in the agency review sessions that had been set up to gauge how well the account was being handled. For Chresta, this was a way of giving customers a voice in the individual performance assessments.

Chresta felt that there was much to do in terms of designing the right kind of performance system. But, at this stage of Allcomm's existence, using performance measuring rods as coaxing and controlling instruments was important only up to a point. Survival was the predominant word at Allcomm at this time. Chresta could see its effects everywhere: Most of the lights in the Allcomm building, for instance, were typically on till 8 or 9 PM, while those at the Ciba building across the road were almost all off by 4, and definitely so by 5. As well, two-thirds of his employees had purchased shares in Allcomm. At SF 500 each, the gesture was mostly symbolic, but it did say something. What mattered was that they all showed up at the board meetings, and made their opinions as owners and members of the company—as well as employees—heard and taken seriously. "It's rather like Israel," he mused. "We have an urgent sense of mutual survival which is caused by having a collective understanding that we're living in a hostile environment. Under these circumstances, people automatically work together and work harder."

Costing and Pricing Services

"Overall, then," Chresta concluded the meeting, "I think that we have made headway in some very choppy seas. Fred, since this is your first meeting, perhaps you would like to give us the benefit of some of your impressions." Chresta looked at Wagner expectantly and found him eager and ready to respond. Wagner picked up a pen and began to scribble some figures on the white board. (Refer to Exhibit 4.)

"I must say I'm impressed. For instance, we had a total turnover of SF 20.2 million in 1991 and just over 15% came from the external 10% of the client base. So, though our business with Ciba was worth 17.5 million in 1991, we only had to use part of the guarantee.

"In addition, we achieved this laden with overhead costs. These costs—SF 2 million in all—are not transparent. Twenty percent I can trace; the rest is a mess. My instinct tells me, though, that many of them are unnecessary. And those we do need we can probably find more cheaply outside."

Sounds of concern came from the group, but Wagner went on: "The whole question of costs is incredibly complex. The truth is that we don't understand any of them or how they should be allocated. But, we must get them straight so we can ascertain once and for all which services and customers are profitable and which aren't."

"You're right about that," Chresta said. "We know what a person costs by the hour, but we don't know what an hour of machine use costs. We know what a piece of cardboard costs, but we don't what a person's experience should be costed at. A lot of the costs are hidden, they simply can't be tracked and traced, and it's difficult, if at all possible, to decide with any degree of accuracy what goes where.

"Customers have different ideas about the way they want to pay. Some want to work on an agency commission system; others have a global amount available and they want to achieve something with it—without spending one cent more. And still others want to work on an hourly fee basis. What it all boils down to is

---

EXHIBIT 4   Figures for Allcomm

Income	
Operating turnover	20,233,485
Nonoperating income	1,324,344
Total	21,557,829
Expenses	
Salaries and wages	14,324,294
Other, including taxes	7,194,829
Total	21,519,123
Profit	38,706

that, if we want to be truly customer oriented, we have to devise a financial system that lets us work with all these requests and understand our true profitability.'' At this point, Chresta restlessly sprang up. ''We also have to be concerned about our capacity. As we grow, we are going to have to look for alliances and for freelancers to fill the gaps. I'm in the process of talking to one or two competitors about the possibility of their coming in on some of our work. If we want to give our customers communications solutions, we've got to pull in all the talent we can muster.''

Murmurs arose from the group. ''Isn't that unusual, Jurg?'' Fred remarked.

Chresta smiled. ''This is an unusual company, Fred . . . ''

26 ALTO CHEMICALS EUROPE (A)

Eberhard Graaff had held the position of headquarters marketing manager for stabilizers at Alto Chemicals Europe (ACE) for only two months when problems with subsidiary sales managers began to surface. It was December 1980 and the end of an eight-week period in which Graaff had spent time studying the industry and the company's several European subsidiary sales organizations to familiarize himself with the challenges of his new job. In the preceding week, a number of important decisions had been made by Graaff that would have long-term strategic implications for ACE's stabilizer business. He had informed the subsidiary sales organizations that stabilizers, a chemical used in making plastic products, were no longer to be sold based on low or even competitive prices, and that share gaining at the expense of profitability of sales was no longer an acceptable policy. They were also informed that headquarters marketing was to take on a more active role in setting prices and determining target sales volumes for the various subsidiaries.

Reactions from the field to Graaff's decisions were immediate. Subsidiary sales managers were unanimous in their opposition. Expressions used by the managers to describe the new headquarters policies ranged from ''unworkable'' and ''contradictory'' to ''theoretical'' and ''dictatorial.'' What the sales managers appeared to resent most was the notion that their own local judgment on sales matters had to be subordinate to that of headquarters. In the past, they had enjoyed relative autonomy in these areas.

Graaff was not overly perturbed by the negative reaction of the sales organization. He was, however, concerned about the steps needed to assure sound implementation of the revised strategy for stabilizers.

This case was prepared by Professor Kamran Kashani. Copyright © 1986 by the IMD, Lausanne, Switzerland. Not to be used or reproduced without permission. IMD case 313.

Company Background

ACE was the regional headquarters for Alto Chemicals Corporation's operations in Europe. Alto was a major North American-based multinational whose principal activities included production and marketing of commodity and specialty chemicals. With its headquarters and production facilities located in Switzerland and France, ACE accounted for more than a third of Alto's global production and sales volume.

Nine wholly owned subsidiaries, each serving one or more countries in Western Europe, reported to ACE.[1] The products produced and sold by the subsidiaries in the region ranged from finished compounds such as agricultural chemicals to "building blocks" used in the production of other products such as solvents, elastomers, and stabilizers.

ACE's headquarters organization was by product group. Five directors, each responsible for one or more products, reported to the company's president. Functions such as marketing, manufacturing, and planning were included under each product organization. Every director, in addition to having a regionwide product management responsibility, also supervised one or more of Alto's subsidiaries in Europe. The subsidiary managing directors, who reported to their assigned "associate" director, were in turn responsible for ACE's operations in their respective national markets. These included sales of all products produced in the region as well as any local production. The subsidiaries were typically organized by function.

The headquarters–subsidiary interaction was best described as a matrix relationship. The "dual boss system" was a common expression used to portray the dual sources of influence on product and subsidiary management.

Stabilizers

Stabilizers were a category of chemicals used to make plastic products. When mixed with PVC (polyvinylchloride) resins and dyes, the stabilizers helped prevent the breakdown of polymers in the finished product caused by environmental factors such as temperature, light, and general aging. A plastic product not adequately treated with stabilizers was likely to become brittle and discolored over time. For example, the plastic covering of an electrical cable would lose its flexibility and disintegrate eventually if not protected by stabilizers. Management estimated that close to 40% of all PVC uses in Europe were in applications requiring the addition of a stabilizer.

Product management had identified eight end-use and process segments for the stabilizer market. These segments produced a wide range of goods from plastic bags and upholstery to wall covering, cables, hoses, and shoes. Although the share of each segment in total market varied from one country to another, the

---

[1] Alto's subsidiaries operated in the United Kingdom, France, Belgium, West Germany, the Netherlands, Italy, Spain, Portugal, and Sweden.

three largest segments accounted for more than 50% of the market Europe-wide. (Refer to Exhibit 1.)

In 1980, an estimated 600,000 tons of stabilizers of all types, valued at approximately $600 million, were sold by the industry to approximately 1,100 plastic fabricators in Europe. This was considered one of the most fragmented markets served by ACE. Stabilizers had experienced an annual growth rate averaging less than 3% in tonnage during the 1970s. The market was expected to remain stagnant, however, for most of the 1980s. As one member of product management explained, "Stabilizers have matured as an industry. All potential applications have been discovered, and we do not see any prospect for rapid growth among the existing uses.

The recessionary conditions prevailing in many European user industries during the past year were blamed for the 15% decline in total consumption from the 1979 level. The industry's unutilized plant capacity was estimated at about one-third.

More than 20 companies competed in the European stabilizer market. The four largest producers were Ciba-Geigy (Switzerland); ACE; Berlocher (West Germany); and Lankro (United Kingdom). Together they accounted for approximately one-half of the market in 1980. ACE management pointed out that most competitors had a home base where they were particularly strong. All companies, however, tried to sell their stabilizers regionwide.

The chemical properties of the stabilizers produced by ACE differed from those made by others in Europe. The company's variety was referred to in the trade as "Tin" (Sn)—the generic name representing its chemical structure. The stabilizers most frequently produced by competitors had a different structure and were generically referred to as "Barium" (Ba). Both varieties were general-purpose products with large end-use applications. Differences in properties—such as

---

EXHIBIT 1   Stabilizer Market Segments (1979)

End-Use or Process Segments	Sample Products	Consumption (% of Total)	Number of Fabricators (Estimate)
Coated fabrics	Upholstery	17%	180
Flooring	Cushion flooring Sheets/tiles	20	160
Wire and cables	Cable jackets and insulation	17	235
Compounds	Shoes	11	55
Plastisole	Wall covering, gloves, balls	5	90
Calendering	Very broad: dresses, housing, etc.	13	180
Extrusion	Hoses	11	130
Injection molding	Shoes	6	70
		100%	1,100

heat and light resistance, and weathering and oil absorption—were considered by many in management to be minor between the two varieties. Although in theory general purpose stabilizers could substitute for one another in most applications, in practice plastic fabricators could not switch easily from one type to another, as the process technologies required were considerably different. Barium was by far the most commonly used stabilizer in Europe.

Entry Strategy

ACE's decision to enter the European stabilizer market was made in 1970. The original strategy called for a step-by-step penetration of the market toward a long-term market share objective of 20%, projected at 160,000 tons by 1979. The main elements of the entry strategy are described below:

1. *Market exploration:* As ACE did not have any working knowledge of the European stabilizer industry, the first few years after entry were to be spent exploring "the possibility of becoming a major fully integrated stabilizer supplier by 1980." The long-term choice of stabilizers for ACE was Tin, for which the company's European subsidiaries had ample feedstock or the needed raw material. However, beginning in 1970, ACE entered the market with Barium purchased from European producers.

2. *Third-party production:* Due to the high level of start-up investment in production facilities, ACE's supply of Barium initially, and of Tin later on, was to be secured through production agreements with established European producers. A member of the management closely involved with supply negotiations referred to the process as "difficult—something you can do when you have a strong heart and lots of guts." The company foresaw eventual European production once sufficient sales volume was attained.

3. *Conversion:* Barium was to be an entry product in Europe; ACE management intended to gradually convert its customers to Tin. Conversion was to be encouraged through lower initial prices, but also through assuring better product performance. Initial discounts of 2–3% below Barium prices were deemed necessary, as conversion required changes in process and machinery that had to be justified economically.

4. *Segmentation:* Product management was keenly aware of the differences among various segments in the stabilizer market. For some, performance was more important than price; for others, the reverse held true. In wire and cables, for example, stabilizer costs were less than 2% of the total cost. As a result, these producers were less sensitive to price than those in flooring for whom the cost ratio was around 10%.

Size also played an important role: Large firms purchasing in excess of 500 tons per month paid lower prices than small and medium-sized firms purchasing one truckload or more at a time. The difference in price could be as large as 5%.

The entry strategy placed its sales emphasis on those segments for which price played a relatively more significant role. As one subsidiary sales manager explained, "We had to get the attention of people when we first started up. We used the tools we had, and price was an important tool."

Selling Stabilizers

ACE's Tin stabilizers, branded as Polystab, were sold through a specialized sales force in all the subsidiaries. They were assisted in technical matters by the staff from technical service located in Geneva. The service was thought to be of particular importance for small and medium-sized clients who did not have one in-house. Management believed that the specialized salespeople and the highly competent technical service, both unique in the industry, had allowed the company to gain and build in-depth knowledge of the various industries and processes using stabilizers.

For selling purposes, the subsidiaries grouped their accounts according to the following classifications:

1. *Base:* Regular Polystab customers mostly converted from Barium.
2. *Strategic:* Important prospects; usually trendsetters in their industry, currently using Barium.
3. *Swing:* "In and out" customers; price-oriented.

In 1980, the *base* accounts provided the bulk of Polystab sales. The *strategic* accounts, on the other hand, were key targets for conversion and hence long-term sources of sales. They required intensive attention from management and often a highly technical type of selling. The *swing* accounts were usually converted, but could not be counted on as regular customers because of their low-price orientation.

The task of converting from Barium to Tin fell on the sales force. The sales management pointed out that selling revolved around establishing tangible advantages for the client to justify the changes in equipment and process that were usually needed. They also mentioned that, in certain applications, conversion held only small benefits that were hard to demonstrate. In all cases, conversion was a time-consuming process. Product management estimated that it took, on average, 18 months to convert an account. The actual time spent could vary from six months to several years. In every case, a minimum of 8 to 10 visits from the technical service staff in Geneva was required.

For all the subsidiaries, the proportion of selling time spent on conversion had declined since the mid-1970s. In a typical case, in 1980 the sales force spent only a quarter of its time on conversion prospects, whereas in 1975 the ratio was close to 60%.

Since ACE was not the sole supplier of Tin in the market,[2] most converted customers compared prices before placing an order—usually done on a monthly

---

[2] For all other producers, Tin accounted for a minor share of their stabilizer sales, as they did not have their own feedstock required for its production.

basis. The sales force, therefore, was intimately aware of the importance of price in making sales.

One subsidiary sales manager explained the buying behavior of stabilizer customers: "The larger companies have a professional buying practice. They check with two or three regular suppliers and then place their order. The smaller firms, on the other hand, tend to contact a multitude of producers, trying to negotiate a low price. They often wait till the middle or end of the month hoping for a general deterioration in prices." He added that Barium producers were the price setters in the market, and therefore a knowledge of their prices, as well as those for Tin, was essential in selling. "Prices do fluctuate during the month, depending on the level of demand and the producers' eagerness to sell their inventory. So timing is critical. When you set your prices high at the beginning of the month and you don't get an order by the 10th, you get pretty nervous. You can easily overreact and then destroy your average price level for the rest of the month." Typically, about two-thirds of each month's sales were made in the first two weeks of the month.

A stabilizer salesman in the subsidiaries had between 10 and 25 accounts to look after. His days were spent partly in the office, preparing reports and reaching customers by phone, and partly on the road, visiting companies. Some sales managers insisted on visiting each account a minimum of once a month.

Stabilizer Marketing Organization

The marketing organization for stabilizers is shown in Exhibit 2. Partial job descriptions for key executives in the organization are given in Exhibit 3.

Graaff, who was new to the stabilizer organization, described the matrix structure as one built on "interaction and positive confrontation." Another executive, Peter Hansen, director for stabilizers, referred to the dual boss system as working well: "In the old days before the system arrived, the subsidiaries wouldn't even let us into their offices!" A sales manager with many years in the company also commented on the system: "The dual boss relationship can be useful or painful. It depends on the chiefs."

Headquarters marketing had profit responsibility for stabilizers. Graaff described the product line's profitability as a function of production costs, average prices received by the subsidiaries, and the total volume of sales. Management at the subsidiary, on the other hand, was held accountable primarily for the volume of sales generated in their market, in addition to the cost of selling and the level of receivables. Subsidiaries paid a transfer price for stabilizers sold in their market.

The performance of sales managers was evaluated jointly by the subsidiary managing director and headquarters marketing manager. Whenever a manager was responsible for the sales of a number of products, a joint performance appraisal would be undertaken for each line. Company executives pointed out that a superior overall performance could mean an increase in annual salary of up to 10% for the sales managers. This merit raise was said to be a "big carrot" and an important incentive.

Exhibit 2 *Stabilizer marketing organization*

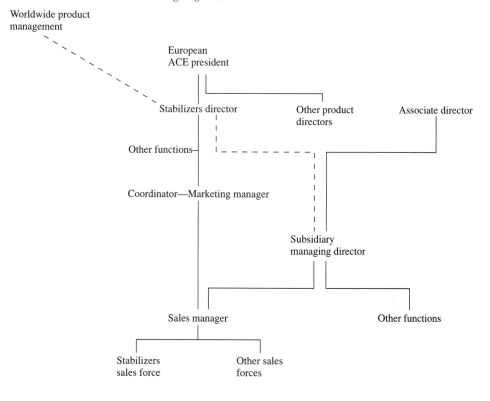

Worldwide product management

European ACE president

Stabilizers director

Other product directors

Associate director

Other functions

Coordinator—Marketing manager

Subsidiary managing director

Sales manager

Other functions

Stabilizers sales force

Other sales forces

Exhibit 3 **Partial Job Definitions**

Director, stabilizers	Serves as regional product manager, responsible for all phases of the region's stabilizer business, including technology, manufacturing, marketing and supply, and transportation; establishes regional goals, objectives, plans, and action steps and works with worldwide product manager to assure that these are consistent with the worldwide plan and resources; responsible for proper execution of approved plans; must coordinate his conduct of business with and seek guidance from worldwide product line manager and the regional president.
Stabilizers, marketing manager	Responsible for all marketing activities within stabilizers; consults subsidiary marketing and sales personnel to develop the marketing inputs for the stabilizer business plan; responsible for proper execution of approved marketing plan and regionwide results; shares responsibility with subsidiary sales manager for development of sales staff.
Subsidiary managing director	Is accountable for all of the chemical businesses in the subsidiary; shares responsibility with each of the regional product line directors for planning and conduct of each of the businesses within the subsidiary.
Subsidiary sales manager	Shares responsibility with each of the regional product line marketing managers for planning and conduct of the businesses within the subsidiary; must play an important role in high level contacts with key customers; will advise on overall strategy within the country including the economic outlook as well as opportunities for new businesses; will encourage a close working relationship between salesmen and the regional product line marketing managers.

Before Graaff joined stabilizer marketing, quarterly and annual sales quotas were used as bases for performance evaluation. Quarterly meetings in Geneva between the marketing and sales managers compared the progress in stabilizer sales against quotas.

By company policy, all ACE executives and members of the sales organization were compensated by a fixed salary. This policy also applied to the 10-man specialized stabilizer sales force in Europe, whose salaries and performance evaluation procedures were determined at the subsidiary level.

Eberhard Graaff

Eberhard Graaff had been with Alto for 15 years before being assigned to stabilizer marketing. A chemical engineer by training, he had filled various positions in Europe and the Far East as a business analyst, design engineer, plant supervisor, and subsidiary sales manager. This was his first appointment in Geneva; his predecessor had recently retired from the company. In 1980, Graaff was 40 years old and the second youngest member of the stabilizer marketing organization.

"We felt we needed a man with positive leadership," explained Peter Hansen, Graaff's immediate boss. Graaff's outstanding performance as sales manager in France was considered as one factor in his promotion to the marketing position. Graaff himself believed that his "tough name" in the company was also instrumental in his selection.

ACE executives were aware of the difficulties inherent in Graaff's new assignment. Hansen explained, "The job of headquarters marketing is complicated not only by the different market and competitive conditions of each subsidiary, but also by the diversity in personalities and cultures of their management." He felt that the job required, in addition to marketing expertise, skills in establishing a dialogue with the subsidiaries and in building a sales team.

Strategy Revised

The stabilizer strategy set in motion in 1970 had achieved most of its objectives by 1980. ACE's stabilizer share in Western Europe was nearly 18%. Predictably, the proportion of Barium in total company sales had declined over the years. As of mid-1979, Tin stabilizers were being produced by the company's own facilities in France. In that year, the stabilizer sales force was calling on a total of 170 accounts in the region.

Graaff's first couple of months in the new job was taken up with visits to each of the nine subsidiaries and a review of marketing and sales practices regionwide. By December, Graaff had reached a number of conclusions regarding the current Polystab strategy as implemented in the field:

1. *Overreliance on price:* Selling was too price oriented; Barium prices were matched or undercut by two to three percentage points even for the converted Tin accounts.

2. *Narrow market base:* Price-oriented selling had led to emphasis on those segments where it played an important role (i.e., the larger companies and Swing accounts).

3. *Low profitability:* Low prices in the region meant low profitability for the stabilizer business. The current regional average contribution margin of $40 per ton was deemed as an unsatisfactory return for the recently completed facilities in France.

4. *Price discrepancies:* In the absence of central coordination, differences in subsidiary prices were encouraging the larger, geographically diversified clients to buy their entire requirements from cheaper subsidiaries and transfer them for use to other subsidiary markets. Price differentials among subsidiaries were partly due to different average market prices in each country. Traditionally, for example, German stabilizer prices were a few percentage points above those of other European countries.

Graaff commented on the conclusions of his eight-week study:

The picture became rather clear to me. We are a volume-oriented organization, from here all the way down. This is a legacy of the original strategy which gave us a chance to compete in this market. So as long as the quarterly sales quotas were met, nobody complained. And to meet the quotas, subsidiaries had a fairly open hand in setting prices. Headquarters price guidelines were only good for the first few days of each month. Afterwards, the sales pressure from the field forced the people in Geneva to give in, leading to low average prices for the whole month. This cycle would repeat itself 12 times a year.

Graaff was convinced that a revision of the successful stabilizer strategy was in order. "Product management and top ACE executives have been increasingly concerned with the return on our heavy investment in stabilizer facilities," he explained. "My understanding of this market leads me to believe that improved profitability is possible, provided we have the right segments and selling approach."

In December 1980, Graaff communicated in writing the following elements of the revised stabilizers strategy to the subsidiary sales managers and asked them to incorporate these points into their future sales plans. A summary of the revised strategy follows:

1. *Non-price selling:* Price to play a subsidiary role in selling; instead, emphasis to be placed on areas where ACE held a competitive edge such as expert sales force, superior technical service, and general corporate reputation for supplier reliability.

2. *New accounts:* Selling aimed at conversion of new accounts to receive added impetus; new accounts to come primarily from small and medium-sized firms, and segments that were less price sensitive such as wire and cable.

3. *Price leadership:* Discounting or merely "meeting Barium prices" will no longer be an acceptable pricing policy for converted accounts; sales

management to watch for opportunities to initiate price leadership vis-à-vis other suppliers.

4. *Central coordination:* Geneva was to take a more active part in setting price and volume targets for subsidiaries; the highly competitive low-price markets were to receive less sales emphasis than those enjoying higher average prices; headquarters coordination to aim at regional optimization.

The average price improvement was expected to yield immediate results. For the 1981–1982 planning period, Graaff was projecting a doubling of contribution margins to $80 per ton.

In his communication to the sales organization, Graaff also mentioned that, although he was willing to accept a slight short-term drop in sales due to price improvement, the longer-term objective remained a growth in volume. This, he maintained, was essential if the new stabilizer plant were to operate at an economical utilization rate.

Sales Management Response

Reactions from the field were not long in coming. Communicating their sentiments to Graaff mostly by phone, sales managers were unanimously against the announced changes in the business strategy. "To speak of price improvement at a time when the whole market is declining is just absurd," was a typical comment from the field. Another manager responded, "Your strategy of improving both price *and* volume is unrealistic and contradictory." Still another commented, "The smaller accounts take the same amount of selling time as the larger ones. If we added them to our customer list, we would be running after more accounts for the same volume of sales. That wouldn't make sense." Another manager labeled the revised strategy as "not market oriented, but rather inward looking."

Sales management also expressed concern about their future relationship with clients. One manager explained, "We have gained our customer base through conversion and the promise of savings to the client. They did not scream when we gradually raised our prices to the Barium level during the past few years. At least they know that they won't be paying more than their Barium-using competitors. Now, if you were a user of Barium for 25 years and I succeeded in converting you, how would you react if I came around a few months later and told you that from now on you will be paying a premium over their prices? You'd probably ask me—whatever happened to the savings you promised? The money is in your pocket not mine!" This executive added that problems of this kind would have a detrimental effect on sales force motivation.

Underlying most managers' complaints was another concern—that the initiative in key decision areas was shifting away from subsidiaries toward Geneva. One subsidiary sales manager explained what was felt by many:

So far, we have succeeded in stabilizers because of local initiative; we knew our markets well enough to have confidence in headquarters marketing. They trusted our best judgment. We are professionals in this field and should be allowed to harmonize our own performance. Headquarters can help by synthesizing and giving broad guidelines. That's all. Rigid rules go against management harmony.

Implementation

Graaff was not surprised by the sales organization's reactions to his proposals. He explained, "I myself was in the subsidiaries for a number of years, so I know how they feel."

Graaff intended to take steps toward implementing the strategy, which he believed was sound and consistent with market realities. "I am convinced the strategy will work," he added in defense of his decisions. "It aims at changing our customer mix, which in turn allows us some pricing leverage in the long run. It also aims at enlarging the base, which reduces our risk with a few large customers, and, finally, it takes a regional view of the stabilizer business, where all competitors and a number of customers are operating in more than one national market. A regional strategy gives us the flexibility of shifting our volumes toward those markets where we earn better margins."

Graaff did not minimize the implementation task ahead of him: "The job won't be easy, but I have always been sent into jobs with difficult problems." He added that, although he believed Hansen was in favor of improved profitability, he had not cleared the specifics of his strategy with the director and was certainly not going to ask for his help in implementing it in the field. "I am not the type who would seek advice from the boss on everything," he emphasized. "I have always followed the things I believe in."

ALTO CHEMICALS
EUROPE (B)

In the first six months of 1981, Graaff had undertaken a number of steps that he believed were necessary to implement the revised stabilizers strategy. He was reviewing the results to date with the purpose of deciding what to do next.

Graaff's Actions

Between January and June of 1981, Graaff had taken the following measures:

• *HQ presentation:* Early in January, Graaff invited the subsidiary sales managers to a planning meeting where he made a presentation on the main elements of the revised strategy. Central "monitoring" on price and volume, in addition to new emphasis on smaller accounts for the less price-sensitive segments, were highlighted in the presentation. He also underlined that selling should become more technical in nature, with emphasis on quality and performance arguments. The need for closer collaboration between the sales force and technical service staff was similarly underscored.

• *Monthly meetings:* Subsidiary sales managers were asked to meet monthly with Graaff at headquarters to set price and volume targets and review progress to date. Graaff explained later, "The meetings were necessary to have better control of the business but also to give the subsidiaries a chance to talk to each other and see the whole picture."

• *Account targets:* Along with price and volume targets, the monthly meetings resulted in a "rolling list" of named accounts for each subsidiary's sales force to pursue. The accounts were segmented by size, end use, and whether they deserved a special effort for conversion. Accounts known for "price cutting"

This case was prepared by Professor Kamran Kashani. Copyright © 1986 by IMD, Lausanne, Switzerland. Not to be used or reproduced without permission. IMD case 327.

were left off the list, even the larger ones. Some rules were established for division of the selling effort between old accounts and new ones.

   • *Volume redistribution:* To improve average prices received in the region, lower sales targets were set for historically competitive markets such as Holland. With higher target volumes for less price-oriented markets such as Germany, Graaff intended to shift the total volume toward the more profitable subsidiaries.

Results to Date

Although Graaff considered the first six months to be too short a time to determine the effectiveness of the new strategy, a few results had begun to surface. The company had gained a number of new accounts among the medium-sized and smaller companies. This had been achieved despite the absence of discounts. On the other hand, several medium-sized and large accounts had been lost, some going to competitors and others reverting to Barium.

The overall impact on total volume of changes in the customer base was difficult to assess, as the industry sales had declined by about 8% during this period. Also, in some markets the contribution margins had increased slightly—in others not.

Meanwhile, the relationship between Graaff and the subsidiary sales managers had deteriorated significantly. The monthly meetings had often turned into shouting matches between Graaff and the more outspoken sales managers. The complaints voiced by the latter centered around the inherent wisdom of the new strategy and its impact on short-term results. Typical among these complaints were statements such as the following:

   • "You show us numbers and ratios to argue why a higher price is better than a lower price. But, the market doesn't have to follow your logic. Our customers don't understand our ratios; they don't even care. What they want is a lower price."
   • "For every key account I lose, I have to run after several smaller ones."
   • "You are destroying what took me years to build."

Conclusion

Graaff did not enjoy his monthly encounters with the sales managers, but he was not overly concerned. He felt it was "part of the job." What was beginning to concern him, however, were signs that his boss was losing patience. On some recent occasions, Hansen had mentioned that sales-force motivation should not be sacrificed for the sake of a strategy and that a more consensus-oriented approach might be more effective in winning subsidiary support. Evidently, some subsidiary managing directors had been in touch with him regarding complaints from the field.

Although agreeing with the merits of a consensus approach, Graaff was not totally convinced that it would work in this situation: "Consensus is fine. But, at the end of the day someone has to make a difficult decision, and, in this case, that someone is me.'' Graaff was, however, more profoundly concerned about whether Hansen really believed in what he was trying to accomplish. ''There are times I think even Hansen doesn't believe the strategy is going to work. It's difficult to change things when people have been around a long time and used to a different thinking,'' he complained.

Despite certain signs of unease, Hansen had not tried to stop Graaff. On the contrary, he had given him a free hand to proceed.

THE COCHLEAR BIONIC EAR: CREATING A HIGH-TECH MARKET (A)

"It's mystifying," he muttered, gazing out at the bright June light across the Rhine to Germany, which was just visible from the Basel-based European headquarters. "Our system works better than any other surgical procedure. We have a failure rate of 1%. No other kind of surgery offers that sort of result. Why aren't we selling more?" By June 1990 Mike Hirshorn, CEO Worldwide, was getting increasingly concerned about the drop in sales of the Cochlear hearing implant device.

He had been with the Australian company since its inception and had experienced all the ups and downs of getting regulatory approval and carving out an entirely new market. As one of the original members of the project team, Mike had helped take the ear implant invention of a university professor and transform it into a commercially viable product for the profoundly deaf.

"Look," he declared, "we've managed to get rid of 3M, our biggest competitor. But still we've only succeeded in selling 3,500 units worldwide. Do you realize there are another 50,000 adults out there, if not more, who need us? Yet we can't seem to break through!"

After a brief silence Brigette Berg, CEO for Europe, responded, "Maybe we just have to face the fact that the market is smaller than we think. The only place we're still growing is in Europe, and that's only because new countries are finally beginning to include us in their health coverage schemes." Brigette had set up the Basel office in 1987 to market and distribute the Cochlear hearing system, the most technologically advanced in the world.

She went on. "Maybe we should stop worrying about volumes. After all, we've got 90% of the market in the United States and 60% in Europe, and the best

This case was prepared by Professor Sandra Vandermerwe and Research Fellow Marika Taishoff. Copyright © 1991 by the International Institute for Management Development (IMD), Lausanne, Switzerland. Not to be used or reproduced without permission. IMD case 381.

product in the world. Why shouldn't the market be prepared to pay more for it? It makes more sense to me to consider raising the price." She looked across at Dennis Wheeler, her American counterpart, for a reaction.

"Perhaps in Europe, where most countries just fix quotas and aren't that price sensitive," Dennis said quickly. "But then we'll risk losing the 25% of the US market which depends on government support. In my opinion, if we want to stay ahead of the competition, we've got to bring down the price even if it means finding ways to cut back on spending."

"We've got to be careful there, Dennis," Mike replied. "I would hate to hold back now. There's no way we can survive without opening up the market. Which means we must invest in marketing our implant better. At the moment, 95% of our potential customer base still doesn't even know we exist."

Cochlear's Background and Financial Profile

In 1979, after 10 years of researching the possibility of implanting hearing devices into the cochlea, or inner ear, Professor Graeme Clark, head of the Department of Otolaryngology at the University of Melbourne, Australia, looked for an industry partner to help further his project. The Australian government, seeking to encourage high-tech development, called for tenders from companies able to perform a market study and write a development cost plan for commercialization. Nucleus Limited, a local company specializing in cardiac pacemakers and diagnostic ultrasound imaging equipment, won the tender.

Nucleus quickly put together a project team to engineer the product's evolution. This entailed three tasks: development of the product itself, filing the necessary patents, and developing a strategy. By September 1982, they were ready to perform the first implant, which proved to be a huge success. The following year Cochlear Pty Limited was formed in Sydney to handle the new innovation's research and development, manufacturing, and sales. The first US implant took place in 1983, and in the following year, the subsidiary Cochlear Corporation was established outside Denver, Colorado.

Real momentum began two years later when the US Food and Drug Administration (FDA) gave its approval. Only when this had been granted would US health insurers provide coverage for the product and the surgical procedure necessary to implant it. Unit sales in the United States increased from 409 in 1987 to 596 the following year, although they decreased to 553 in 1989. In that same year, Cochlear produced and began clinical tests on the world's first inner-ear implant for children.

Cochlear began to cultivate the European market in 1986 and in 1987 set up an office, Cochlear AG, in Basel, Switzerland. Although European countries did not have regulatory bodies such as the FDA for medical devices, the FDA's opinion was regularly adopted by the European medical authorities. By 1989, when the national health systems in certain countries began to reimburse patients in full or on a quota basis, the company's European position strengthened, with

---

EXHIBIT 1   **Unit Sales and Financial Data**

	1987	*1988*	*1989*
Unit Sales (Including Clinical Trials)			
United States	409	596	553
Worldwide	574	798	839
Dollar Sales (Excluding Upgrades)			
Worldwide (in $ millions)	$8.7	$13.0	$14.2
R&D (in $ millions)	1.1	2.3	3.2
General and administration expenses (in $ millions)	5.9	7.1	7.0
Promotion expenses	0.6	0.6	0.6
Cost of goods sold	Constant	Constant	Constant

198 units sold that year. This led to worldwide growth from 1988 to 1989 despite the decrease in US unit sales.

In an attempt to open up the Japanese market, a four-man operation called Nihon Cochlear was established in Tokyo in 1988; the company was the only player in that market. Clinical tests had been in progress since 1986, with 17 implants completed to date. However, the FDA was not valid there, and a governmental import license, which Cochlear was waiting for, had to be obtained. The Japanese trials cost $1.5 million. In order to get the import license, Cochlear had to provide implants free of charge.

The company reached financial breakeven for the first time in 1986. Beginning in 1987 profits improved steadily, and in 1988 Cochlear became a cash-generating unit for the parent company. In 1987, R&D expenditure increased significantly while operating expenses decreased as a percentage of sales. During this time, the sales and promotion expenses remained constant at 80% of general and administration expenses. The worldwide promotion budget was steady at half a million dollars a year.

The cost of goods was maintained at a relatively low level in order to fund research and clinical support. Sales-force expenses were about 25% of the sales budget. The policy of allocating 15% of sales revenue to R&D was exceeded in 1989 due to the urgency of bringing out a new speech processor and a fall in anticipated sales volume. As a guideline, the company tried to spend 15% of its R&D budget on applications research for other developments. Any additional R&D expense had to be cleared by Nucleus, which insisted on a 20% return for all investments. (Refer to Exhibit 1 for unit sales and financial data.)

On Deafness and Being Deaf

There were two categories of deaf people, about equal in size: "postlingually" deaf (deaf as a result of illness, age, or accident after having learned to hear) and "pre-lingually" deaf (deaf at birth). This hearing-impaired market was comprised of the *profoundly deaf* and the *severely deaf.*

Severely deaf people could be helped, to a greater or lesser extent, by a hearing aid which amplified sound. The customer bought this device, which cost approximately $1,000, after consulting a doctor or by going directly to a hearing aid retailer. These retailers, who were very commercialized, tended to regard Cochlear as a competitor and therefore a threat. Research showed that less than 20% of the people who needed a hearing aid actually bought one, and, of those who did, only 50% used it. The rest put it in a bottom drawer either because it "failed to help," or because it "looked bad" and "made their handicap too evident."

People whose hearing problems were not being satisfactorily improved by hearing aids could have become a market for implants. But as long as they could hear at all, such consumers were usually not prepared to risk surgery. In addition, they tended to mix frequently with profoundly deaf people and thus had an important influence on them as well as in the political arena.

Research was commissioned to assess the extent of the deaf phenomenon. It was estimated that approximately 500,000 *adults* worldwide were profoundly deaf, and that another 500,000 were severely deaf. Applying the rule of thumb for high-tech medical markets, it was assumed that the United States accounted for roughly half of this amount.

Ordinary devices such as hearing aids were useless for the profoundly deaf, as the inner ear had become so damaged that surgical intervention was necessary. In ascertaining the real size of the profoundly deaf market, Cochlear took into account psychological and medical factors. Many people who became deaf early in life did not consider themselves "sick" and therefore saw no need for surgery. People with heart problems had no choice; without surgery they could die. But, typically, deaf people would try to live with their deafness.

Many potential users were wary of the concept of an ear implantation, especially of having an electronic device inside the body. One piece of research showed that over 40% of potential users were against the idea of "having wires in their head," "were afraid of doctors and hospitals," or "saw the procedure as far too risky to justify."

Cochlear therefore estimated that only about 10% of the profoundly deaf, or about 50,000 patients worldwide, were possible implant candidates. Apart from this backlog, the data suggested that another 3,000 new cases occurred each year worldwide. In 1990 there were about 10,000 profoundly deaf *children* in the Western world, with approximately 1,200 new cases per year. As of that time, only 50 children had been recruited to the clinical trials in the United States. These trials showed good results, particularly for the postlingually deaf and for children implanted very early in life. While deaf children had to go to special schools, those who had had the Cochlear implant could often attend normal schools, although teachers had to be briefed and trained.

Generally, deaf people tended to be less well off economically than those with normal hearing; Cochlear assumed that about 10% were able to fund the implant themselves. Widely dispersed geographically, there were deaf people in all age categories, although 25% of the profoundly deaf were over 65 years of age.

Decision Making and Influences for Hearing Implants

The decision-making process for an ear implant could be complex, as there were many actors and influences well beyond just the end user. These included regulatory authorities, families, insurance companies, deaf associations and the media. Typically, patients would visit a doctor about a hearing problem. He would refer them to audiologists or ear-nose-and-throat (ENT) surgeons in hospital implant centers, where they would then be examined to see if they were suitable candidates for an implant operation.

The characteristics of patients and doctors differed in the United States, Europe, and Japan. American patients tended to be litigation prone and self-directed in their decisions. Although they were concerned about the implant's appearance, the prime consideration in their decison making was whether and how much it would improve their earning potential. American specialists characteristically offered patients options rather than dictating what had to be done. European deaf patients were more influenced by the surgeon, were not as litigation minded, and the quality of life was more pivotal in their decision making than were professional prospects. They were somewhat swayed by the look of the device, although less so than Americans. Since the main motive for Japanese patients was to cure the problem, they tended to do as their doctors told them.

To illustrate: An American doctor would typically say, "You've got three options—do nothing, have it although it's not great cosmetically, or wait till there's something better on the market." A European doctor's approach would have been more along the line, "I know it looks awful, but it's good for you." The typical Japanese patient would never have asked any questions.

Doctors in America tended to adopt new medical technologies before anyone else, and so, despite the stringency of the FDA, the United States was always considered the most important market. In fact, it was taken for granted that, in order to succeed worldwide, a firm first had to become established there.

Of the 7,000 American ENT specialists, who were predominantly self-employed or worked for free enterprise hospitals, 200 fitted Cochlear devices in the implant centers, of which 100 did so at least once a year. The doctor was strongly influenced by the need to make a profit, while the hospital hoped to at least break even. Audiologists, a profession unique to the United States, would diagnose hearing loss as well as fit hearing aids and speech processors. The doctor and audiologist worked closely with the patient before, during, and after the operation, diagnosing, fine-tuning the system, counseling, and training.

Private or government insurance covered most Americans, with 60 private health insurers providing coverage for about 75% of those insured; the government welfare programs, Medicare and Medicaid, insured the rest. These reimbursement schemes invariably fell a few thousand dollars short of the average $30,000 necessary for the product and procedure. It was then either left to the patient to find the money or for the hospital to agree to carry the shortfall. Of the 200 US hospitals that purchased the product, about half funded the shortfall either for reasons of prestige or for furthering medical research.

Because of the changes that were anticipated as a result of 1992, regulatory medical bodies similar to the FDA, but less well funded, were expected to emerge in Europe. After six years of lobbying by Cochlear, the UK's Department of Health and Social Security decided in 1990 to fund 100 units per year for three years. With Sweden beginning in 1983 and Norway in 1986, Scandinavia sponsored about 20 units per year. Workers' disability insurance covered relevant cases in Switzerland. Germany, which accounted for 60% of all European units sold, was the only country whose medical insurance system provided 100% coverage to anyone who needed the implant. In the remaining European countries, implants were funded by research and charity institutions and were motivated on a case-by-case basis.

Most European surgeons, typically affiliated with state-run universities and hospitals, were not as profit oriented as the American doctors. Although held in high esteem, they were subject to "hospital politics" and were more conservative and slower to adopt new innovations. The more adventurous, who had sufficient decision-making experience and were influential politically, tended to be in their 60s. Since audiology was not usually a separate specialization in Europe, all diagnosis and fitting was done by the surgeons themselves. Of the 2,500 European ENT specialists, 40 regularly implanted and fitted the device.

In Japan, surgeons also worked primarily at state-run hospitals, which were often poorly funded. These hospitals lacked audiologists, and only a small number of surgeons specialized in ear surgery. Ear surgeons were usually university professors with high status but conservative in outlook and slow to adopt innovations. The more aggressive doctors tended to be in their 60s, but those with political influence were the 80-year-olds. As of mid-1990, eight surgeons had been involved in clinical trials in Japan.

Deaf people's associations were organized on state, national, and worldwide levels, and although membership was limited to 10,000 to 20,000, their influence was widespread. In certain cases (in Germany, for instance), families were part of the lobby for government support. Some associations or charities, such as the Royal National Institute for the Deaf in the United Kingdom, were continuously lobbying on behalf of the deaf to obtain more funding from the national health system.

Encouragement from families and friends of potential patients to seek help and undergo surgery depended largely on whether those families and friends were also hearing impaired and part of the strong "nonhearing" communities which were growing worldwide.

The "deaf pride" movement had become a powerful force in the 80s with various factions. Extremists went so far as to suggest that Cochlear was experimenting with deaf people's brains. Mainstream members emphasized that deaf people constituted an ethnic community with their own languages and culture. Many were opposed to any pressure or opportunity for individuals to hear. They claimed it was better to have perfect communication with sign language than imperfect communication with an implant, which they said relegated them to the status of second-class citizens in the "speaking" world. There were as many sign languages as languages, and because of increased mobility and the rapid internationalization of deaf associations, a move was on to develop a global version.

During the 80s, public awareness about deaf pride had grown. The film *Children of a Lesser God* had raised public consciousness on an emotional level because it dealt with the philosophic issue as to whether profoundly deaf people should *want* to change. At that time, there was also widespread media coverage of the Washington-based Gallaudet University, exclusively for the deaf, where students could follow a full university program in sign language. Public interest in this institution was enhanced when students protested over the nomination of a non-deaf president, forcing him to resign.

The Cochlear Hearing Implant System

The Cochlear implant was named after the *cochlea,* a part of the inner ear about the size of a pea and shaped like a snail shell. *Cochlea,* in fact, is the Greek term for "snail shell," which is what the product implant resembled. (Refer to Exhibit 2 for an illustration of its technical characteristics.)

EXHIBIT 2

Technical characteristics

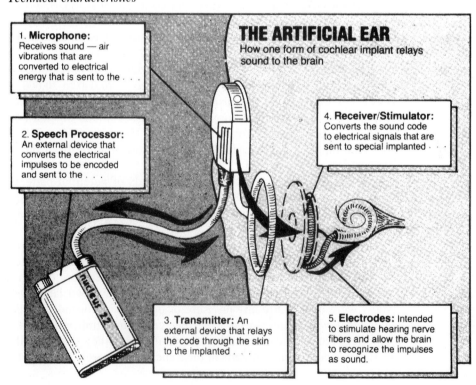

THE ARTIFICIAL EAR
How one form of cochlear implant relays sound to the brain

1. **Microphone:** Receives sound — air vibrations that are converted to electrical energy that is sent to the . . .

2. **Speech Processor:** An external device that converts the electrical impulses to be encoded and sent to the . . .

3. **Transmitter:** An external device that relays the code through the skin to the implanted . . .

4. **Receiver/Stimulator:** Converts the sound code to electrical signals that are sent to special implanted . . .

5. **Electrodes:** Intended to stimulate hearing nerve fibers and allow the brain to recognize the impulses as sound.

People could become profoundly deaf either at birth or later in life due to injury or an illness such as bacterial meningitis or mumps. The inner ear has a multitude of sensory cells, or hair cells, each one connected to the hearing nerve, which transmits sound in electrical messages to the brain. Profoundly deaf people lack or lose such sensory cells.

Hearing aids amplified sound. This instrument was only adequate for the "hard of hearing" or, in some cases, the severely deaf. The Cochlear "Bionic Ear" was for the profoundly deaf who could not hear at all. Microelectronic engineering had been adapted to the latest research on hearing physiology to produce a high-tech system which consisted of five parts, all of which were necessary to enable the deaf person to hear:

> The *directional microphone* (fastened onto the ear) picked up sounds and converted them into electrical energy impulses, which were sent to the speech processor.
>
> The *speech processor* (resembling a Walkman and worn externally on a belt, shoulder pouch, or in a pocket) was a computer that selected the most important electrical impulses needed for hearing noises and words, coded them, and sent them to the transmitter.
>
> The *transmitter* (placed behind the ear) relayed the coded noises and words through the skin to the receiver/stimulator in the implant.
>
> The *implant* itself (surgically placed in the bone behind the ear) consisted of a *receiver and electrodes*. The receiver, comprised of an integrated circuit with more than 1,000 transistors (similar to those in a pacemaker), converted the codes into electrical signals and sent them to the electrodes. The electrodes, which substituted for the damaged sensory "hair cells," electrically stimulated the hearing nerve fibres and thus allowed individuals to hear a variety of high and low sound pitches, which were subsequently transmitted to the brain to be deciphered. (See Exhibit 3 on the following page for illustrations of the product in use.)

Cochlear was the only company to have a 22-channel electrode. Unlike its earlier 1-channel unit, the multichannel device enabled more sounds to be heard and could be fine-tuned for a particular pitch and loudness by the surgeon, thereby catering to the individual hearing needs of each patient. But, no matter how much customizing was done, people who had become deaf could not hear in the same way as before the impairment. They would hear new sounds that had to be correlated with ones they had heard in predeaf years. This process was like learning to speak a foreign language, and it took, on average, three months of training and practice. For children, this process was even longer. It could take years for those who were born deaf to be able to hear and speak.

Despite Cochlear's technological superiority, it remained impossible to predict before a surgical operation how each individual patient would respond. Research showed that about 50% of patients who had the operation were eventually able to understand speech without lip-reading and could even use the telephone. The remaining 50% benefited as well, but to significantly varying degrees—from

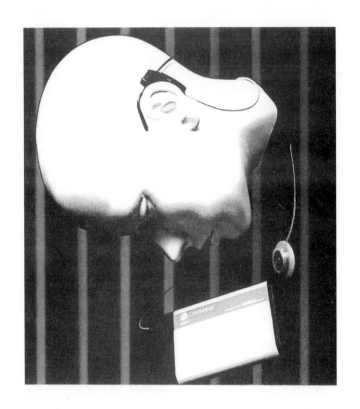

EXHIBIT 3
Illustrations of products in use

the worst cases, where only noises and warning signals were audible, to those who could follow speech only by lip-reading. The result depended on each individual—the state of the ear as well as the brain's learning capacity, neither of which could be assessed at the outset.

All R&D in Australia was done by 25 people. R&D was grouped into three areas: implant technology, electronic engineering, and mechanical design. Aware that many patients would be hesitant to undergo successive surgery because of improvements in technology, Cochlear's R&D team deliberately designed its first implant version in 1982 with much more capacity than the speech processor could then handle. The idea was to enable the patient's hearing ability to be improved at some future date, without having to undergo further surgery, by updating and modifying the speech processor.

Since then, most R&D efforts had gone into improving the speech processor, with rewarding results. In the first six months of 1990, the firm sold $4 million worth of upgrades and modifications to its existing customer base. Every new model or improvement of an existing model had to go through the FDA approval procedure. New-product developments could not be heavily publicized because users would put off any buying decision when they anticipated a model change, which caused serious inventory problems.

All manufacturing was done in Sydney. Using a manual process with extensive computer testing, the 50 highly skilled and specially trained plant workers produced approximately 1,400 systems annually, but there was capacity for twice that amount. The components used were very specialized and tended to come from single-goods suppliers worldwide. A constant stock was kept to eliminate delays in the event of problems in the suppliers' market and in order to get bulk prices.

There were two main areas in Cochlear's factory: the section where the implant was made under "clean room" procedures and the nonenvironmentally controlled area where the speech processor "externals" were made. For the implant, subassembled parts were first manufactured and then put together in small batches of 20 to 30 units. The entire cycle, which required using microscopes, would take at least three months. Discrete electrical components and custom integrated circuits were soldered onto circuit boards. The external parts of the system were made using standard assembly techniques similar to those used by any small-volume high-tech electronics equipment manufacturer. Staff turnover in the external area was very low, whereas in the implant section it was high.

Improving reliability of the units and the performance of the system were key priorities. It required ongoing upgrading of the electrode manufacturing methods. Although the staff generated many ideas, 99% of them could not be used because of the difficulties of working with an item as small as .6 mm in diameter.

Over the years, Cochlear looked at three other applications for its technology: implantable hearing aids, tinnitus, and functional electrical stimulation (FES). In 1986 it seemed that hearing aids had considerable synergy with its product. However, after having spent $1 million up to 1989, the company decided that the technology, marketing, manufacturing, and profit margin formula were too different to warrant further investment. In 1989, Cochlear started work on the treatment of tinnitus ("ringing in the ears" syndrome), a condition experienced by 1 in 7 people. By mid-1990, half a million dollars had been spent. A large investment would have been necessary to perfect an FES device, an implant that electronically stimulated the nerves of paraplegics. Cochlear carried out some R&D but decided, after losing a tender to supply the US Department of Veterans Affairs, to give the FES only low-level research support.

Overview of Cochlear's Competitive Position

The American multinational 3M had entered the market at approximately the same time as Cochlear, with a lower technology product that the company believed would yield a similar hearing benefit. As 3M's price was one-third lower than Cochlear's, 3M initially dominated the market. Once Cochlear entered, however, the US firm gradually lost market share and faded from the scene late in 1989.

Although there were five major players in the worldwide market, Cochlear was the only one with FDA approval. The others—Hochmair, Hortmann, Symbion, and Minimed—were all developing similar devices and intended to get the required approval. Because some European doctors protested that Cochlear was making too much money, one or two university medical schools in Europe, including the University College of London, developed their own low-budget version of the implant. Although such hearing systems, distributed only through the universities' clinics, were only 1/10 the price of Cochlear's device, they were not regarded as sufficiently reliable to pose a serious competitive problem.

While Cochlear was confident—given its 3,500 satisfied patients worldwide and the FDA stamp—that it had a clear competitive advantage, the company constantly monitored the competitive strength of the main manufacturers, using four criteria: (1) organization, size, and professionalism; (2) technology; (3) clinical benefit and effectiveness; and (4) safety.

Neither the Hochmairs, an Austrian team, nor Hortmann of Germany were considered serious opponents by Cochlear, given their lag in the important categories of clinical benefit, effectiveness, and safety. However, the two American firms, Symbion and Minimed, were both perceived as potential threats to future sales.

Symbion, a firm associated with the University of Utah, was in the clinical trial stage. It had managed to produce a unit which, while using a much lower level of implant technology, nonetheless achieved the same hearing performance, and at the same price as Cochlear's device. Symbion's accomplishment was due to putting considerably more effort into the speech processor than into the implant. A plug which connected the microphone headset to the implant by penetrating the skin created both an aesthetic and a safety disadvantage as the passageway could permit infection to enter the inner ear and the brain. It was considered a flexible product, however, because any kind of stimulation could be used, whereas the Cochlear device only allowed radio wave transmission.

EXHIBIT 4

Market share and 1990 projections

% Market share

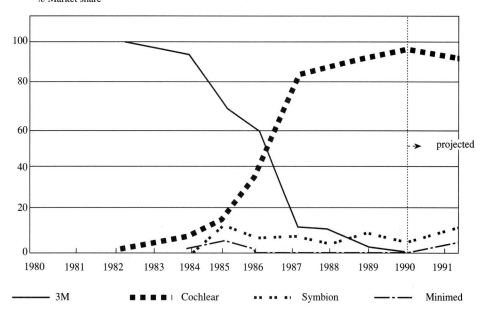

Affiliated with the well-known University of California at San Francisco medical school, Minimed began its research in 1966. Although its device had only 16 channels, Minimed's performance could potentially be as good as Cochlear's due to its capacity to better represent certain nonspeech sounds. Because of problems with its microchip technology, the company had not yet been able to begin clinical trials because it first needed to receive FDA approval and medical coverage. There were rumours that the problem would soon be solved and by 1991 Minimed would be making clinical trials.

The company annually analyzed market share. With doctors eager for more players to enter the field, Cochlear had, in making its projections for 1990 and 1991, factored in the entry of Minimed and a growth in market share for Symbion. (Refer to Exhibit 4 for market shares from 1982 to 1989 and projections for 1990 and 1991.)

Cochlear's Marketing Strategy

Cochlear treated the ear implant market as a single one. The logic was that the medical profession and deaf associations were linked internationally through medical conferences and medical journals.

The product was identical worldwide. All units and promotional material clearly identified the Cochlear brand name and logo, and the 22-channel feature was used extensively to differentiate the product as the one with maximum clinical benefits.

Cochlear decided early on that it could not devote equal time and resources to both aesthethics and performance. Convinced that the latter would be the more important criterion for the market, the company decided to position itself as the most technologically sophisticated and clinically superior.

In early 1990, market research confirmed what top management had suspected: performance was more important than either price or appearance. This survey, which was intended to gain a better understanding of the needs and wants of the implant market, was conducted among 14 Cochlear implant patients, 11 audiologists, a surgeon, and the director of an implant center in one of the US hospitals that fitted Cochlear devices. The results revealed that implant patients considered performance to be the most important factor. In fact, on a scale of 1 to 10, performance was ranked 8 out of 10, price 5, and appearance 3.

These people were extremely happy to be able to hear and, if given a choice, would have opted for an implant system that allowed them to hear speech, music, and environmental sounds over one where the external units were either cordless or worn behind the ear but offered lower performance. Nevertheless, the patients did acknowledge that a segment of the deaf market would consider a Cochlear implant if a behind-the-ear system became available and would probably accept a lower performance level to get a device so small and unobtrusive.

Cochlear had given some thought to the cosmetic appeal of its external units, particularly the speech processor. Initially, it had been made from plastic pipe, then from stainless steel, and, in September 1989, a more contemporary design was developed using molded plastic.

For three months after surgery, patients had to return to the hospital or the doctor for training; checkups were then repeated annually. The nonusage rate of all implant patients worldwide was 1%. For the very few patients who experienced a problem with their unit, there were doctors trained by Cochlear to troubleshoot. If a unit proved faulty, it was sent back to the regional office for repair. While the implant was guaranteed for five years, it was expected to last a lifetime. The speech processor had an average breakdown time of three years, and each system had a three-year warranty. Hospitals had to maintain adequate supplies of spare units at all times to avoid any risk that the patient could be incapacitated due to a faulty product.

A premium price strategy was deliberately used and strictly maintained in order to highlight the Cochlear system's unique technology. The average $30,000 cost to patients included the Cochlear system as well as all hospital and surgical expenses. On average, the Cochlear device was priced at $17,000 for both adults and children, although it was slightly more in Europe and even higher in Japan. The figure was three times the price of the 3M model when it had been on the market. Symbion's price was equal to Cochlear's, and it was rumoured that Minimed would enter clinical trials at the same price level. Hochmair and Hortmann were priced in the middle range.

Cochlear distributed its products directly in three regions—Denver, Basel, and Tokyo—each one headed by its own CEO reporting to the Sydney head office. The salespeople, clinically trained audiologists and engineers, called on doctors and hospitals. They were supported by a team of clinical experts who advised, counseled, and handled any problems that arose, using clinical support centers in each region. These support centers would also work with patients who wanted an implant but were unsure how to handle the finances or apply for insurance. Every office also maintained a technical service team, reimbursement specialists, and two to three marketing people to organize conferences, handle PR, and prepare brochures.

In the United States, some private audiologists who had fitted and tested hearing devices would leave their own practices and, on a part-commission basis to help cope with the workload, sell Cochlear implants. Some extra audiologists in hospitals were funded by Cochlear. In Europe, where the ENT surgeon was also the audiologist, the Basel-based European headquarters oversaw all sales except for the United Kingdom, Scandinavia, and Israel, which were handled in London. Any direct selling by doctors would have been regarded as unethical in Europe. In Germany, Cochlear managed to persuade one of the largest hearing aid retailers to stock its cables and spare batteries.

Upgraded units became an important part of Cochlear's marketing activities. The $4 million in sales in 1990 was achieved by reaching users through doctors and offering a special reduction in price (from $6,000 to $4,000) if a decision were made by a particular date. The upgrade was introduced and launched at a promotional event hosted on a riverboat. This event was followed by direct mail and by papers presented at conferences by doctors who had experienced improved performance during clinical trials. Most patients paid for their own new units in the United States because the insurance companies refused to pay. In Europe, they were funded by the national health systems.

Publicity was aimed at patients and doctors. Initially, the novelty of the implant innovation made it relatively easy to get media attention, and, on the whole, newspapers, radio, magazines, and TV provided reasonable coverage, particularly of successful cases. Although no formal market research had been done, the Cochlear top team estimated that company awareness worldwide was 70–80% among ENT surgeons and around 5% among potential users.

The company encouraged medical and scientific journal articles about its product and occasionally paid doctors' travel expenses when they delivered papers at conferences. The system was exhibited at major worldwide medical conferences, while local community forums and meetings with education departments and school authorities were routinely organized. Because it could be considered unethical to directly approach such supporting charities as the Rotary Club, Cochlear only provided information when needed.

Promotional material was distributed to doctors, hospitals, audiologists, and hearing aid retailers to enable them to respond to queries. Postoperative instructional booklets were provided for patients, and a newsletter was sent out from each sales office to doctors, to the existing patient base, as well as to local family self-help events. (See Exhibit 5 on the following page for examples of promotional material.) Lectures were given to any deaf association on request, and papers were presented at conferences on deafness whenever possible. Inevitably, though, these activities engendered a certain amount of antagonism, such as walkouts or other forms of protest from "deaf pride" members in the audience.

EXHIBIT 5

Examples of promotional material

A.

B.

A. Information newsletter sent to hospitals, doctors, and audiologists.
B. Brochure for audiologists, doctors, and children and their families—sent during clinical trials.

Mike Hirshorn continued talking. "The FDA is on the verge of giving us the go-ahead for children. That's a market worth another 10,000 units, provided we do the job right. Parents will do anything to help their children, so I expect that market to be much easier and quicker to penetrate than it was for adults."

He stood up and walked to the window, watching the last rays of sunshine disappearing over the horizon. "For a start, we could increase our sales force. That way, we could break into new territories and increase the call rates with existing doctors."

"What about the additional costs?" Brigette inquired.

"It's not a big deal," Mike answered. "Even if we doubled our sales force worldwide, we would only have to sell 15% more units. The Sydney factory can easily handle the extra volumes."

"We could, of course, use the capacity to make a cheaper second model instead," Dennis Wheeler suddenly suggested. "Maybe then we could get into some new countries like Turkey, Greece, the Middle East, and Southeast Asia.

Come to think of it, that could also push up our numbers in the States and maybe even in Europe.''

"That would ruin our image," Brigette responded. "If we want to keep our position, we have to stick to making the highest performance quality even if it means raising our price. Isn't there a section of the US market that could take a price hike, Dennis?"

"Yeah, maybe 10%, max 20%, but of the privately insured market," Dennis replied hesitantly. "Don't forget, though, that this may be exactly what Symbion and Minimed are waiting for—to grab market share."

Mike listened carefully. He knew that he would soon have to recommend to his board ways to maintain profitability despite sagging sales and more threatening competition. He agreed that Cochlear's future hope was its hearing technology. But, somehow the company had to get that technology used and appreciated.

THE PROCTER & GAMBLE COMPANY

Lenor Refill Package

In July 1987, Kathy Stadler, assistant brand manager for Lenor—Procter & Gamble GmbH's (P&G Germany) profitable fabric softener brand—was preparing for an upper-level management meeting to discuss a proposal for the national launch of a Lenor refill package. The refill package represented an innovative solution to West Germany's growing environmental concerns by promising to reduce by 85% the packaging materials used in Lenor's standard plastic container. Management hoped that this line extension would help stem Lenor's eroding sales volume and market share.

Stadler recalled a memo written two years earlier by Rolf Kunisch, the general manager for P&G Germany, in which he advocated ''moving the company's attitudes from defensive thinking in environmental terms toward proactive and successful approaches.'' While Stadler felt that the Lenor refill package met this mandate, she was uncertain about the consumer response. Stadler knew that the refill package would not address many German consumers' concerns that fabric softeners were ''superfluous'' products. A ''biodegradable'' version of Lenor still needed three years of development. The refill package seemed to offer an interim response to consumers. Would the public hail it as an attempt to protect the environment? Or would they view it as an effort to avoid addressing the public's underlying concern with Lenor's product formula?

Stadler's brand manager, Leonard Phillippe, felt that an aggressive promotion of an existing concentrated formula of Lenor, which used less packaging materials than the more popular fully diluted version, would be less risky than the refill package introduction. Stadler, however, believed that this strategy would not stem Lenor's eroding sales volume. Nevertheless, she knew that both options would be hotly debated at the forthcoming meeting with Rolf Kunisch.

This case was prepared by Julie L. Yao, MBA '91, under the direction of Professors John A. Quelch and Minette E. Drumwright. Copyright © 1991 by the President and Fellows of Harvard College. Harvard Business School case 592-016 (Revised 1993).

The Procter & Gamble Company

In 1987,[1] the Procter & Gamble Company (P&G), a leading consumer products company, had more than $13.7 billion in assets, generated $17 billion in worldwide revenues, and delivered $617 million in pretax earnings. P&G sold products in 125 countries, marketing more than 100 brands of laundry, household cleaning, personal care, food, and beverage products. International operations, which included Europe, South America, and Asia, accounted for over 30% of P&G's 1987 sales and earnings. In 1987, international sales grew 38%, almost five times as much as US domestic sales.

P&G had a long-standing reputation for superior products, marketing expertise, talented employees, conservative management, and high integrity in its business dealings. A strong corporate culture pervaded the firm. The 1987 annual report stated the company's philosophy as follows:

> We will provide products of superior quality and value that best fill the needs of the world's consumers. We will achieve that purpose through an organization and a working environment which attracts the finest people; fully develops and challenges our individual talents; encourages our free and spirited collaboration to drive the business ahead; and maintains the Company's historic principles of integrity and doing the right thing. Through the successful pursuit of our commitment, we expect our brands to achieve leadership share and profit positions and that, as a result, our business, our people, our shareholders, and the communities in which we live and work, will prosper.

To develop these superior products, P&G relied on continual product development. In 1987, more than 3.3% of its revenues were spent on research. In addition, P&G believed in extensive product and market testing. P&G frequently took two to three years to test a new product and its marketing strategy before a major launch.

Procter & Gamble GmbH

Procter & Gamble GmbH was established in 1960 following the acquisition of a local detergent manufacturer. By 1987, P&G Germany generated DM 1,037 million in revenues.[2] P&G Germany sold more than 30 brands, including Ariel, a top-selling detergent, and Lenor, West Germany's leading fabric softener. Seventy-seven percent of its revenues and 60% of its earning came from the Laundry and Cleaning Division, which included detergents, cleaners, and fabric softener.

P&G Germany's 6,700-person subsidiary comprised four divisions: Laundry and Cleaning, Paper, Beverages, and Health and Beauty Care. Each division had Sales, Finance, Manufacturing, and Product Development organizations. Every major P&G Germany product also had its own brand management team, which

---

[1] P&G operated on a July 1 to June 30 fiscal year basis; at the time of this case, P&G had just entered its 1988 fiscal year. Unless otherwise specified, all P&G company data are on a fiscal year basis.

[2] One US dollar was equivalent to 1.9 deutsche marks (DM).

developed and implemented the brand's marketing strategy against sales and profit targets approved by top management. A brand team generally consisted of a brand manager, an assistant brand manager, and one or two brand assistants, who all worked closely with the division's other departments as well as with staff groups specializing in advertising services, management information systems, and personnel.

A 320-person sales force marketed P&G Germany products to the retail trade. Key account managers called on the headquarters of the large retail grocery chains year-round, while field salespeople serviced both independent stores as well as chain outlets.

P&G Germany manufactured most of its products locally. While some production was outsourced, P&G Germany generally preferred to manufacture its own products to ensure the highest level of quality control.

The Fabric Softener Industry

Fabric softener products first appeared during the 1950s to combat the perceived harsh effects of detergents; when added to the wash, fabric softener produced soft, scented, and static-free clothes. It was particularly popular in Europe, where hard-water washing conditions were common. In 1987, consumers could purchase fabric softener in one of the three forms: a diluted liquid; a concentrated liquid, three times stronger than the dilute; or woven sheets that were used during machine drying. The regular user's average purchase cycle was two months. Dosage varied according to the type and volume of laundry, but an average washload required 100 ml of dilute or 35 ml of concentrate.

Fabric softener liquids combined 5% softening ingredients, called cationic tensides, with 95% water. Fabric softener concentrates included 15% softening ingredients. Fabric softeners were packaged in hard, high-density polyethylene plastic containers. Users added liquid fabric softener during a washing machine's wash cycle or poured it into a convenient special dispenser built into the machine before the start of the wash.

Like many other household chemical products, fabric softeners, with 2% inert nonbiodegradable ingredients, were considered by some environmentally conscious consumers to be unnecessary. An increasing number of consumers believed that a buildup of nonbiodegradable chemicals could affect their water supply and that the benefit delivered by fabric softeners was superfluous. P&G and its competitors were working on the development of totally biodegradable fabric softeners, but it was thought unlikely that such products would be brought to market before 1991.

Environmental Concern

During the 1980s, public anxiety about environmental problems escalated in Europe. A 1986 survey of 11,800 Western European consumers revealed that 72% were "somewhat" or "very" concerned about ecological problems such as acid rain, toxic waste, landfill capacity, and the greenhouse effect. The media attributed these growing concerns to Europe's high population density, its centuries-old exploitation of natural resources, and the impact on public awareness of the Chernobyl nuclear power plant accident in the former Soviet Union.[3]

West German attitudes were consistently "greener" than those of neighboring countries. In 1987, an opinion poll entitled "Sorrows of the Nation" found that 53% of West Germans surveyed were concerned with the protection of the environment, up from 16% four years earlier. Concern for the environment ranked as their second most common concern, behind unemployment. Environmental issues also affected the German political arena, as evidenced by the rising popularity of the proenvironment Green Party.

A 1987 opinion poll showed that 47% of German households agreed that they used fewer environmentally problematic goods than previously, versus 21% who agreed with the same statement in 1985. Both consumer awareness of environmental issues and the percentage of consumers claiming a willingness to pay more for environmentally friendly packaging had increased. In practice, however, consumers traded off price against environmental safety; there was a limit to the price premium they were prepared to pay. In addition, many consumers indicated that they were not willing to give up product quality for the environment. Nevertheless, environmentally uncontroversial products such as phosphate-free detergents had become increasingly popular.

In 1984, a West German federal government agency publicly denounced allegedly environmentally harmful products, including P&G Germany's laundry booster, Top Job. A consumer boycott to force the removal of these from the market caused Top Job's sales volume to drop by 50% in the following year. In 1986, the government passed the Waste Avoidance, Utilization, and Disposal Act, which gave authorities the power to restrict or even ban materials with problematic toxicity or waste volume.

The West German government also supported a nationwide eco-labeling initiative, called the Blue Angel program, to promote environmentally compatible products through labeling. By 1987, more than 2,000 products in 50 categories bore the Blue Angel seal; fabric softener products had never qualified. By 1987, the Blue Angel seal was recognized by 80% of West German consumers.[4] Industry experts believed that products "blessed" with the Blue Angel seal enjoyed increased sales of up to 10%.

Though public and media attention centered more on a product's contents and less on its packaging, the issue of solid waste reduction was rapidly capturing the German public's attention. Land was scarce; West Germany burned 34% of its trash, compared to only 3% in the United States. In some German communities, there was a social stigma associated with a household's use of larger trash bins. About 20% of municipalities charged citizens for garbage collection based on

---

[3] A. Hussein, *Eco-labels: Product Management in a Greener Europe,* Environmental Data Services, Ltd., Finsbury Business Center, p. 53.

[4] Lori K. Carswell, *Environmental Labeling in the United States Background Research, Issues and Recommendations,* Draft Report, Applied Decision Analysis, 1989, p. 10.

volume. By 1985, West Germans recycled more than one-third of their paper, glass and aluminum waste; however, plastic recycling was limited. Focus group research indicated consumers would be receptive to products with reduced packaging.

Market Size and Trends

The average West German homemaker used eight different products, such as bleach and fabric softener, for washing and cleaning. The German fabric softener consumer enjoyed "fresh" clothes, which combined the characteristics of a soft touch, "clean" smell, and bright appearance. A 1986 P&G Germany market research study concluded that fabric softener usage and dosage were relatively uniform across all age groups, irrespective of brand. Fabric softener users, however, spent more effort on pretreating and prewashing their laundry than nonusers.

In 1987, West Germany was the largest fabric softener market in Europe, with retail sales totaling DM 346 million ($182 million), compared with almost $1 billion in the US market, with a population four times West Germany's. Although the value of retail sales had increased due to price rises, market volume had fallen from a peak of 18,200 MSUs in 1983 to 16,700 MSUs in 1987.[5] Forecasters predicted further volume decreases of 1% to 3% per year.

Research had shown that this decline was attributed to a shrinking base of fabric softener users. Table A shows usage trends from periodic diary studies:[6]

TABLE A   **Fabric Softener Usage Trends (Percentage Surveyed)**

	1982	1984	1986
Fabric softener users	89%	84%	72%
Total wash loads softened*	72	67	57
Wash loads softened among users†	75	73	74

* Percentage of all wash loads recorded in diary study that had fabric softener added.
† Among fabric softener users, average percentage of wash loads per user that had fabric softener added.

Results from a 1986 telephone survey found that many consumers had ceased using fabric softener due to environmental concerns highlighted by the news media. Research revealed that West German consumers were concerned about

---

[5] An MSU, or thousand statistical units, was a standardized P&G measure that permitted comparison of products on the basis of an equal number of uses. Consequently, a 1-liter bottle of 4:1 Lenor concentrate and a 4-liter bottle of Lenor dilute were equivalent on an MSU basis because both gave the consumer the same number of uses. Costs and unit volumes are presented per SU (abbreviation for statistical unit) for comparison purposes.

[6] Each participant was asked to keep a diary of his or her usage habits during a two-week time period, from which results were tabulated.

EXHIBIT 1   **Selected Results from Fabric Softener Usage Monitoring Studies**

	June 1985	*February 1986*
Percentage of Respondents Who Were:		
Fabric softener users*	60.0%	60.0%
Nonusers	40.0	40.0
Homemakers Aware That Fabric Softener Allegedly Harms the Environment		
Fabric softener users	55.0%	74.0%
Nonusers	66.0	70.0
Fabric Softener Users Claiming to:†		
Use less fabric softener per load	18.0%	24.0%
Soften fewer loads	16.0	14.0
Total (unduplicated)	26.0	27.0
Reasons Nonusers Never Used/Stopped Using Fabric Softener		
Environmental reasons	42.0%	48.0%
Softness dissatisfaction	26.0	13.0
Effects on skin	29.0	23.0
Drying on clothesline	20.0	29.0

* Fabric softener users had used the product at least once in the previous three months before the interview; nonusers had not.
† Seventy-two percent of the users who used less softener or softened fewer loads claimed to be doing so for environmental reasons.

the environmental effects of using supplementary household products such as fabric softener than consumers in other West European countries. Exhibit 1 presents key results from this study.

Competition

In 1987, four competitors sold 78% of the volume in the West German fabric softener market.[7] P&G Germany's Lenor led the market with a 37% volume share, followed by Colgate-Palmolive's Softlan (20%), Unilever's Kuschelweich (Snuggle) (13%), and Henkel's Vernel (8%). General and private-label brands accounted for the remaining 22% of the market.

All four multinationals sold their fabric softener brands throughout Western Europe. Each competitor promoted similar product benefits: freshness, softness, ease of ironing, and elimination of static cling. Lenor's distinctive, 4-liter blue container appeared in the mid-1970s and quickly became the standard package size and shape imitated by competitors. By 1987, all brands were sold in both diluted and concentrated formulas, in 4-liter and 1-liter sizes, respectively. In addition, in 1987 Henkel and P&G introduced dryer sheets, which accounted for less than 1% of market volume. All brands were broadly distributed throughout the retail trade.

---

[7] All market share figures were based on statistical unit (MSUs) volume.

Vernel followed a low-budget advertising strategy. Softlan, on the other hand, was aggressively advertised through the media. Kuschelweich gained high consumer awareness through its "stuffed bear" advertising mascot. Lenor emphasized its "Aprilfrisch" scent. In newspaper and handbill copy, Lenor led in share of fabric softener features in retail newspaper ads and handbills (42% for May/June 1987), followed by Softlan (21%), Kuschelweich (15%), and Vernel (5%).[8]

The materials cost for each brand varied due to different chemical formulations. Table B shows selected relative costs and pricing for the top four brands of diluted fabric softener in 1987:

TABLE B   **1987 Indexed Costs and Prices for Leading German Fabric Softener Brands**

	P&G	*Colgate*	*Lever*	*Henkel*
Brand name	Lenor	Softlan	Kuschelweich	Vernel
Packaging	100	106	106	106
Chemicals	100	85	93	92
Media expenses	100	136	85	40
Total costs	100	105	94	82
Recommended retail price	100	87	88	85

NOTE: The index is based on a 4-liter package of dilute.

Consumers perceived little differentiation among fabric softener brands except on the basis of price and scent. Consequently, fabric softener brands were frequently involved in price and promotion wars to defend or capture market share, which depressed manufacturer and trade margins. For example, the average profit margin realized by retailers on Lenor declined from 12.7% in 1984 to 2.5% in 1986.

Henkel, a prominent German household products company with 1987 sales of DM 9.9 billion, rapidly imitated innovative product ideas and marketed them globally. Henkel also strongly emphasized environmental protection, spending nearly 25% of its DM 285 million research budget on this issue in 1987. Colgate-Palmolive (DM 10.6 billion in 1987 sales) and Unilever (DM 57 billion) devoted less than 2% of their revenues to R&D.

In early 1987, Henkel acquired Lesieur-Cotelle SA, a French detergent manufacturer that produced Minidou, a fabric softener concentrate that since the early 1980s had been sold in 250-ml flat plastic pouches. Minidou users emptied the pouch's contents into any 1-liter container and then diluted the concentrate with water. Some P&G executives suspected that Henkel might try either to extend the successful Minidou concept, which had captured 29% of the French market by

---

[8] Feature share, calculated from a survey of 200 West German newspapers and 2,000 grocery handbills, represented the percentage of times a particular brand was featured in retail trade promotions for fabric softeners.

1987, to other markets or to license the use of the technology to Colgate-Palmolive, which was pursuing lower-cost packaging alternatives.

Distribution

Fabric softener was sold through West Germany's highly concentrated retail market; five major chains together controlled more than 75% of total grocery sales (DM 127 billion in 1987). Manufacturers sold their products through several classes of trade: mass merchandisers (more than 53,800 sq. ft. in size), hypermarkets (16,000–53,800 sq. ft.), supermarkets (8,600–16,100 sq. ft.), convenience stores (under 8,600 sq. ft.), and discounters (various sizes). West German consumers shopped for fabric softener in all types of stores, although it was less likely than other grocery items to be purchased in convenience stores.

Fierce competition meant that grocery retailers achieved total after-tax profit margins of only 1% to 1.5%. Because they focused increasingly on the direct product profitability (DPP) of their stock per linear foot of shelf space, retailers were especially keen on high-margin, space-efficient products with rapid turnover. The emphasis placed on DPP resulted in a selective product assortment; only the large mass merchandisers and hypermarkets maintained a complete selection of brands and package sizes for any product category. Supermarkets kept a full range of brand names, but with limited size selection, whereas convenience stores and discounters sold only one or two brands. All classes of trade, except for convenience stores, also sold their own private-label brands in many high-turnover categories.

Every August, manufacturer account representatives negotiated with each major retailer the following year's major target purchase levels, volume discounts, and new-product listing agreements. Manufacturers needed a retailer's listing for each new product, even for product line extensions; individual retail stores could purchase products only from their chain headquarters' approved list. Although manufacturers could introduce new products throughout the year, listing agreements were easier to obtain during the August meetings. Approved products generally reached store shelves within two weeks of an order being placed. In addition to account representatives, each manufacturer also had field salespeople who serviced individual stores, both chain-owned and independents, by taking stock orders, suggesting shelf arrangements, and implementing local sales promotions.

To minimize handling and reshelving costs, many retail stores sought to display products in their original shipping cartons and stressed convenient packaging to the manufacturers. A set of product packaging guidelines, known as the ''ten commandments,'' was developed by a retail trade association for manufacturers. These guidelines defined the dimensions, weight, and appearance of the shipping cartons that retailers preferred. Few products met all 10 guidelines.

Advertising and Promotion

In 1987, most television advertising reached German consumers via the two state-run national channels. Each September, manufacturers reapplied for time slots;

the television stations then allocated specific commercial spots to each firm for the upcoming year. P&G Germany would then allocate the time slots it had been granted among its brands.

Regulations limited the consumer promotions that West German manufacturers could use. Coupons and refund offers were not permitted; the value of on-pack and in-pack premiums (gifts attached to or included in product packages) could not exceed DM 0.30 in value. Bonus packs, which gave consumers extra volume of product for the same price, were difficult to implement on liquid products such as Lenor. Price packs (products with a lower-than-normal recommended retail price preprinted on the package) were allowed but were rarely used due to trade opposition. Some manufacturers did run sweepstakes and contests, although they were tightly regulated by government agencies.

Volume discounts and trade promotion allowances for each product were traditionally negotiated with individual retailers. P&G Germany instituted account-specific promotion plans based on total sales volume rather than the sales of each brand. This approach was considered more effective in building trade relationships because it gave retailers more flexibility in what they promoted.

Lenor Fabric Softener

Lenor, launched in West Germany in 1963, was the first nationally marketed brand of fabric softener. By 1987, Lenor had achieved 98% store penetration. More than half of Lenor's total volume was sold through mass merchandisers, as indicated in Exhibit 2. Sales revenue and unit volume in 1987 were DM 180 million and 6,200 MSUs, respectively.

At first, Lenor was sold as a specialty item in small 500 ml containers, at a price nearly 10 times higher than the 1987 inflation-adjusted price for the same quantity. In 1965, P&G Germany broadened Lenor's appeal by lowering its price

Exhibit 2 Lenor Sales Volume by Store Type in 1987

Store Type (by Size)	Number of Stores	Percent of Stores	Grocery Market Turnover* (Billion DM)	Percent of Market Turnover	Lenor Volume Breakdown†	
					4-Liter Dilute	1-Liter Concentrate
Mass merchandisers	412	0.6%	17.2	13.6%	62.0%	36.0%
Hypermarkets	1,195	1.6	17.2	13.6	20.0	20.0
Supermarkets	2,542	3.5	18.6	14.7	9.0	13.0
Convenience stores	64,409	88.2	59.9	47.3	6.0	16.0
Discounters	4,442	6.1	13.8	10.9	3.0	14.0
Total	73,000	100.0%	126.7	100.0%	100.0%	100.0%

* Market turnover is defined as sales volume times retail value. 1.9 DM = $1
† Percentages are based on statistical unit volume for the first six months of 1987.

and developing a highly successful advertising campaign that remained in use for the following 18 years.

The 1-liter Lenor concentrate (Lenor CT) joined Lenor dilute on retail shelves in 1983. By 1987, 30% of Lenor's volume was sold in this 3:1 concentrated form. The package cap doubled as a measuring cup, which the consumer could use to determine how much liquid to add, in undiluted form, to the wash. Brand management believed that some fabric softener users regarded the concentrate's performance as inferior to the dilute's, although laboratory tests demonstrated no difference in efficacy. These users questioned whether "so little could perform as well." One P&G executive explained, "Although the concentrate is less awkward to carry home from the store, many consumers are wedded to the 4-liter package." Advertising for Lenor concentrate stressed the number of wash loads that could be softened with the contents of the small 1-liter package. Dryer sheets, introduced in the spring of 1987, sold to a limited market (0.4% of Lenor's 1987 sales volume) because 75% of West German households line-dried their laundry rather than using electric clothes dryers.

P&G Germany promoted Lenor heavily to the retail trade and consumers, spending 25% of the product's yearly manufacturer's sales on television and radio advertising, consumer promotions, trade promotions, and indirect brand support.[9] Table C indicates the percentage breakdowns of Lenor's advertising and promotion expenses for 1986 and 1987:

TABLE C Percentage Breakdown of Advertising and Sales Budget

	Dilute 1986	Dilute 1987	CT 1986	CT 1987
Media	20%	23%	20%	21%
Consumer promotion	4	1	1	1
Trade promotion	74	74	77	75
Indirect brand support	2	2	2	2
Total	100%	100%	100%	100%

Approximately 30% of the brand's total marketing budget was allocated to the concentrate.

In 1987, liquid Lenor was available in the package sizes and prices shown in Exhibit 3 on the following page. Recommended retail prices were at least 10% higher than those of its competitors. However, Lenor was a popular loss leader among retailers.[10] Ninety percent of Lenor dilute volume and 25% of concentrate volume were sold by retailers at feature prices in 1987.

---

[9] Indirect brand support included development costs for advertisements and commercials, production expenses associated with store displays, and other expenses incurred for consumer and trade promotions.

[10] Loss leaders (products retailers sold at prices below cost to attract consumers) were usually popular brands in frequently purchased product categories.

EXHIBIT 3 **Lenor Liquid Package Sizes and Prices, 1987**

Formulation	Size	Number of Units per Case	Number of Stat. Units per Case*	Suggested Retail Price (DM)	Average Feature Price (DM)	Suggested Retail Price Per SU (DM)	Average Feature Price Per SU (DM)	Percent of Lenor Sales Volume
Dilute	4 Liters	4	0.68	5.53	4.64	32.53	27.29	70%
Concentrate (3:1)	1 Liter	16	2.01	4.75	4.08	37.81	32.48	30%

* Statistical Units (SUs) convert different sizes and products to an equivalent use basis. Thus, two items with the same number of SU will deliver an equivalent number of uses to the consumer.

Between 1984 and 1986, Lenor's sales volume had declined by 7.5% annually, with an actual loss of more than 1,000 MSUs. Sales volume in 1988 was predicted to decline similarly if nothing was done to revive the brand. Brand management attributed this loss to increasingly aggressive competitive price promotion, which eroded Lenor's market share, and to a shrinking market due to unfavorable consumer sentiment. Lenor brand management had to develop a marketing strategy that would combat Lenor's eroding sales and market share in the face of consumers' increasing environmental concerns.

Lenor's Strategic Options

Stadler reviewed the strategic options her brand management team had developed in the last few months.

Relaunch the 3:1 Concentrate

One option explored was the aggressive relaunch of Lenor concentrate, promoting waste reduction benefits similar to those of a refill package. The 1-liter concentrate used approximately 45% less packaging materials than the 4-liter bottle on an equivalent use basis. Lenor's 1988 advertising and promotion budget (DM 45.2 million) could be increased by DM 2.9 million and be reallocated so that 40% would be spent on the dilute and 60% on the concentrate. Brand management estimated that this change would increase the concentrate's sales by 780 MSUs, 400 MSUs of which would result from cannibalization of the dilute. The finance department felt that the cannibalization rate would be even higher, with up to 480 MSUs of lost dilute sales.

The Lenor Refill package

A second option was introducing a new, more potent form of Lenor concentrate in a refill package. With the 4-from-1 concentrate, consumers would pour 1 liter of the concentrate into an empty 4-liter Lenor dilute bottle at home and add three liters of water to produce the original Lenor dilute formula. The Lenor brand group believed that the waste reduction benefits gained both from packaging

EXHIBIT 4   Consumer Panel Results, March 1987

	1-Liter Carton	*1-Liter Doypack*
Number of users	205	205
Participants who would buy the alternative regularly at 4.98 DM	53%	49%
Favorable/unfavorable comments on handling	88%/33%	88%/41%
Percentage of reused containers that were "smeary" after transfer	10%	28%
Packaging ratings		
Ease of opening	57%	52%
Transferability of product	63%	46%
Environmental friendliness	74%	65%
Ease of disposal	79%	75%
Incidence of spillage	8%	25%

reduction and bottle reuse would appeal to environmentally conscious consumers. The refill idea was not new to West Germans; many shoppers purchased milk packaged in flat plastic bags that were then slotted inside a permanent container at home. Stadler also felt that "German consumers were ready to bear the extra trouble associated with refilling to help their environment."

Preliminary Research.   In the fall of 1986, P&G conducted two focus group interviews of 8 to 12 fabric softener users to explore their attitudes toward a refill concept and determine how to market such a product. Several users expressed interest in trying a refill product that they felt would reduce waste through container reuse. When asked how they would sell this idea to their neighbors, many said that they would stress waste reduction.

Next, a consumer panel test explored the acceptance of specific refill package ideas. Participants used different types of trial refill Lenor packages for four weeks, and afterward answered a survey about their likes, dislikes, and purchase intentions. From the Results, researchers concluded that the refill concept had significant business-building potential.

Package Design.   In the spring of 1987, P&G Germany explored two specific refill package options. Technical researchers suggested two designs: (1) a laminated cardboard carton, similar in design to a milk carton and (2) a stand-alone soft plastic package, known as a "doypack" pouch, already used in West Germany to sell single servings of fruit juice. The technical staff believed that they could expand the size of this package to hold fabric softener concentrate.

In March 1987, P&G Germany tested these refill options in a consumer panel test. Participants were asked to test one of two package designs for Lenor concentrate: a 1-liter laminated "milk" carton or a 1-liter doypack pouch. Users rated the laminated carton highest for its environmental compatibility, ease of use, and convenience; the doypack pouch ratings followed closely behind. Messiness was also a significant factor in preference for either package; participants who spilled the product when transferring it into the larger container rated both packages lower in terms of handling. Exhibit 4 summarizes the test results.

Laminated Cartons versus Doypack Pouches.   Brand management investigated further the advantages and disadvantages of the two refill package designs. Both designs promised the same 85% reduction in package materials volume. In either case, P&G Germany had no facility that could produce the new packaging and would therefore need to hire subcontractors to meet a September launch date. This posed additional costs and risks. P&G Germany had not worked with any of the potential packaging suppliers before; consequently, Lenor's management did not have firsthand experience with their reliability in terms of delivery or quality. In addition, Lenor's product development group felt that there might be future capacity problems, since none of the potential subcontractors had ever handled the quantity of product P&G Germany was asking for.

Laminated Cartons.   Laminated carton technology had existed for 20 years. The cartons rarely leaked, and consumers spilled a minimum of product during refill tests. Retailers could easily display the rigid carton on their shelves; the product would not require a customized shipping case. Each case would hold ten 1-liter cartons of Lenor.

West German safety regulations, focusing on the potential for accidental misuse of products, strongly discouraged packaging nonfood substances in containers generally used for food items. Consequently, P&G Germany ran some risk of government intervention if it used the laminated carton for its refill package. In addition, although the general public considered the carton as environmentally friendly, environmental experts regarded the wax-coated cardboard materials as difficult to recycle.

Doypack Pouch.   Adapting the doypack pouch to Lenor's requirements provide difficult; the largest pouch size previously produced was 500 ml, half the size needed for Lenor. The first prototypes leaked, and more than 10% of the packages burst when dropped. Lenor's product development group felt optimistic, however, that these issues would be resolved within two months. Furthermore, a product-handling test in June 1987 revealed spillage difficulties. Participants in studio tests were asked to open the pouch and pour its contents into a 4-liter Lenor container. Although the least spillage occurred after the doypack's entire top was cut off with scissors, researchers found that users preferred to clip off only a corner of the package top. Lenor's brand management was concerned that the refill package would prove to be too messy for many consumers.

P&G Germany would need to produce customized shipping containers that would display the product attractively while following the stringent criteria determined by retailers. A picture of the doypack and the proposed case design are presented in Exhibit 5.

Comparative Production Costs.   The laminated carton and doypack pouch would achieve, respectively, 5% and 14% cost savings per SU over Lenor dilute, due to reduced package materials and lower delivery costs. Exhibit 6 shows a detailed cost breakdown for the proposed and existing Lenor product line. Lenor's allo-

EXHIBIT 5

Case of doypack refill pouches

EXHIBIT 6   1988 Breakdown of Direct Materials and Manufacturing Costs (DM per Statistical Unit)

	1-Liter Carton*	*1-Liter Doypack**	*4-Liter Dilute*	*1-Liter Concentrate*
Fabric softener chemicals	DM 4.60	DM 4.60	DM 4.69	DM 4.77
Packaging materials	1.84	1.82	3.40	2.72
Manufacturing	3.33	3.19	2.93	2.60
Delivery	0.86	0.76	1.79	1.01
Contractor expense	1.52	0.65	—	—
Total direct costs (DM)	12.15	11.02	12.81	11.10
Cost index				
(Lenor Dilute = 100)	95	86	100	87
SU per container	0.17	0.17	0.17	0.126
Total costs/container (DM)	2.06	1.87	2.18	1.40

* P&G Germany expected that the first 400 MSU produced would cost 33% and 41% more for the carton and doypack, respectively, due to initial start-up costs.

cated fixed costs were approximately DM 68 million per year.[11] The first 400 MSUs would cost an extra 33% and 41% for the carton and doypack, respectively.

Pricing.   Exhibit 7 shows the breakdown of 1988 proposed prices and trade margins for the Lenor product line. Brand management wanted the suggested retail price for the refill package to be at least DM 1.5/SU lower than that for the 4-liter dilute to reflect packaging cost savings. This would provide the price incentive

[11] Fixed costs included general sales/marketing, administrative, and distribution costs (80% of total); fixed manufacturing (17%); and product research and development costs (3%).

EXHIBIT 7   1988 Proposed Retail Price and Trade Margins

	1-Liter Refill	4-Liter Dilute	1-Liter Concentrate
Expected retail price (DM)	5.49	5.79	4.89
Expected retail margin	9%	0%	9%
Manufacturer's selling price (DM)	5.04	5.79	4.49
SU per container	0.17	0.17	0.126
Retail revenues (DM/SU)	32.29	34.06	38.81
Manufacturer's revenues (DM/SU)	29.65	34.06	35.64

needed to motivate consumers to buy the refill packs. The savings were 5% of manufacturer's list price.

Volume Forecasts.   The brand group forecast a 1988 sales volume of 1,500 MSU for the refill pouch; however, the team predicted that 60% of the refill package sales would come from canibalization of existing Lenor sales. The finance department was less optimistic, forecasting an 80% cannibalization rate and a sales volume of 750 MSUs, resulting in only a 150 MSU net increase in total sales. For the launch, P&G would need 400 MSUs to stock 70% of West Germany's retail chain stores.

Promotion and Advertising.   Brand management proposed a 6.5% increase over its original 1988 advertising and promotion budget, with DM 6.5 million to be allocated specifically to the refill package relaunch. At estimated refill sales of 1,500 MSUs, this budget equaled DM 4.31/SU. Table D breaks down the Lenor marketing budget with and without the refill package introduction:

TABLE D   Alternative 1988 Advertising and Promotion Budgets

	Without Launch	With Launch	Difference
Media	DM 10,849	DM 12,227	DM 1,378
Consumer promotion	1,957	1,976	19
Trade promotion	92,830	31,350	1,520
Indirect brand support	2,546	2,565	19
Total	DM 45,182	DM 48,118	DM 2,936

The Lenor brand group proposed to focus all Lenor advertising on the refill package for the first three months after launch. P&G Germany's advertising agency developed and tested two commercials called *Splish-Splash* and *Perspectives,* based on the doypack pouch option (see Exhibits 8 and 9). *Splish-Splash* and *Perspectives* achieved unaided recall ratings of 37% and 47%, respectively, exceeding P&G Germany's 35% average unaided recall score for acceptable new

---

EXHIBIT 8   Advertising Copy for Lenor Pouch:
***Splish-Splash* Commercial**

(Music begins, with young male and female dancers, brightly
dressed, dancing while holding Lenor containers and the Lenor
pouch.)

Singing to the 1960's tune of *Splish-Splash*:

Splish, Splash,
We're up-to-date,
Use Lenor in the refill pouch.

Just take your empty bottle,
Refilling is not difficult.
Just add water

Splish, Splash,
You feel it immediately,
Everything April-fresh and soft.
New Lenor in the
Environmentally safe refill pouch.

Splish, Splash,
The pouch is great,
Makes itself really small for the garbage

Splish, Splash,
Be up-to-date,
Use Lenor in the refill pouch.

---

copy.[12] Product labeling would highlight the environmental benefits of the packaging, in particular the 85% volume reduction in packaging materials, and would carry the phrase *refill pack*. Stadler hoped that the refill package would qualify for a Blue Angel label, which could help increase Lenor's sales, but felt uncertain that the improved packaging alone would gain the Blue Angel program's endorsement.

Proposed sales literature emphasized reductions in the retailer's warehousing (48% less), transportation (72%), and handling costs (70%) compared with the 4-liter Lenor dilute. The case container designs for both the carton and the doypack met 8 of the trade's 10 commandments, more than did any existing P&G Germany product. Finally, brand management felt that the opportunity to realize higher retail margins than could currently be obtained on the heavily promoted 4-liter dilute (9% vs. 0%) would also appeal to the trade.[13]

---

[12] Day-after recall testing measured communication effectiveness. Consumers who had watched television at the time when a test commercial spot was being shown were interviewed by telephone the following day. Unaided recall occurred when a consumer remembered the brand and message content of the test commercial without prompting. Aided recall involved prompting.

[13] Retail trade margins of 0% were due to the frequent use of the Lenor 4-liter dilute as a loss leader. Retail margins on Lenor sold at feature prices were often negative.

EXHIBIT 9

Storyboard for "Perspectives" commercial

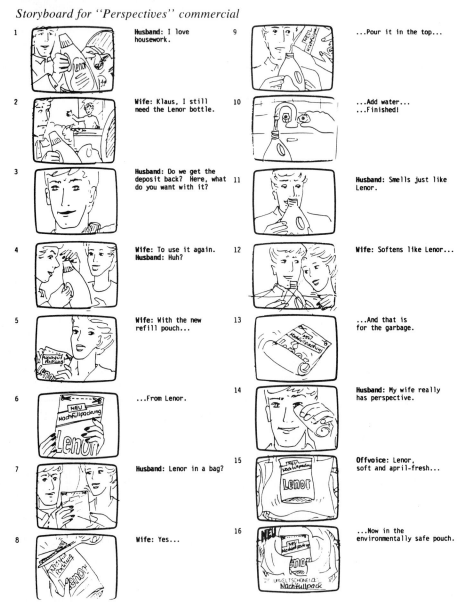

1 — **Husband:** I love housework.

2 — **Wife:** Klaus, I still need the Lenor bottle.

3 — **Husband:** Do we get the deposit back? Here, what do you want with it?

4 — **Wife:** To use it again. **Husband:** Huh?

5 — **Wife:** With the new refill pouch...

6 — ...From Lenor.

7 — **Husband:** Lenor in a bag?

8 — **Wife:** Yes...

9 — ...Pour it in the top...

10 — ...Add water... ...Finished!

11 — **Husband:** Smells just like Lenor.

12 — **Wife:** Softens like Lenor...

13 — ...And that is for the garbage.

14 — **Husband:** My wife really has perspective.

15 — **Offvoice:** Lenor, soft and april-fresh...

16 — ...Now in the environmentally safe pouch.

An Integrated Marketing Option

As Stadler pondered the pros and cons for the refill package, Daniel Knower, the assistant brand manager for Vizir, P&G Germany's liquid detergent brand, stopped by her office to discuss a new marketing concept he wanted to pursue. He said, "You know, we are struggling with the same environmental issues. I think that this refill concept is great and could be expanded to other brands, such as Vizir. We could market the products more efficiently under a new brand name, such as *Eco-pak*. Advertising copy could focus on the refill package as a product form that spanned multiple brands—Lenor, Vizir, and other liquid products.'' Realistically, both Stadler and Knower speculated that the manufacturing complications, larger marketing scope, and increased coordination associated with such a strategy would add at least three months to the Lenor refill package's September introduction date. However, both felt that the idea merited discussion with their respective brand managers.

Conclusion

At the next day's meeting, Rolf Kunisch discussed several issues with the Lenor brand management team. First was the possibility that any effort P&G made to address environmental issues could backfire. The Public Relations Department had warned of ''waking a sleeping dog.'' P&G had many highly visible products that might attract opposition from environmentalists. Although the Lenor refill package might raise the firm's profile as an environmentally conscious corporate citizen, it might also draw attention to other P&G products for which environmental and cost-effective improvements were not readily available.

Kunisch was also concerned about the rapidity with which brand management had developed the refill package proposal. Had the product been tested enough? Were there hidden issues that might have been missed in the rush to launch? Was there really an urgent need for action? No other German consumer goods company had addressed environmental issues through innovative packaging. With such a novel and relatively untested idea, what risks would P&G Germany run as the first to market?

Several other P&G country managers in Europe had scoffed at the ''crazy German ideas about the environment,'' seeing little applicability of the refill-package idea to their own markets. Kunisch wondered if P&G Europe headquarters would also conclude that P&G Germany was overreacting to the environmental concerns of some West Germany consumers. Stadler left the meeting, uncertain of the final outcome for the refill package's future.

After the meeting, Lenor's brand manager, Phillippe, asked Stadler to prepare a revised set of recommendations for Lenor, addressing some of Kunisch's concerns. Stadler continued to be positive about the new packaging concept; however, she realized that the internal sell would be tougher than she had anticipated.